Innovation in Music

Innovation in Music: Future Opportunities brings together cutting-edge research on new innovations in the field of music production, technology, performance and business. Including contributions from a host of well-respected researchers and practitioners, this volume provides crucial coverage on a range of topics from cybersecurity, to accessible music technology, performance techniques and the role of talent shows within music business.

Innovation in Music: Future Opportunities is the perfect companion for professionals and researchers alike with an interest in the music industry.

Russ Hepworth-Sawyer is co-chair of the UK Mastering Group, a freelance mastering engineer, writer and consultant through MOTTOsound (www.mottosound.com) and part-time lecturer at York St John University, UK.

Justin Paterson is Professor of Music Production at London College of Music, University of West London, UK.

Rob Toulson is Founder and Director of RT60 Ltd, specializing in technology development for the audio and music industries.

Perspectives on Music Production

This series collects detailed and experientially informed considerations of record production from a multitude of perspectives, by authors working in a wide array of academic, creative and professional contexts. We solicit the perspectives of scholars of every disciplinary stripe, alongside recordists and recording musicians themselves, to provide a fully comprehensive analytic point-of-view on each component stage of music production. Each volume in the series thus focuses directly on a distinct stage of music production, from pre-production through recording (audio engineering), mixing, mastering, to marketing and promotions.

Series Editors
Russ Hepworth-Sawyer, York St John University, UK
Jay Hodgson, Western University, Ontario, Canada
Mark Marrington, York St John University, UK

Titles in the Series

Producing Music
Edited by Russ Hepworth-Sawyer, Jay Hodgson and Mark Marrington

Innovation in Music
Performance, Production, Technology, and Business
Edited by Russ Hepworth-Sawyer, Jay Hodgson, Justin Paterson and Rob Toulson

Pop Music Production
Manufactured Pop and BoyBands of the 1990s
Phil Harding
Edited by Mike Collins

Cloud-Based Music Production
Sampling, Synthesis, and Hip-Hop
Matthew T. Shelvock

Gender in Music Production
Edited by Russ Hepworth-Sawyer, Jay Hodgson, Liesl King and Mark Marrington

Mastering in Music
Edited by John Paul Braddock, Russ Hepworth-Sawyer, Jay Hodgson, Matthew Shelvock and Rob Toulson

Innovation in Music
Future Opportunities
Edited by Russ Hepworth-Sawyer, Justin Paterson and Rob Toulson

For more information about this series, please visit: www.routledge.com/Perspectives-on-Music-Production/book-series/POMP

Innovation in Music
Future Opportunities

Edited by Russ Hepworth-Sawyer, Justin Paterson and Rob Toulson

LONDON AND NEW YORK

First published 2021
by Routledge
2 Park Square, Milton Park, Abingdon, Oxon OX14 4RN

and by Routledge
52 Vanderbilt Avenue, New York, NY 10017

Routledge is an imprint of the Taylor & Francis Group, an informa business

© 2021 selection and editorial matter, Russ Hepworth-Sawyer, Justin Paterson and Rob Toulson; individual chapters, the contributors

The right of Russ Hepworth-Sawyer, Justin Paterson and Rob Toulson to be identified as the authors of the editorial material, and of the authors for their individual chapters, has been asserted in accordance with sections 77 and 78 of the Copyright, Designs and Patents Act 1988.

All rights reserved. No part of this book may be reprinted or reproduced or utilised in any form or by any electronic, mechanical, or other means, now known or hereafter invented, including photocopying and recording, or in any information storage or retrieval system, without permission in writing from the publishers.

Trademark notice: Product or corporate names may be trademarks or registered trademarks, and are used only for identification and explanation without intent to infringe.

British Library Cataloguing-in-Publication Data
A catalogue record for this book is available from the British Library

Library of Congress Cataloging-in-Publication Data
Names: Hepworth-Sawyer, Russ, editor. | Paterson, Justin, editor. | Toulson, Rob, editor.
Title: Innovation in music : future opportunities / edited by Russ Hepworth-Sawyer, Justin Paterson and Rob Toulson.
Description: New York : Routledge, 2021. | Series: Perspectives on music production | Includes bibliographical references and index.
Subjects: LCSH: Music and technology. | Music—Performance. | Sound recordings—Production and direction. | Music trade.
Classification: LCC ML55 .I568 2021 (print) | LCC ML55 (ebook) | DDC 781.4—dc23
LC record available at https://lccn.loc.gov/2020029016
LC ebook record available at https://lccn.loc.gov/2020029017

ISBN: 978-0-367-36337-6 (hbk)
ISBN: 978-0-367-36335-2 (pbk)
ISBN: 978-0-429-34538-8 (ebk)

Typeset in Times New Roman
by Apex CoVantage, LLC

Contents

About the editors   viii
Preface   x

PART I MUSIC PRODUCTION INNOVATION

1. Country & Eastern: Contextual and cultural mediation in the recording studio – two producers, two artists, two cultures   3
   RICHARD LIGHTMAN

2. Defining and developing a sonic signature in music mixing: A practice-based approach as modern-day studio mentorship   17
   ANDREA SUCCI

3. Making records within records: Manufacturing phonographic 'otherness' in sample-based Hip Hop production   37
   MICHAIL EXARCHOS

4. Motormouth: An essay in sonic recontextualization   56
   JEZ NASH

5. The Individualist: Todd Rundgren's approach to innovation and his 1993 interactive album *No World Order*   70
   TIM HUGHES

6. Ground control and cloud booths: Using Dante to break geographical barriers to music production   89
   PAUL FERGUSON AND DAVE HOOK

7. Music production utilising Internet of Things technologies   106
   MARQUES HARDIN AND ROB TOULSON

PART II MUSIC TECHNOLOGY INNOVATION

8. **Development of an Ambisonic Guitar System**   125
   DUNCAN WERNER, BRUCE WIGGINS AND EMMA FITZMAURICE

9. **Retaining pianistic virtuosity in #MIs: Exploring pre-existing gestural nuances for live sound modulation through a comparative study**   146
   NICCOLÒ GRANIERI, JAMES DOOLEY AND TYCHONAS MICHAILIDIS

10. **Improvising song writing and composition within a hybrid modular synthesis system**   162
    HUSSEIN BOON

11. **Speaker Park: An intersection of loudspeaker design and post-acousmatic composition**   175
    JON PIGOTT AND ANTTI SAKARI SAARIO

12. **Sound objects: Exploring procedural audio for theatre**   188
    MAT DALGLEISH AND SARAH WHITFIELD

13. **Hearing and feeling memories: Connecting image, sound and haptic feedback to create a multisensory experience of photographs**   206
    MATTHEW D.F. EVANS, JAMES DOOLEY AND SIMON HALL

14. **Concepts for the design of accessible music technology**   219
    JOE WRIGHT

15. **Security engineering in the arts**   235
    ANDY FARNELL

PART III PERFORMANCE INNOVATION

16. **Transparency and authenticity in the live arena: An exploration of electronic music performance techniques**   247
    DAVE FORTUNE

17. **BTS' "Speak Yourself" world tour as an intermedial spectacle of attachment**   260
    ALICJA SULKOWSKA

18. **A review of contemporary practices incorporating digital technologies with live classical music**   273
    CLARA COLOTTI

19. **Free ensembles and small (chamber) orchestras as innovative drivers of classical music in Germany**   290
    ALENKA BARBER-KERSOVAN AND VOLKER KIRCHBERG

Contents

20. Transforming musical performance: Activating the audience as digital collaborators — 306
    ADRIAN YORK

21. The online composer–audience collaboration — 331
    LUIS RAMIREZ

22. New instruments as creativity triggers in composer–performer collaboration — 342
    AGATA KUBIAK-KENWORTHY

23. "My avatar and me": Technology-enhanced mirror in monitoring music performance practice — 355
    GIUSY CARUSO, LUC NIJS AND MARC LEMAN

24. Creative considerations for on-screen visuals in electronic pop music performances — 370
    KIRSTEN HERMES

PART IV MUSIC BUSINESS AND ARTIST DEVELOPMENT INNOVATION

25. Towards a quantum theory of musical creativity — 389
    MATTHEW LOVETT

26. Observing mood-based patterns and commonalities in music using machine learning algorithms — 403
    JEFFREY LUPKER AND WILLIAM J. TURKEL

27. The role of contests and talent shows as part of the artist development process within the music industry — 414
    STEFAN LALCHEV AND PAUL G. OLIVER

28. Music: Leeds – supporting a regionalised music sector and scene — 432
    PAUL THOMPSON AND SAM NICHOLLS

Index — 445

About the editors

The co-chairs of the 2019 Innovation in Music Conference (www.music innovation.co.uk) also acted as editors for this volume.

Russ Hepworth-Sawyer is a mastering engineer for MOTTOsound.com serving artists and labels internationally and has developed specialist remastering techniques to restore the back catalogues of many leading artists. Russ also co-mastered multi-stream audio specifically for the variPlay interactive-music system developed by Rob Toulson and Justin Paterson (below). Additionally, Russ is also a long-serving part-time academic at York St John University, UK, and now delivers bespoke professional-level training to many in the industry through the newly formed www.makeitsoundright.com. Russ is co-chair of the Mastering Group for the Audio Engineering Society and co-founded the UK's first Mastering Conference. Russ has written several books on audio and mastering for Routledge including *Logic Pro: Audio & Music Production, Demo To Delivery, What is Music Production?, Practical Mastering*, and *Audio Mastering: The Artists*. Russ is also a founding editor of the Perspectives on Music Production series where this book proudly resides. Russ's current research centres around the learning journeys of the professional mastering engineer.

Justin Paterson is Professor of Music Production at London College of Music, University of West London, UK. He has numerous research publications ranging through journal articles, conference presentations and book chapters, and is author of the *Drum Programming Handbook*. He is also an active music producer. Research interests include 3-D audio and interactive music, fields that he has investigated with prominent industrial organizations such as Warner Music Group. Together with Professor Rob Toulson, he developed the variPlay interactive-music system. He currently leads a team at UWL as part of the HAPPIE consortium (Haptic Authoring Pipeline for the Production of Immersive Experiences), funded by the Innovate-UK 'Audience of the Future' initiative. In this, he is developing a novel music-production control interface in mixed reality, based upon high-resolution haptic feedback.

Rob Toulson is Founder and Director of RT60 Ltd, specializing in technology development for the audio and music industries. He was previously Professor of Creative Industries and Commercial Music at

About the editors

University of Westminster and Director of the Cultures of the Digital Economy Research Institute at Anglia Ruskin University in Cambridge. Rob holds a first degree in Mechanical Engineering and a Doctorate in Acoustics and Vibration Analysis; he is also an innovative musician, music producer and sound engineer working across most music genres. Rob is inventor of the unique iDrumTune Pro mobile app, which assists percussionists with drum tuning and has reached the position of number one music app in over 60 different countries on the iPhone App Store.

Preface

The Innovation in Music network brings together practitioners, experts and academics in the rapidly evolving and connected disciplines of music performance, music production, audio technologies and music business. In 2019, the Innovation in Music Conference (InMusic19) was held at the University of West London and included keynote interviews, performances and panel discussions with Trevor Horn, Lula XYZ, Bruce Wooley, Rhiannon Mair, Sarah Yule, Matan Berkowitz, Rhiannon McLaren and the Radio Science Orchestra among others. The network and conference acts as a forum for industry experts and professionals to mix with researchers and academics to report on the latest advances and exchange ideas, crossing boundaries between music disciplines and bridging academia with industry. After the conference, contributors were invited to submit articles for this book, *Innovation in Music: Future Possibilities* – which showcases the event. Accordingly, this book gives a broad and detailed overview of modern and cross-disciplinary innovations in the world of music.

The conference itself demonstrated a 'world first' via its performance keynote, whereby the Radio Science Orchestra ensemble played live in separate studios in London, and were joined in real time by musicians in Edinburgh, using GPS clocking via satellite to maintain data integrity over distance and keep latency within a naturalistic experience for the performers. The combined result was spatialized in 3-D, with interactive live video of all the musicians being projected onto the audience, using them as human pixels, then VJ-ed and re-projected onto the walls. Bruce Woolley interspersed his keynote dialogue over the music, and was joined by Matan Berkowitz, who improvised further musical layers using his self-built gestural controllers. This event encapsulated much of the spirit of this book and technical details are offered in Chapter 6.

The book is divided into four parts, representing innovations around each of music production, technology, performance and business. In Part I, innovative examples of music production are presented, which ranges from low latency musical transmission to genre-boundary-breaking production techniques. Part II discusses innovation in music performance, discussing innovations from development of a unique ambisonic guitar system to procedural audio for theatre. Part III presents a number of new technologies for performance, from use of motion capture to aid classical piano-performance, to audience influence of live jazz-band improvisation via smart real-time electronic feedback. Finally, Part IV considers innovation in music business and artist development. Topics range from the quantum theory of musical creativity, to observation of mood-based patterns in music.

We thank all chapter authors, conference speakers, delegates and conference-sponsors for their support, and intend that the chapters of this book will be a lasting record of contemporary music innovations and a resource of research information for the future.

Russ Hepworth-Sawyer, Justin Paterson and Rob Toulson

Part I
Music production innovation

1

Country & Eastern

Contextual and cultural mediation in the recording studio – two producers, two artists, two cultures

Richard Lightman

1.1 INTRODUCTION AND BACKGROUND

The social and creative hierarchical positioning of the record producer in a studio context is determined by the technological and cultural dynamics within the studio and the relationship between the producer and the artist (Burgess, 2013:130–145). However, this relationship between the parties concerned seems to be weighted differently depending on cultural associations and cultural commonalities. Cultural differences appear to exacerbate incidences of insecurity and there are external, internal and stakeholder perceived pressures on the producer to meet diverse expectations. These same pressures exist within the framework of the same-culture producer/artist creative process, but there are elements of translation and interpretation removed from the transaction that are of additional concern to those outside of these parameters, (Frith and Zagorski-Thomas, 2012:149–160). There is the constant questioning as to whether either party is understood and on a creative level, the creative ideas and influences, objectives and outputs are not necessarily articulated in a fully comprehendible form (Glossop, 2014). This can be a positive contributory element to the creative process but does inject an additional dynamic into the interactions. Kerrigan (2013: 111–127) posits that cultural transference is embedded into an individual's understanding of codes and practices within a culture and that this then gets transformed into creativity. The practitioner's understanding of the process is not necessarily shared with other collaborators and unless the codes and practices are clearly defined between the parties concerned at the outset of a project, there can be a confusion of objectives and approaches to the qualitative, creative or commercial assessment of the output.

The analysis of the functions and outcomes of the mediation process within music production, within a mixed cultural context, provides further insight into the required negotiations and methodologies employed in the recording studio between artist and producer. The following outlines some of those processes through an auto-ethnographic case study of an album recording. This may help future recording artists and their producers to understand the cultural motivations and circumstances that inform the expectations of both parties within the production process, which can then be applied positively to enhance the end product.

As I had explored, experienced and researched this dynamic from both sides of the relationship as a practicing bhangra producer in the 1990s and a researcher of South Asian production techniques, it became apparent that it would be an invaluable addition to the research to experience and evaluate the relationships and dynamics from an equitable stance as both producer and artist in a modern-day context. This could then be evaluated as to how or whether the process had progressed from both an external and internal perspective.

It was an accidental opportunity that allowed this further exploration. I had arranged for a concert performance of bhangra artists for students at the University of Kent. The musical director was my former associate and bhangra producer, Kuljit Bhamra, MBE, who had provided some research material via interview and with whom I had worked in the capacity of engineer and as a session musician in the early 1990s. We both worked with some of the same artists as producers in the past and this has provided an opportunity to compare styles, approaches and cultural interactions. It was during the programming of the event that Bhamra suggested that the two of us play together as an opening act to the concert. We had played on each other's productions as session musicians over the years, overdubbing parts onto existing arrangements, but had actually never played together before. The idea was that I would play a style on guitar (my first instrument) that would sit comfortably within my musical lexicon and that Bhamra would accompany me on tabla and Indian percussion. To test the concept, we met at his studio where we played together, extemporising and moving in and out of Western and Eastern styles. Being so enthused by this, we decided that after the concert, we would record an album together with the working title of 'Country & Eastern'. This would afford an additional opportunity to investigate from within, the relationships between the two cultures but with a balanced sense of production skills from the two protagonists, acting as both producers and artists. There was an awareness that this could create friction, however it could also create an intensity within the creative process that came from a position of technical and musical expertise with the possibility of creating a new genre. The success of this collaboration would depend on both an understanding of each other's cultural influences and a tolerance, or acceptance of breaches of each party's musical forms and the framework that surrounded this. The other contexts that needed to be incorporated into the equation, with a requirement for negotiation, mediation, tolerance and eventual consensus, were the technical procedures and habitual processes employed by each of the parties from a production perspective. Both of us were accustomed to different procedural methodologies when addressing our recordings and the differences could cause frustration or conversely, might be the interventions that could break both of us out of our technical comfort zones, creating new sonic vistas through non-familiar approaches to the production process.

As we sat and played together, we recorded our ideas. These recordings acted as a notepad for the musical concepts and structures that we

Figure 1.1 Richard Lightman and Kuljit Bhamra, MBE

could draw upon later when embarking on recording the album. The initial plan was to record basic backing tracks within the studio and then take the tracks away to our own studios where parts could be added on to the tracks. These additions could then be compared and adapted for the final recordings.

The element of trust was rooted in the target final product and the commercial viability of the project. We were both aware that apart from the research element, the end game was also profitability. The objectives outweighed any creative misunderstandings of form and by doing so, provided the creative tension and space required to create something bigger and better than either of the parties concerned could create independently. All parties had something to gain and it is partly this dynamic that mediated any of the internal power struggles that existed between us. Even when creative differences become untenable, there is still the end goal that can bring a project back from the brink of failure. In this particular case there was the basic understanding that neither of us were going to waste our time on just creative pursuits and that ultimately, we needed to generate an equitable remuneration for our efforts. World music producer, Ben Mandelson states that although he is always in a situation where he is looking to exploit the market through his artist's creativity, he is always looking for a fair deal for all (Cottrell, 2010).

After much negotiation over time availability and diarising, I went to Bhamra's studio, taking fourteen different guitars with me. The sole purpose of this was to have a palate of sounds that could be employed if they were sonically compatible with Bhamra's extensive tabla set up. This was not done consciously to be competitive, but in retrospect it was a way of setting one's store out to show versatility. Bhamra's studio houses over 100 percussion instruments and drums and it could be argued that I did not want to be outdone. It references the observation that musicians will jostle to claim geographic possession of space when arriving in a recording studio, often placing instruments or cases in awkward positions near the console to establish territory. Once the lines have been drawn and the session settles down, these areas in some way become a safe space for the musicians who will invade or wander into the producer's 'space' in a form of territorial confrontation. This was not my intention during this writing session, but there may have been an underlying personal agenda that even I was unaware of at the time.

Bhamra was initially unsure as to whether this project would really work and voiced his apprehension of bringing me into his world, at the same time recognising that I was intent on dragging him into mine. He played a few motifs on the harmonium and after listening to them, an instrument was selected that would best represent what he was doing. I copied the motif and he would assist me further by suggesting the bends and inflections that I should play to further incorporate the Eastern flavour of the music, even if it were to be played on a Western styled instrument such as a banjo guitar. It was too early to definitively state that we were creating a new genre, but it was obvious to both of us that something different and 'magical' was happening.

After six hours, we had over twenty collaborative compositions; some driven by my guitar constructs and some by his tabla rhythms melodies augmented with the occasional harmonium melody. We agreed to review these and reduce the output to ten compositions, constructed so that they could be cut down or extended to useable lengths to support usage by moving image producers and editors – a key target market.

1.2 THE STUDIO RECORDINGS

1.2.1 Day 1

For the initial recordings I arrived early at the studio with my arsenal of guitars. Bhamra arrived two hours after the start of the booking so that guitars and amplifiers could be miked up in advance. When he arrived, we set up and miked his percussion instruments under his direction in acknowledgement of the experience that he had with recording his own instruments in his studio in Southall. There was much relaxed banter at this point, which was a way of easing any tension of the impending recording.

By the early afternoon, we had reviewed the structures and musical arrangements that came out of our jam session and decided to try to record a couple of tracks. Most of the recordings were first takes. It was agreed that the tracks would benefit from additional bass, percussion, bansuri flute and guitar overdubs and that an organic approach to the recordings, by not using midi instruments, should be maintained. Both of our experience of years in studios was evident as the playing and approach was very relaxed. We were able to musically 'bounce' off each other creatively as if we had been playing together for many years, which was not the case. Nods and hand signals were instantly acknowledged and the whole experience was extremely enjoyable.

1.2.2 Day 2

On this day, we recorded four tracks. The arrangements were done 'on the fly' and we played the different sections of the songs by signalling to each other, knowing that should anything need to be changed at a later date, sections could be cut and pasted during an editing stage. Initially, there was a difference of opinion as to how to structure compositions. Bhamra veered towards repetition to encourage dance as per bhangra dance music, whereas I veered towards traditional Western A/B, A/B/C arrangements. A compromise was achieved very quickly as it was understood that there were opportunities for editing the individual compositions after recording. There are many examples where producers have not necessarily been able to agree with the artist or another producer on the final performances. In the case of Steely Dan (4 Comments, 2018), many different solos or performances by different musicians on a track would be recorded and then the decision as to which take to use would be made after much discussion between Donald Fagan and Walter Becker and their engineer.

1.2.3 Day 3

On this day we started with repairing some of the performances on the tracks that we had recorded. The microphones and instruments were still in place and so we were able to overdub any replacement parts with the same sounds. Most of the repairs were done as a result of my reviewing the recordings at my home studio. Both guitar and tablas were addressed. The arrangements were also edited; extending their lengths by cutting and pasting sections into the songs.

Three new tracks and additional overdub percussion such as shaker, dhol drum, bell and pot were recorded. At this point it was agreed that two more tracks, along with additional percussion overdubs, would be recorded on Day 4, leaving Day 5 for guitar overdubs.

1.2.4 Day 4

The last two tracks were recorded and this was the easiest workflow in terms of agreeing on arrangements or finding the relevant percussion patterns to compliment the guitars. On reflection, we had now settled into a routine and the studio working environment was now more familiar to both of us. Perhaps we should have started the process of recording the first few tracks again to improve on the initial recordings but time allocation and other commitments did not allow for this.

All initial percussion overdubs were finished and this left the fifth day for some of the guitar overdubs that I thought would benefit from having been done in the studio rather than in my own studio. This included acoustic guitars utilising the ambience of the room and numerous microphone placements, and electric guitars requiring the use of the amplifier set up in the room, again with ambient mics.

1.2.5 Day 5

This day was attended by just an engineer and me. Again, there was a relaxed atmosphere but on reflection, the inclusion of an engineer in the session added another element and distraction to the process of my producing my own performances, something that I had grown accustomed to doing on my own in my own private studio environment. Some tensions started to emerge in terms of procedure of recording as I have very set routines in recording my own performance, but this was mitigated by my hierarchal position as the producer. We then completed rough mixes of all the material.

The initial recordings in the studio were deemed a success, but observationally, much of what I needed to play involved syncopated rhythms and although it was easy to play all my guitar parts on my own or against a click track, as soon as the tablas were playing with me, I found it much more difficult to keep in time and 'feel'. The musical meeting of East and West and the musical communication between the two musicians had elements of confusion from a very base level. This could be attributed to the differing cultural roots that not only contributed to the creative process, but also hindered creativity as it needed to be addressed at all times within the playing. This then highlights a possible situation that may generally permeate through to intercultural interactions within production and the basic forms of music communication and that they are impacted by these very basic understandings or misunderstandings; a sort of give and take.

The next step was to add the bansuri flute.

1.3 THE BANSURI FLUTE RECORDINGS

It was decided that it would be easier if the bansuri flute was recorded at Bhamra's Red Fort Studios in Southall, as it would be easier for the flautist to get to the studio and as Bhamra was to be in charge of this part of the recording, it would be more convenient and faster in his own environment. Part of the discipline of recording is negotiating the space and if one feels very familiar with that space, it usually eases the workflow of the recording. However, sometimes the familiarity aspect creates too much of a relaxed atmosphere and less is achieved in the allotted time. Gibson (2005) states that recorded music is a product of more that the artist-producer relationship. It is additionally affected by all the stakeholders and more specifically, the space where the recording takes place. The space is employed as an additional contributor to the creative process.

The bansuri flautist, Robin Christian arrived with a collection of thirty-five bamboo flutes. I subsequently learned from him that they were built to facilitate different scales, flourishes and tunings. The tuning element was interesting as apparently, bansuri flutes made in India are either made during the monsoon season or in the heat of summer as the tuning will be affected by weather conditions. Although there was purportedly an adjustment made of any tuning inconsistencies through the choice of instrument, the flutes in question were all hand carved from bamboo and susceptible to warping, shrinking or expanding, relative to humidity and temperature changes and this needed to be addressed with the mild use of tuning software to ensure that the takes were in tune with the backing tracks and each other.

Bhamra was quite dictatorial with Christian and gave him exact melodies to play with very little freedom of expression. I intervened for the last two tracks and asked him to extemporise. This resulted in some interesting additions, some of which we kept in the final recordings.

The verbal reference to notes and musical descriptions that were used during the session related to the classical Indian scale and Christian kept trying to describe what he was doing in English to include me in the conversation. During the recording, if he was asked to change a grace note or flourish, he would then get another flute out. This was difficult as the sound of each flute was slightly different and we kept asking him not to change flutes in the middle of a song. This was to ensure that we maintained the integrity of the original flute timbre on the track. Bhamra kept making snide remarks about this in the studio control room out of earshot of Christian which seemed to help Bhamra in dealing with the frustration of guiding the musician's performance. This is a common occurrence that I have encountered in studios between producers and engineers whilst recording artists. It is a form of reinforcing the stature of hegemony and technical pecking order within a studio context. Although the artist is mostly unaware of this, it helps to alleviate the frustrations and tempers the approach from the engineer and producer in dealing with the artist's demands, inconsistencies and moods. Most of the outward approach by producers and engineers is geared to ensuring that the artist or performer feels comfortable. The case studies in Farinella's *Producing Hit Records – Secrets from the Studio* (2006) and Massey's *Behind the Glass: V.2* (2009) document the approach of producers and the techniques used to alleviate tension and insecurities that the artist might be experiencing in order to get the best performance. However, there are producer and engineer stresses that are often bypassed when analysing the creative recording experience.

To further research this, Mike Paxman, producer of Judy Tzuke and Status Quo, was asked how he related to the stresses of recording with insecure, demanding and non-compliant artists, and what techniques and interventions he used to address the producer's frustrations, insecurities, self-doubt and having to deal with difficulties in the studio. He revealed that he knew of some producers who would go home after a session and drown their frustrations with a bottle of wine, but it was interesting that he avoided his own personal and emotional reactions to this and deferred to the methods employed in dealing with the artist in order to achieve the best recorded results.

> The 'producer's vision' can be a contentious area. The producer's planned direction for a recording's outcome has to be in most cases, fluid, and you have to allow for some wiggle room; otherwise you're always going to be frustrated or displeased with the outcome. Recorded music, as live performance, has a life of its own and invariably the way to get the best outcome is to direct things as much as possible then allow the piece to grow of its own accord. This of course means that you must always be prepared to change your mind or to adapt if something comes up that looks like it will change the course of things for the better.
>
> I don't often suffer from self-doubt when in the studio, but I have various techniques to deal with periods of tension and frustration. The good thing about being the one 'in the chair' is just that . . . you can make decisions to shape the project, not that your approach will ever be the 'only' way to approach the task at hand, but if you proceed down the path of your choosing with a degree of skill, confidence and belief, hopefully that will lead to a good outcome. It's really important to be well prepared, to know the music you are working on inside out and to have more than one option in mind.
>
> (Paxman, 2019)

In contacting other producers, even more evasive or deflective answers were given that addressed the outcome of the recording and the qualitative results achieved, but revealed little about their own well-being and dispositions. It is perhaps the role of the producer to remain impersonal and private in order to get the best results in the studio, and this then is reflected in their outward public facing, even with people that have a commonality of experience. My own method of relieving the intense frustration of working with some artists was to go home and play guitar very loudly and aggressively.

1.4 THE BANSURI FLUTE EDIT PROCESS

The next process, after having recorded the bansuri flute at Bhamra's studio, entailed a further act of trust. Many different takes were recorded and Bhamra was left to choose the best performances and phrasing. He then provided me with an edit which I could import into the original recording software project. The editorial control, at this time, was entrusted to him which relied on his in-depth understanding of the South Asian approach to flute performance, phrasing and tuning. When Bhamra had finalised his edits, he sent the files over to me with the proviso that I could further adjust the placement and timing of the files to best suit the overall track. What was refreshing in this case, was that there was a total understanding of the technological process between us and that this did not interfere with the creative process. The choice of performance was left to Bhamra and the overall decision on timing placement was left to me. This method of remote collaboration, with the use of three different studios highlighted the change and malleability of localisation of the technology, but also supported the idea that the creative cultural collaboration needed to include a large element of trust. That trust can be evaluated in terms of the cultural expertise and understanding of the parties concerned. The more cultural expertise that exists, the more artistic freedom and relevancy can be exercised. Cultural metacognition, is used as a benchmark and indicator for the success of cultural collaborations within business contexts. The greater the understanding of the other cultures participating; the greater the chance of success, (Chua, Morris and Mor, 2012). Although there was also a cultural assimilation of technology for the implementation of creativity, the main focus was on the creative collaboration itself and the technology was simply a facilitator.

1.5 OVERDUBBING ADDITIONAL GUITARS

The next step was to take the amalgamated project files to my own studio and overdub additional guitars. This enabled me to experiment without any time or financial pressures. I was aware that I did not want to 'over cook' the production by layering the recordings with too many instruments and was careful to not dominate or obscure the percussion on the tracks which played such a key part of the compositions. The idea was that on completion of my recordings, Bhamra would have a right of veto of any of the additional guitar parts subject to negotiation. Again, a sensitivity of the cultural integrity of the project and the knowledge that some creative and cultural negotiations would ensue, influenced the creative decisions taken in putting additional instruments on the tracks. In this instance, it was Bhamra's turn to trust that I would make the correct decisions in the parts that I put onto the individual compositions and that I would not corrupt the initial creative dynamic that existed when we originally recorded just guitar and tabla. During this process, there was a sense of self-reflection as to my validity as a cultural expert exerting my own cultural influences on the recording and performances, much as I had felt when producing bhangra recordings in the 1990s. There were times when I tried to emulate South Asian phrasing, but I pulled back from this approach as I felt it was inappropriate and not authentic. The question of two completely different creative cultural influences meeting in the middle brought up the question of authenticity. At what point would my approach, or even Bhamra's approach be considered not authentic, as the end product was to be, in effect, a new genre? I decided to take a less contentious approach and follow the route of being true to my own cultural roots, letting the music evolve through the confluence of strong Eastern and Western influences finding common ground in an almost combative fashion.

1.6 THE HARMONICA SESSION

To further the cultural mix, I wanted to try to balance some of the bansuri flute with another Western instrument for three of the songs. I thought I would attempt to use harmonica on these tracks and contacted harmonica player, Tim Staffel, who I had previously produced two albums for. Staffell was the original singer and bass player in the band Smile, introducing Freddie Mercury to the band that then became Queen.

I invited Staffell to come down to the studio and suggested that we make this an informal social occasion. Above and beyond the social interactivity, having worked with him in the past, I knew that this was an almost guaranteed method to get him relaxed in anticipation of recording in the studio, in order to achieve the best performance.

The difficulty I encountered in the session was that of the rhythmical feel of the track from Staffell's perspective. Even though the three tracks he was playing on were of a Country or Blues root, he found it difficult to play against the syncopated rhythms of the table-based percussion. Whereas on the whole, I felt comfortable with this when I was playing guitar, Staffell would drift and lose focus as to where he was within the bar relative to his musical phrasing. The solution to this was to give him a 'four beats to the bar' click track, playing in addition to the other instruments, so that he felt more grounded in a Western musical environment. This was surprising as Staffell is well versed in jazz and syncopated funk rhythms, but he felt uncomfortable with the Eastern approach. This gave me further insight into the creation of cross-cultural genres. Each contributor must feel comfortable in their own creative cultures, but must also feel comfortable in those creative cultures that come from being immersed in another musical background. It is more than just an intellectual understanding of the 'other' genre, it is also an emotional and creative cultural adaptation that is required for the cross-cultural interaction to be mutually acceptable and ultimately successful.

1.7 THE REVIEW SESSION

In reviewing the final recordings and compiling the harmonica takes in the appropriate tracks, I then tried to step back from the process in terms of my creative contribution and reviewed the tracks with a view to their commercial viability rather than just the enjoyment and reflective analysis of having played on the recordings.

I then embarked on a first mix. This involved careful scrutiny of instrument volume levels, EQ, panning, effects and some judicious editing of instruments that might be interfering with other instrumental performances. One of the main technical difficulties was the sonic interference between the bass tabla or 'baya' and the bass guitar. Both of these instruments occupy a similar frequency bandwidth and as the bass tabla has a sustain that is not found in Western musical genres with bass drums or other percussion instruments, it created an unpleasant bass tonality when playing with the bass guitar that was not easily addressed though equalisation or side chaining, a compression effect used to limit the volume of one instrument when another is playing. This effect is often employed when mixing bass drums and bass synths or guitars in dance music. My solution was to use a multipressor that compresses only certain frequencies of an audio signal. This had the effect of taming the bass guitar on the frequencies that clashed with the tabla.

The mixes were completed and then checked on many different audio systems. This part of the process included an assessment of the sonic continuity and compatibility between the tracks. After some adjustments, to ensure level, equalisation continuity, the tracks were then sent to Bhamra for his comments. Some of these were contained within an email as follows:

> Hi Richard
> I think it all sounds fantastic!!!! Here are some notes, which I think will help to create some contrasting textures and narrative arcs.
>
> TRACK 1:
> I find the flute overpowered by the **guitars** during the 3 main themes.
> It could be that the **guitars** need to be lowered and the flute raised in volume.
>
> TRACK 2:
> I love this track!
> Again, I find the flute too low (or not present enough compared to the **guitars**).
>
> TRACK 3:
> I love this track too!
> It's a bit of a shock when the **guitars** first come in.
>
> TRACK 10:
> Lovely and soothing!!
> Again, I think that the flute is fighting to be heard above the **guitars** . . . Is it possible to remove the **sitar/guitar** until 1:03? (sorry!)
> . . . and then perhaps one of the other **guitars** 3:24–4:02 and then at the outro 5:42 onwards.
> I feel that the layered **guitars** could be structured so that they're not all playing at the same time throughout.
>
> Hooray - it all sounds fab!!!
>
> (Bhamra, 2019)

My reaction to this email was that apart from some of the constructive suggestions of more space and dynamics, Bhamra was now trying to exert some additional Eastern influence on the end product, whereas I had purposefully oriented the mixes towards a Western approach to meet, what I conceived to be, the market expectations particularly of film and television editors; my perceived key target market for this recording.

I replied in a friendly tone suggesting that Bhamra was doing what all producers do on sessions and use the familiar set routine of 'I really liked that take. It was fantastic but could we just try another one?'. This was all done in the interests of comradery and collaboration, but there was an underlying cultural power struggle here that exists within all producer-artist relationships and especially when there are two producers who are from differing cultural backgrounds collaborating.

When two distinct cultures merge to try to collaborate and both parties are not only producers but also the artists, the dynamics and relational roles from a technological, musical, hierarchical and cultural perspective become fluid. Within this scenario the boundaries that define the roles of engineers, producers and artists are amplified, questioned and redefined at almost every juncture. The subtexts of culturally diverse difference and technological prowess create unspoken power struggles between the protagonists. The unspoken struggle for genre dominance within the production process seemed to come to the fore at the mixing stage. The race for the finish line seemed to exacerbate the tensions and inherent worries of both collaborators. This was the final negotiation and whatever happened at this point would be final and could not easily be amended. Our objective was to maintain the integrity of the output and ourselves as producers.

This tension and struggle for dominance was tempered by mutual respect, but it was still there as an undercurrent to our interactions. It seems that all the jostling for position in the recording studio including territorial placement of instruments, along with taking control of the recordings at different junctures, were all precursors to the final unstated but most important negotiation; which side of the West or the East was the final product going to lean towards.

I phoned Bhamra to discuss this. He took a very apologetic stance, saying that these were not dictates and that I could ignore them if I wanted to. It was as if the negotiating balance had shifted due to some form of insecurity relative to the tracks submitted from the artist's perspective and not the producer. Even with all the technological expertise, a lifetime of experience, shared values, collaborative intent, peer acknowledgement and successful past achievements, the artist/performer insecurities rise to the surface.

1.8 THE FINAL MIX

I completed the mix incorporating Bhamra's comments, using some discretion as I didn't fully agree with every point, but I appreciated that his comments would have been initial reactions and that we would both have addressed this process in a similar manner. It has been my experience that the first reaction, rather than a laboured considered reaction to mixes is more intuitive, and although there may be inconsistencies in the comments, there is more validity to this than if it was tempered by consideration, review and polite protocol. I have also found this generally to be the case with numerous takes of one performance; the first performance in the studio needs to be captured as it is the most intuitive and expressive. It may contain mistakes, but that can be rectified. The essence of the performance is lost in the more calculated and planned ensuing performances, the more the performer retakes and rerecords.

The reaction to the mixes was positive. He expressed a deep emotional reaction to the overall sound, stating that he 'loved it' and was extremely proud of what we had done.

The making of this album was an entirely enjoyable experience and both of us were very happy with the results. The exchange of ideas, compromises and cultural referencing was both exhilarating and challenging and a number of unexpected musical interventions were required to enable the recording of this project. The exchange of musical cultures and the pure enjoyment of music making was enriching and – we may have created a new genre: Country & Eastern.

Country & Eastern served to further support the hypothesis that the confluence of two creative minds, and in this case also cultures, results in an output that is greater than the sum of its parts (Copleston, 1999). It also provided an opportunity to explore the artist/producer relationship and observed further that despite the experience and wisdom of, in this case, two record producers, artist insecurities will always surface during the creative process, but there is also the inherent stress element of the responsibility of the overall recording that is borne by the producer. When the producer(s) is also the artist(s), this can cause an internalised conflict that needs to be addressed. The project also further underpinned the theory that a practitioner's cultural expertise has a significant proportional impact on the creative success and implementation of a production. The creative contributions and performances are easier to facilitate and become more effective with a greater understanding and absorption of cultural values. To create a musical environment in which all participants are comfortable and interacting, within one set of cultural parameters, is often difficult. However, creating a unified and mutually acceptable collaborative result between different cultures, an activity often accompanied by tensions and disagreements, requires the negotiation and management of expectations and an acknowledgement and understanding of the different cultural values. Producers and artists should make further efforts to engage with the different cultural values as well as the mutual collaborative objectives set out when embarking on a recording.

BIBLIOGRAPHY

4 Comments (3 August 2018). How Steely Dan Went Through Seven Guitarists and Dozens of Hours of Tape to Get the Perfect Guitar Solo on 'Peg'. *Open Culture* (blog). Available from: http://www.openculture.com/2018/08/steely-dan-went-seven-guitarists-dozens-hours-tape-get-perfect-guitar-solo-peg.html [Accessed 27 February 2019].

Bhamra, K. Interviewed by: Lightman, R. (2014). Southall, Middlesex (interviewed 14 August 2014).

Bhamra, K. (10 May 2019). Country & Easter mixes [email].

Burgess, R. (2013). *The Art of Music Production, the Theory and Practice*. 4th edition. New York: Oxford University Press.

Burgess, R.J. (2014). *The History of Music Production*. New York: Oxford University Press.

Buskin, R. (1999). *Insidetracks: A First-hand History of Popular Music from the World's Greatest Record Producers and Engineers*. New York: Spike.

Christian. R. (n.d.). Robin Christian. Available from: http://www.robin-christian.com/new-page-4 [Accessed 28 February 2019].

Chua, R.Y.J., Morris, M.W., and Mor. S. (2012) 'Collaborating Across Cultures: Cultural Metacognition & Affect-Based Trust in Creative Collaboration'. SSRN Electronic Journal, 2012. Available from: https://doi.org/10.2139/ssrn.1861054 [Accessed 21 February 2019].

Copleston, F.C. (1999). *A History of Philosophy, Volume 8.* Tunbridge Wells; Burns & Oats. Available at: https://www.amazon.co.uk/History-Philosophy-Bentham-Russell-v/dp/0860123014/ref=sr_1_1?keywords=9780860123019&linkCode=qs&qid=1583692390&s=books&sr=1-1 [Accessed 8 March 2020].

Cottrell, S. (2010). 'An Interview with Ben Mandelson'. *Ethnomusicology Forum* 19, no. 1: 57–68. *Academic Search Complete*, EBSCO*host* (Accessed 4 August 2014).

Farinella, D.J. (2006). *Producing Hit Records: Secrets from the Big Chair*. New York: Schirmer Trade Books. Available at: http://www.loc.gov/catdir/toc/ecip0512/2005013954.html [Accessed 24 August 2015].

Frith, S. and Zagorski-Thomas, S. (eds) (2012). *The Art of Record Production: An Introductory Reader for a New Academic Field*. Farnham: Ashgate.

Gibson, C. (2005). Recording Studios: Relational Spaces of Creativity in the City. *Built Environment (1978–)* 31, 192–207.

Glossop, M. Interviewed by: Lightman, R. (2014) Shepherd's Bush, London (interviewed 8 August 2014).

Hepworth-Sawyer, R. and Golding, C. (2011). *What Is Music Production?: A Producer's Guide: The Role, the People, the Process*. London: Focal. Available at: http://capitadiscovery.co.uk/medway-ac/items/692010 [Accessed 2 August 2015].

Hitchins, R. (2014). *Vibe Merchants: The Sound Creators of Jamaican Popular Music*. Surrey and Burlington, VT: Ashgate.

Howard, D.N. (2004). *Sonic alchemy: Visionary Music Producers and their Maverick Recordings*. Milwaukee, WI: Hal Leonard Corp.

Kerrigan, S. (2013). 'Accommodating Creative Documentary Practice Within a Revised Systems Model of Creativity'. *Journal of Media Practice* 14, no. 2, pp. 111–127, doi: 10.1386/jmpr.14.2.111_1

Massey, H. (2009). *Behind the Glass: V. 2: Top Record Producers Tell How They Craft the Hits*. San Francisco, Berkeley, CA and Milwaukee, WI, Backbeat Books.

Nolasco, S. (2018). Freddie Mercury's Pal Tim Staffell Says 'Bohemian Rhapsody' Was 'The Right Way To Do It'. *Fox News*, 9 November 2018. Available from: https://www.foxnews.com/entertainment/freddie-mercurys-pal-tim-staffell-says-bohemian-rhapsody-was-the-right-way-to-do-it [Accessed 2 March 2019].

Paxman, M. (2019). *Producer Research Question*. Correspondence with Richard Lightman [Email].

Savona, A. (2005). *Console Confessions: Insights & Opinions From the Great Music Producers*. San Francisco, CA: Backbeat.

2

Defining and developing a sonic signature in music mixing

A practice-based approach as modern-day studio mentorship

Andrea Succi

2.1 INTRODUCTION

Previous research into defining sonic signatures shows the existence of categories that they tend to fall into, based on the determining factor for their existence. Agents such as technology/equipment, places (both geographical locations and recording studios), and people (producers, record labels and audience) all contribute to the overall identity of a recording. Gottinger (2007), Seay (2016) and Zak (2001) explain how studio equipment possesses distinct tonal qualities that inevitably affect the character of the sound that is being recorded. This gets combined with the acoustic properties of the live room where the recording is being made, which denotes how a recording studio can acquire its own distinct sound and transfer it onto a record, as discussed by Schmidt Horning (2012). Likewise, the people who are involved in the recording process all have the ability to impart their own trademarks, altering the character of the final product, as explained by Gillespie (2007) and Zagorski-Thomas (2016) – the concept can be extended to audience and record industry too (Howlett, 2012a, 2012b). The research also shows how another prominent external factor that influences the imprint of a sonic signature is musical style – the so-called tropes of the genre (Zak, 2001; Zagorski-Thomas, 2010) – and, finally, the issue of creative collaboration is equally seen as significant to the development of a recording's aural footprint, with authors such as Carter (2005) and Howlett (2019) recognising the collaborative nature of the recording process and Davis (2009) warning of the difficulty in attributing the 'ownership' of a signature.

A review of key literature determines that there is no single definition of sonic signatures and that there is no currently set framework for creating one either. Sonic signatures are multifaceted agents, intrinsic in nature, but that can also be systematically developed. The issue at the heart of this study is that, currently, literary sources are only concerned with the emergence of sonic identities during the recording phase, not addressing the impact of the penultimate step of the process that is mixing, considering that mix engineers are commonly known to have a distinctive style and are hired for it. The task of mixing involves treating and combining multiple tracks of recorded, sampled or synthesised material into a multichannel (normally stereo) format (Izhaki, 2012, p.5). In the music production chain, mixing happens after the recording (or tracking) session has taken place and before the final mastering stage. It is the chance for an engineer to reassess the overall balance of each individual element in the composition, solve any problems with the tracks and apply processes and effects to the recording that enhance its sonic quality. As Izhaki (2012, pp.5–8) suggests, it is also the time for the engineer to create a final product that conveys the emotion of the recorded performance and delivers their own aesthetic vision for the song.

The deduction from the research is that out of the numerous causes for the presence of mixing trademarks, many of them are not dependent on the engineer's specific practice and others are shaped through their workflow. There is also an assumption that these traits are something that mixers become known for *through* their work and that gets attributed to them by an expert audience and the record industry at a later stage. This chapter aims to propose a system for consciously creating a mixing sonic signature, where the engineer gains awareness of their practice and builds upon it. It does so by integrating a practice-based element into the multi-methodological design of action research and autoethnography, that resembles the historical apprenticeship model of learning from a mentor. A sample of four mix engineers was chosen based on the two criteria that are most relevant to the researcher's current professional practice: style and setup. By analysing video tutorials of these engineers, a set of techniques, concepts and workflows were created and evaluated in a series of sixteen test mixes, with further evaluation and selection of ten final mixes that showcase the sonic signature developed by the author.

The emphasis on the practice-led nature of this project is important to highlight that the study puts the researcher's work at the forefront, becoming an active participant in the research. This links to the issue of measuring success and assessing the validity of the results, which is addressed by acknowledging the great degree of subjectivity that is afforded by action research and resting on the assumption that it is quite challenging to prove aesthetic choices on a universal level. Whilst action research is the primary methodology in this work, the lack of external participants posed a concern as to whether the study followed a single paradigm. The emphasis on individual self-reflection and the exploratory nature of the project resonated more with an autoethnographic framework and, therefore, the use of multiple methodologies felt more appropriate to ensure greater validity of the claims. The study relied on qualitative data collection and analysis, through both primary and secondary sources. The latter formed the starting point of the data-gathering process and consisted of academic literature and video recordings of professional mixing engineers. Primary data is in the form of video recordings of the author's mixing practice and subsequent evaluation of the footage through the technique of critical incidents.

2.2 BACKGROUND

The research background is centred around three key concepts, that are intended as sub-questions for the study, as follows:

2.2.1 What is a sonic signature and how does it relate to mixing?

The concept of sonic signature in record production is one that cannot be defined in one single, 'universal' way. Instead, it is dependent on several determining factors and on the context in which it is applied. What the research will agree on is that a sonic signature is an identifiable characteristic in the sound of a piece of recorded music, which originates from different aspects. The idea of 'having a sound', seen as an aesthetic trait, became part of the vocabulary of popular culture in the early 1960s and is a concept that is commonly associated with "the names of record producers, record companies, and urban centres of musical production" (Théberge, 1997, pp.192–193). Zagorski-Thomas (2016, p.68) provides an overview of the notion of signature sounds, suggesting that they would have to be defined according to their schematic nature, so based on what features apply in any given circumstance. The author recognises the impact of technology, spatial characteristics, types of sound sources, instruments, processing, and even certain elements in the musical performance itself, as agents that can influence the sound of a record and leave an audible mark. Seay (2012) quotes John Covach:

> Different recordings have what might be thought of as 'sonic signatures' – features that mark them in terms of where and when they were recorded, as well as by whom.
>
> (Seay, 2012)

Being that an overall definition is difficult to attain, the chosen framework for gaining a holistic understanding of sonic signatures is to break them down into the various categories that emerged through the research and explore the impact of each of them.

Equipment

The idea that a piece of equipment possesses a distinct sonic identity has been extensively documented. Gottinger (2007) based his doctorate work on the sound properties of every electronic component in a recording studio's signal chain, describing how 'harmonic distortion' is the responsible factor for the characteristic sound of recording equipment. This distortion happens with every element that is introduced throughout the recording process and, as the author mentions (ibid., p.35), the colouration that equipment brings to the original sound source is oftentimes desirable and purposely chosen for a particular application. Gottinger (2007, p.384) states that, originally, sonic signatures were caused by the limitations of the available technology and, as a result, they became an integral part of commercially successful records. Thus, nowadays, these aural properties of equipment are sought after by music professionals wanting to use them to creatively shape their trademark sounds.

The process of applying a sonic signature to a record, therefore, starts – consciously or not – with the gear choices made by an engineer or producer. Seay (2016, p.348) discusses a process of transformation of sound that takes place in a recording, explaining how, as soon as a microphone is placed in front of a source, "a translation of reality is underway" (ibid.). Moreover, the signal path leading to the recording medium, which typically may include any preamplifiers (which amplify the signal coming from a microphone), dynamic processors (such as compressors, for instance, that reduce the dynamic range of the signal) and tonal shaping tools (such as equalisers, that modify the frequency response of the signal) all add to the distortion of the sound source and create a "a new artistic reality as a new object with its own aesthetic character" (Seay, 2016, p.348). Gottinger (2007, p.252) goes a step further by taking into account the role of loudspeakers in this process of sound colouration, explaining how studio monitors will reproduce the sonic traces accumulated throughout the entire signal chain, as well as then adding their own. Zak (2001, p.115) also warns that the sound of a recording can vary greatly when played through different speakers, leaving no absolute standard for accuracy of sound reproduction. The influence of studio monitors is particularly important at the mixing stage when final decisions on the overall tonal balance of a record have to be made based exclusively on the sound coming from the speakers. To this extent, Zak (2001, p.117) explains that to create mixes that translate well across various listening means and environments, "recordists reference their work on several monitors of differing size and quality and in different environments" (ibid.), all of which is going to contribute to the final sonic results.

It is clear that avoiding any sort of audible footprint from recording equipment is impossible and, therefore, Zak (2001, p.109) considers the process of selecting a signal chain for recording – or indeed for mixing – a task that requires aesthetic judgement, as well as technical expertise. Often, once a particular chain has been established for an artist, it will be kept consistent from one record to another – especially on lead vocals, as brought to light by Zak (2001, p.111) – implying how the colouration created by equipment plays a considerable role in determining a sonic trademark. Moore (2019, p.224) quotes producers Warren Huart and Chris Lord Alge who argue that for a mixing engineer, it is desirable to build upon an existing signature, as opposed to starting from a blank canvas. Tracking with processing, therefore, "allows the artist and producer to hear the aesthetic of the production as it is being developed" (Moore, 2019, p.223). The underlying thought here is that there is always an 'actor' behind the choices of appropriate forms of recording technology, who can actively use tools to shape the sonic fingerprint of the recording. The notion of 'actor' stems from Zagorski-Thomas' (2016) concept of 'actor-network theory' (ANT), which Paterson (2017, p.87) applies to mixing practice, stating that any elements (such as technology in this case) that are consciously allowed to influence artistic direction, gain a degree of autonomy, becoming actors that form a signature.

Places

Just as the choice of a microphone and recording chain will influence the sonic output of a record, the placement of said microphones within the space in which the session is taking place, will also greatly alter the character of the sound. It is what Gottinger (2007, p.109) refers to as 'acoustic signatures', or in other words, the distinct sound of a studio's live room. Schmidt Horning (2012, p.34) talks about the recording studio effectively becoming "the *final instrument* that is recorded" (ibid.), with engineers as far back as the 1950s acknowledging its impact on their records. This acoustic trace, coupled with the use of certain recording technology, created iconic signature studio sounds that have been documented over the years. Gottinger (2007, p.97) describes the peculiar sound of Elvis Presley's vocal as a mixture of Sun Studio's room acoustics and the slap-back echo (which is a short single repeat echo) that was added to the tracks, and similarly, Chess Records in Chicago produced recordings that bear traits of their studios' rooms mixed with the specially treated EMT 140 plate reverb unit (which adds resonance to a sound source).

Seay (2016, p.351) focused his work on the signature of Sigma Sound Studios in Philadelphia, which seemed to be a combination of the live rooms' acoustics and the use of a pre-delay in front of their EMT 140 plate reverb unit. In this case, the author refers to this combination of space and equipment as the "Sound of Philadelphia" (Seay, 2016, p.350), introducing the theory of a studio becoming responsible for the sound of an entire city, notion that he applies to the town of Nashville too (Seay, 2016, p.347). On that same wavelength, Théberge (1997, p.193) – quoting the work of William Ivey – explains that Nashville became one of the first centres to have its own labelled sound, which came from the need for creating a permanent niche (country music) within the music market in the USA. The features of this new sound were, for the most part, musical, however, a contributing factor was also, on the technical side, the emphasised sonic clarity of the recordings. The author stresses the importance of the local network of sound engineers, producers and studio musicians that created this system, which became so structured that it could later also be replicated in other cities (Théberge, 1997, p.194).

Zagorski-Thomas (2012, p.60) expanded on this idea by analysing differences between the sound of records made in the UK and the USA in the 1970s. Other than some aesthetic considerations, the main differentiations came down to the use of space (i.e. acoustic treatment and microphone placement) in the recordings, as well the sounds of the available technology being quite distinct between the two countries; differences that the author found in mixing practice as well.

Thus, the acoustic signature is another sonic characteristic of a recording that cannot be eliminated and, in fact, for most established commercial studios, it is an integral component of their output, which distinguishes one live room from another. Hodgson (2019, p.43) explains that "when recordists add a room mic to a mix, they also add the acoustic character of the tracking environment" (ibid.). It comes back down to the 'actor' behind the planning of the session to choose which spatial fingerprint is going to be the most appropriate for a particular project – a decision which, together with the equipment used, can immediately give the record an initial trademark. Zak (2001, p.100) describes how much of Phil Spector's 'wall of sound' production was derived from the acoustics of Gold Star Studios in Hollywood, where the producer kept going back to incorporate the sound of those spaces into his records. The author quotes Larry Levine, one of Spector's engineers, who revealed that once Spector moved away from that particular studio, his production style changed too.

Gottinger (2007, p.107) explains that a room with a strong frequency imbalance can even mask signatures created by the equipment used, becoming the most audible sonic trace in the record. When it comes to mixing, having a control room that gives a neutral response and avoids colouration is paramount, to create mixes that sound consistent across different environments (Zak, 2001, p.104). Nonetheless, there will still be a degree of influence from the mixing space, which becomes part of the engineer's signature.

People

The sonic traces that accumulate throughout the recording process are ultimately linked with the people who are working on the session and, for the most part, it is the producer out of the studio personnel that is attributed to a sonic trademark. In a typical major label scenario, the producer would be responsible for overseeing all aspects of the project, often being involved in the production and arrangement of the musical material too, however, rarely taking on full engineering duties during the tracking and, later, mixing of the record. Separate recording and mixing engineers are respectively hired for these tasks. In smaller studios or independent productions, the lines are much more blurred, and tasks tend to cross over. Although existing literature almost exclusively focuses on producer signatures, the principles discussed in this section apply to mix engineers too, as they are similarly selected for their unique identity.

Trademarks of music producers come in different forms. For Zagorski-Thomas (2016, p.67), the key is for an individual to "consistently do something dramatically different from 'common practice'" (ibid.), be it innovatively using technology or space, or calling the same session musicians for every project. Gillespie (2007, pp.30–39) recognises the existence of musical forms of sonic signatures for producers, which he considers a "means of identifying production authorship on a purely sonic level within musical texts" (Gillespie, 2007, p.30). These could be certain types of sounds (both instruments and/or effects) that are continually utilised in a particular producer's recordings, as well as rhythmic or structural patterns across different tracks, or even embedding samples of other songs into their own productions, for instance.

Carter (2005) acknowledges the presence of 'people' signatures too, describing how certain producers have immediately identifiable sounds, echoing the argument presented so far that most producers' identity will be a combination of musical, aesthetic and technological elements – the recurring example being Phil Spector's 'wall of sound'. The author quotes Dallas Austin: "Some producers have a sound . . . and they do every other record out of that same sound. So, it develops a brand as far as the sound is concerned" (Carter, 2005). Zak (2001, p.178) calls this the producer 'auteur', who very much becomes an artist in their own right, bringing a larger vision and extra 'voice' to the project. However, Carter (2005) also takes a contrasting stance to the notion of the producer being the sole 'sonic architect' of a record, explaining that their exact role varies depending on the needs of the project and, in some instances, a producer may have little to no impact on the sonic outcome of the record, depending on their level of technical expertise and modus operandi. This introduces the thought that the studio process is a collaborative one in nature and the extent to which this affects the imprint of a sonic signature is analysed further in this work.

The research into sonic signatures brought to light a paper by Jarrett (2012) that introduces an antagonistic view to the main point discussed here, and that is that a producer should *not* leave a sonic imprint – it is the idea of the 'invisible producer' (Jarrett, 2012, p.129). According to the author, it is best to let the music and the artistry shine through, without any audible contribution from the recordists. Whilst it can be agreed that the primary role of the producer is to be a "servant of the project" (Zak, 2001, p.178), and that it is not always desirable to be a producer 'auteur', the firm belief is that sonic traces are inevitably left along the recording process, as it has been demonstrated through the literature reviewed thus far. Howlett (2012a, p.189) shares his point of view in response to Jarrett's thoughts, which neatly sums up the concepts explored in this work. The role of a producer can best be described as a 'nexus' – or link – between "the creative inspiration of the artist, the technology of the recording studio, and the commercial aspirations of the record company" (Howlett, 2012a, p.189). In essence, the producer (and this encompasses anyone else involved in the recording process) can never really be transparent, as the choices of recording studio, gear, engineering, arrangement, and even selection of the best performances, require a great deal of critical evaluation and, consequently, "affect the character of the outcome" (Howlett, 2012a, p.189).

Business

The last category in this taxonomy of sonic signatures links on from the concept of the producer as 'nexus', as explained by Howlett (2012a, p.190, 2012b). It refers to a series of external factors that may influence the record-making process and which ultimately play a role in the sonic outcome. Howlett (2012a, p.190) describes the limitations imposed by a record company, for example, on a project: financial constraints, which determine the choice of studio, as well as the pressure to produce a record that will meet commercial standards and aspirations. Although these are not factors that can actively create a sonic signature, they still can have an indirect effect on the people involved in the project and impact on the overall footprint. This thought extends to the work of a mixing engineer, as, generally, a final mix is a combination of the mixer's original vision, together with the feedback received from the artist or record label, and anyone else involved in the project. Conducting mix revisions means allowing other people's opinions (which perhaps are signatures in itself?) to sway sonic results.

Another concept that fits well in this category comes from Bromham (2017, p.251), who discusses the practice of selling a famous mixing engineer's sonic trademark. This could be through releasing a series of signature audio plugins, all containing presets created by established mixers. The idea of selling a particular sound is not unreasonable and gives the user more possibility of experimentation, however, what Bromham is concerned about, is the way this model promotes the use of presets to achieve a particular sound or style, instead of relying on knowledge and understanding of mixing practice. The author also warns of what selling a pre-existing sonic signature can do to developing a unique one: "It could be argued that the use of presets limits creativity. A paint-by-numbers approach to using presets in mixing can easily produce similar generic results in people's mixes" (ibid).

2.2.2 Is there as degree of stylistic (genre-specific) influence into a mixer's sonic signature?

Having a sonic signature essentially means having a unique style that defines one's work. Style in music is not just about aesthetics, it is also linked to the concept of genre. In order to fully understand how to create an original sonic identity, there needs to be an analysis of the degree to which genre influences the development of a signature sound. On the whole, producers (and mixers) typically get chosen for the particular style of music they have specialised in (Gillespie, 2007, p.28), and Burgess (2013, p.210) recommends choosing a niche, rather than 'genre-hopping', to maximise commercial success and industry recognition. The same principle applies to recording studios, whereby artists or labels may select a particular studio for the affinity with their genre (Schmidt Horning, 2012, p.36).

When discussing mixing specifically, Zak (2001, p.143) recognises the impact of musical style as one of the determining facets of building a mix. Certain aspects are considered conventions for a style of music, which influence the development of a sonic signature, in the sense that they are characteristics that need to be followed to conform with the tropes of the genre. Although not strictly mixing related, Zak (2001, p.153) makes the case of the Roland 808 kick drum being considered the sound of hip-hop.

This particular instrument (or any of its variations) is a determining attribute of the genre, which must be taken into consideration when building a sonic identity in this type of music.

Similarly, staging concepts also follow stylistic conventions, with genres such as heavy metal featuring distorted guitars as the most prominent element of the mix, to quote an example brought forward by Zak (2001, p.159). Zagorski-Thomas (2010, p.253) talks about 'functional staging', explaining how 1970s music was mixed according to the place where it was going to be reproduced. For the case of disco music, to overcome the issue of added reverberation originating from the large rooms of nightclubs, engineers would keep drum sounds very dry to accentuate the rhythmical elements of the tracks and add artificial ambience to parts that welcomed audience participation, such as vocal hooks and handclaps. Conversely, rock music was typically being consumed on small home hi-fi systems, therefore engineers would add considerable amounts of ambience to simulate the stadium rock experience (Zagorski-Thomas, 2010, pp.253–256). The author's concepts on staging not only show the impact of genre on mixing a record, but also demonstrate how consumers influence the production of recorded music, which refers back to the business category.

This discourse raises the question of where 'authenticity', as theorised by Moore (2002), connects with genre and sonic signatures. Zagorski-Thomas (2010, p.259), Morey (2009), Shepherd (2007) and Brackett (1995) all acknowledge that following stylistic traditions leads to authenticity in that particular genre, therefore, producing and mixing music according to style conventions is desirable to create an end product that is considered genuine by the consumers and the music industry. Brackett (1995, p.77) brings the example of country music and how authenticity there starts with the lyrics of a song and is then closely followed by the "forward placement of the vocal in the recorded mix" (ibid.) – a guideline to adhere to when mixing in this genre.

2.2.3 Are mixing sonic signatures the result of a collaborative or individual process?

Zak (2001, p.163) states: "Making records is intrinsically a collaborative creative process, involving the efforts of a 'composition team' whose members interact in various ways" (ibid.). With this in mind, and considering that every person who contributes to the making of a record can add their own sonic footprint, who does the signature that is heard on the final product belong to? Carter (2005) also recognises that the production process is a collaborative one and as a direct result of that, there is a sonic residue left by *every* contributor along the way.

> Responsibility for both sonic and aesthetic outcomes is, at the most basic level, the result of a creative collaboration between the composer and/or arranger, performer, recording and mastering engineers, producer and, in some cases, record company.
>
> (Carter, 2005)

It needs to be noted that Carter (2005) applies this concept to popular music only and acknowledges that other genres, such as electronic music, are characterised by more individualistic work. Nevertheless, Sawyer (2017, p.147) argues that collaboration facilitates the creative process, leading to overall greater results. The author also underlines the importance of collaboration over a period of time to achieve what he calls 'group genius', which translates to the production process in music. In a follow-up paper to the 'producer as nexus' concept, Howlett (2019, p.91) identifies the collaborative engagement that takes place during every step of the recording process, including mixing. The author infers that this kind of creative teamwork leads to a more satisfactory outcome.

One last insight into the concept of collaboration comes from Davis (2009), who admits that obtaining the 'creative ownership' of a sonic signature is an arduous task, given the many inputs from people throughout, and, therefore, the answer to this question has to be left slightly open-ended at this point. It is clear from the literature that the final signature is not purely the result of an individual's work, but assessing whose trace is the most prominent has yet to be established. It could be argued that a mixing engineer, being the penultimate figure involved in the shaping of the overall sound, leaves a 'fresher' and more distinguishable footprint.

2.2.4 Evaluation

The taxonomy of sonic signatures presented in this work helps to understand some of the elements that characterise them and the overarching concept is that they exist through the combination of *all* those individual parts added together. Everything that happens throughout the recording process and everyone who is involved in it leaves a trace, which shapes the overall sonic identity of the music. It comes down to a combination of individuals (musicians, producers, engineers) creatively collaborating in a particular recording studio, in a particular location, using particular equipment, whilst also adhering to stylistic conventions. Thus, in the case of a mixing engineer, creating a sonic signature means considering all these aspects and applying them to their own practice, making informed choices of equipment, workflows and techniques. This idea is summarised through Table 2.1, showing how crafting a signature is dictated by both external and internal factors.

Table 2.1 External and internal factors defining a mixing engineer's sonic signature

External Factors	**Internal Factors**
Equipment	Aesthetic Vision
Control Room / Studio	Professional Background / Training
Production Team / Colleagues	Personal Background
Client Revisions	
Genre	

2.3 DEVELOPING A FRAMEWORK FOR CREATING A SONIC SIGNATURE

2.3.1 The modern-day studio mentorship

Given that there are so many aspects influencing a sonic identity, creating a definitive one is unlikely. A change of genre, gear and workflow, for instance, would automatically impact on one's trademark. It seems more appropriate to work towards shaping the signature that is most relevant to one's current professional practice, allowing for it to develop and adapt as circumstances vary. With this in mind, the proposed model for crafting a signature is to follow a practice-based approach involving a variant of the studio apprenticeship method. Traditionally, engineers would acquire their mixing skills through assisting their mentor – assimilating tacit knowledge through practical experience in the studio (Horning, 2004, p.707). This way of learning is regarded as instrumental to the development of an engineer's career (Horning, 2004, p.719) and is considered a determining component in the creation of a sonic identity (Seay, 2012). Therefore, referring back to Table 2.1, the intention is to build upon the internal factors, expanding on the engineer's training by following their mentors and utilising that as the vehicle to form the basis of their own signature. The twist on the old model that is presented in this project sees the analysis of online video tutorials from professional engineers, in which mix sessions get broken down and concepts and workflows are explained in detail. Choosing mentors is a critical feat, as there are a great number of tutorials available. The rationale for this is to utilise genre and setup as criteria, selecting engineers who work with the same style of music and similar equipment, as well as using a comparable workflow, to the researcher. In the case of this particular project, the genre niche is country/pop music and the setup is ITB (in the box) mixing, which involves working entirely inside a DAW (digital audio workstation – software), as opposed to using hardware equipment.

2.3.2 Results from the studio mentorship phase

Analysing video recordings of tutorials from the selected sample of four mixing engineers (Mix With The Masters, 2019a, 2019b, 2019c, 2019d and pureMix.net, 2019a, 2019b, 2019c), provided technical knowledge, concepts and workflows to later test in the creative mix practice phase, following the model of learning from a mentor. In these videos, the engineers essentially share a broken-down account of their sonic signature, explaining the key elements and mixing decisions that lead to their trademark sound. The chosen engineers were F. Reid Shippen, Andrew Scheps, Chris Lord-Alge (CLA) and Michael Brauer. The results from this analysis are presented in Table 2.2 and only show the characteristics that are considered to be most representative of the mixer's signature. Specific technical concepts, such as plug-in/outboard gear choices and parameters were also noted in the videos' examination but omitted from this table in an effort to generalise findings and present a blueprint for mix analysis.

Table 2.2 Results from video tutorials analysis

	F. Reid Shippen	Andrew Scheps	Chris Lord-Alge	Michael Brauer
Setup	Hybrid	ITB	Hardware	Hybrid
Genre – Country/Pop?	Yes	Yes	Yes	Yes
Workflow	- Vocals first, then follows session. - Has outboard gear set to same settings and mixes 'into' it.	- Drums first and vocal last. - Parallel compression is the preferred tool.	- Drums first and vocals last. - Console approach: routing is setup and ready to use. - Fixed outboard settings.	- Drums first and vocals last. - Console approach: set routing with multi-bus technique. - Fixed outboard settings.
Dynamic Processing	- Vocal sent to four pre-determined compressors, then blended.	- Multiple parallel compressors on drums, vocals and bass. - Multi-band compression trick on vocals.	- Compression from console or outboard. A lot of the time the compressors are used only to add character.	- Vocal sent to four pre-determined compressors, then blended. - Parallel compression used for tone.
Tonal Shaping	- Heavy use of high-pass filters. - Heavy use of harmonic colouration.	- EQ used sparingly and to add character. - Heavy use of harmonic colouration.	- Heavy use of high-pass filters. - Generally very aggressive EQ.	- EQ used sparingly and to add character. - Heavy use of harmonic colouration.
Spatial Processing	- Haas effect on guitars. - Reverbs or delays to add ambience on top of general stereo reverb.	- Minimal use of reverb and delays.	- Heavy use of reverbs and delays. - Multiple reverbs for tone.	- Heavy use of reverbs and delays. - Multiple reverbs for tone.

Staging	Prefers LCR-style panning (100% left, centre, 100% right).	Leaves panning and levels as they are on original session.	Conventional panning, even spread across stereo field.	Conventional panning, even spread across stereo field.
Automation	Light. Would rather build the dynamic.	Light. Would rather use clip gain.	Heavy. Both on mix and FX returns.	Heavy. Both on mix and effect returns.
Use of Drum Samples	Yes – to reinforce kick, snare and cymbal hits.	No	Yes – to reinforce kick and snare.	Yes – to reinforce kick and snare.
Special Processing	Parallel compressor for the whole mix ('Back Bus'), blended into 2-Bus.	Parallel compressor for everything except drums ('Rear Bus'), blended into 2-Bus.	Parallel EQ and widener on whole mix to boost certain sections.	Parallel compressor for certain elements of the mix, blended into 2-Bus.

2.3.3 Integrating the practical element

The practical element of the project included producing sixteen test mixes (four per engineer), aimed at exploring the different aspects that emerged in the previous phase – either a specific technique, or generally speaking a mixing workflow, or even theoretical concepts. The material for twelve out of the sixteen test mixes was obtained through free commercial multitracks sourced online from Dueling Mixes (2019), David Glenn Recording (2019), Cambridge MT (2019), Telefunken Elektroakustik (2019) and MixOff Forum (2019). The remaining four sessions were obtained through a colleague's own recording project. The mixing sessions were filmed, producing visual accounts of the creative practice, which were subsequently analysed, to assess the outcome of each session. The idea of filming the sessions was inspired by Davis (2009) and Anthony (2017), who utilised this ethnographic approach in both their studies in a similar fashion. Evaluating the footage enabled the extrapolation of salient moments in the mixing process where the set objectives for that session had been achieved (or not achieved). The process of video analysis was facilitated by keeping a journal whilst mixing, noting any key events or thoughts.

2.3.4 Results from the practical phase

Table 2.3 presents a detailed description of the processes that were evaluated in the test mix phase, dividing them by engineer and preference.

On the whole, processes that appeared useful from the text mix phase were (1) the console approach to setting up and carrying out a mix, (2) the greater use of parallel processing, (3) and the use of harmonic distortion.

The console approach follows CLA and Brauer and enables the implementation of a structure in ITB mixing too. It was extremely useful having the entire mix laid out in such a way that a certain number of auxiliary track always corresponded to the same instrument, for example, and that all sends were already pre-assigned – it made the mixing process a lot quicker and smoother, minimising time spent adjusting the signal routing and just focusing on performing the mix. In addition to this, using the same plug-in emulation of an SSL 4000 E console channel strip across all tracks seemed to add a certain colour and glue to the mix, especially in the low end of the song. The specific plugin was the Brainworx bx_console SSL 4000 E (Plugin Alliance, 2019), which was created in collaboration with SSL and features TMT (Tolerance Modeling Technology), that faithfully emulates the character of each of the seventy-two channels of the original console, giving slight variations between the channels, as would be expected in the hardware.

The increased parallel processing was inspired by all four engineers, with the implementation of both dynamic and tonal tricks. The main advantage here was that sharing parallel processes across various elements of the mix increases the interaction between those elements, giving the song more 'life', whilst also being less intrusive than applying those same processes directly onto the tracks.

Modern-day studio mentorship

Table 2.3 Evaluation of processes carried out in the test mixes phase

	Positive	Negative
F. Reid Shippen	- Use of drum samples - 'Back Bus' (Parallel Mix Bus) - Use of harmonic distortion - Haas effect as a widener - Starting mix with vocals	- Not enough use of reverb - Panning LCR is too extreme, too much gap between centre and sides of the mix - Not enough use of automation to make the mix grow dynamically
Andrew Scheps	- 'Rear Bus' (Parallel Mix Bus) - Working at low volumes - Parallel processes on drums (compression and saturation) - Parallel widener effect - Multi-band compression trick on vocals - Favouriting delays over reverbs - Gated snare reverb	- Building mix entirely on parallel processes makes it difficult to manage levels and makes it too aggressive - Starting with drums and working in solo means having no sense of context - Lacking samples to reinforce drums - Not enough use of automation or effects
Chris Lord-Alge	- Use of drum samples - Console approach in DAW - Parallel EQ and widener on whole mix - Extensive use of automation and effects	- EQ approach too aggressive - Lack of dedicated reverbs
Michael Brauer	- Use of drum samples - Console approach in DAW - Multiple parallel compression on vocals - Use of harmonic distortion - Spring reverb on guitars - Extensive use of automation	- The Multi-Bus approach is difficult to manage, would take some time to master, but generally speaking, does not suit my aesthetic.

Finally, the use of harmonic distortion, mostly influenced by Shippen, really changed the colour of the mixes, becoming an extra tool to shape the tone and character of the song.

Other elements had been explored previously, such as the use of drum samples to reinforce kick and snare and starting the mix with vocals. Both these processes are typical of country/pop music, which is a contributing factor as to why they had been integrated before this study. Interestingly, out of the four mentors, F. Reid Shippen was the only mixer to feature both these processes in his practice and he is almost exclusively involved with country music, thus showing a tendency to follow style conventions. In a similar fashion, producer Phil Harding (2017, p.65) shares his preference for mixing 'top down', that is starting with the lead vocal. This is largely due to his involvement with 1990s boy-band pop music, which stylistically requires the vocals to be the most prominent feature to please the audience and industry.

The final part of the practical process involved selecting ten out of the sixteen test mixes, which, following the evaluation stage, are the closest to reaching the overall sonic aesthetic sought after in this work and expanding on those mixes in a process of triangulation, where all the successful concepts and techniques were explored further. This enabled the creation of a mixing template to work from, which forms the basis of the current sonic signature. The advantage of following a pre-determined structure when mixing ITB is underlined by Paterson (2017, p.87), who introduces the concept of 'mixMacros', that is a set of plug-in chains, automation curves and signal routing configurations, that can be replicated across different mixes to ensure a sense of continuity in the sound and mixing style. It is rooted in the idea of an engineer continually turning to the same hardware equipment, for instance, or utilising a particular analogue console. Harding (2017, p.74) echoes the importance of a mixing template, devised through the author's '12-step mixing program', which much like this study, seeks to offer a system for structuring a mix – the emphasis in that case being on mixing pop music. Thus, the mixing template provides a tangible account of a sonic signature and forms the foundation of it, holding information about the mixer's preferred workflow, gear, and overall aesthetic. The intention is to keep updating the template along the way, as elements of this aural fingerprint will develop over time.

2.4 CONCLUSION

This chapter defined the concept of sonic signatures and focused on identifying their role in music mixing, proposing a structure for analysing one's own professional practice and implementing a sonic trademark in their work.

Having a recognisable sound is a desirable trait for a mixing engineer and the development of this sonic identity comes from a mixture of external and internal factors. It is valuable for the engineer to be aware of how their current equipment and working environment actively influence the sound of their mixes; how there are sonic residues left by the earlier actors of the recording process; and how stylistic conventions and industry/consumer expectations further dictate their work. These external factors are then combined with the ones that come from within the mixer, namely their aesthetic vision, musical upbringing and training, all of which lead to the engineer making informed choices about their mixing practice. The internal factors, particularly the training aspect, are the ones that the mixer can use to consciously shape their signature. In this study, the proposed model for this was to follow a practice-based approach, through a modern-day version of the traditional studio mentorship method. It involved analysing the work of influential established mixers, testing and evaluating elements of their workflow and practice, in order to come up with a set of technical concepts (a template) that provides the starting point of the engineer's sonic signature. It has become apparent through this project how a big component of a mixing engineer's signature is, in fact, their workflow and having a template can ensure this sonic mark keeps being imprinted onto their mixes. The goal is for the template to keep evolving as circumstances change, as there is no definitive signature, only one that is relevant to one's current working situation.

Whilst the focus of this project was the subject of mixing, in an attempt to conceptualise mixing practice and contribute to academic knowledge in this field, the belief is that this structure can be applied to other music areas as well. The study encourages professionals to reflect on their practice and understand the factors and processes that influence it, whilst also making conscious decisions about what elements they can take from their mentors and implement in their workflow, to develop an identity and a trademark sound. The proposition is that a signature can be actively crafted by following a systematic process and the framework utilised in this project lays the foundation to what is going to be an ongoing study in the field.

REFERENCES

Anthony, B. (2017) 'Mixing as a Performance: Creative Approaches to the Popular Music Mix Process', *Journal on the Art of Record Production*, (11). Available at: https://www.arpjournal.com/asarpwp/mixing-as-a-performance-creative-approaches-to-the-popular-music-mix-process/ (Accessed: 31 August 2019).

Brackett, D. (1995) *Interpreting Popular Music*. Cambridge; New York: Cambridge University Press.

Bromham, B. (2017) How Can Academic Practice Inform Mix Craft? in: *Mixing Music*. Edited by R. Hepworth-Sawyer and J. Hodgson. New York; London: Routledge., pp. 245–256.

Burgess, R.J. (2013) *The Art of Music Production: The Theory and Practice*. Fourth edition. Oxford; New York: Oxford University Press.

Cambridge MT (2019) *Mixing Secrets For The Small Studio (Cambridge Music Technology) | Free Multitrack Download Library*. Available at: http://www.cambridge-mt.com/ms-mtk.htm (Accessed: 1 September 2019).

Carter, D. (2005) 'Well Past Time: Notes on a Musicology of Audio Recording Production', in: *Art of Record Production Conference*, Griffith University, Brisbane. Available at: https://www.artofrecordproduction.com/aorpjoom/arp-conferences/arp-archive-conference-papers/17-arp-2005/57-carter-2005 (Accessed: 3 September 2019).

Davis, R. (2009) 'Creative Ownership and the Case of the Sonic Signature or, "I'm listening to this record and wondering whodunit?"', *Journal on the Art of Record Production*, (4). Available at: https://www.arpjournal.com/asarpwp/creative-ownership-and-the-case-of-the-sonic-signature-or-%e2%80%98i%e2%80%99m-listening-to-this-record-and-wondering-whodunit%e2%80%99/ (Accessed: 29 August 2019).

Dueling Mixes (2019) *Dueling Mixes*. Available at: https://www.duelingmixes.com/ (Accessed: 1 September 2019).

Gillespie, M. (2007) *'Another Darkchild Classic': Phonographic Forgery and Producer Rodney Jerkins' Sonic Signature*. MMus Thesis. Université Laval Québec.

Glenn, D. (2019) *David Glenn Recording*. Available at: https://www.davidglennrecording.com/ (Accessed: 1 September 2019).

Gottinger, B. (2007) *Rethinking Distortion: Towards a Theory of 'Sonic Signatures'*. PhD Thesis. New York University.

Harding, P. (2017) Top-Down Mixing – A 12-Step Mixing Program, in: *Mixing Music*. Edited by R. Hepworth-Sawyer and J. Hodgson. New York; London: Routledge.

Hodgson, J. (2019) *Understanding Records: A Field Guide to Recording Practice*. New York: Bloomsbury Academic, pp. 62–76.

Horning, S.S. (2004) 'Engineering the Performance: Recording Engineers, Tacit Knowledge and the Art of Controlling Sound', *Social Studies of Science*, 34(5), pp. 703–731. doi: 10.1177/0306312704047536.

Howlett, M. (2012a) *The Art of Record Production: An Introductory Reader for a New Academic Field*. Edited by S. Frith and S. Zagorski-Thomas. Burlington, VT: Ashgate.

Howlett, M. (2012b) 'The Record Producer as a Nexus', *Journal on the Art of Record Production*. Available at: https://www.arpjournal.com/asarpwp/the-record-producer-as-nexus/ (Accessed: 26 August 2019).

Howlett, M. (2019) *Art of Record Production: Creative Practice in the Studio*. Edited by S. Zagorski-Thomas et al. London; New York: Routledge.

Izhaki, R. (2012) *Mixing Audio: Concepts, Practices and Tools*. 2nd ed. Amsterdam; Boston: Focal Press.

Jarrett, M. (2012) *The Art of Record Production: An Introductory Reader for a New Academic Field*. Edited by S. Frith and S. Zagorski-Thomas. Burlington, VT: Ashgate.

Mix With The Masters (2019a) *Andrew Scheps | Halloway 'Crossfire' | Deconstructing a Mix #7 | Mix With The Masters*. Available at: https://mixwiththemasters.com/dm7 (Accessed: 1 September 2019).

Mix With The Masters (2019b) *Chris Lord-Alge | Carrie Underwood 'Smoke Bereak' | Deconstructing a Mix #27 | Mix With The Masters*. Available at: https://mixwiththemasters.com/dm27 (Accessed: 1 September 2019).

Mix With The Masters (2019c) *Michael Brauer | Elle King 'Ex's & Oh's' | Inside the Track #3 | Mix With The Masters*. Available at: https://mixwiththemasters.com/itt3 (Accessed: 1 September 2019).

Mix With The Masters (2019d) *Michael Brauer | Mixing Setup #1 | Mix With The Masters*. Available at: https://mixwiththemasters.com/ms1 (Accessed: 1 September 2019).

MixOff Forum (2019) *MixOff Forum*. Available at: http://mixoff.org/index.php (Accessed: 2 September 2019).

Moore, A. (2002) 'Authenticity as Authentication', *Popular Music; Cambridge*, 21(2), p. 209.

Moore, A. (2019) *Producing Music*. Edited by R. Hepworth-Sawyer, J. Hodgson, and M. Marrington. New York: Routledge.

Morey, J. (2009) 'Arctic Monkeys – The Demos vs. The Album', *Journal on the Art of Record Production*, (4). Available at: https://www.arpjournal.com/asarpwp/arctic-monkeys-the-demos-vs-the-album-2/ (Accessed: 29 August 2019).

Paterson, J. (2017) *Mixing Music*. Edited by R. Hepworth-Sawyer and J. Hodgson. New York; London: Routledge.

Plugin Alliance (2019) *Brainworx bx_console SSL 4000 E, Plugin Alliance*. Available at: https://www.plugin-alliance.com/en/products/bx_console_ssl_4000_e.html (Accessed: 3 September 2019).

pureMix.net (2019a) *Andrew Scheps Mixing Template | pureMix.net*. Available at: https://www.puremix.net/video/andrew-scheps-mixing-template.html (Accessed: 1 September 2019).

pureMix.net (2019b) *F. Reid Shippen Mixing Dierks Bentley | pureMix.net*. Available at: https://www.puremix.net/video/f-reid-shippen-mixing-dierks-bentley.html (Accessed: 1 September 2019).

pureMix.net (2019c) *Inside The Mix: Zac Brown Band w/ Andrew Scheps | pureMix.net*. Available at: https://www.puremix.net/video/inside-the-mix-zac-brown-band-with-andrew-scheps.html (Accessed: 1 September 2019).

Sawyer, R.K. (2017) *Group Genius: The Creative Power of Collaboration*. Revised edition. New York: Basic Books.

Schmidt Horning, S. (2012) *The Art of Record Production: An Introductory Reader for a New Academic Field*. Edited by S. Frith and S. Zagorski-Thomas. Burlington, VT: Ashgate.

Seay, T. (2012) 'Capturing that Philadelphia Sound: A Technical Exploration of Sigma Sound Studios', *Journal on the Art of Record Production*, (6). Available at: https://www.arpjournal.com/asarpwp/capturing-that-philadelphia-sound-a-technical-exploration-of-sigma-sound-studios/ (Accessed: 28 August 2019).

Seay, T. (2016) *Sound as Popular Culture: A Research Companion*. Edited by J.G. Papenburg and H. Schulze. Cambridge, MA: The MIT Press.

Shepherd, B. (2007) 'The White Stripes, Garage Rock and the Production of Retrospectivity', *Proceedings of the Art of Record Production Conference*, Brisbane, December 2007. Available at: http://www.artofrecordproduction.com/aorpjoom/symposiums/19-arp-2007/120-shepherd-2007 (Accessed: 10 September 2020).

Telefunken Elektroakustik (2019) 'Multitracks', *TELEFUNKEN Elektroakustik*. Available at: https://www.telefunken-elektroakustik.com/multitracks (Accessed: 1 September 2019).

Théberge, P. (1997) *Any Sound You Can Imagine: Making Music/Consuming Technology*. Hanover, NH: Wesleyan University Press: University Press of New England.

Zagorski-Thomas, S. (2010) 'The Stadium in Your Bedroom: Functional Staging, Authenticity and the Audience-led Aesthetic in Record Production', *Popular Music*, 29(2), pp. 251–266. doi: 10.1017/S0261143010000061.

Zagorski-Thomas, S. (2012) *The Art of Record Production: An Introductory Reader For a New Academic Field.* Edited by S. Frith and S. Zagorski-Thomas. Burlington, VT: Ashgate.

Zagorski-Thomas, S. (2016) *The Musicology of Record Production.* First paperback edition. Cambridge: Cambridge University Press.

Zak, A. (2001) *The Poetics of Rock: Cutting Tracks, Making Records.* Berkeley, CA: University of California Press.

3

Making records within records

Manufacturing phonographic 'otherness' in sample-based Hip Hop production

Michail Exarchos (a.k.a. Stereo Mike)

3.1 INTRODUCTION

Charles Mudede (2003) explains that in the context of Hip Hop "a turntable is forced to [...] make meta-music (music about music) instead of playing previously recorded music," and expands that the sampler is "repurposed to turn one DJ repurposing two turntables into a thousand mini DJs repurposing two thousand virtual, mini turntables." Looking at sample-based record production through such a lens highlights both the theoretical complexities inherent in pursuing a comprehensive musicological understanding of the artform, as well as the material implications this poses for its practitioners, who continue to explore alternatives to copyrighted samples as their source material. Alongside the numerous creative approaches that out of legal and financial necessity sprung out in Hip Hop practice in the early 1990s,[1] resorting to sample *construction* brings about its own set of poetic-aesthetic issues (see, for example, Exarchos, 2019). The predicament is accurately resounded by The Bomb Squad's Hank Shocklee in the following interview excerpt:

> We were forced to start using different organic instruments, but you can't really get the right kind of compression that way. A guitar sampled off a record is going to hit differently than a guitar sampled in the studio [...] So those things change your mood, the feeling you can get off of a record. If you notice that by the early 1990s, the sound has gotten a lot softer.
>
> (McLeod, 2004)

In reminiscing about his own creative reaction to the shifting sample-licensing landscape of the 1990s, the Public Enemy producer highlights two important considerations, which will remain key foci for this chapter. Firstly, he makes a clear delineation between the sonics that can be acquired from 'recordings,' as opposed to those that can be acquired from 'records.' Secondly, he associates the effect of the acquired (sampled) sonics with both *feeling* and the ensuing aesthetic (*the sound*) of Hip Hop outputs produced in an era inevitably defined by these changing practices.

The first point highlights samplists' preoccupation with phonographic sound as an essential source variable that facilitates the sample-based aesthetic. It is not a stretch to suggest that the second point, with its inferred triangle of *sonics-feeling-output*, refers to the impact the qualities of the source material will have on the practitioner's ensuing sample-based creative *process*. Shocklee's delineation, therefore, underlines that even the descriptor 'sample-based' in the context of Hip Hop music requires careful consideration and arguably only tells half the story: that of process, not of the qualities of the source. Furthermore, if all digital sonic capture can be described as a form of sampling (Kvifte, 2007), then it is essential to enquire what differentiates outputs that can be described as belonging to the sample-based aesthetic, from any other digitally recorded form of contemporary music.

The questions acquire increased urgency with the global uptake of maverick sample-creating strategies combating a worldwide crisis of access to 'raw sonic materials' in contemporary *beat-making*.[2] This is best captured by Wayne Marshall in his aptly titled article, 'Giving up Hip-Hop's Firstborn: A Quest for the Real after the Death of Sampling':

> Producers working for large record labels, enjoy production budgets that permit them to license any sample they like [. . .] Independent and largely local artists, operate well enough under the radar to evade scrutiny or harassment and continue to sample with impunity [. . .] Acts with a sizeable national, if not international, following but who lack the resources of a "major label" [. . .] find themselves in a tight spot: to sample or not, to be real or not, to be sued or not?
> (Marshall, 2006, p. 869)

The problem therefore becomes political, and the creative reaction to it—through a radical reimagining of what a *sample* can be—an ingenious survival mechanism by the beat-making community to continue practicing authentic forms of sample-based music-making.

Less, then, a collective "death of sampling" and more so "a quest for the real" (ibid.), the issues sample-*creating*-based practitioners now face become the comparisons their works will inevitably attract against an aesthetic bar set by almost four decades of phonographically sourced sample-based Hip Hop (if we consider Marley Marl's experiments with affordable samplers around 1984 as the starting point see, for example, Kajikawa, 2015, pp. 164–165). In other words, the question becomes whether self-created source objects can suffice as effective triggers to sample-based production practices; and what qualities should be infused into these source objects, should they prove inspirational to—rather than simply functional for—the beat-making process. Arguably, there was less need to discuss the phonographic qualities of a source when the source was by default phonographic. But the context framed by these alternative practices necessitates an investigation into both the source's qualities, and the mechanics of the interaction between these and ensuing sample-based processes.

Using a predominantly autoethnographic approach, I will draw insights from two creative practice stages involving, first, the construction of original samples that strive to convey phonographic signatures, and, subsequently, sample-based composition that has been inspired, facilitated by, and built from these samples. The autoethnographic interpretations will be triangulated with literary and aural analysis (of relevant discography in the case of the latter) aiming at a reflexive extrapolation of the solo discoveries within a wider beat-making context. One of the critical insights that will emerge from the autoethnographic approach, as will be shown next, is the notion of phonographic 'otherness.' Grappling with this concept, defining it, and examining its mechanics in the context of sample-based Hip Hop will provide the underlying thread to the chapter.

3.2 SOUND LITERATURE

Although a lot has been written about sample-based music practices, the majority of literature on Hip Hop focuses on the motivic aspects of what has been described as "musical borrowing" (Williams, 2013). This focus on the musical qualities of the source, and the ensuing discussion of sampling processes predominantly as means of compositional manipulation, however, miss out on essential *material* dimensions underlying the sonic phenomena that define sample-based musics. As Kyle Adams warns regarding the problems of Hip Hop analysis:

> The techniques developed for the analysis of Western art music, even when they can provide accurate descriptions of some of hip-hop's surface phenomena, often leave the analyst without a deeper sense of how hip-hop operates and why it seems to communicate so effectively with such a broad audience.
>
> (Adams, 2015, p. 118)

A number of authors, thus, have been digging deeper into sample-based poetics to arrive at more meaningful theorizations of their aesthetic effect. Many of these efforts pursue sonic (concrete) priorities over musical abstraction and explore embodied manifestations of sample-based sound—such as "gesture and impact" (Goldberg, 2004, p. 130)—to paint a more holistic picture of the perceptual phenomena on hand. Starting with Tricia Rose's *Black Noise*, her seminal analysis of Public Enemy and The Bomb Squad's late-1980s/early-1990s production processes reveals how African-American beat-makers' selection (*sampling*) and manipulation (*processing/mixing*) rationale bridges era/style-signifying phonographic qualities in source samples, with sonic utterances of political consequence in the final outputs (Rose, 1994, pp. 74–77). Yet, Rose leaves questions about the sources' qualities unanswered: "you really can't replicate those sounds" (Stephney, cited in ibid., p. 40).

In *Making Beats*, his ethnographic examination of Golden Era beat-making practices, Joseph Schloss (2014) offers an exhaustive mapping of Hip Hop producers' modus operandi, expressed as the manifestation of sonic traits collectively defining the sample-based aesthetic. Schloss discusses at length the choice of source materials (records), tools (samplers), and preferred approaches in sample-based Hip Hop composition,[3] refreshingly suggesting that "symbolic meaning (as opposed to pragmatic value within the musical system) is almost universally overstated by scholars as a motive for sampling" (ibid., pp. 135–168). Nevertheless, his technical discussion stops with the isolation of percussive sounds via filtering, and he soon returns his attention to rhythmic and melodic manipulation such as quantization and 'chopping'—the latter defined as the "practice of dividing a long sample into smaller pieces and then rearranging those pieces in a different order to create a new *melody*" (ibid., p. 151, emphasis added). Delving more scholastically into sample-based layering, Amanda Sewell (2013, pp. 26–67) constructs a detailed typology of sampling in Hip Hop, delineating samples into "structural" (main groove), "surface," and "lyric" categories, and these into further subcategories according to their source qualities and function.[4] Her typology allows for a more systematic discussion of how the juxtaposed layers in sample-based music interact, as well as their stylistic ramifications, but stops at a structural representation of sample-based layers rather than an exploration of the mechanics underlying their sonic juxtaposition and mixing.

In *Sounding Race in Rap Songs*, Loren Kajikawa (2015) fuses musical analysis with critical race theory to provide a fascinating re-reading of beat-making practices as sonic/musical representations of identity. But as the project's objective is not an examination of what defines sample-based aesthetics per se, it only goes as far as deploying surface/musical elements (motifs, rhythms) as the exemplifiers of these expressive mechanisms. Adam Krims (2000, pp. 41–54) perhaps comes closest to an effective description of sample-based phenomena with his notion of the "hip-hop sublime," which he defines as "a combination of incommensurable musical layers" that "are selectively and dramatically brought into conflict with each other." Although Krims understands "timbre [. . .] as a crucial means of organization," he nevertheless associates his notion of the sublime with layering maximalism and, thus, the project manages to accurately express the phenomenon, but not the underlying mechanics responsible for the sample-based aesthetic as a whole (ibid.).

David Goldberg (2004, p. 129) pinpoints where the missing link may lie; citing Costello and Wallace (1990, p. 85) in his chapter 'The Scratch is Hip-Hop: Appropriating the Phonographic Medium,' he offers a crucial insight: "Rap/hip-hop has been the first important American pop to use digital recording and mixing techniques in the music's *composition*, its *soul*" (emphasis in original). He goes on to attribute the defining characteristic of rap music to "spatial modification" expressed via "exploding kicks," "echoing snares, and the sometimes terrifying sonic manipulations of DJ scratches," mapping the creation (composition) and essence (soul) of the sample-based aesthetic to the interaction of sampling and *mixing* processes (Goldberg, 2004, p. 130). Combined with Mudede's interpretation of sample-based Hip Hop as meta-music, this interaction assumes exponential dimensions for the sample-*creating*-based practitioner. Not

Making records within records

only have the mixing practices of sample-based record production not received sufficient attention, but an alternative approach that involves the construction of source content first, inevitably poses questions about the mixing and manipulation of source objects that themselves require prior recording, mixing, and production development. The pursuit of the newly constructed 'phonographic' in a meta context, therefore, necessitates a bidimensional examination of mixing theory as it applies to sample-based Hip Hop from the perspective of both the 'source' and that of (its interaction with) the end output. The creative practice experiments that follow, alongside reflective insights drawn from the project's research journal, will attempt to illustrate some of these complex phenomena, the analysis drawing out what is essential about the sample-based aesthetic via the use of autoethnographic strategies.

3.3 ON 'PHONOGRAPHIC OTHERNESS'

3.3.1 Hearing otherness

The following section is extracted from a journal entry entitled 'Songwriting for Sound' and it illustrates the first of a progressive trajectory of insights that has led to coining the term 'phonographic otherness.' In it, I am reflecting on being immersed in the process of attempting to create *adequate* source material for subsequent sample-based composition:

> It hit me that what I have been doing is, creating music in order to create sound. The recent 'songs' made this clear [. . .] I have always felt that the issue was never one of borrowing motifs/phrases that gives sample-based Hip Hop its unique signature; or, I should say it is not solely a musical argument [. . .] This would not explain why samplists go for *records*, rather than *recordings*. My pursuit throughout this journey has been to understand the sonic variables that explain this differentiation. My process, it seems, has focused on creating musical excuses, so to speak, in order to be able to make *mini records*—phonographic moments, or ephemera. I have been creating riffs, jams, overdubs, even songs, as musical seeds that allow me to then create, capture, and manipulate the *sound* that carries these musical ideas [. . .] looking back at all the instruments laid down at the end of these long sessions, I see sonifying tools which needed musical ideas—musical context—in order to produce meaningful sounds that could then be captured and made phonographic [. . .] The full immersion into these moments has given the resulting objects [. . .] a musical, stylistic, and *sonic* coherency that makes them feel as *separate* entities even when they are/become part of a new beat (emphasis in original).

To illustrate this *alterity* between a sampled 'object' and the new beat that uses it, it may be worth analyzing, first, an example from discography: Westside Gunn's 'Stefflon Don' from *Supreme Blientele* (2018)—produced by SadhuGold and Hesh—provides a case of highly accentuated difference between new and sampled (previously recorded) elements. Westside Gunn's voice carries markers of contemporary recording and production techniques (close-mic recording, enhanced 'presence' and 'air' in the equalization, and compression stability) all of which differentiate it clearly from the vocal samples included in the looped phonographic sample. Whether the latter is sampled from vinyl or another format resulting in a lo-fi characteristic (or processed with the intention of sounding old and otherworldly), the combination of tremolo/delayed guitar and haunting vocals that it consists of feel decidedly 'other' to the rap, drums, and sub bass that comprise the new elements. Furthermore, the source sample sounds slowed/pitched down, which adds to the less pronounced top end of its spectral content. The two 'streams' so to speak (old and new), become clear at 0'43", when the sample momentarily cuts out.

From a mix perspective—beyond the clear spectral differences perceptible between the new (present, defined) and sampled elements (featuring less clarity, presence, and high frequency content)—there are also differences on the *depth* axis of the sonic image (as well as the 'speed' of the sounds in terms of their transient/envelope characteristics): the sample feels rather three-dimensional and infused with notable spatial resonances (particularly on the modulated guitar, but also around the vocals). The whole sonic 'bubble' of the sample—to use a visualization from Gibson (2008)—is held together by its harmonic distortion, the coloration from the master medium, the recording/mixing signal paths deployed in its making, and any playback/recording devices used during sampling. Little effort seems spent on 'gluing' the samples with the new elements (this seems intentional, part of a lo-fi statement), apart from one heavy-handed but effective strategy: the notable compression applied to the whole beat (new and old elements combined) most likely courtesy of SadhuGold's Roland SP-404 sampler (Mlynar, 2018). This strategy makes the featured sample 'pump,' expanding and contracting in terms of volume, reacting to the sub and drums, at times drowning the kick drum and, at others, allowing the hi-hat to jump out of the combined balance. The effect feels extreme but intentional, paying dues to lo-fi influences (such as RZA's production style and contemporary lo-fi Hip Hop), but also rhythmically and dynamically 'marrying' the two streams together in the end production. The sample is indeed treated as a 'featured' entity within the full beat: dynamically pumped, cut twice, kept separate, kept 'other' whilst, at the same time, integrated through the heavy compression approach. The ambience surrounding the sample expands and contracts in tandem, creating a haunting dynamic-spatial effect. The following journal entry provides a personal reflection upon the resulting sonic experience:

> This belonging together of the elements that comprise the sample, this retainment of the sonic world of the sample whilst featuring it within a new beat, and the simultaneous celebration (in terms of production choices) of its 'otherness' whilst integrating it into the new

musical context (e.g. chopping, pumping with the beat) is a defining sonic characteristic of sample-based Hip Hop. Sample-based Hip Hop borrows, features, and manipulates not elements, but full masters, expanding and reshaping complete mix 'staging'[5] that has already been committed to a master. As a form of not just music-making but also music *mixing*, sample-based Hip Hop is defined by the sound of the coming together of full mix 'stages' against manipulation possible through sample-based processes. We are actually hearing both new programming and new mixing interacting with previously committed mix stages. So, it is not just the sound of 're-imagined' sequences or phrases, but also the sound of creative ways of integrating phonographic sonic objects (whole 'mix architectures') into *meta* phonographic processes

(emphasis in original).

Perhaps, SadhuGold's collaborator, rapper Estee Nack, summarizes the effect most succinctly when describing the beat-maker's style as "some old outer space shit" (Mlynar, 2018). In this laconic—if somewhat street—characterization he zones in on two important conditions for the perception of sonic otherness, as will be examined next: manifestations of time (*old*) and space (*outer space*) featured within the sonic discourse of the sample-based composition.

3.3.2 Defining sonic otherness

I have been using the notion of phonographic 'otherness' to refer to sonic characteristics of source objects in the context of a form of music/making that has been described as meta-music (music about music) (Mudede, 2003). From an autoethnographic perspective, it is important to reflexively interpret my use of the term as a sample-*creating*-based practitioner, but also to define otherness more widely. Dictionaries range in their definitions of otherness, from "the quality or *fact* of being different" (Lexico, 2019, emphasis added) through to "being or *feeling* different in appearance or character *from what is familiar, expected, or generally accepted*" (Cambridge Dictionary, 2019, emphasis added). As may be extrapolated just from these two definitions, interpretations of otherness refer to some notion of alterity or difference, but there is no consensus on whether the inferred quality is regarded as absolute or relative. Furthermore, there are multiple understandings of the term in philosophy, psychology, sociology, and anthropology linking otherness to intersubjectivity and social identity, with implications that range from the construction of a self-image, through to attributing otherness "less to the difference of the Other than to the point of view and the discourse of the person who perceives the Other as such" (Staszak, 2008, p. 1). Applying characterizations of otherness to a group, thus, may also be driven by discrimination and so the term has assumed negative connotations in disciplines such as anthropogeography. Staszak (2008, p. 2) provides a helpful delineation, however, stating that "difference belongs to the realm of fact and otherness belongs to the realm of discourse."

For a musicological understanding of otherness, it is useful to turn to Weheliye (2005) who offers a fascinating link between the possibilities offered by the mechanical reproduction of sound (e.g. the phonograph) and notions of (inter)subjectivity as expressed by contemporary black artists. In *Phonographies: Grooves in Sonic Afro-Modernity*, he demonstrates how fictional characters in modern film/literary narratives:

> control and manage the contingencies of sonic otherness by locating it in the sounds of specific subjects [. . .] Music, and sound in general, roots subjects in their environment by making that environment audible, while the immersion that comes with the listening experience is always tied to a space from whence it originates, thereby spatially marking the sound.
>
> (ibid., pp. 111–112)

Weheliye here not only demonstrates how the process of mechanically capturing and reproducing human sounds (e.g. music) transfers the energy of a subject onto a localized source, but also illustrates the spatial implications of this sonification. Although Weheliye is primarily concerned with how the sonic reproduction of music expresses the representation of identities negotiating social spaces, it will be interesting to expand on the implications of this idea beyond music consumption/reception/playback and onto music *making*.

In his exposition of the turntable as a repurposed or estranged object, Mudede (2003) helpfully explains that: "For Heidegger, a broken object exposes its thingness; for Marx, it exposes its source, the laborer, the one who has transferred his/her body's energy into the substance of the object." The estranged, broken, or repurposed object here is the turntable—Hip Hop's original instrument—transcending from playback tool to music-making instrument, and the source it exposes is the original laborer (the musician/s) whose energy has been materially and physically engraved onto the phonographic record being manipulated. Mudede illustrates the concept on his blog by depicting Hip Hop producer Eric Sermon operating a mixing board, on top of an image of a DJ scratching a record, itself sitting above a picture of Marvin Gaye playing the piano (ibid.). The illustration could easily be reimagined to feature a beat-maker operating a sampler (with mixing functionality), itself replacing multiple turntablists manipulating/scratching a number of records, which in turn contain recordings (*productions* to be accurate) of live performances (see Figure 3.1). This visualization helps conceptualize the meta levels of sonification involved in sample-based Hip Hop, as well as an illustration of otherness as the sonic alterity of a/multiple subject/s whose essence has been transferred onto material form (the phonographic groove).

It is important to note that Weheliye (2005, pp. 111–112) ties the listening experience to a "space from whence it originates [. . .] spatially marking the sound" and that he refers to "contingencies of sonic otherness" in relation to *control*. It would not be a stretch then to reimagine

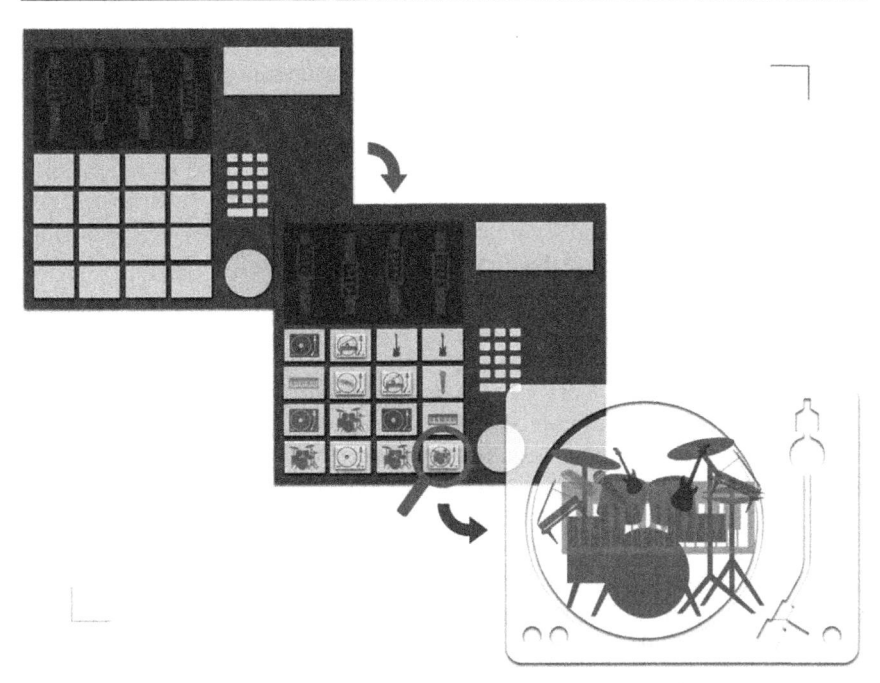

Figure 3.1 A schematic representation of a digital sampler (with mixing functionality), enabling the manipulation of multiple record segments, which in turn contain productions of live performances

a sample-based producer's (e.g. SadhuGold's) manipulation of a sonic object (for example, a previously released record), not only as an abstract/ motivic manipulation of musical material, but as a form of "discourse" (Staszak, 2008, p. 2), in the context of which the beat-maker exercises control over the material manifestations of recorded subjects' labor. The leap from social spaces to sonic objects is made possible via Weheliye's idea of sound rooting subjects in particular environments (via phonographic playback). The notion of environment, though, can be expanded beyond the spatial to all types of context 'marked' by the phonographic process (geographical location and/or hyperreal space, as well as the era, style, or time communicated by the record). The variables "marking the sound" (ibid.) become indicators of sonic otherness, a phonographic 'territory' that may resonate both time *and* space (alongside further musicological signifiers). Pickering (2012, pp. 25–26) coins the term "elsewhen" to highlight "the temporal distance brought about by recorded music" noting that: "Musical repeatability means that we are able to hear music from various previous periods and identify them, even on a decade-by-decade basis, by their *characteristic musical sounds*" (emphasis added). Simon Zagorski-Thomas (2014, p. 68) offers a useful definition of these characteristic sounds as 'sonic signatures' that "can relate to particular types of performance or programming characteristics [...] to spatial characteristics, to particular types of distortion, to the characteristics of particular types of sound sources or instruments or to the type of processing." It follows, that the sample-*creating*-based practitioner is tasked with the dual objective of not only manipulating (discoursing with, exercising control over) sonic objects that carry identifiable phonographic context, but also with creating and infusing these objects with sufficient sonic 'identity' (character), so that they feature as 'other' against the meta (sample-based) process. But how does this infusion manifest in practice?

3.3.3 Featuring otherness

For the practice-based part of this investigation an original Hip Hop production has been conceived built upon two groups of constructed samples. The two-stage process has involved creating and producing the samples as fully committed productions (records) of specific and different stylistic foci (at different times), and without a preconception of what form the ensuing Hip Hop production would take. The first of the samples has been sourced out of a multitrack production for a forthcoming release with rock band Asympt Man (of which I am a co-producing member, bassist and keyboardist, therefore ensuring access to the source material). The second sample is a segment taken from an original blues composition for which I have performed and overdubbed all the instrumental layers (drums, electric bass, electric guitar, piano and harmonica), recorded, mixed, mastered, and produced with particular attention paid to achieving late-1950s Chicago Blues timbral and spatial signatures. The two source scenarios have been purposefully included, in the first case, to allow access to individual multitrack elements and, in the second, to limit access to the full blues 'master' alone. The intention has been to create an applied context of sources being featured within a new phonographic construct, illustrating consciously featured phonographic contrast as a key aesthetic driver for the envisioned sample-based Hip Hop output. Additionally, the different degrees of access (individual multitrack elements vs. full master), allow both the construction of "aggregate" and the use of "intact" structures if one was to deploy Sewell's (2013, pp. 26–67) typological descriptors. As there has been little analysis in literature so far that focuses on the sonic (mixing) aspects of the phenomenon, the creative practice experiment has provided an opportunity to study the mechanics of sample layering beyond their structural functionality (i.e. also in terms of the mix architecture). Table 3.1 provides a summarized description of the sample layers, their types, as well as the creative processes (layering and manipulation) that have led to their mix placement in the final Hip Hop production. Figures 3.2a and 3.2b offer a schematic representation of how the individual layers are 'staged' in the final production. Video 1[6] showcases the individual sample segments as well as the complete instrumental production.

Table 3.1 provides a neat delineation between musical/abstract processes (surface phenomena) such as re-pitching, chopping, and layering noted in

Making records within records

Table 3.1 A summarized description of the sample layers, their types, as well as the creative processes (layering and manipulation) that have led to their mix placement in the final Hip Hop production. Samples 1–4 feature in the main (verse) section of the end production, while the remainder samples (highlighted by shaded cells) are added layers brought in for structural variation and the differentiation of the chorus section

Sample/type	Description	Processing
1: Aggregate main (structural)	Aggregate structure functioning as the main groove (riff/hook) of the new production, constructed out of chopped and pitched-down Hammond B3 organ, acoustic drums and electric bass performances from the Asympt Man multitrack, plus added vinyl crackle. (The syncopated organ part in the verse is replaced by a legato variation for the chorus sections)	Organ sampled through Red Panda Tensor (tape effects emulator) pedal, processed through Akai MPC X amp distortion (emulation), and sent to backwards tape reverb on the sampler; drums sampled through Tensor pedal, processed through VCA-style compression and sent to a drum room reverb on the sampler; electric bass sampled through Tensor pedal
2: Intact 1 (constituent, surface)	Intact sample taken from the blues production/master and used as a constituent surface sample. (The severe filtering focuses the spectrum on the piano part contained within the intact sample)	Late-1950s Chicago Blues (e.g. Chess Records) inspired recording, mixing, and production process, deploying real recording spaces, a tiled bathroom as echo chamber in post-production, and hardware/software emulations of vintage pre-amps, channels, and outboard processors in both the tracking and mixing phases; end output low- and high-pass filtered, then sent through drum room reverb on the sampler
3. Non-percussion live layer 1 (constituent, surface)	A directly recorded, then pitched up and reversed lead Telecaster guitar performance layer taken from another production; used as a constituent surface sample	Processed through MPC X amp distortion (emulation), and sent to backwards tape reverb and a triplet (dub) delay on the sampler

(*continued*)

Table 3.1 (continued)

Sample/type	Description	Processing
4. Voice (constituent, surface)	Vocal sample from MPC X onboard library	Sent to backwards tape reverb and a longer non-linear reverb on the sampler
5. Non-percussion live layer 2 (aggregate, structural)	A directly recorded, and then pitched up and reversed rhythm Telecaster guitar performance layer taken from the same production as sample 3 above; used as an additional layer to the main aggregate structure for variation	Processed through MPC X amp distortion (emulation), and sent to the longer non-linear reverb and the triplet (dub) delay on the sampler
6. Intact 2 (aggregate, structural)	Another intact sample taken from the blues production/master, this time used as an additional layer to the aggregate structure	Production master achieved as described in 2 above; then processed through amp distortion (emulation), equalized, and sent to the drum room reverb and triplet (dub) delay on the sampler
7. Intact 3 (aggregate, structural)	As above, equalized and filtered to accentuate the piano part, and used as an additional layer to the aggregate structure	As above, then processed through amp distortion (emulation), equalized, high pass filtered, and sent to the drum room reverb and triplet (dub) delay on the sampler

Making records within records 49

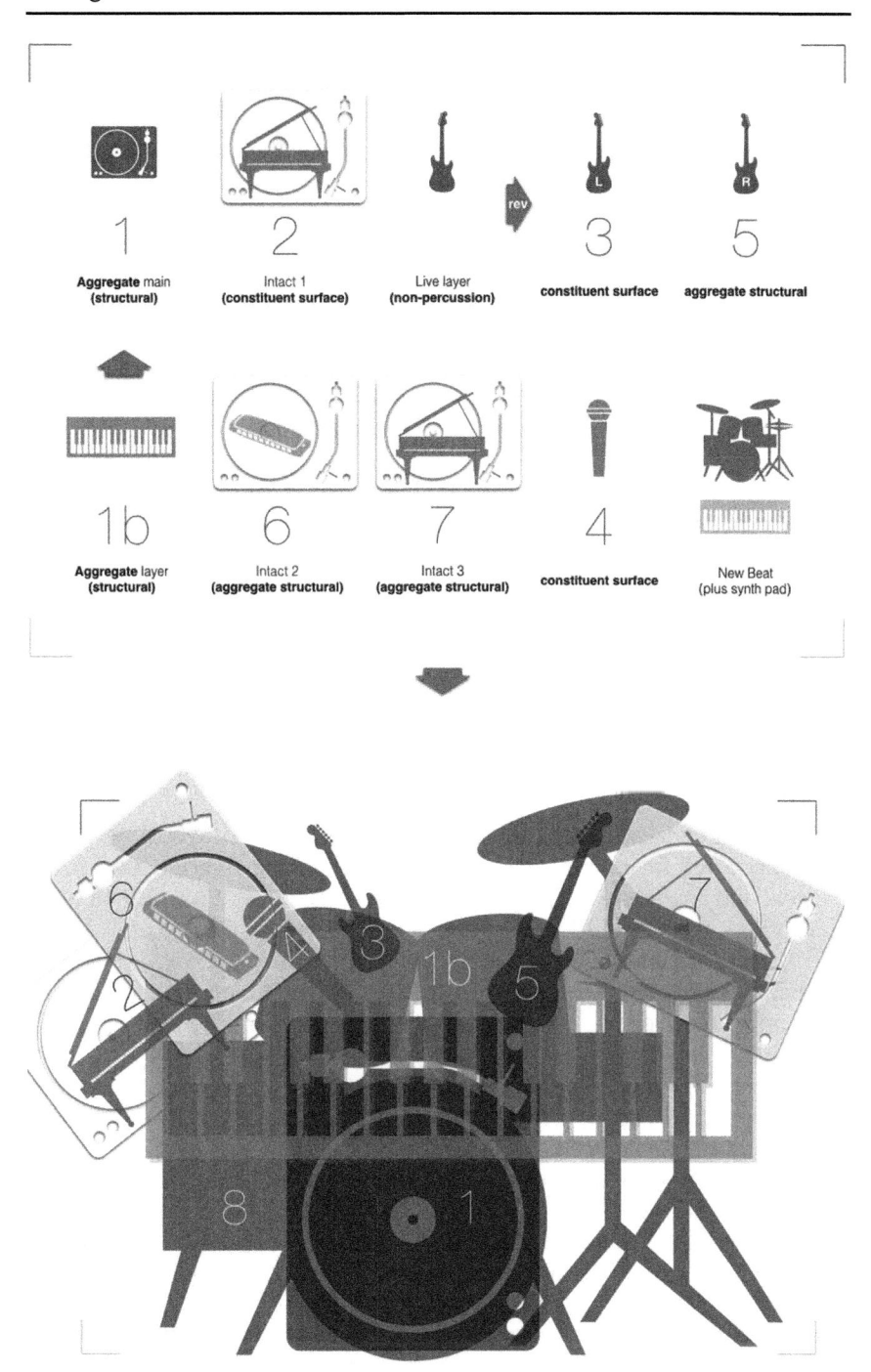

Figures 3.2a and 3.2b A schematic representation of the individual sample layers and their staging in the final sample-based production (the numbering of the sample representations corresponds to Table 3.1)

Note that samples 2, 6, and 7 are represented by a turntable framing the instrument most accentuated by filtering, indicating *intact* structures (mini records within the record) the 'description' column, and mixing/material processes (resulting in staging phenomena), such as the spatial and timbral manipulations detailed in the 'processing' column. It can be summarized that the processing choices associated with both the creation and manipulation of the samples have focused on two overarching strategies:

1. The *narrative/aesthetic*: infusing the samples with characteristic timbral and spatial qualities. For example, the blues 'master' has been created with considerable effort dedicated to reconstructing not just the spatial qualities of late-1950s Chicago blues recordings, but also timbral/tonal signatures reminiscent of the era and representative record label aesthetics. This has been achieved through the choice of instruments, recording equipment, microphones, and spaces deployed, as well as the emulation of vintage processors (and workflows) used in post-production. On the other hand, the main aggregate (structural) sample made out of band multitrack elements has been sampled through a tape effects emulation pedal and layered with vinyl crackle to construct a non-specific, yet clearly *vintage* record illusion. By way of a tape machine implied as both recording and mixing medium, and vinyl as the final/master format, the recording space shared by the drums and organ, and the matching tracking equipment signatures imprinted on both the drums and electric bass (via Universal Audio hardware compressors), have been accentuated and 'glued' back into a unified sonic experience inferring a shared phonographic time and space.
2. The *pragmatic*: ensuring the samples work as part of a coherent mix balance and fit in its overall staging. Much of the filtering, equalization, and spatial processing decisions have aimed at allowing the juxtaposed samples' full mix/master spectra, stereo images, and depth illusions to fit—in a coherent sense—over each other *and* in combination with the new beat elements (the electric guitar, drum hits, and synthesizer pads).

Returning to the notions of 'elsewhen' and 'elsewhere' as key characteristics of sonic otherness, it is clear to see that the first strategy is responsible for, initially, imbuing the source material with narrative signifiers that tie them to particular eras and styles (specific or unidentified), as well as spaces (whether geographical, actual, or hyperreal); followed by manipulating the sources to negotiate (amplify/intensify or control/limit) these sonifications in the context of the full sample-based production. The second strategy is concerned with integrating the ensuing sonic contrasts back into a phonographic whole, but the primary objective here is 'architectural'—the elements have to be mixed so that the actual frequency spectra, stereo width, and illusory depth of the 'collage' function in a sound-engineering sense.

Although the two strategies are not as clearly-cut or always consciously deployed during creative practice, this theoretical delineation helps illustrate the rationale behind the mechanics communicating aspects of sonic otherness in a phonographic context. The following table provides a typology of the perceivable sample characteristics that define this featured, phonographic otherness:

Table 3.2 A typology of sonic characteristics communicating featured 'otherness' in source samples

Sample characteristics defining featured 'otherness'	Examples
Limitations in the source's frequency range	vinyl resolution
Recording signal path colorations	microphones used, sound of mixing desk, recording media, outboard equipment
Mixing signal path colorations	sound of mixing desk, recording media used in playback mode, outboard equipment
End format/medium/master sound (coloration, distortion)	master tape, vinyl
Shared captured spaces over recorded elements	recording (live) rooms, echo chambers
Shared spaces applied in the mix/post-production	spatial processors, echo chambers
Playback devices/formats used to record samples	vinyl player, DJ mixer, YouTube/Spotify codecs
Sampling devices/formats used to record, manipulate and play back samples	phono inputs on sampler, digital extraction codec, virtual software sampler algorithm, filtering, pitch shifting
Surface noise resulting from various mechanical/magnetic production phases	vinyl crackle
Staging architecture achieved as a result of mixing decisions on three dimensions	stereo width, frequency 'height', (spatial) depth illusion
Mix-buss processing, and coloration when hardware/emulation is used	shared equalization, dynamic processing, stereo enhancement, sound of outboard
Mastering processing, and coloration when hardware/emulation is used	shared equalization, dynamic processing, stereo enhancement, sound of outboard
Purposeful accentuation of source's lo-fi-qualities	quality/resolution reduction, increase/addition of surface noise

3.4 CONCLUSIONS

The characteristics above are extracted from the aural analysis and creative practice stages of this study in an attempt to systematize the processes and ensuing signatures that infuse sources with a particular sonic identity. The resulting character differentiates them from new beat-making elements and fuels the sample-based sonic discourse by enabling the interaction of meta-process, and sources perceived as 'other.' This is the aesthetic condition that Schloss (2014, p. 159) refers to when pointing out that "to appreciate the music, a listener must hear both the original interactions and how they have been organized into new relationships with each other." Although each of these characteristics communicates some aspect of sonic otherness, it is important not to think of them as defining variables that explicitly or individually ensure its perception. Instead, collectively, they represent sonic manifestations of 'original interactions' that have taken place as part of a (mini) record-making process: it is the construction of the sources as part of a phonographic vision (a record-making context) that makes them stand out from mere 'recordings' (and, arguably, sample libraries, too), even if instrumental elements/layers end up being used in isolation by way of equalization, filtering, or access to multitracks. Albin Zak III (2018, p. 304) illustrates this quality best by providing the following disclaimer about record production after the post-war era: "Instead of simply *recording* performances, the idea was to *make records*, with the intent of imbuing the disc with a distinctive personality" (emphasis in original).

Of course, the otherness that is communicated by these sonic characteristics works in tandem with musical (harmonic, melodic, rhythmic, stylistic) coherency and structural manifestations (cuts, looping/repetition) that further tie the source utterances together. Furthermore, the difference can become accentuated by other bipolarities typically delineating contrast between sample sources and additional beat-making elements, such as: live feel versus programmed quantization (rhythmic); acoustic and/or electromechanical versus synthesized textures; analog versus digital coloration (timbral); and spatial decays shared over source elements versus the gated ambient envelopes inherent in drum hits frequently deployed for beat construction (spatial). Finally, the majority of the variables listed in Table 3.2, as well as the signatures enforced by the sample-based production environment (sampler/DAW), may also describe the ways in which the final production of the sample-based artifact integrates the contrasts back into a cohesive end phonographic construct (when the respective techniques are reenlisted as part of the sample-based engineering process).

The sample-based Hip Hop aesthetic is the sound of manipulating and recontextualizing characteristics (sonic signatures) derived from phonographic ephemera. These characteristics include signal flow colorations and staging phenomena. But if otherness equates perspective rather than just difference, the *meta* process (sample-based composition/production) has to sonically manifest 'perspective-ness': the sound of discursive workflow, manipulation, a meta-phonographic process interacting with manifestations of—past/other—phonographic processes. In other words, for recontextualization to function, it has to assume an initial context and, therefore, source samples need to carry markers of having first belonged to a sonic 'elsewhen' and 'elsewhere.' Echoing Schloss, the sample-based artifact has to sonify the process of (re)contextualization—as perspective, as meta-process—within the temporal confines of its structure. However, this sonification does not only manifest in the musical interactions between meta-organization and original interactions, but also in the mixing (sonic) mechanics that carefully negotiate the dynamics of *contrast* and *integration* through the materiality of textural and spatial manipulation. The autoethnographic lens deployed here has provided opportunities for "thick descriptions" (Ellis et al, 2011, p. 277) over intrinsic aspects of the creative practice that attempts to construct convincing phonographic 'others' in a sample-based context (making records within records). The examination potentially illustrates how simply making a record is conceptually different to making a record that will feel 'other' within another record, at the same time highlighting the opportunity—and need—to further study the rich sonic phenomena that lie under the surface of contemporary, technologically interdependent musical forms.

NOTES

1. Such as 'interpolation' (the mechanical recreation of existing phonographic motifs—for example, Dr. Dre's celebrated take on P-funk signatures with *The Chronic* [1992]); predominantly live (as in the style of The Roots); and/or heavily synthesized rap subgenres (such as Crunk and other southern US divergences).
2. The term will be used interchangeably with 'sample-based Hip Hop production' from here on: in Hip Hop parlance 'beat' refers to a complete instrumental music production or backing, not just the organization of percussive/drum elements, highlighting the genre's rhythmic priorities. Williams (2014) extends Schloss's (2014) definition of beat as a sample-based instrumental collage to also include non-sample-based elements in the instrumental production.
3. For example, cyclic/Afrological priorities, attention to percussive detail, layering, juxtaposition, a communal "interpretive context," as well as chopping/flipping strategies (Schloss, 2014, pp. 135–168).
4. Sewell (2013, pp. 26–67) categorizes structural samples into "percussion-only," "non-percussion," "intact," and "aggregate" structures—the latter "derived from multiple component samples" or "different parts from the same song"; and surface samples into "momentary," emphatic," and "constituent" types—the latter described as "only a beat or a second long," appearing "only once every measure or two," and "layered against the groove."
5. A number of scholars (for example: Moylan, 2014 [1992]; Lacasse, 2000; Zagorski-Thomas, 2009; 2010; Liu-Rosenbaum, 2012; Holland, 2013) have theorized on the placement of musical elements within the space of a popular music mix, and the concept of 'staging' has emerged as a useful theoretical notion: in essence, it suggests conceptualizing a music mix as a 'stage' where

the placement—but also the dynamic movement and manipulation—of musical elements (mediation) has thematic and narrative implications (meaning) for both listeners and producers.
6. Available online from https://youtu.be/hu5ERs78gTw

REFERENCES

Adams, K. (2015). The Musical Analysis of Hip-Hop, in Williams, J. A. (ed.) *The Cambridge Companion to Hip-Hop*, Cambridge, Cambridge University Press, pp. 118–134.

Cambridge Dictionary (2019). Otherness, *Cambridge Dictionary* (website), available online from https://dictionary.cambridge.org/dictionary/english/otherness [accessed December 2019].

Costello, M. and Wallace, D. F. (1990). *Signifying Rappers*, London, Penguin Books.

Ellis, C., Adams, T. E. and Bochner, A. P. (2011). Autoethnography: An Overview, *Historical Social Research/Historische Sozialforschung*, pp. 273–290.

Exarchos, M. (2019). (Re)Engineering the Cultural Object: Sonic Pasts in Hip-Hop's Future, in Hepworth-Sawyer, R., Hodgson, J., Paterson, J. and Toulson, R. (eds.) *Innovation in Music: Performance, Production, Technology, and Business*, New York, Routledge, pp. 437–454.

Gibson, D. (2008). *The Art of Mixing: A Visual Guide to Recording, Engineering and Production*, 2nd edition, Boston, Course Technology.

Goldberg, D. A. M. (2004). The Scratch is Hip-Hop: Appropriating the Phonographic Medium, in Eglash, R., Croissant, J. L., Di Chiro, G. and Fouché, R. (eds.) *Appropriating Technology: Vernacular Science and Social Power*, Minneapolis, University of Minnesota Press, pp. 107–144.

Holland, M. (2013). Rock Production and Staging in Non-studio Spaces: Presentations of Space in Left Or Right's Buzzy, *Journal of the Art of Record Production*, Vol. 8.

Kajikawa, L. (2015). *Sounding Race in Rap Songs*, California, University of California Press.

Krims, A. (2000). *Rap Music and the Poetics of Identity*, Cambridge, Cambridge University Press.

Kvifte, T. (2007). Digital Sampling and Analogue Aesthetics, *Aesthetics at Work*, pp. 105–128.

Lacasse, S. (2000). *'Listen to My Voice': The Evocative Power of Vocal Staging in Recorded Rock Music and Other Forms of Vocal Expression*, PhD thesis, University of Liverpool.

Lexico (2019). Otherness, *Lexico Powered by Oxford* (website), available online from https://www.lexico.com/definition/otherness [accessed December 2019].

Liu-Rosenbaum, A. (2012) The Meaning in the Mix: Tracing a Sonic Narrative in 'When The Levee Breaks,' *Journal on the Art of Record Production*, Vol. 7.

Marshall, W. (2006). Giving up Hip-hop's Firstborn: A Quest for the Real after the Death of Sampling, *Callaloo*, Vol. 29, No. 3, pp. 868–892.

McLeod, K. (2004). How Copyright Law Changed Hip Hop: An Interview with Public Enemy's Chuck D and Hank Shocklee, *AlterNet* (website), available online from http://www.alternet.org/story/18830/how_copyright_law_changed_hip_hop [accessed December 2019].

Mlynar, P. (2018). Hip-Hop Producer Sadhugold is Quickly Becoming a Name You Should Know, *Bandcamp* (website), available online from https://daily.bandcamp.com/features/sadhugold-interview [accessed December 2019].

Moylan, W. (2014) [1992]. *Understanding and Crafting the Mix: The Art of Recording*, 3rd edition, London, Focal Press.

Mudede, C. (2003). The Turntable, *CTheory* (website), available online from http://www.ctheory.net/articles.aspx?id=382 [accessed November 2019].

Pickering M. (2012) Sonic Horizons: Phonograph Aesthetics and the Experience of Time, in Keightley, E. (ed.) *Time, Media and Modernity*, London, Palgrave Macmillan, pp. 25–44.

Rose, T. (1994). *Black Noise: Rap Music and Black Culture in Contemporary America*, Middletown, Wesleyan University Press.

Schloss, J.G. (2014). *Making Beats: The Art of Sampled-Based Hip-Hop*, 2nd edition, Middletown, Wesleyan University Press.

Sewell, A. (2013). *A Typology of Sampling in Hip-Hop*, Unpublished PhD Thesis, Indiana University.

Staszak, J.F. (2008). Other/otherness. *International Encyclopaedia of Human Geography*, Elsevier, available online from https://scholar.google.com/scholar?hl=en&as_sdt=0%2C5&q=Staszak%2C+J.F.%2C+2009.+Other%2Fotherness.&btnG=.

Stereo Mike. (2019). Making Records within Records, *YouTube* (website), available online from https://youtu.be/hu5ERs78gTw [accessed December 2019].

Weheliye, A.G. (2005). *Phonographies: Grooves in Sonic Afro-Modernity*, Durham and London, Duke University Press.

Williams, J.A. (2013). *Rhymin' and Stealin': Musical Borrowing in Hip-hop*, Ann Arbor, University of Michigan Press.

Williams, J.A. (2014). Theoretical Approaches to Quotation in Hip-hop Recordings, *Contemporary Music Review*, Vol. 33, No. 2, pp. 188–209.

Zagorski-Thomas, S. (2009). The Medium in the Message: Phonographic Staging Techniques that Utilize the Sonic Characteristics of Reproduction Media, *Journal of the Art of Record Production*, Vol. 4.

Zagorski-Thomas, S. (2010). The Stadium in your Bedroom: Functional Staging, Authenticity and the Audience-led Aesthetic in Record Production, *Popular Music*, Vol. 29, No. 2, pp. 251–266.

Zagorski-Thomas, S. (2014). *The Musicology of Record Production*, Cambridge, Cambridge University Press.

Zak III, A.J. (2018). The Death of a Laughing Hyena: The Sound of Musical Democracy, in Fink, R., Latour, M. and Wallmark, Z. (eds.) *The Relentless Pursuit of Tone: Timbre in Popular Music*, New York, Oxford University Press, pp. 300–322.

1. DISCOGRAPHY

Dr. Dre (1992), [CD] *The Chronic*, Interscope Records.

Westside Gunn (2018), [digital release] *Supreme Blientele*, Griselda Records.

4

Motormouth

An essay in sonic recontextualization

Jez Nash

4.1 INTRODUCTION

The Motormouth project seeks to exploit the use of found sound recordings in popular music composition and production. It has at its heart a recontextualization of field recordings of motorcars. These recordings include running and revving engines, indicator relays, horns, opening and closing of doors, bonnets, boot lids, gloveboxes, electric windows, and cooling fans. One would normally consider these sounds as noise. In order for this 'noise' to become popular music, we need to explore the ways in which it can be acted upon in order to take on this new role.

Sanglid (2002) states that when noise is repurposed or infused into a new context, the original potentially negative aural experience is recalled and challenged, presenting new potential for meaning. This is a common technique in artistic endeavor, popularized through movements such as Dadaism. The subject is thenceforth viewed from an objective standpoint rather than from a first-hand encounter at source.

Herbert (2005) sets out a manifesto for composition encouraging originality in production through forbidding the use of preset or existing sounds. In his compositions he creates music using only field recordings of the subject of the work to support the narrative.

Berlyne (1970) and Stang (1974) suggest that an unexpected or challenging artifact, (in this case car noises in pop production) can be seen as both a threat and a catalyst to 'arousal potential.' However, if the artifact is too threatening, often through being too 'novel,' then this novelty factor needs to be mediated in order for liking to occur. Zajonc (1968) states that exposure to an *unfamiliar* artifact in a *familiar* context can instigate attitudinal enhancement. Smalley's notion of spectromorphological gestural surrogacy explores the extent and nature of the link between sound and gesture, the link being weakened through orders of surrogacy (Smalley, 1997).

The Motormouth project suggests that a methodology which incorporates the findings of Zajonc and Smalley can be used to mediate the novelty factor in sonic recontextualization, increasing the likelihood of liking, arousal potential and attitudinal enhancement, and, hopefully therefore, musical enjoyment.

The cars used in the project, together with the songs they resulted in are as follows:

- VW Golf 1.8 GL: *Playing Tonight*
- VW Sharan 1.9 TDi: *Long Way to Grandma's*
- Jaguar XK 140: *Friday (Jonesy in the Jag)*
- Westfield SEi: *Glory Days*

The productions are available for listening at soundcloud.com/motormouth-4/tracks.

4.2 BACKGROUND TO THE PROJECT

Théberge (1997) states that musicians using technology now have to contend with the driving forces of an industry that seems to homogenize music production. He also points out that the music technology industry, by definition, sees the musician as consumer. The proliferation of the Digital Audio Workstation (DAW) has meant that swathes of creatives, old and new, have been double clicking an icon which, for decades, placed in front of them a default piece of music with a default key, time signature, and tempo: C Major, 4/4, 120BPM. Any deviation from this default state is an edit (Herbert, 2015).

On discovering the affordances of tape, composers were able to 'cross a Rubicon' of compositional affordances. On one side of this duality was the grand canon of Western Art music; the other, uncharted plains of Avant-garde sonic exploration and experimentation. Examples include turning a tape reel upside down and rewinding it so that it can be played in reverse; cutting and splicing using razor blades and sticky tape; increasing or decreasing playback speed. These new methods of recording and writing, instantiated by Pierre Schaeffer through *musique concrète* (Schaeffer, 1952), were not to everybody's post-war conservative taste. But, through the pioneering and open-minded work of composers and producers in the mid-1960s onward, these ingredients would become fused with rock and roll, to bring experimental music into mainstream popular music through works such as Pet Sounds (The Beach Boys, 1966), Piper at the Gates of Dawn (Pink Floyd, 1967), and Sgt. Pepper's Lonely Hearts Club Band (The Beatles, 1967). This metamorphosis is expounded in great detail by Manning (2013).

In a bid to make these pioneering methods available to the masses, a significant thrust of the music technology industry throughout the years appears to have been an encapsulation of experimental music methodology, packaged and presented as consumable commodity, such that any one of us can plug in a piece of gear or dial up a patch and we can sound like any number of electronic music composers, past and present. Templates and presets appear to represent alarmingly good value for money considering the amount of sheer sonic variety they afford and, therefore, also represent good business.

The composer Matthew Herbert's P.C.C.O.M. Manifesto (Herbert, 2005) sets out a template for his compositions. The manifesto includes a set of rules which prohibit using presets and previously existing music, thereby ensuring a level of originality and authenticity in his work. Much of his work necessitates that the sounds used give voice to their origins, often with sociopolitical subtext. One Pig, for example, utilizes a set of field recordings documenting the life cycle of a pig, from birth right through to the dinner plate. Herbert's reasoning is to encourage deeper listening and thinking, urging the listener to include the point-of-view of the source material, in this case, a pig, and that which needs to happen to it in order to become consumable commodity (ibid). The pig is both the subject of the production and the source material.

Motormouth seeks to draw on the potential for field recordings to convey a sense of subtext through relating the lyrical content to a specific journey which has (or may have) been taken in the car. In 'Playing Tonight,' the lyric tells of the author's frantic journey to a nightclub where he is due to perform, and the car in which he is traveling, a 1994 VW Golf, is used as the source audio for the backing track. In 'Long Way to Grandma's,' a VW Sharan people carrier is used as the source material, and the song depicts an eventful family journey to the West Country to visit relatives. The car is both the subject of the song, and the source material.

4.3 NOISE INTO MUSIC: EXPANDING THE SONIC PALETTE: AFFORDANCES

The possibility of using noise to compose music raises the question: what is the difference between noise and music, or rather, what needs to happen to noise in order for it to become music? And in order to be able to answer this, one must first tackle the question: what is noise?

4.3.1 Defining noise

The Old English Dictionary (OED) definition reads 'a sound, especially one that is loud or unpleasant or that causes disturbance.' Apparently, the origin of the word is the Latin *nausea*. Another OED definition of 'noise' relates to *discord*. Scholars of Bach's Chorales are at pains to avoid double 3rds, parallel 5ths, etc. However, by the time of the Romantics, these discrepancies were no longer heard as discordant. Later, the Impressionists were regularly using parallel 5th movement as compositional features, for example the depiction of church bells in Debussy's 'La Cathédrale Engloutie' (Debussy, 1910).

Post-industrial use of the word often refers to interference, e.g. noise on an electrical signal reducing its clarity. The term 'signal to noise ratio' used in audio and visual electronic apparatus suggests opposing entities whereby one is desirable (signal), and the other, not (noise). The term 'noise' often, therefore, has negative connotations and so could be defined thus: an unsolicited sonic side effect often resulting from mechanical, electrical or human activity.

4.3.2 Sampling

Prior to its software plugin counterpart, the word 'sampler' commonly referred to a standalone piece of audio hardware that is capable of taking an analog input and recording and storing it as digital audio. This could then be edited in a number of ways, and 'keymapped,' i.e., mapped to a MIDI note number, which could be used by a MIDI sequencer to trigger playback of the audio. I define the process as: capture, edit, keymap, trigger.

It should be noted that the incorporation of samplers into DAWs in the form of plugins has, by necessity, removed the direct 'audio in' functionality of the standalone sampler. Analog to digital conversion (A to D) and *vice versa* (D to A) are facilitated by linking to the circuits of the DAWs own inputs and outputs via an audio interface. More recently drag-and-drop functionality has been incorporated, such that pre-existing audio files can be immediately available for editing and MIDI triggering. The functionality of a sampler is, of course, still there within the DAW. However, the 'capture' element is now a little more convoluted than merely connecting a sound source to a direct input. There is now an extra step in the workflow of 'capture' and, perhaps therefore, one less reason to incorporate sound from outside the DAW, such as field recordings or found sound.

The development of the sampler began in the late 1970s with the onset of semi-affordable A to D and D to A technology, employed in the Fairlight CMI system and also in New England Digital's Synclavier. This development cumulated in more affordable units such as the Akai S-series, the EMU Emulators and SP12s, Ensoniq's Mirage, and, coupled with on-board sequencers, the Akai MPC range beginning with the Akai-Linn collaboration unit, the MPC 60. Samplers were not particularly fussy about what was presented at their analog input jacks (although, many devices featured RIAA equalization circuits preferable for receipt of signals direct from phonograph turntables). Amongst the affordances of these 'tape-less studios' (as described in Synclavier promotional material) was the ability to extract grooves and breaks from existing recorded material for recontextualization into new compositions, the practice going on to form a cornerstone of hip hop, and feeding many other forms of pop production, once subsequent devices became more affordable. Also, however, one could make a field recording on a portable tape recorder, bring it back to the sampler-equipped studio, and incorporate it into production workflow, thereby instantiating Varèse's notion of organizing sound (Varèse and Wen-Chung, 1966).

Our sound libraries of multi-sampled, velocity-layered, multiple articulation, multi-mic complexity occupy vast storage space, and are presented to us through elaborate GUIs populating a significant majority of user menus. How, then, might we go about composing music using 'noise' and sound captured from outside of the DAW? The tools for this do exist, but are often hidden in sub-menus. Plugins such as EXS24 (Logic), and NN-XT (Reason) feature the ability to import (as opposed to capture), edit, keymap and trigger digital audio. These tools, however, are not promoted to the same extent as the populated versions thereof residing in the instrument presets menus. One has to specifically look for and instantiate the 'empty' versions of these devices. They do not appear on default templates, but they are there, albeit they are several mouse clicks away.

4.3.3 Repetition theory

Perhaps, an explanation of how discordant noise can become musically acceptable lies in the research of Deutch et al. (2008), namely, that repetition affords musicality. Their work suggests that the neural circuitry is involved when listening to speech associates' pitch information with expressivity, therefore the brain's focus is on the meaning of the verbal communication aided by this expressivity. The relationship between this pitching and music is largely an irrelevance, a side effect. Aligning this with our definition in Section 4.3.1, we could consider this side effect as noise. However, if a section of a phrase is extracted and repeated there is a modulation in the temporal lobe. Meaning has been ascertained and subsequent hearings lift the restriction of the focus on meaning, affording a freedom to enjoy the pitch and rhythm of the loop, i.e., the music. It can be argued, therefore, that repetition is a tool for turning noise into music.

"Believe" (Cher, 1998) features what would previously have been considered an unwanted artifact of digital vocal pitch correction – the 'yodel' effect which happens when using extreme settings across a moving pitch. The judicious repetition of this effect within the song itself, coupled with the heavy rotation on commercial radio, preceded an uptake of the process which went on to become ubiquitous to the point of cliché, and, even then never relenting, such that the sound is now an intrinsic, almost memetic, component within certain genres. It could be said, therefore that *repetition* garners *familiarity*.

4.3.4 Exposure, familiarity and attitudinal enhancement

In his research around 'mere exposure,' Zajonc (1968) points out that music which, on first encounter, is regarded as unfamiliar and challenging, can, through repetition, become more favorable to the listener. He states that this phenomenon is especially prevalent if there is no likely prior associational familiarity, i.e., the artifact is *novel*. He notes the corollary that if there has been a prior conceptual understanding of the artifact, then the extent to which the music becomes favorable is negligible.

The 'liking' of the unfamiliar and challenging artifact is, according to Berlyne (1970) and later Stang (1974), instantiated by its 'arousal potential.' However, if the arousal potential is too high *or* too low, liking is far less likely to occur. They also point out that it is in fact the novelty factor of an artifact which can lead to very high arousal potential based on the idea that it can be perceived as a threat. If, however, this threat turns out to be benign, then the arousal potential is attenuated back into the zone where liking is more likely to happen.

Zajonc also states that if the exposure to a new and unconventional artifact occurs within the context of something which is familiar, then the potential for attitudinal enhancement is great. So, presumably, if one were to expose a listener to a novel artifact within the safety of a familiar context, then, combining the ideas of Zajonc with Berlyne and Stang, one could postulate that the potential for attitudinal enhancement and subsequent liking is relatively high. If so, then this novelty factor could potentially be used as a catalyst, rather than a threat, to musical enjoyment.

4.3.5 Context

When the band Art of Noise formed in 1984, their work incorporated significant use of a Fairlight CMI. This device facilitated capture, editing, keymapping and polyphonic triggering of any sound presented at input. It also featured an interactive screen on which waveforms could be edited with a pen and sequenced. Their first album release (following an EP) entitled "Who's Afraid Of The Art Of Noise" (Art of Noise, 1984) featured extensive use of the Fairlight CMI. With it, they were able to incorporate unconventional sound sources into an emerging but familiar genre. One can assume, in the light of Zajonc's findings, that the popularity of this work was due to the fact that it heavily utilized such widely diverse sounds as starter motors and revving engines, retuned excerpts of speech, footsteps, church bells, gun shots and 'industrial' noises, that it did so in a familiar context – that of dance music. The single "Beat Box" featuring on both the EP (Into Battle with . . .) and the first album, went to number 1 in the US Dance chart in 1984. Much of this first album contains at least suggestions of familiar harmonic, melodic and rhythmic patterns. Indeed 'Beat Box' is based loosely around a 12-bar blues, although the orchestration is far from what one would traditionally associate with blues.

4.3.6 Noise into music: summary

A distillation of the above exploration into the relationship between noise and music yields the following points:

- Noise, when used repetitiously becomes familiar;
- Familiarity often leads to attitudinal enhancement;
- This attitudinal enhancement is most significant if the context in which the 'noise' is placed already has some form of familiarity.

Of course, this distillation fails to take into account factors such as negative association with the initial noise and, of course, the effect of overexposure. The latter is widely explored by Hunter and Schellenberg (2010, p. 175), together with Zajonc et al. (1972); Schellenberg et al. (2008), and concluding in the main that overexposure can lead to satiation and boredom. Nevertheless, the point remains that it is through the interplay between repetition, familiarity and context that *noise* has the potential to become *music*.

4.4 MOTORMOUTH: ARRANGING, MIXING AND PRODUCTION

Thus far we have considered a justification for expanding the sonic palette, whereby sound not traditionally considered to be musical could be effectively recontextualized to do so. Considering the three points in the previous section, concerning repetition, familiarity and attitudinal enhancement, the production methodology associated with the Motormouth artifact is outlined as follows. The initial intent of the overall 'sound' of the production was to create from field recordings a production which would be recognized ('liked,' even) by an audience familiar with sub-genres of pop. The design would feature elements of hip hop, ska / 2 Tone and Oi!, and, as such, the orchestration would need to resemble, or at least suggest, the musical elements found therein. Kick, snare, hi-hats, together with bass, organ, brass and sound effects would need to be approximated from the raw material.

The extent to which this raw material can be manipulated is relatively limitless within the sample level editing capabilities of the DAW. Afterall, a sound wave, whether it is a kick drum or an indicator relay, is simply a digital representation of positive and negative electrical energy occurring at editable frequency and amplitude. Sonically speaking, an indicator relay can be morphed into a convincing kick drum relatively easily, but what would be the point of that, i.e., why not just load up a kick drum from the built-in sample library? To answer this question, part of the intent of the audio artifact is to leave as much of the original sound intact so as to enable the audience to have some reminder as to the origin of the sounds wherever possible. Processing has been done, but a balance has been sought, such that there is still a resemblance to the original source.

4.4.1 'Synth' sounds

An obvious starting point for generating pitched material was the sound of the exhaust of a running (and revving) engine. These were trimmed in 'loop mode,' a feature of sampling hardware and software which facilitates matching the end of a sound loop with the beginning in order to create a seamless playback loop. This was problematic for recording sounds of any engine that was not running at its idle (or 'tick-over') state. Despite extremely careful use of the accelerator pedals on all of the cars, it was impossible to maintain a completely steady RPM count. This became evident in the looping process where within the space of half a second the pitch of the 'note' would fluctuate by at least 25 cents. This necessitated the use of relatively short loops. Furthermore, in order to loop seamlessly, the start and end of the sample would need to be at the same point in the piston firing sequence. With short samples the opportunities for getting a loop point in the correct point in the firing sequence and at the same pitch at which the sample started was very limited indeed. Cross-fading within the sample playback device alleviated the issue to a certain extent, but the loop points are, nevertheless, clearly audible in many of the exhaust notes utilized throughout the production.

4.4.2 'Drum' sounds

Sounds used as kick drums were largely derived from doors or bonnet lids closing, but in all cases these recordings needed a great deal of processing in the form of enveloping to facilitate harder attack, and EQ to enhance energy in low frequencies.

Sounds to replicate 'snare'- type functionality emanated either from closing gloveboxes or, again, closing doors pitched up. Again, a great deal of processing was required to enable these sounds to work as a snare component. As the intention for the audio artifact was to achieve a work which would be accessible to pop aficionados, it was not enough to simply place the raw recordings on the 'two' and the 'four'; they needed to be processed such that they took on some of the 'rattle' elements of a snare drum, and this was often done by means of applying distortion, and boosting upper-mid-frequencies to add 'crack.'

In order to provide the kind of higher-frequency percussive qualities 'traditionally' reserved for hi-hats, there were a number of sounds to choose from. The preferred raw recordings were of indicator relays, which were then pitched an octave or so higher.

4.4.3 Arranging

Once the source material had been crafted into sounds which could take on the duties of the more conventional sounds expected in this genre, the work of arrangement could begin. This was done largely along the same lines as a traditional arrangement – a beat was created followed by a hook and a bass line. Then lyrics were written, inspired by the energy of the beat and related to a particular journey in that car.

4.4.4 Mixing and production

The arrangements were such that they largely resembled more traditional pre-mix recordings. The organization of sequenced tracks into, e.g., 'kick,' 'snare,' 'hats,' 'bass,' 'synth,' facilitated a familiar approach to mixing. A balance was assembled with further EQ treatments to enable each element of the track to have its own sonic 'space' in the mix. This was followed by application of dynamics control routines and time-based effects processing.

One of the key aims of the mixing process was to preserve as much as possible of the 'car-ness' of the source material, bearing in mind the composer Matthew Herbert's statement regarding the over-manipulation of sound, i.e., the pointlessness of making one sound become another entirely (Herbert, 2008). This has not been entirely successful in that many of the sounds are, in fact, more like their 'traditional' counterparts than the original field recordings. Some of the original recording samples are recognizable in the works but some are not, due to the amount of processing applied to achieve the contextual familiarity. However, the fact remains that the work does have a uniqueness in that all of the sounds, however heavily treated, did start off as recordings from cars, and that, as such, the resemblance of sounds to their traditional counterparts is by no means absolute.

4.5 SONIC CARTOONING

Zagorski-Thomas (2014) points out that much of contemporary record production, particularly in the mix process, entails a considerable distortion of original source material, such that merely the salient aspects of each individual source can be perceived (as opposed, perhaps, to actually *heard*), and that perception of these salient characteristics is enhanced in varying degrees, dependent on their intended meaning in the production as a whole. He uses the analogy of a 3D line drawing of a box: the viewer will 'see' a box in three dimensions even though subsequent analysis reveals a series of lines in two dimensions. In acoustic country / folk /acoustic music (or any music where the listener expects to hear 'traditional' orchestration) this cartooning is such that the original source recordings retain enough information through the production to render them irrefutably representative of the source, yet enhanced (distorted) to give them a 'caricature' status in the mix. In the case of the Motormouth production methodology, this cartooning goes a step further in that the source recordings are rendered only partially (but, still, definitely) associated with the original, but 'dressed up' to suggest instrumentation and timbre expected in the genre.

4.6 SPECTROMORPHOLOGICAL GESTURAL SURROGACY: MEDIATING THE NOVELTY FACTOR IN SONIC RECONTEXTUALIZATION

Another way of looking at this aspect of the production is to consider the idea of gestural surrogacy, as posited by Smalley (1997). Smalley reminds us that a listener's perception of an instrument being played is such that it is subject to a subconscious audio-visual conditioning. (ibid., 1997). The sound of a drum being hit, for example, conjures not only the sound itself but also a motor-sensory and psychological response in the listener. It is not just the ears that are stimulated, but also a brain impulse analogous to that which caused the performer to strike the drum in the first place – see Lakoff and Johnson (1999) and Mahon and Caramazza (2008). This goes some way to explaining the temptation in a listener to mime the drum solo in Phil Collins' "In the Air Tonight" (Phil Collins, 1980), or the electric guitar intro to Derek and the Dominos' "Layla" (Derek and the Dominos, 1970). However, this phenomenon is significantly dependent on the necessity that the listener recognizes the sound being performed, otherwise there would be no 'decryption algorithm' to enable the listener to decode the gestural intent. If this facility for decryption is removed then the listening experience potentially becomes detached from perception of gesture, leading to a remoteness to which Smalley refers as *surrogacy* (p. 112). The extent to this detachment depends on a number of factors. *First order surrogacy* denotes a direct link between the gesture and the sound, but without musical meaning. *Second order surrogacy* denotes a musical instantiation of "traditional instrumental gesture," whereby the instrument is either real or a synthetic clone of the real (such as a string patch on a synthesizer). *Third order surrogacy* refers to a sense of opaqueness in the perception of source and / or cause, facilitating ambiguity in the music. *Remote surrogacy* is the detachment of perception of source and cause, but Smalley points out that "some vestiges of gesture might still remain," but that this may require "propagating or reinjected energy in the spectromorphology."

4.7 ANALYSIS

Here follows a non-exhaustive breakdown of the intro to one of the pieces in the audio artifact, and how the concepts of cartooning and spectromorphology can be applied by way of analysis. The purpose of this is to demonstrate how, in several of the pieces, the 'arousal potential' is addressed by way of establishing an element of familiarity.

4.7.1 Motormouth: 'Playing Tonight'. Source recordings: 1992 VW Golf 1.8L Automatic (green)

0:00 to 0:06 (minutes:seconds)

SPECTROMORPHOLOGY: FIRST ORDER SURROGACY

The initial sounds of the track consist of the sound of the door closing and the starter motor attempting to fire the engine. At this stage there is no real suggestion that these sounds have musical meaning, but there is a clear link between the portrayal of the sound and the gestures that created them. It could be argued therefore that at this stage these sounds are, in fact, noise.

Cartooning: minimal distortion – light use of EQ and dynamics, purely to increase loudness such that there is little doubt as to their origin.

0:06 to 0:15

SPECTROMORPHOLOGY: SECOND ORDER SURROGACY

The original sounds have started to become 'organized' using repetition, context, and attitudinal enhancement; noise taking on a form of musicality, but the link with the original gesture and sound source is still preserved. The lower, punchier sound of the door closing has been contextualized as fulfilling the spectromorphological purpose of a kick drum due to its *familiar* location in the arrangement. Likewise, a glovebox slamming shut represents a snare, and the indicator relay, a hi-hat. This representation is facilitated by triggering these source recordings commensurate with kick, snare and hat samples sequenced as they might well be in a pop production. The engaging and familiar backbeat rhythm potentially starts to induce attitudinal enhancement.

Cartooning: Increasing distortion. Towards the end of this passage the indicator relay is processed using an automated EQ, which removes low frequencies and enhances the highs such that the presentation is much more akin to an EDM hi-hat. However, the memory of its origin is preserved as the listener gets to hear the metamorphosis in progress.

0:15 to 0:31

SPECTROMORPHOLOGY: THIRD ORDER SURROGACY

The link between source and cause is starting to become weakened as the processing ramps up. The link is now only really there due to the trajectory of the processing carried out in the previous section. The sounds are familiar due to this, but they are no longer direct associations of source and cause. Of course, the fact that the listener does have a very good idea as to the link between cause and source (due to the contiguity with the processing) could suggest that this section is, in fact, more second order. The deliberate pitching of the sustained exhaust note, again, takes the listener on a journey from second to third order surrogacy, in that the mere pitching alone detaches gesture from source. To reach the high note in this section, the car would have to be revved far beyond its capability. Whilst the pitch is not unheard of in, say, a high-performance race engine, the initial passage of the piece suggests that this is anything but, to even a novice motorist.

Cartooning: Heavy distortion. The exhaust notes have been dynamically and sonically enhanced such that, although there is still some resemblance to the original (albeit through the familiarity with the antecedent passage), they take on a 'Pimp My Ride' caricature (Pimp My Ride 2004–2007), sounding more like a large-bore exhaust pipe such that might be retrofitted to a customized car in order to give it more sonic presence. The door (kick) and the glovebox (snare) have been processed in much the same way that their 'real' counterparts would have and, as such, have taken on much of the characteristics of a kick and snare. One would, for example, tend to shape the frequency curve of a kick so as to ensure that low-end punch, together with high-end attack are the caricatures. The 'snare' is also treated to a gated reverb – a not un-common approach to a 'real' snare, further supporting familiarity.

0:31 to 0:45

SPECTROMORPHOLOGY: THIRD ORDER AND REMOTE SURROGACY

Some of the source recordings have been processed so much that they retain little of the association between cause and source. The high 'ska' is actually another high-pitched exhaust note which was judged to have just enough similarity with a brass section so as to fulfill this role. Other than reading a sleeve note, the listener would have very little idea of the source of this sound. However, the virtually untreated 'handbrake' sound does its best to remind the listener of the origin of the source material.

Cartooning: Extreme distortion. The exhaust notes are very highly pitched and treated to rapid re-triggering, chromatic re-pitching and time-based effects, notably delay. They now function as the 'ska' element of the arrangement and orchestration.

0:45 to 1:15

SPECTROMORPHOLOGY: LARGELY REMOTE SURROGACY

Virtually no use of unprocessed sounds exists in this passage so there is little chance of linking source with gesture; but the intention is that the listener will have been able to establish context and familiarity enough by this point to then engage with the lyrical content in the first verse.

Cartooning: Virtually all of the sounds are now so distorted from the original that they have become not just caricatures, but almost parodies of their 'conventional' counterparts.

4.8 SUMMARY

We have seen how the point at which noise becomes music is characterized by a number of factors: familiarity, context, arousal potential, repetition and recontextualized sociological meaning. In the case of this particular project, these characteristics have been applied to field recordings of cars with a view to demonstrating that the hyphenated musician's (Théberge 1997, p. 221) sonic palette need not be limited to factory presets, or even edited versions thereof. Moreover, we have seen that sounds traditionally termed 'noise' can be used to create pop music, capitalizing on the novelty factor (appropriately mediated) of the sources, to instantiate arousal potential and 'liking.'

REFERENCES

Berlyne, D.E. (1970). Novelty, complexity, and hedonic value. *Perception and Psychophysics*, 8, pp. 279–286.

Debussy, C. (1910) *La Cathédrale Engloutie*: Paris: Durand et Cie., 1910. Plate D. & F. 7687.

Deutsch, D., Henthorn, T., and Lapidis, R. (2011) Illusory transformation from speech to song. *Journal of the Acoustical Society of America* 129, 2245–2252. Available at: http://scitation.aip.org/content/asa/journal/jasa/129/4/10.1121/1.3562174

Herbert, M. (2005) *Personal Contract for the Composition of Music (Incorporating the Manifesto of Mistakes)*. Available at: http://matthewherbert.com/about-contact/manifesto/

Herbert, M. (2008) Interview with iDJ. Available at: http://www.ianroullier.com/interviews_and_features/matthewherbert.htm

Herbert, M. (2015) *On Creative Manifesto: A Conversation with Matthew Herbert*: Interview with Shaun Curtiss: Ableton Loop Conference: October 31, 2015, Funkhaus, Berlin.

Hunter, P., Schellenberg, E. (2010) Interactive Effects of Personality and Frequency of Exposure on Liking for Music. *Personality and Individual Differences*, 50(2011), pp. 175–179.

Lakoff, G., Johnson M. (2003) *Metaphors We Live By*. 2nd ed., Chicago, University of Chicago Press.

Mahon, B., Caramazza, A. (2008) A Critical Look at the Embodied Cognition Hypothesis and a New Proposal for Grounding Conceptual Content. *Journal of Physiology-Paris*, 102(1–3), pp. 59–70.

Manning, P. (2013) *Electronic and Computer Music*. New York, Oxford University Press.

Pimp My Ride (2004–2007) MTV, first shown 4/3/2004.

Sanglid, T. (2002) The Aesthetics of Noise: DATANOM. Available at http://www.ubu.com/papers/noise.html [accessed 8/18/2014].

Schaeffer, P. (1952) *À la recherche d'une musique concrete*: Éditions du Seuil, Paris.

Schellenberg, E.G., Peretz, I., and Vieillard, S. (2008). Liking for Happy and Sad Sounding Music: Effects of Exposure. *Cognition and Emotion*, 22, pp. 218–237.

Smalley, D. (1997). Spectromorphology: Explaining Sound-shapes. *Organised Sound*, 2, pp. 107–126 doi:10.1017/S1355771897009059.

Stang, D.J. (1974). Methodological factors in mere exposure research. *Psychological Bulletin*, 81, pp. 1014–1025.

Théberge, P (1997) *Any Sound You Can Imagine: Making Music / Consuming Technology*. Wesleyan, University Press of New England.

Varèse, E., Wen-chung, C. (1966). The Liberation of Sound. *Perspectives of New Music*, 5(1), pp. 11–19. doi:10.2307/832385.

Zajonc, R.B. (1968) Attitudinal Effects of Mere Exposure. *Journal of Personality and Social Psychology Monograph Supplement*, 9(2), pt 2: June 1968.

Zajonc, R.B., Shaver, P., Tavris, C., and Van Kreveld, D. (1972) Exposure, Satiation, and Stimulus Discriminability. *Journal of Personality and Social Psychology*, 21, pp. 270–280.

Zagorski-Thomas, S. (2014) The Spectromorphology Of Recorded Popular Music: The Shaping of Sonic Cartoons Through Record Production. In *The Relentless Pursuit of Tone: Timbre in Popular Music*. Eds. Fink, R., LaTour, M.O., Wallmark, Z. New York, Oxford University Press.

DISCOGRAPHY

Art of Noise, The, (1984) *(Who's Afraid Of) The Art of Noise*: ZTT / Island.
Beach Boys, The, (1966) *Pet Sounds*: Capitol.
Beatles, The, (1967) *Sgt. Pepper's Lonely Hearts Club Band*: Parlophone.
Cher, (1998) *Believe*: Warner Bros.
Derek and the Dominos, (1971) *Layla*: Atco / RSO / Polydor.
Matthew Herbert, (2011) *One Pig* : Accidental Records.
Phil Collins, (1980) *In the Air Tonight*: Virgin / Atlantic.
Pink Floyd, (1967) *Piper at the Gates of Dawn*: EMI Columbia / Tower.

5

The Individualist

Todd Rundgren's approach to innovation and his 1993 interactive album *No World Order*

Tim Hughes

5.1 INTRODUCTION

In 1993 Todd Rundgren released *No World Order*, an album-length, interactive piece of music. *No World Order* was among the very first releases in the initial wave of 'enhanced' or 'interactive' albums in the early 1990s. These releases were designed to take advantage of several new, CD-based formats developed by Phillips and Sony, including CD-ROM, CD-i, and CD+. The intent was to expand commercial music further into the emerging markets of CD-based home computer software and interactive home consumer devices. At the time of its release, *No World Order* represented a considerable leap forward in both the digital recombination of music and the development of musical interactivity. Yet it was a commercial failure and was generally disregarded by critics.

This chapter examines *No World Order* amidst several intertwined subjects: Rundgren's long career as a musical and technical innovator, the recent history of digital interactive music, the construction of *No World Order* and how it followed several themes from Rundgren's earlier innovations, and the reasons for its commercial failure and limited popularity. It concludes with a discussion of some of the lessons that can be learned from it with respect to interactive music and innovation, and especially Rundgren's career-long approach of working with emerging technologies – both to avoid stylistic, conceptual, and technical limitations *and* as a way of limiting possibilities in order to fuel creativity.

5.2 TODD RUNDGREN, *THE INDIVIDUALIST*

> He didn't want to go backward in time, and neither did we. Actually, in my observation, the cool thing about Todd, and what keeps him going, so to speak, is that he likes to throw everything out and start all over again . . .
> (David Johansen, quoted in Meyers, 2010, 304)

Todd Rundgren's career as an artist, songwriter/composer, producer, engineer, and technological pioneer has spanned fifty-three years at the time of writing. He has released forty-one studio albums – including twenty-six as a solo artist and ten more with Utopia – many of which were double-length. These albums include 404 original songs that he either wrote or co-wrote.

Rundgren began his professional career in 1966 as a guitarist with the blues-rock group Woody's Truckstop, before leaving to found The Nazz in 1967. The Nazz provided Rundgren with his first experience making studio recordings and music videos. It also marked the beginning of his career as a songwriter, and Rundgren quickly established the twin styles of piano-based torch ballads and guitar-driven pop for which he was known (Rundgren, 2013b). In 1970 he began releasing a long string of self-produced albums as a solo artist, for which he typically wrote all the songs and often performed all the instruments. He reached his commercial peak as an artist relatively quickly with *Something/Anything*, a two-disc gold record which provided his biggest hit, 'Hello, It's Me,' which reached Number 5 on the *Billboard Hot 100 Chart* in September 1973 (Billboard, 2020).

At this crucial point in his career, poised on the verge of stardom (Myers, 2010), Rundgren did two highly unusual things that confounded the industry but revealed his approach as a musical and technical innovator. First, he radically altered his musical style, largely abandoning mainstream pop for a series of stylistic shifts through heavily synthesised Progressive Rock, guitar-driven Glam Rock, Soul-based balladry, New Wave, Electronic Dance Music, and other styles much more difficult to characterise. In essence, and in a manner similar to several contemporaries such as Frank Zappa or Joni Mitchell, he began to eschew compromise for the sake of an expanded audience whenever doing so meant imposing creative barriers. He has continued to make highly idiosyncratic, self-produced music at a steady pace to the present day, frequently working in multiple styles, roles, and media. Second, in 1973 Rundgren also began a parallel artistic career as the frontman, producer, and principal songwriter of Utopia, which transformed from a Progressive Rock/Jazz Rock sextet with three keyboardists in 1973 to a New Wave/Synth Pop quartet of singer-songwriters from the late 1970s through 1986, when they disbanded.

Rundgren also embarked on a *third* parallel career in 1970 as a producer and audio engineer, achieving much greater commercial success as a producer than he ever gained as an artist. He started as the house engineer at Bearsville Studio, where he recorded albums by artists including The Band and Jesse Winchester. He then moved into freelance production in 1971 with Badfinger's *Straight Up*. Rundgren eventually produced albums for over sixty artists, across a broad range of styles – many of which either achieved major commercial success or are regarded as landmark works (see Table 5.1).

The range of artists represented in this table demonstrates Rundgren's creativity and stylistic diversity. Of these, however, Meat Loaf's *Bat Out of Hell* unquestionably had the biggest impact on Rundgren's career. Sales figures for albums are notoriously inaccurate, but the label that released it claims that *Bat Out of Hell* has reached 'more than 50 million copies sold

Table 5.1 A selection of Todd Rundgren's production credits across different styles

Year	Artist	Album	Style/Genre
1970	Jesse Winchester	*Jesse Winchester*	Country Rock
1970	The Band	*Stage Fright*	Americana
1971	Badfinger	*Straight Up*	Pop Rock
1973	New York Dolls	*New York Dolls*	Glam Rock/Proto-Punk
1973	Grand Funk	*We're An American Band*	Rock
1974	Grand Funk	*Shinin' On*	Rock
1974	Daryl Hall and John Oates	*War Babies*	Pop/Soul
1977	Meat Loaf	*Bat Out of Hell*	Theatrical Rock
1979	Tom Robinson Band	*TRB Two*	Punk Rock
1979	Patti Smith Group	*Wave*	Punk Rock
1982	The Psychedelic Furs	*Forever Now*	New Wave
1983	Cheap Trick	*Next Position Please*	Theatrical Rock
1986	XTC	*Skylarking*	New Wave
1990	Jill Sobule	*Things Here Are Different*	Alternative
2000	Bad Religion	*The New America*	Punk Rock

worldwide' (*Cleveland International*, 2019). The unusual history of *Bat Out Of Hell* made it particularly profitable for Rundgren, who personally funded the recording in exchange for a large royalty percentage:

> The actual number is contested although it is generally considered to be in the top five-selling albums of all time . . . I originally took the job on under duress. Meat Loaf dumped his record label on the eve of us going into the studio and that meant I was the ultimate underwriter of the whole project. That's why in the end I did so well. By some estimation better than Meat Loaf and [songwriter] Jim Steinman . . . my very first royalty cheque was for three-quarters of a million. I haven't seen one like it since.
>
> (Rundgren, 2013a)

Rundgren's profits from this and other productions allowed him the freedom as an artist to work without typical financial concerns:

> That liberated me musically . . . I was making so much money from production that I never had to worry about surviving in music. I never had to worry about having a hit.
>
> (Rundgren, quoted in Derisso, 2018)

The breadth and length of Rundgren's creative output as an artist and producer is striking, but his role as a musical and technical innovator is equally impressive. As an artist, Rundgren has always been an early adopter of new technologies that expand the palette of available sounds and songwriting techniques: Even before the beginning of his professional career, Rundgren had discovered how to create a phasing effect by altering the timing of two synchronised tape players. In 1968 he added this effect to the outro of 'Open My Eyes' (Nazz, 1968), the very first song he recorded and an early example of phasing (Blair, 2008). Rundgren was also among the first artists to take full advantage of extensive overdubbing. Although this technique had been used by Les Paul from the very first days of multi-track recording, it was still quite rare by February 1972, when Rundgren released *Something/Anything*. He had recorded the first three sides of this double album entirely by himself, in many cases with heavy layers of over-dubbed instrumentation. *Something/Anything* was just released before Stevie Wonder's *Music of My Mind* and *Talking Book* (March and October 1972, respectively) and Mike Oldfield's *Tubular Bells* (1973) popularised the concept of the one-man studio orchestra.

Rundgren also used complex tape effects, including extreme editing, looping, and speed manipulation on many albums to create effects similar to musique concrete. This began with *Runt* in 1971 but continued even as late as 'Pretending to Care' on *A Capella* (1985). And, much like Zappa, he saw many creative possibilities in the use of large-scale musical collage – regardless of the technology employed in its construction. Both made extensive use of analogue tape effects in the 1970s, but also continued the practice well in the digital era, using digital editing, manipulation, synthesis, and other effects to extend their use of collage. The entire first side of 1973's *A Wizard, A True Star*, for instance, is a single tape-based collage of songs, song fragments, and sound effects. *No World Order*, recorded twenty years later, is very similar to *A Wizard, A True Star* in many ways – in effect a digital, interactive music collage:

> *No World Order* . . . actually continues ideas dating as far back as *A Wizard, A True Star*. Todd played all the instruments, cutting and pasting hundreds of song snippets into a (semi-)cohesive whole.
> (Kopp, 2019)

Rundgren has also long experimented with recontextualised and interpolated sounds. On *Bat Out of Hell*, for instance, he used an electric guitar to mimic a motorcycle crash on the title track and employed Phil Rizutto, the baseball announcer for the New York Yankees, to provide 'play-by-play' descriptions of the makeout scene in 'Paradise by the Dashboard Light'. An equally famous example is his use of a child's voice in the opening and closing of XTC's 'Dear God' (from *Skylarking*, 1986), in place of the voice of lead singer Andy Partridge, as a way of connoting a sense of lost innocence. He also occasionally employs intertextuality and pluralism in highly unusual ways. Examples include *Faithful* (1976), one side of which featured studio recreations of landmark songs from the mid-1960s, and Utopia's *Deface the Music* (1980), an entire album of newly written and recorded Beatles pastiches.

Rundgren was also an early and extensive user of sound synthesis, particularly for a mainstream American rock artist. He began using them on *Something/Anything*, toured with at least one synthesiser player from 1972 on (and as many as three with Utopia), and has often built entire albums around them. His synthesiser-based 1975 album *Initiation* included 'Born to Synthesize', a song defending their use at a time when it was still somewhat controversial. He began using sequencing as early as 1972 on 'Breathless', employing an EMS VCS3:

> It was complex, but this was 1972. There was no MIDI. . . . I would have been manually sequencing with an EMS 'Putney' [VCS3] with a little keyboard
>
> (Rundgren, quoted in Blair, 2008).

Rundgren was also an early adopter of digital sampling. His 1985 album *A Capella* consists entirely of recordings of his voice – often, though not always, digitally sampled – which were then used in a variety of ways, ranging from multi-part vocal harmony to digitally edited and electronic transformed samples. Many of these sounds would reappear on *No World Order*.

Even in less obvious ways Rundgren could be highly innovative. For instance, he increased the use of compression on his own recordings. This allowed him to record songs that were much longer and had louder bass sounds than was previously possible for vinyl LPs. A good example is 'A Treatise on Cosmic Fire', a thirty-five minute and twenty-three second instrumental with a Soul-based dance beat and prominent bass parts that he was able to fit on a single side of *Initiation* in 1975. Rundgren also often experimented with highly unusual approaches to recording, combining more established techniques with new technology. For *Nearly Human* (1989), he replicated Phil Spector's 'Wall of Sound' approach from twenty-five years earlier. But in this case he combined the live recording of large ensembles with fully digital recording, to allow for better separation and more modern editing techniques. On his subsequent album, *Second Wind* (1991), he again wrote for a large ensemble to be recorded live in the studio. But in this case the studio sessions took place *onstage* at San Francisco's Golden Gate Park, in front of an audience that was instructed to remain silent during the takes. So, rather than a typical recording of a concert, the events were recording sessions in which an audience was invited to eavesdrop.

In addition to these innovations as an artist and producer, Rundgren also made key contributions to new or developing technologies in video, music video, microwave and satellite broadcasting of concerts, interactive television, computer graphics, computer animation, 3-D animation, and Internet-based patronage and distribution of music. (See Table 5.2 for a partial list of Rundgren's technical innovations.) For instance, Rundgren

The Individualist

developed the idea of a satellite-based music video network well before MTV. He and his manager Eric Gardner made a deposit for a transponder in order to secure a channel on RCA's SATCOM 3 satellite. They had signed or licensed numerous performances, promotional videos, and music videos for broadcast, well before MTV's first broadcast in August 1981. But SATCOM 3 failed to reach a geosynchronous orbit after its launch in

Table 5.2 Some of Todd Rundgren's innovations in video, programming, animation, and distribution

Year	Innovation
1978	The first interactive television concert broadcast over the Warner/QUBE system
1978	The first live nationally broadcast radio concert in stereo (by microwave), linking forty cities across the United States
1979	The first demonstration software for RCA SelectaVision's videodisc format
1979	Developed with Eric Gardner a satellite-based, 24-hour music television channel, to be broadcast on a channel on RCA's SATCOM 3 geosynchronous satellite. (The satellite failed to reach geosynchronous orbit, costing Rundgren and Gardner their access to a transponder.)
1980	The first music video to utilise compositing of live action and computer graphics 'Time Heals'. ('Time Heals' was eighth video shown in MTV's initial rotation.)
1981	The first color graphics tablet for a personal computer (*The Utopia Graphics Tablet System*)
1982	The first live national cablecast of a rock concert (USA Network), simulcast in stereo
1982	The first two commercially released music videos
1983	Nomination for the first-ever *Grammy* for 'Best Short Form Video'
1990	Development of a computer-generated, kinetic-art screensaver, *Flowfazer*
1990	Development with New Tek of *Toaster Link*, a device for linking multiple Commodore *Amiga* home computers employing New Tek's *Video Toaster* to run their *Lightwave 3D* animation software. Rundgren himself created three music videos, 'Change Myself' (*Second Wind*, 1990), 'Theology' (1992), and 'Fascist Christ' (*No World Order*, 1993) which were used to demonstrate the graphic possibilities of *Lightwave 3D* and the *Amiga*.
1993	The first interactive music album, *No World Order*, for the Phillips CD-I, or 'Green Book', interactive format
1994	One of the first 'Enhanced CDs', *The Individualist*, for the CD+, or 'Blue Book', format for audio CD plus computer programming data.
1994	Adaptation of *No World Order* for Time-Warner Cable's experimental interactive television network in Orlando, FL.
2000	Launching of a subscription-based music downloading service, *Patronet*.

December 1979, resulting in the loss of the transponder and ending this development (James, 2008).

All of these technical innovations by Rundgren are directly connected to his creative practice. Certainly, it is easier to avoid repeating yourself if you are continually working with new or developing technologies, musical styles, media, and distribution systems. But one of the key aspects of this practice is that it is also a useful way for an artist to escape what Harold Bloom called 'the anxiety of influence' (Bloom, 1973). This escape is possible because, simply put, artistic antecedents are limited or non-existent in new media. Additionally, and of perhaps equal importance, the *limitations inherent in emerging technologies can be useful in fuelling the creative process*. *No World Order* exemplifies the effectiveness of this creative strategy.

5.3 THE RECENT HISTORY OF DIGITAL INTERACTIVE MUSIC

One of the most interesting areas in the sonic arts currently is interactive sound. Thanks to new technologies, support networks, and audiences, interactive sound has grown explosively in recent years. Much of this development has been in categories such as Interactive Sound Installations, Interactive Sound Design, Interactive Video Art with Sonic Components, Soundtoys and online instruments, Locative Audio and Location-Aware Sound Design, Interactive Scenography, and Instructive Technology (Collins et al., 2014).

But *interactive music*, more specifically, has developed more slowly. With the digitisation of commercial music in the late 1980s, there was considerable industry interest in enhanced or interactive CDs as a method for delivering additional content – and additional profits. Toulson and Paterson (2018) have broken Interactive Recorded Music (IRM) into three large categories:

- Recorded music that allows the listener to manipulate musical or technical aspects of the playback
- Playback of recorded music that might autonomously vary on each listen (adaptive/dynamic music are terms that might overlap here)
- The results of reappropriation after elements of recorded music are made openly available to listener, producer, artist or DJ

While adaptive playback and reappropriation of recordings are certainly important and are a form of interaction, it is primarily the first category that relates to what is typically marketed as 'interactive music'.

A number of forward-thinking artists released enhanced CDs between 1993–1995 after the Green Book and Blue Book formats were developed (see Table 5.3). These enhanced CDs typically allowed the user a great deal of freedom in interacting *with the artist*, in the role of a fan or consumer.

Table 5.3 Early enhanced CD releases by popular artists, 1993–1995

Artist	Title	Year
TR-I (Todd Rundgren)	*No World Order*	1993
Peter Gabriel	*Xplora1*	1993
David Bowie	*Jump*	1994
Prince	*Interactive*	1994
Brain Eno	*Headcandy*	1994
Sarah McLachlan	*Freedom Sessions*	1994
Sting	*All This Time*	1995
TR-i	*The Individualist*	1995

But they generally were not designed for the user to be able to interact *with the music*. For instance, Prince's CD-ROM *Interactive* (1994) allowed the user to virtually tour his Paisley Park Studios, listen to songs and song clips, and watch a selection of music videos or a series of interviews with other artists about Prince's music.

After the initial interest in these interactive enhanced CDs faded—possibly because there were no significant commercial successes—the idea of interactive releases was revived with music apps in the late 2000s (see Table 5.4 for some prominent early examples). The music app has been a more persistent medium, partly because it is connected to the digital downloading of content, which has become the primary means of delivering musical content to audiences. For instance, Jay-Z's app *Magna Carta* (2013) was developed as part of a promotional deal with Samsung. Its function was to allow the first million fans to download his album *Magna Carta Holy Grail* for free, through the app. Similarly, Paul McCartney's group Wings re-released five albums from the 1970s in 2014 for delivery via iPad apps.

As with enhanced CDs, however, the additional content that the apps provided typically consisted of programs designed to provide access to outtakes, photos, videos, interaction with other fans, and/or privileges such as early downloads of new or supplemental material. Yet, while there was a higher level of interactivity in many apps, few allowed listeners any sort of ability to shape the music (Morris, 2016, 483–485).

There were, however, some apps that legitimately explored musical interactivity rather than interactive consumption. For instance, Peter Gabriel's *MusicTiles* (2013), released to mark the twenty-fifth anniversary of his album *So* (1988), allowed users to rearrange stems from the original recording sessions of *So* through a *Tetris*-like interface (Sandhana, 2013). Composer Phillip Glass's *REWORK_* (2012) had a similar app that allowed users to recombine two different musical elements by manipulating a pair of discs onscreen. Most notable of the early interactive music apps was Björk's *Biophilia* (2011), which included a series of different apps housed within a larger interface. Most of the apps within

Table 5.4 App-based music releases by popular artists, 2009–2014

Artist	Title	Year
U2	U2 Mobile App	2009
Kristin Hersh	Crooked	2010
Björk	Biophilia	2011
Phillip Glass	REWORK_	2012
Lady Gaga	Artpop	2013
Peter Gabriel	MusicTiles	2013
Jay-Z	Magna Carta	2013
Bernhoft	Islander	2014

Biophilia allowed some interaction with the music through video games. However, four of them allowed the user to significantly recompose elements of songs through different kinds of interfaces — one like a harp, one like a keyboard, etc. This bundled collection of apps afforded a fairly significant amount of music-making by the user, albeit only as part of an existing musical environment.

In addition to enhanced CDs and app-based albums, of course, there is another important form of interactive music that is often overlooked, but is far more common and pervasive: music for video games. Game music has *always* been highly interactive because it is a component of an interactive environment, triggered as a direct response to a player action. However, the music is generally a supplementary element, rather than the focus of the work. Yet even in such cases the music is still interactive simply because the actions of the user change the music to a significant degree, albeit indirectly: 'Music performance games such as *Guitar Hero* (2005) and *Rock Band* (2007) proved very popular and although the result was music, gaming was the core ethos with control coming from hardware controllers that, in part, emulated real instruments' (Toulson and Paterson, 2018).

Additionally, in many traditions musical performance has always incorporated something of an interactive element. Examples range from the interaction between spontaneous calls and responses in the African-American Gospel, Blues, and Jazz traditions or student-teacher interactions in classrooms, to the in-concert audience sing-alongs with modern pop artists like Queen or Lady Gaga, and even Zappa's notorious 'audience-participation time' from his live concerts (as can be heard on the recordings of his residency at the New York Palladium, *Halloween 77*). In more recent years, highly responsive tools for spontaneously generation (e.g. *Max/MSP/Jitter*) and control (e.g. *Ableton Live*) of sound have been developed for live music performance. These tools enable improvisational interaction between multiple performer-improvisors and other sonic elements, such as ambient sonic responses, real-time samples, or generative software – which can include interactions based upon audience responses.

However, in almost all of these examples, the *listener's* control of the music is either highly constrained or limited to a small role as part of a larger piece of music. Considerably less development has occurred in the creation of music that gives the audience the ability to transform the music as a whole. Rundgren's *No World Order*, the first interactive enhanced CD ever released, is a significant exception to this overall rule because it allowed its users to substantially alter the form of all or part of a large-scale, highly varied piece of music in a variety of ways, drawing the users more fully into the creative process itself:

> At least one of these projects, however—Todd Rundgren's CD-I version of *No World Order*—allows users to manipulate and reassemble various components of the musical recordings themselves. In this way not only are notions of 'passive' consumption called into question but, also, the integrity of the musical work and claims of authorship and originality—key components of the star system itself.
>
> (Théberge, 1997, 253)

5.4 *NO WORLD ORDER*

Although it was perceived as an abrupt stylistic shift at the time, *No World Order* represented the culmination of a number of themes that had already appeared earlier in Rundgren's career. These included Musique Concrète, Collage, Sonic Recontextualisation, Intertextuality, Sequencing, and Digital Sampling, as discussed above. Another theme that was developed in *No World Order* was audience interaction. As early as 1973, Rundgren was thinking of practical ways to allow his fans to participate in his music. For instance, his song 'Sons of 1984' (from the 1974 album *Todd*) combined interactive recordings of two entirely separate live audiences singing along with his band. The first interaction occurred during a concert at New York's Wollman Skating Rink in Central Park in August of 1973. The audience was taught a vocal part for the chorus and recorded on microphones suspended from trees in the park, while the band onstage was recorded in a more conventional manner. The second interaction occurred at a later concert in San Francisco, when a different audience was recorded singing a different, responsive vocal part while listening to a playback of the previous recordings. The two audience interactions were then combined to create an antiphonal chorus for the album's closing track, in an almost Venetian Polychoral style (Myers, 2010, 106).

On *No World Order* Rundgren extended and combined each of these themes in a modern, digitally edited context. His approach was directly inspired by the then-current style of digital remixes popularised by producers like Arthur Baker and Trevor, British artists like Frankie Goes to Hollywood or The KLF, and early sample-based Hip Hop constructions. While the repeated, recontextualised riffs of artists like MC Hammer were pervasive in the late 1980s to early 1990s, the clearest influence on *No World Order* is the style of elaborate digital collages developed by Public Enemy's production team, The Bomb Squad (Walser, 1995). As Rundgren put it:

> Music was constantly being recontextualized via sampling or remixing, into a product that was called a 'new song'. My thought was that, if the audience was responding to this, then this is something where you could use technology to actually emulate in real time.
>
> (Myers, 2010, 295)

When combined with the advent of a dedicated interactive platform, the Phillips CD-i, Rundgren saw a clear creative direction.

Rundgren programmed *No World Order* with his collaborator from *Grokgazer*, programmer Aaron David Levine. It consisted of 933 discrete musical fragments, each of which came in five different mixes. The fragments varied in length but were typically four bars long. Each fragment was designed to be recombined in any order with some semblance of coherence. Rundgren sang with a rap vocal style – for which he was very much *not* known at the time – because his more conventional legato sung vocals made digital cutting and splicing much more difficult:

> The implicitly poetic nature of rap music made it easier to create these little modules that could be switched around and they would still have meaning, in spite of the reordering. Sometimes it would sound like rap of some kind, but then in a different context it could be [word jazz] like Ken Nordine, something like that. I wasn't thinking, 'Oh, I'm trying to gain validity as a rapper here,' I was thinking more in terms of the possibilities it afforded in this new experimental context.
>
> (Rundgren, quoted in Myers 2010, 296)

In addition to the vocals, the modular nature of the project mandated certain musical characteristics for the fragments:

> This forced me to think in terms of every piece of music having a discrete beginning and end, which could be cut out and pasted into a different context . . . So much of the *No World Order* record was the process of tooling all of the sound that had been recorded to accommodate interactive technology.
>
> (ibid.)

Some of the fragments were based on modified samples from Rundgren's more recent recordings, such as the Michael Jackson-like 'Huh!' from the opening of 'Feel It' (*Nearly Human*, 1989) or the sound of the trollish character from 'Lockjaw' (*A Capella*, 1985).

Rundgren also embraced the idea of digital remixing to such an extent that he asked four other producer friends, Jerry Harrison, Don Was, Hal Willner, and Bob Clearmountain, to create unique digital remixes of the 933 fragments: 'These producers' mixes became the basic versions, so you could start with their versions and apply various programmatic filters and stuff like that on it to change it into something you wanted' (ibid.). Essentially these digital mixes provided an expanded set of raw musical materials for the listeners themselves to use as the basis for their own remixes, using the interface designed by Rundgren and Levine as the tool for chopping and screwing the music. And by incorporating so many fragments that can be combined in so many ways, *No World Order* is a very large-scale piece, at least equivalent to a double album. (The conventional album version of *No World Order* alone is 53:12 in length, well over the conventional length of a commercially released album, and there is substantially more material included in the interactive version.)

Each musical fragment was assigned values for seven different parameters, or 'flavours':

- 'Program' referred to the position of the fragment in a specific producer's remix.
- 'Direction' allowed you to control how the program would transport through the possible selections. Choices included 'Fast Forward', 'Very Fast Forward', 'Hold', and 'Reverse'.
- 'Form' had three simple selections, 'Creative', 'Standard', and 'Conservative', which served to either loosen or constrain the interface.
- 'Tempo' had seven different values, ranging from 96–132 BPM.
- 'Mood' had five different emotional settings such as 'Bright' or 'Sad'.
- 'Mix' referred to the five versions of each fragment. The values were 'Thick', 'Natural', 'Spacious', 'Sparse', and 'Karaoke'. The last allowed the user to easily create a vocal-free version of the album to sing along with.
- 'Video' allowed the user to select display options such as 'Blank', 'Swarm', or 'Title'.

Rundgren and Levine then wrote a clean parametric interface that allowed the user to control both the centre point on a range of values and the width across that range for each parameter. They also created 'conditions for an intelligence that would select clips automatically . . .' and 'algorithms for gaussian randomization' (Rundgren, 2018, 220) so that the program would assemble a musical output based in highly varied ways upon the user's inputted parameters.

The result was a large-scale piece of music that gave the listener useful control over a large extent of the shape and construction of the music itself, drawing from a diverse menu of raw materials. It was entirely possible to control the parameters to generate highly specific kinds of outputs (for instance, to listen to each producer's remix as a stand-alone album with a single 'mix' setting or to listen only to outputs at a specific tempo), or simply to choose very loose guidelines and give the program almost complete control. Perhaps the most significant element of the program is that the controls could be changed *on the fly*, so that it would seamlessly adapt to the new instructions as soon as the current fragment finished playing.

All of this contrasted quite substantially with other 'interactive' releases of the time. Of the early Enhanced CD releases listed in Table 5.3, for instance, only *No World Order* allowed 'the listener to manipulate musical or technical aspects of the playback' (Paterson and Toulson, 2018). The rest primarily functioned to allow the user to interact as a consumer, rather than to alter playback itself. However, the second wave of interactive music releases – the App-based music releases that began to emerge this century, listed in Table 5.4 – did offer some useful examples of musical interaction. Gabriel's *Music Tiles* and Glass's *REWORK_* both offered limited interaction through a game-like interface, but with some very striking musical results. Björk's *Biophilia* is so far perhaps the only release to *exceed* the level of interactivity Rundgren provided with *No World Order*, even if it is only through the use of multiple different tools bundled into a single app. The game-like interfaces that all three artists employed proved much more successful than Rundgren's very direct interface in coaxing uncertain listeners to experiment with new technology. In many ways, these differences of interface design reflect the different musical approaches of the artists. Rundgren has long eschewed any compromise for the sake of accessibility, which has allowed him greater freedom while limiting his appeal to a small, core audience. By contrast, Gabriel, Björk and Glass – unusually for a Postmodernist composer – have all persistently developed creative ways to draw new listeners to their work, while trying to limit the extent of the impingement upon their creative practice. As a result, although their experiments with interactivity generally curtail the level of user control in comparison with Rundgren's approach, at the same time far more users have been drawn to experiment with interactive music through these three apps than the relatively small number of users of *No World Order*.

5.5 REACTION

Upon its release, the interactive version of *No World Order* achieved very limited commercial success, for a variety of possible reasons: First, *No World Order* was designed for a new platform, Phillips' CD-I format, which was expensive, commercially unsuccessful, and quickly abandoned. While it was swiftly adapted for the PC and Mac systems, it was not as well suited to them. Additionally, in 1993 consumers were not yet accustomed to using their computers as primary listening devices. Third, listening to *No World Order* was not easy for many listeners, either technically or stylistically. Creating anything other than a conventional album with the program required some work on the part of the listener. As many interactive artists have discovered, not everyone *wants* to control their music to such an extent, particularly in a home consumer setting. And Rundgren's use of rap vocals was off-putting to a large segment of his older, rock-oriented audience (Myers 2010, 296). This was particularly true since the highly electronic nature of the backing tracks was also an extreme stylistic departure from the more traditional large ensembles used on Rundgren's previous two albums (*Nearly Human* and *Second Wind*).

Fourth, the program was promoted with a complicated tour that was fraught with technical difficulties from the beginning. His performances were accompanied by heavily hyped but relatively transparent 'interactive' gimmickry, such as passing out silly string or video cameras for the audience to use, or using traffic lights to instruct them when they were allowed to come onto the edge of the stage to dance. Fifth, in celebration of his use of interactivity, Rundgren changed his artistic name to 'TR-i' for two years, a move which was widely mocked and which created considerable confusion. (This came one year before Prince similarly changed his professional name to the unpronounceable Love symbol, a move that was also derided.)

Finally, Rundgren's record label, Forward, insisted that he also release a conventional album version of *No World Order*. This caused considerable confusion. Was *No World Order* an interactive album, or a regular one? Then in 1994, after both the CD-I and album versions had been relatively unsuccessful, Forward insisted upon another, even more conventional version that Rundgren called *No World Order Lite*. That meant in just two years *No World Order* had been released five times: as a CD-I, as a 16-track audio CD, as a CD-ROM for PC and Mac, and then as a 10-track 'Lite' version. For these reasons and others, *No World Order* did not become the paradigm-altering success that it had the potential to be and, as can be seen from the history of interactive music, has led to few successful follow-ups.

5.6 CONCLUSION

While *No World Order* was not a hit, it remains nonetheless a remarkable achievement. Judging the success of such a work is somewhat different than for more conventional music. Transformative innovations like this are often not enormously successful, simply because they are so different. They can be perceived as 'fake' or 'gimmicky'. For instance, Les Paul's early multi-track recordings were not universally accepted, as Jeff Beck later recalled:

> I remember my mum saying "You shouldn't listen to this music. It's fake ... It's one guy tricking us." So I said, "That's it. That's the music for me".
>
> (Soundbreaking, 2016)

Additionally, because Rundgren had abandoned any aims of conventional commercial success nearly two decades before, judging his project by that criteria alone is overly facile. Rundgren in fact achieved what *he* set out to do: He created a large-scale, complex piece of truly interactive popular music. It does what few other interactive compositions have done to date:

It allows the listener to control the music itself to a significant degree, with highly varied results. And *No World Order* does have its admirers:

> It challenges listeners at every turn; even in its de-fanged *Lite* version it's not "easy listening." But for the . . . faithful, *No World Order* is as compelling a work as Todd Rundgren has ever produced . . . Much maligned—even ridiculed in some quarters—on its release and not generally considered among his best works, Todd Rundgren's *No World Order* remains a fascinating example of the groundbreaking artist who's unafraid to try new things. And beyond that, if one approaches it with an open mind, it's a great listen.
>
> (Kopp, 2019)

As the first large-scale interactive piece of popular music, much can be learned from it about interactivity, which can be quite useful going forward. First, while providing the user with control over the music itself is an interesting ideal, the reality of exercising that control can also be an obstacle for some. As a result, it can be helpful to allow the user the opportunity to decide *not* to interact with the music, or to do so in a limited way. Designing a clean, simple, and intuitive interface is one way to build a piece that combines the *option* of interactive control without forcing it upon the user.

> Admittedly, the kind of far-reaching control represented by 'NWO' isn't for everyone . . . But for people itching to get behind the wheel, 'NWO' represents a watershed event.
>
> (Fisher, 1994)

Second, in any use of new technology, it's important to recognise the limitations of the form and embrace them creatively. Rundgren's exclusive use of rap vocals, samples, and electronically generated sounds on *No World Order*, for instance, was a self-imposed limitation that allowed him to exceed the perceived limits of early digital sequencing technology by working within delineated four-bar fragments. But that decision also opened a large new chapter for him stylistically, as he continued to use rap vocals on his next couple of albums even though there was no technological need for them. Indeed, Rundgren has continued to work in an evolving, heavily EDM-based manner ever since then.

Third, rather than adapting an already-existing work and making it more interactive (as other artists such as Peter Gabriel, Prince, and David Bowie did at the time), it's better to design something expressly for the purpose of interactive use. It may not be as successful commercially, but it will be that much more likely to invite true interaction from the audience.

Fourth, making interactive music is *already* a radical change to the musical form – even in 2020 when interactivity is more familiar to most listeners. While it might make the music more effective interactively, aggressively changing your musical style or attitude might make it seem too alien or remote to your audience – as was the case with *No World Order*.

Similarly, a great deal can be learned about innovation from Rundgren's career in general and from *No World Order* specifically. These lessons include perhaps the central one to be learned from Rundgren's career: It's best, *as a creative artist*, to avoid repeating yourself. On a recent tour to support his autobiography, Rundgren claimed that when his ability to write pop songs had become formulaic in the early 1970s, he discovered that 'I found my comfort zone to be very uncomfortable'. His success as a producer allowed him a good deal of freedom in this respect:

> Through my constant production work I had become free of the economic pressures most artists felt when in the studio. My singular challenge was not to repeat myself, something that my peers were nearly obligated to do if they were going to hang on to the attention of a flighty and fickle audience that simultaneously considered change a kind of treason.
>
> (Rundgren 2018, 126)

In a related way, it's important not just to change from time to time, but to *keep* changing. Whenever Rundgren has gained mastery of a new style, tool, or technique, he has almost immediately moved onto something new:

> There are no rules. I suppose it's because I do have a certain experimental element, that's a proactive way of continuing to move, but then there's also sort of reactive ways that cause you to move. That's me not wanting to repeat myself . . . My constant need to change is really just my short attention span. Once I finish a record I listen to it copiously so that I can figure out exactly what I've done right and what I've done wrong. Then I move on.
>
> (Rundgren, 2010)

It's also important not to easily accept technological limitations. Rundgren has often been frustrated by such limitations in his ability to fulfil his artistic vision. Where possible, though, he has attempted to circumvent these limitations by developing or expanding that technology. In the case of *No World Order*, there was no existing system for delivering interactive music. So Rundgren and Levine simply set about creating their own system, taking advantage of the newly available CD-I protocol and machine.

At the same time, however, it is important for creative reasons *to limit yourself*. There is a good bit of research support for the use of limitation as a tool for fostering creativity. A number of successful artists of different sorts have consciously limited themselves, erected challenging boundaries, or embraced rigid sets of rules in order to open up creative possibilities:

> Sometimes restrictions get the mind going. If you've got tons and tons of money, you may relax and figure you can throw money at any

problem that comes along. You don't have to think so hard. But when you have limitations, sometimes you come up with very creative, inexpensive ideas.

(Lynch 2007, 115)

In his conversations with Robert Kraft, the composer Igor Stravinsky discussed how the rigid rules of serial counterpoint opened his mind by limiting it: 'The serial technique I use impels me to greater discipline than ever before' (Craft and Stravinsky, 1959, 22). This sentiment is perhaps most succinctly expressed by The White Stripes' Jack White, who said 'Ease of use is the death of creativity' (*It Might Get Loud*, 2008). As a result, Rundgren's refusal to repeat himself prevents him from developing too much 'ease of use' with any given style, technology, or technique.

These last two points – refusing to accept limitations yet at the same time choosing to limit yourself – seem to generate a paradox. But one way Rundgren has managed to resolve this paradox is by *working with emerging technologies*. By using technologies that are still being developed, or by developing them yourself, the limitations come from the technology *and not from existing traditions*. This means that you have relative freedom to use them in your own way, avoiding the 'anxiety of influence' from others (within the possibilities of the technology). Yet at the same time the *technological* limitations still provide significant barriers for the artist to overcome, fuelling creativity.

Todd Rundgren's *No World Order* represented a great advance in the development of interactive music technology, one which has yet to be surpassed in the 27 years since its release. The biggest criticism of it, and the likely cause of its commercial failure, is that it made its users, those who were meant to interact *with* the music and not just consume it, somewhat uncomfortable. This was, however, by design. As Rundgren himself might put it, it's best not to get comfortable in your comfort zone. While other artists have experimented with interactive music in ways that make the users more comfortable with the new technology, this seems to have considerably constrained the creative possibilities afforded by that technology. As other artists and engineers develop new tools to allow users to interact with music, such as the *variPlay* music app (Paterson et al., 2019), this balance between creative possibility and consumer accessibility will have to be considered very carefully.

REFERENCES

Billboard (2020). *Todd Rundgren*, available online from https://www.billboard.com/music/todd-rundgren [accessed: 3 December 2019].

Blair, J.J. (2008). Todd Rundgren, *Electronic Musician*, available online from https://www.emusician.com/gear/todd-rundgren [accessed December 2019].

Bloom, Harold (1973). *The Anxiety of Influence: A Theory of Poetry*. Oxford: Oxford University Press.

Cleveland International (2019). Bat Out Of Hell Hits the Stage: An Album Born in Cleveland Is Now a Musical, *Clevelandinternational.com* (website) [12 August]

Available online from https://www.clevelandinternational.com/news/-bat-out-of-hell-hits-the-stage-an-album-born-in-cleveland-is-now-a-musical-photos- [accessed: 3 December 2019].

Collins, K., Kapralos, B. and Tessler (2014). *The Oxford Handbook of Interactive Audio*. Oxford: Oxford University Press.

Craft, R. and Stravinsky, I. (1959). *Conversations with Igor Stravinsky*. New York, Doubleday.

Fisher, M. (1994). Multimedia Review: No World Order, *Variety*, 17 October, available online from https://variety.com/1994/film/reviews/multimedia-review-no-world-order-1200409149/ [accessed: 3 December 2019].

It Might Get Loud (2008). Directed by Davis Guggenheim [feature film], New York, Sony Pictures Classics.

James, B. (2008). *A Dream Goes On Forever—The Continuing Story of Todd Rundgren (Volume 2): The Utopia Years*, with a foreword by Kasim Sulton, Bentonville, Arkansas, Golden Treasures Publishing.

Kopp, B. (2019). Todd Rundgren, *Trouser Press*, available online from: http://www.trouserpress.com/entry.php?a=todd_rundgren [accessed: 3 December 2019].

Lynch, D. (2007). *Catching the Big Fish: Meditation, Consciousness and Creativity*. London, Tarcher/Penguin.

Myers, P. (2010). *A Wizard A True Star: Todd Rundgren in the Studio*. London, Jawbone Press.

Morris, J. (2016). App Music, *The Oxford Handbook of Music and Virtuality*, ed. by Sheila Whiteley and Shara Rambarran. Oxford, Oxford University Press, 477–492.

Paterson, J. and Toulson, R. (2018) Interactive Recorded Music: Past, Present and Future. In *Audio Engineering Society Convention 145*, 17–20 October 2018, New York City, US.

Rundgren, T. (2010). Excerpt From my Interview with Todd Rundgren, Interviewed by Gene Meyers for *The Rattle Bag*, available online from https://genemyers.wordpress.com/2010/12/23/excerpt-from-my-forthcoming-interview-with-todd-rundgren/ [accessed 3 December 2019].

Rundgren, T. (2013a). Todd Rundgren: 'Every Once in a While I Took a Trip and Never Came Back', interviewed by Paul Lester for *The Guardian* 1 May 2013, available online from https://www.theguardian.com/culture/2013/may/01/todd-rundgren-interview [accessed 3 December 2019].

Rundgren, T. (2013b). Todd Rundgren on Songwriting, Meat Loaf, and Utopia, Interviewed by Torsten Schmidt for *Red Bull Music Academy* (website), available online from https://www.redbullmusicacademy.com/lectures/todd-rundgren [accessed 3 December 2019].

Rundgren, T. (2018). *The Individualist: Digressions, Dreams & Dissertations*. Los Angeles, Cleopatra Press.

Sandhana, Lakshmi (2013). Peter Gabriel's Latest App *MusicTiles* is 'So' 2.0. *Fast Company* 1 July, available online from https://www.fastcompany.com/3004537/peter-gabriels-latest-app-musictiles-so-20 [accessed: 3 December 2019].

Soundbreaking (2016) *Painting with Sound*. Directed by James Manera [television programme]. New York, NY, Show of Force Productions.

Théberge, Paul (1997). *Any Sound You Can Imagine: Making Music, Consuming Technology*. Hanover, NH, Wesleyan University Press.

Walser, Robert (1995) Rhythm, Rhyme, and Rhetoric in the Music of Public Enemy, *Ethnomusicology*, Spring/Summer 1995, 193–217.

DISCOGRAPHY

Badfinger (1971), [vinyl LP] *Straight Up*, Apple.
The Band (1970), [vinyl LP] *Stage Fright*, Capitol.
Björk (2011), [app] *Biophilia*, One Little Indian Records.
Gabriel, Peter (2013), [app] *MusicTiles*, Real World.
Glass, Phillip (2012), [app] *REWORK_*, Orange Mountain.
Jay-Z (2013), [app] *Magna Carta*, Roc-A-Fella.
Meat Loaf (1977), [vinyl LP] *Bat Out Of Hell*, Cleveland International.
Nazz (1968), [vinyl LP] *Open My Eyes,* SGC Records.
Oldfield, Mike (1973), [vinyl LP] *Tubular Bells*, Virgin.
Prince (1994), [CD-ROM] *Interactive*, Compton's New Media.
Rundgren, Todd (1972), [vinyl LP] *Something/Anything*, Bearsville.
Rundgren, Todd (1973), [vinyl LP] *A Wizard, A True Star*, Bearsville.
Rundgren, Todd (1974), [vinyl LP] *Todd*, Bearsville.
Rundgren, Todd (1975), [vinyl LP] *Initiation*, Bearsville.
Rundgren, Todd (1976), [vinyl LP] *Faithful*, Bearsville.
Rundgren, Todd (1985), [vinyl LP] *A Capella*, Warner Brothers.
Rundgren, Todd (1989), [vinyl LP] *Nearly Human*, Warner Brothers.
Rundgren, Todd (1991), [vinyl LP] *Second Wind*, Warner Brothers.
Rundgren, Todd (1992), [music video] 'Theology', *The Desktop Collection*, Direct.
Rundgren, Todd (as "TR-I") (1993), [CD-Rom] *No World Order*, Electronic Arts.
Rundgren, Todd (1993), [CD] *No World Order*, Forward.
Rundgren, Todd (1994), [CD] *No World Order Lite*, Forward.
Rundgren, Todd (1995), [CD+] *The Individualist*, Digital Entertainment.
Utopia (1980), [vinyl LP] *Deface the Music*, Bearsville.
Wonder, Stevie (1972), [vinyl LP] *Talking Book*, Motown.
Wonder, Stevie (1972), [vinyl LP] *Music of My Mind*, Motown.
XTC (1986), [vinyl LP] *Skylarking*, Virgin.
Zappa, Frank (2017), [CD] *Halloween '77*, Universal.

6

Ground control and cloud booths

Using Dante to break geographical barriers to music production

Paul Ferguson and Dave Hook

6.1 INTRODUCTION

This chapter concerns the idea of long-distance, real-time music collaboration in contemporary music production contexts. The practical application of the work described in this chapter was demonstrated during the keynote performance by the 'Radio Science Orchestra' at *Innovation in Music 2019*, hosted by the University of West London (UWL). The Innovation In Music Conference bridges academia and the music industry and has been a strong supporter of research into long-distance, real-time performance. Demonstrations have taken place during the 2013 and 2015 conferences that led directly to industry collaboration with audio manufacturers Focusrite and Audinate (Ferguson, 2015). The keynote was the inspiration of Professor Justin Paterson at UWL, allowing the authors to work with Focusrite to produce a world first for long-distance, interactive performance: a method by which commercially available Dante hardware and software can be used to achieve what was previously limited to a research environment.

In 2007, Carot *et al.* (2007, p. 131) noted that there are "several technical and cultural barriers that need to be overcome in order to bring networked music performance in the mainstream". In the thirteen years since, the networked audio landscape has developed significantly. This chapter contributes to both those technical and cultural conversations, addressing two specific areas. Firstly, through discussion of a practical case study, we will investigate our new format for long-distance, real-time work – namely Audinate's Dante Audio Over IP with its new multi-zone capabilities. Secondly, we will consider and discuss concepts, terminology and nomenclature in relation to the experience of music production in a long-distance, real-time context. Through this discussion we propose a terminology that supports the experience, represents the technical process and makes use of existing terms and concepts already part of wider culture to bridge academic research with mainstream usage. Concluding this, we will consider music industry responses to this breakthrough demonstration.

6.2 CONTEXT

An increasing number of studies are being conducted regarding the possibilities of networked music collaboration. From nascent considerations around the introduction of high-quality streaming audio (Chafe *et al.* 2000), to useful discussions highlighting the differences and similarities between telematic and networked music, interest in this area is demonstrably growing both within the academic community and in industry. Many commercial applications are now available for uni-directional streaming, allowing access to live events from other/ multiple locations around the world. This is evident in large-scale ventures such as National Theatre's *NT Live*, and live-streamed concerts from the London Symphony Orchestra. Companies, such as Inner Ear (Scotland), provide solutions for live streaming services. Although these are sometimes described as interactive streaming events, in reality they are uni-directional, long-distance events, that allow people to experience live events happening in other places around the world. There is currently less commercial activity in the development of multi-directional, interactive live streaming, this being the area where further technological and workflow development are required before it can be implemented and taken up by a wider audience.

Consider these statements taken from discussion with a range of people within the music industry:

> When can I record a drummer in Ireland without having to leave my studio in Scotland.
>
> Calum Malcolm (2018) Producer/ Engineer
> (Blue Nile, Mark Knopfler, Simple Minds)

> So, can I just plug into a booth somewhere and join in the session?
> Zack Moir (2019) Musician/ Academic

> What is a cloud? It's just someone else's server
> Chris Chafe (2019) Academic / Director
> of CCRMA (Stanford)

From these quotes, we have a producer and engineer who would make use of the technology (with sufficient reliability and ease of use) to engineer from his own studio space in one country but make use of musicians elsewhere around the world; a musician and an academic who is interested in being able to join recording sessions, rehearsals and performances from his own institution by just booking a booth and connecting; and a long-established scholar of time-based, real-time activity examining the word "cloud" that is so well established in popular culture. Introducing the topic through these quotes is useful as it establishes some of the different needs and expectations that musicians, engineers and academics might have about what they want from real-time networked music production.

The term *music production* is being used in this article in order to include recording, performance, engineering and collaboration. Carot *et al.*'s paper from AES *30th International Conference* (2007) on the state of the art for networked music performance identifies areas being examined to include network latency, other technological issues and sociological issues, including its usefulness and cultural implications. It is hoped that this chapter contributes to current conversations relating to all of these issues.

6.3 WHAT DO WE ALREADY KNOW?

To address this project, the first stage is to recognise both the work done by academics that has got us to this stage, their achievements and also the problems that still require attention. In 1998, Everhart's "asynchronous web jams" provided opportunities for people to perform in a non-real-time fashion with other musicians around the world through downloading material, adding to it and re-uploading it. Pignato and Begany's "technologically mediated distance collaborations" (2015, p. 113), took this further with live performers from around the world (USA, Canada, Ireland, Germany, New Zealand, Israel) contributing to a live ensemble performance taking place in State of New York University. In this case the performers were reacting to the live performance. However, they were connected by Voice Over IP (VOIP) service, Skype, and as such would have incurred latency such that it wasn't possible to maintain timing elements with other distance performers. VOIP helps to build a musical understanding of the acceptable limits of latency in a digital system and further to this, is the issue of audio quality. Additionally, the audio over VOIP is dynamic-range compressed and low quality. Chafe and Gurevich's (2004) study into temporal displacement is useful in pinpointing maximum delay times between locations where musicians can still react musically to each other in real time.

Systems such as Jack-Trip and LOLA (Ferguson, 2013) provide very fast transfer of audio (and video) between long-distance locations. The issue that arises here is that the speed of audio transfer is prioritised over the quality of the audio received. A continuous, uninterrupted audio stream is achieved, but it contains the clicks and pops of digital errors, rendering it of no use in a recording-studio context for high-quality audio capture. Another problem in the workflows being created for this emerging technology has been the centring, hosting and controlling of signals. Up until now, most experiments into real-time, long-distance studio sessions have been operated with both a studio control room and an engineer at each end, meaning transport running in two places, DAWs running in two places and essentially two recording or digital mixing sessions running at once. For this study, we propose a new format using the new multi-zone capabilities of Audinate's Dante Audio Over IP to 're-centre' the recording studio control room into a single 'Ground' location, with a number of 'Cloud Booths' digitally linking into the session that can potentially be connected from a range of other geographic locations.

6.4 BREAKING GEOGRAPHICAL BARRIERS TO MUSIC PRODUCTION

As mentioned previously, Moir, Ferguson and Smith (2019) described their long-distance recording sessions focused on a model whereby the audio was sent with very low latency via LOLA, while simultaneously being recorded at high quality through Avid Pro Tools Cloud Collaboration (Figure 6.1). This dual-stream approach was required as LOLA ensures its low latency at the detriment of its audio quality, while the Avid Cloud audio ensures its quality, but is not real-time. By combining the two, Ferguson was able to provide fast enough audio transfer to satisfy musicians response times and high-enough audio quality for recording engineering purposes. While the dual-stream approach was effective, it would obviously be even more beneficial for there to be only a single stream that can

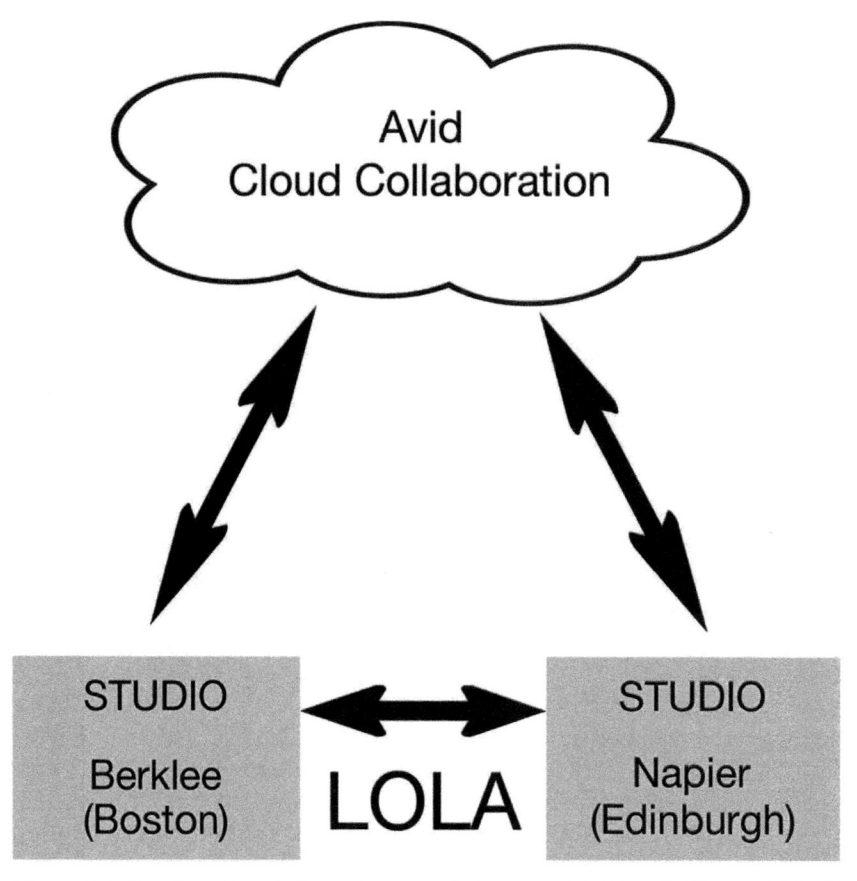

Figure 6.1 Previous 'dual stream' approach between Berklee College of Music and Edinburgh Napier University

(Moir, Ferguson and Smith, 2019)

Ground control and cloud booths

achieve both high-quality audio and low-latency transfer, simplifying and improving the process.

A number of issues arose with the previous dual-stream method. Running two Pro Tools systems (one at each point) means that there was no transport synchronisation and a rudimentary 'count down' was required to record with manual transport control at each end. Audio quality for musicians is of the lower, 'glitchy', format in order to maintain low latency. The remote engineer cannot monitor quality of audio while tracking, as the audio is added via the Cloud afterwards.

In an effort to address these issues, we proposed a new method utilising Audinate's Dante audio over IP, which, as of September 2019, became capable of operating over multiple zones. Dante is a leading digital networking format for Audio Over IP, and can be found at the forefront of live sound, broadcast and connecting multiple recording studios. By enabling distribution across multiple zones, it opens up the possibility of transferring high quality, uncompressed multi-channel audio over long distances, during interactive recording sessions. This step forward creates opportunities for music creation over distance, providing accessibility to music facilities for those that may be unable to access them, reducing carbon footprints through negating the need to travel great distances for recording sessions, and allowing collaboration between artists all over the world that may otherwise not be possible. In order to achieve this, a number of technical factors require consideration including Dante on single subnets (IT departments typically split their Local Area Network into smaller sub-networks called subnets), using Dante Domain Manager to bridge local subnets, clocking over distance, buffering and jitter. With this being a world first in its novel use of Dante and DDM over academic networks, there follows an analysis of the processes involved in successfully connecting, clocking and running the session on 5 December 2019 between University of West London and Edinburgh Napier University.

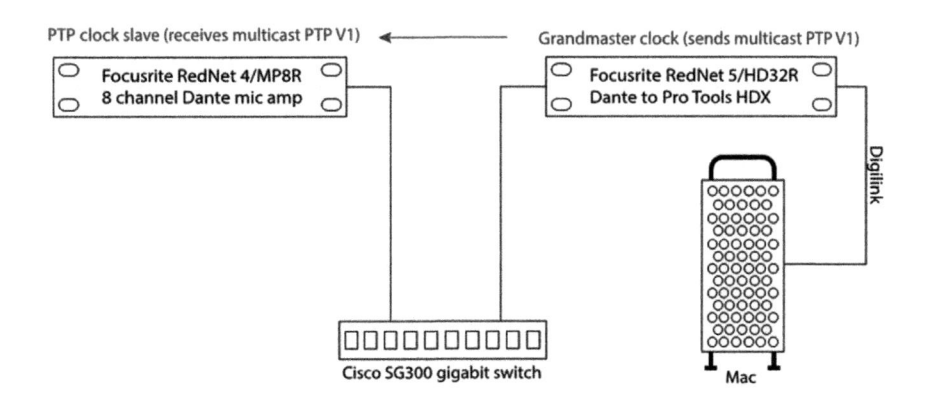

Figure 6.2 A single subnet Dante system

6.5 CONVENTIONAL SINGLE SUBNET DANTE

Before considering what must *change* to allow Dante to operate over distance, first consider a conventional deployment of Dante where the devices are on the same subnet. Figure 6.2 shows a simple system where the Dante devices are plugged into a single switch. Typically, the devices will self-assign themselves a link-local IP address in the 169.254.xx.xx range and one of the devices will establish itself as the Grandmaster Clock as determined by the Best Master Clock (BMC) Algorithm described in the IEEE1588-2002 Precision Time Protocol specification (Commonly referred to as PTP version 1). The elected Grandmaster will then act as a clock master and will transmit multicast PTPv1 clock messages for the other Dante devices to follow. Unlike a unicast message that is sent from one device to another, multicast messages are transmitted to all devices and a network switch will normally ensure that multicast messages do not pass beyond the subnet. As an example, the discovery mechanism that causes a Dante device to be visible to the Dante Controller software application uses multicast and therefore the device would not see beyond the subnet.

The direct consequence of the above is that if two subnets are used to deploy Dante equipment in two areas of a building, (for example Studio 1 and Studio 2), then those Dante networks are truly isolated – a device on Studio 1's subnet is not visible on Studio 2's subnet and the two subnets each have their own Grandmaster Clock.

6.6 USING DANTE DOMAIN MANAGER TO BRIDGE TWO LOCAL SUBNETS

Although isolation between two studio subnets could be desirable, a situation may arise where we need to connect a Dante device on Studio 1's network to a Dante device in Studio 2. If multicast messages do not pass between the subnets, how do we clock and discover the Studio 2 device? Dante Domain Manager (DDM) provides a solution based on the concept of a boundary clock introduced in the 2008 revision of IEEE1588 (commonly referred to as PTP version 2). Each studio subnet (referred to as a Domain in DDM) has a device acting as a boundary clock that either transmits or receives unicast PTP clock messages.

In Figure 6.3 the Studio 1 subnet now includes a computer running DDM software. As before, the RedNet 5 continues to send multicast PTPv1 clock messages to any Dante slave devices within its subnet. In addition, the RedNet 5 device has been configured by DDM to send unicast PTPv2 clock to a device on the Studio 2 subnet that has been 'enrolled' into the Studio 1 'Domain' and has been designated as a boundary clock slave. In essence, this Studio 2 device has been removed from the Studio 2 Dante network and will no longer be visible to Dante Controller users in Studio 2. It is clocked by the Studio 1 Grandmaster Clock and audio can be routed to and from it as though it were part of the Studio 1 subnet.

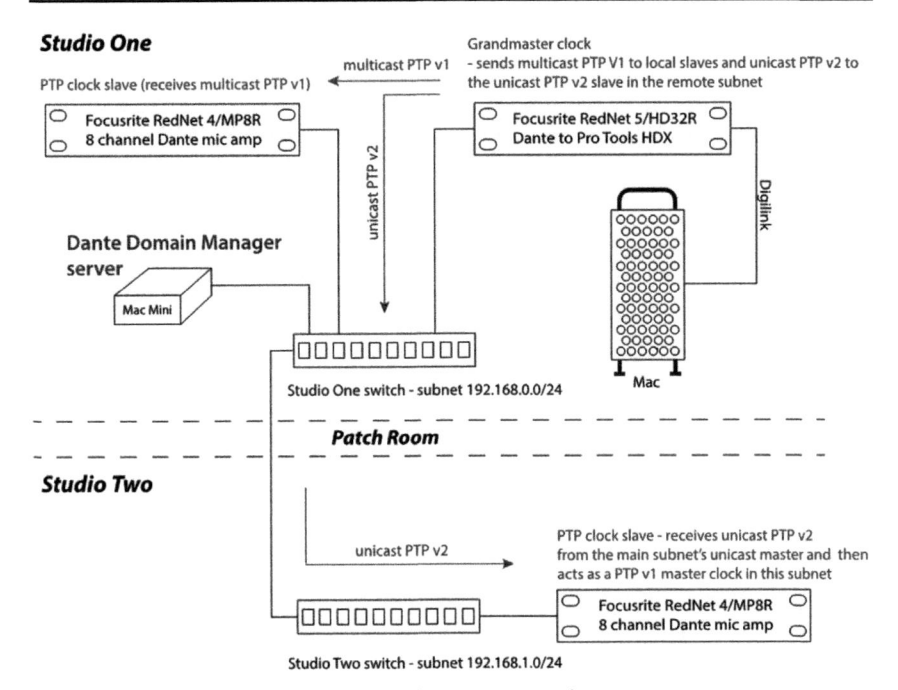

Figure 6.3 Bridging two subnets with Dante Domain Manager

6.7 LONG-DISTANCE DANTE

During beta trials of DDM in 2017, Ferguson posed the following research question to Focusrite and Audinate: "What might we expect if Studio 1 and Studio 2 were in universities in different cities, joined by the academic network, instead of the same building?". Edinburgh Napier University's work with the LOLA system showed that Jisc's Janet National Research and Education Network (NREN) provided bandwidth and jitter performance that allowed low-latency audio and video to successfully traverse between universities. However, LOLA is not a syntonous system (i.e. the transmitter and receiver will not be running at exactly the same speed) and has no mechanism equivalent to PTP to lock together the audio clocks at either end. At that stage, it was anticipated that network-induced jitter between Edinburgh and London would be too great for the two Dante clocks to lock but this will be examined further in this chapter. In February 2019, Audinate approached Ferguson with details about the 'zoning' feature to be incorporated into the forthcoming version 1.1 release of DDM. The DDM 'Zone' extends the concept of enrolment described earlier by allowing the device to be declared as being in another (geographic) zone as well as another subnet. DDM assumes that each zone separately derives its PTP clock from a GPS satellite. Thus, both the local and remote-zone Grandmaster clocks are derived from GPS and are, therefore, syntonous. It is no longer necessary to transmit jitter-prone unicast PTP to the remote device.

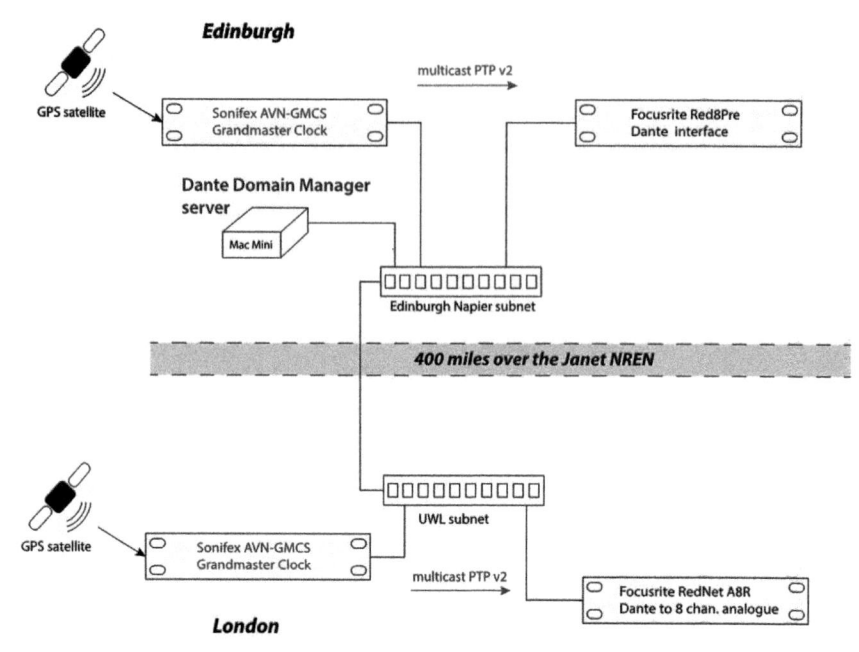

Figure 6.4 Two-zone Dante Domain Manager configuration

Figure 6.5 Two-zone clocking between Edinburgh and London

Figure 6.4 shows the two-zone configuration used for the *Innovation In Music 2019* Keynote performance. In this example, a *Napier Domain* was created in DDM and then an 'Edinburgh Zone' and 'London Zone' established within that. The Focusrite Red8Pre was enrolled into the *Napier Domain* and placed in the default 'Edinburgh Zone'. The Focusrite A8R in the University of West London was then enrolled into the *Napier Domain* and placed in the 'London Zone'.

GPS-derived Grandmaster clocks in each site have won the PTP Best Master Clock Algorithm and provide multicast PTPv2 clocks for those sites. Figure 6.5 is a screenshot taken from Dante Controller and shows the clocking for the Figure 6.4 two-zone DDM configuration. Three things can be noted:

1. The Grandmaster clocks are shown as 'unknown devices' (Actually Sonifex GMC GPS-derived PTPv2 clocks)

2. The Edinburgh Napier Focusrite Red8Pre and UWL RedNet A8R appear as PTPv2 slaves (to the Sonifexes)
3. The Red4Pre and RedNet A8R are also acting as PTPv1 multicast masters bridging PTPv2 for any local Dante devices requiring PTPv1.

6.8 NETWORK-INDUCED JITTER AND DANTE BUFFER SIZE

Before considering network jitter during the trials, we must first examine the network connection between Edinburgh and London. The Edinburgh Napier University connection was via a dedicated 1Gbit research link and was not subject to any firewall traffic shaping or stateful packet inspection. The connection at the University of West London went through a firewall and although given highest priority it was seen to be affected by the volume of network traffic in and out of UWL depending on the time of day. As a result, a round-trip (RTT) network ping between Edinburgh Napier University and the University of West London varied between 12 ms and 45 ms with an average around 15 ms.

The Focusrite Red8Pre and RedNet A8R were chosen for the keynote performance because they both use the Audinate Brooklyn II Dante module. Dante Domain Manager allows the Brooklyn II's maximum buffer size of 2000 samples per channel to be selected which equates to 40 ms

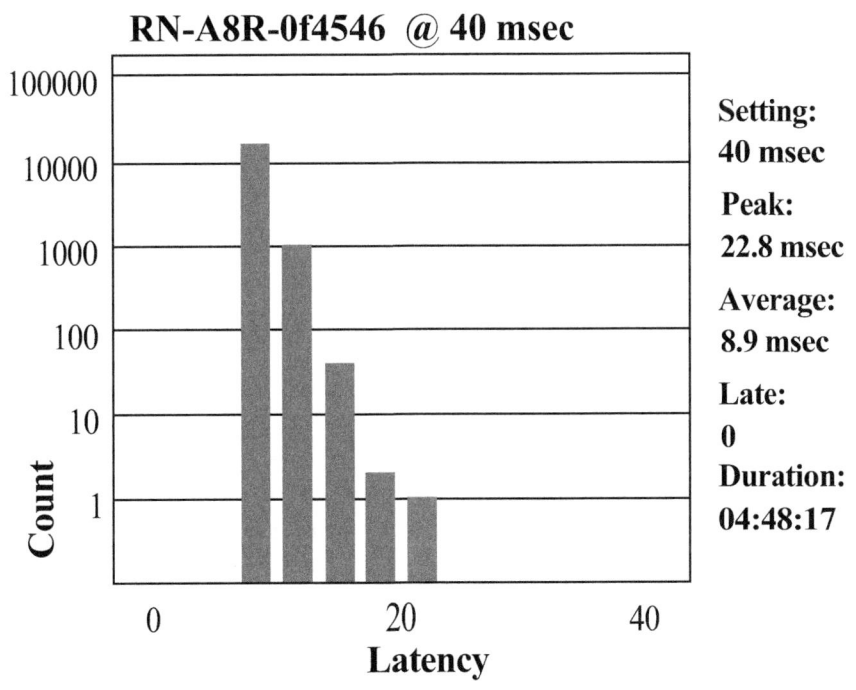

Figure 6.6 Edinburgh to London received packet latency (in ms) over a four hour test period

at 48 kHz sample rate and is therefore large enough to accommodate the largest (RTT divided by two) network delays seen above. The graph in Figure 6.6 shows the latency spread seen over a four-hour period. No audio packets arrive outside the 40 ms buffer maximum and the average is below 10 ms. In a future study the authors will test the theory that bypassing the firewalls at both ends will allow a buffer size of 20 ms and potentially 10 ms, thus below Chafe's 25 ms upper limit for best synchronous performance (Chafe *et al.*, 2010) and opening up the real-time potential of the 'Cloud Booth' distance space to be further discussed later in this chapter.

6.9 UNICAST PTP OVER DISTANCE

Returning to the question posed in 2017, the testbed in Figure 6.4 also allows us to test the assumption that network jitter would be too great

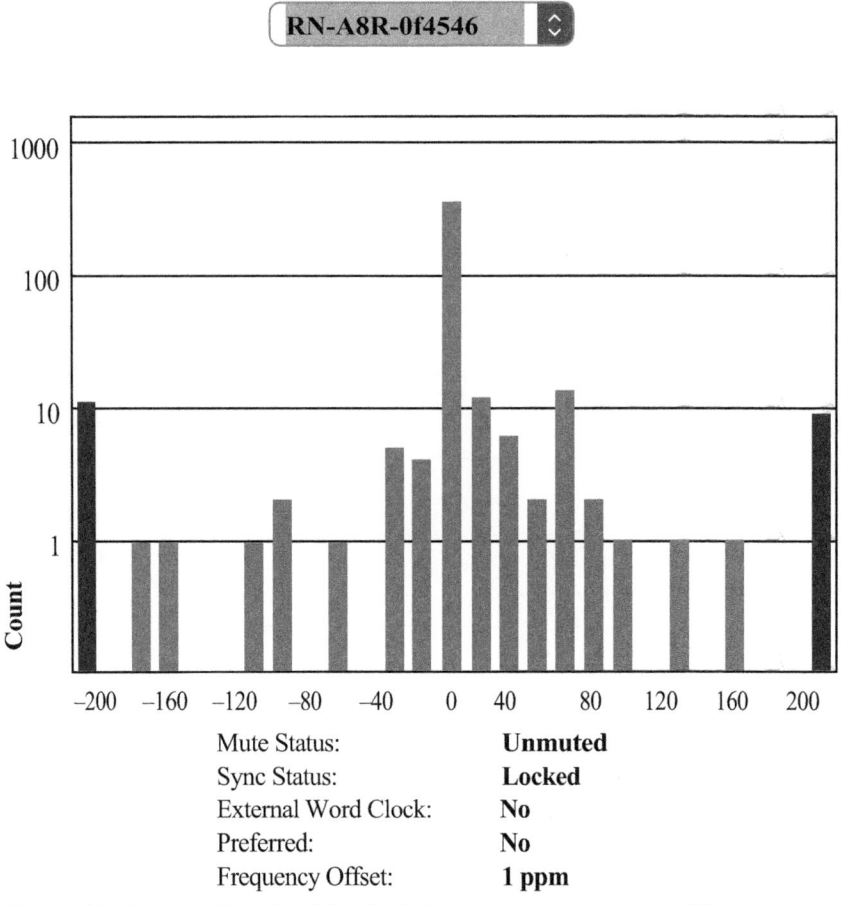

Figure 6.7 Observed London (slave) clock variation in parts per million

to achieve device synchronisation by sending unicast PTP clock over the Janet network. If we place the Edinburgh and London device in the same default zone, DDM will no longer assume GPS-based clock synchronisation and will elect a PTPv2 boundary-clock master and slave and send unicast PTPv2 between Edinburgh and London. Figure 6.7 shows the Focusrite A8R Voltage-controlled Crystal Oscillator (VXCO) attempting to follow the high-jitter PTPv2 clock coming from Edinburgh. When the VXCO frequency offset exceeds ± 200ppm the device mutes its audio and the unit indicates an unlocked state in Dante Controller. This muting and subsequent unmuting could occur within one minute when UWL network traffic was high.

The key point here, is that we have bridged the academic and commercial worlds. Although DDM zones were intended for use over an isolated network (e.g. connecting a broadcaster with studios in two different cities), we have successfully established that the Janet academic network offers sufficient performance to do this between London and Edinburgh without requiring a dedicated point-to-point link. Through experiments carried out in these areas encompassing Dante on single subnets, the use of Dante Domain Manager over subnets, clocking over distance, buffering and jitter, we arrived at the stable and functional system-design that provided the backbone for the *InMusic19* Keynote Performance at University of West London in December 2019.

6.10 CURRENT LANGUAGE AROUND LONG-DISTANCE SPACES CONNECTED BY TECHNOLOGY

Having established the imminent viability of long-distance, real-time production using Dante equipment that is commonly found in commercial studios, it becomes useful to also discuss and propose terminology and nomenclature that assist in conceptualising and practically applying the technology if we are to successfully bridge academic research with mainstream usage. The terms used in academic papers (much like "long-distance real-time music production" in this chapter) do not translate into easy ways of discussing the activities. For example, it is unlikely that music creators are going to use phrases such as, "want to get together for a technologically mediated distance collaboration?", or "I'll catch you later for some real-time, remote, interactivity". As such, there is an opportunity here to look at the concepts behind the technical elements of the process, the concepts behind some of the sociological and philosophical discussions around the topic, and current terms that are already fully integrated into mainstream culture. Through a consideration of these three, we wish to propose a very simple model that provides a naming-structure and underlying concept for how to consider the inclusion of distance collaboration within the existing recording studio model.

6.11 STEPS TOWARDS DEFINING LONG-DISTANCE SPACES LINKED BY TECHNOLOGY

Some discussion has taken place that considers the connection of musicians over networked audio as the creation of a *virtual* space (Moir *et al.*, 2019). The reality of real-time low-latency studio recording over distance is that it connects musicians in *physical* spaces, temporarily removing the distance between them. Each musician remains in a physical space, not a virtual space, and they can see, hear and perceive the world around them. The technology erases the geography between them, expanding the shared headspace that a headphone cue mix provides. From this perspective, it is a cue mix that creates a 'shared headspace' where musicians can meet sonically when they are in different rooms or other physical spaces. We have had video and audio in studios for a long time as a means of connecting people without being in the same physical space. In this context, the distance technology is just allowing that pre-existing headspace to expand geographically.

The 'virtual space' acts as a nexus. It interconnects a range of sources and multiplexes them into a new collective whole; this nexus is normally the mixing desk, or more likely the DAW. Consider the addition of long-distance connection to this system similar to a Wide Area Network versus a Local Area Network. Existing recording studios are generally closed-circuit local area networks. This technology provides the opportunity for recording studios to be truly open, multi-zone Wide Area Networks. If this is taken as a foundational metaphor, the studio experience is not necessarily "decentred" as described by Pignato and Begany (2015) but "re-centred" – with the studio control room, where mixing and recording takes place, at the core and a series of booths and live spaces orbiting the space like satellites. The recording studio revolves around, and is centred on, the control room – the space where all signals, performances and musicians converge, combine and are woven together into a stereo image.

In a long-distance, multi-location scenario, spaces can be separated into 'Ground' spaces, connected by geography, and 'Cloud' spaces, connected by technology. In this scenario, you might have:

- Ground Control (Room) (Edinburgh)
- Ground Studio/ Live Room (Edinburgh)
- Ground Booth (Edinburgh)
- Cloud Booth 1 (London)
- Cloud Booth 2 (Berlin)

The Ground studio spaces are defined by the location of the master control space. Any distance-spaces connected to this become Cloud Booths. The 'virtual' space is still the cue mix as has been the case in studios for decades. Figure 6.8 shows the configuration for a session running in Edinburgh with a Cloud Booth transmitting in from London.

One aspect of this terminology and configuration is that control rooms and booths can all be 'floated'. For example, if the central tracking space

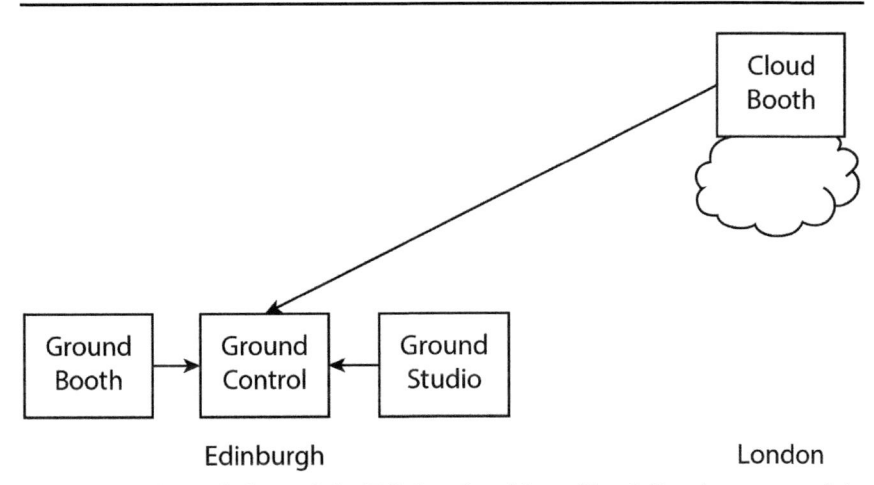

Figure 6.8 Ground Control in Edinburgh with a Cloud Booth connected in London

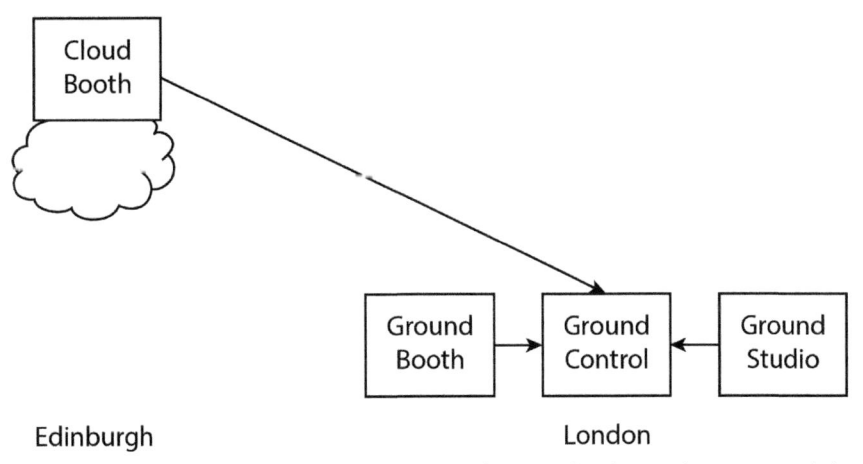

Figure 6.9 Ground Control in London with a Cloud Booth connected in Edinburgh

shifts in the example above from Edinburgh to London, the Edinburgh spaces become Cloud Booths and the London spaces take on the role of Ground Control, Ground Booth etc, as demonstrated in Figure 6.9.

For the keynote performance detailed in this article, in the preparatory weeks commencing 25 November 2019 up until the 4 December 2019, ENU's studios were Ground Control, with UWL taking the role of a Cloud Booth. On the day of the keynote concert, control of the session was in London and that became the location of the Ground Control room. Subsequently, ENU became Cloud Booth 1.

Why does this matter? It matters because it is helpful in considering both simple technical terminology to explain the roles of the spaces involved;

terminology that uses and connects to existing terms for both music industry and digital communication. It is also significant because it contributes to conversations about multilocality, deterritorialism, and the untethering of a person's physical location due to digital communication over distance. This perspective assists in anchoring the recording-studio experience, providing a potential stability through joining/ attaching musicians over distance with existing cultural phenomena. It is not proposed that by simply naming spaces and providing a philosophical reasoning for their names that issues of distance collaboration such isolation, 'outsider-dom', and miscommunication will disappear, but it is hoped that steps towards an organised definition of the spaces will support the process of improving the experience for those transmitting in from a Cloud Booth. Other simple solutions such as Skype screens running in every Ground and Cloud space would provide interim solutions to the loss of synchronous communication when recordings stop.

6.12 CONCLUSIONS

The live keynote performance successfully tested and confirmed the prediction made by Ferguson during his InMusic 2015 LOLA demonstration that the academic research and industry development would ultimately align. We have shown that the NREN can be used to connect ENU and UWL across two Dante zones that were separately clocked using GPS. In relation to previous research incarnations (Moir *et al.*, 2019) benefits from this system include:

- No need for transport synchronisation as the entire 'master' session is being tracked into one studio machine, at one end of the session
- High-quality audio is monitored in real time to ensure quality for engineering and tracking purposes
- High-quality audio is available with very low latency for musicians to hear and interact with each other

A number of issues and considerations should also be noted. Firstly, with a buffer set to 40 ms to accommodate traversal of UWL's firewall, the latency exceeded the 25 ms identified as being the point at which it is problematic for musicians to play to (Chafe, 2004). Secondly, there are some areas that require consideration to further support this such as what happens when the music stops for musicians in the Cloud Booth? Harry Docherty, distance musician in Edinburgh noted:

> I could hear everything very well and it was good having Skype visuals too. I would've liked a wee bit more communication . . . [It was] Overall very enjoyable.

Docherty's "Skype visuals" is actually referring to Hook's use of WhatsApp to send photos and video clips from the concert venue to give the Edinburgh team some sense of how the concert looked from the perspective of the London audience.

Similarly, Jamie McLardy, overseeing the Cloud Booth in Edinburgh from a technical viewpoint observed:

> From an engineer's perspective, this could've been happening right above us, the distance wasn't felt at all . . . no audio issues . . . thus the immersion wasn't broken. Further video for myself would've been good . . . the only material we had to give scope and depth was the photos and videos sent by yourself and Paul (via Whatsapp). It's strange to send a feed not knowing exactly the process beyond Napier. It's like being blindfolded and sat in a room, anyone could be watching but you wouldn't know.

In terms of implications for sound engineers, Pignato and Begany (2015) observed the role of "tech coordinator or technician" in establishing and maintaining distribution system. Moir *et al.* (2019) observe a need to separate distance technology and the role of engineer, feeling that the networking and technical requirements of distance connectivity should not impact on the role of the engineer. It is worth considering how engineers react to this. In reality, this is becoming part of the engineer's toolkit (and therefore will become as invisible to the musician as patching or syncing equipment within the ground control space). Method changes but content and needs remain the same. Whilst using the 'dual stream' approach shown in Figure 6.1 Ferguson stated that he "moved from being a sound engineer to a network engineer more concerned with packet loss than audio quality and performance" (Moir *et al.*, 2019). Neither Ferguson or UWL Engineer Scott Harker felt this using commercial Dante-based equipment in the 2019 keynote at UWL, indicating a shift towards less intrusive requirements in terms of network connections.

6.13 MUSIC INDUSTRY RESPONSES AND NEXT STEPS

Following the successful keynote demonstration at the Innovation in Music 2019 Conference, Focusrite (2020) have produced a case study that documents the project and states that its demonstrated ability to collaborate between institutions using Dante goes beyond education and has clear equivalents in commercial studios, broadcast and post production. Resurface Audio (2020) have issued a news feature about the keynote entitled "Dante over Distance: Remote is a Reality" and say that excitingly, this isn't a sci-fi glimpse into the future. Most of the customers they have spoken with who lamented the single-site limitation and were excited by the possibilities of Dante over distance already had the necessary high-performance network connectivity between their sites.

Inspired by the success of the keynote project, the authors have been working with Audinate, Focusrite and Professor Chris Chafe (Stanford University) and have now successfully tested Focusrite Rednet, GPS, and Dante between Edinburgh Napier University and Technischen Universität Berlin using the Janet and Geant NRENs. Audinate (2020), the developers of Dante, have scheduled a live webinar interview plus Q&A to share the authors' Dante-over-Distance research with the user community. The next tests will investigate network optimisation to reduce the end-to-end latency to 10 ms for sites less than 1000 kilometres apart.

REFERENCES

Audinate (2020). Dante over Distance: Achieving multi-site, long distance, real-time collaboration with full-resolution audio using Dante. Webinar 12 May 2020. Retrieved from http://go.audinate.com/lp-events/webinar-series-20. Accessed 23 April 2020.

Carot, A., Renaud, A. and Rebelo, P. (2007). Networked music performance: state of the art. *AES 30th International Conference*. Audio Engineering Society.

Chafe, C. and Gurevich, M. (2004). Network Time Delay and Ensemble Accuracy: Effects of Latency, Asymmetry. 117th Audio Engineering Society Convention, Audio Engineering Society.

Chafe, C., Caceres, J. and Gurevich, M. (2010). Effect of temporal separation on synchronization in rhythmic performance. *Perception*, 39(7): 982–992.

Chafe, C., Wilson, S., Leistikow, R., Chisholm, D. and Scavone, G. (2000). A Simplified Approach to High Quality Music and Sound Over IP. *Proceedings of the COST G-6 Conference on Digital Audio Effects (DAFX-00)*, Verona, Italy, 7–9 December.

Everhart, D. (1998). 'Collaborative dance, interactive music, folklore preservation: High-bandwidth applications with global implications', paper presented at INET '98, Geneva Switzerland. Retrieved from www.faculty.georgetown.edu/everhart/works/inet.html. Accessed 12 March 2015.

Ferguson, P. (2013). Using Low-Latency Net-Based Solutions to Extend the Audio and Video Capabilities of a Studio Complex. 134th Audio Engineering Society Convention, Rome, Italy.

Ferguson, P. (2015). Real-Time Long-Distance Music Collaboration Using the Internet. In R. Hepworth-Sawyer, J. Hodgson, J. L. Paterson, and R. Toulson (eds.), *Innovation in Music II*. Shoreham-by-Sea, UK: Future Technology Press, 174–178.

Focusrite (2020). RedNet Enables 'World-First' Cross-Border Interactive Performance. Retrieved from https://pro.focusrite.com/case-studies/live-sound/rednet-enables-'worldfirst'-crossborder-interactive-performance. Accessed 28 February 2020.

IEEE Standard No. 1588–2002 (2002). IEEE Standard for a Precision Clock Synchronization Protocol for Networked Measurement and Control Systems. IEEE.

Moir, Z., Ferguson, P. and Smith, G. (2019). *Real-Time, Remote, Interactive Recording Sessions: Music Production Without Boundaries in Producing Music*. Taylor Francis Group.

Pignato, J. M., and Begany, G. M. (2015). Deterritorialized, Multilocated and Distributed: Musical Space, Poietic Domains and Cognition in Distance Collaboration. *Journal of Music, Technology and Education* 8(2): 111–128.

Resurface Audio (2020). Dante over Distance: Remote is a Reality. Retrieved from https://resurface.audio/dante-over-distance-remote-is-a-reality/. Accessed 28 February 2020.

7

Music production utilising Internet of Things technologies

Marques Hardin and Rob Toulson

7.1 INTRODUCTION

The Internet of Things (IoT) paradigm consists of ubiquitous, interconnected devices that freely communicate and exchange data worldwide utilising the internet and widespread computing networks. IoT has delivered major impacts in commercial areas such as smart housing and enterprise, healthcare, as well as industry and manufacturing, but to date has seen little mainstream investigations within creative-driven fields. Exploring creativity, the music industry is one proposed area that can benefit from an embedded IoT architecture. Lacey (2015) highlights four areas that can be augmented by interconnected smart devices: remote performances, remote recording, remote live mixing, and generative and algorithmic music composition.

Whalley (2015) feels that real-time and networked data streams can make electronic musicianship "part of our artistic landscape", and, as part of his advocacy of greater roles of intelligent machines in affective music making, he also proposes a shift from the older remote performance led focuses of networked music. Regarding music production, interconnected musical devices have the potential to encourage greater engagement with rare, bespoke, and professional hardware that is remotely distributed through computing networks, and ultimately help preserve desirable sounds or creative processes that may become lost in modern production techniques. This form of remote engagement fuels the concept of the *virtually extended music studio*, where greater diversity in music composition and expression can be achieved within personal, home and non-professional working environments. The development and normalisation of IoT-enabled music processes can therefore enable novel advances in music production and impact future standards in the production process.

7.2 BACKGROUND

A shift in music production approaches has evolved from hardware dominated techniques to widely accessible digital processes, complemented by the aid of computer software and hardware-emulating plugins. Software has allowed high-quality music production tools to become available in hobbyist spaces and have helped professional sounds traditionally developed in studio spaces become replicable on personal computing devices.

While audio software has brought huge benefits and flexibility to music production, there is still an existing appeal for the creation, recording and manipulation of music using analogue and physical production devices; for example, analogue valve compressors, spring and plate reverb units, retro synthesizers and electronic drum machines. In an interview with Mack Wilson, tech editor of DJ Mag, he mentions that music makers "are sticking to analogue because the sound is softer and it brings a bit of the past into the future, which is something that can't be achieved with new apps and soft synths" (Reidy, 2014).

One deterring factor in the modern day use of physical hardware is accessibility. Physical music production devices can often be limited to production spaces and studios, and are sometimes large, difficult to transport, and costly for consumers to purchase and own. An opportunity to network physical music devices, however, could potentially grant greater accessibility to these less accessible tools and impact modern techniques for music production incorporating analogue audio hardware. IoT can present a useful option for addressing a lack of accessibility to physical musical devices by embedding them with computing technology, effectively granting the opportunity to be engaged, controlled, and manipulated remotely through the use of interconnected and internet-facilitated communication protocols. Arguably, with the aid of IoT, new tools can be developed to help better bridge the music producer to the music production process.

7.3 RESEARCH

The background of this research indicates that music production using hardware and analogue technology still has value in modern music, and greater accessibility to hardware production devices would be a welcome complement to more accessible software-driven techniques. This research proposes that the Internet of Things and networked music technologies provides a method to increase the utility of hardware music devices. Proper exploration of this concept required a better understanding of modern IoT architectures that could help realise an IoT-enabled music system, and the subsequent investigation of opportunities and benefits that these systems can provide for music and producers themselves.

7.3.1 Research questions and methodology

In order to understand the impact that IoT can have on music production, three research questions are proposed. Firstly, what are the current capabilities of IoT infrastructures to support distributed audio system networks, and what improvements can be identified and evaluated? And secondly, how can IoT-enabled music systems facilitate new music production engagement, workflows, and collaboration methods? Additionally, what cultural, enterprise, and creative benefits do IoT-based music systems present?

The first research question investigates and explores how a practical IoT-enabled music system can be developed by uncovering key IoT technologies that could be tested, evaluated, and analysed to successfully achieve such a system. An iterative, design-build methodology was followed that required researching available IoT technologies, and following incremental stages of prototyping, building, and testing until a full IoT music system was implemented, following a similar approach to that described by Paterson *et al.* (2015, p. 198).

Once a prototype of an IoT-enabled music system was successfully achieved, the second and third questions sought to understand how these types of systems could impact music producers; exploring how they can affect the current production standards and workflows of music producers and uncovering benefits and challenges that may arise. To facilitate this evaluation, the prototyped IoT music system was presented and its functionality demonstrated to music producers of different backgrounds. After the demonstrations, questionnaires were distributed to the participants and a select number of interviews with accomplished music practitioners were conducted to gain insight into their production backgrounds, experience and preferences with software and hardware processing techniques, and opinions concerning the impacts widespread IoT music systems could have on their individual production practices.

The culmination of the practical design and build of an IoT-enabled music system in addition to the feedback shared among interview and survey respondents helped develop insights into opportunities and challenges that the systems can provide, and can further shape a future vision of distributed, interconnected music production.

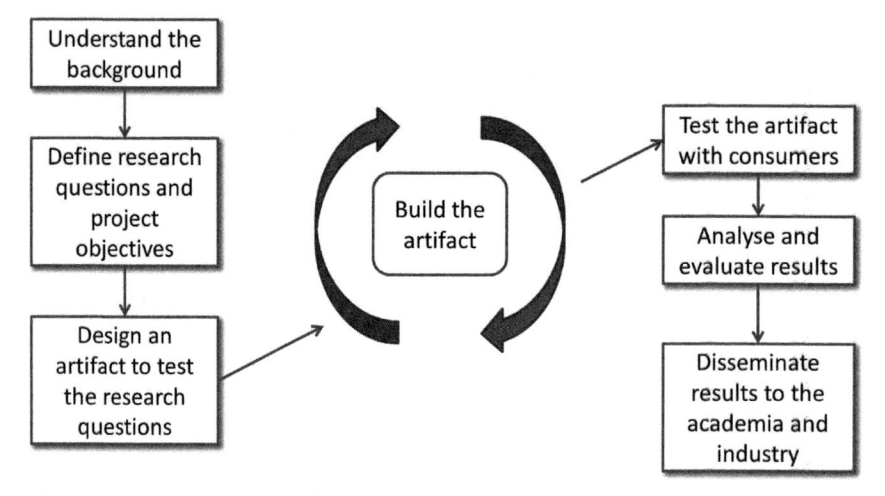

Figure 7.1 Iterative design-build methodology

Paterson *et al.* 2015

7.3.2 Practice-based IoT music system development

The practical design of the IoT music system focused on the development of a proof-of-concept IoT-enabled application that can control a minimum of two physical audio processors in real time. The concept centred on a virtual model where recorded audio is transferred to a networked musical device, and the device is controlled using a user interface accessed by a personal PC in order to remotely process and manipulate audio. The newly processed audio is then delivered to the second device where further audio processing can occur before returning back to the user. The round-trip process is represented in Figure 7.2.

The design-build stage followed an iterative, inspect-and-adopt model outlined by Keith (2010, p. 30) that consisted of setting small goals and building in stages to reach set targets, taking into account changes that may occur along the way. For this research, four targets were established: research of embedded systems and fundamental IoT processes that can enable a networked music system; designing and prototyping and IoT-based control system, investing; testing, and incorporating audio streaming functionality; and designing and prototyping a complete hybrid, analogue-digital IoT audio system.

Two processing techniques were chosen for implementation of the IoT music system due to their noticeable effects: equalisation (EQ) and reverb. Networkable microcontrollers were utilised for controlling motors and actuators that were connected to the processors. The HTML5 Websockets communication protocol was incorporated into a web-based user interface

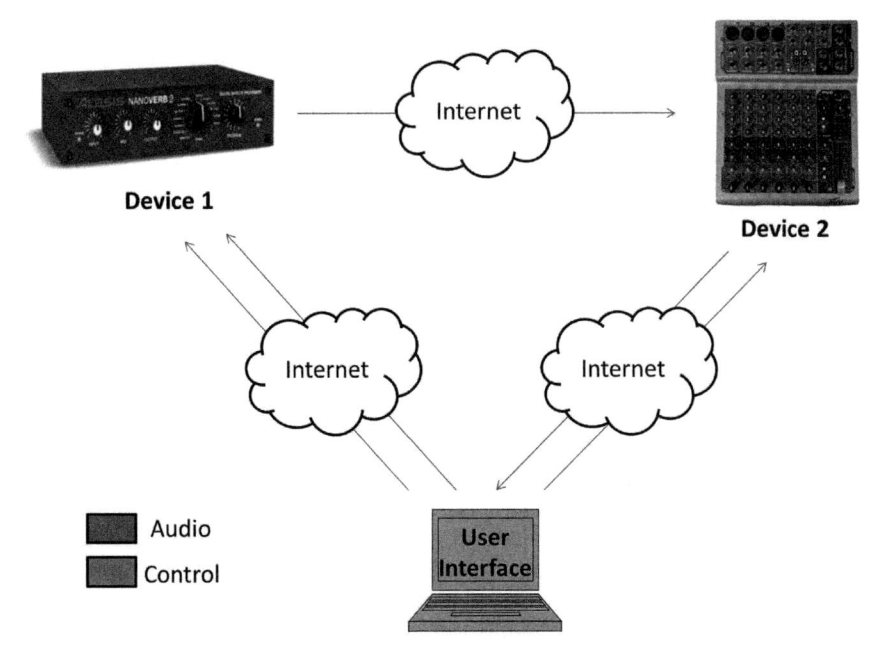

Figure 7.2 IoT-enabled music production concept

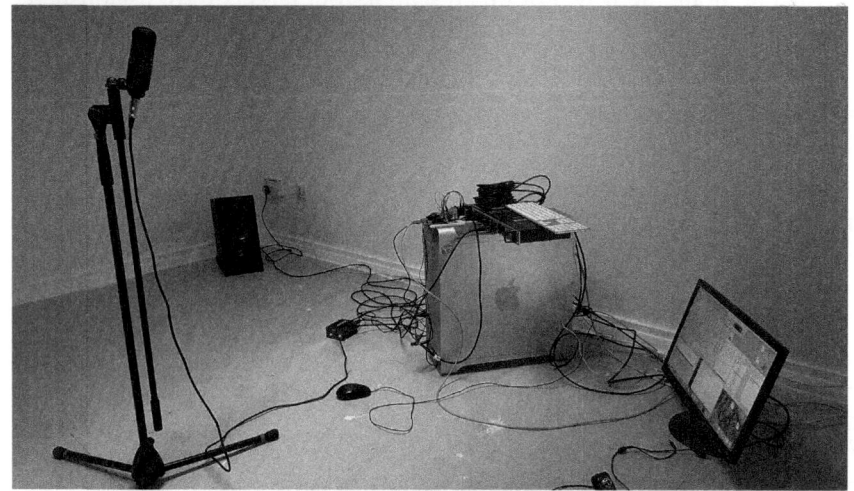

Figure 7.3 IoT music EQ (a) and reverb (b) processors

to allow remote transfer of control data from a personal computer to the embedded microcontrollers that manipulated the physical devices. The final design resulted in two applications: an audio mixing board that was modified with motorised potentiometers attached to its EQ knobs, and a physical hardware reverb unit that adapted motorised potentiometers to its wet and dry mixing knob. Reverb processing was further expanded by adding virtually controllable gain outputs to a speaker and microphone system that could be placed in an echoic space to create remotely produced real-time, natural reverb.

Once IoT-based control of the networked devices was achieved, the next step was investigating platforms that could deliver real-time audio to the controlled devices. The CCRMA-developed platform *JackTrip* (Cáceres, and Chafe, 2010) was used after a thorough investigation of streaming performance and robustness over distributed computing networks (Hardin and Toulson, 2019). The combination of networked control and real-time,

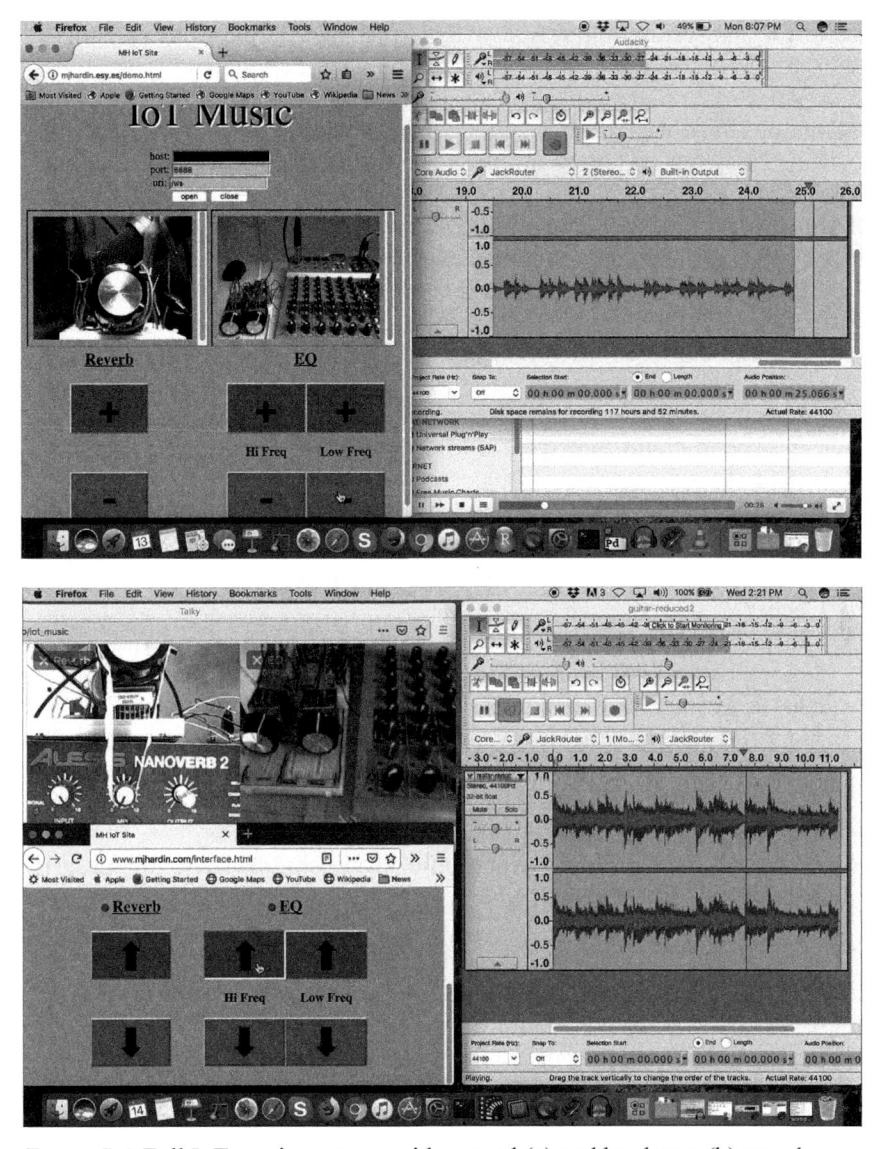

Utilising Internet of Things technologies 111

Figure 7.4 Full IoT music systems with natural (a) and hardware (b) reverb

high fidelity audio streaming allowed a complete IoT-enabled music system to be fully realised and evaluated.

7.3.3 Music producer evaluations

After completion of the proof-of-concept IoT music system, evaluations were conducted to both observe and understand the possible impacts of these systems on music production. User insight evaluations were designed and created to be qualitative driven, aiming to "provide illumination and understanding of complex psychosocial issues" that were "most useful for answering humanistic 'why?' and 'how?' questions (Marshall, 1996, p. 552). The user insight evaluations were conducted by two types of surveys: open and closed-ended questionnaire questions that gathered anonymous feedback from a range of music producers, and interviews focusing on richer and more in-depth views from professional and experienced music producers.

Anonymised questionnaires targeted producers from a variety of production backgrounds and experiences, and the respondents were categorised into two groups, *music producers* and *casual music makers*, based upon their self-identifying preferences. The first six questions of the questionnaire explored the producers' backgrounds in production, asking where and how they typically produce music, and gathered insight into both their experiences and preferences for using analogue and physical devices as compared to software equivalents. The questionnaire questions are listed below:

1. Describe Your Musical Status.
2. If You Mix and Process Your Own Music, Where Does This Normally Occur?
3. If You Mix Music, How Likely Are You to Use Physical Audio Processing Systems to Process Music in Comparison to Software Equivalents (e.g. Hardware Compression vs. Software Compression)?
4. Do You Feel That Physical Processing Hardware Give Better Results Than Their Software Equivalent?
5. With Regards to Physical Hardware, Do You Feel Analogue Components Provide Better Results than Digital Counterparts?
6. Would Your Use of Physical Audio Processing Systems Increase If They Were More Accessible?

The remaining questions collected insights specifically regarding the respondents' impressions and views of an IoT-enabled music system. These questions presented more opportunities for open-ended feedback that addressed potential opportunities and challenges that music producers perceive from widespread adoption of these systems. There remaining questions are listed below:

7. Do You Feel an IoT-Based Music Processing System Adds Greater Accessibility to Analogue or Professional Audio Processing Hardware?
8. Briefly Describe Your Impression of an IoT-Based Music Processing System.
9. If Available, How Interested Would You Be In Incorporating IoT-Based Music Processing Systems Into Your Own Music Workflows?
10. Are There Any Pros and Cons You Can Envision From IoT Extensions to Music and/or Other Creative Fields?

Interviews were conducted in conjunction with the questionnaires that specifically targeted music professionals with more developed experience in the fields of music production and sound engineering. The interview questions were completely qualitative and presented open-ended variations of the questionnaire questions. This prompted deeper conversations among the respondents and provided richer views to emerge about the systems.

7.3.4 Results and discussion

The questionnaire and interviews provided two types of data: quantitative, numerical data from the multiple choice answers regarding the sample groups' production methods and qualitative discussions from the open questions. The multiple choice selection of the closed-ended questionnaire questions were statistically broken down by each question and the qualitative data from the open-ended conversations were thematically analysed and categorically coded into groups. The questionnaire received 56 responses and encountered data saturation, a point where no new data emerged and the responses were believed to satisfy the aims of the research questions. Among the questionnaires, 20 (36%) respondents identified as casual music makers and 36 (64%) respondents identified as music producers. Key statistics from the questionnaire data are presented below:

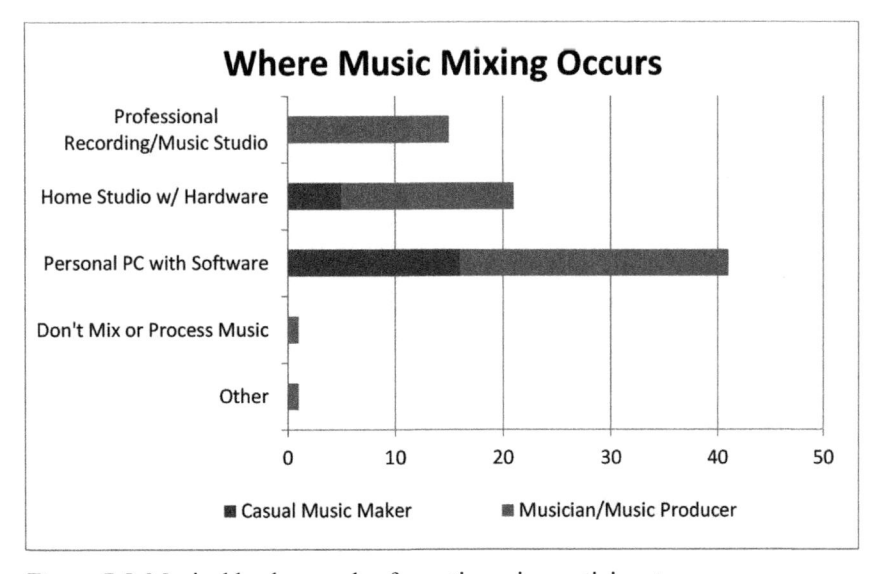

Figure 7.5 Musical backgrounds of questionnaire participants

Among the respondents 73% reported using a personal computer with software as their main process to produce music. This shows that a large percentage of music producers work within a personal production environment and may not regularly access physical music production hardware.

Although Figure 7.5 proves that modern trends of production tend to rely on software techniques, Figure 7.6 shows that all of the respondents felt analogue and physical hardware produce either the equivalent or better results than their software equivalents:

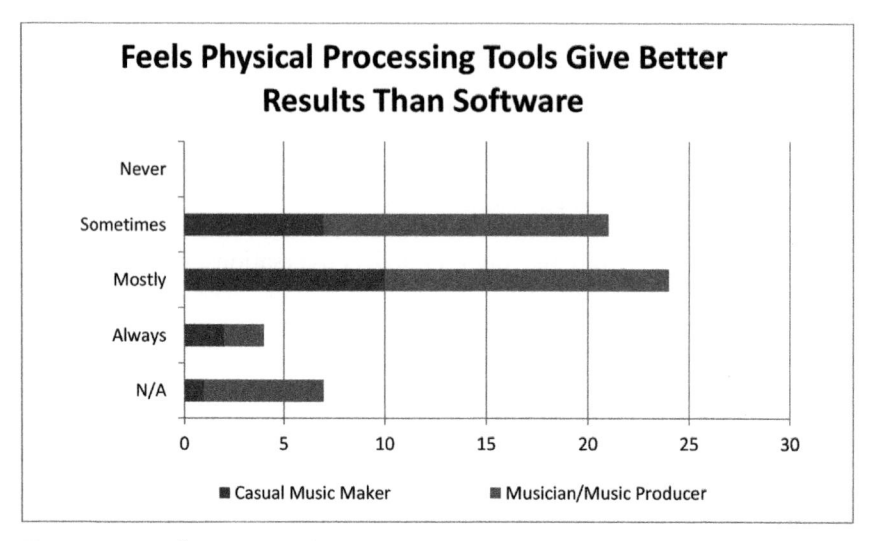

Figure 7.6 Feelings concerning analogue processing tools providing better results than software equivalent

Furthermore, when asked if their use of physical audio processors would increase if they became more available, 89% of respondents confirmed they would use more physical audio processors in Figure 7.7 below:

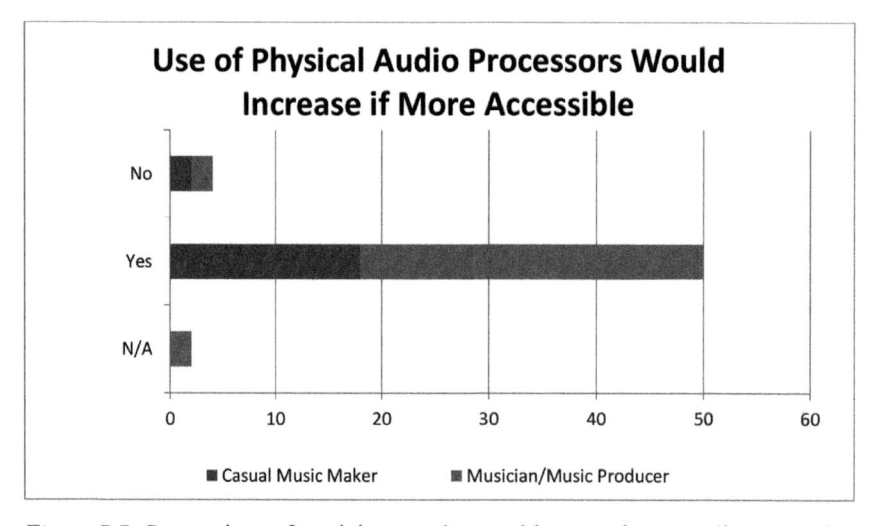

Figure 7.7 Comparison of participants who would use analogue audio processing systems if they were more accessible

Feels an IoT-Based Music Processor Adds Greater Accessibility to Processing Hardware

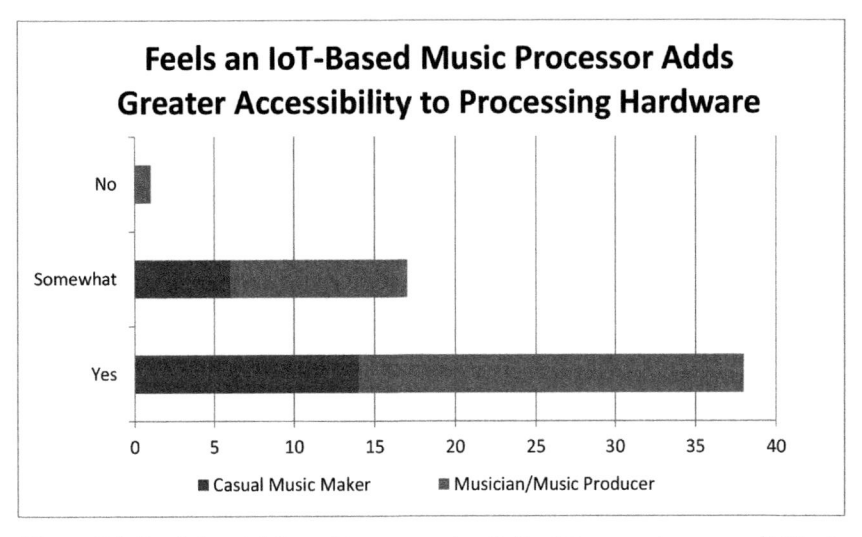

Figure 7.8 Participants' thoughts concerning IoT adding greater accessibility to analogue audio processing systems

In comparison, respondents were asked about their potential to incorporate IoT-enabled music production hardware specifically into their production workflows if the devices became publicly available and mainstream. In the responses, 89% of respondents reported they would in some way incorporate IoT-enabled music processes into their work flows.

The closed-ended questions helped provide a baseline understanding of the music producers' engagement with physical audio processing tools and their appeal to utilise IoT-enabled music production techniques. The open-ended questionnaire questions and interviews allowed a richer subset of data to emerge regarding IoT-music systems, and prompted conversations that explored both the opportunities and challenges these systems could present. The professional interviews drew from the expertise of individuals across a spectrum of audio backgrounds, from musicians, songwriters, producers, and engineers, and coupled with the producer questionnaires gave a clearer understanding of how IoT-enabled music processing can presently impact professionals in the field. The following music professionals were interviewed as part of the research:

1. Simon Gogerly – University lecturer, Grammy award winner, and leading UK music producer and mix engineer.
2. Alan Branch – Grammy award winning audio engineer, producer, musician, and writer.
3. Gary Bromham – Professional music producer, mix engineer, guitarist, and songwriter.
4. Dr. Bill Campbell – University lecturer, sound engineer, and audio producer for music, film, and gaming.
5. Dan Wilde – UK singer, songwriter, and music producer.

6. Mat Skidmore – Freelance live recording and mix engineer.
7. Todd Reitzell – Musician and sound engineer. Founder and managing director of an international creative agency.

Following the transcription of the interviews, the open-ended feedback was thoroughly reviewed and analysed, pulling out reoccurring themes that were either shared across each of the data sets or specifically addressed the second and third research questions. The resulting themes were categorised into the following groups: hardware/software appreciation, accessibility and engagement, new and augmented workflows, creative benefits, cultural benefits, enterprise benefits, educational benefits, reliability concerns, and the availability/limitation of resources. Each theme is discussed further in the following subsections.

Hardware/software appreciation

A leading draw for the use of software production techniques based on the surveys responses was recallability. With software plugins constantly improving and becoming more indistinguishable from their hardware components, many music producers valued the ability to save a production setting and return to it both at a later time and in the convenience of their personal production environments. On the opposite end, while software has granted access to reliable, high-quality production techniques, many music producers reported that they still value the unique sound experiences achieved from hardware. Some felt that hardware cannot fully be replicated by software. Branch mentions:

> But some stuff, you know synthesisers or certain valve compressors that have got kind of non-linearities or certain things about it, there are times when you plug in a real hardware piece of gear and you just know that it sounds real.

Additionally, there are producers who simply prefer the sound of hardware over software. Some questionnaire respondents reported that while better may not be the correct term, hardware is "different and mostly richer", and "have a more organic sound, in comparison to their software equivalent . . .".

Accessibility and engagement

Survey respondents commented on IoT-enabled production devices allowing hardware to become more accessible, and Bromham contributed his thoughts adding:

> When I started producing music, it was common to hire in equipment on sessions and I see this [IoT-enabled music] as an extension of this principle. It means that someone that would not otherwise have access

to a well-known piece of equipment, due to cost or size considerations, might subsequently have access to this world!

For individuals who have limited access to hardware, respondents argued that IoT could take "away the location barrier when it comes to audio recording". Additionally IoT was seen to present opportunities for individuals with special mobility requirements to access physical hardware, as one questionnaire respondent alluded, "it has potential for curious producers but most notably, people with disabilities".

New and augmented workflows

The opportunity to access more musical resources inherently changes the way individuals can conduct and perform their standard productions. Gogerly reveals:

> I would definitely embrace [IoT-enabled music] in a big way I think because it's almost like having an extended studio where you can access pieces of equipment that you don't have or you don't own and you can't afford to buy necessarily or just don't have physical access to . . .

IoT can allow music producers to develop new production techniques based upon remote access to hardware and impact the process in which they compose music. Reitzell shares feedback on how he feels IoT can optimise recording sessions within a studio:

> I'm an engineer in a control room recording someone and instead of going through 4 sound proof doors to get to a knob that's in a room with the performer, I can do it using IoT. This is a massive time saving for everyone, time saver for the engineer . . . it doesn't disturb the performer and you can more quickly, well with less disruption, adjust a parameter that might be causing possible ear damage or possible equipment damage.

Lastly, other survey respondents felt IoT can offer producers completely new sound experiences as current, isolated production processes might mean some people "may never get to experience certain types of physical equipment".

Creative benefits

Having new methods and techniques available to produce music has underlying creative benefits. Skidmore exclaims:

> Anything that can give access to more kinds of equipment and sounds is useful for creativity . . . especially if you have a specific thing that you think you're after but you don't have access to it.

Survey respondents reflected on using IoT to have greater opportunities to experiment with hardware that they wouldn't normally utilise. Additionally using new technology and processes for producing music allows unique sound experiences to be generated. One example is related natural real-time reverb, where one questionnaire respondent mentions that IoT "will enable producers to find their own sound while using different responses in places such as frequency responses". Campbell similarly sees value in a real-time reverb scenario, adding:

> So that speaking on a live scenario, where you probably wouldn't get that same effect . . . you wouldn't get the musician playing in exactly the same way if you're doing it through convolution. So in that sense, if you would have the real-time Internet of Things where you would actually have a drummer playing and hearing themselves playing in an amazing space that would probably be something that would be spectacular in itself.

Additionally these creative benefits are not only exclusive to individuals of specific financial means, but can allow greater accessibility to music hardware for the general public and add an additional layer of democratisation to the music production process. One producer sums up this point in the questionnaire by saying "IoT Based processing can create a new platform for the new generation of producers to expand their creativity whether in a bedroom studio or professional studio".

Cultural benefits

In correlation to the creative benefits, IoT could offer broader production options to wider populations of music producers, such as the bedroom musician, and provide them with open access to the musical hardware they desire to use. In the questionnaires one music producer reports:

> I believe that, if accomplished, it would be an amazing breakthrough as a business and as a product. The idea of being able to obtain all these hardware or physical sound obtained properties [sic] from my "bedroom" studio would be great. I happen to match the description of the bedroom studio and being able to use synthesizers and other tools would become an essential in my production.

Similarly, IoT-enabled access to hardware can be appealing to an identifiable generation of *post-modern* producers who romanticise about the quality and techniques of the past while simultaneously co-existing in the present digital environment. Wilde reminisces about recording on tape when thinking about additional opportunities of IoT:

> And maybe there's a shift, especially as people like grow up with all this technology like plug-ins . . . when I recorded my first album on tape . . . there's still this nostalgia for all that vintage stuff.

Lastly, Branch feels that collaboration facilitated by the internet and networked music can create a "beauty of joining" between different cultural communities, which as a result "maybe we could create more because of that."

Enterprise benefits

If musical hardware can be accessed and shared across remote networks then it can influence a new market of monetised music resources distributed across the internet. In regards to new monetary opportunities arising from sharing pre-owned hardware, Wilde mentions:

> I think everybody even if you really enjoy your job, most people would say if they could work a little bit less and still make money from their assets or whatever they would do that. So I think, yeah, there would be a lot of people who would say, right ok this allows me to a little bit less production and just have these hours where I rent out my equipment.

IoT may also allow producers with lower incomes to have more affordable options for renting hardware instead of purchasing the devices or booking studio space. Bromham shares that:

> The [IoT-enabled music] concept and process almost certainly have a place in post-production and mastering where select pieces of hardware might easily cost far more than those used in traditional recording and mixing environments.

Similarly the opportunity to network vintage equipment and underutilised material spaces may bring them added value. Lastly, IoT can aid in the preservation of hardware devices, as Reitzell mentions:

> So you spend thousands and thousands on a mixing desk and as soon as someone gets their little greasy fingers on it we start beating up. So if it could be completely robot controlled that would mean that it would take less abuse and might last longer.

Educational benefits

Another perceived benefit of IoT-enabled music production is that it can allow musicians to remotely observe and learn more about the hardware devices they wish to engage with. Music producers researching hardware can conduct real tests with the devices to learn about their capabilities and performance. Gogerly fondly mentions:

> I would say that it would be a very attractive proposition to most producers and mixers, especially those of more sort of technical leaning

> I guess who, you know, theoretically you could try out pretty much anything you can think of if every sort of device available was there just via your browser, it would be a really impressive thing.

Campbell feels IoT-enabled music devices can be used as a comparative tool to "compare digital to analogue", and useful for research-based listening tests where "you could actually get people from all over to be able to do these experiments for you or this research to test their abilities". Similarly Skidmore shares how IoT-enabled music devices can serve academia outside of personal and market research by offering an educational tool that can "show students an actual piece of equipment and actually run audio through it".

Reliability concerns

With the presented opportunities of IoT also come perceived challenges. Several survey respondents worried about the dependency on a stable internet connection arguing that "latency and encoding/decoding seem like big hurdles". Also, one questionnaire respondent mentioned IoT-enable music production may present difficulties to implement in "less fortunate countries [that] don't have direct access to internet or limited access to internet". While the research exploring real-time music transfer over robust networks has yielded positive results (Drioli, Allocchio, Buso, 2013; Ferguson, 2015; Hardin and Toulson, 2019) the survey responses showed that network reliability and latency are still prevalent concerns regarding any networked music application.

Availability/limitation of resources

A last concern is the limitation of available music production resources. Gogerly poses concern mentioning:

> I mean the only thing that I can see as a downside to the audio thing is that, you know, obviously because you're connecting to something physical in a different location you can only have one person using it at a time.

Unlike software that can be duplicated and owned by multiple users, only one person can utilise a hardware device at a time. IoT can present a dilemma where hardware that was regularly accessible may become consistently unavailable as universal access potentially oversaturates device demand. Whether the hardware consists of bespoke networked devices developed by a manufacture for sole online consumption, or is provided by a recording studio offering online availability to their devices in conjunction with shared physical access, access to IoT-enabled music hardware would need some level of regulation to allow fair and controlled access to these devices.

7.4 CONCLUSIONS

Conducting and implementing this research helped gather insight into the viability of IoT-enabled music processing for production and composition and shared potential advantages and consequences it could pose for the music producer. With respect to the three research questions, the main conclusions drawn are the following.

The practical design and build of an IoT-enabled music system showed that, with existing communication infrastructures, it is possible to remotely connect and engage with physical music production devices through the effective transmission of data over the internet. Resources such as Websockets and JackTrip provided open and low-cost methods to virtually send control and media information to remote devices, and offered insight that IoT music production can occur without high, overhead costs.

More noteworthy are the possible opportunities that IoT can have on the actual music producer. Distributed music hardware can help better bridge the musician to musical devices, and give more flexibility in production techniques with the aid of remote processing. Greater access to physical devices means that producers can engage in more experimentation, have greater opportunities to collaborate, and utilise more resources to produce desired sounds.

Lastly, while concerns about network stability do exist, IoT-enabled music has a number of foreseeable benefits as perceived by surveyed music producers in this research. For cultures of musicians who exist outside of the traditional music studio, IoT allows them to extend professional hardware virtually into their personal and preferred production environments. This can allow them to utilise new tools while maintaining the aesthetics of the personal workspaces. The options to have more production tools available can also influence creativity, as producers can test, play with, and experience new sounds which may not have been traditionally available to them. Additionally, new creative techniques can emerge, like the possibility of networking material spaces with speakers and microphones and using their acoustic qualities are physical, real-time reverb chambers. The added ability to remotely test hardware, understand their characteristics, and even compare them to software equivalents opens new educational opportunities that can benefit research and academia alike. Finally, a model of exchanging networked music devices to consumers can help develop new enterprise ventures for providers and collectors of music technology. Schemes to virtually hire musical equipment can become an added source of income for providers while simultaneously offering affordable options for consumers, and the ability to network desired but underutilised devices and spaces can grant them an increase in value.

REFERENCES

Cáceres, J.P. and Chafe, C. (2010). JackTrip: Under the hood of an engine for network audio. *Journal of New Music Research*, 39(3), pp.183–187.

Drioli, C., Allocchio, C. and Buso, N. (2013). Networked performances and natural interaction via LOLA: Low latency high quality A/V streaming system. In *Information Technologies for Performing Arts, Media Access, and Entertainment*. Berlin: Springer, pp. 240–250.

Ferguson, P. (2015). Real-time long-distance music collaboration using the Internet. In: Hepworth-Sawyer, R., Hodgson, J., Toulson, R. and Paterson, J.L. (2016). *Innovation in music II*. Future Technology Press, UK, pp. 174–178.

Hardin, M. and Toulson, R. (2019). Quantitative Analysis of Streaming Protocols for Enabling Internet of Things (IoT) Audio Hardware. *Proceedings of the 146th Audio Engineering Society Convention*, Dublin.

Keith, C. (2010). *Agile game development with Scrum*. New Jersey: Pearson Education.

Lacey, L. (2015). How the Internet of Things Could Impact Music Composition, Production & Performance. Ask.Audio. [online] Available at https://ask.audio/articles/how-theinternet-of-things-could-impact-music-composition-production-performance

Marshall, M.N. (1996). Sampling for qualitative research. *Family practice*, 13(6), pp. 522–526.

Paterson, J., Toulson, E.R., Lexer, S., Webster, T., Massey, S. and Ritter, J. (2015). Interactive digital music: enhancing listener engagement with commercial music. In: Hepworth-Sawyer, R., Hodgson, J., Toulson, R. and Paterson, J.L. (2016). *Innovation in music II*. Future Technology Press, UK, pp. 193–209.

Reidy, T. (2014). Retro electronics still popular – but why not just use modern software? *The Guardian*. [online] Available at https://www.theguardian.com/music/2014/feb/15/oldelectronic-instruments-popular-software

Whalley, I. (2015). Developing Telematic Electroacoustic Music: Complex networks, machine intelligence and affective data stream sonification. *Organised Sound*, 20(1), pp. 90–98.

Part II
Music technology innovation

8

Development of an Ambisonic Guitar System

Duncan Werner, Bruce Wiggins and Emma Fitzmaurice

8.1 INTRODUCTION

The term *sound spatialisation* indicates a group of techniques for organising and manipulating the spatial projection and movement of sound in a physical or virtual listening environment (Valiquet, 2012). In addition to pitch, timbre, intensity and duration, an understanding of space is a significant musical parameter and as such, spatial sound controllers should be regarded as instruments of musical expression (Pysiewicz and Weinzierl, 2016); spatialiser design should therefore include immediacy, liveness, and learnability. Perez-Lopez (2015) identifies several design considerations for spatialisation systems, including: Is the performer exclusively controlling spatial parameters (in contrast to one who controls both spatialisation and sound generation)? What is the required level of expertise for expressivity and virtuosity? Is the spatial control made by an individual, or shared by a group of performers? Does the system provide a graphical user interface for real-time visual feedback? Many of these observations and questions have informed our approach to the development of the GASP project.

8.2 GASP SYSTEM OVERVIEW

An Ambisonic Guitar System has been devised and realised, with the project name GASP: 'Guitars with Ambisonic Spatial Performance'. GASP is an ongoing University of Derby research project, where our interest in Ambisonic algorithmic research and guitar sound production is combined with off-the-shelf hardware and bespoke software to create an Ambisonic based immersive guitar sound system. It is an innovative audio project, fusing the musical with the technical, combining individual string timbralisation with Ambisonic immersive sound. GASP also extends into an artistic musical project, where 'space' becomes a performance parameter, providing new experimental immersive sound production techniques for the guitarist and music producer. The project was initially research for post-production; however, the system can also be used within the live performance domain in large format theatre/concert systems. Additionally,

Figure 8.1 GASP hardware photograph (excluding Ambisonic speaker system)

Copyright R. Johnson 2019

the audio may be downmixed to work with traditional stereo sound installations or personal playback over headphones i.e. binaural or google 360° virtual reality (VR) sound via web streaming.

The GASP project is a guitar based 2D Ambisonic instrument and performance system. Work began using hexaphonic pickups in 2010 (for example, see Randell, 2011). The current configuration, as shown in Figure 8.1, consists of two interconnected computers (Mac Pro and iMac), three visual monitors, eight loudspeakers, audio interfacing, and three guitars (two Strat type and an electro-acoustic) with various hex/multichannel pickups fitted.

8.3 GASP SYSTEM DETAIL

The key features of the GASP system shown in Figure 8.2 and Figure 8.3 comprise of:

- Multichannel guitar pickups to facilitate the processing of individual strings independently for timbre, spatial location and other production processes.
- An eight-speaker circular array which supports a 2D, 360° spatial representation, with a choice of first, second or third order Ambisonic encoding/decoding.
- Timbral effects, which are achieved with commercial sound processing software, configured for individual string timbralisation.

Development of an Ambisonic Guitar System

- Spatial positioning and dynamic movement is achieved using bespoke WigWare plug-ins; auditioned over an array of circular loudspeakers or using binaural decoder output on headphones.
- Arpeggiation effects using audio gate switching on individual strings using the 'Guitarpeggiator'; a means of creating arpeggiation like effects, such that simple or complex polyrhythms can be realised for recording or live performance.
- A range of GASP Auditory Scenes, which combine spatial, timbral, and arpeggiation presets.

8.3.1 Guitars

The GASP guitars have multichannel pickups (aka hex, hexaphonic or divided pickups) installed. Two of the guitars, a black Yamaha APX500 electro-acoustic and maroon Mexican Fender Stratocaster are retrofitted with Ubertar hex passive pickups (Rubenstein, 2019). A third guitar, a sage green Mexican Fender Stratocaster with pau ferro neck (a wood which does not threaten the health of species and ecosystems (Fender, 2017, 2020)), is retrofitted with Cycfi Nu-Series Modular Active Pickups (Cycfi Research, 2019). The Fender Stratocasters were chosen as they enable straightforward installation of the multichannel pickup as it simply replaces the bridge pickup. This positioning has the advantage of generating minimal crossover into the pickup area of the neighbouring string when string bending occurs, although there are tonal considerations for this positioning which produce a slightly thinner timbre than other pickup locations. The exception to this is the Yamaha electro-acoustic which has an Ubertar hex pickup mounted across the sound hole.

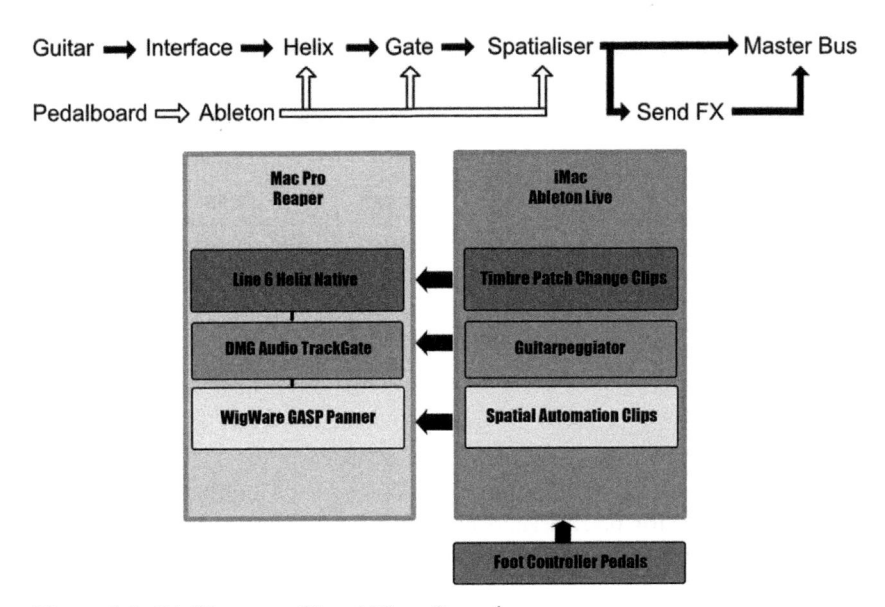

Figure 8.2 GASP system Signal Flow Overview

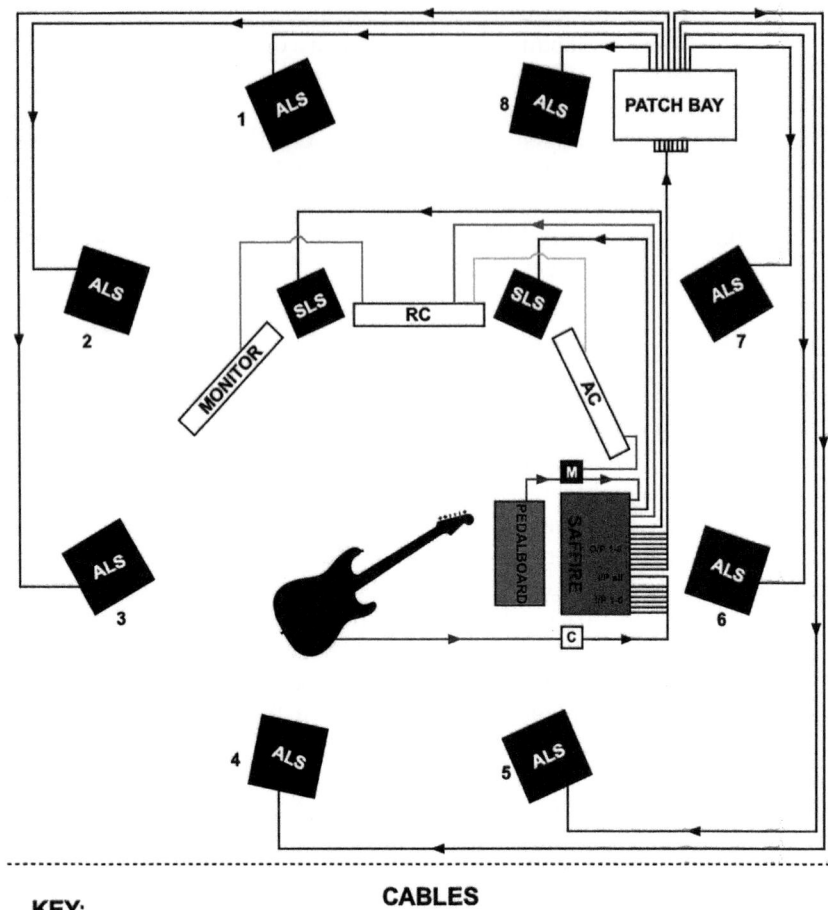

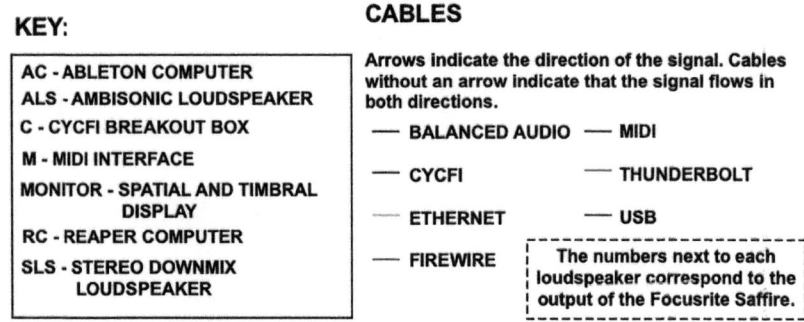

Figure 8.3 GASP lab interconnections overview

Courtesy of H. Dale 2019

Due to their modular design, the Cycfi Nu-Series Modular Active pickups are available for 6, 7, 8 (and upwards) string guitars. In comparing the Ubertar with Cycfi pickups it is noted there are some variations with consistency of output; the active Cycfi pickups provides a more consistent output level across all strings with a high output and transparent timbral clarity, whereas the individual outputs of the passive Ubertar pickups require some level balancing before further processing. The current system uses a Focusrite Liquid Saffire 56 to route the individual signal from each string to the computer for processing.

8.3.2 Spatialisation

Spatially, the system is based around Ambisonics, pioneered by Michael Gerzon in the 1970s (Gerzon, 1974a) as an improvement to the, then, state of the art system, Quadraphonics (Gerzon, 1974b). It was important for the GASP system to be both spatially accurate and flexible in its presentation to the user. Ambisonics is a system based around the spherical harmonic decomposition of a sound field in two, or three dimensions and the reconstruction of this sound field using loudspeakers or headphones where headphone playback makes use of head-related transfer functions, with or without head-tracking. This flexibility made it ideal for the GASP project. More recently, Ambisonics has been utilised as one of the standard playback formats for virtual reality and 360-degree video, further expanding the possibilities of the system (Wiggins, 2017). The GASP system currently operates in two dimensions (using circular, rather than spherical harmonics) and uses panners of up to 3rd order. With increasing Ambisonic order, the accuracy of the spatial reproduction improves, but more loudspeakers and channels per track are required. 3rd order requires 8 speakers arranged in an octagon as a minimum and needs 16 channels per track for the encoding for full 3D (7 channels are all that's necessary for 2D reproduction at 3rd order, but the full 16 channels are used in the system to allow for future expansion to 3D).

Currently, the GASP system has the following playback modes:

- Minimum of eight speakers arranged in an octagon (for 3rd order playback)
- Minimum of six speakers arranged in a hexagon (for 2nd order playback)
- Minimum of four speakers arranged in a square (for 1st order playback)
- 5.1 or 7.1 decodes (3rd order using irregular optimised decoders [Wiggins, 2007])
- Two-channel stereo mix-down using the UHJ format (Gerzon, 1985)
- Binaural output (with or without head-tracking, up to 3rd order resolution)

Ambisonics differs from many other formats in that the encoding of the sound field is separated from the decoding, or presentation, of that sound field to the listener. To encode an audio source in a particular direction (which is the core function of a *panner* or *spatialiser* tool), the audio signal is multiplied by the coefficient of each spherical harmonic channel at the required angle (although the panner's graphical user interface shows a 2D plane, the plug-in does implement panning in three dimensions, allowing for future expansion). The GASP panner pre-dates Ambisonics being standardised for virtual reality, which uses the ambiX standard of channel ordering and normalisation (Nachbar *et al.*, 2011) so uses the Furse-Malham normalisation and channel ordering scheme (Malham, 2003). Conversion to the newer ambiX scheme is simply a change of channel order and gain, and can be realised using free plug-ins (Wiggins, 2016).

The signal processing elements of the system are hosted in Reaper (Reaper.fm, 2019) DAW running on a Mac Pro. Reaper is utilised to manage routing and sequencing of the audio due to its flexibility in terms of channel count, routing possibilities and its support for multiple plug-in standards (Wiggins, 2008). Each track requires 16 channels for the

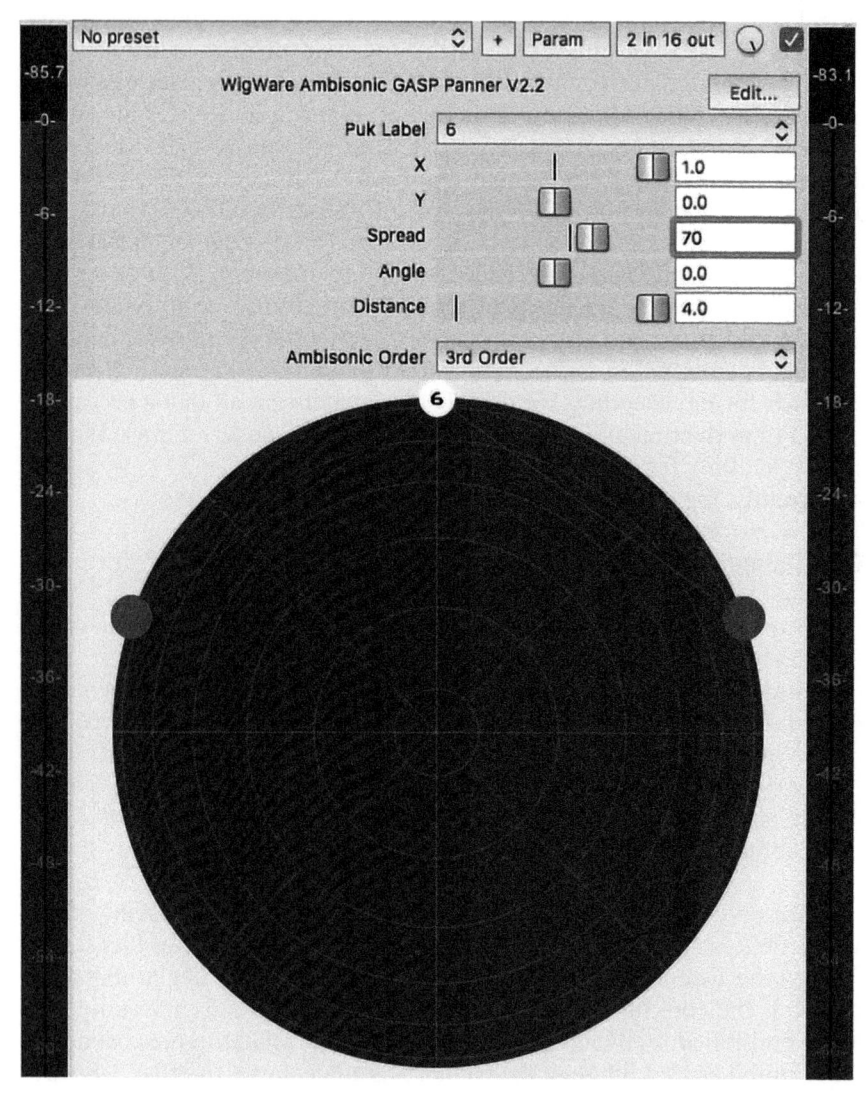

Figure 8.4 A single string spatialiser with 'stereo' image shown as red and blue dots

3rd order Ambisonic signals that are created by the spatialising panner as shown in Figure 8.4.

8.3.3 Timbralisation

The intensive real-time timbral processing and spatialisation for each individual string is carried out in the Mac Pro computer, the sound processing (timbralising) software is Line 6 Helix Native (Line 6, 2018). Each string is processed individually by a Helix Native preset, this simulates a typical guitar rig to provide amp simulation and effects, creating the core timbre of the sound. In the early stages of the GASP project Native Instruments Guitar Rig (Native-instruments.com, 2019a) was used but was later switched to Line 6 Helix Native which appears to be more computationally efficient with a greater variety and quality of effects. An instance of a Helix preset on each string produces a two-channel stereo output, as many patches have some form of a stereo effect on them such as reverbs, delays or chorus. It is worth noting that when applying amp distortion, having each string processed individually as opposed to processing the combined output, generates a more transparent timbre. This is a function of each individual string benefitting from the full bandwidth and dynamic range of the amp simulation processor. Any Helix presets can be used in the GASP system, although 28 presets have been identified and stored which facilitate sounds for a wide range of performance genres. These are currently categorised into five sets; the presets are selectable from the GASP Timbral Presets Clip Bank within Ableton:

1. Clean/Chorus x 4
2. Amp Crunch x 4
3. Distortion x 4
4. FX x 5
5. Extreme FX x 11

The stereo signals from Helix Native are sent to WigWare GASP Panners, which position each stereo pair in 2D space using 1st, 2nd or 3rd order Ambisonics encoding. The variable parameters for the panners are Spread, Angle and Distance. Spread controls the angle between the two channels of the stereo Helix output signal so they can be positioned at either the same point in space or directly opposite each other or anywhere in between. Angle controls the lateral angle of the centre of the stereo image defined anticlockwise from the front. The distance parameter is slightly mislabelled and is more accurately related to the directivity index of the resulting decoded signal. At the maximum 'distance', the polar pattern on replay is as directional as it can be (limited by the Ambisonic order used). As the distance is reduced, the directivity becomes wider, spreading the sound across more of the loudspeakers (essentially lowering the order continually from 3rd to 0th order, allowing for fractional orders in between). At a distance of zero, the sound comes out of all loudspeakers equally. Snapshots of the reproduced directional response of a single sound source can be seen in Figure 8.5. This variable directivity control is well suited to a music production context whereas *true* distance encoding, which is possible in Ambisonics using distance filtering and other psychoacoustic cues (Wiggins and Spenceley, 2009), would make mixing and production more difficult as the level, frequency response and other factors would change when altering this parameter. The encoding equations used to enable this feature can be seen in Table 8.1. The standard equations (Furse, 2014) are shown in column 3 and the altered equations to enable directivity panning used within GASP are shown in column 4. The standard encoding equations are based on simulating a plane wave and have been altered to allow for a distance control that affects the directivity of the audio source where each signal's components are scaled by the distance raised to the order (d^n). As we are panning only in the horizontal plane, currently, then z will always be 0 and x and y will be the co-ordinates of the source position on the panners graphical user interface (between -1 and 1). The full set of 3D 3rd order equations are shown for completeness.

When horizontal panning/spatialisation is used, only the channels W, X, Y, U, V, P and Q are needed (when the *z* coordinate is 0, the other channels

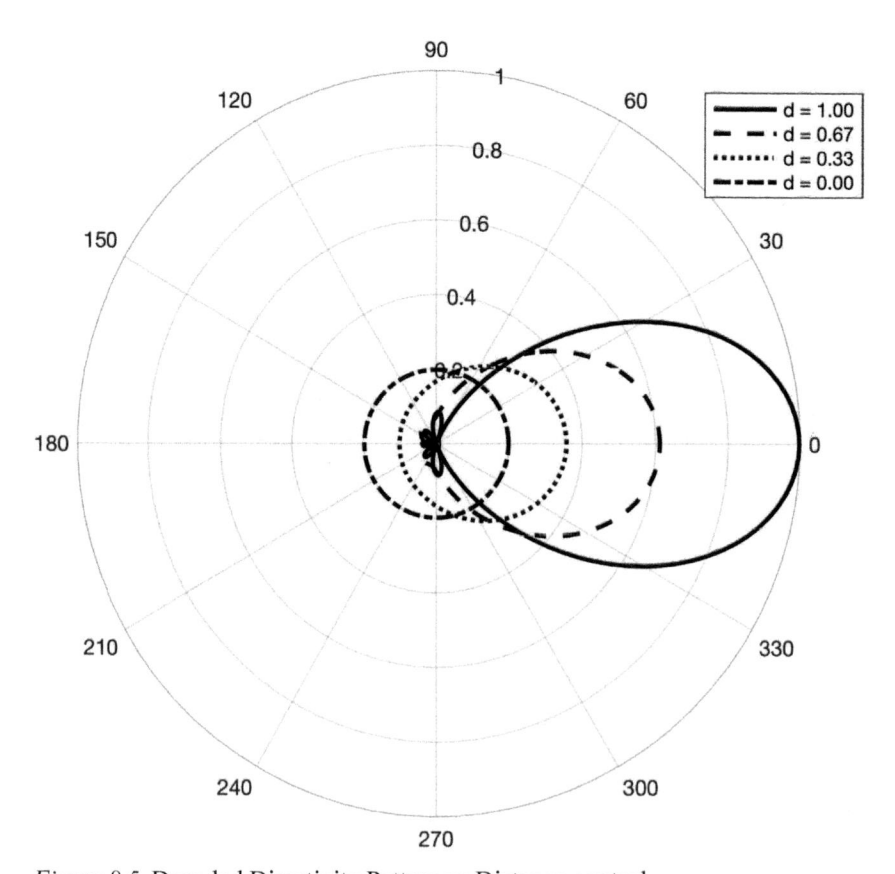

Figure 8.5 Decoded Directivity Pattern vs Distance control

Table 8.1 Ambisonic encoding equations with and without 'distance' parameter

Channel Name	Ambisonic Order	Encoding Equations (x,y,z on surface of a sphere)	Encoding Equations using distance 'd'
		$\sqrt{x^2+y^2+z^2}=1$	$d=\min\left(1,\sqrt{x^2+y^2+z^2}\right)$
W	0	$\dfrac{1}{\sqrt{2}}$	$\dfrac{1}{\sqrt{2}}$
X	1	$x(-1\ to+1)$	$x(-1\ to+1)$
Y	1	$x(-1\ to+1)$	$x(-1\ to+1)$
Z	1	$x(-1\ to+1)$	$x(-1\ to+1)$
R	2	$1.5\times z^2 - 0.5$	$1.5\times z^2 - 0.5\times d^2$
S	2	$2\times z\times x$	$2\times z\times x$
T	2	$2\times y\times z$	$2\times y\times z$
U	2	x^2-y^2	x^2-y^2
V	2	$2\times x\times y$	$2\times x\times y$
K	3	$\dfrac{z(5\times z^2 - 3)}{2}$	$\dfrac{z(5\times z^2 - 3\times d^2)}{2}$
L	3	$\dfrac{8x(5\times z^2 - 1)}{11}$	$\dfrac{8x(5\times z^2 - d^2)}{11}$
M	3	$\dfrac{8y(5\times z^2 - 1)}{11}$	$\dfrac{8y(5\times z^2 - d^2)}{11}$
N	3	$2.5981\times z(x^2-y^2)$	$2.5981\times z(x^2-y^2)$
O	3	$5.1962\times x\times y\times z$	$5.1962\times x\times y\times z$
P	3	$x(x^2-3y^2)$	$x(x^2-3y^2)$
Q	3	$y(3\times x^2-y^2)$	$y(3\times x^2-y^2)$

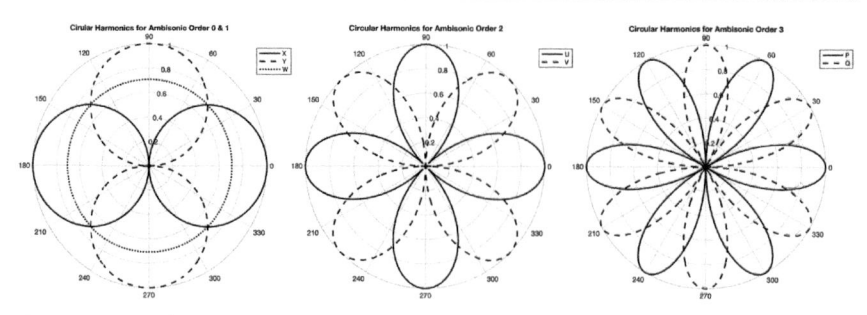

Figure 8.6 Gain versus angle plots for 2D Ambisonic encoding equations

exhibit 0 or fixed gain). The gain verses angle for these channels are shown above in Figure 8.6. The Ambisonic decoder creates a directional response for each loudspeaker position using a linear combination of these signals.

In order to easily select various dynamic variations of the Space, Angle and Distance spatialisers, several spatial preset clips have been created in Ableton, a snapshot is shown in Figure 8.7.

- Pseudo Mono – All Strings together with minimal spread.
    - Static front
    - Rotating Clockwise
    - Stepping motion Anticlockwise
    - Stepping motion Anticlockwise, Wider Spread

- Circle – All strings spaced approximately equally around the circle.
    - Static, Narrow spread
    - Static, Wide spread
    - Rotating Clockwise, Narrow Spread
    - Rotating Clockwise, Wide Spread
    - Rotating Clockwise, Spread oscillating
    - Rotating Clockwise, Spread oscillating, Distance oscillating
    - Strings 1,3,5 rotating clockwise, Strings 2,4,6 rotating anticlockwise, Narrow Spread
    - Strings 1,3,5 rotating clockwise, Strings 2,4,6 rotating anticlockwise, Wide Spread
    - 1,3,5 clockwise, 2,4,6 anticlockwise, Spread oscillating
    - 1,3,5 clockwise, 2,4,6 anticlockwise, Spread oscillating, Distance oscillating
    - Stepping clockwise, Wide Spread

- Ping Pong – Strings crossing between opposite sides.
    - Instant Switch, All Strings Together
    - Instant Switch, String 1,3,5 opposite 2,4,6
    - Smooth motion over Strings 1,3,5 opposite 2,4,6
    - Smooth motion over 1 opposite 2, 3 opposite 4, 5 opposite 6, each pair offset by 45°.

Development of an Ambisonic Guitar System 135

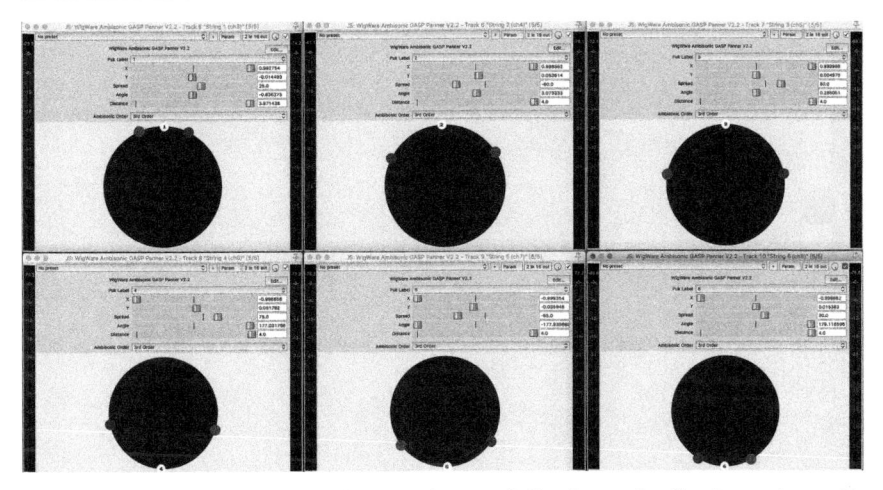

Figure 8.7 Screenshot showing static spatialisation of all six strings: In performance mode, dynamic modulation of spatial parameters can be applied

Each spatial preset can have its own speed of rotation, or speed of location switching, which is mapped to a continuous controller on a rocker pedal on the Behringer FCB1010 foot controller.

8.3.4 Arpeggiation

A further feature of the system is a set of individually MIDI triggered audio gates which facilitate programmable rhythmic muting and unmuting of individual strings. This has been named the 'GuitArpeggiator'; as it produces an effect reminiscent of arpeggiators found on many synthesisers.

The audio gates are triggered by a MIDI note sequence from an Ableton clip; a MIDI note filter on each channel is setup to filter the single note that relates to that string. This filtered note signal is sent to an instance of DMG TrackGate (Dmgaudio.com, 2019), which is set to receive a MIDI note on/off sidechain associated with each individual string, as shown in Figure 8.8. The individual string's gate attack and release times can be adjusted; it should be noted there are optimal settings required to avoid harsh switching and audible glitching. The MIDI note-on message triggers the gate's attack, the gate then stays open until the note off message triggers the release phase. The arpeggiation effect can also be blended with the output from the other mono guitar pickups such that a sustained strummed chord can be output from the mono pickup output, whilst the MIDI sequence picks out and enhances the selected programmed rhythmic notes.

8.3.5 Ambisonic send effects

Two Ambisonic effects (i.e. effects that process Ambisonic B-format signals directly) are setup on bus sends that receive the signals after the

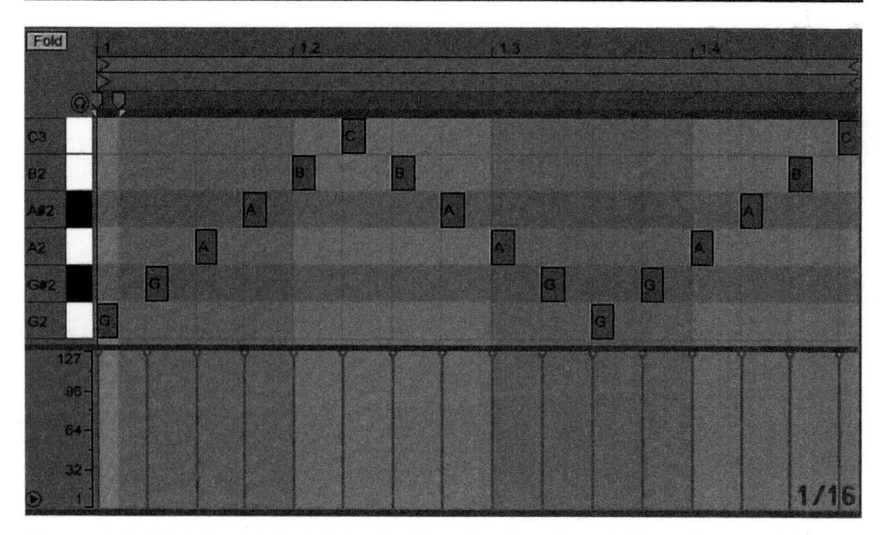

Figure 8.8 'GuitArpeggiator' screenshot showing the MIDI notes (G2 – C3) on/off switching of six Trackgates, each of which are assigned to individual strings

spatialisation process has taken place; these are WigWare AmbiFreeVerb 2 and Blue Ripple 03A Spatial Delay.

AmbiFreeVerb 2 (Wiggins, 2016) provides a full 3D spatial reverb operating at 1st order. The reverb processing is novel as the processing in the spatial domain allows the reverb to be applied to the entire sound field, but processing different areas of the sound field separately, demonstrating good spatial and immersive properties that react to the spatial panning and information contained within the sound field. Although the reverb works at 1st order resolution, the 3rd order direct sound (supplied by the panners) provides the higher directional impression of the dry audio (Wiggins, 2016).

Blue Ripple spatial delay provides a delay effect for the whole 2D sound field with a rotation effect in the feedback loop so every repeat from the delay can come at a different angle. This has a particularly interesting effect in conjunction with some of the GASP spatialisation patterns (Blue Ripple, 2019).

8.3.6 System control

For live use, a control system is required, which can be used to select presets in real-time either by the performing guitarist with a foot controller, or even a 'live producer' working in conjunction with the performer. Given the large number of parameters in each signal path, and when each of these is multiplied by seven (one for each isolated string and one for the mono output of the middle pickups), it is clear some form of intermediate macro control system is required. In order to unify the timbral, spatial and other parameters, a second computer (iMac) running Ableton

Development of an Ambisonic Guitar System   137

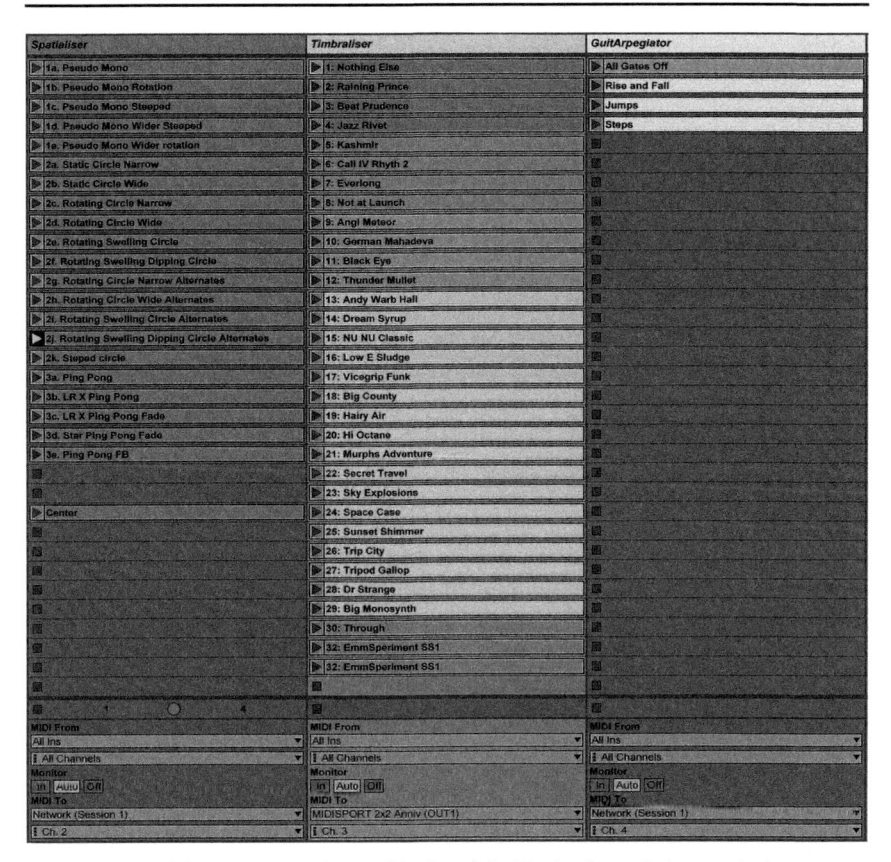

Figure 8.9 Ableton screenshot with Spatial, Timbral, and Arpeggiation preset clips

Live (Ableton.com, 2019) has been programmed to function as the macro controller. Ableton clips, as shown in Figure 8.9, are implemented to facilitate the three core elements of GASP processing, i.e. spatialisers, timbralisers, and arpeggiation presets; collectively referred to as GASP Auditory Scenes.

The clip structures in Ableton create looping sequences of MIDI continuous controller messages. The loops are effectively functioning as low frequency oscillators controlling the parameters of the spatialisers. Additionally, there are a bank of clips which contain program change messages to enable timbre selection and arpeggiation presets.

For the system to be controlled by a performing guitarist, a Behringer FCB1010 MIDI pedalboard is employed (Behringer.com, 2019); this allows the performer to independently select timbre, spatial and arpeggiation preset clips which are stored in Ableton. The FCB board is configured to allow the guitarist to both select Ableton clips and operate the continuous controller pedals to enable variations in spatialisation. Each pedalboard footswitch is setup to send out a unique MIDI message which can then be assigned to trigger any Ableton clip, including master clips. One of the expression pedals on the FCB foot controller is assigned to control the tempo of the Ableton session, which is directly related to the spatialisation parameters. The spatialisers position audio to a given location and are controllable via the tempo of Ableton's sequencer, which is in turn mapped to continuous controller pedals of the FCB foot controller, allowing real-time user control. As the clip length is set in bars, this speeds up or slows down the rate of the spatialiser, thus facilitating interesting spatial rotation and/or fast locational switching effects of individual strings. It is worth noting, the FCB1010 is notoriously challenging to program, so firmware upgrades to UNO/FCB (Control Fcb1010.uno, 2019) have been installed, enabling improvements in this regard.

8.3.7 Spatial effects and control

In the current configuration, we have noted some interesting phenomena associated with control of the Spread, Angle, Distance (SAD) spatialisers. The control of movement of the SAD spatialisers are currently all simultaneously directly mapped to Ableton's tempo, such that as the tempo is increased, the parameter values for all SAD spatialiser parameters also increase pro-rata. The tempo control is mapped to the FCB foot controller allowing the performer to vary the SAD spatialisation values using FCB's continuous controller (CC) rocker pedal. Ableton's available tempo values range from 20–999 bpm, which are mapped to CC pedal values 0–127, which is a numerically linear mapping. Given this current configuration, some investigations into the performative aspects of real-time spatial manipulation have been carried out. Whilst the current linear mapping generates some interesting spatial effects, there are also some limitations for real-time live performance control. It is noted that around the mid-range of the tempo values there are some particularly interesting spatial effects which exist around a narrow band of tempo values. However, this narrow band is not well suited to the CC foot controller, as a finer resolution of rocker pedal movement is required. Work being currently undertaken should enable this to be investigated further; a linear to non-linear look-up table for continuous controller values has been created, which will facilitate the mid-range SAD values to effectively be expanded. This should allow a more nuanced investigation of the spatial effects at these mid-range tempo values. Example non-linear mappings are shown in Figure 8.10.

All SAD values are currently simultaneously affected by Ableton's tempo setting, such that *independent* control of the individual Spread, Angle or Distance parameter movements with CC foot controller pedals are unavailable. This provides the next challenge for future work; to investigate ways in which to facilitate individual and independent control of SAD parameters. This would also enable additional features such as LFO and EG controllers for each SAD parameter to be a programmable or real-time performative feature.

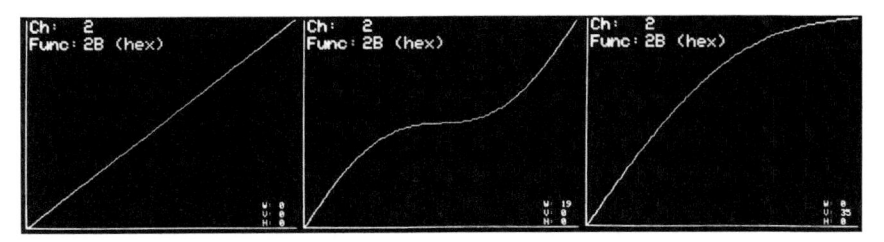

Figure 8.10 Examples of transfer function curves for CC modulation of SAD parameters (future work)

Courtesy S. Thackery 2019

8.4 REFLECTIONS OF GASP POST-PRODUCTIONS

GASP productions of *Elliot's Joy, Prelude to Life* (Baker, 2014) and *Pale Aura* were first presented at the Technical University of Hamburg, Germany, 'Klingt Gut' international conference June 2017. *Cat Fantastic* was first presented at University of Derby, UK, 'Sounds in Space' symposium, June 2019. Examples of productions, using YouTube spatial audio (optimised for headphone listening using 1st, rather than 3rd, order Ambsionics) can be found on the GASP YouTube channel (https://tinyurl.com/GASPYouTube, Werner and Wiggins, 2019).

Some comments received from interested parties include guitarist Roman Rappak (Miroshot, 2019) who upon hearing of the project, commented:

> it's exciting to think of the kind of creative options this would open to guitarists, and as a live band that is focused so heavily on tech and the future, this could be exactly the kind of sound we are looking for . . .
>
> (Rappak, 2018)

Music Producer David Ward, Executive Director of JAMES (Joint Audio Media Educational Support) (Jamesonline.org.uk, 2019):

> of particular interest, on our [accreditation] visit, was the Guitar based Ambisonic Spatial Performance project where we became aware of the myriad commercial, theatrical, performance and educational potentials of this project.
>
> (Ward, 2018)

Guitarist and Educator Fred T. Baker (En.wikipedia.org, 2019):

> The first time hearing my tracks back I was amazed by the quality of the spatial sound, it really had the WOW factor. I feel it has much potential for future development, it would be fantastic in a larger theatre. I think this system is unique, it gave my composition a whole new dimension.
>
> (Baker, 2018)

Elliot's Joy: composed and performed by Fred T. Baker, production by Jack Hooley and Dominic Dallali. This was the first of a series of GASP productions; the recording was made with our Yamaha APX400 electro-acoustic fitted with Ubertar hex pickup, and recorded directly into ProTools, with timbralisation subsequently applied using NI Guitar Rig and spatialisation production completed in Reaper using WigWare. Upon reflection, the 'phasey' guitar timbre is probably a little overdone, and there are some sections (e.g. bridge part) of the mix which seem to 'pop-out' level wise, a little too much. The lower strings as the bass part work well, although there is little spatial movement in the low frequency content.

Prelude to Life: composed and performed by Fred T. Baker, production by Charlie Box and Duncan Werner. The recording was made with our Yamaha APX400 electro-acoustic, recorded directly into ProTools. Timbralisation is a mix of both NI Guitar Rig and instrument samples. Melodyne's (Celemony.com, 2019) pitch to MIDI conversion was applied, the MIDI note events were then arranged to trigger various instrument samples in NI Komplete (Native-instruments.com, 2019b). Upon reflection, the timing of pitch to MIDI conversion worked very well, such that the nuances of the guitar performance are precisely captured. The production was experimental, and again, upon reflection the choice of instrumentation could be refined, perhaps with a less diverse range of timbres, which may better suit the performance genre.

Pale Aura: performed by Dominic Dallali, production by Jack Hooley and Dominic Dallali. The recording was made with our Fender Stratocaster fitted with Ubertar hex pickups, recorded directly into ProTools, then timbralised with NI Guitar Rig. The spatialisation production was completed in Reaper using WigWare. This track is the guitar part of Pale Aura by the band Periphery, it is in the genre of progressive metal. It turned out to be quite a dramatic production, with rapid changes in location for close temporal events. The guitar part consists of some highly syncopated timing elements, which have been mapped to rapid location switching. There is a good range of amp distortion timbres employed for different parts of the performance. An unfortunate hiss is noticeable during both the intro and outro, which would also benefit from better creative spatialisation. A low kick drum was included to provide the listener with a sense of meter as the guitar performance includes several syncopated elements, and upon reflection the kick is an unwelcome distraction from the performance in places.

Cat Fantastic (CF): performed by Jack Hooley, production by Duncan Werner and Emma Fitzmaurice. The initial recording was made using our Fender Stratocaster fitted with Ubertar hex pickups. Two very different mixes of the track were made, both using Helix Native for timbralisation.

CF Mix 1 has a fixed timbre with dynamic spatialisation. Using the same timbre throughout, several spatial presets were applied during different sections of the arrangement, this enabled critical listening of the variations of the spatial production of the mix. However, upon reflection a greater sense of spatial modulation could have been achieved by implementing tempo (speed) variations in the SAD spatialisation.

CF Mix 2 applies post-production timbral morphing and dynamic spatialisation. Initial ideas for timbral morphing included some investigation into real-time continuous controller messages mapped to timbral parameters, e.g. chorus modulation values or reverberation. However, this proved problematic as the number of continuous controllers requiring real-time modulation was far greater than Helix would allow access. 'Pmix plugin preset interpolator' (Olilarkin.co.uk, 2019) was investigated; however, this supports VST2 only, whereas Helix works with VST3, AAX or AU formats. Nevertheless, real-time timbral morphing remains an area for future investigation. However, in order to demonstrate proof of concept, multiple versions of each string, each with different timbres were printed on time-synchronised parallel tracks, thus allowing crossfading between individual string timbres, then mixing the respective tracks. The timbral morphing works well although future mixes using this technique would benefit from longer morphing time durations.

A general observation relating to GASP post-production is identified where the musical nature of differing guitar performance styles (an example could be acoustic picking vs thrash metal) can benefit from potentially extreme variations in timbral and spatial production, such that *the more complex the performance technique, the greater the creative potential for the GASP production*.

8.5 CRITICAL ANALYSIS AND FUTURE WORK

8.5.1 System rationalisation

Techniques for system rationalisation are sought, which will mean a rethink of the current configuration; considerations include combining sound processing actions (Reaper, Helix, WigWare, currently on Mac Pro) and system control (Ableton currently on iMac) into one application and be able to run on one computer. The most demanding data processing is Helix, so any rationalisation process would look here first.

8.5.2 Expansion to 3D

The current system operates in a 2D immersive environment; however, future work will look towards GASP productions which include height information for a deeper immersive experience. This then begs the questions, how might our current 2D guitar production techniques be expanded to 3D, and does this enhance the aesthetic immersive experience of a guitar performance further than a 2D experience? Further questions then arise, such as how does the stylistic performance technique of a specific genre of guitar performance map into 3D.

8.5.3 Live performance control

Given the current spatial parameters of Spread, Angle and Distance, leads us to consider enhancement possibilities for interface and control. Pysiewicz and Weinzierl (2016) suggest a taxonomy of spatialisation with three categorisations; controller type/interface, control of spatial parameters, and scope of the control. The document provides consideration for further creative options, which may be applied for GASP enhancement. One way we have considered how the GASP system may be controlled in a performance environment is through a dedicated 'live GASP producer' who would provide control over timbral, spatial and other performance realisation parameters, independently of the guitarist. This then leads to the idea of an interactive sound arts performance where the guitarist responds to changes initiated by the live producer, the outcome being potentially unpredictable depending on the imaginative response of the performing guitarist. Further, the live production control parameters could be made available to an audience who may also contribute to the performative outcome, resulting in an audience/guitarist interactive performance.

The live production work to date has focussed on spatial manipulation of individual strings, each with the same timbral processing. Future work will investigate Reaper Project templates to include individual and differing timbres across different strings, or probably more usefully across groups of strings, e.g. strings 1,2,3 with timbre A, strings 4,5,6 timbre B. This technique can then be expanded to include different spatial presets on individual, or other alternative grouping of strings.

Additionally, real-time timbral morphing remains a key area for future work. Investigations into accessing multiple parameters of timbral processing via CC messages continue to take place with both Helix and Guitar Rig.

8.5.4 Frequency band splitting

An alternative approach without the use of hex pickups is to take the standard mono guitar output and divide into a range of frequency bands, which can then be independently processed, either timbrally, spatially or both. To achieve this, a six-way crossover (frequency splitter) network was implemented on the main mono guitar input. As the system configuration is already optimised for six channels of guitar, the six frequency bands can be mapped to these channels. The output of each band of the crossover is then fed to the same processing channel setup as is used for the individual string processing system, which allows for all the same patches to be used along with the same control system. The crossover points are chosen to have equal octave spacing and be within the range of frequencies that are produced by an electric guitar. Whilst this approach has been tested, we have not yet examined the spatial effects and possibilities in as much detail as individual string processing.

ACKNOWLEDGEMENTS

Since the inception of the GASP project, there have been both technical and musical contributions from staff and students at the University of Derby, so big thanks to: Charlie Middlicott, Sam Speakman, Mark Randell, Alex Wardle, Joe Callister, Tom Lawson, Tom Weightman, Dominic Dallali, Jack Hooley, Charlie Box, Emma Fitzmaurice, Beth Mansfield, Thomas Nash, Harry Dale, Steve Thackery, Emiliano Bonanomi (session guitarist), and others. . . .

REFERENCES

Ableton.com. (2019). *Music Production with Live and Push | Ableton*. [online] Available at: https://www.ableton.com/en/ [Accessed 26 November 2019].

Baker, F. (2018). *Comment on the GASP System*. [email].

Behringer.com. (2019). *|FCB1010|Behringer|P0089*. [online] Available at: https://www.behringer.com/Categories/Behringer/Accessories/Midi-Foot Controllers/FCB1010/p/P0089 [Accessed 26 November 2019].

Blue Ripple Sound. (2019). *O3A Core*. [online] Available at: http://www.blueripplesound.com/products/o3a-core [Accessed 26 Nov. 2019].

Celemony.com. (2019). *Celemony*. [online] Available at: https://www.celemony.com/en/start [Accessed 26 November 2019].

Cycfi Research. (2019). *Cycfi Research*. [online] Available at: https://www.cycfi.com/ [Accessed 26 November 2019].

Dmgaudio.com. (2019). *DMG Audio: Products: TrackGate*. [online] Available at: https://dmgaudio.com/products_trackgate.php [Accessed 26 November 2019].

En.wikipedia.org. (2019). *Fred Thelonious Baker*. [online] Available at: https://en.wikipedia.org/wiki/Fred_Thelonious_Baker [Accessed 28 November 2019].

Fcb1010.uno. (2019). *FCB/UnO Control Center for the Behringer FCB1010*. [online] Available at: https://www.fcb1010.uno/ [Accessed 26 November 2019].

Fender (2017). *CITES Regulations For The Importation And Exportation Of Rosewood Effective* 2 January 2017. [online] Available at: https://support.fender.com/hc/en-us/articles/115000867426-CITES-Regulations-For-The-Importation-And-Exportation-Of-Rosewood-Effective-January-2-2017 [Accessed 8 March 2020].

Fender (2020). *Pau Ferro Guitars | Fender Guitars*. [online] Available at: https://www.fender.com/articles/tech-talk/what-is-pau-ferro [Accessed 8 March 2020].

Furse, R. (2014). *HOA Technical Notes - B-Format*. [online] Blue Ripple Sound. Available at: https://web.archive.org/web/20141020063947/http://www.blueripplesound.com/b-format [Accessed 28 November 2019].

Gerzon, M.A. (1974a) *Sound Reproduction Systems*. Patent No. 1494751.

Gerzon, M.A. (1974b) What's wrong with Quadraphonics. [online] Available at: http://audiosignal.co.uk/Resources/What_is_wrong_with_quadraphonics_A4.pdf [Accessed 26 May 2016].

Gerzon, Michael A. (November 1985). Ambisonics in Multichannel Broadcasting and Video. *Journal of the Audio Engineering Society*, AES, 33 (11): 859–871.

Jamesonline.org.uk. (2019). *JAMES*. [online] Available at: http://www.jamesonline.org.uk/ [Accessed 28 November 2019].

Line 6 (2018). Helix Native. [Online] Available at: https://uk.line6.com/helix/helixnative.html

Malham, D. (2003), "Higher Order Ambisonic Systems," abstracted from 'Space in Music - Music in Space', an Mphil thesis by Dave Malham, submitted to the University of York in April 2003, [online]. Available at: http://www.york.ac.uk/inst/mustech/3d_audio/higher_order_ambisonics.pdf [Accessed 9 September 2011].

Miroshot. (2019). *Miro Shot – AR/VR Band/Collective*. [online] Available at: https://miroshot.com/ [Accessed 28 November 2019].

Nachbar, C., Zotter, F., Deleflie, E. and Sontacchi, A. (2011). Ambix-a suggested ambisonics format. In *Ambisonics Symposium*, Lexington.

Native-instruments.com. (2019a). *GUITAR RIG 5 PRO*. [online] Available at: https://www.native-instruments.com/en/products/komplete/guitar/guitar-rig-5-pro/ [Accessed 27 November 2019].

Native-instruments.com. (2019b). *KOMPLETE 12*. [online] Available at: https://www.native-instruments.com/en/products/komplete/bundles/komplete-12/ [Accessed 27 Nov. 2019].

Olilarkin.co.uk. (2019). *Audio Software by Oli Larkin*. [online] Available at: https://olilarkin.co.uk/index.php?p=pmix [Accessed 26 November 2019].

Perez-Lopez, A., (2015). *3DJ: A Supercollider Framework for Real-time Sound Spatialization*. Georgia Institute of Technology.

Pysiewicz, A. and Weinzierl, S. (2016). Instruments for Spatial Sound Control in Real Time Music Performances. A Review. In *Musical Instruments in the 21st Century* (pp. 273–296). Springer, Singapore.

Randell, M. (2011). *Report on a Technological and Aesthetic Exploration of a Multichannel Guitar System*. [online] Academia.edu. Available at: https://www.academia.edu/11735503/Report_on_a_technological_and_aesthetic_exploration_of_a_multichannel_guitar_system [Accessed 2 December 2019].

Rappak, R. (2018). *Audience of the Future: 3D Guitar Production System*. [email].

Reaper.fm. (2019). *REAPER | Audio Production Without Limits*. [online] Available at: https://www.reaper.fm/index.php [Accessed 26 November 2019].

Rubenstein, P. (2019). *Ubertar Hexaphonic Guitar Pickups*. [online] Ubertar.com. Available at: http://www.ubertar.com/hexaphonic/ [Accessed 25 November 2019].

Sounds in Space. (2019). *Sounds in Space*. [online] Available at: http://soundsinspace.co.uk/ [Accessed 26 November 2019].

Valiquet, P., (2012). The Spatialisation of Stereophony: Taking Positions in Postwar Electroacoustic Music. *International Review of the Aesthetics and Sociology of Music*, pp.403–421.

Ward, D. (2018). *James Accreditation Visit*. [email].

Werner, D. and Wiggins, B. (2019). *GASP*. [online] YouTube. Available at: https://tinyurl.com/GASPYouTube [Accessed 2 December 2019].

Wiggins, B. (2007) The Generation of Panning Laws for Irregular Speaker Arrays Using Heuristic Methods. *Audio Engineering Society Conference: 31st*

International Conference: New Directions in High Resolution Audio. Audio Engineering Society.

Wiggins, B. (2008). Reproduced Sound 24 – Proceedings of the Institute of Acoustics, Vol 30. Pt 6.

Wiggins, B. (2016). *YouTube, Ambisonics and VR.* [online] The Blog of Bruce. Available at: https://www.brucewiggins.co.uk/?p=666#more-666 [Accessed 26 November 2019].

Wiggins, B. (2017) Analysis of Binaural Cue Matching using Ambisonics to Binaural Decoding Techniques. *4th International Conference on Spatial Audio*, 7–10 September, Graz, Austria.

Wiggins, B., Spenceley, T. (2009) Distance Coding and Performance of the Mark 5 and st350 SoundField Microphones and Their Suitability for Ambisonic Reproduction. *Reproduced Sound 25 – Proceeding of the Institute of Acoustics, Vol 31, Pt 4.*

DISCOGRAPHY

Fred T. Baker (2014), [CD] *Life Suite*, First Hand Records. https://www.youtube.com/watch?v=hDJfv-Hft_s

9

Retaining pianistic virtuosity in #MIs

Exploring pre-existing gestural nuances for live sound modulation through a comparative study

Niccolò Granieri, James Dooley and Tychonas Michailidis

9.1 INTRODUCTION AND AIMS

This chapter looks at the evaluation of *Reach*, an augmented keyboard instrument that provides control over the sound modulation of a live piano feed. The chapter builds upon existing research previously presented at the Innovation in Music conference that took place in London, September 2017 (Granieri, Dooley and Michailidis, 2019). The comparative user testing discussed here investigates if and to what extent invasiveness in Digital and Augmented Musical Instruments (#MIs) affected the ability of pianists to improvise at a first encounter with the instrument freely. To do so, the Reach v1.0 system, mounted on an acoustic grand piano, was compared with two existing keyboard interfaces. The keyboard interfaces chosen, TouchKeys (McPherson, 2012) and ROLI Seaboard (Lamb and Robertson, 2011), enable real-time sound modulation with different levels of invasiveness. Six jazz pianists took part in the test.

The user test investigates different aspects of the relationship between pianists and the musical instruments playing through two improvisational scenarios. There were different aspects of this relationship that were a focal point of this study. These ranged from the ability of users to improvise freely on a keyboard-based #MI without extensive prior experience with it, to the importance of the means of interaction provided by the instrument itself. While different gestural controllers have varying levels of precision and control over the sound, the tests also examine, through final interviews with the participants, the importance of dimensionality (Zappi and McPherson, 2014) of the instrument when compared to the affordance provided. The concept of dimensionality, as used by Zappi and McPherson, is intended as the number of dimensions of control over sound that an instrument or interface provides. The ability of the pianists to freely improvise at a first encounter with the instrument was also compared with the low degree of invasiveness, providing a fertile ground to transfer the instrumental technique developed.

The first two key points sought to investigate three concepts regarding instrument interaction: *freedom of playing*, *learning curve* and *aural invasiveness*. While these elements require longitudinal studies with the tracked progression of the musicians, in this user study these concepts are to be applied solely to the first encounter that the musician has with the instrument. In this specific user-testing, freedom of playing describes the amount of freedom that the user felt in the first encounter with each particular interface and is directly linked with the ability of the pianists to use their pianistic technique to control the novel interface. The freedom of playing also explores and facilitates the spontaneous exploration of extramusical gestures. Extramusical gestures, in this context, are gestures that do not directly contribute to the traditional instrumental sound generation, yet can be uniquely recognised by the interface and subsequently interact with the sound. Video recordings of the improvisations and the responses during a semi-structured interview will explore these aspects.

Similarly, the concept of learning curve can be interpreted as the amount of time needed for the user to get acquainted with the interface during the first encounter. This point was investigated mainly throughout the interview process and ties back to the freedom of playing. The aural invasiveness aspect of this exploration followed the results of the initial user testing, as described in (Granieri, Dooley and Michailidis, 2019). Classical pianists struggle more with the aural elements of the system than the gestural ones. In this comparative scenario, further exploration of the topic with all the proposed interfaces aimed to elicit the importance of aural invasiveness.

9.1.1 Instrument choice

The study compared three instruments that pertained to three distinct keyboard-based digital instrument categories. The Seaboard was chosen to represent a keyboard-based Digital Musical Instrument (DMI) with some major changes regarding both the hardware and the interaction. The instrument – apart from taking the keyboard layout as inspiration – modifies everything else: from the key spacing – smaller than a classical keyboard layout – to the wedge shaped keys (Dahlstedt, 2017), all the way to the key interaction, which shifts from the traditional moving keys of a keyboard to a pressure and position-sensitive silicone slate. With this different interaction plane, the Seaboard was chosen to be the instrument in the test that provided control over the piano sound with the greatest gestural learning curve. Being so different from a traditional keyboard, it has been noted previously by researchers like Dahlstedt (2017) that the technique required was not that of a pianist, making it an instrument tailored mainly to non-specialist keyboard players.

The TouchKeys, an augmentation of an existing keyboard, was chosen to represent the apparent gap between Reach, an augmentation of an acoustic piano, and Seaboard, a keyboard-based DMI. While both the TouchKeys and the Reach system could *potentially* be mounted both on a digital keyboard and an acoustic piano, the choice of having them mounted on two different instruments was purposeful. While TouchKeys is marketed as being able to transform any piano-style keyboard into an expressive multi-touch control surface, most of the use cases showcasing the system in action used the system applied to a MIDI keyboard.

There are multiple prototype systems that provide the user with gestural control over sound modulation and these will be explored in next section of this chapter, however the test was aimed at considering only instruments that could have been used in a real-world scenario. For this reason, prototypes not easily available to the general public were not taken into consideration and the TouchKeys used was the one sold pre-mounted on a Novation Impulse 49.

9.2 BACKGROUND AND PREVIOUS WORK

The ability of performers to communicate through their instrument depends on the fluency that the performer has with the instrument itself (Tanaka, 2000). Fluency, in this case, is seen as a combination of technical proficiency and expressive charisma, which in turn depend on the time spent practising an instrument and ways of incorporating ancillary movements that are known to convey expressiveness in musical performance (Miranda and Wanderley, 2006).

In recent years, several innovative keyboard interfaces have been developed that range from augmented keyboard interfaces to redesigns of the traditional keyboard interface. The ROLI Seaboard redesigns the keyboard interface entirely by maintaining its layout, but by using discrete sound activators merged into a continuous controller within a touch-responsive silicone overlay. The TouchKeys augments an existing keyboard's interface by covering the keys with capacitive sensors, allowing the position of the finger on the key and indeed the amount of contact area to modulate musical parameters.

Alongside these two commercial devices, many prototype devices exist. One such device is the system developed by Yang and Essl (2012), providing the pianist with multi-axial gesture controls over audio processing of the keyboard sound using a combination camera-based hand detection and visual projections. Another device is the PiaF (Zandt-Escobar, Caramiaux and Tanaka, 2014) that combines machine learning with camera based technology to recognise body gestures providing control over audio-processing parameters, noting how a pianist's interpretation is communicated both by the sound produced and the supporting body gestures. The ancillary gestures used in this research show a potential for the intuitive control of audio processing with movements not directly related to sound production. Reach develops this concept further by focusing entirely on ancillary hand gestures as a means of manipulating sound-processing.

The Reach system was used to conduct four case studies with creative practitioners of different musical background (Granieri, Dooley and Michailidis, 2019). Through collaborative design workshops, the creative practitioners, a composer and two songwriters, helped define the current state of the Reach system. The gesture-sound mappings implemented in the Reach system for this test were investigated and used in the live performances resulting from the case studies (Knibbs and Granieri, 2018; Stenton and Granieri, 2018a, 2018b; Tunley and Granieri, 2018).

9.3 THE REACH SYSTEM

Figure 9.1 presents an overview of the Reach system. The Reach v1.0 system uses a custom-made homonymous application, written in C++ using the JUCE framework, and Leap Motion's VR-oriented Orion SDK (Guna *et al.*, 2014) to capture hand-tracking data from a Leap Motion sensor. The Reach was developed to work on a variety of computers, including embeddable development boards such as the LattePanda (2019), to provide the broadest options to the users in terms of computational power.

The Leap Motion is placed approximately 30cm above the piano keyboard, where positional data is tracked by Reach, encoded and transmitted as OSC messages. The OSC transfer protocol has been chosen over MIDI because of its ability to transmit data with a higher resolution, thus maintaining a higher level of precision when mapping the gestural data to sound-modulation parameters. This tracking data, coming from the joints of the fingers, palms and wrists, is then received by a Pure Data patch, and mapped to sound-modulation parameters. For this comparative study, the Reach system had a fixed set of gesture-sound-effect couplings to make the comparison with the other instruments coherent.

Due to the high level of precision of the Orion SDK, there was no need to de-noise the data. Instead, real-time peak-detection audio analysis was conducted on the incoming piano signal in Pure Data. When hitting a note, the positional data received from the Leap Motion was 're-centred', meaning that no audio modulation would occur unless the hand moved away from the current position. If the hand moved and a key was struck, the process repeated. This approach prevented erratic behaviour in the audio processing.

A description of the mapping of gestural data to sound-modulation parameters follows. Lateral movement of the hand after a note had been played were mapped to a pitch-shifting algorithm ranging +/- 75 cents of a tone, where movements to the right raised the pitch and movements to the left lowered the pitch, creating a vibrato effect. The height of the palm

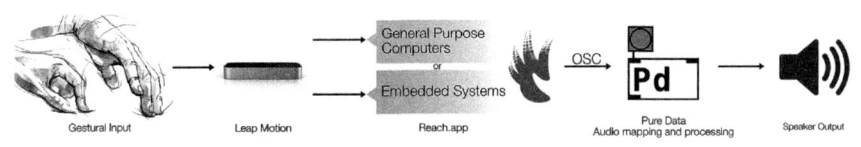

Figure 9.1 Overview of the Reach system

when fingers touch the keys on the keyboard was inversely mapped to the amplitude modulation and the reverb effect. When the pianist's hands were positioned in a regular playing position, a clean, unprocessed piano sound was sent to the loudspeakers. As the pianist moves his or her hands vertically away from the piano, reverberation is applied to the live piano sound, with the amplitude of the unprocessed piano sound being inversely proportional to this.

9.4 THE COMPARATIVE USER TESTING

9.4.1 The setup

The three systems used in the testing, the Reach system mounted on a Steinway & Sons grand piano, the Seaboard and the TouchKeys, were placed in a triangular arrangement, in order to accommodate the pianist in the centre and comfortably switch from one system to the other as seen in Figure 9.2. All three systems were active at all times, to limit the amount of setup time during the actual test. Three Genelec 8030A speakers were positioned at each end of all three keyboards. One speaker was placed at each vertex of the triangle, meaning that each system shared one speaker that was switched between one and the other via software routing in between the individual tests.

The sound fed into the Reach system was captured by an Audio Technica AT4040 cardioid microphone and fed into a Mac Mini 4,1 through an Edirol UA-25EX. The Leap Motion data, parsed through Reach on a Lenovo ThinkPad Yoga 260, was then fed in via Ethernet to modulate the sound parameters. To split the required computing power between more machines, and to avoid any overloading issues – once processed and effected – the audio was sent out to a Macbook Pro 11,4 through a TC Electronics Impact Twin audio interface to be recorded. The recording was solely a precautionary

Figure 9.2 Comparative testing keyboard and speaker setup

measure to avoid losing data during the tests; the system had previously been successfully run through a single laptop setup. The latency of the system was below the perceivable threshold of 15 milliseconds and was thus disregarded; the destructive nature of the effects and the loudness of the acoustic piano itself had been observed to mask any delay occurring in previous tests and case studies.

Both the Seaboard and the TouchKeys were configured to play piano samples. The sample library included with the ROLI Equator software was used due to the good quality of the samples, ease of setup, mapping of parameters and compatibility of the software itself with other MIDI Polyphonic Expression (MPE) devices.

9.4.2 The effects

The effects used to modulate the sound were consistent across the three systems, with minor adjustments to each keyboard interface as detailed below. This choice enabled the user to be aware of the trade-off between the three keyboard interfaces; the more invasive the interface, the more control and options. The Seaboard, which was considered the most invasive interface of the three because of the complete redesign of the keyboard itself, covered in touch and pressure-sensitive material, was set up to enable sound modulation with four different gestures:

- Vibrato Effect – Lateral swaying of the finger(s)
- Amplitude modulation – Pressure of the finger(s) (if done fast enough, tremolo effect)
- Detuning Effect – Vertical slide of the finger(s)
- Continuous Glissando – Glissando on the bar above and below the keys

The TouchKeys was set up to enable sound modulation with three different gestures:

- Vibrato Effect – Lateral swaying of the finger(s)
- Amplitude modulation – Pressure of the Finger(s) (if done fast enough, tremolo effect)
- Detuning Effect – Vertical Slide of the finger(s)

The Reach system maintains two gestures in common with the other systems while offering a third gesture. This approach makes users aware that while touch-free interfaces lose control and precision when modulating effects, as shown by Wilson (2010), they can expand the range of useful gestures; in this case, the ability to track the natural leaps of the hand above the keyboard and controlling the amount of reverb. The gestures that were implemented were the following:

- Vibrato Effect – Lateral swaying of the hand(s)
- Tremolo Effect – Height of the palm(s)
- Reverberation – Height of the hand from the keyboard

9.4.3 Methodology

Each test was designed to last approximately one hour, although in practice, the shortest test lasted 52 minutes and the longest 1 hour 30 minutes (due to some software issues). Subjects were briefly interviewed about their pianistic background, current knowledge and experience with electronic music and #MIs. They were also asked to describe any prior knowledge of the three systems, and if they had previously played or performed with them. This background information was later linked to the ease of use, learnability and approachability questions. In addition, users were also asked if they had played and/or improvised any of the two proposed pieces: *Goodbye Pork Pie Hat* by Charles Mingus, and *Musica Ricercata n.7* by György Ligeti.

While considering the common background between all the users, the decision was made to push the two improvisations in two different directions to elicit different ways of playing from the musical performances.

The first piece shown in Figure 9.3, Goodbye Pork Pie Hat, was chosen as representative of a jazz standard. Moreover, the blues connotation of the piece containing a 'blues-like' melody is usually associated with wind or brass instruments due to its original version being played on the saxophone, making the tune hard to play expressively on a piano. This melodic line with vocal characteristics aimed to encourage expressive playing. Users were expected to be familiar with the piece and thus able to perform a typical jazz improvisation. This approach intended to boost confidence while improvising and engage with jazz vocabulary automatisms that would have triggered the three systems in different ways, without asking the pianist to think about the gestures to perform. On the other hand, Musica Ricercata n.7 was chosen for the modal nature of the melody and supposed unfamiliarity of the tune. All the elements apart from the melodic line had been removed from the score, as seen in Figure 9.4. The intention was to lay the ground for a freer improvisation, that explored all the encountered effects in the previous ten minutes of playing on the instrument.

After the pre-test interview and a brief explanation of the system, the order in which the users would have played the three systems was revealed. The order in which each pianist played the three #MIs was randomised to reduce the effect that playing one keyboard first could have on the following. Having three separate systems and six pianists, each pianist

Figure 9.3 Excerpt from the Goodbye Pork Pie Hat score

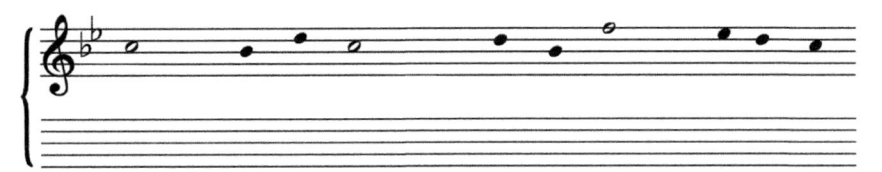

Figure 9.4 Excerpt from the Musica Ricercata No. VII score

played the three systems in a different order. The pianists had five minutes to try the system and get comfortable with the sound and effects coming from the speakers. When the users felt comfortable with the systems and all the gesture-effect couplings, the pianists were asked to perform two five-minute improvisations.

The first improvisation was on Goodbye Pork Pie Hat. The user was asked to play the main theme and follow the score once, and then to improvise freely for the remaining time. All of the users were asked to play the theme once in order to have a similar baseline that could be compared side by side. The second improvisation was on Musica Ricercata n.7 and followed the same process as the first. After each test, users were asked to complete a User Experience Questionnaire (UEQ) (Schrepp, Hinderks and Thomaschewski, 2014) to evaluate the experience. The post-test interviews provided further information about their experience and level of invasiveness of each system.

9.5 RESULTS AND DISCUSSION

When they first tried it, most of the pianists appreciated the ability to modulate sound parameters with their gestures on all three instruments. This happened consistently across all three keyboards, regardless of the order in which the pianists were asked to play them. This result was also independent of the musical background of the musicians, whether they owned electronic gear, or were completely naive to the environment. Ubiquitously, kind of gesture recognition technology appeared fascinating.

The UEQ evaluated the user experience through attractiveness, efficiency, perspicuity, and dependability, novelty and stimulation. Responses were mapped to a Likert scale between -3 and +3. Figure 9.5 below shows the average values from all the six users, for each keyboard. The y-axis of the plot represents the mean of the data gathered through the UEQ questionnaire. This questionnaire, comprised of 26 items, assigned a score between -3 and 3 to every question with 0 being the neutral answer.

In the same graph, as noted in the legend, the three interfaces are represented with three different shades: darkest for Reach and lightest for the

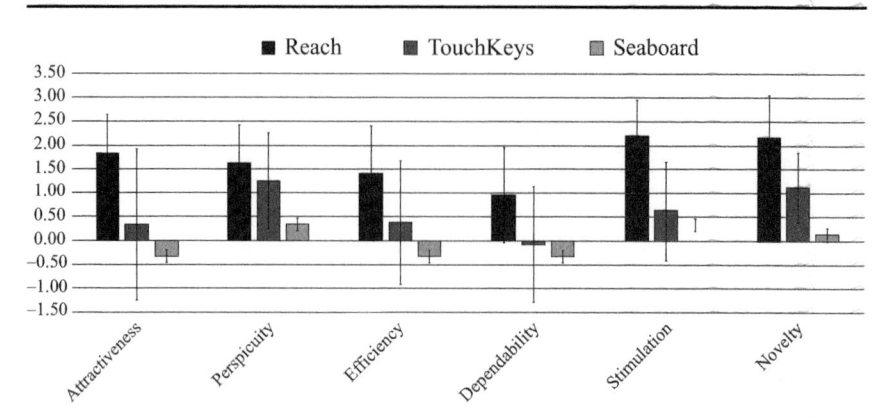

Figure 9.5 UEQ interface comparison showcasing mean and standard deviation for each value analysed

Table 9.1 Interface ranking according to three factors

	Interest		
Ranking	**Reach**	**TouchKeys**	**Seaboard**
First	5	1	2
Second	1	2	1
Third	0	3	3
	Freedom of Playing		
Ranking	**Reach**	**TouchKeys**	**Seaboard**
First	6	0	0
Second	0	5	1
Third	0	1	5
	Learning Curve		
Ranking	**Reach**	**TouchKeys**	**Seaboard**
First	4	3	0
Second	2	2	1
Third	0	1	5

Seaboard. Overall, the Reach system was considered the best user interface, especially for playing and being able to modulate a piano sound in real time. It is clear that as for the first test iteration, the high values across the criteria were due to the non-invasive character of the system and the ability to play on an acoustic piano.

A similar trend can be seen in the rankings, shown above in Table 9.1, of the three systems according to three factors: interest, freedom of playing and learning curve. The users ranked the three interfaces according to these factors during the interview. While overall the Reach system was ranked higher than the others, one user considered it tied with the Touch-Keys both regarding the interest factor and the ease of learning. In the table, a tied ranking has been arbitrarily shown as the highest rank for both the tied interfaces. For example, in the case where Reach and Touch-Keys were considered equal regarding the learning curve, a 'first' mark was assigned to both interfaces in the table. The same can be seen between the Seaboard and Reach where the two interfaces tied on the interest factor, while the TouchKeys was considered the easiest interface to learn and approach. The data, while not statistically valid due to the limited pool of users, suggests a possible outline of what the data from a larger user group might look like.

9.5.1 The feel of the acoustic piano

During the interview process, at the end of each test, several topics surfaced that shone a light on the results of the questionnaire. In particular, one user said:

> The first thing I notice about an instrument is the feel [of the keys]. That's the reason why I find many keyboard instruments really bothering to play. You don't have the same feel of a piano or a Rhodes for example, that has much more (tactile) feedback. I notice the difference of feel also from piano to piano.
>
> (Participant No. 1)

This appeared to be a recurring theme throughout all the tests and interviews where all users were drawn towards the Reach system because of the ability to play on an acoustic piano along with the flexibility of live sound manipulation. While at first this element could be seen as source of bias in the test results, it is nonetheless a verification of the limited ability of the current state of keyboard-based #MIs. Reach is seen by most of the participants as a first step in improving the lack of keyboard-based Augmented Musical Instruments (AMIs) by taking full advantage of the accessibility and non-invasiveness of both an acoustic piano sound and feel. As explored by Dahl (2016, p. 77) this kind of practice could be considered a *design exploration*; "[d]esign exploration seeks to explore possibilities outside of current paradigms, to transcend and provoke".

The provocation, in this research, is to incite and push the development of keyboard-based AMIs alongside the development of the existing paradigms: whether referring to innovative DMIs such as the Seaboard or more niche AMIs such as the TouchKeys. The test aimed to look at keyboard-based #MIs in a more holistic way. As discussed in the introduction, one of the main goals was to analyse how performers would approach the proposed instruments at the first encounter, and to what extent they would be able to improvise on two different pieces: a known jazz standard, and a modal melody. With the improvisation at a first encounter as the main focus of the comparative test, the learning curve of the interfaces and precision in sound modulation have been considered and analysed throughout the semi-structured interviews.

In response to a question that sought to investigate why the ease of use of the Reach system was better for him, compared to the other two interfaces, another user said:

> Because the touch and everything is so familiar and feels good, the new elements are much easier to control because you don't have to think about that as well as the interface itself.
>
> (Participant No. 5)

The same user underlined how the familiar interface of the acoustic piano helped him shift attention on the novelty of the gesturally controlled interface without having to focus also on his pianistic technique.

9.5.2 Degree of invasiveness, learning curve and additional technique

Closely tied to the feel of the instrument itself, another aspect that was investigated was how the invasiveness of the interfaces affected the ability to approach the instrument, learn the instrument and to what extent pre-existing instrumental technique could be implemented. On multiple occasions, users commented on this aspect throughout the testing phase, and the same topics were then dealt more in-depth in the interviews. One user, after having described the TouchKeys as *really hard to control*, described his first approach with the Reach system saying "Oh loved it! So much easier!". In this specific case, the user found the interaction with the Reach system easier from a cognitive point of view. During the interview, it became apparent that the new sonic elements provided by the Reach system were easier to control because the user felt that he did not have to think about the interface, that the acoustic piano was an environment in which he felt completely comfortable. The pianists were able to just focus on exploring the system and its effects, forgetting about the actual pianistic technique that had been consolidated in many years of study. Regarding the additional technique usually required to play AMIs and DMIs, one user said:

> My technique doesn't work there, I need to take one week with it, after one week I can go and play it. But I have one concert today, and if I need a piano, I don't take this and this (pointing at the Seaboard and the TouchKeys).
>
> (Participant No. 2)

Similar comments were made by other users, pointing to the need for additional practice to build up the required technique to play the instruments. None of these comments were made regarding the Reach system. On the other hand, two users out of six spontaneously asked if they could employ extramusical technique on the Reach system to trigger it in various ways. One user later explained his experiments by saying:

> there were times when I was trying to do two gestures at once: I was trying to get the reverb to stay on and put some pitch bend in there (he was covering one hand with the other).
>
> (Participant No. 6)

This spontaneous search for additional technique reflects the level of accessibility and ease of use of the Reach system. It also highlights an emergent feature of the system and shows how the transparency of the interface allowed the user to explore musical and gestural ideas. Transparency in this context is the ability of an interface to disappear in the eyes of the performer enabling him or her to interact directly with the sonic and musical output. Similarly, the accessibility of the interface combined with the confidence of the user to approach the described interactions led to an exploration of possible extended technique outside of the proposed gestural nuances. These extramusical gestures – sought by the participants themselves – did not cause any disruption to the performance. The affordance provided by the instrument itself helped the user transition from the nuanced gestures embedded in the pianistic technique towards sound controlling gestures beyond traditional performance motions.

The verbal reactions around how the users approached the three systems were also diverse. All of the reactions of the users when trying the Reach system for the first time were positive and of interest towards the sounds and processes behind it. Most of the immediate reactions of the same users when approaching the other two interfaces were referring to the difficulty of transferring their skills to that environment, or to the unconventional design of the interfaces themselves.

9.5.3 Control precision

Analysing the data revealed that regarding the level of precision in terms of parameter modulation, the Reach system was the least precise. For this reason, it was essential to investigate whether this difference in precision was an acceptable trade-off considering the low degree of invasiveness. When asked, five out of six users mentioned that they would prefer a less precise system that would give them more freedom of playing. A user specifically stated:

> I would definitely go for the Reach system. I am all about the sound and feel. If we're speaking about piano sound, there are no keyboards that will hold up the comparison. If I play here (indicates the piano) I feel so much better. It's not only a question of control, but it's also a question of aesthetics and inspiration. How can you be inspired or play the piano on something like this (indicates the Seaboard).
>
> (Participant No. 1)

Another user also stated:

> I thought that precision matched the freedom on your system. I feel like it was easier to be precise on your (Reach) system compared to the others.
>
> (Participant No. 5)

This quote could be linked to the limitation regarding the balance between wet and dry signal. This will be discussed in the following section.

9.6 USER TESTING LIMITATIONS

Even though the test provided useful insight around the relationship between interfaces with a low degree of invasiveness and the ability to play freely and improvise at a first encounter, it presented a few limitations that need to be addressed. This section aims to acknowledge the limitations and explain the reasoning behind certain structural choices.

9.6.1 Sound balancing

One of the main limitations was the balancing between the wet sound (or processed live piano sound) and the dry sound (or unprocessed live piano sound). When designing the test tasks and structure, a decision was made to leave the digital piano sound to its default settings. This choice was made keeping in mind that the default state of the plugin for the piano sound would have been crafted and designed to work well with the Seaboard and any other MIDI Polyphonic Expression (MPE) devices (i.e. TouchKeys).

During the test we uncovered that the difference in sound balance between the three systems had an effect on the perception of the system itself. The Reach system, with a prominent clean sound coming from the acoustic grand piano and a more nuanced effected sound coming through the stereo speaker combined with the natural ability to hear clearly both the wet and dry sound, provided the pianists with a different aural experience compared to the other two systems.

In retrospect, to provide a more equal sound experience to the users, a second audio track playing back the clean piano sound without any modulation could have been created in the Digital Audio Workstation (DAW) providing the Seaboard and the TouchKeys with a similar sonic experience in terms of dry/wet balance.

9.7 IDEAS FOR FUTURE DEVELOPMENT

Feedback received from the users was directed not only to the specifics of interaction and invasiveness, but also to the more practical aspects of the instrument itself. One user that took part in the user testing, towards the very end of the interview, asked about the actual setup of the system. After having explained the inner workings of the system, the pianist discussed the importance of having an all-round accessible musical instrument. As soon as the word *software* was mentioned, the user reacted by saying:

> You still need a software? I am speaking as a musician. The cool thing about a contact mic is that it's immediate. You stick a microphone on the piano, plug it into a pedal, and you're set. So, I'm wondering, how would you go and make it even more "compact"? [. . .] It would be really cool to have something really small without too many things. I hate computers in live settings. You are dependent to something that could crash every second.
>
> (Participant No. 1)

The elements that make an instrument accessible are not limited to the interaction with the instrument itself: accessibility is an all-round feature – from the most practical elements – such as portability, size, setup time and reliability, to the most musical elements, such as interaction, and freedom of expression. This concept was clear for every participant in the test. Each of the musicians had an aspect of the instrument that they considered extremely important for the instrument to be considered accessible.

9.8 CONCLUSIONS

Having analysed all the results from the comparative testing, a connection has been established between the invasiveness of the digital system, comfortableness of the instrumentalist to approach the instrument, and the ability to freely improvise and transfer previously learned skills and technique. There have also been cases where this experience has led to a spontaneous exploration of extramusical technique to control the system in different ways. Out of the investigated topics, the most surprising results were gathered when asking about the trade-off between precision of modulation in relation to the invasiveness of the system. All of the jazz players that took part in the test seemed to prefer a less precise mean of modulation in favour of a less invasive interface. This was later linked to two main factors: the first one being that an overly precise mapping of the fingers resulted in disrupting the flow of the improvisation, and a second one being that not being able to precisely predict the outcome of the modulation, the pianists treated the system almost like another musician with which they could interact. From the comparison of the results from both the user testing sessions, it is clear that users are more likely to prefer less invasive AMIs or DMIs in favour of a less disruptive experience.

During the first round of user testing (Granieri, Dooley and Michailidis, 2019), when testing Reach alone, users noticed that the system put a strain on the aural aspect of playing, making it difficult for users to predict the outcome of their gestures. When compared with existing interfaces, the Reach system was seen as the least invasive instrument to play an effected piano, displaying an acceptable comparison between a low degree of invasiveness and control precision.

Even though initially there was no particular musical genre suited for the system, user data suggests a tendency toward a compositional and improvisatory approach with the Reach system. When compared to existing keyboard-based systems, the Reach system has been identified as the most user friendly, and easiest to approach and explore at a first encounter. However, the current setup has been seen as not yet being fully developed in this regard, and there is a need to develop the accessibility of the system.

The UEQ data from both rounds of testing have shown how the approach of lowering the degree of invasiveness of the system by ensuring that its operating mode does not conflict with pre-existing instrumental technique, is not only valid, but inspiring and useful. Even users who are unfamiliar with the system, were quickly able to take control of it and effect the sound with a minimal amount of guidance.

REFERENCES

Dahl, L. (2016) 'Designing New Musical Interfaces as Research: What's the Problem?', *Leonardo*, 49(1), pp. 76–77. doi: 10.1162/LEON_a_01118.

Dahlstedt, P. (2017) 'Physical Interactions with Digital Strings – A hybrid approach to a digital keyboard instrument', in *Proceedings of the International Conference on New Interfaces for Musical Expression*. Copenhagen, Denmark: Aalborg University Copenhagen, pp. 115–120. Available at: http://www.nime.org/proceedings/2017/nime2017_paper0023.pdf.

Granieri, N., Dooley, J. and Michailidis, T. (2019) 'Harnessing Ancillary Microgestures in Piano Technique: Implementing Microgestural Control in to an Expressive Keyboard-based Hyper-instrument', in *Innovation in Music - Performance, Production, Technology and Business.* 1st edn. Routledge. Available at: https://www.routledge.com/Innovation-in-Music-Performance-Production-Technology-and-Business/Hepworth-Sawyer-Hodgson-Paterson-Toulson/p/book/9781138498198.

Guna, J. *et al.* (2014) 'An Analysis of the Precision and Reliability of the Leap Motion Sensor and its Suitability for Static and Dynamic Tracking', *Sensors*. Multidisciplinary Digital Publishing Institute, 14(2), pp. 3702–3720.

Knibbs, C. and Granieri, N. (2018) *Listen*. Available at: https://youtu.be/pC8Fze2sJVs.

Lamb, R. and Robertson, A. (2011) 'Seaboard : a New Piano Keyboard-related Interface Combining Discrete and Continuous Control', in *Proc. of NIME'11. International Conference on New Interfaces for Musical Expression*, Oslo, Norway, pp. 503–506. Available at: http://www.nime.org/proceedings/2011/nime2011_503.pdf.

McPherson, A. (2012) 'TouchKeys: Capacitive Multi-Touch Sensing on a Physical Keyboard', in *Proceedings of the International Conference on New Interfaces for Musical Expression*. Ann Arbor, Michigan: University of Michigan. Available at: http://www.nime.org/proceedings/2012/nime2012_195.pdf.

Miranda, E.R. and Wanderley, M. (2006) *New Digital Musical Instruments: Control And Interaction Beyond the Keyboard (Computer Music and Digital Audio Series)*. Madison, WI, USA: A-R Editions, Inc.

Schrepp, M., Hinderks, A. and Thomaschewski, J. (2014) 'Applying the User Experience Questionnaire (UEQ) in Different Evaluation Scenarios', in Marcus, A. (ed.) *Design, User Experience, and Usability. Theories, Methods, and Tools for Designing the User Experience*. Springer International Publishing, pp. 383–392.

Stenton, R. and Granieri, N. (2018a) *12.jpg*. Available at: https://youtu.be/X2F MMex2LKI.

Stenton, R. and Granieri, N. (2018b) *//aria alla francese*. Available at: https://youtu.be/gzLTwMbGjxM.

Tanaka, A. (2000) 'Musical Performance Practice on Sensor-based Instruments', *Trends in Gestural Control of Music*. IRCAM París, 13(389–405), p. 284.

Tunley, R. and Granieri, N. (2018) *Wax & Wane*. Available at: https://youtu.be/a0wCGydfons.

Wilson, A.D. (2010) 'Using a Depth Camera As a Touch Sensor', in *ACM International Conference on Interactive Tabletops and Surfaces*. Saarbrücken, Germany: ACM (ITS '10), pp. 69–72. doi: 10.1145/1936652.1936665.

Yang, Q. and Essl, G. (2012) 'Augmented Piano Performance using a Depth Camera', in *Proc. of NIME'12. International Conference on New Interfaces for Musical Expression*, Ann Arbor, Michigan: University of Michigan. Available at: http://www.nime.org/proceedings/2012/nime2012_203.pdf.

Zandt-Escobar, A.V., Caramiaux, B. and Tanaka, A. (2014) 'PiaF: A Tool for Augmented Piano Performance Using Gesture Variation Following', in *Proc. of NIME'14. International Conference on New Interfaces for Musical Expression*, London, United Kingdom: Goldsmiths, University of London, pp. 167–170. Available at: http://www.nime.org/proceedings/2014/nime2014_511.pdf.

Zappi, V. and McPherson, A. (2014) 'Dimensionality and Appropriation in Digital Musical Instrument Design', in *Proceedings of the International Conference on New Interfaces for Musical Expression*. London, United Kingdom: Goldsmiths, University of London, pp. 455–460. Available at: http://www.nime.org/proceedings/2014/nime2014_409.pdf.

10

Improvising song writing and composition within a hybrid modular synthesis system

Hussein Boon

10.1 INTRODUCTION

This chapter focuses on the use of modular synthesizer rack-units Ornament and Crime (o_C) CopierMaschine. These are implementations of an Analogue Shift Register as a performative and writing/composition tool. Included alongside this will be some of the history of Shift Registers, general information concerning their operation, discussion of potential applications and example case studies from my own improvising and writing approaches.

It is best to keep in mind that whilst the modules under discussion here are in the domain of modular synthesis, Shift Registers are also available as plugins for Ableton Live, Native Instruments Reaktor Blocks and in the free VCV Rack. There is no initial requirement to invest in an expensive modular system to explore this process, assuming one has access to any or all of these software environments.

10.2 HISTORY

The Shift Register is in the domain of sequencing technologies and yet has probably escaped the attention of most practitioners as to its potential utility. The Analogue Shift Register (ASR) emerged during the early 1970s; there is evidence that custom modules were built by Fukushi Kawakami for the composer Barry Schrader (Shrader, 2019) possibly as early as 1972. The first available commercial unit was for the Serge Synthesizer System (Hard Sync, 2009) and released in the mid 1970s. Serge's catalogue described the ASR as a "sequential sample and hold module for producing arabesque-like forms in musical space" (Hard Sync, 2009) and its origins can be found within two previous devices, the Bucket Brigade Device (BBD), sometimes known as Bucket Brigade Delay, and the Sample and Hold (S&H) module (Bjorn and Meyer, 2018, p.253).

Although analogue delay lines were first developed in the 1920s, the Phillips Research Labs BBD (Computer Music, 2019) appeared towards the end of the 1960s, allowed a stored analogue signal to be shifted, or 'shuttled', through a series of capacitors updated each clock cycle – effectively forming a discrete-time (i.e. non-continuous, or 'quantized') analogue delay line. The number of possible outputs was from 1 to 1+N. The name came from lines of people who used to pass buckets of water along the lines. Of course, as water would be spilt or lost along the way, so the BBD's signals would degrade as the signal passed through many capacitors. More capacitors meant longer delay times, but with the trade-off of signal degradation. However, this side effect did imbue a certain character to the audio signal, popular with some guitar pedals.

The S&H circuit (Waltari and Halonen, 2003, p.19) captures (samples) a dynamic voltage source updated every clock cycle. Typical voltage sources include both varieties of noise and waveforms such as sine, saw, and triangle, however anything that generates a voltage is fair game.

> the S/H can "look" at a continually changing voltage source such as the output of an audio oscillator or LFO, noise, an envelope, keyboards, etc.
>
> (Strange, 1972, p.80)

The classic use of a S&H function to open and close filter circuits is a good example of typical application. Sample sources can also undergo a variety of operations such as wavefolding, rectification, and other sorts of wave distortion and wave mixing might be applied to derive further new dynamic wave shapes. This is key to producing varying types of output.

10.3 A VARIETY OF SHIFT REGISTERS

The Shift Register essentially combines the dynamic voltage values of the S&H module with the delayed output of the BBD. The Serge module had three outputs, also available as a Dual ASR (2ASR), and much like the BBD, the sampled value would be passed down the line to the next output and discarded once no more outputs were available. Boon's (2020b) arabesques result from passing a dynamic source, such as Sine, Triangle, or envelope, sampled with a fast-enough clock or gate signal to produce an output that closely mirrors the original waveform shape. This produces rhythmically interlaced and spiralling patterns forming "meandering themes in music" (Grove Art Online, no date). When outputs are patched to two or more oscillators these will appear to 'chase' each other in sync very much like a Quadrature LFO or 'leaping salmon'. However, instead of being correlated by phase, the outputs are related by clock pulse or musical time divisions, and a classic analogy is to consider the Shift Register as a sort of canonic utility device. The output can be shaped by a combination of waveform shape, waveform amplitude and clock interval cycle, but will always have some semi-randomness due to it being "designed as a sequencer that you can steer in one direction or another, not one that you can program precisely" (Whitwell, 2012a). By altering any one of these three aspects either separately or in combination, users are able to structure source material to better direct the output. The unit also allows for a more exploratory 'throwing paint at the wall' approach whereby arbitrary clock, LFO, or both, can be passed into the unit to see what comes out.

A highly dynamic waveform sampled with a slow clock cycle will result in a greater degree of variation between sampled states, more so than where the waveform speed is roughly in sync with the clock pulse. A fast clock source with a slow amplitude waveform will result in smoother voltage changes over time. It is in these sorts of areas where a more experimental approach can be adopted, using wildly different sources to elicit melodic outputs controlled by using either a manual or voltage-controlled switch. Again, this approach allows for the 'throwing' variety but also allows for voltages to be prepared in advance. To assist in this there are many control voltage (CV) tools available that provide for precise recall of voltages, and where performances require aspects to be 'repeatable', these will be a necessary solution.

In the domain of the DAW, Ableton's CV Tools (Ableton, 2019) allows for very precise voltage values to be recorded and saved within individual projects. Being able to save these as Ableton Live Clip (.alc) files is advantageous and allows for work to be reused across projects. When combined with a DC-coupled interface or solution such as Expert Sleepers ES-8, this will provide a very robust, recallable system. Whilst this discussion has covered how source material can be 'designed' on its way into the module, values passed to the outputs will be semi-randomized and it is in this area where the ASR differs significantly from the more precise approach to sequencing available in a DAW or hardware sequencer.

When considering using a Shift Register or S&H device, users will have to accept that randomness will be formulated as part of their working practice in respect of melodic outputs. There are various Shift Register implementations with the Serge module either available under licence, such as the Turing Machine from Music Thing Modular as a kit, or built by a variety of makers, with variations available from companies such as 2hp. Implementations will vary between modules and companies, and for the rest of this discussion we will be concerned with the MXMXMX module Ornament and Crime (o_C), and in particular the CopierMaschine app.

The Shift Register is broadly applicable to any style or genre and is an equally interesting tool from which to make samples especially applicable to styles such as Liquid Drum and Bass or for those requiring an immediate Reich/Glass-like composition tool. If freeform jamming is a preferred mode of exploration then it's best to leave the DAW in record to capture outputs that might be edited later. With the ever-growing sophistication and capabilities of audio to MIDI transcription, e.g. Ableton's audio to MIDI conversion options, recorded outputs can be converted into MIDI data relatively easily, edited and refined to one's taste. With a CV to MIDI Converter the outputs can be captured directly in real time and passed to a DAW for capture or editing, or to a sampler perhaps for additional orchestration.

10.4 ORNAMENT AND CRIME

The o_C module is described as a polymorphic CV generator including features such as quad envelopes, quadrature lfos, quad quantizers, dual step sequencers, neo-Riemannian Tonnetz transformation, dual Lorenz and Rössler (strange attractor) modulation generators. The CopierMaschine app is a digital representation of the Analogue Shift Register, originally developed by Max Stadler in 2014 and subsequently updated and extended by Patrick Dowling and Tim Churches in 2016. At its core it is a

> DAC breakout board for the teensy 3.1/3.2 ARM development board (cortex M4), with an OLED display: somewhat like a pimped-up "ardcore", though its focus is on generating precision control voltages.
> (Stadler et.al., 2016b).

The module is not commercially available but is instead distributed as an open source project with build documentation available on GitHub. There is a community of Eurorack makers around the world and modules are sold on Ebay, Reverb, and Modular Grid. Makers can also be found via forum websites such as Modular Grid and Muff Wiggler. Regardless of whom builds the module, it will have the following:

- four Trigger (TR) inputs labelled TR1 ... TR4
- four CV inputs labelled CV1 ... CV4
- four CV outputs
- two rotary encoders, with built-in push switches
- two push buttons.

As well as displaying parameter information, the OLED display can switch to a screensaver mode that offers a visual representation of the app currently in use (Boon, 2020b).

10.4.1 CopierMaschine

The CopierMaschine app extends the original Shift Register concept beyond its BBD and S&H roots and its "ASR mode works as a cascaded, four-stage sample-and-hold module" (Stadler et.al., 2016a) with developments such as three types of self-generating internal sampling CV sources:

- Linear Feedback Shift Register (LFSR) – an adaptation of Whitwell's code for his Turing Machine
- ByteB – five different bytebeat equations generating semi-fractal note values rather than audio signals
- IntSq – ten integer sequences introducing several classes of random and fractal integers.

The LFSR offers some differences to using an LFO as source, since it is a mathematical function that is state based, generating linear values that are determined by the previously held value or state.

The second enhancement are the quantization algorithms which offer a comprehensive set of choices and also provides some memory space (four slots) for users to edit their own scales. Amongst the available scales include Major (Ionian), Natural Minor (Aeolian) as well as other modes, the various pentatonic and blues scales, folk, Spanish, Middle Eastern, Wendy Carlos' Alpha, Beta and Gamma scales, Quartertone scales and the Tritaval Tuning (Bohlen-Pierce), and more. It is worth considering what advantages the internal quantization of CV values affords in terms of devising pitch classes for innovative composition and performance within an accessible, modular environment.

10.4.2 Design elements

Beyond scale quantization, there are also a number of features that offer additional scope to organize and prepare melodic outputs for performance. These are:

- define which notes should be active within the selected scale, termed the scale mask in relation to the root note
- scale rotations (CV3)
- the addition of a freeze (TR2 or down button) function, much like the loop lock in the original Turing Machine
- variable buffer size (CV2) and buffer length
- internal transposition either by octaves or semitone.

The scale mask enables notes to be active or 'muted' within the selected scale/quantization algorithm. It can be as simple as defining a sequence of notes such as an arpeggio of R, 3, 5 or R, 5, b7, or R, 2, b3, b7 or more complex relationships such as Quartal or Pandiatonic (Persichetti, 1961, pp.223–225). Sources such as Slonimsky's Thesaurus of Scales and Melodic Patterns (Slonimsky, 1999), perhaps using the first few notes of a folk melody or bass line will produce almost limitless variations. Scale rotations allow users to create still more variation, enabling the scale mask to be shifted through the different degrees of the scale or selected notes. Rotations can be placed under manual control or under the control of an LFO or voltage source (CV3). The scale mask can also be reversed and this allows for a more extended, almost binary like aspect to be introduced when dealing with pattern variations.

The freeze function (TR2 or down button), places the current configuration into memory as a repeating figure. Once frozen, the figure can still be rotated, transposed and scaled. Scaling (the parameter 'igain') can be thought of as a means of managing head room or dynamic range of the melodic outputs. By managing this it is possible to 'focus' on certain parts of the motif and is one of the vital controlling mechanisms to influence melodic outputs to exhibit a more dynamic relationship for performances.

Buffer size and buffer length will determine the sort of outputs, and the Ornament and Crime online manual states:

> the ASR is a ring-buffer (buffer size = 256), and (to simplify things) by default outputs the sampled values S[x] stored at the buffer locations index * output-stage, ie A = S[i * 1], B = S[i * 2], C = S[i * 3], and D = S[i * 4]. The default index setting (buf. index) is 0 (internally i = 1), in which case things boil down to standard ASR behaviour. . . .
>
> (Stadler et.al., 2016a)

However, if buffer length is changed to a different value then:

> say, i = 8, the ASR in that case would output the values stored in the buffer at locations S[8], S[16], S[24], and S[32], thus delaying output A by 8 clocks, B by 16 clocks, and so on. Thus, modulating the index parameter doesn't just delay the output on channels B to D, but also allows different patterns to be created (based on the contents of the buffer).
>
> (Stadler et.al., 2016a)

Buffers can be set to unequal ratios such as 5 and 7 or 11 and 9 and with the freeze function activated, this relationship will be audible, creating an additional level of variety to be considered as part of the composition process. Overall, the developers have taken the idea of the ASR, enhanced it, and provided practitioners with a potentially expressive realization applicable to all types of writing and performance contexts.

10.5 PERFORMANCE APPROACHES

Having covered much of the basic mechanical detail and operation, for the rest of this chapter I will present some performance and writing approaches to use as the basis for improvising using CopierMaschine. Some have been mentioned already, but it should be noted that there are many ways of devising solutions and working within these systems. The requirement to have an o_C module aside, there will be little discussed here that cannot be replicated with even the most modest setup and that a small module case with a desktop semi-modular synthesizer will probably be sufficient. Ableton's CV Tools and a DC-coupled audio interface will bridge the computer to module very effectively, and that there are implementations in Ableton using Max for Live, Native Instruments' Reaktor Blocks and VCV Rack, available for free, allowing experimentation to take place without requiring a large outlay.

10.5.1 Performance kit list

The equipment I use for my writing and performance work consists of a 15" Macbook Pro running Ableton Live 10.x; a 4-Channel USB Audio/MIDI interface; an 84hp 12U modular system with a variety of modules.

I tend to play bass lines manually using the QWERTY keyboard from the computer with synth and 'tape loop' elements derived from and modulated within my modular system before returning signals back to the DAW for summing. There isn't much latency and wherever possible I try to keep plugin counts low. This is augmented with a small 25 key USB keyboard used to transpose some of my sequences or for specific function control commands.

As manipulating a modular synthesizer and playing bass at the same time is quite a hands-on task, I use an expression pedal whose output is converted to CV values, enabling me to control an additional set of parameters on the o_C module using my foot. I also use an iPad running Liine's 'Lemur' app and create macros for one-finger performance-control gestures. Lemur offers the advantage of being able to design a UI that exposes only the parts I want to interact with, reduces clutter, and also reduces the possibility of misfiring an element.

Improvisation within this system requires an open-ended approach to both structure and performance duration. One of the goals in using modular systems, due to potential patch complexity, is to devise transitions from one piece to the next, rather than for pieces to necessarily conclude. So, at some point, the performer needs to find a way of steering performance elements towards the newly emerging piece. Structuring those elements should be flexible enough to be adaptable in response to the musical outputs. What this means is that it is probably advisable to have a variety of parts or figures prepared in advance that act as possible raw source material and that these are flexible enough to be set in new contexts. Such approaches include preparing pitch sets to function as a bass line, establishing a harmonic context, or gate outputs that alter the rhythmic content of a part – for example, modulating the strike input of a Make Noise LxD module. In her National Endowment Award report Suzanne Ciani (1976), highlights a number of note-row based selections used as source material structured around the use of several 16-step (stage) sequencers. By combining and recombining these ideas, shifting values, altering start and end points, time bases and clock divisions, this allows for an almost limitless approach to configuring improvisational pieces within a modular synthesizer – where the source material is also modular in concept. In addition to prepared pitch sets I tend to use bass lines drawn from Dub Reggae, 2Step, Afrobeat, Garage and House styles as 'gluing' factors, generally preferring to use sub bass using either Sine or Triangle sources. Variation can also be achieved by superimposing gate patterns on VCAs, or to trigger envelopes that modulate additional parameters to render parts as more multifaceted and layered for performance.

10.5.2 Use case 1 – four voices

This patch tends to offer the most obvious use, and provides immediate gratification when a particular motif is generated that is passed down the line and delivers the arabesques described in the original Serge advertising material (Boon, 2020a).

- Tune all four oscillators to a Unison pitch.
- Patch o_C's four CV outputs to each oscillators' V/Oct input.
- Patch the oscillator outputs to a mixer and balance the volume levels.
- Patch either a) a clock signal from a DAW or b) use a Square wave LFO – as a clock for TR1.
- Select Aeolian as the scale with C as the root.
- Design scale mask as C, D, Eb, G, Bb.
- Select LFSR as CV1 source and leave the rest at their defaults.
- Set Buffer Size to 0 and Buffer Length to 4, which are the defaults.
- Set Gain to 0.70.

With all oscillators tuned to a unison pitch, it is worth exploring pitching them as octaves apart or, as will be discussed next, to other complementary pitches.

10.5.3 Use case 2 – a combinatorial approach and the prominent voice

For this example, a combinatorial style of approach is proposed with the performance goal of revealing each output in turn as the prominent voice. It is possible to achieve this using two oscillators, however, four allows for the piece to be extended due to higher voice-count. Simply put, this is achieved by varying mixer levels at key stages for each voice or group of voices, used in combination with the freeze function, which in my experience acts as a sort of 'glue' to facilitate change.

Using this with four oscillators I have found that three should be tuned to the same pitch, though not necessarily in the same register, with the remaining oscillator tuned to a fifth above the fundamental of oscillator 1, assuming this is the first prominent voice. This tuning will require some thought when designing the scale mask so that parts remain within a complementary harmonic system unless the goal is for a sort of binary composition. Assuming C Aeolian mode, a basic mask of C, Eb, G will produce the notes G, Bb, D in the oscillator tuned a fifth above, likewise Eb, F, G will produce, Bb, C, D and F, G, Ab will produce C, D, Eb.

Once all pitch data is organized, all four o_C outputs can be patched to the four oscillators and patch their outputs to a mixer in output order i.e. OSC 1 to Mix In 1 and so on.

- oscillator 1 tuned to C3 and patched to mix channel 1
- oscillator 2 tuned to C2 and patched to mix channel 2
- oscillator 3 tuned to G3 and patched to mix channel 3
- oscillator 4 tuned to C2 and patched to mix channel 4.

Zero all mixer levels and patch to a PA or DAW etc. The speed of clock source is an individual choice, and likewise whether to use an external or internal source for sampling. There are interesting outputs to be discovered here and there's probably not enough space to go through every available choice.

If one were to now start the clock and fade up Mix channel 1, this will be the main figure and will be treated as the current prominent voice. Now it is a question of fading oscillator 2 up at some point to support the current, prominent voice. The volume level of supporting voices should complement, but not overwhelm the first voice. At this point the freeze function can be deployed and the pattern subjected to variation. Rapidly turning freeze on/off should be explored as this will clear some but not all of the buffer to be overwritten, meaning that some melodic fragments will remain until completely cleared. It is a 'destructive' approach and carries some 'risk' as once the pattern has been replaced it cannot be retrieved whilst parts are frozen, sample source material can also be varied and once freeze is deactivated a new pattern will emerge to mirror the changes in sample source. Depending on which mixer channel has been placed the oscillator tuned to a fifth, an interesting change to the general texture and harmonic implications might be noticed when this is introduced.

At some point, the next phase will be to activate the freeze function and to slowly fade out all voices. I usually do this by starting the fade on the most prominent voice until it starts to merge into the others, and then manipulate a few more faders. Before all channels are at zero, take channel 2 and start to fade this back up so that a new buffer part is heard emerging from the 'quiet' and once again commence the process of unfreezing and fading up as each output becomes the prominent voice in turn. The oscillator tuned to a fifth will emerge as the new prominent voice and impose a 'pseudo change' of key centre.

10.5.4 Use case 3 – single oscillator with filter

The use of four outputs may not be to everyone's taste. The lines can be quite dense when heard as a sort of cluster, but this is by no means the only possible choice. Whilst CopierMaschine's USP tends to be four parts in sync and in harmony together, although it's not a harmonizer, it can still be used with a single oscillator within a small system. The following patch is a good place to start from.

The output from o_C is a CV value quantized to a scale or set of notes of one's choosing. This means other modules capable of receiving pitch information (in V/Oct.), such as filters, can be used to cement a pitch-based connection between oscillator and filter.

If one were to patch output 1 to the V/Oct. of an oscillator, patch the oscillator output to a filter and patch the filter output to the mixer. Take one of the remaining o_C outputs that can be patched into the CV input of the filter to control its frequency. If there is a patch point for Resonance, then one can use one of the other outputs to control this as well. If the oscillator being used also has additional CV-modulation ports, then one can consider patching one of the o_C outputs to here as well.

A relatively straightforward approach such as the above demonstrates the sort of control that can be applied using a small system. The overall impression will be that the notes are tracked closely, followed by filter-frequency changes, and these are perceived as more 'musical'. Variation can be achieved by patching different o_C outputs to the filter.

10.6 CLOCKS, GATES AND TRIGGER SOURCES

In all of the preceding performance scenarios, a continuous clock has been assumed; however, interrupting or disrupting clock cycles is also an aspect to explore in order to derive varied compositional outputs. Clock or gate sources tend to be square waves but can be anything with a rising edge, even audio. Interruption can be achieved using manual or voltage-controlled switches, especially when managing a number of differing clock sources, and in addition to this, there are four categories, discussed below.

Touch-based modules such as Make Noise Pressure Points or Doboz XIIO generate a gate output when touched, allowing the performer to trigger the module – updating clock cycles manually. This type of approach will mean that hold-cycle lengths will vary and allow for performers to make decisions around when conditions are right to trigger a new value.

As I tend to be playing bass parts, each note event generates a gate output which can act as a clock signal to trigger the unit. Rhythmically intense bass parts result in faster sampling sequences whereas sustained notes result in more statically held values.

An arpeggiator can also function as a clock source, especially when its hold function is enabled. Setting the rate to a continuous note-value such as eighths or sixteenths means the o_C module will see eight or sixteen triggers per bar. Of course, the possibility exists to set the arpeggiator rate to a different subdivision (such as three sixteenths) with the advantage that the o_C module will still receive a generally constant set of gates. Varying the arpeggio rate can also be automated in a DAW, or using a plugin such as Max for Live's LFO tool.

Logic, OR combiners and probability modules can also be sources for clock signals. A logical-operator module evaluates a number of signal inputs, usually gates or triggers, and generate an output gate based on the chosen comparison method. A probability module such as Mutable Instruments' Branches, which is a dual Bernouli Gate, takes a single signal source, routing the result of a random coin toss to one of its two outputs. Using this sort of module or approach introduces a bit more uncertainty and 'chaos' to a performance.

10.7 CONCLUSION

This brief introduction and overview of Ornament and Crime's Copier-Maschine implementation of the ASR demonstrates its viability in the domain of performance-based composition. The ASR has perhaps been disregarded in favour of sequencers with more precision-editing capabilities; however, this is to overlook what such a module is capable of, and the strength of the musical outputs possible when using varied sampling sources. o_C's inclusion of quantizing algorithms is both straightforward and effective, facilitating a melodic and/or harmonic context to be devised by the performer/composer and creates a space that allows and encourages experimentation when designing differing pitch-class sets. As such, the o_C has catered for a wide range of possible tastes in respect of quantizing material, expanded further by developments including scale mask, scale-mask inversion and scale rotations, that when coupled with variable buffer settings and the freeze function results in a very powerful performance-creation environment.

Patching a continuous clock and dynamic waveform, what I refer to as 'Electro Continuo', to the Ornament and Crime module will result in always moving, hopefully interesting, patterns. When varying clock sources –whilst a relatively straightforward area – there is a degree of variety achievable that can be applied to manage output periodicity. Clock sources can be an overlooked area given they are less 'glamorous' than some esoteric waveform derived from a function generator such as MATHS. Exploring the ways and means of interfacing the performer with the module, especially where the performer is also a source of clocks, allows for even more variation and individuation when generating new parts.

We have also seen how oscillator tuning will impact scale-mask choices. Once two oscillators (separated by a fifth) receive outputs from the same module then we enter a more complex management space. Yes, one could approach this as some sort of binary composition, but by constructing a scale mask that seeks to fill in the gaps for a more complete pitch set, we can arrive at an interesting, constrained compositional approach. Once a third and perhaps fourth oscillator are added to the mix, then the potential complexity increases. Straightforward, musical solutions such as organising additional voices in octaves as a means of managing this complexity whilst maintaining an 'interesting' sound and reducing potential conflicts. By varying oscillator type, perhaps by even using tuned percussion with short decays, performers will be able to ensure that differences are more audible to the audience.

A combinatorial performance approach to managing four voices was discussed. This demonstrated a good starting point for a performance methodology that goes beyond the 'set-and-forget' approach and, whilst there is nothing intrinsically wrong here, especially where o_C might not be the focus, but more an accompaniment. Such a combinatorial approach allows for aspects of lines to be foregrounded, enabling whole pieces to be performed from seemingly random outputs, organized around a central, determining principle. Tuning one or more oscillators to different pitches will introduce even more variety with 'illusory' tonality changes for added interest!

When I use the freeze function, I tend to be listening out for melodic to lock in and it is at this point where new areas of harmonic interest are opened up for exploration using the aforementioned processes such as rotation, scaling and buffer length. Variations in buffer length and size will be more apparent when using freeze and will suggest different time signatures which the performer can choose to follow or imply as a cross rhythm. It is entirely possible to prepare precise voltages in advance that target specific buffer settings as is also true for scale rotations. Whilst the usual inclination might be to freeze the outputs for extended periods of time, it is also possible to freeze in a sort of manual burst-like mode that, if combined with a variety of sampled waveform under the control of a switch or by rapidly changing LFO speed, can yield different results.

In conclusion, this module opens up a wealth of possibilities in terms of design workflow and experimentation. The various approaches outlined here can be used to generate differently performed compositional outputs that are highly applicable in any contemporary song writing, composition, improvisation, recording or media context – outputs that are not the usual products of more traditional keyboard, guitar or even DAW paradigms. Taking all aspects considered here in diverse combination can result in a level of variety that makes this unit highly explorable, sufficiently configurable, and an immediate source of ideas. For those working in areas of generative composition or looking to integrate such approaches into their performance practice, an ASR such as o_C, is a very viable and performable proposition that might be explored in a greater creative environment.

REFERENCES

Ableton. (2019). *CV Tools Ableton*, 2019. Available online at https://www.ableton.com/en/packs/cv-tools/#? [Accessed 22 March 2020].

Boon, H. (2020a). *Improvisation Demonstration No.1 – YouTube* [2020]. Available online at https://www.youtube.com/watch?v=K53BLAhTc9c&feature=youtu.be [Accessed 22 March 2020].

Boon, H. (2020b). *o_C Demo - Arabesque – YouTube*. Available online at https://www.youtube.com/watch?v=0CWJwJJNz_w&feature=youtu.be [Accessed 22 March 2020].

Bjorn, K. and Meyer, C. (2018). *Patch & Tweak*, Denmark, Bjooks.

Ciani, S. (1976). *Report to National Endowment Re: Composer Grant*, University of Victoria. Available online at https://people.finearts.uvic.ca/~aschloss/course_mat/MU307/MU307%20Labs/Lab3_BUCHLA/Susanne%20Ciani%20Buchla.sm.pdf [Accessed 22 March 2020].

Computer Music. (2019). *A Brief History of Bucket-brigade Delays (and 4 Great Plugin Emulations)*, Music Radar (website). Available online from https://www.musicradar.com/news/a-brief-history-of-bucket-brigade-delays-and-4-great-plugin-emulations [Accessed 22 March 2020].

Doboz. (2016). *XIIO Doboz*, 2016. Available online at http://doboz.audio/xiio/ [Accessed 22 March 2020].

Expert Sleepers. (2016). *ES8 Expert Sleepers*, 2016. Available online at https://www.expert-sleepers.co.uk/es8.html [Accessed 22 March 2020].

Grove Art Online (no date). *Arabesque*. Oxford University Press. Available from https://www.oxfordartonline.com/groveart/view/10.1093/gao/9781884446054.001.0001/oao-9781884446054-e-7000003513?rskey=uMGYyd&result=1 [Accessed 21 March 2020].

Hard Sync. (2019). *A Brief History of Analog Shift Registers (ASR)*, Hard Sync, March 2009. Available online at http://hardsync.blogspot.com/2009/03/brief-history-of-analog-shift-registers.html [Accessed 22 March 2020].

Liine. (2019). *Lemur Overview*, Liine, 2019. Available online at https://liine.net/en/products/lemur/ [Accessed 22 March 2020].

Make Noise. (2010). *Pressure Points,* Make Noise, 2010. Available online at http://www.makenoisemusic.com/modules/pressure-points [Accessed 22 March 2020].

Native Instruments. (2019). *What Is Reaktor Blocks*? Native Instruments, 2019. Available online at https://www.expert-sleepers.co.uk/es8.html [Accessed 22 March 2020].

Persichetti, V. (1961). *Twentieth Century Harmony*, London, W. W. Norton & Company, pp. 223–225.

Shrader, B. (2019). *The Fortune Modules*, Barry Shrader (website). Available online from https://barryschrader.com/the_fortune_modules/ [Accessed 22 March 2020].

Slonimsky, N. (1999). *Thesaurus of Scales and Melodic Patterns*, New York, G. Schirmer.

Stadler, M., Dowling, P. and Churches, T. (2016a) *Ornament and Crime User Manual for v1.3,* Ornament and Crime, 2016. Available online at https://ornament-and-cri.me/user-manual-v1_3/ [Accessed 22 March 2020].

Stadler, M., Dowling, P. and Churches, T. (2016b) *Hardware Basics, Ornament and Crime*, 2016. Available online at https://ornament-and-cri.me/hardware-basics/ [Accessed 22 March 2020].

Strange, A. (1972). *Electronic Music: Systems, Techniques and Controls*, USA, W.C. Brown.

VCV Rack. (2020). *Plugins VCV Rack*. Available online at https://library.vcvrack.com/?query=Shift+Register&brand=&tag=&license= [Accessed 22 March 2020].

Waltari, M., and Halonen, K. (2003) Sample-and-Hold Operation, Circuit Techniques for Low-Voltage and High-Speed A/D Converters. *The International Series in Engineering and Computer Science (Analog Circuits and Signal Processing)*, vol 709. Springer, Boston, MA, pp.19–21.

Whitwell, T. (2012a). *22 Things to Know About the Turing Machine*, Music Thing Modular, 2012. Available online at https://musicthing.co.uk/pages/turing.html [Accessed 22 March 2020].

11

Speaker Park

An intersection of loudspeaker design and post-acousmatic composition

Jon Pigott and Antti Sakari Saario

11.1 INTRODUCTION

Speaker Park was a project which brought together a custom, 24-channel installation of hand built, sculptural loudspeakers made by Roar Sletteland and Jon Pigott, with two composers, Antti Sakari Saario and Mari Kvien Brunvoll, who took up residencies to work with the system. The project, curated by Norwegian producers Leo Preston and Veronica Thorseth, founders of WRAP Kunsthuset, was funded by the city of Bergen and the Norwegian Arts Council (among others). It was premiered at the *Borealis International Festival of Sound Art and Experimental Music* in Bergen in 2019. Preston and Thorseth describe *Speaker Park* as 'a new concert installation that makes us rethink our relationship to musical technology. Bringing together speaker makers, artists, composers and musicians, the project tries to get away from the commercially motivated hi-fi market, and challenge the criteria by which traditional sound systems and listening experiences are evaluated' (Preston and Thorseth 2019).

This chapter will explore the technical and creative opportunities and challenges of *Speaker Park* by Saario and Pigott, through themes of creative collaboration, the physicality of sound, space and materials and the idea of the *assemblage*. For this project, composer Saario developed the 24-channel fixed-media composition *Above the Blackened Skies. Beneath the Remains. (A†BSB†R)* (2019) [duration: 18']. Pigott's contribution to the speakers of *Speaker Park* were 12 rectangular boxes (circa 500mm high) with a sculptural arrangement of internal forms and materials that reflected elements of industrial speaker design (see Figure 11.1) and which appropriated 'cone-less' speaker transducers. This coming together of the sonic, the compositional, the spatial and the material, formed the creative ground for the project and this was reflected in comments by critics:

> What can one actually expect when one mixes something temporal with a more permanent and physically rooted expression?

With drone-like bass sounds and a more rhythmic drive, he [Saario] emphasised the feeling of the sound waves. I say feeling, because it really was a physical experience.

(Synnes Handal 2019)

11.2 A CONTEXT OF CREATIVE LOUDSPEAKERS

The conscious use and misuse of the loudspeaker in compositional and sound-art practice, as well as in musical instrument and technology design has a rich heritage that has become increasingly well documented in recent years (Van Eck 2017). Perhaps unsurprisingly, from the very early days of electrical and electronic music technologies, loudspeakers were incorporated into the sound processing techniques of instruments. Early electronic keyboard instrument, the Ondes Martenot, for example, featured a series of bespoke diffusers – custom loudspeakers which included the appropriation of metal gongs and tuned strings to add characteristic timbre and resonance to the electronically produced sound. A little after the Ondes Martenot, Donald Leslie's rotating-baffle speaker cabinet (the 'Leslie Speaker') appeared for use with electric organs, such as the Hammond. It was also around this time that electromechanical processing devices such as plate and spring reverbs became available which, though not technically loudspeakers, used the same moving coil technology of loudspeakers to acoustically excite materials for sonic effect.

As recording technology and production techniques developed and the space of the recording studio became an increasingly important location for not only the capture but also the creation of music, loudspeakers became a vital component in delivering a reliable, accurate and, where possible, transparent window into a sonic universe. This situation can be linked to a general development of sound recording technologies but also, as Ethan Rose (2013) explains, to the 'distillation of listening' which he identifies as a modernist project, seeking to rationalise and separate the senses, allowing for an 'absolute' music and an objective understanding of sound. It is partly from this context of an ideal loudspeaker listening situation that music composition was able to fully embrace electronic sound synthesis and the manipulation of 'concrete' sounds on tape, with works by Varèse, Schaeffer, Stockhausen, Cage among others from the 1940s onwards.

This tradition of idealised listening and studio-based composition and production has been spurred on over the years by easily accessible and affordable studio technologies. This is especially the case with more recent availability of digital tools where seemingly limitless sonic possibilities are afforded by ever more powerful computers and an ever more competitive market place of available digital tools for use by the creative. As such, studio-based and studio-quality listening that assumes and requires transparent loudspeaker interaction is now deeply embedded across both popular and experimental music composition and production activities.

Beyond this tendency towards transparency and standardisation in stereo loudspeaker listening there also exists a tradition of listening within multi-loudspeaker arrays, the emergence of which can be linked to a concern with the creative spatialisation of sound in composition. Barrett (2007) identifies early examples of this in the activities of Pierre Schaeffer and Pierre Henry in 1950, in Cage's *Imaginary Landscape No 4* (1951) for twelve radios and in Varèse's 1958 *Poeme Electronique* (1958) for a 425-speaker array installed in the Phillips pavilion at the Brussels World's Fair. Barrett claims, however, that the first 'true' spatial composition, conceived prior to the act of performance was Stockhausen's 1960 *Kontakte* (1960). Emmerson, (2007: 151) identifies that the 'rise of multi-loudspeaker diffusion within the "French tradition" of Schaeffer's Musique concrète is not well documented' with the first 'controlled sound-environments' emerging in the mid-1960s. It was not until the early 1970s however, that such systems became formalised and established with Christian Clozier's *Gmebaphone* and François Bayle's *Acousmonium*. These were followed a few years later by systems in other countries such as the Birmingham Electroacoustic Sound Theatre (BEAST) in the UK.

Despite the initial drive for such multi-loudspeaker sound-spatialisation techniques seemingly emerging from creative compositional concerns, Barrett (ibid.) claims that the 'influence of the loudspeaker orchestra on compositional aesthetics is somewhat tenuous'. Certainly, the listening experience of the audience appears as a key emphasis with such systems through considerations such as an audience's three-dimensional immersion in pure sound, and for example, the accurate distribution of stereo fields across large auditoria. This audience impact factor of multi-speaker listening environments is also at play in the more commercial end of the spectrum with surround sound for cinema and multimedia experiences for example.

It is tempting to categorise some of this technical and creative activity into the loudspeaker-as-instrument on the one hand and bespoke listening environments on the other but there are examples that challenge this simple attempt at categorisation. Most notably, David Tudor's 1968 *Rainforest* (Driscoll and Rogalsky 2004) is an installation of sculptural loudspeakers which appropriates found objects (bed springs, cart wheels etc.) as resonant materials attached to cone-less loudspeaker drivers to create highly resonant and colourful timbral responses. Tudor had a particular interest in the individual and unique voice of loudspeakers which certainly can be understood as loudspeaker-as-instrument. But *Rainforest* is also a listening environment, an installation space of prepared and spatially arranged loudspeakers through which an audience is able to explore and interact. Gordon Monahan has also made work that conflates the instrumental/environmental categorisation of loudspeakers including *Speaker Swinging* (1982) a performance piece where loudspeakers are swung by performers creating a kind of human-powered Leslie-speaker-cabinet listening experience, and *Kinetic Audio Transmissions* (2016) where motors are used as loudspeakers through resonant objects in a system not dissimilar to Tudor's *Rainforest*. Also, Andrea Valle's *Rumentarium Project* takes a similar approach of using customised loudspeaker-type arrangements to create an 'acoustic computer music' (Valle 2013). Questions relating to whether or not, and when a loudspeaker may be considered an instrument have also been explored in a range of literature (Sharma and Schultz 2017; Mulder 2010; Emmerson 2007; Van Eck 2017).

11.3 POST-ACOUSMATIC COMPOSITIONAL APPROACH

For Saario, this territory of the creative foregrounding of loudspeakers within *Speaker Park* maps to a post-acousmatic sensibility (Riikonen and Saario 2011b). The composition of *A†BSB†R* was approached through a primary focus on the corporeality of sound, its physical visceral sensations and ability to affect bodies. Such an approach suggests no hierarchical value between live and mediated experiences, and places an emphasis on *tactile listening* and the materiality of sound (Riikonen and Saario 2011a, 2011b).

Through this post-acousmatic frame, the dynamic potential and interaction of all elements of compositional praxis in a given context is more important than their control. As such, listening as sensing and awareness of sound, and other compositional bodies – become key operational modes. To develop the necessary tactile awareness, the composer must seek to understand the ever-shifting relationship associated between the sound, sounding and other bodies of a given work.

Ida Rolf, the creator of the 'structural integration' approach to health and physical wellbeing, states that 'structure is behavior', and that 'in any energy system, however complicated, structure (relationship of units of any size in space) is experienced as behavior' (Rolf 1977). The *Speaker Park* project prompted considering such possibilities alongside, for example, Smalley's (1986, 1997) concept of *spectromorphology* which is 'concerned with perceiving and thinking in terms of spectral energies and shapes of space' along with behaviours, motion and growth processes within a musical context. With an awareness of such positions, Saario's *A†BSB†R* sought to articulate and portray the unique physical qualities of *Speaker Park* through an affective and embodied approach, as opposed to simply a representative one bringing about an experience of multiple levels of sound, sounding structures and materials.

In this sense, the post-acousmatic composition is a political enterprise, one that navigates the interconnected energy systems of human and non-human bodies, with all aspects of the compositional praxis being productive factors in a political *machine* (Deleuze and Guattari 1988). In *A†BSB†R*, Saario is developing a body practice for and applying 'body work' (Rolf 1977; Schultz and Feitis 1996) and 'tissue flow' (Hudis 2006) principles to sound-based fixed-media composition. Just as connective tissue defines the body contour and is the organ of structure and movement in the body (Rolf 1977), sound shapes the 'space contour' and produces a tactile space, albeit temporary and continually unfolding.

This produces a transition from the 'primacy of the ear' (Harrison 1992) to the primacy of bodies in a context where the bodies, space and technologies of *Speaker Park* are 'inextricable of each other' (Riikonen and Saario 2011a), from the odd geometric ports and divided space of sculptural loudspeakers through to the multi-loudspeaker arrangement in the room and to the body of the listener. In this web, sound both affects and touches in 'reciprocal activity unfolding alongside with other diverse socio-material layers of fleshly signification' (Riikonen and Saario 2011b). From this perspective, fixed-media listening is an interactive and sensual practice of being in intense and immediate contact with the recorded past-present-future sound flow and associated 'multiple tactile-aural forms'(Riikonen and Saario 2011b).

The compositional intent of $A\dagger BSB\dagger R$ became focused on effect-production and production of differences of tone, intensity and space, over musical 'content' (Colebrook 2002). Micro-perceptions and micro-differences produced by the inherent 'voice' of each unique loudspeaker were an integral part of the compositional process of this tone production. As such *Speaker Park* as a compositional medium, context and value proposition, affords the post-acousmatic composer an excellent platform and a creative matrix to explore sound-based fixed-media composition, body work, and affective space production.

11.4 SOUND, SPACE AND OBJECTS: DESIGN IN SPEAKER PARK

The speakers designed for *Speaker Park* by Pigott combined the technique of using cone-less drivers coupled to resonant materials found in the examples from Tudor and Monahan, with a sculptural approach which took inspiration from the formal characteristics and materials from the world of standard and industrial loudspeaker design. As can be seen in Figure 11.1 these characteristics include truncated prisms, exponential curves, driver ports, grilles and the standardised rectangular 'box' of industrial loudspeakers. In the context the sculptural speakers of *Speaker Park*, these various tropes from the worlds of public address systems, sound systems and domestic hi-fi took on a new visual identity which somehow also echoes the minimalist sculptures of Robert Morris, Sol Lewitt and Donald Judd from the mid-1960s and later. The choice of simple industrial materials (predominantly wood, metal, plastic) with sharp geometries and repetition across the forms, contributes to this visual connection.

Although there are visual references to standard loudspeaker construction, the sonic voice of each of Pigott's speaker forms is far from standard. Utilising the type of moving coil driver shown in Figure 11.2 each speaker produces a unique and characteristic sound created in part by the materials that these drivers are coupled to, materials which effectively become the speaker cone. In the 1960s, Tudor appropriated these types of cone-less speaker drivers from the world of hobby electronics and engineering, and they are now produced commercially for use in home cinema (for invisible sound propagation through internal drywall interiors) and underwater listening (through the skin of a hot tub for example), among other uses including vending machines and video gaming chairs. In Pigott's speaker designs for *Speaker Park* the drivers excite a range of materials selected for their ability to acoustically broadcast sound in a characteristic way including plywood, plastics and metal, all of which are thin, relatively light and quite stiff.

This choice of materials and acoustic behaviours was informed by one of the collaborative requirements of the *Speaker Park* project which was to create a series of sonically unique and unusual speakers, but that were not too extreme in their resonant distortion. Techniques such as those used by Tudor, Vale and Monahan of attaching large springs

Figure 11.1 A selection of Pigott's sculptural speakers for *Speaker Park*

Figure 11.2 Cone-less speaker driver used in the above speakers

and percussion instruments to speakers and electromechanical drivers resulting in highly coloured and distorted audio was carefully avoided in favour of a slightly more conservative approach of selecting materials that would broadly work as a traditional diaphragm though still add a characteristic tone of, for example, being 'tinny', 'muffled', 'boxy' or 'wooden' sounding or perhaps of having a very limited dynamic range. Further to these speaker-diaphragm characteristics, the boxes themselves also introduced resonances according to the various ways in which their internal voids were divided and subdivided, and were used by any ports that existed between the different chambers and materials. This is of course exactly as would be the case in standard speaker design except with Pigott's *Speaker Park* speakers, the various acoustic chambers and ports were created for visual effect rather than to create a flat frequency response and a transparent listening experience.

In the paper *Objects as Temporary Autonomous Zones*, Timothy Morton (2011) presents an object-oriented ontology whereby there are 'no environment distinct objects' and objects do not exist *in* time and space, but that 'they "time" (a verb) and "space"'. They produce time and space. With the *Speaker Park* composition, *A†BSB†R,* Saario had the sonic-affective intent to produce a *zone* that enables and empowers 'space' for autonomy of experience and subjectivity to emerge, in relation to the presence and experience of the custom loudspeakers. The *Speaker Park* and *A†BSB†R*, as a literal and material composite of sound and sounding objects, 'space', 'time' and 'affect', with sonic space and time emanating from this (sound object) assemblage. Here, a zone is produced where the anti-configuration of *Speaker Park* has disrupted both the standardised production and presentation of fixed-media sonic space, and the anti-spatialisation and non-diffusion of *A†BSB†R*.

The *Speaker Park*◇*A†BSB†R* experience, and the associated spatial effect and affect production resists both the 'downward' and 'upwards' reduction described by Morton (2011). We do not consider the experience to be usefully reducible to either its comprising parts, nor to a holistic 'one'. The installation and composition are, for us, better understood as a rhizomatic, connected and open network of spatial and sonic affect and potential, with the concert installation-design bringing a different, and a difference into, the sonic value economy at play.

The *Speaker Park* presents the composer with an anti-configuration of loudspeakers, in terms of comprising loudspeaker types, numbers, layout, and format (see Figure 11.3). The anti-configuration of the *Speaker Park* loudspeakers, effectively resists the production of stable ('solid') phantom images in a stereo or surround soundfield, and as such challenges ('invites') the composer to seek and produce different spatial *intensities* and relationships than those of the standardised stereo or multichannel loudspeaker systems and formats.

As the *Speaker Park* loudspeaker system has no inherent sense of fixed front, back and sides and thus does not striate the available soundfield by default, it opens up the potential for the production of a smooth space of pure spatial strategy.

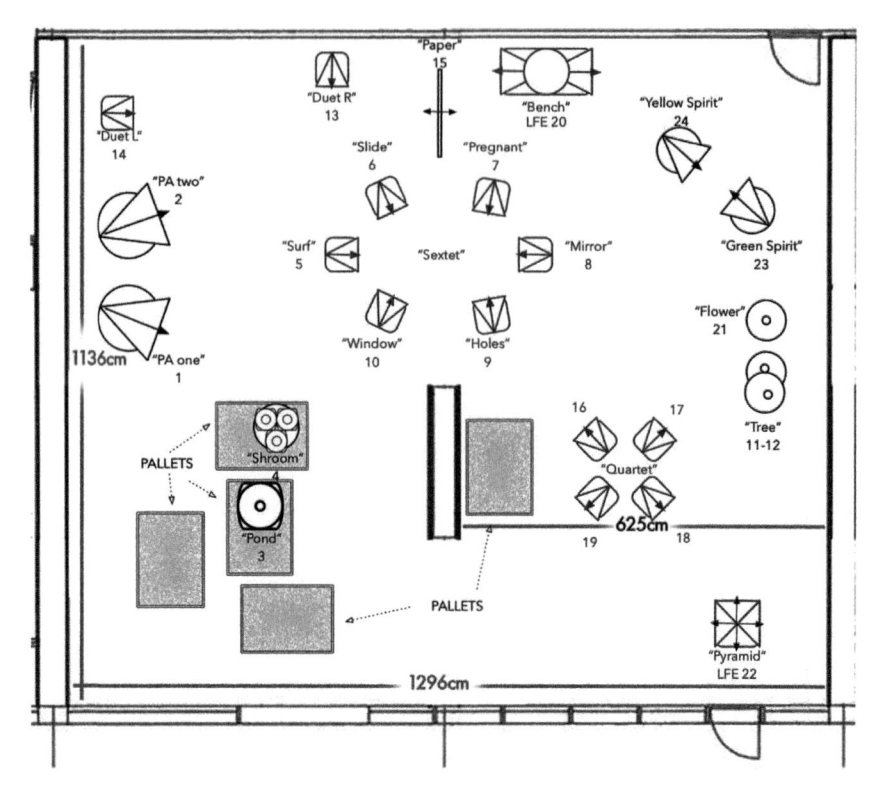

Figure 11.3 WRAP Large Project Room (Speaker Park venue, Borealis 2019). Floor plan. NB speakers 5–10, 13, 14 and 16–19 were made by Pigott

The sound objects associated with Saario's composition practice are typically predicated on the notion of a stereo space, either by the production of stereo space, being in a stereo space, and/or containing a stereo space. This extends to his work in and with surround-sound formats and 'typical' NSML (non-standard multi-loudspeaker) diffusion systems (Deruty 2012), which he tends to approach from the perspective of multiple stereo planes combined with spatialised mono elements and native B-Format surround recordings. Working with *Speaker Park* necessitated a different perception and approach in relation to space production and thus the composition at large.

Harrison (Deruty 2012) raises concerns about isotropy in relation to the associated impossibility of intimacy due to 'random' distances between speakers and a listening audience, the general audio quality, and the distortion of composers' original intent. These imply an assumption of a static audience and/or set seating in relation to the loudspeaker system as well as a notion of fixed perspective in relation to the composition. The effective anisotropy and omni-directional asymmetry of the *Speaker Park* anti-configuration, without any inherent hierarchy or reference to front, back and sides, and with no fixed zone for audience,

Speaker Park: design and composition

was found to produce an environment with high level of potential for intimacy, all on the listener's terms.

With *A†BSB†R* Saario decided to shape the *Speaker Park* installation space so that one's position in the physical room did not matter or produce a hierarchy of positions in relation to the work. To paraphrase, the design brief for the sonic-space-body experience was one of 'disappearing' sweet-spot (Deruty 2012) with the spatial focus being one of continual immersion, irrespective of listener position. The approach empowers the participants to stay static or move in the 'park' and explore the space-continuum as desired, thus creating the potential for a moment of subjective 'autonomy' in a shared relational space, by producing and highlighting the difference *and* interconnectedness, both in and of each spatial perspective in *Speaker Park*; a spatial assemblage of co-existing singularities and reality perspectives. In this seamless, continuous, and literal 'acoustic space' (McLuhan 2005) of *A†BSB†R*, everywhere and nowhere is a sweet-spot and the experience is one of 'all-at-oneness' (Bey 1991; McLuhan 2005).

Saario composed *A†BSB†R* into and in, as well as with and for, the *Speaker Park* speaker-space assemblage. There was no sound projection, spatialisation or sound diffusion typical of a finished composition *per se*. Composition and sound diffusion were coupled into a single production-workflow stage, and both the compositional and spatial considerations plus their associated actions were effectively inseparable from each other. The composition was 'production-of-space' and the work emerged through this process of becoming-composition becoming diffused, or rather 'becoming-sound becoming-space'.

This approach maps to a compositional approach for producing organic, emerging and nomadic structures, and to develop unfolding musical and sonic discourse which follows the basic listening premise outlined by Harrison (1992):

> The starting point is always the sound – the individual sound in all its uniqueness. The details of its internal structure, of its spectral and temporal evolution reveal its potential and hint at what might be. The sensitive ear draws in and evolves other sounds with related potential – unleashed, from micro-structure through to whole pieces.
> (Harrison 1992)

In light of the above, the composer is effectively listening to the perceivable *spectromorpohological* qualities (Smalley 1997). With *Speaker Park* it becomes important to extend the notion of a 'sound object' (Schaeffer 2017) to include all elements of the *loudspeaker-space-fixed-media-playback* assemblage, with the listening focusing on the specific, particular, and unique features of each 'sound event', as enabled by the sound recording and playback assemblage. The uniqueness of each sound, the speakers, the anti-configuration, and individual subjective experience (whether of composer or audience) produce and facilitate a new corporeal ('concrete') interaction with sound. This is a subjective shaping of the sound-space continuum and production of a smooth space.

Also, with the composition of *A†BSB†R*, there was also no 'colouring' of the 'original musical content' (Deruty 2012), as the musical content and the system were of each other. Instead of trying to minimise colouration, loudspeaker colouration was a fundamental feature, process and a medium, of collaborative composition practice between the composer and the 'park'. There was no enhancement, only 'colour'.

Finally, with this spatial strategy of negation of active sound-diffusion, there is no spatial or spectral performance (Deruty 2012) to 'view'. The 'park' and its participants are the only active agents of performance during the concert installation.

11.5 SPEAKER PARK AS AN ASSEMBLAGE

We understand *Speaker Park* neither as an instrument, a listening environment nor loudspeaker orchestra. *Speaker Park* is a collective of sonic collaborators and co-creators both human and non-human, where the ontological category of something 'being' an instrument or an orchestra, with their associated implied notions of authenticity or validation, hold no currency. The nature of the project was to bring together speaker designers and makers with composers and users into a single creative undertaking with a view to uncovering new and creative possibilities through a critique of standardised and industrialised tools and workflow. From this perspective, we see the project as an 'assemblage'.

Typically credited as emerging from the work of Deleuze and Guattari (1998) from the French word *agencement*, an assemblage refers to both an ensemble of parts and the action required to bring those parts together, whilst simultaneously highlighting both materials and processes. The term implies an emphasis on heterogeneous components coming together through ad hoc arrangements that are open to the possibility of change. From a perspective of vital materialism Bennett, (2010) highlights the affective nature of components of an assemblage which have the power both to act and be acted upon, with the potential for these actions to be located in either human or non-human centres. The result here being that agency is distributed across a heterogeneously rich field rather than being localised in human efforts (Bennett 2010: 23). Assemblages are therefore not governed by a single head or single type of material, rather they are a collective, a coming together of different things yet with power distributed across them in uneven and unexpected ways (Bennett 2010: 24).

Law (2004) follows Watson-Verran and Turnbull (1995) in aligning the idea of the assemblage to the notion of the technological 'black box' – a term often used to describe the way in which technologies are made singular, robust, transportable and closed. Reconsidering the black box through a lens of the assemblage highlights the way in which black boxes are more ad hoc than they may seem, more open to interpretation and change, and less closed.

Speaker Park maps onto these themes relating to the assemblage in a number of ways. Firstly, the collaborative and heterogenous nature of the project spans a range of materials, processes and modes of practice. Composition, electronic production technologies and techniques, formal design considerations and material construction techniques are really only the headlines of this heterogeneity in quite general terms. Inside each of these areas the *Speaker Park* assemblage reaches out making unexpected connections, possibilities and constraints in a myriad of ways. It is the unexpected nature of these crossings that allow for the characteristic ad hoc nature of the assemblage to prompt the creative process to find new solutions.

The *Speaker Park* assemblage lent itself 'naturally' to the exploration and development of its intrinsic and emergent qualities, potentials, affordances and constraints, as compositional vehicles. Thus, the design of *A†BSB†R* emerged organically 'as a product of the various forces in play in the milieu' of *Speaker Park* and was 'not be imposed from outside as specified form, but would work with the *grain* of its matter, from within, but also seamlessly with the milieu and networks extending to its horizons' (Ballantyne 2007: 36). *A†BSB†R* is therefore all but one of many potential sonic designs emerging from the immanent properties of the *Speaker Park* assemblage of agents, materials and processes.

Bennett's emphasis of affect within assemblage maps well onto a loudspeaker project such as *Speaker Park* where it might seem that the material constraints and associated resonances of the speakers draw up some hard lines around what is sonically possible and achievable. But without any audio to voice the characteristic sound of the individual speakers these resonances are not brought into being. In this sense, the composed audio and the sculptural speakers are co-constructive of each other. There is no single power-base of composer, instrument designer, or audio source, but rather an unexpected and uneven web of possibilities and constraints. An audio 'source' in *Speaker Park* is located across both digital-audio workstation and loudspeaker; its nature is negotiated between composer/producer and speaker designer/maker.

The undoing of the technological black box through an understanding of assemblage also helps to unpack the *Speaker Park* project. Some of the initial discussions relating to the project emerged as much from questions relating to commercial, high-end studio technology and speaker specification as from the use of loudspeakers in experimental music. The project curators and participants were keen to test the paradigm of the 'transparent' loudspeaker within a context of composition, production and audience reception. For these reasons it was important that the project moved between the different practitioners that were each focused on the different fields of speaker design, composition and curation of the installed *Speaker Park* environment. It was with this broader, collaborative nature of the project in mind that the decision was taken not to make the speakers too extreme in their mechanical distortion and coloration of audio as described earlier. Future iterations of the project could explore this balance further, testing the balance of power and nodes of resonance distributed within the assemblage.

11.6 CONCLUSION

Speaker Park as a 'milieu' was produced by and at the intersection of loudspeaker design and, in the case of *A†BSB†R*, post-acousmatic composition process. *Speaker Park* effectively re-imagined the relationship matrix of a 'designer-maker-materials-work-medium-space' as an ecology of collaboration. Here, composition and design are in collaboration with all subjects – including materials, media, agents, stakeholders, concepts, space and value propositions, amongst others.

This productive assemblage built on Harrison's (1999) notion of composition as collaboration with sound materials as well as on traditions of exploring the sonic potentials of the loudspeaker within musical instruments, musical composition and listening environments. This produced increased complexity in terms of a network of dynamic interaction, connections, immanent potentials and emergent properties, and opened up new mediums – of and for – both creation and creative collaboration between human and non-human agents. Amongst other modes of interaction and collaboration, *Speaker Park* enabled (or called forth) the forming of an 'aesthetic-causal alliance' (Morton 2011) with the non-human loudspeakers, thus innovating speaker design and post-acousmatic composition in tandem.

REFERENCES

Ballantyne, A. (2007). *Deleuze & Guattari for Architects*, New York, London, Routledge.

Barrett, N. (2007). Trends in Electroacoustic Music, in Collins, N. and d'Escrivan, J. (eds.) *The Cambridge Companion to Electronic Music*, Cambridge, Cambridge University Press, pp. 38–54.

Bennett, J. (2010). *Vibrant Matter: A Political Ecology of Things*, Durham and London, Duke University Press.

Bey, H. (1991). *T.A.Z.: The Temporary Autonomous Zone, Ontological Anarchy, Poetic Terrorism*, New York, Autonomedia.

Colebrook, C. (2002). *Gilles Deleuze*, London and New York, Routledge.

Deleuze, G. and Guattari, F. (1988). *A Thousand Plateaus: Capitalism & Schizophrenia*, London, Athlone.

Deruty, E. (2012). *Loudspeaker Orchestras: Non-standard Multi-Loudspeaker Diffusion Systems*, available online from: https://www.soundonsound.com/techniques/loudspeaker-orchestras [accessed March 2020].

Driscoll, J. and Rogalsky, M. (2004). David Tudor's Rainforest: An Evolving Exploration of Resonance, *Leonardo Music Journal*, Vol 14, pp. 25–30.

Emmerson, S. (2007). *Living Electronic Music*, Aldershot, Ashgate.

Harrison, J. (1992). The Primacy of the Ear, in Smalley, D. *Impact Intérieurs*, Empreintes DIGITALes, Montreal, IMED 0409.

Harrison, J. (1999). Diffusion: Theories and Practices, With Particular Reference to the BEAST System, in *eContact 2.4*, available online from: https://econtact.ca/2_4/Beast.htm [accessed March 2020].

Hudis, N. (2006). *Clinical Diploma in Advanced Oriental Body Work* (clinical teaching session), Newcastle-Upon-Tyne, Tissue Flow Institute.

Law, J. (2004). *After Method: Mess in Social Science Research*, New York, Routledge.
McLuhan, M. (2005). *The Medium is the Massage: An Inventory of Effects,* Berkeley, Gingko Press.
Morton, T. (2011). *Objects as Temporary Autonomous Zones*, available online from http://www.continentcontinent.cc/index.php/continent/article/view/46 [accessed March 2020].
Mulder, J. (2010) The Loudspeaker as Musical Instrument, in *Proceedings of the 2010 Conference on New Interfaces for Musical Expression.* Sydney, Australia, available online at: http://www.nime.org/2010/.
Preston, L. and Robles Thorseth, M.V.L. (2019). Speaker Park, Borealis Festival 2019 (website), available online from: https://www.borealisfestival.no/2019/shows/speaker-park-2-en/ [accessed March 2020].
Riikonen, T. and Saario, A.S. (2011a). Listening to the Recorded Touch: A Strata-Aural Manifesto, *Body, Space & Technology*, 10(1), available online from: http://doi/org/10.16995/bst.94 [accessed March 2020].
Riikonen, T. and Saario, A.S. (2011b). Listening to the Recorded Touch: Towards Visceral Methodologies of Mixed Media Sound Making, *sforzando!*, *EMS/EMF Conference*, New York.
Rolf, I.P. (1977). *Rolfing: The Integration of Human Structures*, New York City, Harper and Row.
Rose, E. (2013). Translating Transformations: Object Based Sound Installations, *Leonardo Music Journal*, Vol 23, pp. 65–69.
Schaeffer, P. (2017). *Treatise on Musical Objects: An Essay across Disciplines,* Oakland, CA, University of California Press.
Schultz, R.L. and Feitis. R. (1996). *The Endless Web: Fascial Anatomy and Physical Reality*, Berkley, North Atlantic Books.
Sharma, K. and Schultz, F. (2017). Are Loudspeaker Arrays Musical Instruments?, *4th International Conference on Spatial Audio* (ICSA), Graz.
Smalley, D. (1986). Spectro-morphology and Structuring Processes, in Emmerson, S. (ed.) *The Language of Electroacoustic Music*, London, Macmillan, pp. 61–93.
Smalley D. (1997). Spectro-morphology: Explaining Sound-shapes, *Organised Sound*, Vol 2, No 2, pp. 107–126.
Synnes Handal, R. (2019). Snop for øyne og ører ('Candy for your ears and eyes') *Bergens Tidende*, available online from: https://www.bt.no/kultur/i/K381g7/snop-for-oeyne-og-oerer [accessed March 2020].
Valle, A. (2013). Making Acoustic Computer Music: The Rumentarium project. *Organised Sound*, Vol 18(3), pp. 242–254. doi:10.1017/S1355771813000216
Van Eck, C. (2017). *Between Air and Electricity: Microphones and Loudspeakers as Musical Instruments,* London, Bloomsbury.
Watson-Verran, H. and Turnbull, D. (1995) Science and Other Indigenous Knowledge Systems, in Jasanoff, S. et al. (eds) *Handbook of Science and Technology Studies*, Thousand Oaks, London and New Delhi, SAGE Publications, pp. 115–139.

12

Sound objects

Exploring procedural audio for theatre

Mat Dalgleish and Sarah Whitfield

12.1 INTRODUCTION

This chapter discusses two practical projects that explore the nature and possibilities of sound in theatre and generative audio in particular. The first of these projects, RayGun, is an augmented prop prototype that has potential advantages related to the responsiveness to user interaction and sound localisation. The second project, INTERIOR, consists of a generative audio play embedded in a tangible, radio-like artefact intended to offer an accessible, bi-modal (audio and haptic) experience in a self-contained and portable package. There are potential applications where existing attempts to make theatre accessible are unsuitable, for instance where travel to an audio-described performance is difficult or impossible.

Our approach is informed by two bodies of theory: discourse around sound in theatre and related areas such as film and video-game sound; and research in procedural generation and specifically, procedural audio. As crossover between the two areas has been limited, these are introduced separately. We then move on to discuss a variety of design issues, describe implementational choices, and consider our experiences and initial findings.

12.1.1 Sound for/in theatre

The use of sound in theatre is likely as old as theatre itself: there is at least some evidence that ancient Greek and Roman amphitheatres exploited a range of acoustic characteristics (Rindel, 2011) and that ancient Greek theatre masks were intended to transform the acoustic properties of actors' voices (Vovolis *et al.*, 2013). From these origins, Max Culver (1981) notes that sound effects in particular "increased in number and sophistication throughout all theatre periods". For both Culver (1981) and Susan Bennett (2019, p.93), these technological advances are closely related to developments in theatre architecture. Bennett (2019, p.93) offers the development of a mechanical 'thunder run' for the newly opened Globe theatre in 1599 as a specific example.

The role of sound in theatre is also seen to fundamentally change over time. If use of sound in theatre was initially 'realistic', playwrights eventually moved away from realism (Culver, 1981). This in turn enabled sound to operate more freely. It could: create mood; operate symbolically; fulfil character roles; or enhance spectacle (Culver, 1981).

Nevertheless, sound in theatre has typically been neglected and the "nucleus of theatre is usually the dramatic text, the actor's body or the visual spectacle" (Sahai, 2009). This is reinforced by Bennett (2019, pp.117–118) who, in relation to the 19th century, states that the "theatre created its most spectacular effects from new advances in lighting technology with sound and music relegated to little more than a backdrop to a visually compelling scene". Similarly, Ross Brown (2009) adds that, in reference to more recent developments, "sound, unlike lighting, was not generally considered to be a base-level technical requirement of theatre other than in musicals".

Theatre today exists as part of crowded cultural and entertainment industries, but the national advisory body Theatres Trust (2019) estimates that more than 1300 theatres remain active in the UK and 15.5 million people attended theatre in the West End last year (SOLT, 2018). Nevertheless, despite the size and importance of the industry, MacDonald (2016) emphasises that theatre sound and its practitioners continue to be misunderstood.

12.1.2 Procedural generation

Procedural Generation (PG) relates to any content or structures created by a formal process (Smith, 2015), but is usually assumed to be computerised and is therefore often contrasted with manual creation (Hendrikx *et al.*, 2013). For Farnell (2007) however, a more useful contrast is between the fluid processes of PG and the relative 'fixedness' of non-PG content. The use of PG dates back to early video games (Brewer, 2017), but there has been renewed interest over the last decade. In some instances, PG is seen to enable the real-time creation of entire universes unique to each player (Freiknecht and Effelsberg, 2017). In others, PG is seen to liberate artists from laborious or repetitive content creation. Nevertheless, if PG may have other advantages such as reduced file size compared to pre-rendered content (Hell *et al.*, 2017), and Green (2016) notes that it is not a universal panacea.

Coined or popularised by Farnell (2007), 'procedural audio' relates to "non-linear, often synthetic sound, created in real-time according to a set of programmatic rules and live input". In contrast to the inherent fixedness of recorded sound ('sound qua product'), procedural audio ('sound qua process') is able to be continuously reshaped (Farnell, 2007). This notion of malleability is also articulated by Verron and Drettakis (2012, p. 1):

> Compared to pre-recorded sounds, it [procedural audio] allows interactive manipulations that would be difficult (if not impossible) otherwise. In particular, procedural audio parameters can be linked to motion parameters of graphics objects to enhance the sound/graphics interactions.

Like PG generally, the last decade has seen revived interest in procedural audio and procedurally generated audio features prominently in titles such as *Grand Theft Auto V* (2013) and *No Man's Sky* (2016). Procedural audio has also been used in commercially released music (Collins and Brown, 2009) and sound design for animation (Farnell, 2007) and electric vehicles (Fitzgerald, 2015). Given these diverse applications, it is surprising that bar a few tentative links, the theatre context remains unexplored. For instance, Fry (2019) discusses synthesis in relation to sound design for theatre but makes no explicit connection to procedural audio.

12.2 TOWARDS A CATEGORISATION OF SOUNDS IN THEATRE

While the importance of sound in theatre has (musical theatre excepted) tended to be underplayed, there has also been limited discourse (Curtin and Roesner, 2015; Brown, 2009). Thus, if it is obvious that sound in theatre consists of disparate elements and many are "fully deserving of a theoretical study of their own" (Bennett, 2019, p. 47), how should sound in theatre be approached?

In contrast to the limited material around sound in theatre, there is significant discourse around film and video-game sound. Particularly prescient are the ideas of Michel Chion. Starting broadly, he (Chion, 1994) argues that sound and image are an innately artificial construction, but their fusion enables a suspension of audience disbelief so that sound and image can be perceived as one. Beyond these foundations, Chion (1994, pp. 71–72) introduces notions of acousmatic and visualised sound to refer (respectively) to "sounds one hears without seeing their originating cause" and "accompanied by the sight of its source of cause". Particularly prescient is that Chion (1994) distinguishes three further sound types: 'onscreen sound' relates to a sound source that is onscreen; 'offscreen sound' relates to a sound source that is not present onscreen; 'non-diegetic' sound is acousmatic and its source is not only unseen, but also "external to the story" (Chion, 1994, p. 73).

More than a decade after Chion (1994) and accepting nonlinearity and interactivity as crucial differences, Karen Collins (2008) outlines dialogue, ambience and music as the three basic types of video-game sound. Similar sound types are suggested by Mats Liljedahl (in Grimshaw, 2010, p. 31), but he notes that "in reality, the possible borders between them are floating", and considers ambient sounds to be a distinct subcategory of sound effects.

A provisional classification of types of sound-in-theatre maps quite readily to those suggested by Collins (2008, p. 5) and Liljedahl (in Grimshaw, 2010, p. 31). Theatre also increasingly crosses over into multimedia (Salihbegovic, 2013). However, it is useful to make explicit a distinction between sound effects related to props and more environmentally orientated ambient sounds. This implies that there are four possible categories of sounds in theatre:

- dialogue
- sound effects (prop sounds)

- ambience
- music

To aid subsequent discussion, a synthesised outline of each category is presented below.

12.2.1 Dialogue

Dialogue relates to "human language brought to sound, the sounding counterpart to the visual text" (Liljedahl, in Grimshaw, 2010, p. 31) and more specifically, to the voice. Chion argues that while discussions about the soundtrack have tended to overlook the voice (Chion, 1999), the soundtrack "almost always privileges the voice" (Chion, 1994, p. 5) to the extent that "the other sounds (music and noise) are merely the accompaniment" (Chion, 1994, p. 6).

While Chion (1999) emphasises that vococentrism almost always means that language and its meaning are privileged, he also discusses how the non-semantic properties of the voice (i.e. those not primarily perceived as message) have a certain 'elusive' power. Smith (in Nudds and O'Callaghan, 2009) goes further, arguing that even if a listener cannot hear what is being said, the non-semantic properties of the voice might identify the speaker, or something about the speaker.

12.2.2 Sound effects (prop sounds)

There are substantial histories of performative, materials-based sound design; most notably Foley sound (Keenan and Pauletto, 2017), but the theatre context has been comparatively neglected. Unlike environmental sounds or ambience, sound effects are typically linked to physical objects (props). Props are stage artefacts used to enhance a performance and are usually inert, although there are limited examples of interactive or augmented props (Zhang *et al.*, 2017). Sounds are sometimes produced acoustically (i.e. entirely by the prop-object), but this inertness means that external sound is often added; in turn raising issues of synchronicity, localisation, responsiveness and repetition.

Current approaches to prop sound typically involve recorded sounds (samples) being played back (i.e. triggered), either humanly or automatically, sufficiently precisely that they synchronise to performer-prop interactions. This requirement for coordination creates the potential for significant temporal discrepancy. Sample-based approaches also have the potential for repetition; and as Collins (2008) notes, any sound that displays repetition quickly becomes noticed. Additionally, if acoustic sound generation can produce subtle, near-endless variations (Hunt, 1999), the pre-fixed nature of sampled sounds means that they are limited in their ability to respond to interaction nuances:

> Although, we have access to techniques such as pitch and speed manipulation for a while now (which allows us to manipulate the source material even during application run-time) it still doesn't

change the linear-in-time nature of the prerecorded audio material. Which is essentially, frozen in time.

(Nil, 2019)

Lastly, the use of standard house-sound-systems for sound diffusion instigates a separation of sound from sound-source that emphatically limits sound localisation. Rather than emanating from an object located in a specific position on or off-stage, sounds are 'lost' in an 'outside-in' stereo or multichannel field. Related issues are described by Smallwood and colleagues (2009) in the context of the Princeton Laptop Orchestra (PLOrk).

12.2.3 Ambience

In contrast to the spatial specificity of sound effects (prop sounds), Chion (1994, p. 76) describes ambient sound as amorphous and immersive; it "envelops a scene and inhabits its space, without raising the question of the identification or visual embodiment of its source". However, Chion (1994, p. 76) also posits that ambient sounds are inherently related to site, to the extent that "we might also call them territory sounds, because they serve to identify a particular locale through their pervasive and continuous presence". If Chattopadhyay (2017) notes that this meaning has become standardised, Brian Eno's (1978) less restrictive definition of ambience "as an atmosphere, or a surrounding influence: a tint" implies more creative possibilities.

12.2.4 Music

Chion (1994, pp. 8–9) outlines two models of music for image: 'empathetic' and 'anempathetic'. Empathetic music follows the rhythms, tone, and emotion of the image with which it is presented. By contrast, anempathetic music proceeds steadily and with indifference to the image. He concedes that there "also exist cases of music that is neither empathetic nor anempathetic", but these are downplayed as having "an abstract meaning, or a simple function of presence, a value as a signpost".

12.3 THEORY INTO PRACTICE: RAYGUN

Our interests in sound in theatre and procedural audio were first manifest in RayGun; a prop prototype focussed on embedded, procedurally generated audio and sound effects (prop sounds) specifically.

RayGun is inspired by the iconic ray-guns of mid-20th-century science fiction. Here, the appeal of the ray-gun subject lies in its abstract and relatively simple but immediately recognisable sound. Developed over a two-month period, RayGun has twin focus:

- improved responsiveness relative to sample-based approaches
- highly localised, object-like sound diffusion

To address the responsiveness issue (Verron and Drettakis, 2012), the audio output of RayGun is entirely procedurally generated. This 'audio

Exploring procedural audio for theatre

engine' is implemented in the open source Pure Data (Pd) programming environment and runs on the Bela (2019) embedded computer platform. The Pd patch can be seen in Figure 12.1.

Synthetic gun sounds are not new and the RayGun audio engine extends earlier work by Brooker (1963, pp. 15–17) and Farnell (n.d.). It combines two techniques:

- white noise progressively filtered by two bandpass filters in series
- three-operator Frequency Modulation (FM) synthesis

The two elements share an Attack-Decay envelope generator that jointly modulates the cut-off frequency of the bandpass filters (and effectively the amplitude of the noise), the pitch of the FM modulators and the FM index. Key parameters are randomised to avoid repetition; the bounds determined by the output of a 3-D accelerometer. Two control inputs – trigger and accelerometer – enable the audio engine to be precisely activated but also be influenced by nuances in user interaction (Figure 12.2).

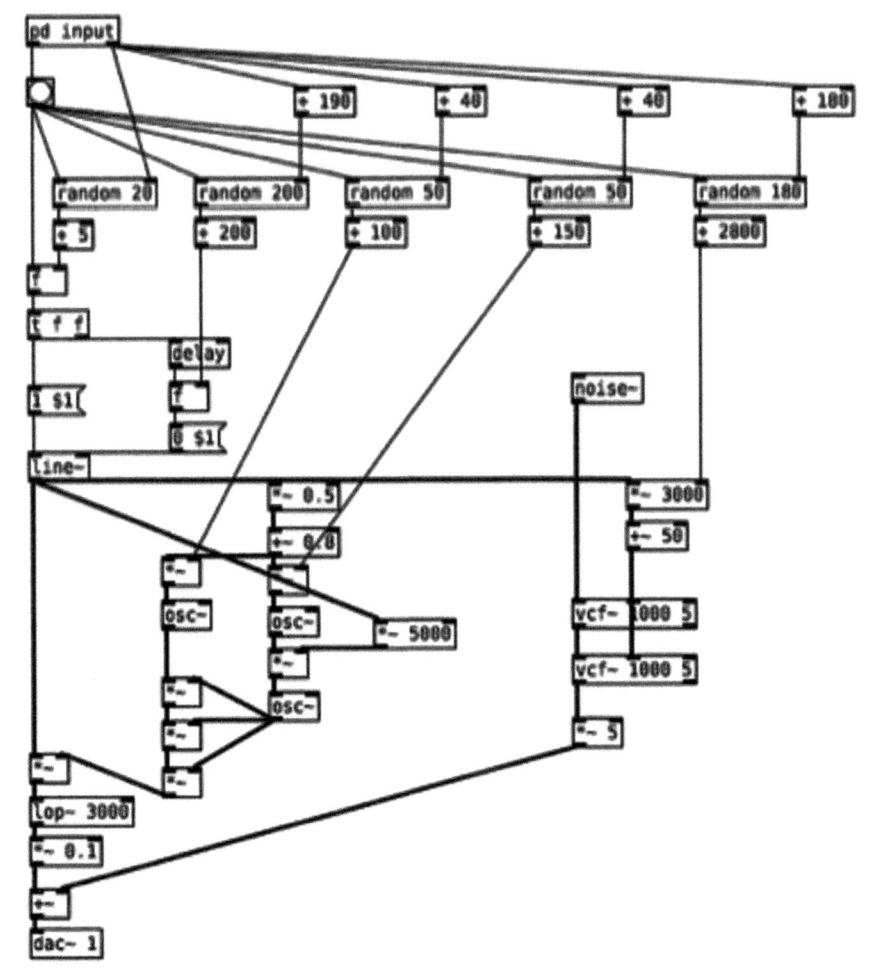

Figure 12.1 The RayGun audio engine as implemented in Pd

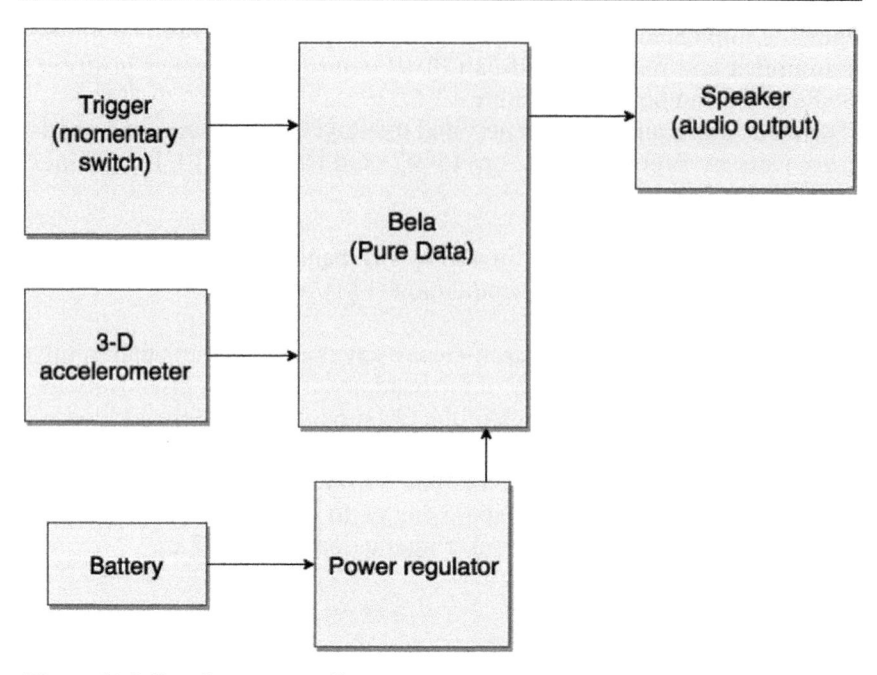

Figure 12.2 RayGun system diagram

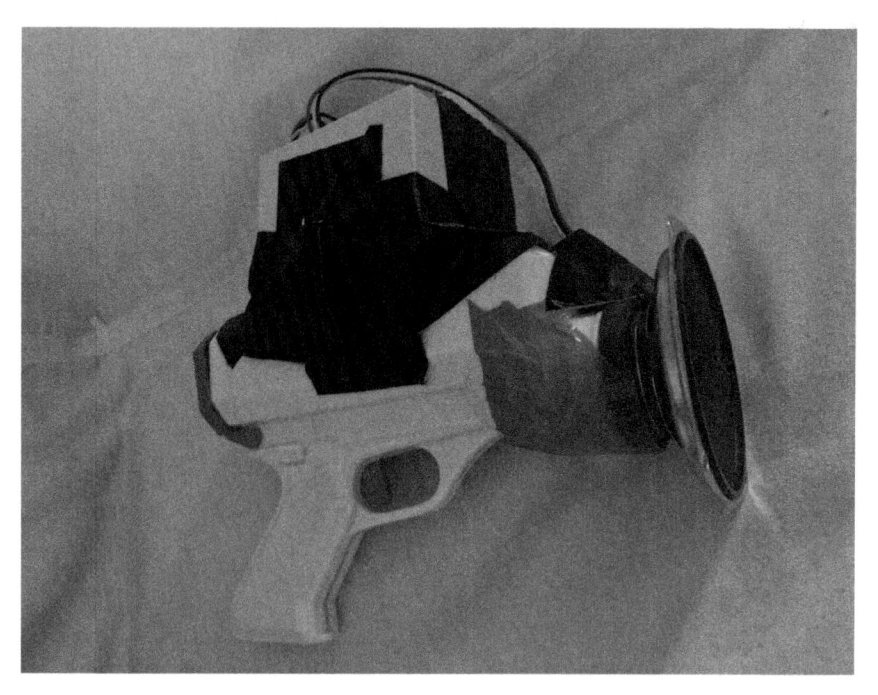

Figure 12.3 The RayGun prop prototype

With little prior work relating to the localisation of object-based sounds in theatre, RayGun draws instead on the localisation solution developed by Smallwood *et al.* (2009) for PLOrk. This uses a hemispherical loudspeaker near each performer to diffuse sound out in all directions from a single point (Smallwood *et al.*, 2009). Informed by this 'inside-out' model, RayGun embeds a single 3" loudspeaker into the prop body (Figure 12.3) so that sound is perceived to emanate from 'inside' the artefact (rather than a house sound system) and come from its location on stage.

The physical coupling between prop and loudspeaker means that vibrations are also passed through the prop body to the hands of the performer as haptic feedback.

12.4 INTERIOR

Theatre's reliance on visual information can be a significant barrier for blind and visually impaired audience members. Blindness and visual impairment encompass a wide variety of conditions and some 360,000 people in the UK are registered as blind and 2,000,000 are estimated to have a visual impairment (RNIB, 2019). Attempts to make theatre accessible to these populations have focussed on audio description (AD); a service that translates the visual aspects of a performance into a succinct spoken commentary (Holland, in Diaz and Andermann, 2009). While 40% of theatres offered at least one audio-described performance between 2013 and 2016 (Cock, 2016), AD for theatre can be problematised in terms of:

- cost of specialist staff and equipment
- setup time and the complexity and/or reliability of equipment
- 'othering' of service users
- attention/distraction issues
- limited opportunities for creativity by describers
- few opportunities for imaginative interpretation by audiences

Court *et al.* (2014) note that a significant number of people with a visual impairment have at least one comorbid impairment; most commonly a mobility impairment, auditory impairment or learning disabilities, and it is likely that AD for theatre is not suitable for all. Additionally, independent travel – for instance to a theatre – is a source of anxiety for many blind people, and is sometimes avoided completely (Johnson and Petrie, 1998).

Against this backdrop, INTERIOR explores alternative modes of accessibility. More specifically, it recasts Maurice Maeterlinck's *Interior* – an 1895 play intended for marionettes – as a generative and largely procedurally generated audio play embedded in a radio-inspired tangible artefact. While RayGun focussed on sound effects (prop sounds), INTERIOR incorporates all four of the sound types from Section 12.2. It provides a multilayered, bi-sensory experience that can be accessed in a number of different ways. Additionally, rather than require users to travel to a specialised venue, it is self-contained and portable so that it can go to users 'in-the-wild'.

12.4.1 Interior (interieur): the context

Belgian playwright Maurice Maeterlinck (b.1862–d.1949), was a writer and playwright who cared little for the demands of the stage and far more for ephemeral nature of theatrical performance as a site for exploration in his creative practice. His 1895 play *Interior* was first performed at the Théâtre de l'Œuvre (where Alfred Jarry's *Ubu Roi* would be performed only a year later), and along with Materlinck's other early plays, is considered an "ancestor of absurdist theatre" (Knapp, 1975, p. 174). This play was specifically written to be performed by marionettes, which Maeterlinck preferred at that stage to actors. He felt that the wooden dolls had the potential for different kinds of meaning, particularly given that the puppeteer would also be visible to the audience. The dolls were for Maeterlinck, as Bettina Knapp (1975, p. 76) argues, able to "[be] inhabitants of two worlds, the real and the unreal, they could be transformed into anything at any time: god or man, saint or sinner". In this play, almost nothing takes place, we simply wait for terrible news to be communicated – when the action is completed, we remain outside of 'the interior' in which the climax is reached.

The play begins with a house, inside of which we can see a living room and a family at peace; outside in the gardens of the property, we see and hear the conversation between an Old Man and a Stranger. The two men consider how to break the terrible news to the family that their daughter has drowned down in the village, and her body has been found (it is never made clear whether this is an accident or on purpose). The men resist telling the family, but they must, since the villagers are bringing her body back to the house. Pressured by the arrival of his granddaughter, the old man does venture inside, only for the mother to realise what his arrival heralds. We are never able to hear what goes on inside the house, all of the dialogue happens in the garden. Bettina Knapp notes that *Interior* is important because of the way in which it carries out a "dissociation of speech and action [which] breaks to a certain extent the conventional empathy usually existing between actor and audience" (1975, p. 82) Even performed by puppets, she notes, "the inevitability of death is so powerful at times as to become unbearable" (Knapp, 1975, p.84).

Maeterlinck went on to win the Nobel Prize in Literature in 1911 (Nobel, 2019) and his complex body of work comprised novels, plays, theoretical essays and explorations of mysticism; often with a recurring theme of the ways in which ordinary life unfolds. Maeterlinck's skill as a writer was "to impose a dreamlike strangeness on the most homely and everyday scenes" (Worth, 1979, p. 164). *Interior* was originally in rhyming couplets, which we have not preserved. In INTERIOR, we have carried out a close adaptation of the 1899 translation to ensure that the rhythm and meaning of the now-dated text does not jolt the listener out of the experience of hearing the unfolding drama. Changes have been made where needed for understanding and for phrasing, keeping close to the intention of the original where possible, but with the goal of allowing the inevitable to unfold over its duration.

While he was to work with actors again, Maeterlinck remained suspicious of their involvement in theatre. In one later essay, 'The Tragical in Daily Life', he writes:

> The mysterious chant of the Infinite, the ominous silence of the soul and of God, the murmur of Eternity on the horizon [. . .] do not all these underlie King Lear, Macbeth, Hamlet? And would it not be possible, by some interchanging of the rôles, to bring them nearer to us, and send the actors farther off?
>
> (Maeterlinck, 1905, pp. 98–99)

He is particularly focussed on the relationship between the "situation of deep seriousness" and the way in which it has to be "unravelled by means of words" (Maeterlinck, 1905, p. 113).

12.4.2 Design concept

The INTERIOR artefact (Figure 12.8) draws heavily on the portable radio. From the motor car to the theremin, there are many examples of how – to increase acceptability – designers choose to imitate familiar designs (Hunt, 1999). In relation to the radio specifically, Nilsson *et al.* (2003) created a radio-like media player for older users (an often-neglected user group). The authors reported that their device had "gained acceptance among the elderly and that they were deeply touched by their use of it". Beyond increased acceptance, familiar design-language is often incorporated to improve ease of use or leverage existing skills. For instance, digital audio workstations such as Pro Tools incorporate extensive skeuomorphic design elements in an attempt to aid the transition from earlier analogue equipment (Bell *et al.*, 2015).

A distinctive feature of the radio interface is its persistence. As Ullmer (2002) describes, the radio has been superseded by a combination of online services and multipurpose devices. However, the radio interface has seemingly endured the loss of the technology itself. For instance, Brazil and Fernström (2004), creators of a radio-like museum exhibit, note that "visitors had no problems in determining how to use the device, or in 'tuning' to hear different recordings" (Brazil and Fernström, 2004).

That this intuitiveness endures beyond the lifespan of the technology perhaps relates to the incorporation of its interaction language into more recent technologies. For instance, the radio interface is a clearly identifiable influence in the user interfaces of digital radios and smartphone applications (Figure 12.4 and Figure 12.5).

INTERIOR reduces the radio interface to a single rotary knob that is used to 'tune into' and 'find' the audio play amongst a radio-like soundscape. This single knob interface is intended to be intuitively operated, but also accessible to a wide variety of users: it offers a persistent, bi-modal representation of the system state, little penalty for recovery from interaction errors, and can be operated one-handed.

Figure 12.4 A Roberts Revival DAB/DAB+ radio

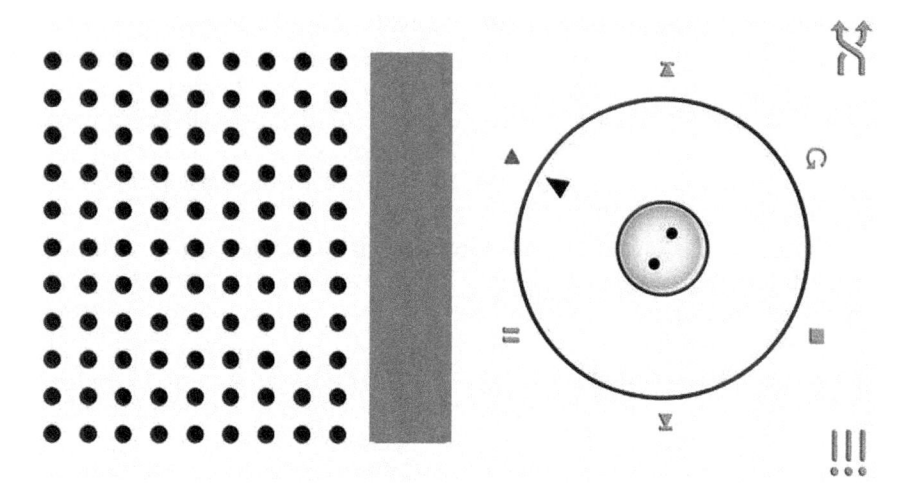

Figure 12.5 The T3 Player for iOS by Motion Pixels

The hiss, hum, static and crackle that characterises the shortwave bands is reproduced throughout. These artefacts are primarily intended to offer additional interaction clues, but, in the post-radio era, may also be of aesthetic interest in their own right (Eno, 1996, p.283).

12.4.3 Implementation

Like RayGun, the INTERIOR prototype utilises the Bela platform (Figure 12.6) and is capable of self-contained operation: external connectivity

Exploring procedural audio for theatre

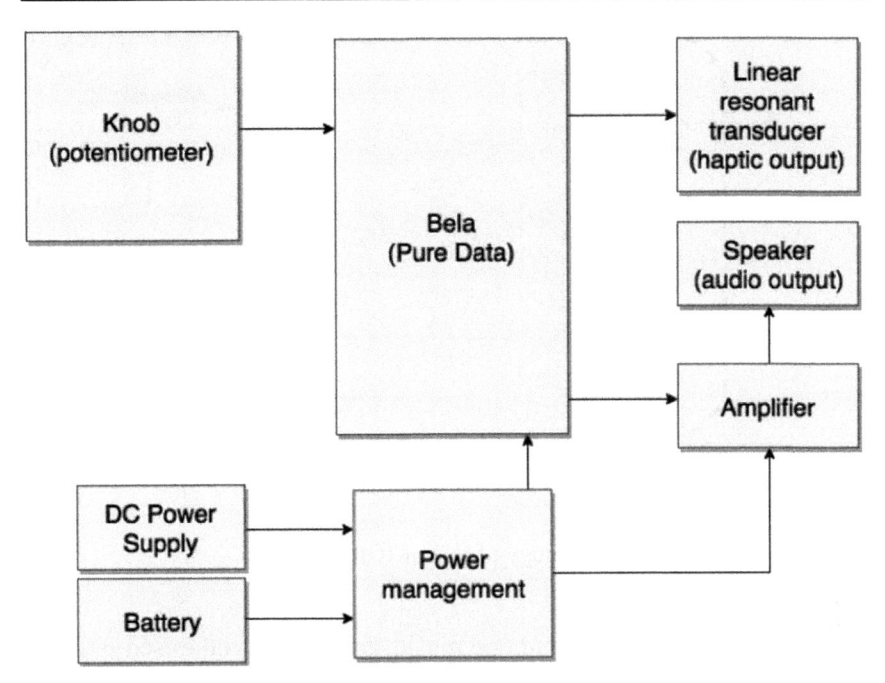

Figure 12.6 INTERIOR system diagram

for power and headphones is provided, but an internal battery and inbuilt loudspeaker are also present.

The software component is again implemented in Pd. The implementation has six layers:

- Input (tuner) layer
- Airwaves layer
- Radio Play layer
- Mix layer
- Artefacts and Distortion layer
- Output layer

Their structure and topology can be seen in Figure 12.7.

The Input (tuner) layer consists of a single knob interface that enables the user to 'tune' the INTERIOR artefact and thereby choose what is heard. The knob is knurled to improve grip and the output of its underlying potentiometer is received inside Pd on the Bela's third input.

The Airwaves layer is informed by the in-game radio stations of *Grand Theft Auto V* (Grand Theft Auto V, 2013) and 'Easter eggs' more generally. It features seven pseudo-radio stations that are encountered as the user 'tunes in' to the audio play. The effect is of reaching in and grasping the audio play through a richly textured gauze. Nine stations are currently implemented:

- five music stations
- three 'numbers' stations
- one news station

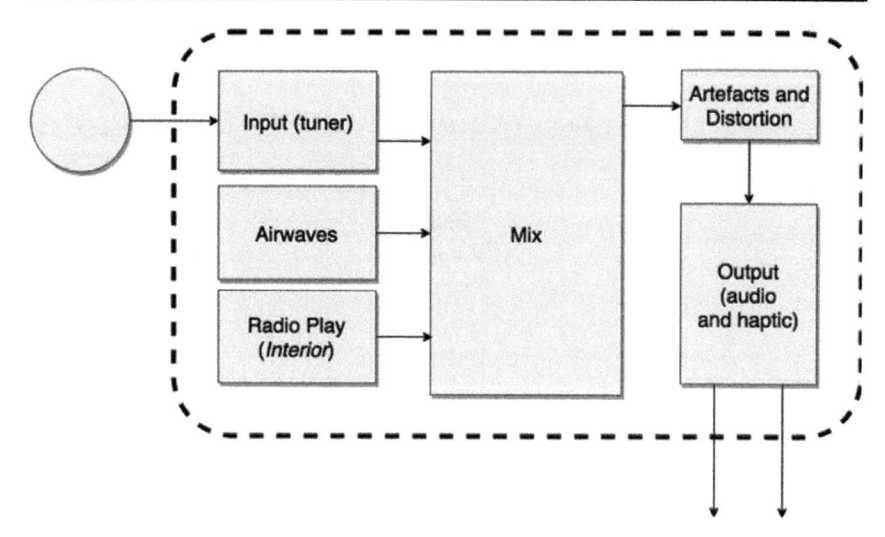

Figure 12.7 The software topology of INTERIOR

All three numbers stations and one music station are synthesised in real-time and are unique each time the system is initialised. The other four music stations and news station (currently) rely on recorded audio but utilise generative playlists to reduce repetition.

The Radio Play layer is intended to be the main user experience and presents a generative version of Maeterlinck's *Interior* that is unique each time it is played. The play consists of a mixture of dialogue, sound effects, ambience and music, and most sounds are procedurally generated. More specifically, all dialogue uses concatenative text-to-speech synthesis to produce 'spoken' sequences on-the-fly from a database of pre-recorded fragments. This dialogue is then extensively processed and combined with additional synthesised sounds to produce a backdrop of ambience and ambient music. More focussed sound effects are also present. They include a fire based on a design by Farnell (2010, pp. 409–418) and footsteps (individual and group).

The Mix layer manages the balance between the Airwaves and Radio Play layers. This balance is largely determined by the Input (tuner) layer, but some random movement is also added.

The Mix layer output passes into the Artefacts and Distortion layer where it is split into wet and dry signals. The dry signal is sent directly to the Output layer. Shortwave-like artefacts are added to the wet signal, and three distortion processes applied:

- hard clipping
- 8-bit transfer functions
- tanh distortion

To add subtle motion, all distortion parameters and the wet/dry balance are slowly modulated by one-dimensional random processes.

Figure 12.8 The prototype INTERIOR artefact

The Output layer is bi-modal (auditory and haptic) and has two channels. The first channel carries the audio output to a MAX98306-based 3.7W Class D amplifier that drives a 3" loudspeaker. The second channel carries low-frequency information to a linear resonant (haptic) actuator fixed to the artefact baseplate.

These elements are housed in a recycled wooden box (Figure 12.8) with removable lid to enable modification and maintenance.

12.5 DISCUSSION

This chapter has introduced RayGun and INTERIOR, in the context of a mixed background in sound in theatre and procedural audio. Further details and documentation of the projects are available online (Dalgleish, 2019). RayGun represented an initial attempt to bring together two previously largely unconnected areas and our own practices. Although relatively simple, it provided useful experience of a new (to us) technological platform and served as a discussion point. Although only tested briefly, its immediacy appears to create interest and encourage actors (who by their own admission would not usually think about technology) to start to consider the creative possibilities of interactive artefacts.

If RayGun instilled confidence in the basic technological platform, its sounds are relatively simple and it is in the more complex INTERIOR that some of the current limitations of procedural audio become evident. For example, a degree of artificiality suits the INTERIOR source material, but it is evident that convincingly naturalistic dialogue generated in real-time using solely procedural techniques remains some way off. It may therefore be useful to consider procedural techniques as part of a broader palette of techniques for synthetic audio that also includes sample playback and hybrid techniques such as granular synthesis. The latter are seen to offer some of the stated advantages of PG around fluidity and reduced file size, but also avoid some of the current limitations of 'pure' PG related to sonic detail.

One area in which procedural audio appears more successful is the production of background or other quiet sounds. These sounds are not usually an attentional focus, but their presence is important and more conventional recorded implementations would (given the need for multiple variations) result in unmanageably large file sizes. Our experiences are that, as Farnell (2007) suggests, PG is also well-suited to sound types that emphasise movement over static detail, but most interesting is the ability to create sounds that move between different types. For instance, numerous sounds in INTERIOR seamlessly crossover between ambience and music. This instability problematises the rigid categories proposed by Chion (1994) and Collins (2008), amongst others: it is likely that the further development and adoption of PG techniques will require new, more flexible theorisation around sound types.

12.6 FUTURE WORK

The next design iteration of INTERIOR will add an LED-based display. This is intended to provide visual feedback as the artefact is 'tuned' and, more generally, supplement the current auditory and haptic modalities. Once implemented, a user study will be carried out to test the efficacy of INTERIOR in-the-wild. Having donated it to the 14/48 Wolverhampton speed theatre festival, we will also receive detailed user feedback on the RayGun prototype in June 2020.

More speculatively, exploration of soft haptics could enable a subsequent INTERIOR iteration to change its shape and mechanical properties. This could in turn facilitate new paradigms of interaction; for example, interaction properties tailored to individual user needs. To similar ends, we are also interested in how virtual reality (VR) can offer users individualised visual stimuli. Soft haptics could also enable the physical form of the artefact to convey information that evolves as part of a narrative journey.

Considered as a platform, INTERIOR has the potential to act as a receiving house for works by others, for instance, as additional 'stations' in its soundscape.

REFERENCES

Bela (2019). Bela: beautifully interactive sensors and sound, *Bela* (website), available online at https://bela.io/ [accessed November 2019].

Bell, A., Hein, E. and Ratcliffe, J. (2015). Beyond Skeuomorphism: The Evolution of Music Production Software User Interface Metaphors, *Journal of the*

Art of Record Production, Vol 9, available online at https://www.arpjournal.com/asarpwp/beyond-skeuomorphism-the-evolution-of-music-production-software-user-interface-metaphors-2/ [accessed October 2019].

Bennett, S. (2019). *Theory for Theatre Studies: Sound*, London, Bloomsbury.

Brazil, E. and Fernström, M. (2004). Interactive Radio: Exploring Visitor Stories Using a Radio Interface, *Proceedings of the Tenth Meeting of the International Conference on Auditory Display (ICAD 04)*, Sydney, Australia.

Brewer, N. (2017). Computerized Dungeons and Randomly Generated Worlds: From Rogue to Minecraft (Scanning Our Past), *Proceedings of the IEEE*, Vol. 105, No. 5, pp. 970–977.

Brooker, F.C. (1963). *Radiophonics in the BBC (monograph number 51)*, London, BBC Engineering Division.

Brown, R. (2009). *Sound: A Reader in Theatre Practice*, New York, Macmillan.

Chattopadhyay, B. (2017). Reconstructing Atmospheres: Ambient Sound in Film and Media Production, *Communication and the Public*, Vol. 2, No. 4, pp. 352–364.

Chion, M. (1994). *Audio-vision Sound on Screen*, New York, Columbia University Press.

Chion, M. (1999). *The Voice in Cinema*, New York, Columbia University Press.

Cock, M. (2016). Dark Performances, *Arts Professional* (website), available online at https://www.artsprofessional.co.uk/magazine/article/dark-performances [accessed October 2019].

Collins, K. (2008). *Game Sound: An Introduction to the History, Theory, and Practice of Video Game Music and Sound Design*, Cambridge, MA, MIT Press.

Collins, N. and Brown, A.R. (2009). Generative Music Editorial, *Contemporary Music Review*, Vol. 28, No. 1, pp. 1–4.

Court, H., McLean, G., Guthrie, B., Mercer, S.W. and Smith, D.J. (2014). Visual impairment is associated with physical and mental comorbidities in older adults: a cross-sectional study, *BMC Medicine*, Vol. 12, No. 181.

Culver, M.K. (1981). *A History of Theatre Sound Effect Devices to 1927*. Doctoral thesis, University of Illinois at Urbana-Champaign.

Curtin, A. and Roesner, D. (2015). Sounding out 'the scenographic turn': eight position statements, *Theatre and Performance Design*, Vol. 1, No. 1–2, pp. 107–125.

Dalgleish, M. (2019). *Sound Objects documentation* (website), available online at https://github.com/matdwlv/soundobjects [accessed November 2019].

Diaz, J. and Andermann, G. (eds.) (2009). *Audiovisual Translation: Language Transfer on Screen*, Basingstoke, Palgrave Macmillan.

Eno, B. (1978). *Music for Airports liner notes* (website), available online at http://music.hyperreal.org/artists/brian_eno/MFA-txt.html [accessed November 2019].

Eno, B. (1996). *A Year with Swollen Appendices*, London, Faber and Faber.

Farnell, A. (2007). An Introduction to Procedural Audio and its Application in Computer Games, *Proceedings of the Audio Mostly Conference*, Röntgenbau, pp. 27–28.

Farnell, A. (2010). *Designing Sound*, Cambridge, MA, MIT Press.

Farnell, A. (n.d.) *Red laser beam* (website), available online at https://www.moz.ac.at/sem/lehre/lib/pd-sounddesign/tutorial_laserbeam.html [accessed November 2019].

Freiknecht, J. and Effelsberg, W. (2017). A Survey on the Procedural Generation of Virtual Worlds, *Multimodal Technologies Interact*, Vol. 1, No. 4, pp. 27.

Fry, G. (2019) *Sound Design for the Stage*. The Crowood Press.

Fitzgerald, R.J. (2015). Sound Design for Electric Vehicles, *Physics Today*, Vol. 68, No. 1, p. 17.

Grand Theft Auto V (standard edition). 2013. PlayStation 4 [Game]. New York: Rockstar Games.

Green, D. (2016). *Procedural Content Generation for C++ Game Development*, Birmingham, Packt Publishing.

Grimshaw, M. (ed.) (2010). *Game Sound Technology and Player Interaction: Concepts and Development*, Hershey, IGI Global.

Hell, J., Clay, M. and Elaarag, H. (2017). Hierarchical dungeon procedural generation and optimal path finding based on user input, *Journal of Computing Sciences in Colleges*, Vol. 33, No. 1, pp. 175–183.

Hendrikx, M., Meijer, S., Van Der Velden, J. and Iosup, A. (2013). Procedural Content Generation for Games, *ACM Transactions on Multimedia Computing, Communications, and Applications*, Vol. 9, No. 1, pp. 1–22.

Hunt, A. (1999). *Radical User Interfaces for Real-time Musical Control*, doctoral thesis, University of York.

Johnson, V. and Petrie, H. (1998). Travelling safely: the problems and concerns of blind pedestrians, *British Journal of Visual Impairment*, Vol. 16, No. 1, pp. 27–31.

Keenan, F. and Pauletto, S. (2017). Listening back: exploring the sonic interactions at the heart of historical sound effects performance, *The New Soundtrack*, Vol. 7, No. 1, pp. 15–30.

Knapp, B. (1975). *Maurice Maeterlinck*, Boston, Twayne Publishers.

MacDonald, P. (2016). Gareth Owen: Theatre Sound Designer, *Sound on Sound* (website), available online at https://www.soundonsound.com/people/gareth-owen-theatre-sound-designer [accessed November 2019].

Maeterlinck, M. (1899). *Alladine And Palomides: Interior, And The Death of Tintagiles: Three Little Dramas for Marionettes* (trans by William Archer and Alfred Sutro), Chicago, Charles H. Sergel Co.

Maeterlinck, M. (1905). *The Treasure of the Humble* (trans. by Alfred Sutro), London, Ballantyne, Hanson and Co.

Nil, B. (2019). Procedural Audio on the Web: Part One, *Medium* (website), available online at https://medium.com/@berraknil/procedural-audio-on-the-web-part-one-166462e7be1c [accessed November 2019].

Nilsson, M., Johansson, S. and Håkansson, M. (2003). Nostalgia: An Evocative Tangible Interface for Elderly Users, *Proceedings of CHI '03 Extended Abstracts on Human Factors in Computing Systems*, Fort Lauderdale, pp. 964–965.

No Man's Sky (standard edition). 2016. PlayStation 4 [Game]. Guildford: Hello Games.

Nobel Prize (2019). *Nobel Prize in Literature 1911* (website), available online at https://www.nobelprize.org/prizes/literature/1911/summary/ [accessed November 2019].

Rindel, J.H. (2011). The ERATO Project and its Contribution to our Understanding of the Acoustics of Ancient Theatres, *Proceedings of the Acoustics of Ancient Theatres Conference*, Patras, Greece.

RNIB (2019). Key information and statistics on sight loss in the UK, *Royal National Institute for the Blind* (website), available online at https://www.rnib.org.uk/professionals/knowledge-and-research-hub/key-information-and-statistics [accessed November 2019].

Sahai, S. (2009). Exploring a Theatre of Sounds, *Proceedings of Sound, Sight, Space and Play 2009: Postgraduate Symposium for the Creative Sonic Arts*, Leicester, UK.

Salihbegovic, F. (2013). Multimedia Theatre Before the Digital Age. *Scene*, Vol. 1, No. 3, pp. 389–403.

Smallwood, S., Cook, P.R., Trueman, D. and McIntyre, L. (2009). Don't Forget the Loudspeaker: A History of Hemispherical Speakers at Princeton, Plus a DIY Guide, *Proceedings of 9th International Conference on New Interfaces for Musical Expression (NIME '09)*, pp. 110–115.

Smith, B.C. (2009). 'Speech Sounds and the Direct Meeting of Minds', in Nudds, M. and O'Callaghan, C. (eds) *Sounds and Perception: New Philosophical Essays*. Oxford, Oxford University Press.

Smith, G. (2015). An Analog History of Procedural Content Generation, *Proceedings of the 10th International Conference on the Foundations of Digital Games (FDG 2015)*, Pacific Grove, CA, USA.

SOLT (2018). *2018 Box Office Figures Released by Society of London Theatre and UK Theatre* (website), available online at https://solt.co.uk/about-london-theatre/press-office/2018-box-office-figures-released-by-society-of-london-theatre-and-uk-theatre/ [Accessed October 2019].

Theatres Trust (2019). Theatres Database, *Theatres Trust* (website), available online at: https://database.theatrestrust.org.uk/ [accessed 09/11/2019].

Ullmer, B.A. (2002). *Tangible Interfaces for Manipulating Aggregates of Digital Information*, Doctoral thesis, Massachusetts Institute of Technology.

Verron, C. and Drettakis, G. (2012). Procedural audio modelling for particle-based environmental effects, *Proceedings of the 133rd AES Convention*, San Francisco, USA.

Vovolis, T., Tsilfidis, A., Georganti, E. and Mouriopoulos, J. (2013). Function and Acoustic Properties of Ancient Greek Theatre Masks vol 2, *Acta Acustica united with Acustica*, Vol. 99, No. 1, pp. 82–90.

Worth, K. (1979). Evolution of European "Drama of the Interior": Maeterlinck, Wilde and Yeats, *Maske und Kothurn*, Vol. 25, No. 1–2, pp. 161–170.

Zhang, Y.X., Ma, P.F. and Zhu, Z.Q. (2017). Magic Props: A Multi-sensory System Fusing Virtual Effects in Live Drama Performance Spatially, *Proceedings of the International Conference on Culture and Computing (Culture and Computing 2017)*, Kyoto, Japan.

13

Hearing and feeling memories

Connecting image, sound and haptic feedback to create a multisensory experience of photographs

Matthew D.F. Evans, James Dooley and Simon Hall

13.1 INTRODUCTION

Photography is a powerful tool for allowing one to preserve and capture a memory. "Images have a deeply ambivalent relationship to time. The single image appears to freeze it, capture it, and memorialize it, and in doing so works against the flow of duration". (Hunt and Schwartz, 2010). With a photograph being frozen in stasis and principally affecting the visual sense, this chapter attempts to investigate how making an image audible can generate a reanimation of a photograph. By using the pixel data from a digitized image as a basis for sonification and generation of haptics from the output, this chapter seeks to explore how an individual can metaphorically feel and hear a person via an image alone.

After the death of Matthew Evans' father in April 2019, photographs of him became a powerful tool for preserving his memory for him and his family. This prompted experimentation into how these photographs could be recycled into new forms.

Matthew's father was a frequent user of social media and this was his first experience of losing a close family member who had a public online presence. Although his father was tangibly gone, there existed an archive that in some ways still felt active. The nature of a public Facebook page also meant that other users could interact with that digital space as they chose fit. This left Matthew feeling as if his father had been left in a kind of digital limbo. Brubecker et al. explain,

> Social network sites provide a new space for the bereaved to engage grief that is socially situated in the daily lives of users. While online grieving might be beneficial for some, the unmarked way in which it is handled by the system presents challenges to others who are not grieving or who are grieving differently. Some find comfort, while others express distress at seeing what they consider private expressions of grief and may even question the authenticity of users' messages, given the medium by which they are expressed.
>
> (Brubaker et al., 2013)

It became clear how few photographs—digital and otherwise—Matthew had of his father, so he was thankful to have this online archive. However, like some of the participants in Brubaker et al.'s research, Matthew felt uncomfortable with the lack of control his father had over the page.

Facebook heightened this duality between comfort and unease even more so due to its cataloguing, organizing, and the sheer amount of accessible data all in one location. This prompted experimenting with how this data could be utilized in a way that allowed a person more control over it.

After downloading his photographs, Matthew deactivated his father's account in search of how his research into interactive art could catalyse this notion of a portal between us and lost loved ones in a way that felt personalized and restored a sense of control to himself as an individual. Yet a photograph can be a promise of the unobtainable. As Gibson explains, about a photograph of her father,

> The absent, yet representationally, present body also haunts the photographic image. The three-dimensional body as a flat surface image on photographic paper, haunts as the substantial, the longed for, and the impossible. In the direct look at the camera lens the photographed subject says: 'Here I am', asserting their existence into the recording of the image. Registered in the image is my father's imminent death. In this photograph, my father is disengaged from the lens and production of the image. Technically, in terms of the image, he is in the photograph but he is not there.
>
> (Gibson, 2004)

In creating sound from image the objective for this chapter has been to uncover whether what Gibson refers to as the 'impossible' could be reconsidered. With death being an unavoidable mark of existence, photographs of our loved ones are a way of creating a sense of permanence from the precarious and fragile experience of being alive. The very nature of being here means that all things are transient, from our thoughts, our feelings and our physical self. Although a photograph may freeze a moment in time, in many ways that artificial construct deviates from the reality of human experience.

A musical note, however, parallels this transient nature more closely. In audio synthesis terms, an ADSR (attack, decay, sustain, release) envelope is an apt metaphor for the nature of a human cycle. There is a sudden attack time of coming into existence, growth and development, a decay time of regulation, a sustain of the main sequences of one's life, and finally a release into not being in existence.

This chapter intends to document research into techniques and approaches that have been uncovered using a cyclical practice-based research methodology (Candy, 2006) through the creation of the installation *A-D-S-R*.

In creating an interdependent, multimodal response from a photograph, this project explores how the compositional form of an image can be used to generate a sonic composition. In translating image to sound, it seeks to explore how different mediums can be connected and how physical and contextual artefacts can be incorporated in the work to further embed the subject of a photograph.

13.2 MAPPING IMAGE TO SOUND

This project uses RGB data, the additive colour mode that is used to digitize real-world colour. A computer realizes a photograph by assigning digital numeric data for red, green and blue to individual points much in the same way that pointillist painters such as Seurut and Signac used individual dots to realize patterns of colour. Via the analysis of pixel data, a photograph can be distilled back to the individual numeric data of which the image is comprised. This repository of data can be then used to generate sound through a variety of mapping techniques. Much like Seurat and Signac, who realized larger paintings from individual brush points, pixel data may be mapped to trigger individual sonic events that contribute to a larger sonic composition.

There are a variety of methods for translating image into sound such as the linear spectrographic process as found in Photosounder (Rouzic, 2018),

> Time goes from left to right, and frequencies from bottom for basses to the top for trebles. The brightness of the pixel define the volume at a specific place in time and frequency, the brighter the louder, the higher in position the higher in frequency, the more to the right the later it occurs in the sound.
>
> (Rouzic, 2018)

This scanning technique has been employed by artists in performative settings, in works such as "Scanline: fp" (Kobayashi, 2016) in which the movement of geometric drawings is mapped to waveforms, and "Soundlines" (Jette, 2013) which scans the movement of a dancer and maps that data to pitch and timbre. In creating an audible relationship between image and sound, Ciciliani states,

> The application of scanline synthesis in audiovisual projects is an interesting method to create a direct correspondence between a digital image and the resulting sound. When it is applied in its pure form, the musical variability is somewhat limited, but methods have been presented that are very suitable for adding sonic variability.
>
> (Ciciliani, 2015)

The sound produced by the scanline approach is often very sonically dense as each pixel in the row is mapped to produce a frequency. As an alternative, the probing approach used by applications such as VOSIS (McGee, 2013) limits the data set resulting in less noisy results. VOSIS takes a raster scan of grayscale pixel data of a section of a chosen image or live video feed. The technique of raster scanning can be used for generating or recording a video image by performing a line-by-line sweep of the image's pixels (Yeo and Berger, 2008).

This scan produces values for each pixel ranging from 0–255 (0 representing black and 225 representing white). This is then processed and filtered to remove noise, scaled and finally processed into an audio wavetable that is used to perform audio synthesis. VOSIS allows the user to generate synthesis from the pixel data from any part of an image or live feed, "Using a multi-touch screen to play image regions of unique frequency content rather than a linear scale of frequencies, it becomes a unique performance tool for experimental and visual music" (McGee, 2013). Applications such as VOSIS can allow for greater compositional control compared with the spectrographic approach, since the user can shift to different areas of focus on the image, for instance as found in the installation "Voice of Sisyphus" (McGee et al., 2012).

Rather than converting pixel data to audio synthesis as mentioned above, this project explores how mapping pixel data to samples can create a cohesive relationship between image and sound that can be used to link the person's digital and physical artefacts, in the case of this installation, a photograph of Matthew's father triggering samples of him playing the guitar.

13.3 VIBROTACTILE EXPERIENCES IN INTERACTIVE ART

Creation of multimodal art installations has been explored in works such as "Sonic Bed London" (Matthews, 2005). This interactive sound installation invited the audience to lie on a bed that had a 12-channel sound system with 6 subwoofers incorporated into the mattress. A similar technique has been adopted in works such as "Wooden Waves" (Perini, 2015) in which sound is output via contact speakers and placed on a wooden floor to create a resonant surface resulting in an audio-tactile installation.

Haptic experiences are also becoming more common in virtual-reality exhibitions. The Touching Masterpieces (2018) exhibition allowed participants to feel sculptural works through the use of haptic gloves, generating a new level of accessibility for people with and without complex disabilities. Other exhibitions such as Haptic Field (Salter and Martinucci, 2016) asked the audience to wear haptic garments that turned the gallery space into a multimodal sensory experience to give users a continually shifting exploration of the relationship between people and technology.

13.3.1 The SUBPAC

The SUBPAC is a tactile audio vest that was initially created to allow music producers to be able to feel the bass frequency spectrum of the music they are making. The device has been used in installation such as "Internal Garden" (Wiggan, 2018) in which the electrical resistance of plants is converted into MIDI note messages with the resulting sound finally processed through the SUBPAC. As Wiggan explains, "by deciphering and registering the impulses and interactions of plants with a device that uses a MIDI interface to transform the impedance from a leaf to the root system of a plant into music, which gives voice to plant perception" (Wiggan, 2018).

Examining the relationship with sound and image through the use of the SUBPAC has been undertaken in events such "Sound in Pictures" (SUBPAC, 2018) in which deaf and hard of hearing participants incorporated the device to gain haptic feedback when creating experimental film and animation. Other interactive installation such as "Seeing Sound and Hearing Frequencies" (Stilon, 2018) uses the SUBPAC to generate a relationship between sound and image. "A music track was chosen and split up into its separate instruments. These instruments were associated with a colour and shape and linked to an Ableton controller so the user could have the ability to choose which instrument to listen to along with seeing visuals associated to that particular instrument" (Stilon, 2018).

Matthew used the SUBPAC in the installation " R e f l e c t" (Evans, 2019), an interactive sound installation. In the case of R e f l e c t, a camera housed in a mirror turned a visual representation into a sonic one through the process of translating pixel data into synthesized sound. The synthesized sound can be then heard on headphones or through loudspeakers. This audio signal was then turned into haptic feedback via the SUBPAC.

13.4 THE SYSTEM

Matthew's father had a deep love for music and was an amateur musician himself, and took a keen interest in writing his own music. This prompted the concept of using his images to catalyse composition, in a sense, having him remain as part of the composition process if only as a source of data. This led to the creation of a generative system (Spiegel, 1985; Eno, 1996; Eigenfeldt and Pasquier, 2013).

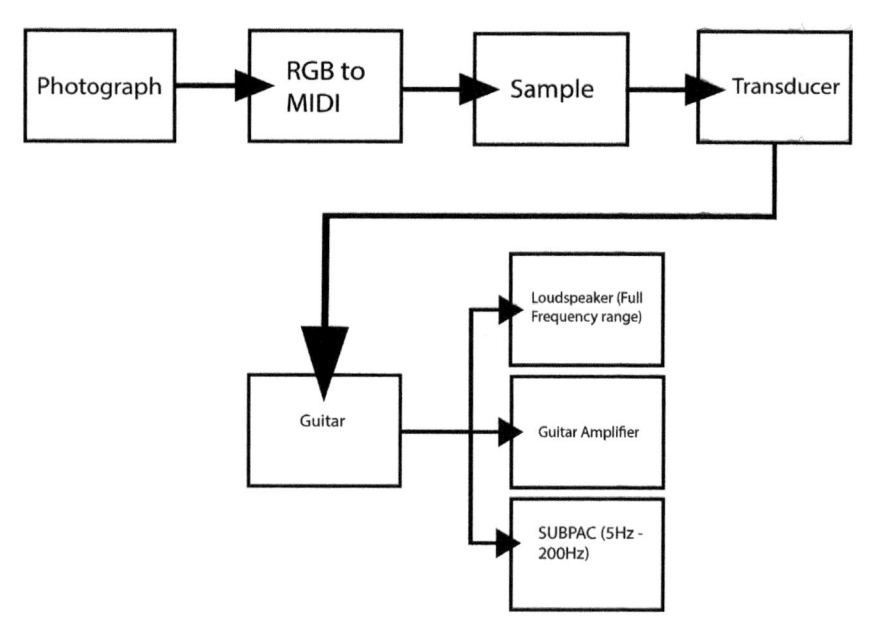

Figure 13.1 Installation process

Hearing and feeling memories

Figure 13.1 explains the process used in the work that translates image to sound to object. RGB pixel data extracted from a photograph of Matthew's late father creates a generative composition by mapping the data to MIDI note messages. These note messages trigger a sample of him playing the guitar, which is output via a vibration transducer. The transducer is attached to the strings of a guitar owned by him, the sound of which is detected by pickups and amplified. The resulting sound is sent through a SUBPAC.

Figure 13.2 outlines the image-to-sound process that has been used in this installation. The system, realized in graphical programming environment Max, begins with the photograph. A probing method (Yeo, 2008) is employed, by which individual pixel data points are read by clicking on the image or raster scanning through it. The spectrographic approach, dependent on image, can produce a very busy sonic output. By implementing the probing approach, the intention has been to create a more nuanced sonic output by selecting individual pixel data points.

The system can be used by clicking on the photograph. Figure 13.3 shows the photograph used in this installation. The probing method allows the user to click on areas of specific interest, for instance the user can 'play' the guitar by clicking on the neck of the instrument. This enables the development of a reflexive and exploratory relationship from the feedback of the sound from the image which can be further informed by the response of the SUBPAC. However, in the case of this installation, an investigation was undertaken into how the mapping of image to sound can establish a paradigm that allows the user to feel more of an audience to the process rather than an active participant.

Each pixel has a red, green and blue value. These three values are gathered and scaled relative to MIDI. (MIDI has a data range of 0–127, the

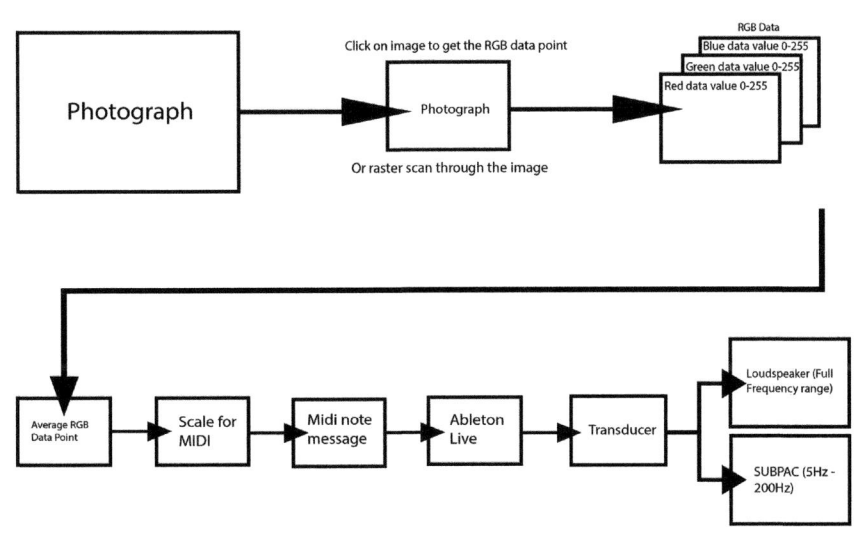

Figure 13.2 Image-to-sound-to-haptic feedback system

Figure 13.3 The photograph of Matthew's father used in the installation

RGB data has range of 0–255, halving this RGB data output allows for the RGB data to be scaled relative to MIDI). This results in the resolution of the image matching the restrictions of the MIDI protocol, meaning no matter what the colour of the pixel is, there is an equivalent note or frequency.

In the case of this installation, the photograph of Matthew's father, triggers a sample of him playing his guitar. The idea of playing the guitar and creating music is embedded in the photograph, therefore how the data is mapped has been chosen to be representative of the meaning of the image. When a person plays an instrument there is a continuous decision process of which note to play, the velocity of those notes, and their duration. Therefore, the average value of each pixel data value is mapped to effect each one of those properties. The photograph used in this installation has a principal set of colours (red, white and black) and by mapping the pixel data points in the ways described, the visual pattern can become a compositional one. For instance, the predominant shade of red of the wall creates the MIDI note G2, the white of the shirt cerates the note G8 and the black of the sofa—although out of the range of piano keys—creates a frequency of 10.91 Hz, which generates a significant response from the SUBPAC.

The initial iterations of the image-to-sound process experiments were undertaken by altering the incoming note pitch based on diatonic scale mapping. This resulted in the sample being pitch shifted to remain in particular modes. However, this reverted far more of the compositional agency to individual and not with the colour or the formation of the pixels of the image. If the user truly wanted to have an experience of being an audience to the image-to-sound process, limiting arbitrary compositional decisions was desirable. Choosing to be less restrictive of areas such as the modality of the sonic output also meant that if the user input a different image there would be a significant difference in the notes that are produced.

Raster scanning as a method of image analysis has been implemented so that the pixel data of the photograph can dictate the rhythm of the composition. Ordinarily raster scanning through an image is done at a steady rate, which when applied in this process produced a monotonous rhythm. To create rhythmic variation, the value of each pixel data point controls the duration of analysis between the data points themselves. This was achieved by mapping the RGB data output of each pixel data point to set the timer of the system. This generates a relationship between each pixel data point and the photograph as a whole and further promotes the model of the image generating the composition.

By using the entirety of the image, the aim has been to preserve the wider contextual information present in the composition of the photograph. For instance, one could crop the photograph to focus more directly on the focal subject matter, however, in doing so a significant amount of data would be removed. In Matthew's case there are a limited number of photographs of his late father, so by incorporating the whole image, the full repository of RGB data is included. Much in the way that *mise en scene* is carefully considered in cinematography and photography, the focal point of the photograph is important, but the location, the lighting, the angle, the colour, all aid in the capturing and preserving of a memory.

Creating a correlation between the subject matter of the photograph and the sonic output is then further integrated through the use of a vibration transducer to output the image-to-sound process through the strings and pickups of Matthew's father's guitar.

13.5 THE SAMPLE

A lot of the image-to-sound applications that have been explored in this study use an internal synthesis algorithm that can result in a sonic output limited to the developer's choice. This can be observed in systems such as "Living Sound Pictures" (Thorborg 2015a), which explores the connection of sounds with images by creating a system that takes a real-time feed of the environment. Thorborg (2015b) states, he aims for the sonic output process to be "aesthetically pleasing". The application generates a polyphonic additive-synthesis output that retains harmony regardless of the visual source, limiting the user concerning the subject. For instance, if one wanted to sonically explore subject matter that would be better represented with noise and discordance, the ability to do so with this application would not be possible. By creating a system that outputs MIDI note messages, the functionality of any digital audio workstation is available, meaning that a potentially greater range of sounds and effects are available. Ableton Live is used in *A-D-S-R*, receiving MIDI data from the Max patch, which is then used to trigger audio events and processing.[1]

In the initial iterations of the compositional output, the translation of image to sound focused on Matthew's memories of his father. On reflecting about their relationship, specific sounds became exceedingly poignant and sonically representative of his relationship with his father. For example, the sound of a dial-up modem connecting to the internet—a familiar sound around his home as a child. An audio clip of dial-up modem was loaded into Ableton Live's "Simpler" and triggered by incoming MIDI messages generated by the pixel data.

Although this provided the work with an output that was sonically rich and complex, this approach of the exploration of personal memory would provide the audience with little correlation between the photograph and sound. It felt more like a therapeutic tool for Matthew himself.

After sifting through other digital artefacts that Matthew had of his father, he came across one recording of him playing the guitar. Much of the audio was unclear, apart from a few seconds of his father strumming. This section of audio was used also used as a sample in Ableton Live, enabling it to become the sonic focal point. By utilizing the RGB data to affect pitch, velocity, duration and rhythm of the sample, this one precious audio clip was able to become far more diverse in its sonic and musical application.

13.6 CONVOLUTION

The final stage of the digital audio processing is the application of convolution reverb. Initial tests with this processing technique were for purely aesthetic reasons, i.e. to provide the composition with a greater sense of ambience and space to create a reflective and meditative environment for the listener. Aesthetically, ambient music is particularly suited for conveying the transitory and ethereal nature of the subject matter within this project. As Adkins explains,

> Whilst ambient music may not rely on traditional functional musical syntax (melody, harmony, and rhythm) it can engender a deep listening experience through slow-moving immersive textures and drones enhanced through the use of noise and fragility to create emergent atmospheres.
>
> (Adkins, 2019)

To further embed Matthew's father as the subject in the work, experimentation was undertaken with what might be used as the impulse response for the convolution process. Drawing on the limited number of digital artefacts related to Matthew's father, there were some recordings of him speaking. Inputting a section of this recording of speech as a sample into Ableton Live's Convolution Reverb plugin gave the composition a novel sonic characteristic by timbrally stamping the triggered samples with Matthew's father's voice. It also provided the composition another way of connecting the subject of the photograph and the and sonic output.

13.7 THE OBJECT

By connecting the digital space and the tangible by the translation of image to sound, a variety of techniques have been implemented to link physical artefacts, and also exploit the physical characteristics of sound through the use of haptic feedback. In doing so, the aim has been to create an immersive sonic and physical experience that provides the audience with a work that allows them to see, hear, and feel this interplay between the multiple media.

Using artefacts in this way in sound art installation has been explored in works such as "Hearing Loss / Cold Atlantic" (Wynne, 2007a) in which the artist uses the hearing aids of his late father to create a feedback field.

> My father died in 2006, leaving behind three pairs of hearing aids and a typically extensive supply of batteries. Hearing aids, like false teeth, are very personal objects which are not only used daily but are actually inserted into bodily orifices. One of the first things that struck me when I began to work with them is that they are made in the shape of my father's ear canals, giving a positive shape to a negative, internal and intimate space that no longer exists. It was literally through these objects that he heard the world during the final years of his life.
>
> (Wynne, 2007b)

Figure 13.4 ADSR installation

One of the physical artefacts that came into Matthew's possession was his father's guitar. This was an instrument that held significant sentimental value. As a child, Matthew and his father went to buy the guitar for his 40th birthday and it was the first instrument that Matthew can remember playing. In connecting the sonic output and posthumous objects, it became of real interest to explore how, through this process of translation, the guitar could be played by 'him' once again. The instrument has been used within the installation in a variety of modes. Firstly, as a physical manifestation of the nature of the situation. Rather than presenting the guitar on a stand, the instrument rests in the open hardcase symbolically evoking a sense of memorial and a final resting place.

The compositional output has been played through a surface vibration speaker, which like *Hearing Loss / Cold Atlantic* generates a feedback field. By mounting the transducer to the strings of his guitar, the strings and the pickups of the instrument colour the output. Like the photograph, this takes the instrument out of stasis. The image is triggering the sound of him playing a guitar and although via an extensive chain, in some sense Matthew's father is playing his instrument again.

13.8 HAPTIC FEEDBACK AND THE CAUSAL CHAIN

The final sonic output of the installation is processed through the SUBPAC. This can be integrated into the translation process to allow for the greater amplification of the tangible qualities of sound, enabling the user to have a more visceral and immersive experience of the installation. The device is placed on a chair and the audience are invited to engage with the installation by sitting whilst the output of the generative composition is played through the device. In doing so the aim is to provide the audience with multisensory experience of the photograph in sound. In creating a haptic response this is to provide a heightened emotional response. As Bonefont explains,

> Sound wave transmission, though on a different level than it, is similar to manual touch in that both are gestures carrying physical energy through space to interact with – to contact - the flesh of another's body. Both seem to be able to generate sensation, and subsequently, emotion, image, and perhaps even meaning for those involved in touch, or sound-touch, relationships with each other. This is a complex and not always linear chain of causality
>
> (Bonenfant, 2008)

In the case of this installation, an attempt has been made to recycle data in a way that can reanimate the digital and the physical. Although a person can never be brought back, the repository of what remains can be used to create new mediums. By using the SUBPAC at the end of this image-to-sound process, a chain can be connected in which a photograph can be both heard and felt.

13.9 CONCLUSION: FUTURE DEVELOPMENTS

In translating an image into sound, multiple modal experiences can be generated. By analysing the digital data stored within an image, it becomes a vast repository of information that can be used creatively. After the death of someone, the digital and the real-world artefacts can be limited, so exploring how new experiences can be generated can provide a new way of experiencing what is left behind. Posthumous photographs become a major source of preserving memories, but they are frozen in time. Through the techniques and approaches explored through this project, the data in an image has been used to catalyse new outputs, reanimating what was locked in stasis.

In future developments of this work, an aim is to explore how these approaches could be used with moving image. In mapping the change of RGB values of a video to a sonic output, a video could create a self-reflexive score, further integrating the relationship between the audio and the visual.

Working on this project has been an extremely helpful tool for Matthew to maintain a relationship with his father. When a sudden loss occurs, there can be an intense feeling of lack of control. This process, however, has allowed Matthew to revisit and reanimate his photographs with a renewed sense of possibility, from circumstances that at the time felt like the end of a process rather than the start of one. At present this research has been focused on Matthew's own relationship with loss. In the future developments of this research, it would be interesting to investigate how this image-to-sound process could be further abstracted as a creative method for others to cope with bereavement.

NOTE

1. The Compositional output can be heard here via Soundcloud: https://soundcloud.com/user-242010528/a-d-s-r

REFERENCES

Adkins, M. (2019) 'Fragility, Noise, And Atmosphere In Ambient Music', in Monty Adkins and Simon Cummings (ed.) *Music Beyond Airports Appraising Ambient Music*. UK: Huddersfield Press, pp. 125.

Bonenfant, Y. (2008). SCAN | journal of media arts culture. [website] Available at: http://scan.net.au/scan/journal/display.php?journal_id=126 [Accessed 31 October 2019].

Brubaker J.R., Hayes G.R. and Dourish, P. (2013) Beyond the Grave: Facebook as a Site for the Expansion of Death and Mourning. *The Information Society*, vol. 29(3): pp. 152–163.

Candy, L. (2006). Practice Based Research: A Guide, CCS Report: 2006-V1.0 November, University of Technology Sydney.

Ciciliani, M. (2015) Scanline Synthesis As a Sonification Method For Digital Images: Techniques and Aesthetic—A Critical Reflection, *Proceedings Of Understanding Visual Music 2015 Symposium*, p. 91.

Eigenfeldt, A. and Pasquier, P. (2013) June. Considering Vertical and Horizontal Context in Corpus-based Generative Electronic Dance Music. In *ICCC* (pp. 72–78).

Eno, B. (1996) Generative Music [website]. Available at: http://www.inmotion magazine.com/eno1.html [Accessed 31 October 2019].

Evans, M. (2019) R e f l e c t [Installation] Birmingham.

Gibson, M., 2004. Melancholy objects. *Mortality*, 9 (4), pp.285–299.

Hunt, L. and Schwartz, V.R. (2010) Capturing the moment: Images and eyewitnessing in history, *Journal of Visual Culture*, Vol. 9, p. 259.

Jette, C. (2013) Soundlines. https://tinyurl.com/y83n4pcg.

Kobayashi, R. (2016) Scanline: Fp [website] Available at: https://player.vimeo.com/video/255927710

Matthews, K. (2005). Sonic Bed_London. [Installation] London.

McGee, R. (2013) VOSIS: A Multi-Touch Image Sonification Interface. In: *NIME*, pp. 460–463.

McGee, R.M., Dickinson, J. and Legrady, G. (2012) Voice of Sisyphus: An Image Sonification Multimedia Installation. Georgia Institute of Technology.

Perini, A. (2015) Wooden Waves. [Installation] Harplinge: BZZZ! international sound art festival.

Rouzic, M. (2018) Photosounder [Software] Available at: https://photosounder.com/

Salter, C. and Martinucci, T. (2016) Haptic Field [Exhibition] Chronus Art Center, Shanghai.

Spiegel, L. (1985) Music Mouse™-An Intelligent Instrument. [Online] Available at: http://retiary.org/ls/programs. html.

Stilon, I. (2018) Seeing Sounds and Feeling Frequency [Installation] Epsom.

SUBPAC. (2018) Sound In Pictures: Visual Music. [Online] Available at: https://subpac.com/sound-in-pictures-visual-music [Accessed 20 November 2019].

Thorborg, J. (2015a) Living Sound Pictures. [Software] Available at: http://www.jthorborg.com/content/lsp/lsp_player.html

Thorborg, J. (2015b) Living Sound Pictures. Sonic College.

Touching Masterpieces (2018) [Exhibition]. National Gallery of Prague.

Wiggan, J. (2018) Internal Garden. [Installation] Birmingham.

Wynne, J. (2007a) Hearing Loss / Cold Atlantic. [Installation] Vancouver.

Wynne, J. (2007b) Hearing_Loss. [website] Available at: http://www.sensitivebrigade.com/Hearing_Loss.htm [Accessed 31 October 2019].

Yeo, W.S. and Berger, J. (2008) Raster scanning: a new approach to image sonification, sound visualization, sound analysis, and synthesis (Doctoral dissertation, Department of Music, Stanford University).

14

Concepts for the design of accessible music technology

Joe Wright

14.1 INTRODUCTION

This chapter explores the concepts and issues arising from research into the design of accessible sonic-play instruments with non-verbal autistic children/young people, and follows on from work previously presented at Innovation in Music in 2017 (Wright, 2019a). This research also draws from inclusive participatory performance practices and aims to increase the breadth of opportunities and choices young people have when interacting with sound and music. Key examples of such practices include projects such as *Sound to Music* (2013) and the *Artism Ensemble* (Bakan, 2015, 2018), where young people shape and/or compose the music made by neurodiverse groups that include neurotypical adults. Bakan's (2015) recollections of the *Artism Ensemble*, perfectly encapsulate the kind of musical context these practices create, he discusses how the neurotypical adults in the ensemble had to be:

> willing to go where the children take them, which is often to places where rhythmic grooves fall apart or fail to emerge, where growing musical momentum and direction suddenly disintegrate for no apparent reason, where they are asked to play things and to play in ways that defy their 'common sense' musical sensibilities, and where they must resist the urge to momentarily take charge of the group to 'fix' the musical problems they encounter.
>
> (Bakan, 2015, p. 120)

These projects could be viewed as attempts on the part of neurotypical adults to engage with music in ways which for them may feel unintuitive, or that in some cases may even clash with their musical enculturation. They are important, as such 'bilingual' (or in these cases bicultural) efforts have been found lacking in society as a whole (Savarese and Savarese, 2010). Parallel arguments have been presented in relation to design as well. In *Design Meets Disability,* Pullin (2009) argues for more radical and critical design approaches in relation to disabled users, where existing designs are predominantly functional or medical in their look and feel.

For Accessible Digital Musical Interfaces (ADMIs), such functional or utilitarian approaches may not meet the aesthetic tastes of a diverse user base either. In her surveys on ADMIs, Frid highlights the diversity among users of accessible instruments, where "[i]ntra-personal differences and preferences may be very dissimilar also for persons *within the same user group* [my emphasis]" (2019, p. 14). This observation is used to highlight the success of highly configurable ADMIs, but this can also be seen as a call to action for designers to come up with a diverse range of new, simple instruments to match a (neuro)diverse population, and a range that has a plurality of musical tastes and needs.

The challenge of this, however, is that design can be seen as an inherently persuasive act, passing biases, intentions and assumptions on the designer's part onto the user (Redström, 2006). Such designs, deliberately persuasive or not, can *push* or *pull* the user, choreographing patterns of human behaviour in both positive and negative ways (Tuuri et al., 2017). Just as Pullin (*ibid.*) has observed medical biases in the design of prosthetics (affecting form, function, look and feel), so too could the design of commercial ADMIs be influenced by music education or therapy, possibly limiting choice for other musical contexts.

The research underpinning this chapter has looked at how ADMIs might be diversified, and at the ways that an instrument might be designed to avoid limiting the user in Artism-esque child-led sessions (Wright, 2019a, 2019b; Wright and Dooley, 2019). The themes discussed below have emerged from this research as prototype sonic-play instruments were put to use in an iterative design process, in collaboration with a group of seven young autistic participants. In light of the group's responses, these themes have potential implications for future ADMI design work, and inclusive musical practice. It is important to stress that the small scale of this study means that the findings presented here can only serve as points for reflection on the design of ADMIs and interactive music technology, and cannot offer concrete solutions or strategies for all situations. Excellent resources do exist elsewhere, however, that provide much more comprehensive design considerations (e.g. Ward et al., 2017), overviews on ADMI research (see Frid, 2018, 2019), or frameworks for inclusive participatory design (e.g. Benton et al., 2012).

14.2 SONIC-PLAY INSTRUMENTS

The desire to explore ADMIs that diverge from musical 'norms' lay at the heart of the design of the first of an ongoing series of sonic-play instruments (Wright, 2019a). Its physical design was simple: a cuboid instrument with a single button-like control surface with LED lights, producing sounds with the *Bela* low latency audio platform (Bela.io, 2019), and an embedded speaker/amplifier (as shown in Figure 14.1). This instrument was designed with two settings: one that enabled clear, replicable control; and another which made the control slightly – but not completely – ambiguous. These congruent and semi-incongruent interaction styles might broadly support *musicking* and *indwelling* orientations of a user towards a musical instrument, the former being concerned with "producing (and precisely controlling) musically organized sounds", and the latter being more about interaction and exploration within a "subjective sonic world" (Tuuri et al., 2017, p. 503).

The prototype was tested in open, child-led musical sessions, which were recorded and later reviewed using methods from play research and inclusive theatre (for details, see: Wright, 2019a). The first phase of testing with this prototype found that, for the small group of participants in the research, both interaction styles could be deeply engaging, depending on the person and the context around the musical activity, affirming the argument made above for the diversification of accessible musical tools.

Drawing from the responses of the group, a second prototype system was developed that could continue to support the diverse playing styles and techniques observed up to that point, but also improve upon the original with superior build quality and additional features (also shown in Figure 14.1). The updated system retained a main cuboid form-factor, with a similar button-like sensor and an embedded speaker, synthesising sound with Bela. The main instrument was also adapted to include an open speaker grille, in the hopes that this would allow more intense engagement with sound, and better sound-projection. The lights that were originally placed above the instrument's sensor were moved inside the instrument, which was diffused by translucent plastic and silicone parts. In addition to this main instrument, five wireless switches were built with a similar, scaled-down appearance that could be used to change the sound and interaction style of the main unit.

The second sonic-play system was tested using similar methods, in open play sessions where the participating young people could explore the instrument on their own terms, with the minimum possible intervention from any accompanying adults (further details of the design and testing of prototypes can be found in: Wright, 2019b). Outlined below

Figure 14.1 Sonic-Play Instruments: Left, first prototype instrument; right, second prototype system

are key concepts and themes that emerged from participants' responses to both prototypes tested in the research. All of the children and young people mentioned below have been given pseudonyms and took part in the research in accordance with ethical guidelines and safeguarding policies at their school, and at Birmingham City University.

14.3 OPENNESS

The term *openness* is used here as a catch all term to describe the relations between a designer's intentions and assumptions for an ADMIs use, and the potential an instrument has to be used in different ways (including those not imagined by the designer). The two sonic-play prototypes had been designed with devices such as the Skoog (Skoog Music, 2019) and BIGmack (Ablenet, 2019) in mind, both have large button or button-like surfaces that can be interacted with. Although a breadth of playing styles had been anticipated, the implicit assumption had been that the prototype would be used as a conventional button, a cube with its sensor facing upwards, to be operated with hands, wrists, and maybe arms. Indeed, this *has* been how the overwhelming majority of neurotypical people have responded to both prototypes during and since this research project. But in reality, the instrument was used by the participants in many more orientations and ways than this, with the four 'unused' faces of the prototypes serving as additional resting points, handholds and supports.

A number of these playing styles are illustrated in Figure 14.2: Anne's pillow technique (Fig.2a), Ben's inverted rock-listen method (Fig.2b), Paul's knee-press technique (Fig.2c), Scott's hug technique (Fig.2d), Tom's head-squeeze technique and co-operative play (Fig.2e and 2f). All illustrate unexpected uses of the instrument during the project. Even when the instrument was used in the expected orientation, it wasn't necessarily operated as expected, as Tom's foot-massage method shows (Fig.2g). With the addition of the switches in later sessions, unexpected modes of use were also seen in Ben's gimbal technique (using a switch as a pivot and pressure point for the instrument as shown in Fig.2h) and stacking methods (Fig.2i). Even the switches alone gave rise to musical and non-musical games. In later sessions, Paul developed what seemed to be a musical gambling method, where he would bounce the switches face-down on the floor, and then line them up to see which ones had turned on or off (Fig.2j), allowing the main unit of the system to musically 'comment' on the outcome. Finally, as an excellent example of how real-world use can subvert expectations or intentions in ADMI design, Stewart – who perhaps wasn't a keen 'sound seeker' (Griffiths, 2019a) – initiated and developed a complicated pattern-matching game using the illuminated switches that came alongside the instrument. This game ended up being a source of great amusement during his sessions. While Stewart never had any trouble matching the patterns he observed, his were lengthy, precise, and fiendishly difficult to replicate.

Even with the explicit aim of making an instrument that would allow people to explore sounds, and with rich prior experiences in inclusive

The design of accessible music technology

theatre supporting the research, the vast breadth of techniques and idiosyncratic playing styles was surprising. This reflected biases assumptions about the ways the instrument may have been used, being reminiscent of adults' experiences playing in the *Artism Ensemble*, as quoted above. If a more complex instrument had been designed for the project, or had a specific kind of interaction been designed for, it is probable that many of these unique practices would not have happened.

It might also be possible, however, to consider in advance how open an instrument may be. For example, the choice of sensor becomes crucial in determining openness for the techniques illustrated below in Figure 14.2. A force sensing resistor (FSR) turned out to be ideal in these situations, as it didn't discriminate against any forces applied to it, regardless of who or what was acting on it. Had a capacitive touch sensor been chosen instead – which may not have been unreasonable for a designer thinking of a button that is operated by hand – many of the above methods would not have worked as there would have been no close-proximity skin contact for the sensor to detect (e.g. Figure 14.2: b, c, d, g, h, i and j).

Figure 14.2 Appropriation of the sonic-play instruments

On the other hand, in some hypothetical situation where a pre-specified action was desired, say in music education or therapy, the use of an FSR would be a hindrance rather than a help, and the capacitive sensor would be a better, more persuasive choice. Of course, a balance can also be struck in this respect, a fine example can be seen in the *Strummi* (Harrison et al., 2019), an ADMI that is designed to be guitar-like in its use, and that is very open within this remit. Any strumming/plucking gestures on this instrument are detected by vibration sensitive piezo transducers, and this means that the instrument can also be explored in other ways that might not be conventionally guitar-like (as a harmonically tuneable drum, a sound amplifying surface, etc.).

Although the idea of persuasion through design is not new, what these responses revealed is just how strong the *push/pull* effects of something as simple as sensor choice can be, having knock-on effects for the un/successful appropriation of an ADMI, and how easily this could have been overlooked. The persuasive or manipulative effects of design choices will ultimately be context specific, with equally context-dependent outcomes for a user. An intriguing outcome of this research was that some choices made the prototype instruments more ambiguous and open, or at least presented conflicting affordances that encouraged players to choose how they felt an instrument should be interacted with. The open, child-led environments that are fostered in groups like the *Artism Ensemble* represent an emerging area where such open or ambiguous musical technologies might have the advantage of allowing young people to discover and express unique embodied relationships with music.

14.4 CONSTRAINTS

In addition to the choice of sensor, a key factor in the prototypes' openness lay in their designed constraints. Anne's pillow method (Figure 14.2a), the co-operative play with Tom (Figure 14.2f), and Ben's gimbal method (Figure 14.2h), are but a few examples where an instrument with additional inputs like Skoog (which has button-like protrusions on five faces of its cubic form) may have become problematic. If the prototype sonic-play instruments had additional sensors added to them in this way, the chances of aligning the instrument consistently for many observed techniques would become more difficult. This is because there are more orientations of the instrument for that technique that will 'work' (i.e. produce sound), but that might produce a different note or sound corresponding with the action: a different sound-event. While a Skoog-style layout might make sound production easier in these observed cases, it also makes it difficult to hold the instrument *without* making a sound, reducing a player's capacity for silence. To enforce this point, a side-by-side comparison of the prototype and Skoog layouts with observed techniques is shown in Figure 14.3, where the former has fewer 'working' orientations, but the latter is far more complex. Again, there is no 'correct' choice to be made here that will suit all contexts. The single button layout was useful for the research outlined above, as it allowed the participating group to explore and form

The design of accessible music technology   225

embodied associations between actions and sounds, which would have been confused by the possibility of triggering extra or other buttons. This comes with a higher potential for error, however, as the blank faces will clearly not produce any sound if the instrument is not oriented properly for the technique. In situations where it is preferable that a user can easily make sounds, without needing to be specific about what those sounds are, the Skoog-like layout would be much more suitable.

Another area that became important to consider during the research was on stylistic constraints, where the output of an ADMI might be restricted prior to use according to some aesthetic criteria. For situations where a young person would ideally be free to choose the ways they make music, as in my study, such constraints – which can be influenced by a designer or music provider – can be very problematic.

This became particularly evident while testing the sonic-play prototypes, where, in spite of a strong commitment to creating a musically open environment, assumptions and biases restricted the musical possibilities for one of the participants. In an early session with the second prototype, for example, Anne had discovered the white noise and sloshing water sounds that the system could make, and lay down on a beanbag with the instruments speaker grille to hear ear (as the 'pillow technique' illustration

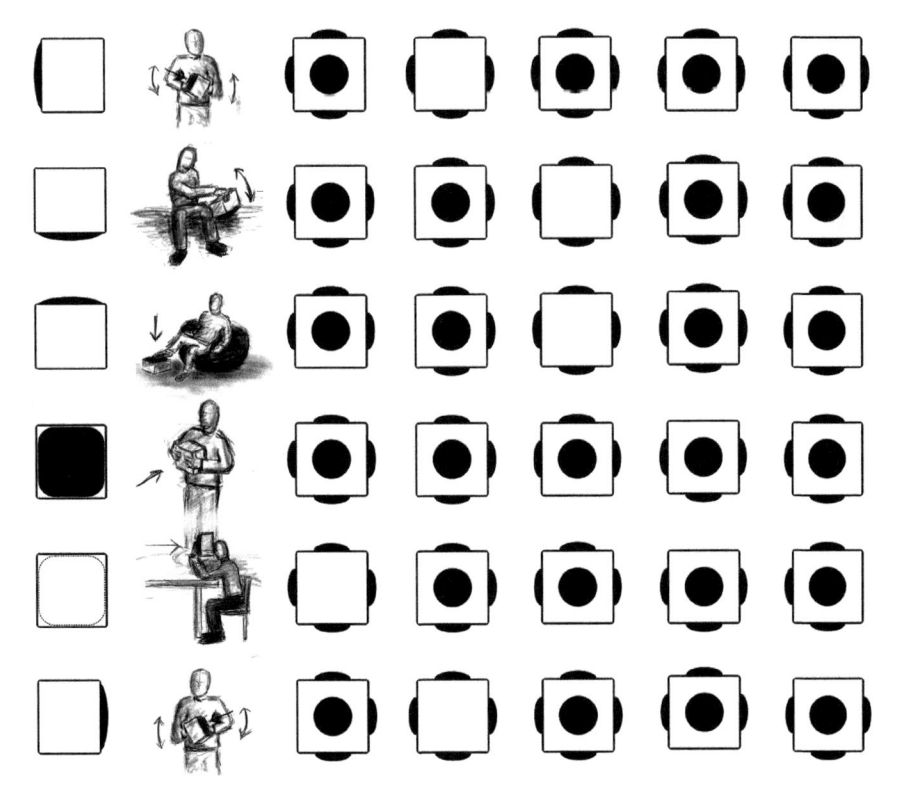

Figure 14.3 'Working' orientations of a 1-button and 5-button ADMI in techniques used during research sessions

in Fig.2a shows). This activity was a breakthrough moment of intense positive engagement with the prototypes: she spent the next few minutes giggling, smiling and laughing at the sounds as they were produced from the weight and movements of her head. At the time, it seemed important to support this new method for playing the instrument for Anne's future sessions, but there were also concerns that the sounds might be too loud in such close proximity to the open speaker grille of the prototype. The sounds were turned down a little, and high frequencies of those sounds were attenuated for the sessions that followed. In those subsequent sessions, however, Anne no longer showed any interest in the prototype as she had done before.

It was only by accident in a later session that it became evident that it was precisely those louder, harsher sounds that were at the heart of Anne's initial positive responses, and her interest in the sounds returned when those kinds of sounds were reintroduced later on in the project. This mistake was made in spite of the wealth of practical experience that went into the planning and delivery of the research. Once again, it illustrates how easily assumptions and biases can affect the delivery and openness of a design process, regardless of the experience and awareness of the researcher.

There may, of course, be situations where it may be appropriate for an instrument to be configured in a pre-defined way (to fit in with a particular ensemble or composition, for example). In a more open situation such as this, however, the more an ADMI can or must be configured by someone other than the actual player of that instrument, the more risk there is of this kind of misunderstanding taking place. Whether or not the actions of a music provider are well intentioned, pre-configuration of the sort described above does risk disempowering the user. Of course, this also comes hand-in-hand with the risk that a more unusual and stylistically constrained instrument could be unpleasant or uninteresting for a user. Thus, considerations of constraints, and the various types of risks associated with them, need to be taken hand-in-hand with the environment in which an ADMI will be used. Seemingly 'risky' stylistic constraints, for example, may be fine in an environment where a person feels safe, or has the option to reject an instrument. Consideration of the musical environment, however, does extend beyond the scope of this chapter.

Broadly, the responses towards the physical and stylistic constraints discussed so far have been reminiscent of previous studies with deliberately constrained instruments (Gurevich et al., 2010; Zappi and McPherson, 2014). Findings of these studies showed that highly constrained instruments elicited highly creative responses and diverse playing styles from participants: this is an area fitting for further research in relation to ADMIs.

One further aspect of constraints was very relevant to the research: the constraints arising from designed interaction styles. That is, the way that an instrument is designed to respond to gestures, and the resulting relationship that forms between a user's gestures, expectations, and experiences. This relationship, interaction-congruence, was the focus of early research with the first prototype instrument (Wright, 2019a). As the research progressed further, however, the constraining effects of interaction styles in these instruments became yet more apparent.

The most notable example of this was seen in Ben's use of the second prototype system. In general, he continued to use the second prototype as he had done the first, by rocking the instrument upside-down, allowing it to 'play itself' under its own weight, and occasionally intervening to make changes or tweaks to the resulting clusters of sounds. As was the case with the first prototype, this practice was aided by sound settings designed to be slightly (but not excessively) chaotic, and by the added indeterminacy introduced by 'hidden affordances' (see Gurevich et al., 2010) in the instrument's material design that caused it to wobble back and forth. This consistency of style was contrasted with one stand out session, in which Ben discovered a technique where the instrument was played by pushing the sensor face-down onto the corner of one of the wireless switches (as shown in Fig.2h). In this moment, the instrument happened to be configured to give congruent control over a looping bell sample, and Ben spent an uncharacteristically long period of time manipulating the bell sounds using this novel technique. Although it is not possible to know how or why the interactions might have been meaningful for Ben, the two interaction styles encouraged certain ways of interacting with the instrument and constrained others: direct control in the congruent style resulted in simultaneous listening and control over the sounds, while the semi-incongruent style encouraged a more indirect, play-listen-play interaction within a bed of somewhat chaotic sounds. These active and indirect approaches might be considered analogues of the *musicking* and *indwelling* stances described by Tuuri et al. (2017).

Both of these techniques were engaging for Ben, and each designed interaction style encouraged a different type of relationship with the prototype system. This shows that both approaches to sound/gesture design have value, and as with many of the features listed above, these styles could be selected for an ADMI based on the type of musical situation (open/pre-defined) an instrument will be used in. As Frid (2019) points out, the approach to sound design/sound synthesis is surprisingly lacking in ADMI literature. The ideas around interaction-congruence are just a small starting point (see: Wright 2019a, 2019b), with only a small amount of field research associated with it at the time of writing. The area of constraints arising from sound design in ADMIs, then, is also area that is rich in potential for further investigation.

14.5 SENSORY COHERENCE AND DIRECTIONALITY

Another interesting area that is underexplored, according to Frid (2018), is in ADMIs that offer multiple modes of sensory feedback. Her surveys have found that ADMIs are more likely to have unimodal feedback or bimodal feedback, and that in her view, vibrotactile feedback is underutilized in inclusive musical instruments. The copresence of auditory, vibrotactile and visual feedback in the updated sonic-play prototypes continued to be an engaging feature in the research sessions with prototype sonic-play instruments. This sensory coherence was probably a major draw for Scott's hugging technique (where the vibrotactile feedback of the instrument can be felt very strongly, see Fig.2d) or in later developments of Tom's head-press method (where both vibration and visual information could be intensely experienced, see Fig.2e). Ward et al. (2017, p. 218) have pointed out that while "the dislocation of excitation and sonification" can be exciting for some, this kind of sensory incoherence can also cause problems for others in understanding cause-effect relationships between gestures and sounds. As well as helping to focus interaction on the instrument, then, instruments with high sensory coherence may help to make such causal relationships clearer. In spite of this, sensorially coherent ADMIs – where multi-modal stimuli are located alongside gestures – are relatively rare: notable exceptions being the Musii (Musii, 2015) and VESBALL (Nath and Young, 2015).

However, it was not just the coherence of sensory feedback that had noteworthy effects on the use of the prototypes in my research, but also the directionality of this feedback. In tests with the first prototype, only Ben had spent any significant time using the instrument upside-down with the sensor on the floor, and this was lessened when the LED lights that were placed on the sensor of the instrument were turned on in later sessions. The appeal of this visual feedback served as a discouragement from techniques that oriented the lights away from view. Changes were made to the second prototype's design in the hope of supporting Ben's activities without limiting those of other participants: an open speaker grille was added at the bottom as opposed to having a speaker inside a sealed, resonant box; and the visual elements were moved inside the instrument, meaning the instrument glowed from the sides, rather than only shining on its top.

The diffusion of the visual feedback had the expected effect of not limiting Ben's inverted-rocking practice with the instrument, but there were unexpected side-effects of changing the second prototype's design in this way. In tests with the second prototype, all but one of the participants explored the instrument oriented both upside-down, as well as in a more typical position. In many cases, this was because the visual details of the speaker grille, and/or the intensity of the sound and vibrations at that point seem to have been just as interesting as the push-button was on the opposite side. It's possible that the accidental 'balancing' of these features, being oriented facing outward on opposite faces of the cube, provided *pull-factors* that encouraged interaction, but didn't *push* the user into a particular orientation of the instrument (as illustrated in Figure 14.4).

For cases like this, the diffusion of stimuli, and the balancing of stimuli in opposite directions, helped to avoid any particular orientation towards the instrument being imposed on a user. The designs became more open after the changes made for the second-iteration prototype. But where a particular orientation *is* desirable, these same strategies could be employed in reverse, though care would need to be taken to ensure the instrument encourages, rather than coerces, the user into a 'correct' action.

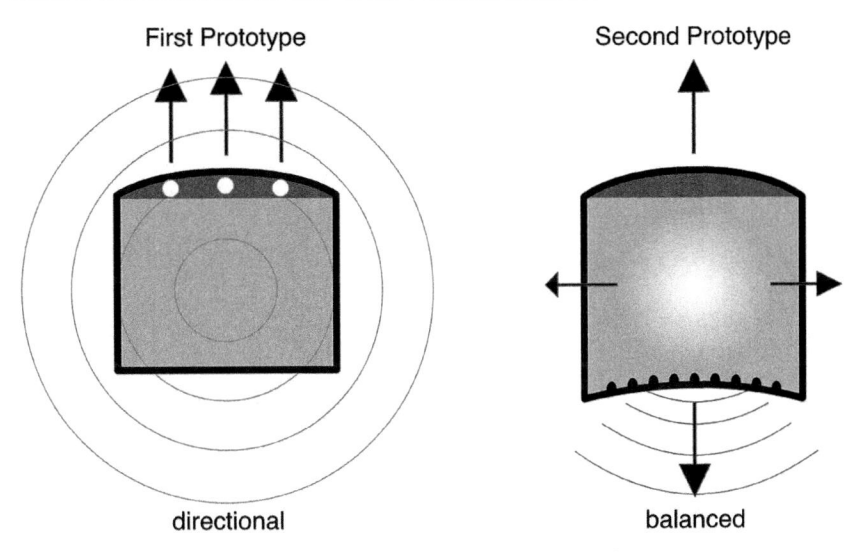

Figure 14.4 Sensory balance in the sonic-play prototype instruments

14.6 ACCESSIBLE CHOICE

The second prototype developed for the research added a small collection of wireless switches to the original design. This allowed some of the same configurability that can be seen in many commercial instruments to be available to the players in research sessions. Following on from the discussion on constraints, however, the range of sounds and interaction styles made available through these switches was far more limited than in commercial ADMIs, taking inspiration from VESBALL's accessible pull-string chord, that could switch the instrument between melodic and rhythmic modes (Nath and Young, 2015). The hope was to provide choices for configuration in an accessible user-ready format, rather than providing a wide range of options that necessitate the pre-configuration of the instrument by someone other than the intended player.

A variety of approaches were taken when testing the second prototype system with the participating group. For some, the switches were swapped out one by one, and participants were able to learn which sounds were associated with them. This was helped by additional consideration of sensory cues, and where those cues were located on the instrument (Wright, 2019b). In other cases, the switches introduced all at once, and were quickly understood and adopted into play with the instrument. Ben, for instance, had understood that the switches changed how the instrument behaved, and mid-way through his exploration of the sounds with his gimbal method, he reached out to the switches, and then thought otherwise. For whatever reason, he had decided not to change the state of the instrument, and therefore left the switches alone.

It is clearly very important that some accessible instruments can be precisely configured for use, and that not every young person will be able to make choices of this kind. However, the accessible choices presented by the switches might offer some users the chance to configure, or to learn to configure, an instrument for themselves. This might in turn open up opportunities for more young people to experience likes and dislikes in sound, and to take charge over the sounds used in musical play, even if the choices made are from a limited set of options as a starting point.

14.7 APPLICATIONS

The above are emergent themes based on the responses to the two prototype instruments that were developed and tested during the research. As has been discussed, the application of these themes is context specific, but could have broad application. Indeed, these themes have carried forward into many recent projects, and into projects planned for the future. This chapter concludes with a few outlines of such projects, and their relation to the themes above.

Ideas around openness applied equally to two inclusive theatre productions – *Sound Symphony* (Independent Arts Projects, 2019) and *Jamboree* (Griffiths, 2019b) – which aimed to create environments where young neurodiverse audiences can interact with, and co-produce the music in performances. For *Sound Symphony* in particular, a lot of time was taken to balance conventional ways of making and experiencing music with less conventional sounds and sound-making objects. The use of more unconventional objects in *Sound Symphony* also ended up highlighting themes in this chapter, independently of the research outlined above. Sound-making props, such as a jacket made from luminescent plastic spoons (in which the visual, haptic and sonic information is all co-located on the garment), had very high sensory coherence. Portable speakers were also used throughout the show to play with the (dis)location of sounds: sometimes to allow recorded sounds to be co-located amidst the live musical elements (rather than coming from a PA system), and at other times to play with the deliberate dislocation of sounds (i.e. where an actors recorded voice projects from the loudspeaker he's holding, rather than being spoken in real time).

The deliberate dislocation of sensory feedback was also key in a recent installation developed for Birmingham-based group, *Ideas of Noise*. The installation featured three central light-sensitive flowers and loudspeakers, surrounded by lights that visually feedback control data to the flowers. The system dislocated the visual feedback from the sensors and sounds, but encouraged interaction in the space between these interdependent sensory elements. Sounds could be manipulated through the casting of shadows onto the flowers. Although this contradicts the thinking behind many features of the prototype sonic-play instruments, the installation serves as a useful counterexample where the dislocation of actions and sounds was exciting for visitors to the sound workshop. The system encouraged exploratory movement and dance that related to the sounds, to space and to visuals. The system also offered accessible choice in the form of a large red button which re-routed the various elements of the system and changed

Figure 14.5 New sonic-play instruments for ongoing research

its sonic behaviour (a rather disruptive element that was a source of mischievous delight for some young workshop goers).

One significant area of work in relation to these themes is in subsequent research on affordable and replicable accessible sonic-play instruments, shown in Figure 14.5. At the time of writing, these instruments can be made at a fraction of the cost of the sonic-play instruments shown above, and, once suitable instructions have been completed, should be replicable by any organization with a 3D printer, or using an inexpensive kit of printed parts. These instruments are built along very similar lines to these original sonic-play prototypes: with a similar form-factor, constrained button-like input (as a starter input device), and coherent auditory/ vibrotactile feedback from an embedded speaker.

Finally, the design concerns have also fed into musical practice beyond the field of inclusive arts. Contributions to a forthcoming duo album of experimental electronic music were performed on a pseudo-modular instrument designed with a constrained set of six one-dimensional controls, and synth design that very closely mirrored that of the second prototype in my study (Onin, 2020).

14.8 SUMMARY

This chapter has discussed some simple themes that, for the research on sonic-play instruments, were both crucial in supporting young peoples' musical play, and difficult to anticipate in advance. One over-arching theme is the *openness* of an ADMI, where high openness might be well suited to child-led ensembles and contexts, but less so where particular skills or actions are choreographed in advance. Constraints were large contributors to the openness of prototypes used in this research, as was the *sensory balance* of the second-iteration instrument. The study also reflects arguments made by Frid (2018, 2019), that sensorially coherent, multi-modal feedback can be an asset to an ADMI, and that it may be worth giving more consideration to the role of sound synthesis in ADMI research. Finally, accessible choices may strike a balance between the high degree of configurability found in commercial ADMIs, and highly constrained instruments, which may be more limited in their broad appeal. Such choices could also play an important role in allowing users to make aesthetic choices for their own music. These themes have continued to be relevant in my subsequent work as a researcher, maker, and musician, and are not limited to inclusive musical contexts. Most importantly, the applications of these concepts are highly context specific; the 'right' choices with regard to openness, constraints, sensory coherence and choice may differ depending on the person, group, time, context, and countless other factors. Crucially, this chapter does not seek to impart 'correct' design choices that will work for all cases, but instead, it aims to illustrate that these are ideas best explored in collaboration and conversation with the people and the environment in which a musical design will be used.

14.9 ACKNOWLEDGEMENTS

The research that underpins this chapter would not have been possible without the contributions, and collaborative efforts of the staff and students in a participating special school. For safeguarding reasons, neither the school nor the individuals within it can be named here. Nonetheless, the hard work, knowledge, creativity and curiosity shown by students and staff alike was a vital source of inspiration and learning throughout the research project. A heartfelt thanks to all who were involved.

REFERENCES

Ablenet, 2019. BIGmack. Available at: https://www.ablenetinc.com/bigmack [accessed 03/11/2019].

Bakan, M., 2015. "Don't Go Changing to Try and Please Me": Combating Essentialism through Ethnography in the Ethnomusicology of Autism. *Ethnomusicology* 59, 116. https://doi.org/10.5406/ethnomusicology.59.1.0116

Bakan, M.B., 2018. *Speaking for Ourselves: Conversations on Life, Music, and Autism*, 1st ed. Oxford University Press, New York.

Bela.io, 2019. Bela: The platform for beautiful interaction. Available at: https://bela.io/ [accessed 11.16.19].

Benton, L., Johnson, H., Ashwin, E., Brosnan, M., Grawemeyer, B., 2012. Developing IDEAS, in: *Proceedings of the 2012 ACM Annual Conference on Human Factors in Computing Systems - CHI '12*. ACM Press, p. 2599. https://doi.org/10.1145/2207676.2208650

Frid, E., 2018. Accessible Digital Musical Instruments-A Survey of Inclusive Instruments, in: *Proceedings of the International Computer Music Conference*. The International Computer Music Association, San Francisco. pp. 53–59.

Frid, E., 2019. Accessible Digital Musical Instruments—A Review of Musical Interfaces in Inclusive Music Practice. *Multimodal Technol. Interact.* 3, 57.

Griffiths, E., 2019a. Keynote Presentation for All Young Stories. Keele University, 26 June 2019.

Griffiths, E., 2019b. Making Jamboree: A Blog from Ellie. Available at: http://www.oilycart.org.uk/about_us/news/making_jamboree/ [accessed 11.15.19].

Gurevich, M., Stapleton, P., Marquez-Borbon, A., 2010. Style and constraint in electronic musical instruments, in: *NIME '10 Proceedings of the 2010 Conference on New Interfaces for Musical Expression*. University of Technology Sydney, pp. 106–111.

Harrison, J., Chamberlain, A., McPherson, A.P., 2019. Accessible Instruments in the Wild: Engaging with a Community of Learning-Disabled Musicians, in: Extended Abstracts of the 2019 CHI Conference on Human Factors in Computing Systems. ACM, p. LBW0247.

Independent Arts Projects, 2019. Sound Symphony by Ellie Griffiths. Available at: http://www.soundsymphony.co.uk/ [accessed 11.15.19].

Musii, 2015. Product Info | Musii – Multisensory Interactive Inflatable.

Nath, A., Young, S., 2015. VESBALL: A ball-shaped instrument for music therapy, in: *Proceedings of the International Conference on New Interfaces for Musical Expression*. Louisiana State University, pp. 387–391.

Pullin, G., 2009. *Design Meets Disability*. MIT Press, Cambridge, MA.

Redström, J., 2006. Persuasive Design: Fringes and Foundations, in: W.A. IJsselsteijin, Y. de Kort., C. Midden, B. Eggen, E., van den Hoven (Eds.), *Persuasive Technology. PERSUASIVE 2006. Lecture Notes in Computer Science*, Vol 3962. Springer, Berlin, Heidelberg, pp. 112–122. https://doi.org/10.1007/11755494_17

Savarese, E.T., Savarese, R.J., 2010. "The Superior Half of Speaking": An Introduction. *Disabil. Stud. Q.* 30. http://dx.doi.org/10.18061/dsq.v30i1.1062

Skoog Music, 2019. Skoogmusic | Accessible Musical Instrument for Everyone!. Available at: http://skoogmusic.com/ [accessed 03/11/19].

Sound to Music, 2013. SOUND to MUSIC – Trailer.

Tuuri, K., Parviainen, J., Pirhonen, A., 2017. Who Controls Who? Embodied Control Within Human–technology Choreographies. *Interact. Comput.* 29, 494–511.

Ward, A., Woodbury, L., Davis, T., 2017. Design Considerations for Instruments for Users with Complex Needs in SEN Settings., in: *NIME '17 Proceedings of the 2017 Conference on New Interfaces for Musical Expression*. Aalborg University.

Wright, J., 2019a. Interaction-Congruence in the Design of Exploratory Sonic Play Instruments With Young People on the Autistic Spectrum, in: Hepworth-Sawyer, Russ., Hodgson, Jay., Paterson, Justin., Toulson, Rob. (Eds.), *Innovation in Music : Performance, Production, Technology, and Business*. Routledge, London.

Wright, J., 2019b. *The Design of Exploratory Sonic-Play Instruments With Non-Verbal Young People on the Autistic Spectrum* (Ph.D. thesis). Royal Birmingham Conservatoire, Birmingham City University, Birmingham, UK.

Wright, J., Dooley, J., 2019. On the Inclusivity of Constraint: Creative Appropriation in Instruments for Neurodiverse Children and Young People, in: Queiroz, M., Sedó, A.X. (Eds.), *Proceedings of the International Conference on New Interfaces for Musical Expression*. UFRGS, Porto Alegre, Brazil, pp. 162–167.

Zappi, V., McPherson, A.P., 2014. Dimensionality and Appropriation in Digital Musical Instrument Design, in: NIME '14 Proceedings of the 2014 Conference on New Interfaces for Musical Expression. Goldsmiths, University of London, pp. 455–460. https://doi.org/10.1055/s-2007-970587

DISCOGRAPHY

Onin (2020), [digital release] *O1N111U1,* FD.

15

Security engineering in the arts

Andy Farnell

15.1 INTRODUCTION

Creative digital arts, comprising film, game and music, have mostly been able to ignore computer security threats. Historically, professional music and media production has used dedicated equipment, processors, consoles, synthesisers, effects racks, and transcoders optimised for DSP. Production processes have been mostly off-line, personal or built around the small production company. Furthermore, there have been few motives to attack creative producers.

By comparison to traditional targets like banks and the military, this combination of low profile and low value assets against which it was hard or impossible to find exploits, made us marginal targets in the last century. But the past two decades have seen production processes move online, become collaborative, distributed and built around commodity general purpose networked computing. Today, international projects are produced using audio and video over IP and complex asset management databases.

Creative media platforms have also become intensely politicised, with increasing cultural divisions between media companies and participants whether as artists or audiences. Starting with the 2014 Sony hack a series of high profile incidents are bringing the vulnerability of creative industries into sharper focus (Melvin and Botelho, 2015).

During the past decade the nature of hacking and the geopolitical environment for digital arts has also changed considerably. A principle text, Anderson's Security Engineering (Anderson, 2008) has been revised through three editions to reflect this. 'Influence' agents of nation state military and quasi-governmental organisations now operate at the level of 'cultural manipulation' – seeding memes, spreading 'fake news', malware, manipulated images and sound. The integrity, provenance and independence of production processes has never been so important to monitor and protect.

15.2 TYPES OF CYBER-THREAT

As for all crime, there is a distinct chemistry to computer crime. Neither victims nor perpetrators are generalists. There are certain kinds of perpetrators with specific motives, tools and opportunities and certain kinds of victims with vulnerabilities and assets. When the right victim finds the right perpetrator, with the right conditions or catalyst, a transgression may take place (Zedner, 2002). For the criminologist it is most important to understand the cultural relationships that set the conditions for crime.

As common examples; Advance fee scammers prey on greed and willingness to collude in a crime, for instance, the classic '419 Nigerian Letter' ruse (Mikkelson, 2001). Blackmail, especially involving sexually explicit photos, leverages shame or fear of exposure (Ellsberg, 1968). Whereas blackmail was once considered a rare and difficult crime to commit, changing conditions of over-sharing, anonymous cryptocurrency, and proliferation of personal data have caused a sharp rise. Some attacks are straightforward revenge or 'hacktivism', which use pranks or exposure (*doxing*) to embarrass overconfident organisations, for example the LulzSec attacks on Stratfor and HB-Gary. Some seek to specifically damage an enemy or competitor's capacity to function, for example the Stuxnet attack by US cyber-command on Iranian nuclear capabilities (Langner, 2011).

By the same logic there are no general solutions to cyber-security. Understanding the chemistry (taxonomy) of a hack can help defenders understand motives and mechanisms, what attractive assets we have that are exposed, and our vulnerabilities. This is how we develop future operational security (opsec) and information security (infosec) strategies. So, what is the chemistry of the 'creative industry' with respect to cyber-crime?

15.2.1 Historical errors

The relation of the arts and entertainments business to digital security has always been rocky. One of the reasons that media producers have much catching up to do in the area of cyber-security lies in the nature of business practices, including some very poorly motivated and misguided efforts over the past 40 years to place focus almost entirely on content protection. A fool's errand of 'copy protection' has squandered the efforts of many smart people whose talents in cryptography and signal processing would have been better employed in more fruitful areas.

In the big picture, one could argue that it is not wasted effort, since nothing has done more to drive development of censorship resistant massively distributed network overlays than the challenge provided by the big entertainments publishers. But pouring money into research and public relations against so-called 'piracy', (an unfortunate misappropriation of an ancient legal term dealing with serious harms), has mainly served to demonstrate a textbook case of sunk cost bias.

More to our point here, arms races driven by 'wars' on abstract ideals tend to produce weaponised code and promote design thinking distorted towards belligerence rather than cultivation or protection. Whereas a 'golden era' of the music business (Krueger, 2019) may have existed from the 1940s to about 1990, in which record companies invested heavily in artist welfare and career development under extended contracts, today media businesses, being 'mediators', tend to treat artists much like customers, as externalities. In the post studio era, as creators of 'works for hire' the artist enjoys little protection and bears all of the responsibility for project delivery.

By taking up opposition to the natural trajectory of the internet as a peer-to-peer information sharing structure, organisations such as the BPI, RIAA and MPAA have made many powerful enemies. Except for companies such as Virgin Media where Internet Service Providers (ISPs) and content creators share corporate ancestry, system administrators are mainly unsympathetic to the needs of an industry they see as entitled. In many quarters, the Sony Pictures Hack of 2014 hack was seen as fair payback for the Sony BMG Rootkit scandal of 2005 in which 20 million infected CDs were released.

15.3 PRE-RELEASE RANSOM

To describe an emerging pattern in attacks affecting the creative industry, which we shall call the premature release threat (or pre-release hack) let us first examine, in vernacular language, some key concepts in information security threat analysis.

The pre-release attack is a form of blackmail with a non-typical execution. To understand the difference between pre-release, classic ransomware, and plain theft, let's note how these superficially similar attacks work with respect to different kinds of value (extrinsic or intrinsic value, and instrumental or market value).

Recall that theft cannot occur when a victim is not deprived of the use of an asset (or in the case of conversion is inadvertently deprived of utility without intent to cause permanent loss). Despite persistent disinformation by politicians and the mass media aimed at conflating copyright infringement with theft, (and widespread ignorance amongst 'expert' internet pundits), we must as computer security thinkers remain clear and precise about words. Not just because of their legal meaning, but because distinct concepts deserve distinct treatments. (This is important because casting the harm as a copyright issue only leads us to the wrong response – trying to use copyright tort law as a remedy against criminals who are not motivated by content. If nothing else, misapplication damages copyright law, as when copyright is used to attack speech. For an example of this consider the European Union's widely criticised Article 13, which is seen by some as back door for corporate control of speech (discussed by Rosati (2019)).

If an attacker gains access to a system, and is able to exfiltrate data, she may then have the additional opportunity to destroy or cryptographically lock the data in-situ. Assuming there is no viable backup of the data this does indeed amount to theft. She can then proceed to ransoming. The attacker offers to return the data, for a price, but this only works if the ransomable value of the stolen goods is more than the market value – otherwise the victim would just buy them afresh rather than give the criminal satisfaction.

The attacker has several choices, depending on her motive. If the data has value to a third party it can be sold. If exfiltration for sale is the objective then destruction of the victim's copy rarely gives any advantage, except out of spite. Indeed, it is probably to the attacker's disadvantage to draw attention to the fact that the data has been accessed.

Alternatively, the data may have no value to a third party, but is uniquely valuable to the victim. This scenario is what has come to be called a ransomware attack. The attacker can either copy the data and destroy the original files, or leave them in place but scramble them with a reversible cryptographic method. The victim must then pay the attacker for access to the key that will get their data back.

In another scenario, the data has intrinsic value because it is sensitive. Here, our victim would not want it widely spread, but not because it is extrinsically valuable enough to sell to a third party. These are the necessary conditions for blackmail. The attacker threatens to widely publish the data, perhaps to social media or to a leaks site, unless money is paid. Of course, the victim is unable to verify whether the blackmailer has destroyed all copies, so blackmail is often an ongoing and escalating crime. However, this means that a blackmail motive is changed when the data sensitivity is time limited. An alternative twist is that the attacker may indeed want to sell the data to a third party who is the actual blackmailer, in which case the data is seen to have instrumental value (and may be commissioned by bounty).

15.4 ISSUES UNIQUE TO THE CREATIVE INDUSTRY

Potentially thousands of hours work go into a creative project. Film edits, mixdowns, and other processes that are intensive in labour or computing cycles have a high extrinsic value. Furthermore, irreplaceable work such as sessions with famous (or deceased) musicians or actors, are unrepeatable performances that have very high non-extrinsic value. Interestingly, such data does not really have a high market value. Watermarking technologies can help thwart resale, although all are removable with some effort, but more practically it's risky and hard to untraceably solicit a buyer for niche data. There is no 'fence' for such specialist wares.

Thus the attack we would most commonly expect to see against creative industries is the ransomware attack. It is easily automated by malware and would be very effective against creative producers because of the high intrinsic asset value. But that is not what we have seen in the Disney or Radiohead attacks. One reason is that many creative producers are unusually good at backups. Ransomware attacks totally fail if there are off-line backups. Indeed, musicians and filmmakers seem to be way ahead of other businesses, even banks, in their diligent valuation of their work. Here is a clue as to why attacks on creative producers fall into a slightly new class.

Blackmail is where the attacker threatens to violate the secrecy of the victim. Normally, for blackmail to work, there must be a psychological dimension of shame. The attacker knows that the victim would suffer reputational damage if the data were made public. The victim is compatible with the attack because negatively sensitive data constitutes evidence that they have done something bad. More rarely blackmail works because the victim would suffer financial damage from publication of the data. It's not that they have done something wrong, but that it would advantage a competitor, perhaps by revealing a manufacturing secret or trade relationship. The 'premature release threat' seen in recent blackmail incidents against creative producers are also *exposure* threats, but are a little different. They rely on the fact that what the victim has done is really good! It works in an industry where holding back positively sensitive information is vital to creating value.

Throughout the history of music recording and filmmaking, artists have worked to a pattern of *'releasing'* a record or movie. Building public anticipation and controlling knowledge about upcoming products avoids spoilers and premature critical analysis. To do that, the work must be kept under wraps. Due to a limited palette of narrative forms, and long production cycles, the game industry is extraordinarily sensitive (to the point of self-defeating paranoia) about this.

Security engineers without experience of the creative industry may find it harder to understand this threat model, and why certain works are more sensitive than they might appear. Imagine if, as conspiracy theorists enjoin us, all sporting events were rigged. Releasing the scores for a season of upcoming football games would utterly ruin that industry because it is enmeshed with gambling and other industries. Yet the football games themselves would be no different, and just as entertaining to a naive observer.

This reliance on adding non-extrinsic value by creating an 'event' or *'experience'* has grown enormously in the entertainments industry due to competition. It is getting harder to differentiate products at the level of mere market value or artistic quality. This opens an opportunity for a new kind of blackmail that has more in common with kidnap than ordinary theft.

15.5 ULTERIOR MOTIVES AND DECEPTIONS

The above analysis only touches the surface values. There are deeper game theoretical elements of bluff to consider. 'Did Disney really get hacked?', was the question widely asked in the media following news that the latest instalment of Pirates of the Caribbean had been snarfed.

With a kidnap it is traditional to offer the ransom payer some evidence that the hostage is indeed captive and alive, such as a lock of hair or item of clothing. Apart from a short clip, Disney got no proof that the movie had been exfiltrated substantially or in its entirety.

It's quite possible for a sophisticated attacker who cannot complete the heist to leave deliberate evidence, misdirection telling a false story. Real-life virtual kidnapping scams, where the situation does not allow the ransom payer to verify the abductor's claims can be mirrored in the digital realm. For example, a network may be taken down or a DNS or authentication host disabled while a spurious claim is proffered. Now, because IT diagnostics, and incident response take time, executives may be panicked into making a payment for a non-existent incident. In this case it seems Disney called the attacker's bluff, and it paid off.

To make things more difficult for security engineers there is the further problem that the entertainments business plays games with disclosure. It tantalises audiences with 'sneak previews', candid exclusive interviews, and 'guerrilla trailers'. This means that hacks can be tacitly endorsed 'inside jobs'. As in real life, kidnappings can be faked, as collusions between the abductee and kidnapper to defraud a third party.

This can be played out in the digital realm too. Due to great structural complexity and tensions between parts of the business – directors, production houses, publishers, distributors, regions, and marketing departments – anyone who knows how this industry really works knows that sometimes leaks are orchestrated. Hacks are even tacitly approved in order to 'create a buzz'. Whether or not anybody would admit this, Hollywood is a tangle of political machinations. At the present time, with cyber-security in the news again, it seems that 'getting hacked' is the latest cool thing. This dangerous game of crying wolf makes the already hard job of securing creative assets even harder.

15.6 ART, POLITICS AND CONFLICT

Art and politics have always been entwined. Painters have lost their heads for unflattering portraits of kings and queens. Music and film played a vital role in the propaganda efforts of the Nazis, Soviet and Cuban regimes, and on the Allied side in World War II. More recently Vladislav Surkov, Vladimir Putin's strategic information warfare adviser has revived artistic 'non-linear warfare' and taken it to a new level of sophistication (Curtis, 2016).

By comparison the Seth Rogen comedy *The Interview*, which popular analysts (Elkind, 2015) claim precipitated the 2014 Sony attack, seems unsophisticated and clumsy. Nonetheless it would be naive to mistake Hollywood as nothing but an entertainments industry, and that the film was innocent buffoonery. Who controls the culture of a nation controls its economy and stability. Post-war New Deal era films painted the USA as 'courageous world saviours', then the Cold War and Vietnam eras gave way to fear-based messaging. This agenda ran until about a decade after 9/11 World Trade Center bombings after which 'anxiety fatigue', economic decline and self-doubt rendered it ineffective for cultural sintering. Starting with Parker and Stone's 2004 Team America, up to the Trump era of 'post truth', ridicule, radical cynicism and contempt (Waller, 2006) form the new coding through which Rogen's mocking of Kim Jong-un must be understood.

What does this mean for cyber-security? As forms of expression, Art and Literature can be a serious business. Apparent cyber-crime may really be cultural conflict. We already accept that journalists and their organisations face ongoing threats to life and liberty for their writing. Most recently (June 2019) *The Intercept* came under cyber-attack by ex-NSA employees acting as mercenaries for the UAE government attempting to expose critical (dissident) writers (Biddle and Cole, 2019). Textbook authors and academics are now coming under scrutiny in the USA, as intellectuals attending conferences or giving visiting talks find their visa applications mysteriously blocked.

In the absence of working diplomacy, rule of international law and respectful inter-cultural norms, it seems that any media production company can now be targeted by state actors, including hacking by foreign or domestic intelligence agencies intent on influencing or sabotaging a cultural work. Is this a realistic scenario?

Consider the impact of Salman Rushdie's *Satanic Verses* (Rushdie, 1988), and the response of some Muslims to what were otherwise considered mild satirical cartoons by the Danish artist Kurt Westergaard. It sent shockwaves through the West. And yet we ourselves are edging toward the same censorship against which our cultural identity of 'freedom and tolerance' is predicated. If the West continues to shut down explicit free speech in its written and spoken forms, more provocative forms of art are likely to emerge along with friction between various groups. 'Speech' is therefore a new battleground on which the values of liberal democracy as 21st Century Occidental 'Anglo-Saxon' culture will be fought, and it will encompass music, lyrics, film, games, and fictional literature.

15.7 HACKING AS ART

This brings us back to LulzSec and the reasons why we need to be careful not to cast some actions that are not crimes (in the criminological sense) as such. In addition to its ambivalence around leaks I feel the entertainments industry faces a far more complex relation with 'hacking' in its future.

'Employees logging on to (Sony's) network were met with the sound of gunfire, scrolling threats, and the menacing image of a fiery skeleton looming over the tiny zombified heads of the studio's top two executives' (Elkind, 2015).

What is interesting about this report of the Sony hack is that such high melodramatics and theatrical flourish of the hackers does not accord with the conduct of disciplined state actors. Attribution is notoriously unreliable in forensic cyber-security, and as the Vault-7 releases revealed there are accessible toolkits specifically designed for misdirection. For infosec experts how the hack was pulled off is the most important part of the story. For politicians the most important question should be why? But it is not. What they really care about is: who gets the blame? Thus 'attribution engineering' is a growing concern.

Indeed, the *Fortune Magazine* analysis concludes that the Sony attack could have been carried out by 'practically any sophomore cyber-security student'. Let's not avoid pointing out that Sony 'had it coming' for many reasons, and had many enemies for whom laying the stunt at the feet of the North Koreans would be a sweet cherry on the cake. The fact that it cost Sony millions may just be 'collateral damage' (ibid).

Elements of irony and poetic justice abound in hacking. The Stratfor attack, on the face of it was a minor website defacement and leak designed to cause embarrassment, but the real payload was the transfer of hundreds of thousands of dollars from large corporations with 'suspect ethics' running 'worldwide networks of informants engaged in intrusive and possibly illegal surveillance activities' (Sledge and Minkovski (2013) quoting hacker Jeremy Hammond) to charities – creating widespread sympathy for the hackers who were dubbed 'Robin Hood Hackers' by the mainstream press.

It would be remiss of security engineers not to recognise that hacking as political art lies outside the conceptual frameworks of cyber-crime or state surveillance as described in the first section. It does not fit within the same moral framework of harms and motives. Again, despite concerted mass media effort to conflate hacking with cyber-crime, vernacular use of the word encompasses all kinds of appropriation, subversion, self-determination, recycling, creative construction and destruction. Even if none of these acts in fact constitute protest or dissent, let alone computer intrusion (network penetration) there is a creeping project to redefine ownership so that users are ever more disenfranchised from their own property, thus redefining such simple legitimate activities as repairing, modifying and sharing as 'hacking'.

This is typified by the case of John Deere, still locked in battle opposing US citizens 'right to repair'. Artists should soon expect this controlling megalomania to extend to their use of proprietary creative tools, perhaps placing limits such as 'approved creative work-flows' – the games industry is already dominated by a small number of 'engines' whose licences effectively police what can and cannot be made. In October 2018, Adobe unilaterally shut off the entire creative cloud infrastructure of a whole country after US President Trump issued a trade diktat against Venezuela, an event that should serve as a warning to any creative organisation or individual using 'cloud based software as a service'.

Art viz. subversion, subterfuge, juxtaposition, trolling, lampooning, and caricature, is intimately enmeshed with political discourse which underwrites a free democracy, a point exquisitely made by Hislop and Newman (2019) in their dramatisation of satirist William Hone's 1817 trial by a British kangaroo court. To that end, the arts have many traditional legal protections forming the basis on which a liberal entertainments industry is able to exist in the first place. Despite 'incoherent attacks on free speech' (Malik, 2018), comedy and satire have always been protected – culturally as well as legally – to the extent that Jewish comedians and stalwart opponents of anti-Semitism flocked to the defence of silly 'Nazi Pug' joker Mark Meechan. This expression in problematic digital forms is only going to increase in direct proportion to clampdowns on more traditional speech as entrenched power encounters more challenges to its legitimacy and competence.

Security engineers must therefore take note that the entertainments industry is not a stable ecosystem. In the battle between Art and speech qua authentic expression and the entertainment 'industry' qua marketable produce acceptable to advertisers, the first battle was over control of the means of production. The artists won by adopting enabling digital technologies, while the industry maintained substantial control over the means of dissemination by buying laws to effectively restructure the internet away from a peered model.

The second major conflict was over copyright. It was a fight the publishers (MPAA, RIAA, BPI etc.) ostensibly won. They won because the artists were ambivalent about monetising their products, and ultimately 'consumer' audiences were satiated more by the carrot of cheap and convenient products than by the stick of legal threats. This can be seen as a purely economic market adjustment, long overdue for an industry with extraordinary profit margins. The real copyright battle regarding use, is yet to be decided. As a tactical prospect the industrialists may declare victory by way of legal purchase (DMCA etc.), but they have wholeheartedly lost at the strategic moral level, and that blow-back is yet to come.

If content qua 'speech' becomes the new cause célèbre it seems unlikely that state actors will actually have any direct involvement, other than in their legitimate role as glacially slow legislators. Kim Jong-un's cyber army are less of a threat than the Hollywood tales tell. In reality, these kinds of hacks are just dry runs for much more devastating and subtle 'interferences' by agencies in China, Russia and the USA.

A risk for cyber-security personnel will be that we are entering a battle between an industry, its own customers, and its own artists, as the tools and targets of influence conducted by digital subterfuge, likely to be a complex and un-civil intra-cultural war. If security engineers are set up as soldiers without understanding the culture and history of this battleground it will be a Vietnam or Afghanistan. Artists can help mitigate this by thinking carefully about their production security, who owns and controls their tools, to what ends their work is being turned, and by whom.

15.8 CONCLUSIONS

For the most part, the digital revolution in the arts has been about tools, but technology affects much more, bringing enabling and disabling effects to other areas. In the digital age, our arts and entertainments industry is built upon a tension, since security and creativity do not happily occupy the same space. Our film, game and music businesses enjoy a privileged position, unique in history and world culture, for tremendous freedom of expression, afforded by so many sacrifices made in defence of liberal democracy. With authoritarianism on the rise again the same industry needs to meet its obligation to defend those values by taking greater care with its use of technology.

However, it currently acts only in pursuit of self-interest and control. By advancing problematic technologies for copy protection, tracking, over-connectedness and surveillance which serve its publishers, advertisers and spies – rather than promoting privacy and freedom-enabling creative technologies – it acts to undermine and deny those same freedoms to its audiences and artists. Hollywood and the mass media, by conflating all hackers with criminals acts to alienate a creative mindset with which they ought to be allied. As its dependence on technology makes it ever more vulnerable the industry lags in capability, is naive in its understanding of geopolitical complexity, and falls supplicant to malevolent seats of power. There is much to be done in the future to help those working in arts and entertainments manage technology more thoughtfully.

REFERENCES

Anderson, R. (2008) *Security Engineering: A Guide to Building Dependable Distributed Systems*. Wiley.

Biddle, S. and Cole, M. 'Project Raven: Team of American Hackers and Emirati Spies Discussed Attacking The Intercept'. *The Intercept*, 12 June 2019. First Look Media.

BBC News (2019) 'Adobe Shuts down Photoshop in Venezuela'. 8 October 2019. BBC.

Curtis, Adam. (2016) 'HyperNormalisation'. BBC documentary.

Elkind, P. (June 2015) 'Sony Pictures: Inside the Hack of the Century'. In: *Fortune Magazine*.

Ellsberg, D. (1968) 'The Theory and Practice of Blackmail'. RAND Corporation, Document P-3883.

Hislop, I. and Newman, N. (2019) 'Trial by Laughter', BBC Radio Drama.

Krueger, A. (2019) *Rockonomics How Music Explains Everything About the Economy*. John Murray.

Langner, R. (2011). 'Stuxnet: Dissecting a Cyberwarfare Weapon'. In: *IEEE Symposium on Security and Privacy*.

Malik, K. (2018) 'The "Nazi Pug": Giving Offence is Inevitable and Often Necessary in a Plural Society', *The Guardian*, 25 March 2018.

Melvin, D. and Botelho, G. (Apr. 2015) 'Cyberattack Disables 11 French TV Channels and Takes Over Social Media Sites'. In: CNN.

Mikkelson, D. (2001) 'Nigerian (419) Scam'. In: *Snopes* (August edition).

Rosati, E. (2019) 'The EU's Long Journey Toward Banning Memes', *Slate Future Tense*, 19 September, Slate Group LLC.

Rushdie, S. (1988). *The Satanic Verses*. Vintage.

Sledge, M. and Minkovski, A. (2013) 'Jeremy Hammond Sentenced To 10 Years In Prison', *Huffington Post*, November 15, 2013.

Waller, J. M. (2006) 'Ridicule as a Weapon'. In: *Public Diplomacy White Papers*, 7 January.

Wiens, K. and Chamberlain, E. (2019) 'John Deere Just Swindled Farmers out of Their Right to Repair'. WIRED September 2018. Condé Nast Group.

Zedner, L. (2002) 'Victims'. In: ed. by R. Morgan, M. Maguire and R. Reiner. *The Oxford Handbook of Criminology*. Oxford University Press.

Part III
Performance Innovation

16

Transparency and authenticity in the live arena

An exploration of electronic music performance techniques

Dave Fortune

16.1 INTRODUCTION

> The means to create electronic music didn't happen in real time; it was well thought out and calculated, finely detailed and labored [sic] over in studios for countless hours. Replicating this material in a live setting is a challenging task, and most electronic artists have historically been happy to stick to DJing as their method of performance.
>
> (Jones, 2016)

For practitioners within the field of contemporary electronic music performance who attempt to respond to this particular challenge, there is a diverse range of existing conventions and methodologies that bring with them their own unique benefits and flaws. This chapter focuses on the interaction between the physical, visual, and audio elements of electronic music performance, and addresses questions regarding authenticity and transparency within the works of many current performers. These issues are particularly evident when compared to established conventions of what constitutes a 'live' performance, where a physical movement typically engenders a specific sound, and the audience is able to identify an obvious link between the two. In response to observations of certain practitioners, a number of alternative paradigms to live electronic performance are proposed that augment the methodologies examined herein.

These alternatives are realised by extending the functionality of pre-existing hardware MIDI controllers using the software platform Max to create new musical interfaces; the interfaces are then employed to create multi-part performances of electronic music works. The traditional model of 'live' instrumental performance is mainly eschewed in favour of techniques, which are more commonly used in the creation of contemporary popular electronic music, specifically sequencing, loop manipulation and signal processing; with a focus on the visual communication of these processes to the audience.

In addition to these practical aims, this practice-based study is highly motivated by the almost limitless options offered by the discipline of live electronic performance. Alfred Darlington aka Daedelus has discussed this within the context of his own transition from being a composer and performer of jazz music, to carrying out those same roles within the field of electronic music. He argues that, for him, "that emphasis on electronics is an infinite possibility" (Darlington, 2015), apparently not sonically or physically limited by the constraints and limitations of acoustic instrumentation. He describes his chosen path as being "thrilling but also very challenging to find [his] performance ends", and affirms that "it's hard sometimes to Figure out where you fit into that infinity" (Ibid.). This project's primary aim is to present alternatives to previously explored methodologies, but in doing so also aims to ascertain where an individual user's performance repertoire might fit into *that infinity*, and establish a unique identity within the field of electronic music performance.

16.2 BACKGROUND AND RELATED WORK

As Jones has remarked, many electronic music practitioners opt for DJing as their preferred method of live performance; while certainly not without artistic merit, the role of DJ is usually concerned more with the curation of existing musical works than the creation of original musical material. In addition to this, DJing employs methods that are fairly well established and understood by their audiences. For live electronic performance this is generally not the case and, perhaps because of this, it has frequently attracted scepticism and criticism, even for some of the most revered artists in the history of the genre. When Kraftwerk began bringing their music to a live arena, the notion of 'machines' replacing 'conventional instruments' on stage was widely considered to be "a cheat perpetrated by people that couldn't play proper instruments, or a plot to deprive regular musicians from earning a living" (Bussy, 2005, p.54). Bussy describes technical issues, and disappointment from fans and critics alike during both their Autobahn and Radio-Activity tours in the mid-70s. He suggests that it was only in the 80s when their live shows became far more regimented, and virtually indiscernible from their studio recordings (to all intents and purposes not particularly 'live'), that they began to receive universal acclaim for their performances (Ibid.). Cunningham (1999, pp.191–192) details the frequent technical issues that Jean Michel Jarre experienced during his debut European tour and claims that "the show lacked emotion in part and relied on the impact of the visuals, but what does one expect from a vocal-less synthesizer act, regardless of its unquestionable musical skills?" When discussing the live shows performed by the likes of Orbital and Underworld in the 90s, Reynolds (2013, p.193) neglects to even comment on the quality of their performances, simply dismissing their live shows as one of a "resurgence of rock notions".

In recent years audiences and critics may have become more open-minded to live electronic music, however performers themselves are still far from establishing a unified methodology for their practice, and as such there seems to be considerable discrepancies between opinions on what constitutes a 'live' electronic performance. For analytical purposes, the broad spectrum of existing methodologies are separated in this chapter into two categories: the *'Band with Backing Track'* and *'Studio on Stage'*. The former tends to be favoured by mainstream electronic acts, often those whose appeal crosses over to pop and rock audiences; this aesthetic approach is adopted in Faithless and Moby's live shows in the late 90s, and more recently by Netsky and Rudimental. These artists appear to presume that their audiences will identify more with a 'traditional' live band setup, and employ live instrumentation, often accompanied by backing tracks. Given that these artists' studio productions are often characterised by heavily sequenced and processed elements, one could question the choice to reproduce this with live instrumentation.

The latter approach, employed by artists including Orbital and Octave One, adheres more to a DJ-like aesthetic, where the artist spends most of the performance adjusting parameters on various pieces of studio hardware or software, often too subtle for their exact function to be perceived by the audience. While this method could be considered more 'authentic', in that it strongly reflects the actual music creation process, it does not offer as strong a connection between the visual and audio elements of the performance as the aforementioned approach. In the section that follows, these methodologies are examined further, alongside ways in which they have inspired performance methodologies within this project.

16.3 AUTHENTICITY VS. VISUAL STIMULI

While the two methodologies discussed above are not without considerable merit, they also present clear shortcomings: the 'Band with Backing Track' offers strong visual elements but it is questionable whether these elements actually reflect what is being heard, which risks alienating audiences that demand authenticity of performance from an artist. The 'Studio on Stage', by contrast, represents a truer, more honest performance that can lack sufficient visual stimuli. Further exploration is therefore warranted of what can be achieved by focusing on the most successful elements from these two methodologies, or as Golden (2012) summarises, "a healthy balance of playing live and sequencing that will create a memorable experience for both audiences and performers". With the 'Studio on Stage' methodology, much of the focus is on creating an authentic representation of the studio techniques that were employed in the creation of a piece, most notably sequencing and audio manipulation. It is worth noting the minimal presence of 'traditional' musical performance in live shows of many such artists; this makes perfect sense in that it reflects the methods employed in the studio. The former approach, while lacking in the same level of authenticity, has more of a focus on visual elements that the audience can connect to audio events that they are hearing.

To elucidate the principle aims at this stage in the project, it was intended that a performance system is created that:

1. Allows the user to perform a multi-part musical work that utilises techniques which characterise the initial studio composition and

production process (specifically sequencing, audio manipulation and signal processing)
2. Executes the above processes in ways that provide sufficient visual stimuli for the audience to perceive the processes that are taking place

16.4 DEVELOPMENT AND INSPIRATION – DRUM SEQUENCER

The first of the two instruments that form the system was born out of a previous research project where Max was employed to create a MIDI step sequencer that was controlled by, and offered basic visual feedback to, a rotary-encoder-based MIDI controller. While intended as a studio tool, it became apparent that it was highly intuitive and efficient for programming rhythmic patterns, something that could be exploited in a live context. Such devices are commonplace in live electronic performance, however typically do not provide the necessary visual stimuli for the audience to accurately perceive their operation. In order for this to be achieved, all steps of a given sequence would need to be clearly visible, and crucially they should be simultaneously displayed in multiple instances to represent the different drum parts that make up a sequence. Previous practice-based research of such devices determined that 8 tracks of 16 steps each would be the ideal configuration here; significantly more would be too complex for the audience to accurately perceive and for the user to quickly programme during a performance, while fewer would not be able to provide sufficient rhythmic complexity and timbral diversity.

The most satisfactory solution identified for the above criteria was that of a large multicolour light-up grid-based interface; despite the prevalence of these devices, after thorough research it was found that that there were very few devices on the market that began to approach the required specifications in terms of visible tracks and sequencer steps. Perhaps this is a result of most devices being aimed towards a studio environment, or more explicitly "a real failure from other music software [and hardware] developers to even attempt to approach live performance in their designs head-on" (Kirn, 2012). The devices chosen for this purpose were two Akai APC20s: MIDI controllers which are intended to perform pre-determined functions within Ableton Live, but also capable of sending and receiving standard MIDI data, and therefore ideal for the needs of this project. When placed side-by-side they offer an 8x16 grid matrix in addition to MIDI faders and rotary encoders (it was later discovered that only five of the eight rows supported multicolour illumination, and a 'scroll' function therefore had to be implemented to incorporate the eight drum tracks).

A key, innovative feature which was crucial to the capabilities of this instrument was regarding the pattern loop points. It is fairly common for a step sequencer to have the option to adjust the end point of a loop allowing shorter patterns or even irregular loop lengths, but not the additional capability to adjust the start *and* end points of a loop 'on the fly'. While this would have limited use in a studio context, it opens up vast potential for embellishment and improvisation in a live environment; at any given time, the user can choose to repeat any section of the available pattern at the press of a button. This is further augmented by the unusual capability to do this on a per-track basis, so that any of the eight drum tracks can be looped in different places, to produce complex evolving rhythmic patterns, or have short two or three step motifs looped to create fills and syncopated variations.

16.5 'THE TOUCH SCREEN REVOLUTION'

At this stage it is appropriate to briefly mention another popular control device that that was ruled out, and the justification behind this. The device in question is the 'touch screen controller' – commonly an iPad or Android-based tablet. Max has the capability to communicate very effectively (even wirelessly) with apps such as TouchOSC, Lemur or Mira, which allow the user to design their own configuration of buttons, dials and sliders; far more versatile, one might argue, than using a pre-determined hardware control surface with a fixed layout of controls. Despite this versatility, such apps exhibit a considerable shortcoming – one that is crucial to the requirements of this project. This is, somewhat ironically given the "TouchOSC" moniker, the fact that the user cannot actually touch or feel any of such 'virtual' controls. This requires the user to be constantly looking at the screen of the device at nearly every moment the device is being operated to make sure their fingers are in the right place. This would make it virtually impossible to look at, and operate multiple devices simultaneously (as occurred often during the practical performance), as well as looking at one of the most important elements of a live performance – the audience.

16.6 DEVELOPMENT AND INSPIRATION – LOOP SEQUENCER

With the drum sequencer handling the majority of the drum and percussion elements of a given performance, methods of performing the melodic and harmonic elements were also required, which for many electronic artists mainly consist of the use of synthesiser motifs and audio loops. Again, given considerations of the performance reflecting the production process, traditional 'live' playing will often be rejected in favour of using some type of sequenced technique. During production sessions for musical material that would form part of the live performance for this project, it became apparent that many of the working methods employed are not conducive to being replicated accurately in a live environment using a setup that would be an accurate recreation of the exact studio methods. Some of these include complex audio routing patterns, reliance on meticulously programmed MIDI CC (continuous controller) or automation data, or simply doing far more things than it would be possible to achieve with two hands, and therefore incredibly difficult to convincingly reproduce in a performance context.

There is also the consideration of which processes will actually enhance the audience's experience if performed live. The audience may appreciate seeing live manipulation of a parameter that is being audibly changed, such as a drastic filter sweep, however there is little benefit to performing complex signal processing or editing that remains static throughout a piece, certainly without accompanying 'live' visual movements with which to form meaningful constructs. While both examples are crucial to a composition, there is little benefit to incorporating the latter into a performance. In a live context it is therefore more useful to use stems, or audio mixdowns of material that retain the necessary audio processing, but can be triggered and further manipulated. The triggering of audio stems enables the user to retain complex editing and signal processing in a performance, but without actually performing the signal processing live, something that would be laborious and add little or nothing to an audience's enjoyment of the performance.

The above perspective is consistent with that discussed by Ferreira (2012, p.4) who argues that "performance in EDM [electronic dance music] is not a question of localized agency, but of the effective mediation between recorded sounds and collective movements" or more plainly "human movements making visible what machine sounds are making audible" (Ibid.). It is therefore entirely logical to manipulate pre-prepared audio stems, as long as the actions that provide the manipulation can be perceived by the audience.

The triggering of audio loops and samples is the premise that many electronic performers, including Scanner, Archie Pelago, Debruit and Four Tet base their live set around, albeit using Ableton Live's session view (Fitoni, 2013; Johnstone, 2017). It was therefore imperative that the loop sequencer in this project not only incorporates additional functionality beyond Ableton Live's capabilities in this respect, but more importantly does so in a way that visually reflects its functionality so that it can be perceived and understood by the audience. Furthermore, this approach avoids attracting a criticism which is sometimes aimed at users of this method, that they conform to "the pseudo-live norm in which artists turn up, plug in and trigger . . . pre-recorded loops in a carefully programmed sequence" (Caryl, 2013), and forgo the live spontaneity that is so crucial to a live performance.

The inspiration for this additional functionality came as a result of performing practical tests of the aforementioned drum sequencer, upon reaching near-completion of its development. After employing the capability to instantly change start and end loop points, with some very pleasing creative results, a logical conclusion formed to apply the same functionality to an audio loop; the means to apply this technique to not just a sequenced drum pattern, but any available audio loop, offered huge creative potential. Furthermore, by exploiting the visual capabilities of the illuminated grid on the APC20, it was possible to create a similar animated visual pattern to that of the drum sequencer to give the (albeit slightly misleading) impression that the loop sequencer was processing 16 individual 'slices' of audio, and therefore communicate the actions of the loop sequencer in a way that would be accurately perceived by the audience. Given the slightly more abstruse functionality compared to the drum sequencer, the multicolour lights of the APC20 were exploited to make the functionality as transparent as possible; for an active track green lights would indicate sections between the currently selected loop points, while a red light would indicate the step currently being played. For a muted track these would be replaced by amber lights and unilluminated lights respectively; while perhaps not essential for the audience's perception, the indication of muted tracks is invaluable for the performer to identify a track's status prior to unmuting (Figure 16.1).

So that multiple clips can be triggered on individual tracks, to allow different motifs to be performed in different sections of songs, a similar system to Ableton Live's session view is implemented. This is accessed by pressing a button to enter a 'Clip Launch' mode, where clips are arranged in horizontal instead of vertical configuration for consistency with the usual "Loop Mode" display.

In further response to the prior discussion of manipulating audio stems in a creative fashion, the loop sequencer also incorporates filters, perhaps the most commonly automated signal processor in electronic music, on both a per-track and master basis. Again, a level of innovation was incorporated in this respect by implementing an 'intelligent' dual-mode filter. The 'dual-mode' capability involved a design where the upper half of a fader's throw controlled the cut-off frequency of a high pass filter, while the bottom half did the same for a low pass filter, and in the centre position both filters are bypassed. The 'intelligent' aspect implemented a feature where both filters' resonance controls are increased around a 'sweet spot', which for most audio sources tested was found to be at cut-off frequencies around 4kHz, and decreased at higher and lower values where high resonance might sound too harsh or muddy; this resulted in achieving a highly 'musical' and expressive filter, especially given that it is controlled with only a single fader. The further capability to allow tracks to be routed to different analogue outputs, in the event that a multi-output audio interface is used, allows the user to apply additional hardware signal processing if desired; in the performance which accompanies this project, this feature was exploited through the use of reverb and delay effects.

Figure 16.1 The 'loop sequencer' display

In addition to the features outlined above, the two instruments feature a number of capabilities which, while not insignificant, do not warrant further detailed examination in this chapter. These features are detailed in Table 16.1 below, while the layout of functions on the physical controllers are identified in the accompanying image (Figure 16.2). Where two features are indicated for a single button these are usually different features for the loop sequencer and drum step sequencer respectively.

Table 16.1 Key to controls and features

1	Step/Clip buttons – *input drum patterns, set loop points, launch clips*	14	Loop Start/End Mode – *allows loop start/end to be adjusted simultaneously*
2	Metronome – *flashes to indicate pulse, displays scroll anchor points*	15	Loop Single Mode – *allows single step to be looped*
3	Quantize – *sets quantise value for triggering and looping*	16	Scroll Buttons – *scrolls step/clip buttons up/down*
4	Master Step/Scene – *master control of loop and clip launch*	17	Bank A/B/Sync – *toggles between clip banks, toggles sync on/off*
5	Clear All – *clears all note data from drum sequencer*	18	Track ON/OFF – *toggles tracks between active and muted*
6	Play – *plays and restarts play of both devices independently*	19	Accent – *indicates which drum sequencer steps are accented*
7	Stop – *stops play of both devices*	20	MIDI Channel/Filter ON/OFF – *changes MIDI channel/toggles filter*
8	Restart – *restarts master clock independent of quantize*	21	Swing amount – *adjusts swing amount*
9	MIDI Note – *volume faders will change drum MIDI note number*	22	Tempo – *adjusts tempo (BPM)*
10	Swing ON/OFF – *turns swing mode on/off*	23	Volume/MIDI note # - *adjusts volume of individual tracks/ drum MIDI note*
11	Clip Launch/Step Edit – *activates clip launch/step edit modes*	24	Cutoff Frequency – *adjusts cutoff frequency of HPF and LPF*
12	Loop Start Mode – *allows loop start to be adjusted*	25	Off-Accent Amount – *controls volume of off-accent notes*
13	Loop End Mode – *allows loop end to be adjusted*		

Electronic music performance techniques

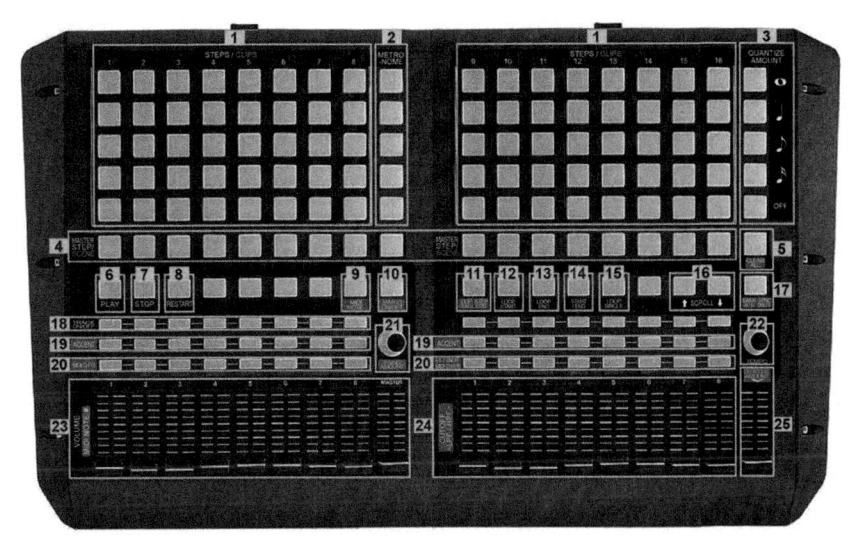

Figure 16.2 The APC20 Control Surface

Figure 16.3 The Live setup

16.7 'ON-STAGE' AESTHETICS

As stated previously, a crucial premise of the performance setup is the communication of intent and process to the audience, and therefore the physical position of interfaces in relation to the performer and audience is an important consideration. Some performers of electronic instruments choose to have their keyboards or control devices in front of them and tilted forward towards the audience so that they can observe the physical movements made by the performer; this could be considered to be slightly unsatisfactory in that this is clearly done purely for the audiences' benefit, and could actually slightly inhibit playing ability and physical dexterity. A more agreeable solution is to have any devices positioned behind the performer at an angle so that from a physical perspective they are easily accessed by the performer, and are also clearly visible to both performer and audience. A further benefit in this instance, given that the setup features two devices that look identical, is that this configuration creates a pleasing symmetry which makes for an even more striking aesthetic (Figure 16.3).

16.8 CONCLUSIONS

This research project culminated in the performance of three musical works using the performance interfaces described above, which were video recorded in a studio setting, and can be viewed at https://vimeo.com/cloudmines. This experience was highly valuable for the purposes of critical reflection for several reasons; the footage was viewed by a number of individuals and from their reactions, insights could be gained as to what extent the aims outlined previously had been achieved. From a personal standpoint, I was able to view the performance from an audience perspective and gain further insight in this respect. Furthermore, the experience of utilising the instruments in a performance context allowed for evaluation of their practical effectiveness, identify potential for further refinement and outline areas for further research.

The video footage was played to a selection of academics, fellow electronic practitioners and experienced instrumentalists who are not particularly knowledgeable regarding music technology. Feedback from these individuals was generally very favourable; most commented that the performance had successfully achieved the aims of communicating to the audience the processes that were taking place, and how physical actions were affecting the resultant audio. In the instances where observers were unsure of the details of some of the specific performance processes, they suggested that despite this ambiguity, it was clearly apparent that the actions were of crucial importance to what was being heard. Furthermore, rather than this ambiguity detracting from the performance, it actually enhanced it, adding a sense of intrigue to what was actually happening. This slight uncertainty could be perceived to be a partial failure of the initial aim of transparency, since the audience might not understand every facet of the performance, however given that this can be the case in many other highly credible forms of musical performance, this can still be considered to be a positive outcome. One example of this is the vibrato technique used on a string instrument such as a violin or cello. While many non-musicians do not understand the exact function of this technique, they will recognise the hand movement used, acknowledge its importance, and associate it with someone who is highly proficient on their instrument; as such it will still contribute significantly to the observer's appreciation of the performance as a whole.

Given these audience responses, it can be concluded with some confidence that this project was successful with regard to fulfilling the criteria of authenticity, in that the live performance techniques accurately reflect studio methods; as well as providing visual stimuli which accurately and transparently communicate to the audience the audio processes that are taking place. Given this observation, it is entirely possible that this work could, as originally hoped, go some way to establishing an alternative paradigm to current methodologies in live performance. Historically, many electronic musical instruments have yielded their most profound results when aspects of their functionality have been 'borrowed' by other practitioners who have then developed or extended this functionality, or even when used in ways not necessarily intended by their creators. This might, therefore, suggest that other practitioners could extend the concepts of the devices explored herein, and further extend repertoires within the field of electronic performance.

In addition to the observations made by others, reflections from a personal perspective have highlighted some areas for potential improvements, the most significant one being with regard to the aforementioned 'clip launch' feature of the loop sequencer. This undoubtedly performs an essential function, given that it allows the user to load different audio files for different sections of a piece, however it could be implemented more elegantly. It currently requires the user to access an alternative display mode where the buttons of the APC20's grid represent the currently available audio clips, which can be selected by pressing them; active clips are displayed in red while all others are amber. The issue is that in this mode there is very little visual movement in the light display, especially in comparison with the 'loop sequencer' mode, which provides multiple layers of rhythmically animated light movements, something that adds a feeling of momentum to the performance (a perspective shared by several individuals who viewed the performance). In the performances there were sections where the 'clip launch' mode was required to be visible for long sections, and this was far less visually stimulating than when the 'loop sequencer' mode was active. Given that it is not essential for the audience to observe the 'clip launch' view, a logical amendment would be to have this function performed by an additional APC20 or similar controller, which would not necessarily be in view of the audience.

In addition to the visual perception of the audience, an important area of reflection is the experience of utilising the instruments from a first-person perspective. While the instruments were largely successful in creating a cohesive final performance, this was not without its considerable challenges. The video recordings that were captured were the product of many attempts or 'takes' where multiple mistakes were made. Most of these were the result of human error; the task of simply programming and triggering parts in the correct places, before even incorporating any improvisation or embellishment was found to be very challenging indeed. Furthermore, in contrast with an instrumentalist in the traditional sense, whose mistakes might consist of a few wrong notes that might be forgiven or even not perceived by the audience, a small error in this scenario could be far more destructive to the performance as a whole. In some cases, it might involve missing a cue that would require the performer to repeat a 16-bar section that would cause some loss in momentum in the piece as a whole, in others the results would be so chaotic and catastrophic that the performance would be rendered somewhat of a disaster. While some of these issues could be simply resolved with some more intensive practice, it may be that certain features may need to be streamlined to improve their usability. Until further rehearsal and testing takes place, it cannot be concluded with certainty whether the current system is ready for use in front of a live audience, where there is only one chance to perform correctly, and a multitude of other factors that can elicit performance errors.

One final area of reflection is the extent to which the devices created as part of this project contributes to the user's own artistic identity. Given that there is a uniqueness to both the methodologies employed and the aesthetic qualities of the live setup, this has been achieved with considerable success. Furthermore, it was observed during performance that certain sections could have been performed more effectively had they been composed differently, and it is therefore likely that these considerations could influence the composition and production of future works, further contributing to the individual's artistic identity. Again, further practical usage of the instruments is likely to yield more definitive conclusions here.

16.9 AREAS FOR FURTHER RESEARCH

Given the points discussed above, a logical direction following this project is to perform further field research; applying the performance methodologies that have been devised to a wider range of repertoire from a variety of composers and producers, as well as collaborating with others as part of larger ensembles. This would be invaluable to establish which facets of the design would benefit from further refinement, and to implement these as required. Essentially, that is to extend the process of practice-based research that formed much of this project and produce a more refined and streamlined solution.

Another viable (and obvious) development is to adapt this project for the *Max For Live* platform, which allows integration of Max with Ableton Live. The benefits of this are that Ableton Live already offers very robust implementation of aspects such as synchronisation and file management – areas that are not as reliable as desired in the current design. Furthermore, the additional capabilities of Ableton Live, as well as its ubiquity within the electronic music community could make for a more adaptable and versatile system, as well as one which might be more attractive to other practitioners who may wish to adopt and further augment the methodologies devised herein.

REFERENCES

Bussy, P. (2005). *Kraftwerk: Man, Machine and Music*, 3rd edition, London, SAF Publishing Limited.

Caryl, K. (2013). What is [Live]? – The New Generation of Live Techno, *Attack Magazine* (website), available online from https://www.attackmagazine.com/features/long-read/what-is-live-new-generation-live-techno/ [accessed October 2019]

Cunningham, M. (1999). *Live & Kicking*, London, Sanctuary Publishing Limited.

Darlington, A. (2015). INPUT EPISODES: Daedelus (Brainfeeder / Ninja Tune) on live performance, *Liveschool Music Training* (video) available online from https://www.youtube.com/watch?v=7Z1UKNt4ve4 [accessed October 2019].

Ferreira, P. (2012). When Sound Meets Movement: Performance in Electronic Dance Music, *Electronica, Dance and Club Music*, 1st edition, Surrey, Ashgate.

Fitoni, L. (2013). The Great Live Music Roundtable, *FACT Magazine* (website), available online from https://www.factmag.com/2013/10/31/the-great-live-music-roundtable-six-producers-debate-the-future-of-live-electronic-music/ [accessed October 2019].

Golden, E. (2012). The Age Of The EDM Rockstar, *DJ TechTools* (website), available online from http://djtechtools.com/2012/06/17/the-age-of-the-edm-rockstar/ [accessed October 2019].

Johnstone, H. (2017). The highly revered electronic producer spills the digital beans at RBMA NYC, *Red Bull* (website), available online from https://www.redbull.com/au-en/watch-four-tet-reveal-the-secrets-of-his-live-show [accessed October 2019].

Jones, C. (2016). A Live Performance Revolution is Taking Over Electronic Music, *Magnetic Magazine* (website), available online from https://www.magneticmag.com/2016/06/live-performance-revolution-taking-over-electronic-music/ [accessed October 2019].

Kirn, P. (2012). Playing Live, Dangerously: Mouse on Mars as Augmented Band, *CDM* (website), available online from https://cdm.link/2012/06/playing-live-dangerously-mouse-on-mars-as-augmented-band-video/ [accessed October 2019].

Reynolds, S. (2013). *Energy Flash*, Revised edition, London, Faber & Faber Ltd.

17

BTS' "Speak Yourself" world tour as an intermedial spectacle of attachment

Alicja Sulkowska

17.1 INTRODUCTION

Described by *Time Magazine* as the "next-generation leaders" (Time Magazine 2018), the Korean boy-group BTS managed to successfully modify the approved schemes of medial presence of musical collectives, at the same time supporting K-pop in its gradual migration from the exotic niche to the relatable intermedial construction the fans were not only able to identify with but, in the first place, actively co-created. Revised and extended during fan events, live shows, and v-lives (live streaming held by group members *via* V-Live website and mobile app), this impression of the direct connection to the idols finds its communicative escalation during the concert, when the actual artistic performance serves as an emotional trigger for the once established bond between individual and the band. The following text offers an insight into medial solutions with the help of which BTS stabilizes its position in this musical hierarchy. All these schemes namely, analyzed from both medial and performative perspective, take part in motivating an emotional reaction among the recipients, contributing to their continuous support for the group. Examining the creative and economic outcomes of such communicative interdependence crystallized during the live show, the study discusses their significance for K-pop and the music industry in general.

17.2 HALLYU 3.0 AND THE RECIPIENT-COMPLEMENTED CONTENT

Differing to the majority of popular music genres, a K-pop show is rarely viewed as an isolated experience and becomes more often an active manifestation and summary of all the artistic tropes, which the group (BTS) developed and established in the span of their whole career, additionally complementing them with individually recognized links to experiences and memories of audience members. Because of the significance of these personal impressions, as Youngdae Kim noticed (Kim 2019, pp. 196–206), the interpretations and theories surrounding the group's music significantly exceed the frames of "unofficial culture" (Fiske 1992, pp. 30–49) of fandom. Instead of it, they establish themselves as equals of the actual "officially" created content. As a result, the space of media is being simultaneously shaped with two actively unfolding forces – the one of BTS, and one of the fans – both of which continuously weave their creative products with help of the medial channels they use for mutual interaction.

Due to this intensive exchange, as well as to the impact the performative strategy applied by BTS has on the industry, it is possible to derive the new type of *Hallyu* ("Korean wave") defining the K-pop scene today. While *Hallyu 1.0* had been primarily connected to k-dramas and analog media, the phenomenon of *Hallyu 2.0* refers to Korean music thematized in the space of the Internet, simultaneously strengthening the impression of collectivity among the viewers (Yecies and Shim 2014). As the artists and labels had used social media during the second wave as well, it would be a mistake to associate the current era of Korean entertainment solely with this shift towards social platforms as Twitter or Fancafe. In this sense, it is rather the recent turning point in the positioning of fan/artist-created contents that may serve here as a start of the new *Hallyu 3.0*. Its development is namely not that much dictated by a particular medium, as by the fan-created vision of the audio-visual presence of the artist, then transmitted to the space of the Internet, press, and television, the instances responsible for the legitimization of fan-established contents. Such individualized reflections are then being shared with other fans, constituting a specific dynamic space of band discourses. In this sense, both fans and artists to the same degree contribute to the band's image, later repeated and adequately stylized by the "mainstream" journalists and anchored in the social space.

The level of fan-created content refers as well to the emotional impact which a particular creative product may have on its recipients. There is a reason why the slogan of BigHit Entertainment, the company behind BTS, is "Music and Artists For Healing." It is namely this direct orientation on the audience and their mental wellbeing that defines the actual semantic outcome of the music, at the same time ennobling the recipients, and not the media, to the role of the productive messengers and editors in the process of communication of the once developed contents. Not only the fans and the media switch places in the entire chain of interaction, emancipating the audience to the role of discursive gatekeepers of the band's creative products, but these are the fans and not the actual group collective treated by medial channels as the primary source of information. This performative gesture of content/role exchange (Fischer-Lichte 2004), mediated by particular aesthetically induced feelings of the audience, is here crucial for the establishment of shared communicative space between sender and recipient, useful during the live show for complementation of the multisensory experience.

Despite the importance of the technical components, the structural impact of the so-called "idol-factory phenomenon" (Yecies and Shim 2014) shall not be ignored while discussing the sources of the band's success. Contrary to popular belief, the term "factory" does not refer here to the strict unification of idols' image and control of industry, but, in the first place, designates the seriality of medial products the artists' personas are being transmitted through. "Factory" in the case of the K-pop scene describes the continuity of performative events and their formal similarity in course of medial transmission, due to which the audience may still be able to personally relate to the cohesive level of narration while being aesthetically drawn to its visual layer. Binding the stage image of the artists to the discursive thread their music follows, this newer face of the known mechanisms supports the band collective in the gradual freeing from the common reproach against popular culture and its alleged lack of identity (Fiske 1992, p. 37). If each band member internalizes namely the narration the music follows, they become in the eyes of the recipients more authentic as artists, as well as can discursively control the path of following fan-interactions, while the majority of their interactive gestures remains strictly anchored in the pre-established artistic concept.

17.3 EMOTIONAL MEMORY IMPACT GROUPS (EMI) AND IDENTITY GROUNDING AS BASIS FOR A LONG-TERM INTERACTION

While examining the importance of BTS and searching for the best way to approach their creative products complemented during the circulation of audiences' emotional attachment, one more musical phenomenon deserves to be mentioned. Not strictly connected to K-pop, but much more spreading itself on the whole history of popular music, the so-called EMI-Groups (Emotional Memory Impact Groups) have a significant share in the strong binding of the actual musical content to the cognitive mechanisms of the audience. As EMI-Groups, one designates the creative instances (constituted by the shared influence of stage persona and charisma) motivating the audience to develop an intense emotional attachment to the artists initiated by their processual and repetitive identity grounding. Together with the dispersal of once suggested artistic vision, these image patterns and interpretative mechanisms are being embedded directly in the cognitive mechanisms of the audience, establishing the artists' creative products as the mutual co-creation of fans' intercultural associations and actions of the performers.

The key-characteristic of this particular category is also coding of the most essential significants not so much in the actual audial structure, but in the affectual customs of recipients confronted with musical product. Their impact allows the smooth incorporation of audio-visual content in the natural stream of associations and memories, binding the group's presence to the emotional experiences of the listener/viewer. In the process of interaction and communication on both artistic and medial level, EMI may be described as a secondary genre – exceeding the K-pop scene, the EMI-Groups establish themselves in the reception patterns triggered by particular detail and not music as a complete performative product. Like in the recipient-oriented Hallyu 3.0, it is far more a raw sketch delivered by the artists, which only then is being complemented and discursively defined by the audience: there are no musical characteristics with the help of which one can define EMI-Groups as such, as this category crystallizes itself not on the audial level, but in the interpretation and long-term connection developed among the audience members. The repetition of a message inside the promptly evolving landscape of interaction not only provides the whole with the impression of narrativity, but also diversifies and intensifies the process of reception with focus on particular senses, directly reacting to recognizable details.

What allows to keep such diverse milestones together, is the already mentioned strategy of identity grounding. During this process, the suggested personas of the band members are authenticated and legitimized through their narrative anchoring in the actual audio-visual content and later complemented during performances. Due to these similarities, the fans view the artists as a synecdoche of the content and meanings they already feel emotionally attached to, almost automatically projecting own worries, memories or experiences on the aestheticized matrix represented by a particular group member. The landscape of EMI-Groups, in this case: BTS, is shaped by the regular revisiting of the themes once deemed as relevant and connected to recipient's biography and interpretation mechanisms, gradually leading to the synonymous reception of own experiences and artistic narratives. Each element of the medial presence of the group has here its share in the process of stabilization of fan-created interpretation theories, which continuously mirror the personal level of memory of each recipient in the dynamic landscape of music and performance.

17.4 BTS "SPEAK YOURSELF" TOUR AS CELEBRATION OF INDIVIDUALITY

The significance of the EMI-concept in the case of BTS emphasizes at the first place the diverse media channels used to connect single narrative events into a more complex audio-visual chain. Due to the clear target-orientation of these channels, as well as their individually accustomed reception among the recipients, every stage of the emotional bonding contributes to the attention shift from the single reproduction of recognizable content to a complexity of multisensory and narratively framed landscapes, referring not just to the visible "now" of a stage matrix, but to the already developed durable interpretation patterns of the recipient. In this sense, the narration that BTS applies on their various texts is not completely created on stage through particular technical measures, but much more gradually unfolds in the mind of the recipient, changing such experience into gradually externalized manifestation of own cognitive patterns.

The main difference between a concert and a show, especially visible in the case of the BTS' *SY Tour*, lies precisely in this gradual overshadowing of the actual musical content by the emotionally and aesthetically supported engagement of the audience. The performative strategies are mandatory to complete the encounter, using extra-musical elements to stabilize the intermedially created image. Due to such emotional anchoring of the content in the minds of the recipients, BTS seem to include each of these interpretation schemes and theories into their performance in order to construct a larger narrative image, further repeated and reworked in the shared space of concert. It is because of this variety of recognizable elements interposing to the final appearance of the show, the fans may have an impression, their support significantly contributes to the current position of the band. In the same way, the dancers and singers change into multi-skilled performers, who, simultaneously, due to their stage personas, serve as the emotionally grounded avatars, automatically awakening particular aesthetic/emotional associations among the audience, already familiar with the contexts of the group's presence.

In this sense, every instance of the performance appeals to the fans' personality and their reception of particular events, changing the show into a spectacle on the verge of collective experience (fandom during *Mikrokosmos*, generation in *Baepsae*) and the manifestation of individuality (the universal "love yourself" message). Just as the group mediates between these two instances, so is each of them thought to connect the artists' presence with individual input of recipients, thematizing the bond between BTS and the fans and incorporating it into performance structures. Regarding these events form such perspective, it is possible to say once again, the essence of the *SY Tour* was not defined by the music of the group, but by the fans' medially aestheticized reception of their experiences and both-sided interaction attempts. That BTS during the entire *SY Tour* was performing almost identical set-lists, did not diminish the pleasure of reception or the engagement of the fans in the show itself. On the contrary, such ritornell-inspired repetition (Deleuze and Guattari 1992) accentuated even stronger artists' relationship with the audience, as the already known matrix of songs and choreography was each time differently complemented by the fans' presence and then reworked in these new, show-focused milieus. The space of the stadium in which BTS music and stage presence were seen/heard, became for many fans a haven for own interpretation patterns, willingly unfolding and weaving with the "original" content the group members personified.

Every live show of the *SY Tour* defined in this sense not the borders of the interpretative engagement, but its epicenter, combining and activating all of the suggestions with the help of which fans and artists interacted on the previous levels of the emotional memory development. These had been dynamized in the performance space and overbuilt with personal theories and aestheticized impressions of the audience. Due to such an order of reception, it is not a surprise that the fan activities themselves prominently form the structure of the live show. Because of it, the actual concert atmosphere unfolds up to two days before the event, enabling attendants the assimilation with this new heterotopic reality, slightly altering their perception mechanisms according to the circumstances of the show. The area around the stadium becomes occupied by merch booths, fans giving away freebies, such as pins and stickers, or selling small band-related goods. Clothing or gadgets, such as BTS character-charms, obsolete in every-day situations, turn into cognitive satellites inviting each participant to become acquainted with other attendants, breaking the egocentric bubble characteristic for other genres. The BTS-concert experience is also *a priori* programmed as a collective one, as it pursues the impression of familiarity with other participants as a fusion of personalities and experiences, one more time highlighting the thematic focus of the group's music.

Yet another important ritual of a K-pop concert is queuing. Strengthening the impression of collectivity, the approximately six hours wait (by VIP ticket holders or fans waiting for their turn in BTS photobooth) emphasizes the heterotopic repealing of time among the show attendants, as it starts to get measured not by the conventional means, but much more according to the events bound to the concert structure (gate open, soundcheck, VIP-entry). The particular order of concert-oriented milestones becomes central for the perception of the temporarily closed reality. That the terms of time and space are entirely subordinated the band and its activity, makes the atmosphere of the concert omnipresent and universally relevant for the audience. The bare fact that queuing is often described as the essence of the K-pop show, defines here the strong before-after polarization of the emotionally rooted frames complemented by the audience, in final effect intensifying the concert experience and its narrative components.

17.5 EMOTIONALLY ROOTED INTERACTION AND SUPPORTING MEDIA TECHNIQUES

Similar time brackets aimed at increasing the emotional significance of the show are applied on the actual structure of the concert itself, as BTS performs both group and solo songs, fragmenting the whole into multiple shorter sets. In each case, however, the show is being framed by the group's introductions and their thank you speeches (outside of Korea accompanied by the presence of the interpreter). These solutions do not serve the informative aim anymore, but much more take over the task of identity grounding, reminding the fans of the already known personas of band members, this time anchoring them in particular emotionally prone (and aestheticized) context. Alongside the group and solo songs, BTS (and other groups) tend to use VCRs and interludes during their shows as possibilities of repeated anchoring as both individuals and musicians in the semantic space of the performance, strengthening their bond with the audience and reminding them of the emotional identification with the message the band transmits.

Every BTS show confirms in this manner the collective power of self-affirmation on the side of the viewer. These are the introduction rounds which allow the audience to identify with the message, and to, one more time, bind the level of music to the level of personal experiences and impressions, expressing their fondness of a particular band member or their typified role inside the group narrative (in the case of BTS unfolded in frames of the so called BTS Universe). Due to these strong identification patterns, the emotional reaction to the show is additionally accelerated, as well as is being viewed as an extension of extra-musical and affirmative tropes represented by the members. Because of such framing of the whole construct with non-musical and persona-based presence of the group, the process of communication renews the once applied individual narratives, connecting the world of the show to the materiality of other communicative instances, such as music videos and interviews, already interpreted and classified by the audience.

Although all these observations correspond with the EMI-structures, it would be an overly schematized simplification to state that the two large video display screens on the sides of the stage serve visual purposes solely. They fulfill much more the complementary (during the performances, when they extend the emotional impact of a song) and summarizing role, explaining the previously suggested tropes. Additionally, the stage decorations accentuate the message of particular song (bumpy castle and spontaneity by *Anpanman*), sometimes even directly reconstructing the scenes from the music videos (wall of rain in *Epiphany* or the opening camera shot during *Boy With Luv*), referring directly to the emotional and aesthetic associations awaken among the fans by the previously viewed content. The recipients do not need to pay too detailed attention to the stage events, as it is more than enough for them to rely on the already proven associations and impressions developed on other medial platforms. Their repetition namely, in connection with the unique atmosphere of the show, results in a construction of the complete landscape of emotionally based performance. Knowing oneself becomes for the audience synonymous with knowing and recognizing the developing band-structures, as the previously initiated process of content-incorporation becomes revived in the presence of audio-visual products of the EMI-Group.

The screens are also just as important as the actual material decorations used on stage, as they complement the events defining the performance, at the same time filling possible narrative gaps with the overall dynamics of color and form schemes. An especially interesting example is here RM's solo *Trivia: Love*, where his "real" hand gestures seem to draw glittery hearts on the screens. At the end of the performance, together with his words, "ARMY, I have a gift for you," the screen shows BTS and ARMY symbols created from little hearts and the word "love" written in multiple languages. The virtual reality and medial solutions appear here as the key point of the whole performance, emancipating the screens to the role of creators of new content, and not just mediators and mirrors of the stage events. The entire multimedial performance fulfills here an especially promiscuous role, highlighting the complexity of the message BTS is associated with, as well as referring directly to the need for cooperation between several medial and material platforms in order to preserve and develop certain constellation of meanings. This fusion then appears natural and logical to the viewers, who already expect particular solutions, based on the central message of the group they already know and understand, as well as the context they are being reminded of.

A similar aim, this time directly relying on the performative actions taken up by the audience, may be assigned to the extra-musical activities taking place in each city before and after the show. The fact that the organizers and BigHit itself use these instances to bring official and unofficial events in one place, maximizing their emotional impact, confirms the hypothesis of Hallyu 3.0 being solely a raw sketch and suggestion, fully colored and perfectioned by the audience and its associative attachment itself. The reality created by the band and constituted by the narrative links the group members develop between the main narrative thread and the recipients, is being brought to life by the active participation of the audience, who engage their own cultural and cognitive habitus into this process, strengthening the impression of uniqueness and individuality of each participant during this interaction.

The first of such instances is the so-called BTS Studio, located by the venue on the days of the shows. In its simplest form described as a virtual reality attraction, the photo booth allows the participants to take a picture with an "avatar" of a BTS band member. After entering a booth and receiving instructions from an assistant, the participant stands in front of a large screen, from which they choose the member they want a photo taken with. Once seated on the bench right in front of the screen, one may observe how the "member" seats next to them, speaks a few words, finally encouraging the participant to strike particular poses. Just like in the case of RM's *Trivia: Love* also, the screens constitute here the actual reality of BTS-microcosmos, motivating the audience to dive into this mediatized world entirely while being reassured about the sincerity of stage personas represented by the members even *via* their avatars. It is essential to notice that the poses of the holograms, as well as their pre-recorded behavior, are an exact repetition of the patterns the fans may recognize from v-lives, concerts, or multiple variety shows. A photo taken with Jimin would most likely be described as "cute," while j-hope behaves in the same direct and joyful manner as the fans remember from interviews and performances. The potential structural difference between prototype and reproduction ceases to exist in the mind of the viewer, as the hologram, so similar to the person it represents, becomes during this short period of time an actual matrix for all the associations the viewers would bind with the real person of the musician, following the previously developed discourses (Benjamin [1936] 2017).

That BTS Studio closes 30 minutes before the stadium doors opened, stabilizes it once again as a non-musical prelude to the personal engagement of each participant into concert structures. Experiencing the acknowledged persona of the group member in an almost intimate setting allows the audience to emotionally contribute to the following legitimization of the group's position and impact during the concert itself. Using Benjamin's terminology, one can state, precisely the process of reproduction of both emotional (on the side of the audience) and synthetic (pre-programmed characteristics of media channels) image of the performance emancipates the gesture of multiplication to the role of the productive extra-musical force, crucial for the empiric complementation of the musical message by each recipient. The reproduction, as presented in the "overbuilding" of narrative layers and development of the emotionally connoted narrative, serves in the case of BTS (as an EMI-Group) the expansive extension of audio-visual presence, as each new group's hologram (in sense of persona repetition) in diverse medial surroundings may be viewed as a next step towards universal connection to the audience members.

A similar task has been assigned to the pop-up store, opened in each city a few days before and closed soon after the show dates. That the stores were not located in the proximity of the stadium, but rather in the city center, indicates here the attempts of interactive dynamization of the fans' engagement. As, obviously, most of the attendants indeed wanted to visit the pop-up store, they were in a particular way forced to explore the city they found themselves in, making the BTS Universe a center of this urban landscape. Moreover, while releasing the T-shirts designs exclusive for particular city, the marketing strategy of BTS enriched the group's presence, stylizing it in an almost touristically arranged way, connecting local cultural landmarks (Eiffel's Tower for Paris, Big Ben for London, "The Bean" for Chicago . . .) with the group's message.

The interior of the pop-up store also encouraged the visitors to active co-creation of the group's medial presence. A large "Speak Yourself" slogan, as well as the installation of red microphones, radically contrasting with the white walls, not only harmonized with the color scheme chosen for the whole tour, but also visibly stressed the presence of the visitors, who stood out as actual actors on the plain background, becoming the heroes and actual voices of the event. In this way, the applied solutions appealed to the fans' self-esteem and result in their long-lasting appreciation of the band contents. BTS' music videos played inside the store collected larger groups of fans who not only sang but even danced along, again extending the band's influence on the city structure far beyond the stadium walls. Direct connection of the shop to the music of the group "clears" the space of the store from the economic/consumerist associations and transports it back to the main positive message (reminded *via* the installations) and the medial charisma of the group the fans feel personally attached to.

17.6 FAN ENGAGEMENT: FROM CONCERT TO CONVENTION

As the individual character of the band members is reminded to the audience in various ways during the concert, so do multiple forms of fan engagement reappear during the show, illustrating the dimension of the co-created recipient/artist space. Both purple slogans or phone flashlights raised in the air during *Mikrokosmos*, and official BTS lightsticks (ARMY bombs) are to a certain degree thought to accentuate the shared influence of both sides in the constitution of the final effect. Once synchronized with a mobile app, all of the lightsticks in the venue follow the programmed lighting scheme, changing colors or the tempo of pulsation. The particular stage decorations in the hands of the audience extend the borders of the band's influence, at the same time fastening the impression of their productive engagement into the structure of the concert on the side of the audience. This intermedial expansion of content and its meanings on various artistic spaces of performative and aesthetic origin stabilizes and legitimizes the position of the band in interpretation patterns of the recipients, binding them stronger to the concept of the group. In the final effect, the medium durably connecting these two spheres is, not without reason, the voice. Fanchants, singing the lyrics even louder than the artists on stage – all of that is during the *SY Tour* of both individually validating and collectively emancipating significance. At the end namely, these elements influenced the perception of the show as an unforgettable and validating experience, used by the attendants to express their thoughts, worries, and expectations, as well as to search for the confirmation of own concepts in the multimedially created image by the group. Because every medial instance actively engaged in the construction of the show had created a similar vision of BTS' intermedial narrative while using different aesthetic and rhetoric means of communication, the main aim of the live show, especially by such important K-pop group as BTS, is to combine and unify all of these images, bringing the fans, as productive recipients, as well as their productive interpretations, together in the shared space.

17.7 OUTCOMES AND CONCLUSION

As seen from the example of the discussed case study, the intense attachment of the fans and their engagement in active creation of the performative band landscapes are not bound to the age or gender of the recipients, as many skeptics like to claim. Instead of it, the crucial understanding of the effectivity of these communication patterns lies in the complementation-oriented chain-relation between media the genre uses to establish its presence and in the recognizable image of the performers, unified through the lens of emotional memory of the audience. By constituting a firm semantic space of themes and motives associated with a specific group, the popularity of the band is being revised and recreated by the simulacrum of fans' engagement and their interpretation patterns, highlighting the double importance of each medial platform. On the one hand, social media allow the groups to develop and legitimize their affirmative personas as the central concept of the band. On the other, they enable the recipients constant reviving of all previously acquired impressions and memories connected to the group, linking them, thanks to complex fandom structures, in a cohesive chain of narration, binding their personal experiences to these thematized by the band.

In this sense also, the successful application of intermedial solutions in the case of K-pop groups could not be easily and in an unchanged form be revised by other genres in only one step, as it requires multidimensional preparation on both a personal and collective level. Social media and media in general should namely not be treated as a marketing tool, but much more be viewed as an open space for fans' expression, keeping up the illusion of personal and productive interaction with the artist, directly referring to possible doubts and wishes of the fans, deciphered from the engagement particular episodes of band's activity had caused. What punk and metal fanzines achieved in the 80s and 90s may be deemed as comparable in terms of ennoblement of fan culture – in cases of these two genres, however, due to their unambiguous ideological polarization, it was communication, but not an attachment of the recipients the scene members strived for. Today, on the other hand, in the world where media contribute to the impression of acceleration of the life pace (McLuhan 1994), the recipients expect music to serve as an anchor, stabilizing the medial space and images they surround themselves with. Such a role may be easily played by the EMI-Groups, almost exclusively oriented on the emotional aestheticizing of self by each viewer.

Hallyu does not translate to "wave" without a reason. The music industry cannot view media presence as a finished consumable product anymore, but instead needs to consider the longer process of its complementation and extension, followed by the fans' attachment, who bound their interests to these dynamic structures. The interaction with recipients, instead of being taken for granted after initiation of the medial presence, as through posting a video on YouTube, shall be continuously re-structured while following the main thematic and discursive course chosen for a particular artist, complemented by every next platform. In this sense, the reoccurring presence of the artists is not a typical repetition *per se*, as each of these appearances includes a slight altering of the original (induced by the material differences of media channels and varying ideas of fans), dynamizing the attachment of the recipients and influencing their emotional engagement into the forming of recognizable content.

This engagement of the audience, due to the ongoing processes of complementation, becomes gradually medialized as well, co-existing with the artists in the same spaces, rebuilt and accentuated during the live shows. Not the music alone namely, but much more the form of the whole event, as well as the ambience of the venue or aesthetic/performative solutions applied, are necessary for changing the concert into the multimedial and multisensory show, the actual future of entertainment industry. Whether through the level of instrumentals, charisma of the artists or the conceptual stage presence, the musical layer needs to be extended and translated on other artistic levels and spaces, remaining in narrative connection with the original medium, totalizing the omnipresent aura of the performance.

In this way, the interactive focus laid on the group's contents shall be initiated already on the level of the materiality, enabling the engagement of the audience through gestures or particular activities (as photocard trade or album unboxings), evolving into financial and medial support, consolidating this unique communicative fusion. Accumulation of various engaging media structures in the proximity of the venue not only revives the associations coined by the group but also reminds the fans of each type of activity *via* which they may be able to connect with the band, leading to the emotional escalation during the concert. Today's music, as the impressive success of K-pop and BTS proved, shall not be just enjoyed but much more experienced and co-created, as the growing generation of recipients highly values such form of productive attachment, encouraging further development of genre structures. The importance of the *Briefing With The Community*, planned to be held twice a year by BigHit Entertainment, shall also not much guarantee transparency inside the industry, as Bang Si-Hyuk stated, but much more set the standards for the whole K-pop market. According to these main goals, the EMI-patterns applied by BTS shall be viewed by other companies as especially attractive and effective, potentially promising the intensifying engagement of the audience in the intermedial presence of other artists applying this model on their structures (BigHit Entertainment 2019). The medial dimension of a group's image serves also, to a significant degree, the fans themselves, as the enunciative production of the content (Fiske 1992, p. 37), as a reaction on the artists' interaction attempts, gradually replaces its passive consumption (Flew 2008, p. 113). Thus, the next step in the exploration of the new attachment landscapes would manifest itself through unfolding of new terminology and discourses, out of which the concept of EMI-Groups may become a starting point for further discussion.

Following the same trope, the industry shall develop strategies focusing not just on automatized promoting of the content, but on emotional reassuring of the recipients of validity of their taste and emotions bound to the complex act of perception. While repetitively presenting the music on various medial platforms, these feelings become legitimized, stabilizing the band's position not only inside a specific environment, but in cognitive patterns of the recipient, enabling the feasible and effective revival of these emotions by every new medial instance that the band will express itself through. In this manner, such a performative communication model with aesthetic undertones (as the one of EMI-Groups) could be rebuilt and extended *via* various medial facets produced by the once established image of the artist, defining even the extra-musical space of interaction and emancipating it to the role of the actual warm-up for the performative communication initiated inside the engaging show structures.

REFERENCES

Benjamin, Walter ([1936] 2017). *Kunstwerk im Zeitalter der technischen Reproduzierbarkeit*. Berlin, Fischer Verlag.

BigHit Entertainment (2019). BigHit Corporate Briefing With the Community. YouTube: https://www.youtube.com/watch?v=Yy9mJE0fZas (accessed: 25.08.19).

Deleuze, G. and Guattari, F. (1992). *Tausend Plateaus*, trans. Gabriele Ricke, Ronald Voullie, Berlin, Merve Vergal.

Fischer-Lichte, Erika (2004). *Ästhetik des Performativen*, Frankfurt am Main, Suhrkamp.

Fiske, John (1992). The Cultural Economy of Fandom, in: Lewis, Lisa A., ed. *The Adoring Audience, Fan Culture, and Popular Media*, New York, Routledge.

Flew, Terry (2008). *New Media: An Introduction*, Oxford, Oxford University Press.
Kim, Youngdae (2019). *BTS: The Review*, Seoul, RH Korea.
McLuhan, Marshall (1994). *Understanding Media: The Extension of Men*, Cambridge, MIT University Press.
Yecies, B. Ae-Gyung Shim (2014). *The K-pop Factory Phenomenon*, available online at: https://www.academia.edu/29628690/The_K-pop_Factory_Phenomenon
Time Magazine, 22 October 2018.

18

A review of contemporary practices incorporating digital technologies with live classical music

Clara Colotti

18.1 INTRODUCTION

In live classical music events, digital technologies have been primarily employed in social media, digital marketing and online ticket sales, but they have scarcely been used in connection with visual and aural experiences in relation to live performances (Steijn, 2014). In fact, research on classical music audiences has revealed that new technologies are perceived as not strictly necessary or even invasive by frequent concert goers (Crawford, 2014). Nevertheless, new and younger audiences are fascinated by new formats of live classical music performances incorporating digital technologies (Dobson, 2010).

In addition, the academy and the classical music worlds have expressed increased interest in the relation between orchestral performance and digital technologies, and over the past few decades orchestras have been exploring different ways to incorporate them in live performances. Documentation on individual projects has been featured in print and online in press releases, reviews, featured articles. Digital technology has been employed by orchestras for different purposes. The British Paraorchestra for instance employs digital technology in order to create bespoke musical instruments, which provide access to music performance for musicians with disabilities (Evans, 2018). However, at present no research has attempted to categorise different digital technologies employed in live orchestral contexts. To address this gap, this research uncovers the most frequently employed digital technologies in contemporary practices and organises them into different categories:

- Classical orchestras and electronic music
- Video projections
- Mobile applications
- Augmented reality and virtual reality
- Artificial intelligence

Each category explores how orchestras have incorporated digital technology with their performances to enhance the audiences' experience. The first section investigates contemporary practices and includes an overview of how orchestras have experimented with electronic music, analysing in what way the two genres have been integrated and have been performed together in a concert hall. The section on video screens and 3D projections examines their multi-purpose use in combination with an orchestral performance. This category includes movie screenings in concert, architectural video installations and abstract visuals projected on large screens. The third section analyses mobile technology and shows how orchestras have focused on the development of interactive concert guides for mobile devices, allowing the audience to access information about the works being performed during the live performance. The fourth section focuses on a specific subcategory of technologies related to augmented reality (AR) and virtual reality (VR), bringing together real and virtual worlds. The last part includes evaluations of unique audio-visual installations generated by artificial intelligence (AI) in response to the music performed by an orchestra. This is a relatively new field in classical music and until now few orchestras have explored this tool.

While the literature review and analysis of case studies have presented examples of the relationship between orchestras and digital technology, there are broader, and associated point of questions which this chapter intends to investigate. These include limits and obstacles of integrating digital technologies with live orchestral performances, analogies with live performance formats used in other music genres and exploration of audience's responses. The main objective of this chapter is to discuss the findings in relation to these aspects and understand whether limitations might help future experimentation with digital technologies; to identify how digital technology applications in other genres could inspire orchestras; to interpret the benefits of integrating digital technology for audiences.

The research sets the basis for a clearer overview of the scope of digital technologies employed by orchestras throughout their live concerts and helps to contextualise orchestras in the wider panorama of the music industry in relation to the use of digital technologies. Orchestras involved in future projects featuring digital technologies could benefit from the findings in so far as the analysis gives an intelligible evaluation on the different tools available, but also uncovers potential complications. Digital technologies are evolving at a very fast pace and continue to offer new possibilities, however, it is currently unknown to what extent, why and how orchestras will choose to embrace them.

18.2 CONTEMPORARY PRACTICES IN LIVE ORCHESTRAL MUSIC

This section presents a review of digital technologies adopted by classical orchestras in the context of live performances. Each sub-section opens with a brief description of the technology, followed by evaluation of the motivations behind the choice of each technology. The closing paragraphs discuss the outcome of these incorporation practices.

18.2.1 Exploring new sounds: classical orchestras meet electronic music

This sub-section delineates the first encounters of classical music and electronics, and it then presents and discusses contemporary practices of orchestras integrating elements of electronic music in their live performances.

The end of World War II brought a new wave in music, when composers began to be curious about new sounds. To satisfy this ambition, music studios grew in Paris and Cologne. *Musique concrète*, already under the auspices of French composer Pierre Schaeffer, developed further around 1948. This is a form of music where the composer incorporates natural sounds into a music piece, without limits imposed by long-established instrumentation and theory (Mayuzumi and Cox, 2018). Meanwhile in Cologne, composer Herbert Eimert established a new technique to make music known as *Elektronische Musik* and created artificial sounds in his studio, creating noises which had never been heard before (Kirchmeyer, 2010). In an article published 20 years later, when looking back at his first electronic sound generations in the Cologne Studio, Eimert interestingly remarked that he did not invent anything but opened the doors to "a new way of listening, a new awareness" (1972), reinforcing the assertion on the need of exploring new music in the postwar era.

But the most eminent figure at the early age of electronic music was probably Karlheinz Stockhausen, an intriguing German composer who joined the Cologne Studio in 1953. He composed a series of studies with cutting-edge techniques, widely recognised as the earliest pieces of electronic music. The next paragraphs will revolve around this charismatic figure and delve into his first works combining classical and electronic music.

The première of Stockhausen's *Gesang der Jünglinge* in the auditorium of Cologne's West German Radio on 30 May 1956 marked the first live performance of a music composition featuring acoustic and electronic elements (Böhlandt, 2008). But it was not until a decade later that Stockhausen presented his eminent work for orchestra and electronics, *Hymnen* (Harvey, 1975). Stockhausen left a vast heritage, composing music for instruments and electronic music until the final years of his career in the early 2000s. His pioneering work in electronic music and its incorporation in his classical music compositions earned him a guru status among many artists, who regard him as one of the most influential characters in the panorama of electronic music – yet others consider him a megalomaniac maverick (Stubbs, 2018).

Since Stockhausen's first live performance featuring acoustic and electronic elements back in 1956, composers from all over the world experimented with electronic sounds and began to introduce them into live performances (ibid.). In addition, advancements in electronic sounds made new ways of incorporating orchestral and electronic music possible. A gradual interest in combining orchestral elements with electronics started to spread for instance within the techno music scene. In the last decade, the godfathers of Detroit techno music Carl Craig and Jeff Mills charmed orchestras and their tracks have been arranged and revisited in symphonic keys. These have also been presented with live orchestras in first class concert halls.

Carl Craig's studio album *Versus* premièred in 2008 at the Cité de la Musique, where it was performed with French orchestra Les Siècles conducted by François-Xavier Roth, Moritz von Oswald and pianist Francesco Tristano (Polyarts, no date). This live performance was the first one to combine electronic and classical composition and the audience received it with five standing ovations. In 2017 Carl Craig produced an album of this project, including orchestral and electronically enhanced versions of his music (Ravens, 2017). The project fulfils Carl Craig's ambition to have his tracks revisited in a symphonic key and have them performed by and with an orchestra (ibid.). It took over ten years to see the project's completion, but as the DJ revealed in a recent interview, "there's a time for everything" (ibid.). Indeed there is: the audience received its first performance with five standing ovations and YouTube videos of the performance attracted millions of views. Since *Versus*' première in Paris, Carl Craig has performed live with the Polish National Radio Symphony Orchestra in Katowice, Chineke! Orchestra in London, and Sinfonieorchester Basel in Basel.

Another early project incorporating orchestral elements and techno music is Jeff Mills' collaboration with the Montpellier Philharmonic Orchestra, bringing forth a live recording of their 2006 performance *Blue Potential*. Its video version on YouTube has hit over one million of views, however reviews of this cooperation are mixed. On the classical front, a review published on BBC Music expresses admiration for the orchestra's replication of Mills' beats and synth sequencing (Dene, 2006). From an electronic music perspective, a review on Resident Advisor claims that the orchestral arrangements work well for some pieces as they propose fascinating variations; but the reviewer is a bit sceptical about the arrangements' contribution to the original tracks, because it does not feel they were adding new components (Eeles, 2006). The DVD recording of the live performance certainly shows a very enthusiastic audience and as applauses throughout the video demonstrate, the performance was well received. More recently, Jeff Mills has collaborated on diverse projects and performed with the RTÉ Concert Orchestra in Dublin, RTS Symphony Orchestra in Belgrade, the BBC Symphony Orchestra in London, Roma Sinfonietta in Rome, Orchestre National du Capitole de Toulouse in Toulouse, just to name a few.

Collaborations between electronic music artists and orchestras are growing, and other electronic music DJs have recently performed with orchestras in concert halls. In Germany, the Dortmunder Philharmoniker presented a concert featuring German duo Super Flu and a performance with German DJ and producer Marc Romboy. Frankfurt/Main-based orchestra hr-Sinfonieorchester played along with Berlin-based DJ and producer Oliver Koletzki, and Berlin is where David August and the Deutsches Symphonie-Orchester Berlin performed together.

18.2.2 Video projections

This sub-section exposes in what ways large projections have been embraced to visually intensify the live concert experience in an age where potential audiences seek experiences that are visually as well as aurally compelling.

Orchestras began placing large video screens in concert halls in the early 1990s, with the ambition of persuading younger audiences to attend and add new elements to the concert experience (O'Bannon, no date). These screens had first been used to show close range images of the members of the orchestra and conductor. The concertgoers' response was mixed: part of them appreciated watching images of the orchestra taken at close range and shown on a large screen; others perceived them as distracting (Wise, 2013).

At present orchestras use large projections in different concert formats, combining them with digital effects and video art. A large number of orchestras has incorporated image projections in their live performances; the next paragraphs present these different concert formats and how orchestras have integrated them with their concerts.

Digital Projection Mapping is a visual expression method, a technique where objects act as a display surface for video projection (Murayama *et al.*, 2014). In the context of live orchestral music, these objects may be concert halls façades or the walls of the auditorium. The Los Angeles Philharmonic launched its 2013/2014 season with a performance featuring video installations by British Director/Designer and Video Artist Netia Jones (Wise, 2013). Projections, video installations and live film were combined with a live concert event designed to commemorate the 10th anniversary of Walt Disney Concert Hall, home to the Los Angeles Philharmonic (Walt Disney Concert Hall, no date). The images projected onto the interior walls of Walt Disney Concert Hall changed on the notes of the music played by the orchestra. Jones has been involved in multiple projects with classical music organisations: in 2013 she collaborated with the New World Symphony Miami and its Artistic Director Michael Tilson Thomas to create an installation around a concert performance featuring video and projections (ibid.). Video screens were placed in the auditorium, hanging at the sides of the stage, displaying photographs of zoomed in snowflakes and snowscapes (Wise, 2013). The imagery accompanied the players performing *Inverno in-ver*, a musical poem referring to winter, composed by Italian avant-gardist Niccolò Castiglioni. Further orchestras have worked with Jones on video installations, including the Bergen Philharmonic Orchestra and Swedish Radio Symphony Stockholm.

In 2015, an artistic collaboration between the Sydney Symphony Orchestra, art studio Ample Projects and the Vienna Tourist Board produced a concert tribute to the glorious music of Vienna. Multiple cameras captured the live performance and a combination of imagery commemorating the artistic heritage of the Austrian capital city and images of the orchestra playing were projected live onto the sails of the iconic Sydney Opera House (TDC, no date).

Digital projection mapping add imagery to objects, transforming them into something different; projections reflect on buildings and their architecture becomes a giant canvas. Notwithstanding the powerful visual impact of digital projection mapping, some orchestras have used large screens and have presented live performances incorporating imagery projected on meshes and screens (as they were originally doing in the early 1990s). Imagery range from film screening to abstract visual art. Orchestras from all over the world, for instance, have been displaying motion pictures while playing the score. This turned out into a popular concert format, with sold out performances, particularly for big movie releases (i.e. Star Wars, Harry Potter).

For the 2013/2014 concert season, four leading American orchestras (New World Symphony Miami, Philadelphia Orchestra, San Francisco Symphony and Los Angeles Philarmonic) commissioned a video interpretation of Benjamin Britten's "Four Sea Interludes" from his Opera *Peter Grimes* on the occasion of the composer's centenary. Video designer and director Tal Rosner produced four video/animation scenarios, matching the four movements of the piece; each scenario corresponded to one of the commissioning orchestras' cities (Rosner, no date). The visuals echoed the music played and featured photographs of emblematic landscapes and architecture of each city.

Large screens and Digital Projection Mapping have been incorporated in live performances for more than three decades. Orchestras have been experimenting with different imagery (movies, photographs, abstract images) and have used disparate devices (screens, part of the concert hall, a combination of both). Most probably technology implementation has contributed to the expansion of visuals in live performances and has offered new ways of integrating imagery with music.

18.2.3 Mobile devices

This sub-section presents how the use of mobile devices has been integrated with live orchestral performances from an audience perspective. It reviews current applications on mobile devices designed to enhance the live concert experience, highlighting their purposes, challenges and outcomes.

Over the last decade many studies have focused on the interaction in the context of musical performances, in particular in association with digital technologies, which developed new forms of interactivity in live shows (Hödl *et al.*, 2012). In part these studies concentrate on mobile devices usage by the audience during a live performance, a trending topic considering the number of people possessing a mobile device is high and still increasing (ibid.).

The results of a research on a rock performance indicates that the use of mobile devices for interactive audience participation is a suitable approach in order to involve and entertain the audience (ibid.). Observations of practices throughout the performances showed that members of the audience frequently used their mobile devices in order to take pictures and videos, use social media, send messages or make calls (ibid.). In this framework, Dutch Jazz trio Tin Men and the Telephone created an application enabling the audience to have a direct influence on the concert by collectively choosing the tempo and colour of the music about to be played (Tin Men and the Telephone, no date). The setup of a classical orchestra performance is different: the ordinary setting consists of the orchestra's members playing actively in front of a passive public. Mobile device interaction is discouraged: at the beginning of a performance a message on the loud speaker would advise members of the audience not to use their mobile devices during the concert performance as the light of the screen might disturb and distract other members of the public. Nevertheless, Golan Levin *et al.* (2001) created *Dialtones: A Telesymphony*, a concert featuring sounds generated by the audience's mobile phones. Prior to the performance, participants registered their mobile phone numbers at designated devices and as a result ringtone melodies were automatically sent to the phones, and their assigned seats were generated. During the performance, Levin and his group of performers ringed the previously registered mobile phones through a system triggered by a tailored software. This setup enabled a maximum of 60 phones located in specific parts of the auditorium to ring simultaneously (ibid.). Few years later, mobile phones were brought onto the stage, when Stanford professor Ge Wang founded the Stanford Mobile Phone Orchestra (MoPhO). MoPhO is an academic ensemble employing mobile phones as the primary musical instrument, thus exploring mobile phones as musical instruments. MoPho have presented performances with different stage setups, for example indoor locations where the performers were moving around the space, delivering a unique experience to each member of the audience (Oh *et al.*, 2010). Professor Ge Wang explored further possibilities to integrate music and mobile devices: one year later he created and released Ocarina, a musical application for iPhone "designed to be an expressive musical instrument" (Wang, 2014). In 2005, Dan Trueman and Perry Cook founded the Princeton Laptop Orchestra (PLOrk); as the name suggests, this ensemble employs laptops as musical instruments (Trueman, 2007).

More recently, classical orchestras and technology companies have started to develop applications for mobile devices to enhance the live orchestra experience.

In 2014 the Philadelphia Orchestra launched *LiveNote*, an application sharing background information about the works being played and the orchestra while the performance is taking place (The Philadelphia Orchestra, 2014). The purpose of the app is to present information in a format that can be incorporated with the live performance. The app allows the audience to learn interesting facts about the piece and guarantees access to written programme notes about specific excerpts. It is available only on a selection of concerts and its use during the performance is not compulsory. A crucial component of *LiveNote* is that it has been designed to have the least possible impact on the audience in the auditorium and it has therefore been meticulously tested during rehearsals. To minimise its impact, the app can only be used in specific areas in the auditorium.

In September 2019 the BBC Philharmonic introduced a new web app called *Notes* with the aim of remodelling concertgoers' enjoyment of performances with a new service for mobile devices; *Notes* guides all concertgoers – frequent and new ones – through the performance and helps them understand the works being played (Webb, 2019). During the performance, *Notes* transmits information about the pieces being played to all connected mobile devices, in real time. Prior to the performance, users connect to a Wi-Fi network and open the web app via a browser on their mobile devices. Members of the BBC Philharmonic team then activate tailored facts about the works which are sent to the app in coordination with what is being performed by the orchestra (ibid.). As for the Philadelphia Orchestra's *LiveNote* app, *Notes* users are invited to sit in a specifically designated section of the auditorium where they can use their mobile devices without distracting other members of the audience who favour a more conventional concert experience. As the BBC Philharmonic's Director Simon Webb points out, other orchestras have incorporated the use of mobile devices apps in live performances (ibid.). What is new about *Notes* is its recurrence: it is the first app to be available throughout a whole main concert season. The audience's first reactions have been positive: concertgoers liked the format of the notes (short and engaging) and they confirmed that the app enhanced their concert experience (ibid.).

Dutch cultural entrepreneur Johan Idema, Muziekgebouw aan 't IJ and Dutch design agency Fabrique created *Wolfgang*, a concert guide app providing programme notes synchronised with the concert performance (Gervais, 2019). The app has been embraced by orchestras in the Netherlands and Belgium since the 2016/2017 season, in Germany since the 2018/2019 season. It has been designed to work with reduced display light in order to not disturb other members of the audience. The audience's response has been positive, who appreciate the discreet design and format of the texts (concise and relevant). The concept of *Wolfgang* is to offer a service to a new audience as well as to experienced concertgoers, who might gather new insight about a work. Another mobile application enhancing the audience experience at a live orchestral performance has been developed by *EnCue* in Baltimore. *EnCue* has been designed to make classical music performances accessible to a wider audience and provides new means for the concert experience (Furness, 2017). Orchestras that have incorporated the app include the Royal Philharmonic Orchestra and the London Symphony Orchestra in London, the Baltimore Symphony Orchestra.

All these applications for mobile devices have been developed with the purpose of enhancing the audience concert experience, both for a new public exploring orchestral music for the first time and for expert concertgoers familiar with the repertoire. The challenge lies in presenting engaging content appealing to a wider public.

18.2.4 Real and virtual: mixed reality visual displays

The concept of augmented reality (AR) was first introduced in 1990 by Boeing researcher Tom Caudell and denoted a new technology involving the overlay of computer graphics on the real world (Silva *et al.*, 2003). In the context of a live classical orchestral event this translates into the audience seeing and listening to a real performance enhanced by virtual objects. AR has not been incorporated in a live classical music performance yet, but it has afforded opportunities in other genres. AR techniques have been used at the 2019 edition of the Coachella Valley Music and Arts Festival in Indio, California (Melnick, 2019); American rock band Starset presented a tour integrating AR elements to enhance the live concert experience (Dragani, 2019).

Nonetheless in 2017 a team of designers worked on a project on a conceptual AR experience for the Oakland Symphony. The purpose was to develop an interactive experience that would attract young audiences, and that at the same time would not be invasive for regular concert goers (Webb, 2017). In the same year, conductor and composer Marcel Thomas commissioned a performance featuring AR elements of Gustav Holst's "Mars, the Bringer of War" a movement from the orchestral suite *The Planets*. His mission was to offer a complete experience of the piece by integrating holographic images in order to intensify the storytelling of the music. The project never made it to the concert hall, but evidence can be found on a one-minute long demo video. The video presents the AR concert experience through the lenses of Microsoft Hololens, the technology used for this project (ArtiShock, no date).

A similar path seems to have been followed by VR. In a digital context, the concept of VR first emerged with *The Ultimate Display*, a paper by American computer scientist Ivan Sutherland published in 1965, alongside his project with student Bob Sproull on the first head-mounted display (HMD) for the Bell Helicopter Company (Dixon, 2006). The music industry did not start to experiment with VR technologies until the 2000s, when VR was first adopted to create immersive videos (Smith, 2017). In 2015, YouTube and Facebook launched their 360° video-posting platforms and musicians began to create and post immersive video content (Taghavi *et al.*, 2019). Examples include British virtual band Gorillaz (Melnick, 2017) and Björk (Gordon, 2015).

In classical music, VR projects mostly involve placing a VR headset-wearing user inside a filmed, 360° performance setting. The Los Angeles Philharmonic for example, presented a VR experience offering a full immersive music experience on the notes of Beethoven's *Symphony No. 5* (Ng, 2015). The project, ironically baptised "VAN Beethoven", consisted of a customised truck which included a VR application for mobile devices, used together with a VR headset (ibid.). London-based Philharmonia Orchestra (PO) has been experimenting with VR since 2015 and has been involved in different VR projects ever since. These include digital installations in the UK and Europe; a VR film to commemorate 40 years since the launch of the Voyager 1 and 2 spacecraft, and the Golden Records they transported; and a VR documentation of a live performance (Philharmonia Orchestra, no date). Another London-based orchestra, the Royal Philharmonic Orchestra (RPO), featured exclusive material and excerpts of performances filmed in 360° VR on their official website

(Royal Philharmonic Orchestra, 2018). Konzerthausorchester Berlin presented its first VR project in September 2015. Visitors were able to wear goggles in a small foyer in the Konzerthaus Berlin and find themselves in the middle of the orchestra (Konzerthaus Berlin, no date). The LA Phil, the PO and Konzerthaus Berlin have projected themselves outside the walls of the concert hall, but neither of them has used VR inside the auditorium of a concert hall.

VR technologies have been incorporated in live orchestral performances by the Houston Symphony Orchestra in their programming throughout the 2017/2018 season. For the closing concert the orchestra performed a digital version of Igor Stravinsky's *The Rite of Spring* with a live dancer on stage, whose motion was captured by stereoscopic cameras simulating human binocular vision. A computer software converted the movements into 3D animations and avatar dancers projected on a giant screen suspended above the players; the sound waves of the orchestra playing fed into computers and helped to shape the animations. For a totally immersive VR experience of this powerful piece, the audience was encouraged to wear 3D glasses (Lu, 2018).

18.2.5 Interactive imagery: artificial intelligence

During World War II, English mathematician Alan Turing carried out a task for the British government and realised a code breaking machine called *The Bombe*, intended to decipher the Enigma code used by the German army (Kaplan and Haenlein, 2019). Turing was fascinated by the effectiveness of *The Bombe* and started to question the intelligence of such machines. His ideas resulted in an article illustrating how to create intelligent machines, especially how to test their intelligence (Turing, 1950). Now known as the Turing Test, it still is the reference point to determine whether an artificial system is intelligent and the most widely spread definition of AI: a machine is defined intelligent when a human interacting with another human and the machine is not able to tell the difference between the two (ibid.).

At present AI is a vast area of study, overlapping with many different subject areas, including computer science, psychology, philosophy and linguistics (Cawsey, 1998). As a result of its multi-disciplinarity, AI has been defined from different angles, but no formal definition has yet been produced. In a framework of live orchestral events, AI can be interpreted as a machine reproducing and enhancing a specific aspect of the live performance.

In music, AI has played an important part in computer music since the 1950s, mostly concentrating on composition, improvisation and performance (Mántaras and Arcos, 2002). But it was not until 2018 that AI was introduced in live music shows (Nisi, 2018). Italian musician and producer Alex Braga, together with a team from Roma Tre University, built an AI tool capable of decoding the improvisation pattern of any musician on stage in real time, which made him the first musician to use AI in a live performance (Maker Faire Rome, 2018). The first performances were split between Braga, his machines and AI on one side of the stage, a pianist at the other extremity, and a massive video projection in the middle. These performances start with the pianist playing and AI taking the signal coming from the piano, which is connected via Musical Instrument Digital Interface (MIDI) to the AI. After 100 notes, the AI cracks the code and sends unlimited notes (predicted on what the pianist is playing) to Braga's equipment. Braga then assigns the MIDI notes to virtual instruments and is able to build electronic orchestrations whilst the pianist is playing (ibid).

In a context of live classical orchestral music, a group of researchers from the Johannes Kepler University in Linz and the Austrian Research Institute for Artificial Intelligence in Vienna presented the first application of machine learning in live music at The Royal Concertgebouw, a world renowned concert hall in Amsterdam (Arzt *et al.*, 2015). A music-tracking algorithm listened to the live incoming audio streams created by the orchestra playing Richard Strauss' *Eine Alpensinfonie* and followed its progress in the score. The output was then integrated to extra content (notes on the pieces, artistic imagery) on tablet computers provided to the audience during the live performance and the purpose of the application was to enhance the concert experience of the users (ibid.). In Autumn 2018, the London Contemporary Orchestra (LCO) presented for the first time in the classical music scene a live concert accompanied by visuals generated by an AI algorithm on the notes of Giacinto Scelsi's *Uaxuctum: The Legend of the Mayan City, Destroyed by Themselves for Religious Reasons*, and John Luther Adams' *Become Ocean* (Barbican, no date). The event, hosted at the Barbican in London with the help of installation design studio Universal Assembly Unit, saw the LCO on stage behind a semitransparent mesh (a recursive neural net engineered by AI technology company Artrendex). While the LCO was playing, a newly built AI generated images which were projected onto the mesh, interacting with the music played by the orchestra. Splashes of colour danced in front of the semi-hidden musicians, while conductor and co-Artistic Director Robert Ames stood right in the centre of a spotlight and waved his baton, creating suggestive shadow games with his gestures.

At present AI's appliances in live music performances are still sporadic and no other orchestra has incorporated AI technologies to enhance their performances in front of an audience. The LCO is nevertheless currently involved in other projects featuring AI and will present new live shows in the near future. More than one year will divide the first show they presented and the next project. It will therefore be interesting to see whether there has been any technical implementation, any change in the audience (old vs. new) and read reviews.

18.3 DISCUSSION AND CONCLUSIONS

This chapter explores how orchestras have been incorporating different forms of digital technology with their live performances during the last couple of years. It presents in what ways orchestras have integrated elements of electronic music with the classical repertoire; to what extent they have employed AR and VR technologies, incorporated large screens or mobile devices, have worked with AI. The reviews of contemporary practices integrating digital technologies with live orchestral performances revealed a series of interesting information and this section presents the key findings in the context of the core theoretical concepts outlined earlier in the background and related work paragraphs. It will also explore in more detail the main purposes of combining digital technologies in relation to audience development, to what extent digital technologies have been used by orchestras and which are the obstacles and limitations of using digital technologies in the context of live orchestral music.

Recent performances by the London Contemporary Orchestra (LCO) have integrated AI elements in order to enhance their live concerts and reshape them into both aural and visual experiences, allowing the audience to enjoy a series of AI generated visuals while listening to a classical music piece. The LCO's first project was presented at the Barbican Hall in London in Autumn 2018 and reviews revealed mixed feelings. *The Guardian* journalist Stephen Pritchard (2018) thought that the visuals and screen felt too intrusive, therefore alienating the orchestra from the audience. But according to composer and music journalist Timmy Fisher (2018) a younger audience reacted with enthusiasm to this new marriage between AI and orchestra. Both reviews reflect the findings of research exploring how classical music audiences adapt to new technology. What emerged for example from a study on the audience of the London Symphony Orchestra by Crawford *et al.* (2014) is a scepticism by frequent concertgoers towards new technology tools, perceived as not strictly necessary or even invasive (ibid.). This scepticism was mostly nourished by the widespread belief that the average classical music listener does not need any tool to support a live concert experience (ibid.). In contrast, in his research on digitisation in music, Carboni (2014) explored the impact of technology with the support of different case studies, all of them proving how classical music could embrace technology tools in order to reach its existing or new audiences.

Digital technology tools can also support orchestras to reach a public that for different reasons has never had the opportunity to attend a classical music event. In 2015 the LA Phil launched the VAN Beethoven project, a customised truck featuring the orchestra's virtual reality app showcasing the first minutes of Beethoven's *Symphony No. 5* in an immersive environment. The VAN was brought to various areas in LA with the purpose of bringing the orchestra to the people, rather than expecting audiences to come to see the orchestra playing in a concert hall (Hempel, 2015).

In light of the aforementioned benefits of integrating digital technology with live performances, why have orchestras barely incorporated them in their concerts (if compared to other music genres)? The first barrier of incorporating digital technologies with a live orchestral performance is whether technology tools are financially feasible for an orchestra. In the case of AR technologies, first-rate headsets (i.e. Microsoft Hololens) cost around £2,700 per person, which generates a £8 million price tag for an audience of a 3,000 seat auditorium. The unsustainability of high costs could explain why orchestras have not been investing in AR. Nevertheless, as demonstrated by Webb (2017) in his project with the Oakland Symphony Orchestra, there are cheaper alternatives on the market, i.e. ZapBox for less than £30. At this stage, given this alternative, it is questionable whether AR has not yet been used in live classical music concert because of its unsustainable costs.

On the VR front, tech giants including Google, Sony, Samsung and Facebook rushed to release futuristic headsets promising to spread VR among the general public (Petrock, 2019). VR has not reached its climactic moment yet, held back by high costs which had an impact on VR applications in orchestral live performances. At this stage it still needs to be investigated whether money is the issue; the next stage of the research will analyse different case studies and conduct an in-depth qualitative research through interviews with the organisations involved and participant observation.

On a broader spectrum, developments in digital technologies as well as their accessibility, encouraged their dissemination in live music performances. Mobile devices have been used during rock concerts for interactive audience participation, AR and VR elements have been presented at numerous music festivals, AI has been employed to create holograms, projections on screens have been used in live performances for decades and electronic music has been incorporated into numerous genres. The practices review presented in this chapter demonstrates that orchestras have experimented with digital technologies as well. However, if compared to other music genres, orchestras offer fewer examples of performances featuring digital technologies elements in their live performances. Studies suggest that this is caused by marketing strategies focusing on audience development; other studies point to economic reasons; some reconnect it to format (classical music as a genre does not need digital technologies).

The use of digital technologies is expanding and increasingly growing, as numerous reports have demonstrated (European Commission, 2017; Petrock, 2019). Recent studies have also shown that young consumers prefer to invest money in experiences rather than artefacts (Barton *et al.*, 2014). It will therefore be interesting to see if in the near future more orchestras will experiment with digital technologies and incorporate them in their live performances, or even if the orchestras that have already integrated digital tools will continue to employ them in a live context. In addition, it could be valuable to detect potential common patterns and relevant feedback from different segments of the audience and within the organisations themselves.

REFERENCES

ArtiShock (no date). Holograms fills concert hall!, *ArtiShock* (website), available online from https://www.artishock.com/portfolio/hololens-in-concert/ [accessed August 2019].

Arzt, A., Frostel, H., Gadermaier, T., Gasser, M., Grachten, M., Widmer, G. (2015). Artificial intelligence in the Concertgebouw, *Proceedings of the International Joint Conference on Artificial Intelligence (IJCAI)*. Buenos Aires, Argentina.

Barbican (no date). London Contemporary Orchestra: Other Worlds, *Barbican* (website), available online from https://www.barbican.org.uk/sites/default/files/documents/2018-10/Other%20Worlds%20for%20web.pdf [accessed September 2019].

Barton, C., Koslow, L., Beauchamp, C. (2014). How Millennials Are Changing the Face of Marketing Forever, *Boston Consulting Group* (website), available online from https://www.bcg.com/publications/2014/marketing-center-consumer-customer-insight-how-millennials-changing-marketing-forever.aspx [accessed August 2019].

Böhlandt, M. (2008). "Kontakte" – Reflexionen naturwissenschaftlich- technischer Innovationsprozesse in der frühen Elektronischen Musik Karlheinz Stockhausens (1952–1960). *Ber. Wissenschaftsgesch*, Vol. 31, pp. 226–248.

Carboni, M. (2014). The digitization of music and the accessibility of the artist. *Journal of Professional Communication*, Vol. 3, No. 2, pp. 149–164.

Cawsey, A. (1998). *The essence of artificial intelligence, the essence of computing series*. London, Prentice Hall.

Crawford, G., Gosling, V.K., Bagnall, G., Light, B.A. (2014). An orchestral audience: classical music and continued patterns of distinction. *Cultural Sociology*, Vol. 8, No. 4, pp. 483–500.

Dene, L. (2006). Jeff Mills Blue Potential Review, *BBC* (website), available online from https://www.bbc.co.uk/music/reviews/vxrg/ [accessed September 2019].

Dixon, S. (2006). A history of virtual reality in performance, *International Journal of Performance Arts and Digital Media 2*, Vol. 2, No. 1, pp. 23–54.

Dobson, M.C. (2010). New Audiences for Classical Music: The Experiences of Non-attenders at Live Orchestral Concerts, *Journal of New Music Research*, Vol. 39, No. 2, pp. 111–124.

Dragani, R. (2019). Augmented reality will change concerts forever, *Verizon* (website), available online from https://www.verizon.com/about/our-company/fourth-industrial-revolution/augmented-reality-will-change-concerts-forever [accessed August 2019].

Eeles, C. (2006). Jeff Mills – Blue Potential, *Resident Advisor* (website), available online from https://www.residentadvisor.net/reviews/3883 [accessed September 2019].

European Commission (2017). Augmented and Virtual Reality, *European Commission* (website), available online from https://ec.europa.eu/growth/tools-databases/dem/monitor/content/augmented-and-virtual-reality [accessed August 2019].

Evans, L. (2018). Musicians callout!, *Paraorchestra and Friends* (website), available online from http://paraorchestra.com/musicianscallout/ [accessed March 2020].

Fisher, T. (2018). An apocalyptic spectacle from Robert Ames and the LCO, Bachtrack (website), available online from https://bachtrack.com/review-scelsi-adams-london-contemporary-orchestra-barbican-october-2018 [accessed September 2019].

Furness, H. (2017). Classical music app to send programme notes to your phone as orchestra plays, *The Telegraph* (website), available online from https://www.telegraph.co.uk/news/2017/06/26/classical-music-app-send-programme-notes-phone-orchestra-plays/ [accessed October 2019].

Gervais, S. (2019). Wolfgang, l'appli qui sous-titre les symphonies, *France Musique* (website), available online from https://www.francemusique.fr/emissions/musique-connectee/musique-connectee-du-jeudi-28-fevrier-2019-69439 [accessed October 2019].

Gordon, J. (2015). Björk Shares 360° Virtual Reality "Stonemilker" Video, *Pitchfork* (website), available online from https://pitchfork.com/news/59847-bjork-shares-360-virtual-reality-stonemilker-video/ [accessed August 2019].

Harvey, J. (1975). Stockhausen's 'Hymnen', *The Musical Times*, Vol. 116, No. 1590, pp.705–707.

Hempel, J. (2015). LA's Philharmonic is bringing the symphony to everyone. In VR, *Wired* (website), available online from https://www.wired.com/2015/09/la-philharmonic-vr/ [accessed August 2019].

Hödl, O., Kayali, F., Fitzpatrick, G., (2012). Designing interactive audience participation using smart phones in a musical performance, *Proceedings of the International Computer Music Conference*, Ljubljana.

Kaplan, A., Haenlein, M. (2019). Siri, Siri, in my hand: Who's the fairest in the land? On the interpretations, illustrations, and implications of artificial intelligence, *Business Horizons*, Vol. 62, pp. 15–25.

Kirchmeyer, H. (2010). *Konfliktstoff ‚Pausenzeichen': Ein Kapitel Hamburg-Kölner Rundfunkgeschichte aus der Sicht Herbert Eimerts, nebst einem Nachspann bislang unveröffentlichter Briefe Eimerts und Stockhausens aus dem Jahre 1952.* Archiv für Musikwissenschaft 67, pp. 52–76.

Konzerthaus Berlin (no date). Virtual Konzerthaus, *Konzerthaus Berlin* (website), available online from https://www.konzerthaus.de/en/virtuelles-konzerthaus [accessed August 2019].

Levin G., Gibbons, S., Shakar, G., Sohrawardy Y., Gruber J., Lehner J., Schmidl G., Semlak, E. (2001). *Dialtones: A Telesymphony.* Final Report. *Flong* (website), available online from http://www.flong.com/projects/telesymphony/ [accessed March 2020].

Lu, C. (2018). Houston symphony experiments with live music, dance, and virtual reality, *Houston Public Media* (website), available online from https://www.houstonpublicmedia.org/articles/arts-culture/2018/05/18/286171/houston-symphony-experiments-with-live-music-dance-and-virtual-reality/ [accessed September 2019].

Maker Faire Rome (2018). A-MINT: AI & Music to try MFR18, *Maker Faire Rome* (website), available online from https://2019.makerfairerome.eu/en/a-mint-ai-music-to-try-mfr18/ [accessed September 2019].

Mántaras, R.L., Arcos, J.L. (2002). AI and music: from composition to expressive performance, *AI Magazine*, Vol. 23, pp. 43–58.

Mayuzumi, T., Cox, C.L. (2018). The principles of electronic music (1956). *Contemporary Music Review* 37, pp. 100–120.

Melnick, K. (2017). How to watch the Gorillaz 360° music video on any VR headset, *VRScout* (website), available online from https://vrscout.com/news/watch-gorillaz-360-music-video-vr-headset/ [accessed August 2019].

Melnick, K. (2019). Coachella Debuts Its First Interactive AR Stage, *VRScout* (website), available online from https://vrscout.com/news/coachella-ar-interactive-stage/ [accessed August 2019].

Murayama, S., Torii, I., Ishii, N. (2014). Development of projection mapping with utility of digital signage, In *2014 IIAI 3rd International Conference on Advanced Applied Informatics*, IEEE pp. 895–900.

Ng, D. (2015). L.A. Philharmonic's Van Beethoven takes virtual reality for a classical spin, *Los Angeles Times* (website), available online from https://www.latimes.com/entertainment/arts/la-et-cm-los-angeles-phil-vr-20150924-story.html [accessed September 2019].

Nisi, A. (2018). L'Intelligenza Artificiale? Per la musica è una rivoluzione cosmica, *Ninja Marketing* (website), available online from https://www.ninjamarketing.it/2018/10/06/maker-faire-rome-braga-ai-artificial-intelligence-groundbreakers/ [accessed September 2018].

O'Bannon, R. (no date). Do visuals help classical music? *Baltimore Symphony Orchestra* (website), available online from https://www.bsomusic.org/stories/do-visuals-help-classical-music/ [accessed October 2019].

Oh, J., Herrera, J., Bryan, N., Dahl, L., Wang, G., (2010). Evolving the mobile phone orchestra, *New Interfaces for Musical Expression*, Sydney.

Petrock, V. (2019). Virtual and augmented reality users 2019, *eMarketer* (website), available online from https://www.emarketer.com/content/virtual-and-augmented-reality-users-2019 [accessed August 2019].

Philharmonia Orchestra (no date). Virtual reality & apps, Philharmonia Orchestra (website), available online from https://www.philharmonia.co.uk/digital/virtual_reality_and_apps [accessed August 2019].

Polyarts (no date). Carl Craig: Versus + Orchestra, *Polyarts* (website), available online from https://www.polyarts.co.uk/artists/carl-craig-versus-orchestra [accessed September 2019].

Pritchard, S. (2018). The week in classical: Other Worlds; Cendrillon; St Matthew Passion – review, *The Guardian*, (website), available online from https://www.theguardian.com/music/2018/nov/04/other-worlds-barbican-review-cendrillon-glyndebourne-tour-st-matthew-passion-eto [accessed September 2019].

Ravens, C. (2017). How Carl Craig spent a decade bringing his best tracks to life for orchestra on *Versus*, *FACT Magazine* (website), available online from https://www.factmag.com/2017/04/25/carl-craig-versus-interview/ [accessed September 2019].

Rosner, T. (no date). Britten / Four Sea Interludes / Miami / San Francisco / Philadelphia / LA / 2013–14, *Tal Rosner Video Design + Direction* (website), available online from http://www.talrosner.com/britten/four-sea-interludes/miami/san-francisco/philadelphia/la/2013-14 [accessed October 2019].

Royal Philharmonic Orchestra (2018). Royal Philharmonic Orchestra and Google Arts & Culture forge new partnership to take orchestral music to a new generation, *Royal Philharmonic Orchestra* (website), available online from https://www.rpo.co.uk/about/news-press/95-press/310-royal-philharmonic-orchestra-and-google-arts-culture-forge-new-partnership-to-take-orchestral-music-to-a-new-generation [accessed August 2019].

Silva, R., Oliveira, J., Giraldi, G. (2003). Introduction to augmented reality, *National Laboratory of Scientific Computation*.

Smith, N.K. (2017). How virtual reality is shaking up the music industry, *BBC* (website), available online from https://www.bbc.co.uk/news/business-387 95190 [accessed August 2019].

Steijn, A.M. (2014). Classical music, liveness and digital technologies. In: Richards, G., Marques, L., Mein, K. (eds.) *Event design social perspectives and practices*. London: Routledge, pp. 119–129.

Stubbs, D. (2018). *Mars by 1980: the story of electronic music*. London, Faber & Faber.

Taghavi, A., Samiei, A., Mahzari, A., McMahan, R., Prakash, R., Farias, M., Carvalho, M. (2019). A taxonomy and dataset for 360° videos, *Proceedings of the 10th ACM Multimedia Systems Conference*, Amherst, Massachusetts.

Technical Direction Company (TDC) (no date). TDC brings Visions of Vienna to live, *Technical Direction Company* (website), available online from http://www.tdc.com.au/visionsofvienna [accessed October 2019].

The Philadelphia Orchestra (2014). The Philadelphia Orchestra Launches LiveNote™, An Interactive Concert Guide for Mobile Devices, *The Philadelphia Orchestra* (website), available online from https://tinmenandthetelephone.com/projects/tinmendo/ [accessed October 2019].

Tin Men and the Telephone (no date). Tinmendo interactive concert app, *Tin men and the telephone* (website), available online from https://tinmenandthetelephone.com/projects/tinmendo/ [accessed October 2019].

Trueman, D. (2007). Why a laptop orchestra?, *Organised Sound*, Vol. 12, No. 2, pp. 171–179.

Turing, A.M. (1950). I.—Computing machinery and intelligence, *Mind LIX*, pp. 433–460.

Walt Disney Concert Hall (no date). insideOUT 10th Anniversary Celebration, *Walt Disney Concert Hall* (website), available online from http://wdch10.laphil.com/season/10celebration.html [accessed October 2019].

Wang, G. (2014). Ocarina: Designing the iPhone's Magic Flute. *Computer Music Journal*, Vol. 38, No. 2, pp. 8–21.

Webb, R. (2017). Augmented Reality and the Oakland Symphony, *Medium* (website), available online from https://medium.com/@RylandWebbUX/augmented-reality-and-the-oakland-symphony-3186137853e6 [accessed August 2019].

Webb, S. (2019). Smartphones welcome! BBC Philharmonic transforms concerts with live updates sent to audiences' phones, *BBC* (website), available online from https://www.bbc.co.uk/mediacentre/latestnews/2019/smartphones-welcome-bbc-philharmonic [accessed October 2019].

Wise, B. (2013). Orchestras use new video technology, courting a younger crowd, *WQXR Blog* (website), available online from https://www.wqxr.org/story/311596-orchestras-video-technology-younger-crowd/ [accessed October 2019].

19

Free ensembles and small (chamber) orchestras as innovative drivers of classical music in Germany

Alenka Barber-Kersovan and Volker Kirchberg

19.1 INTRODUCTION

This chapter takes as its theme the current state and development of classical art-music in Germany. This musical arena might be presumed to be in crisis yet has been experiencing transformations that contradict the negative prophecies about the future of this musical genre. Innovations have been emerging from smaller orchestras that are organized in less bureaucratic and informal ways. These might be found in free ensembles and relatively young and small (chamber) orchestras' implementation of innovative and unconventional strategies, on all levels of the musical, performative and organizational practice. However, there is also currently the emergence of 'liquid orchestras' – a term derived from the sociologist Zygmunt Bauman's (2013) 'liquid times' or societies. Here, we transfer his general observation of society to these orchestras. These orchestras often have uncertain, precarious and variable structures, frequently engaging part-time-employed or ad hoc hired musicians and staff. The labelling of these orchestras as "free ensembles" renders the term 'free' – in neoliberal times – absurd.

19.2 THE PRESUMED CRISIS OF CLASSICAL ART-MUSIC

In Germany, over the last couple of decades, the (political) discourse on classical art-music has been dominated by the concern about the future of this musical arena. Symphony orchestras in particular, which are often regarded as the epitome of European high culture and financed accordingly by public and private subsidies, have seemed to be under risk. The most obvious (and often-cited) signs of this threat are the ageing of the listening public and the decline in the sales of recorded media. Among other negative indicators are both growing competition and rising production costs in the face of declining or at least stagnating (state) subsidies. These are sometimes compounded by the reunification of the two German states, and this has led to mergers or even closures of some established orchestras. Cultural policies have responded to this assumed threat of 'disappearance' (cf. Deutsche Orchestervereinigung 2011; Heinen 2013; Gembris and Menze 2018, among others) with massive investments in music mediation and audience development. Target groups of these investments are especially young people (cf. Plank-Baldauf 2019) and people with intercultural backgrounds (cf. Mandel 2014; Allmanritter 2017). A further strategy to strengthen this musical genre was the inclusion of the orchestra scene in the Germany's 'Nationwide Inventory of Intangible Cultural Heritage' (UNESCO, no date; cf. DOV 2014).

Although the concern was partly confirmed by empirical data, the fear did not materialize (cf. Keuchel 2014; Concerti Media GmbH 2016). On the contrary, because a closer look at the classical scene shows that in this field a dramatic transformation has taken place, in which on the one hand some traditional performance formats indeed lost their appeal. On the other hand, this process was accompanied by various innovations around concert life that contradict the pessimistic prophecies about the future of this musical area. In this respect the most important impulses came from free ensembles and (chamber) orchestras with their potentially unconventional performative practices (cf. Lorber and Schick 2019).

Accordingly, the research question that we consider here is to study reasons and consequences of the conspicuous emergence and current significance of these new and often rather non-bureaucratic, and – at least to the outside – 'informal' small orchestras. This appearance is associated with both the renewed interest from new concert audiences, and politicians concerned with culture. However, the appearance is also indicative for a society that emphasizes the uncertainties of 'liquid times' (Bauman 2013) in the late capitalist and neo-liberal era – the structures of labour and working conditions in these orchestras strongly resemble either the general new working environment of start-ups, or network-based projects under temporary or self-employment conditions (cf. Boltanski and Chiapello 2005).

19.3 THEORETICAL FRAMEWORK

According to studies by Braun-Thürmann (2005), Drucker (2006) and Howaldt and Jacobsen (2010), innovations are both multi-layered phenomena of existing social practices, and products of inevitable social changes in our work and life environments. These practices can relate to different aspects of social life, such as technology, economy, or social and cultural issues. Therefore, an innovation is always affected by and embedded in a broader social setting, which in turn confirms or rejects (socially, economically, or symbolically) a given innovation. This theoretical concept of external conditions affecting the production of culture has its basis in the sociological "production-of-culture" approach as developed by Peterson and Anand (2004). In consequence, an innovation is never a novelty *sui generis*, but can be considered as such only in relation to dominant conditions; it refers to issues such as renewal, change or revitalisation and implies a departure from the prevailing conventional system (cf. Piazza 2017). The main conventional organization that the free ensembles significantly differ from is the organization of the 'Kulturorchester', with a very specific (and union-confirmed) legal contract for salaries and tariffs, regulated for 129 publicly subsidized orchestras in Germany (cf. Zieba and O'Hagan 2013).

This chapter presents a preparatory study that is theoretically founded in entrepreneurial, innovational, and work-transformation studies on micro, meso, and macro levels (cf. Moore 2016; Loacker 2013; Gielen et al. 2012). The project as a whole assumes that the appearance of these smaller ensembles are indicators for and results of significant changes in the work and life-organization of late capitalism and neo-liberalism (cf. Sennett 1998; Boltanski and Chiapello 2005; Bröckling 2005). One expression that perhaps most accurately describes these changes not only in the labour market but also of organizing life in late capitalism, is the "gig economy" (Crouch 2019).

Musicians that work in these liquid orchestras are typical of an artistic labour market that is organized as a vertically disintegrated system of production, or as a gig economy. This system encourages innovation, but it also shapes and restricts individual careers and increases uncertainties around their development (cf. Menger 2006). In these liquid times, employability and salary levels depend not only upon a very high professional qualification as a musician, but also on the innovativeness of performance styles, extraordinary compilations of music pieces, and an elastic readiness for project- and network-based teamwork. In our analysis, we focus on the musicians, the staff, and the musical bodies associated with these free ensembles and smaller orchestras, and consider four levels of analysis, which are all closely related to each other:

- Individual characteristics and patterns of musicians (micro level)
- Musical-performative issues (micro to meso level)
- Organizational issues (meso level)
- Societal and policy issues (macro level)

Based on these theoretical foundations, we conducted ethnographic observations and document-analyses (of homepages, newspaper reports and videos) of five prominent free ensembles in Northern Germany (*Ensemble Resonanz, ensemble reflektor, STEGREIF.orchester, Orchester im Treppenhaus* and *junge norddeutsche philharmonie*). They are notable for their strife for musical distinction, their experimental approach towards repertoire, and their enthusiasm and joyful playing appeal – to a younger generation of listeners – who have not previously been concert goers.

19.4 THE GERMAN ORCHESTRA SCENE

Today in Germany, there are estimated to be some 800 orchestras that are capable of performing conventional classical-music concert programmes. However, they play at different levels of quality and work under different organizational, legal and financial conditions. In an international comparison, a special feature of the German orchestral scene represents the so-called 'Kulturorchester' (cultural orchestras; Mertens 2019). This term, which is still often viewed with discomfort, originates from the Nazi era, and was based on an understanding of art, which gave symphonic music, embodied above all in the 'ingenious' work of Ludwig van Beethoven, the status of the highest cultural asset of the 'German nation' (Felbick 2015). At the same time however, this term also implied trade-union demands, which were first laid down in 1938 in the *Tarifordnung für Deutsche Kulturorchester* (Collective Bargaining Regulations for German Cultural Orchestras). Today, the term Kulturorchester is understood predominantly in the legal sense in order to distinguish them from the other professional orchestras by the type of (high) state subsidy (Mertens 2019: 192). According to the *Deutsches Musikinformationszentrum* (MIZ; German Music Information Centre), there are currently 129 *Kulturorchester*, including 81 theatre orchestras, 29 concert orchestras and 11 radio orchestras, four big bands, 7 radio choirs and 8 chamber orchestras (Mertens 2019: 191).

The decisive criterion for this classification is that the mentioned orchestras are publicly financed, have a permanent staff, are active all year round, and play so-called serious music. The working conditions of musicians, whom as a rule, are employed for an indefinite period – yet can still be terminated – are regulated in the *Tarifvertrag für die Musiker in Kulturorchestern* (Collective Bargaining Agreement for Musicians in Cultural Orchestras) and applied across the whole country. Further, the individual orchestras are classified according to their number of players in the so-called remuneration groups A to D, although there are also some deviations from these general guidelines (cf. Mertens 2019).

19.5 FREE ENSEMBLES AND (CHAMBER) ORCHESTRAS

In addition to the Kulturorchester, there are now also numerous ensembles and (chamber) orchestras that are called 'free'. They are put together by mostly young musicians, who earn their living as freelancers; this might be termed a 'portfolio career'. In addition, some of them are shareholders of an ensemble, thus participating directly in its economic success or failure (cf. Holst 2014).

In Great Britain, and especially in London, a similar development has occurred in the last ten years. This vibrant 'alternative classical music scene' is predominantly active in unconventional venues from warehouses to pubs to abandoned underground stations, or even in a multi-story car park in Peckham (by the Multi-Story Orchestra), and presented by promoters such as 'Nonclassical' or on the 'London Contemporary Music Festival' (Djuric and Andrewes 2014). In both Great Britain and Germany, these musical bodies act independently and are increasingly perceived as a separate structure apart from the established orchestras, mostly not receiving (any major) institutional support (cf. FREO 2018).

According to MIZ (the German Music Information Centre) there should be about 180 corresponding free ensembles in Germany, although the number is probably higher (cf. Lorber and Schick 2019) due to many not being reported. These are mostly smaller ensembles, chamber orchestras and in rare cases full-scale symphony orchestras, and the transitions between the different line-ups are fluid. As is still evident from the under-researched history of this field, the first ensembles of this kind formed during the 1920s and 1930s. With their transparent musical texture, they represented a counterweight to the bombastic sound masses of the late Romantic period and put new accents upon the repertoire. On one hand the emphasis was on the rediscovered 'early' music, and on the other, the cultivation of the avant-garde chamber music of that time. Key works that promoted this development were *Pierrot Lunaire* by Arnold Schönberg (1912) and *Die Geschichte vom Soldaten* by Igor Stravinsky (1917) with their perhaps less conventional chamber instrumentations (Flender 2007).

Although the division of the free ensembles into 'old' and 'new' music is only schematic, because this scene is characterized by a remarkable variety of line-ups, programme orientations and presentation forms, the MIZ has maintained the above-mentioned classification. Orchestras dedicated to early music often pursue the concept of 'historically informed performance practice'. They play baroque and early classical music on authentic instruments, make use of the expressions and technical possibilities of past times or devote themselves to the revival of works that have already fallen into oblivion. However, those ensembles specializing in 'modern' music tend to work closely together with composers, encourage new compositions or integrate new works into their programmes, so that – with the exception of some radio orchestras – they can be regarded as the actual promoters of the contemporary musical creativity (cf. Lorber and Schick 2019).

As can be seen from the MIZ statistics, free ensembles have been founded in several waves. Although there were some post-war 'free' chamber orchestras active, it was not until the mid-1980s that this scene experienced a veritable founding boom. At that time *Ensemble Modern*, *ensemble recherche* and the *Freiburger Barockorchester* were formed, and these became role models for numerous successor formations. According to FREO (2018), this wave of foundations could be traced back to the 'inertia' of the large institutions, which relied on the classical-romantic repertoire, performed by large orchestras in large newly built concert halls. The same inertia applied to music academies, which preserved the traditional educational canon and neglected both historical performance practice and the promotion of modern music, which again, prompted many composers to establish their own ensembles.

As a matter of importance, it must be pointed out that during the 1980s and 1990s, the free ensembles did not only play music that differed from the established concert programmes. They also broke with the conventions of the existing concert system in order to modify their performative practices both aesthetically and organizationally – according to their needs. This also largely applied to the new generations of ensembles that were founded around the turn of the millennium. They continue to react flexibly to the dramatic changes in the broader social context, and implement innovative aspects at all levels of musical, performative and organizational practice.

19.6 ENSEMBLES RESEARCHED

Although the outstanding quality of the above ensembles is of enormous importance – for leading the way, setting standards and developing new presentation strategies – up until now they were seldom a subject of actual research. There are some scattered articles dealing with specific aspects of the free musical scene, but empirical studies that would provide a comprehensive overview of this musical field are lacking. Consequently, the outcomes of the research presented here are still explorative, focusing on the musicians involved and the innovative character of their performative practices. Based upon both our ethnographic observations and also the study of documents such as homepages of the ensembles, newspaper reports and videos, the following statements were deduced from the analysis of the following five ensembles:

- ***Ensemble Resonanz*** was founded in 1994 by the members of the *Junge Deutsche Philharmonie* (Young German Philharmonics). The 18-strong core-musician ensemble is based in Hamburg, has the status of the orchestra in residence of the new *Elbphilharmonie* concert hall and owns also a club-like venue of its own, the '*Resonanzbunker*'. The ensemble views itself as an interface between a chamber orchestra and a new-music soloist ensemble. In its concerts, the ensemble draws on the contrast between old and contemporary music, juxtaposing unorthodox interpretations of classical works with the musical avantgarde, offering its public unfamiliar listening experiences. In 2002, the ensemble was awarded the *Orchestra of the Future* award by the *Würth-Stiftung*, followed in 2016 by the *Classical:NEXT Innovation Award* for its project *Urban String*, which situates classical music in a club atmosphere.
- ***Orchester im Treppenhaus*** was established in 2006 by the cellist and conductor Thomas Posth. It is situated in Hannover where it is praised as being 'a sensation'. As with other ensembles researched herein, this group also works with an augmented-performance concept and explores the boundaries of the live concert by opening doors to new listening experiences. The ensemble and its conductor were repeatedly honoured with prestigious awards, e.g. the *pro-vision-Preis* of the *Stiftung Kulturregion Hannover* (amongst others) in 2015.
- ***ensemble reflector*** was founded in 2015 by the conductor Thomas Klug – a well-known figure of this scene: He was the concertmaster of the *Deutschen Kammerphilharmonie Bremen*, and as the conductor and artistic director of *Ensemble Resonanz* for two years. His new orchestra includes some 40 young professional musicians and is situated in Hamburg and Lüneburg. It is self-governed and independent, giving musicians space for participation and the development of a broad

range of programmes without any boundaries. In 2019, the orchestra was awarded the *Max-Brauer-Preis* by the *Alfred-Toepfer-Stiftung*.
- **STEGREIF.orchester** is an international group of some 30 young, versatile musicians with different musical backgrounds. It is led by the artistic director Juri de Marco and based in Berlin. Since 2015, the ensemble creates innovative, musically and visually powerful reinterpretations of well-known repertoire and explores new dimensions of sound. It is an improvising symphony orchestra, which plays by heart and without a conductor. In 2017 the ensemble received its first major award, the *Berlin Startup Music Prize*, followed by the *Würth Prize* from *Jeunesses Musicales Germany*. Further, the orchestra negotiated a three-year partnership with the *Deutsches Symphonie-Orchester* Berlin and the *junge norddeutsche philharmonie*. This collaboration – *Trikestra* – was established in order to unite artistically and organizationally, and close the gap between the independent music scene and the established musical institutions.
- **junge norddeutsche philharmonie** (Young North German Philharmonic) was founded in 2010 and is situated in Northern Germany. It is a project-based young orchestra, predominantly comprised of music-academy students and dedicated to the development of innovative event formats. Working without hierarchy, members are also encouraged to participate in organizational activities and to develop further skills in areas other than music. As with the *STEGREIF. orchester*, the *junge norddeutsche philharmonie* is a member of the Berlin-based project *Trikestra* and realizes some five–six innovative projects each year.

19.7 INNOVATIVE PERFORMATIVE PRACTICES

Cultural innovations affect the subjective, intersubjective and structural level of music making and are detectable in all processes of musical production, distribution and reception. Significant detail of all such aspects is beyond the scope of this chapter, and so it will focus on the various ensembles and their innovative performative practices. The point of departure is the assumption, that the above so-called 'crisis' of classical art-music is de facto a crisis of conventional performance culture and not of crisis of the art-music itself (cf. Tröndle, 2008: 137). This crisis principally resulted from the fact that the concert system is based on a long tradition, during which conventional musical performances degenerated into rigid concert rituals. For example, at the beginning of the 19th century, it was still customary to consume food or drinks or to talk during a musical performance (cf. Tröndle 2014: 21). However, particularly after the 'concert hall reform' of around 1900, music became detached from the usual social contexts (it became 'autonomous music'), and as a "substitute religion" (Heister 1983) with its entertainment function suppressed.

Conversely, the free ensembles and (chamber) orchestras researched here, all apply several different strategies that can be regarded as innovative in comparison to the conventions of the traditional concerts. It is worth noting that not all of these strategies are deployed by all of the ensembles and not all are deployed in the same fashion. They all have idiosyncrasies, but there are also some features that these orchestras all have in common. Thus, the following can be considered:

1. Traditional concerts usually open with an overture, followed by a solo concert, and after the break the evening reaches its peak with the reproduction of a well-known symphony (cf. Kalbhenn 2011). Most ensembles and orchestras discussed here, however, distance themselves from these formal conventions and develop new concert formats and dramaturgical concepts. Thus, for instance *Orchester im Treppenhaus* organizes *Hygge Concerts* – the name was taken from the Swedish feel-good concept – for which the visitors are supposed to bring their own sitting arrangements in order to experience the music in the most comfortable way. At the *Dark Room* concerts by the same orchestra, the audience is blindfolded and guided by the musicians to their designated seats, for an immersive experience in which the ensemble is accompanied by actors' voices. *STEGREIF.orchester* also performs street music, and encourages the public to sing along, and during the *junge norddeutsche philharmonie* performance of *#etruschka (referring to the Ballet Petruschka by Igor Stravinsky)* – the public could dance.

2. In a traditional concert, there is a fixed stage arrangement. Musicians normally sit in a specific order behind their music stands with a conductor standing in the middle of the orchestra on a low podium, controlling all aspects of the performance. They are all dressed in black, which erases the visibility of the ensemble in order to stress the acoustical component of the performance. This whole set up emphasizes the concept of the faithfulness to the 'musical work' that the orchestra is reproducing.

    However, some ensembles broke with this tradition, and especially radical is *STEGREIF.orchester*. The musicians play by heart and move across the stage in a sort of a choreographed dance, which fulfils them with a feeling of freedom and opens space for creativity and improvisation. Further, no concert dress-code is prescribed, and they wear everyday outfits, reflecting their individuality. Sometimes the musicians even mingle with the public, which also listens standing up or moving around, and the constant motion of all parties turns the whole venue into a huge stage.

3. Considering the repertoire, free ensembles and (chamber) orchestras play a broad range of musical works, with standard classical compositions also amongst them. Although the score remains unchanged, their programmes mostly differ from the established conventions, filling the venue with a specific atmosphere, which traditional orchestras celebrating the seriousness of the 'art religion' often miss. Not all musicians choose to work in a freelance ensemble, not because they weren't offered a suitable job in a *Kulturorchester*, but rather that they just wish for independence and artistic freedom which might

otherwise be suppressed in an established institution. In the ensembles highlighted here, musicians play pieces that they choose themselves in the way they want to hear them. This opens new possibilities for expression and self-realization, which in turn elicits a positive impact upon the public.

4. Some ensembles, especially *STEGREIF.orchester*, which in its projects *#freebeethoven*, *#freeschubert* and *#freebrahms (referring to Beethoven's Eroica, Schubert's Great C major Symphony and Brahm's Third Symphony)* exposed the well-known pieces to radical reinterpretation. The interventions of *STEGREIF.orchester* are immense, because after a fundamental de-construction of the above works, the remaining musical fractions serve as departure points for free improvisations. Although the core material of the original compositions remains recognizable, the re-compositions can be characterized as new works in their own right. Since this orchestra encompasses musicians from different musical backgrounds, the improvisational framework also contains a variety of crossovers into other genres such as jazz, rock, folk and klezmer. A similar concept was realized by the *junge norddeutsche philharmonie* in its project *#etruschka*. In the first part of the concert, the Stravinsky's Petruschka was reproduced without any changes of the musical substance. In the second part, it was taken as a source of inspiration and the sound of the classical symphony orchestra was enlarged by live electronics.

5. Traditional concert rituals (cf. Rösing and Barber-Kersovan 1993; Heger 2013) presuppose the primacy of listening as the only legitimate form of reception of classical music and reduce its perception to contemplative immersion in the work. However, due to a perceived sensory overload (cf. Tröndle 2014), such reception does not correspond with the preferences of today's consumers (cf. Schröder 2014; Thorau et al. 2011). In order to meet such contemporary aesthetic expectations, events by these ensembles often include also other arts, such as literature, dance, theatre, performance art or multimedia presentations. Thus, for instance *Orchester im Treppenhaus* presented the tragic story of the film star Renate Müller by actors, performing against the background of gloomy sounds. In its concerts on romanticism, *Ensemble Resonanz* included fragments from the *Romantic Theory* by Novalis. *STEGREIF.orchester* performed its own version of Mozarts *Don Giovanni* together with the *Neuköllner Oper*, *junge*, and *norddeutsche philharmone* includes dancers in its performances.

6. In their search for the "Classical Concept of the Future" all such contemporary ensembles also include different kinds of media. They work with photo, film and video and their trailers are professionally made and of high artistic quality. *Ensemble Resonanz* has its own CD label and presents a monthly classical radio transmission on the digital radio station *ByteFM*. The web-portal *resonance.digital* aims at 'digital natives' and opens new venues on the Internet. Very similarly, the *STEGREIF.orchester* offers a digital education series called *plural*, as

a new approach to present classical music to a young public. *Orchester in Treppenhaus* developed a programme, in which during the first part of a concert (of traditional works) the public can use a special app on their smartphone to mark their favourite parts of the music, which are then subsequently performed by a chamber ensemble in an intimate setting.

7. The above ensembles do not regard classical music as a hermetically sealed exclusive field. They are put together by musicians who are open to various styles of popular music and are capable of combining them with classical music at a high artistic level. *Ensemble Resonanz*, for example, plays their *Urban String* events together with a DJ and merges classical chamber music with electronic dance music. *ensemble reflektor* performed a concert with the jazz saxophone player Malte Schiller and his band, STEGREIF.orchester made a 'flash mob' together with a choir, a rapper and a soul singer, and it is about to write a techno-symphony. In a similar sense, the *junge deutsche philharmonie* explored the possibilities of a crossover between classical music and electronic (dance) music, and *Orchester im Treppenhaus* proved in its title *disco* that classical instruments can also produce a funky groove.

8. Free ensembles are also prone to leaving the usual concert venues and perform at unusual or unconventional places such as harbour quays, bunker rooms, schools in socially problematic districts, staircases in public housing complexes, and metro stations – to name just a few. Unusual performance spaces both facilitate and trigger unusual performance styles and modes that would be not likely be sanctioned in conventional concert houses (cf. Kirchberg 2020). The layout of the traditionally magnificent concert hall implicitly imposes certain behavioural restrains upon performance. Thus, although the ensembles and (chamber) orchestras do not refuse to play in such venues, they are also trying to make a special break out of the rigidity of classical conventions. *Ensemble Resonanz* established its own performance venue called *Resonanzraum*, which is supposed to be the first chamber music club in Europe. It is situated in a former World War II bunker, which is also the home of many start-ups from the pop music scene, in the gentrified Hamburg inner-city neighbourhood "Schanzenviertel". Further, the ensemble is also playing in other clubs around the town and advertising their performances with red text sprayed on the pavement. *Orchester in Treppenhaus* performs often in a museum, *ensemble reflektor* is in residence in Hamburg *Oberhafen Quartier*, where old warehouses were turned into a creative quarter, and *junge norddeutsche philharmonie* chose as the venue for their *DETECT CLASSIC FESTIVAL* the so-called *RWN terrain*, which was a torpedo research station of the Nazi navy during World War II.

9. Some ensembles are also active also beyond mere playing by putting up their own concert series or even festivals. *Ensemble Resonanz* organizes a *Resonanzraum Festival* with a yearly changing theme; in 2019 the festival was devoted to Romantic Music. *ensemble reflektor* also

invites musical friends from different backgrounds to its 'extended' series of festivals, which started in 2019 with *ultraBach*. This took place in Lüneburg and compromised a series of different events, from splendid concerts to intimate home-music, drawing together professionals, amateurs and music students and culminating in an "imaginary cantata", a newly composed chorale, based on Bach's cantatas. A dancing concert in the music school and a club night further brought Bach into the 21st century.

19.8 CONCLUSION AND OUTLOOK

Looking at these examples, classical music is not extinct in Germany, as was feared in the past by parts of the cultural and political establishment. On the contrary, this musical arena seems to be very much alive and has been doing well for some time. Although innovative approaches are noted in all parts of the classic field, the "actual innovation engines" and "creative laboratories for the classical music scene" (cf. Lorber and Schick 2019; FREO 2018) seem to be the free ensembles and (chamber) orchestras, setting new standards for contemporary musical life.

What makes these ensembles innovative are not just the unconventional programmes. Their organizational forms and working methods differ significantly from those of the so-called *Kulturorchester* and affect aesthetic/musical, performative, technical, media, organizational and financial aspects, closely interconnected in a multi-dimensional dynamic system of mutual relationships. An important issue seems to be the fact that these ensembles are "free", not only in that they lack institutional (financial) support, but also that they have a crucial impact on the question of what music is being played – and how.

Free ensembles take the term 'freedom' quite literally and understand their 'free' makeup as playgrounds in which they can try new things, unfold their creativity and create new paths to classical music both through new concert formats and performance practices. Although deeply rooted in the classical tradition, they try to extend it by exploring soundscapes beyond the boundaries of conventions and looking for interrelationships and cross-pollination of different musical worlds. Their joy of experimentation is not self-centred, but public oriented. All of the above ensembles understand the need for recruitment of new public strata beyond the educated bourgeoisie. They view this as their social obligation, and they also organize educational projects or support school classes within that realm. However, contrary to the established orchestras with their mediating programmes aimed at introducing (young) people to the classical tradition, these new ensembles try to also meet the expectations of the public in a bidirectional dialogue. They do not limit themselves to the reproduction of the standard repertoire, but present themselves with a youthful demeanour. They do not put up barriers between the stage and the auditorium, but make sure that their performances still satisfy the need for relaxation and entertainment.

The results of these efforts have not gone unnoticed. Such unconventional performance practices do seem to appeal to young listeners, who are generally interested in music, but would normally not attend a concert of a so-called *Kulturorchester* in a conventional venue such as a *Konzerthalle*. These new musical bodies seem to resonate with the *Zeitgeist* of the present day, to meet the musical taste of younger new listeners, and to reshape their expectations – previously derived from long-term tastes, places and behaviour patterns.

However, the non-conformism and elastic rule-interpretation of the free ensembles brings more than a pinch of new ideas to the classical-music concert scene. This scene was defined by old and stagnant patterns and is therefore perceived by some as going through an existential crisis; however, the optimism related to the neo-innovative and entrepreneurial spirit has sprinkled it with more than a grain of doubt. The dialectics of innovation and neo-liberal constraints, as pointed out by, e.g. Boltanski and Chiapello (2005) or more recently by Crouch (2019), is characteristic of a labour market that is more and more based on sub-contractors. This is exemplified in the construction sector, Uber drivers in the mobility sector, and AirBnB suppliers in the hospitality sector. It is also now found in the classical-art-music world and defines the labour market for young and able musicians of this area.

We therefore end this article with observations by two sociologists of the arts, Pierre-Michel Menger and Angela McRobbie, who for the last two decades have studied these advantages and disadvantages of the artists' (although not specifically of the musicians') labour market. Menger (2018) laments the contingency of the artistic system of rewards. Since innovation is at the core of this artistic success, newness is a threat from the new arrivals – the free ensembles – being levelled at the formerly successful organizations (e.g. *Kulturorchester*):

> And there is nothing more subtly attractive than a professional world where innovation through exploitation of uncertainty is combined with . . . a narrow crest path between the consolidation of . . . reputation and the permanent exposure of these reputations to challenges from new arrivals.
>
> (Menger 2018: 169)

Whereas Menger – from a structuralist perspective – emphasizes the constraints of a neo-liberal society that demand a "liquid" work environment of permanent self-evaluation and individual responsibility, McRobbie (2009) – from an agency-oriented perspective – offers some light at the end of the tunnel.

> [C]reativity has been instrumentalised as a regime of freedom, bringing with it the possibility of happiness at work. . . . [W]e need to pay more analytical attention to not just the subsumption of life by work but to life itself, how . . . can everyday life be used as a possible instrument for critique against the overwhelming authority of work, can life be a source of creative opposition?
>
> (McRobbie 2009: 136f.)

It will be the task of future research to find out how (and how much) these emerging free ensembles are only a product of a neo-liberal society in liquid times, or whether (and how much) they can constitute an ongoing alternative, non-conformist and creative oppositional force to the current cultural hegemony.

REFERENCES

Allmanritter, V. (2017). *Audience Development in der Migrationsgesellschaft: Neue Strategien für Kulturinstitutionen*. Bielefeld: transcript Verlag.

Bauman, Z. (2013). *Liquid Times: Living in an Age of Uncertainty*. Hoboken: John Wiley & Sons.

Boltanski, L. and Chiapello, E. (2005). *The New Spirit of Capitalism*, trans. G. Elliott. London and New York: Verso.

Braun-Thürmann, H. (2005). *Innovation – Eine Einführung*. Bielefeld: transcript.

Bröckling, U. (2015). *The Entrepreneurial Self: Fabricating a New Type of Subject*. Newbury Park: Sage.

Concerti Media GmbH (Ed.) (2016). *„Typisch Klassik!" Concerti Klassikstudie 2016 - Eine Repräsentativbefragung über Interessen, Gewohnheiten und Lebensstile der Klassikhörer in Deutschland*. concerti (website), www.klassikstudie.de [Access November 2019].

Crouch, C. (2019). *Will the Gig Economy Prevail?* Hoboken: John Wiley & Sons.

Deutsche Orchestervereinigung (DOV) und Zentrum für Kulturforschung (ZfKf) (2011). *Präsentation des 9. KulturBarometers*, http://www.miz.org/dokumente/2011_KulturBarometer.pdf [Access November 2019].

Deutsche Orchestervereinigung (DOV) (2014). *UNESCO-Kulturerbe*, https://www.dov.org/aktuelles/unesco-kulturerbe [Access November 2019].

Djuric, D. and Andrewes T. (2014). *We Break Strings: The Alternative Classical Scene in London*. London: Hackney Classical Press.

Drucker, P. (2006). *Innovation and Entrepreneurship*. New York: Harper Business.

Felbick, L. (2015). Das „hohe Kulturgut deutscher Musik" und das „Entartete" – über die Problematik des Kulturorchester-Begriffs. In: *Zeitschrift für Kulturmanagement*, 2/2015, 85–115.

Flender, R. D. (Ed.) (2007). *Freie Ensembles für Neue Musik in Deutschland*. Mainz: Schott.

Freie Ensembles und Orchester (FREO) (2018). *Mission Statement*, https://freo.online/warum-freo/ [Access November 2019].

Gembris, H. and Menzel, J. (2018). Zwischen Publikumsschwund und Publikumsentwicklung. Perspektiven für Musikerberuf, Musikpädagogik und Kulturpolitik. In: Tröndle, Martin (Ed.): *Das Konzert II. Beiträge zum Forschungsfeld der Concert Studies*. Bielefeld: transcript, 305–332.

Gielen, P., De Bruyne, P., and Bruyne, D. (2012). *Teaching Art in the Neoliberal Realm. Realism Versus Cynicism*. Amsterdam: Valiz.

Heger, K. (2013). *Das Konzert (als musikalische Veranstaltung) und sein Publikum: Wandel und neue Modelle*, https://musikwirtschaftsforschung.files.wordpress.com/2009/03/masterarbeit_katharina-heger.pdf [Access November 2019].

Heinen, A. (2013). *Wer will das noch hören? Besucherstrukturen bei niedersächsischen Sinfonieorchestern*. Heidelberg: Springer Verlag.

Heister, H.W. (1983). *Das Konzert. Theorie einer Kulturform*. Wilhelmshaven: Heinrichshofen.

Holst, Ch. (2014). *Kultur unternehmen: Wie junge Musiker das Kulturmanagement neu erfinden*. BoD.

Howaldt, J. and Jacobsen, H. (Eds.) (2010). *Soziale Innovation: Auf dem Weg zu einem postindustriellen Innovationsparadigma*. Weinheim: Verlag für Sozialwissenschaften.

Kalbhenn, D. (2011). *Konzertprogramme. Das Kernprodukt als Chance und Herausforderung für Konzerthäuser*. Frankfurt/Main: Peter Lang.

Keuchel, S. (2014). Ein erster, zusammenfassender Bericht zum 8. KULTURBAROMETER, http://www.orchestermanagement.de/fileadmin/user_upload/pdf/8_Kulturbarometer_Zusammenfassung_02.pdf [Access November 2019].

Kirchberg, V. (2020). A sociological reflection on the concert venue. In: Tröndle. M. (Ed.). *Classical Concert Studies: A Compendium to Contemporary Research and Performance*. London: Routledge.

Loacker, B. (2013). Becoming 'culturpreneur': How the 'neoliberal regime of truth' affects and redefines artistic subject positions. *Culture and Organization*, 19(2), 124–145.

Lorber, R. and Schick, T.E. (2019). Freie Ensembles. In: Deutscher Musikrat (Ed.). *Musikleben in Deutschland*, https://themen.miz.org/fokus-freie-ensembles [Access November 2019].

Mandel, B. (Ed.) (2014). *Interkulturelles Audience Development: Zukunftsstrategien für öffentlich geförderte Kultureinrichtungen*. Bielefeld: transcript Verlag.

McRobbie, A. (2015) 'Governance der Kreativwirtschaft: Diagnosen und Handlungsoptionen', in Lange, B. et al. (Eds.) *Governance der Kreativwirtschaft: Diagnosen und Handlungsoptionen*. Bielefeld, Germany: transcript Verlag.

Menger, P.M. (2006). Artistic labor markets: Contingent work, excess supply and occupational risk management. *Handbook of the Economics of Art and Culture*, 1, 765–811.

Menger, P.M. (2018). Inequalities in the Arts. In: Halley, J.A. and Sonolet, D.E. (Eds.) (2018). *Bourdieu in Question. New Directions in French Sociology of Arts*. Leiden: Brill, 161–180.

Mertens, G. (2019): Orchester, Rundfunkensembles und Chöre, In: Deutscher Musikrat (Ed.) *Musikleben in Deutschland*, http://www.miz.org/static_de/themenportale/einfuehrungstexte_pdf/03_KonzerteMusiktheater/mertens.pdf [Access November 2019].

Moore, A. (2016). Neoliberalism and the musical entrepreneur. *Journal of the Society for American Music*, 10(1), 33–53.

Nationwide Inventory of Intangible Cultural Heritage | German Commission for UNESCO (UNESCO) (no date). Available at: https://www.unesco.de/en/culture-and-nature/intangible-cultural-heritage/nationwide-inventory-intangible-cultural-heritage (Accessed: 20 April 2020).

Peterson, R.A. and Anand, N. (2004). The Production of Culture Perspective. *Annual Review of Sociology* 30, 311–334.

Piazza, L.A. (2017). *The Concept of the New: Framing Production and Value in Contemporary Performing Arts.* Leverkusen: Verlag Barbara Budrich.

Plank-Baldauf, Ch. (Ed) (2019). *Praxishandbuch Musiktheater für junges Publikum: Konzepte–Entwicklungen–Herausforderungen.* Heidelberg: Springer-Verlag.

Rösing, H. and Barber-Kersovan, A. (1993). Konzertbezogene Verhaltensrituale. In: Bruhn, H. and Rösing, H. (Eds.). *Musikpsychologie. Ein Handbuch.* Reinbek: Rowohlt, 136–147.

Schröder, J.H. (2014). *Zur Position der Musikhörenden. Konzeptionen ästhetischer Erfahrung im Konzert.* Hofheim: Wolke Verlag.

Sennett, R. (1998). *The Corrosion of Character: The Personal Consequences of Work in the New Capitalism.* New York: WW Norton & Company.

Thorau, C. and Odenkirchen, A. and Ackermann, P. (Eds.). (2011). *Musik, Bürger, Stadt. Konzertleben und musikalisches Hören.* Regensburg: Con Brio.

Tröndle, M. (2008). Man muss das Konzert verändern, um es zu erhalten. In: Mandel, Birgit (Ed.). *Audience Development, Kulturmanagement, Kulturelle Bildung. Konzeptionen und Handlungsfelder der Kulturvermittlung.* München: kopaed.

Tröndle, Martin (Ed.) (2014). *Das Konzert. Neue Aufführungskonzepte für eine klassische Form.* Berlin: De Gruyter.

Zieba, M. and O'Hagan, J. (2013). Demand for live orchestral music – The case of German Kulturorchester. *Jahrbücher für Nationalökonomie und Statistik*, 233(2), 225–245.

VIDEOGRAPHY

Das Ensemble Resonanz, https://www.ensembleresonanz.com/das-ensemble-resonanz/ [Access November 2019].

Das Ensemble Resonanz, https://www.youtube.com/watch?v=_QoYuWk1tYw [Access November 2019].

ensemble reflektor // Eroica 4. Satz, https://www.youtube.com/watch?v=QZsgTte13Hc [Access November 2019].

ensemble reflektor bei der 22. clubkinder Tagebuchlesung, https://www.youtube.com/watch?v=TjAr3exqZbQ [Access November 2019].

ensemble reflektor // Eroica 4. Satz, https://www.youtube.com/watch?v=nG36w3DtIQA [Access November 2019].

ensemble reflektor, SYRIAB BAND MIT Ensemble reflektor Orchestra: Bnt Al-shalabia, https://www.youtube.com/watch?v=FIPYHwzk4ik [Access November 2019].

ensemble reflektor // Teaser, https://www.youtube.com/watch?v=QZsgTte.13Hc [Access November 2019].

ensemble reflektor, ultraBach – Ein Festival für Lüneburg und Johann Sebastian Bach, https://ensemble-reflektor.de/ultrabach/ [Access November 2019].

Ensemble Resonanz: Arbeit und Struktur, https://www.youtube.com/watch?v=nfCMCuA0nQ0 [Access November 2019].

Ensemble Resonanz, Konzertsaison 2019/20, Pressekonferenz am 8. Mai 2019, 11 Uhr, im resonanzraum St. Pauli https://www.ensembleresonanz.com/app/uploads/2019/05/Presskit-Ensemble-Resonanz-Saison-2019.20.pdf [Access November 2019].

Ensemble Resonanz, KüchenKonzerte #22: Vogel/Hehemann & Ensemble Resonanz, https://www.youtube.com/watch?v=UfC9vLeC1V8 [Access November 2019].

Ensemble Resonanz // urban string, https://www.youtube.com/watch?v=ZXS-Ntl6wvI [Access November 2019].

Ensemble Resonanz, URBAN STRING industry, https://www.youtube.com/watch?v=ZXS-Ntl6wvI [Access November 2019].

Ensemble Resonanz, urban string elbinsel open air, https://www.youtube.com/watch?v=jsNUqSLdGsQ [Access November 2019].

Ensemble Resonanz, »weihnachtsoratorium« https://www.youtube.com/watch?v=eEos8MJEVE0

junge norddeutsche philharmonie, https://junge-norddeutsche.de/ [Access November 2019].

junge norddeutsche philharmonie, detect classic festival, https://detectclassicfestival.de/ [Access November 2019].

Junge norddeutsche philharmonie, Imagefilm – Das Zukunftsorchester, https://www.youtube.com/watch?v=xTsvFBS15ig [Access November 2019].

junge norddeutsche philharmonie, Sommerprojekt Trailer - junge norddeutsche philharmonie, https://www.youtube.com/watch?v=OZEU_xXI3iM [Access November 2019].

Orchester im Treppenhaus, Musikvermittlung, https://treppenhausorchester.de/news/ [Access November 2019].

Orchester im Treppenhaus: Disco – Kostia Rapoport: Squares on the stairs, https://www.youtube.com/watch?v=4h_OLTgo3_8 [Access November 2019].

Orchester im Treppenhaus, Über den Dächern von Hannover, https://www.youtube.com/watch?v=9VRAbdOiXME [Access November 2019].

STEGREIF.orchester, Filmmusik Orchester Eskalation! - Stegreif live im #BongoBoulevard https://www.youtube.com/watch?v=qc6cUzvOuH8 [Access November 2019].

STEGREIF.orchester, #freebrahms - #bebeethoven, https://www.youtube.com/watch?v=793ElQqTe_g [Access November 2019].

STEGREIF.orchester: #freebrahms-trailer, https://www.youtube.com/watch?v=AcyhI4OEdhY [Access November 2019].

STEGREIF.orchester, Homepage of the orchestra, https://www.stegreif-orchester.de/ [Access November 2019].

STEGREIF.orchester im Stummfilmkino Delphi - #freeschubert 2.0, https://www.youtube.com/watch?v=9RBhxgTKzGo [Access November 2019].

STEGREIF.orchester mit dem OMNIBUS am Brandenburger Tor, https://www.youtube.com/watch?v=amkcKjSGygI [Access November 2019].

20

Transforming musical performance

Activating the audience as digital collaborators

Adrian York

20.1 INTRODUCTION

There has been little research found with a focus on exploring the compositional and performance protocols and technological infrastructure that need to be developed to create successful interactive audience participation within an existing popular music genre using pre-existing technology. This research presented here attempts to respond to that and continue "a dialogue between performer, audience, composer and technology" (York, 2019, p.3). The following text presents a structured case study to address the associated research questions:

1) What is the experience of audience members engaging in interactive musical participation within contemporary jazz?
2) What are the opportunities for incorporating interactive musical participation within contemporary jazz?

The composition *Deeper Love* was composed specifically for this research, as a creative vehicle to implement the findings that emerged out of a performance of *The Singularity*, a pilot study presented at the Innovation in Music conference in 2017. Hödl, Kayali and Fitzpatrick (2012) describe Interactive Musical Participation (IMP) as being "when a spectator can take part or at least make a contribution in a live concert through a technically driven system" (Hödl, Kayali and Fitzpatrick, 2012, p.236). Following on from York's (2019) "Transforming Musical Performance: The Audience as Performer", this chapter illustrates the integration of IMP into the author's artistic practice as a jazz musician.

Several novel elements were developed for the performances of *Deeper Love* including the *Deeper Love* Soundpad App (Toulson and York, 2018), compositional protocols for sampled 'improvised' lines, triggered within Ableton Live by the audience-soloists using WiiMote controllers, the conceptions of audience-performers and audience-soloists as new performer categories in jazz, akin to Biles' (2007) "audience-mediated performance" and a new performance context of 'audience takeover'.

The *Deeper Love* performances are designed to investigate whether this research can relocate this artistic practice from the context of an academic conference to something more real-world such as a concert or club. It also seeks to explore the experiences of the participants in the performance and to make critical judgements on the quality of the interactivity, to analyse the usability and scalability of the technological solutions being used, to develop the performance protocols that underpin this practice, and to evaluate whether the compositional and improvisational methodologies were appropriate and successfully applied. The results taken from the performances will also provide data that will be applicable to further research in this area.

20.2 BACKGROUND AND RELATED WORK

Freeman has created three ranks of interactions in his survey and taxonomy of research and artistic practice in the field of IMP (Freeman, 2005, pp.757–760). The first rank features compositions in which the audience feature directly as 'performers', the second has the audience functioning as 'sound transmitters' of "pre-composed or curated sonic material through the medium of ubiquitous personal handheld digital computing devices such as mobile phones" (York, 2019, p.5). Freeman's third rank sees the audience as 'influencers', interacting by methods including voting via handheld digital devices or waving light sticks in the air. "The data from these inputs is then analysed and presented to the performers as some kind of visual cue that triggers a pre-determined sonic gesture" (ibid., p.5).

York (ibid.) has extended Freeman's survey identifying key influences on the research presented in this chapter. The work of Musica Elettronica Viva (MEV), a composer's cooperative set up in 1966 in Rome is notable and in particular Frederic Rzewski's composition *Sound Pool* (1969), which Rzewski describes as "a form in which all the rules are abandoned" (Rzewski and Verken, 1969, p.94). In *Sound Pool*, the audience is asked to bring along their own instruments and to perform with the MEV, thus becoming part of Freeman's first rank – the audience as performers.

> In the context of Sound Pool musicians are no longer elevated to the position of a star but instead work with the audience managing *energies* and enabling the audience to *experience the miracle* without overwhelming the audience/performers with their virtuosity. The outcome of this process is that the audience no longer exists as a discrete entity.
>
> (York, 2019, p.6)

Freeman's second rank of audience participation – the audience as sound transmitters – was mapped in the first systematic study of what has become known as 'distributed music' by Taylor (2017). Golan Levin's *Dialtones: A Telesymphony* (Levin, 2001), a composition that uses the audience's mobile phones as sound sources, is identified by Taylor as a "foundational composition of this emergent genre". The experience of participating in a performance of *birds* (CoSiMa, 2016) at Music Tech Fest in Berlin in

2016 in which the audience downloaded and then triggered sounds from a web application, played a major role in the creation of the technical infrastructure for this project allowing the audience to become both sound transmitters and performers. The author noted the ubiquity of smartphone ownership amongst the participants and the relative ease with which the web applications were downloaded and then triggered.

Paterson *et al.* (2017) demonstrated various audience-interaction methods with pre-recorded music in an iOS app format called variPlay. This system was one of a number that offered complex control over playback permutations of multiple stems inside an app, yet still with a very simple GUI.

Building from Cook's (2001) principle for designing computer music that researchers should "Make a piece, not an instrument or controller" and Rosenkransa's (2010) proposal that interactivity is measured by the 'frequency of engagement' within a 'mediated communication', another objective of the *Deeper Love* performances is to test out the criteria for a successful audience-participatory experience as proposed by Lee and Freeman (2013, p.450):

- To make participation easy (accessibility)
- To collect gestures from the audience and turn them into a single musical composition (musical security)
- To drive audiences to start participation without reservation (initiation)
- To motivate people to participate and sustain the interest (attraction)
- To provide a clear relationship between their gestures and outcome in music (transparency)

Carrying out the research performances in the context of club and concert performances creates the opportunity for data collection in something approaching a real-world performance setting compared with the constraints of an academic conference. The analysis of this data will lead to the creation of 'performance protocols', a framework for compositional design, and suggestions for a technical infrastructure that will give the outcomes of this research the potential to be carried forward into the mainstream of popular music performance.

There are two separate visions driving this research:

1. At large concerts or music festivals, audiences of many thousands could be transformed into audience-performers, moving from a state of alterity to being part of a new homogenous entity with the performer; that instead of using their phones for shining lights, filming or taking photographs, audience members will become sonic collaborators in the performance creating an 'ontogenic' composition in a process of distributed creativity (Sawyer and DeZutter, 2009).
2. At jazz concerts at clubs and festivals, as well as becoming audience-performers as detailed above, volunteer audience members can become audience-soloists, engaging in improvisation and sonic dialogue with each other and with the other performers.

20.3 DESIGN AND IMPLEMENTATION

The compositional construction of *Deeper Love* is partially developed from conclusions drawn from the evaluation of the pilot performances of *The Singularity*. As with *The Singularity* the chosen metre is 4/4 but for *Deeper Love* a hip-hop swung 16ths feel is utilised at a tempo of eighty-two beats per minute. One of the potential outcomes of this research is to move IMP from being a research-based practice to becoming part of mainstream popular music performance practice. Hip-hop was an influence on 89% of songs in the USA Top 100 charts in 2018 (Hit Songs Deconstructed, 2019) so working within a sub-genre such as hip-hop/jazz rather than something more esoteric creates a link to the mainstream of popular culture. Presenting the research in a musical context not too far removed from the mainstream of popular music may be a factor in gaining acceptance for IMP.

The heuristic analysis drawn from the performances of *The Singularity* indicated that the harmonic complexity of the composition created unwanted dissonances when some of the pitches triggered by the audience-soloists using the WiiMote controllers clashed with the chords. By using modal harmony – one of the archetypal methodologies of modern jazz harmony – for the pitches selected for the *Deeper Love* Soundpad App as well as for the melodic and harmonic material in the composition, no problems were created with the chord-scale relationships, which were then able to function without any issues of dissonance across the harmonic structure of the whole piece.

The scale chosen for *Deeper Love* is the Dorian mode (Figure 20.1), a minor scale with a major 6th and a flattened 7th.

The tune is built around a two-bar double bass ostinato figure (Figure 20.2) which is constructed around two three-note motifs. The first motif consists of the tonic (C) followed by the minor 3rd (Eb) and then the perfect 4th (F). The second motif uses the same intervallic relationships but builds from the fifth degree of the scale of C Dorian (G) moving to Bb and then returning to C. The two motifs then repeat with the repetition being rhythmically displaced. The ostinato figure features all the notes from a C minor pentatonic scale (C Eb F G Bb), all notes but one from C blues scale (C Eb F [F#] G Bb) as well as having five notes out of the seven from the

Figure 20.1 Dorian mode in the Key of C

Figure 20.2 Deeper Love Double Bass Ostinato

C Dorian scale (C [D] Eb F G [A] Bb). This ambivalence from a chord-scale perspective allows for improvisation using all three of these scales. The structure of the piece as shown in Table 20.1.

The first solo from one of the two audience-soloists is featured in the third section. As in the performances of *The Singularity*, they are tasked with pressing buttons on a WiiMote controller to trigger sonic events. The first soloist using WiiMote 4 (Table 20.2) has a series of pre-composed samples of vibraphone motifs and improvised lines in the Dorian mode to use as improvisational source material. There are seven samples in all, and the sample set went through several iterations in a heuristic process of development. One of the conclusions drawn from the research performances of *The Singularity* was that sounds triggered by the audience-soloists should have gentle attack envelopes to avoid rhythmic incompatibility.

On reflection it seemed clear that having a slow attack would lead to less 'interesting' performances; 'interesting' being one of the key criteria for this research. The challenge was to develop samples that could:

- be triggered at any point in the bar and still lead to a satisfying musical conclusion
- allow the audience-soloist to improvise with the samples through a process of discovery, playing, retriggering and joining different sample elements together
- create an informal, immediate, accessible and natural experience for the audience-soloist thus addressing more of the key criteria for this research

The outcome that seemed to be most effective was to use trills, scale and pattern-based motifs and lines that *floated over* the rhythm affording

Table 20.1 Deeper Love Structure

i)	Introduction	8 bars
ii)	Head	8 bars
iii)	Vibes solo (*audience-soloist*)	open duration
iv)	Synthesizer solo (*audience-soloist*)	open duration
v)	Audience Participation 1(*audience-performers*)	open duration
vi)	Introduction	8 bars
vii)	Head	8 bars
viii)	Audience Participation 2 (*audience-performers*)	open duration

Figure 20.3 Deeper Love Vocal Melody

Table 20.2 WiiMote Sonic Element Control for *Deeper Love*

WiiMote 3	Triggers arpeggiated synthesizer patterns
WiiMote 4	Triggers pre-prepared improvised vibraphone motif and phrase samples

a freeform approach to *metric displacement* (Love, 2012) rather than being locked into a strict metrical structure. This approach obviated the need to address any issues of latency management because the accuracy of the trigger point was not relevant. The accompaniment for this section kept the same bass and drum feel with a simplified Dorian mode electric piano part creating a less sonically dense texture than in *The Singularity*, thus ensuring that the audience-soloists can identify their own contributions with clarity.

The fourth section is designed to work as the sonic bed for the second of the two audience-soloists to trigger synthesiser patterns via WiiMote 3 (Table 20.2) using a lead-synth-type sound. The bass and percussion accompaniment remain the same as for the previous section, but the electric piano drops out creating even greater sonic clarity for the improvisors.

The fifth audience-participation section creates a clear contrast, with the previous compositional elements being the moment when the rest of the audience are activated as audience-performer participants in the performance – by triggering the audio samples from the *Deeper Love* Soundpad App on their iPhones. The rhythm is defined by a repetitive shaker loop, and harmony and texture are partially provided by a thirty-bar loop featuring Dorian-scale textures using a single-pitched waterphone-esque sample from Live, to create a suitable soundscape bed. The other textural element is a loop of 31-bar and one beat, with an Ableton bell-type sample featuring a lengthy reverb or backwards reverb tail. This was another improvised part using the Dorian mode. Having the two textural elements looping around different bar lengths implies a polymetric approach (Rubbra, 1953) and creates textural variety as the loops do not cycle together. In this section, the samples are played by the audience-performers, who touch the buttons on their GUI, a 5 x 5 Soundpad grid. There are twenty vocal samples, all of which are either single notes or licks. The other five samples are made up of three more ambient soundscapes, a whispered 'Deeper Love' and a whispered 'aaaah' vowel sound. All the pitched samples use the Dorian mode.

The following two sections are reprises of the introduction and vocal head. The tune ends with a repeat of the audience-participation segment of the composition with the programmed loops gradually fading out leaving the sounds from the audience's iPhones as the final moment of the composition.

Deeper Love is an archetypal modal jazz composition with a structure constructed around a head/solos/head model; however, the interactive elements create the novel structural conception of the audience bringing the performance to a close in the novel performance context of 'audience takeover'.

20.4 TECHNICAL INFRASTRUCTURE

The technical infrastructure for the performances of *Deeper Love* builds on the framework that was utilised for the pilot project, with samples being played back via Ableton Live running on a MacBook Pro. However, in the performances of *The Singularity* an audience-performer was controlling an iPhone running TouchOSC (Hexler, 2019) to trigger different sections of the composition. On reflection, use of such a bespoke installation did not seem like an interactive performance element that could realistically be scaled up, another key objective of this research. As a solution to the issue of upscaling of the numbers of interactive performers, *Deeper Love* audience members instead used distributed sound on their mobile phones via the Soundpad app.

Audio .aif files were imported from a Logic Pro X session into Ableton Live (Figure 20.4) as clips into the various tracks and then eight 'scenes' were created to form the master song structure. Two discrete tracks were set up for the two WiiMote audience-soloists. The first marked *Vibes Wii4* is running the Ableton Sampler and hosting the improvised vibraphone samples. The second called *arpeg beep Wii3* contains a synthesiser patch entitled Dual Osc 2 Pure Lead and an arpeggiator with a Classic UpDown 8th setting.

Both vocal and ambient samples for the *Deeper Love Soundpad* were first trialled within Ableton Live (Figure 20.5) to see how they worked with the backing track for the audience-participation scenes.

Figure 20.4 Deeper Love Ableton Live Session

Figure 20.5 Deeper Love Ableton Live Samples for the *Deeper Love Soundpad App*

Figure 20.6 Deeper Love Performance Rig: Push 2, laptop, WiiMote, Roland RD-700

An Ableton Push 2 controller (Figure 20.6) was used within the performances to control the Master Track of Live which made its selection much easier in a performance context, since the buttons on the Push 2 were larger and more accessible for triggering than clicking directly on the track in Live's GUI.

As in *The Singularity*, the WiiMote controllers were connected to the laptop via Bluetooth, which connected to Ableton Live via OSCulator (Osculator, 2019).

The *Deeper Love* Soundpad App (Figure 20.8) was developed in conjunction with Professor Rob Toulson (University of Westminster), who undertook the coding. The app is downloadable from the Apple App Store.

The app enables all members of the audience who have access to an iPhone or iPad to be active participants in a musical performance. This is achieved by the audience-performers triggering pre-prepared audio samples by touching the virtual buttons on the 5 x 5 *S*oundpad grid. The process of IMP mobilises the audience members who are transformed from being 'passive receivers' of information into 'audience-performers' – now able to engage in sonic dialogue both with each other and the on-stage performers. However, the audience-performers have a limited degree of agency since their samples are pre-composed. They do have control over the order in which the samples are triggered, how much of the sample is triggered, its volume, the metric positioning of each sample trigger point, and they have also the ability to retrigger samples and create sample combinations to form new textures.

It is primarily digital technologies that create the possibility for novel types of interactivity such as that presented in this study. Yang and Coffey state that "Digital technology is revolutionizing the way people consume media, creating . . . interactive opportunities such as multimedia

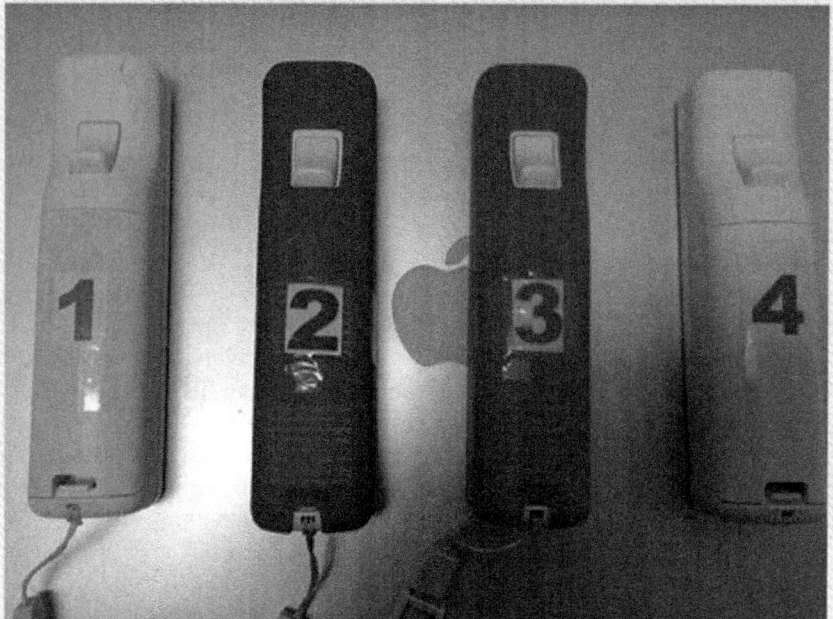

Figure 20.7 WiiMote controllers

offerings and two-way communication" (2014, p.78). They also observe that audiences are familiar with interactive processes and this combination of digital familiarity with the ubiquity of smartphones creates the conditions for straightforward digital interactivity, and the subsequent creation of what has been described as a "communication pathway". The simplistic

Figure 20.8 Deeper Love Soundpad

interface-design of the app and its choice as a container for the audience-performer's interactivity was to enable the research questions to be evaluated in the context of creative practice rather than impose technological process upon the participants.

To enable what Rosenkransa (2010) describes as 'frequency of engagement' for the audience-performers and synthesising the conclusions drawn from previous research, eight principles were developed for the design of the technological infrastructure for this project and were applied to the grid design of the app, which needed to be:

1. informal
2. interesting
3. immediate
4. accessible
5. natural
6. necessary
7. affordable
8. scalable

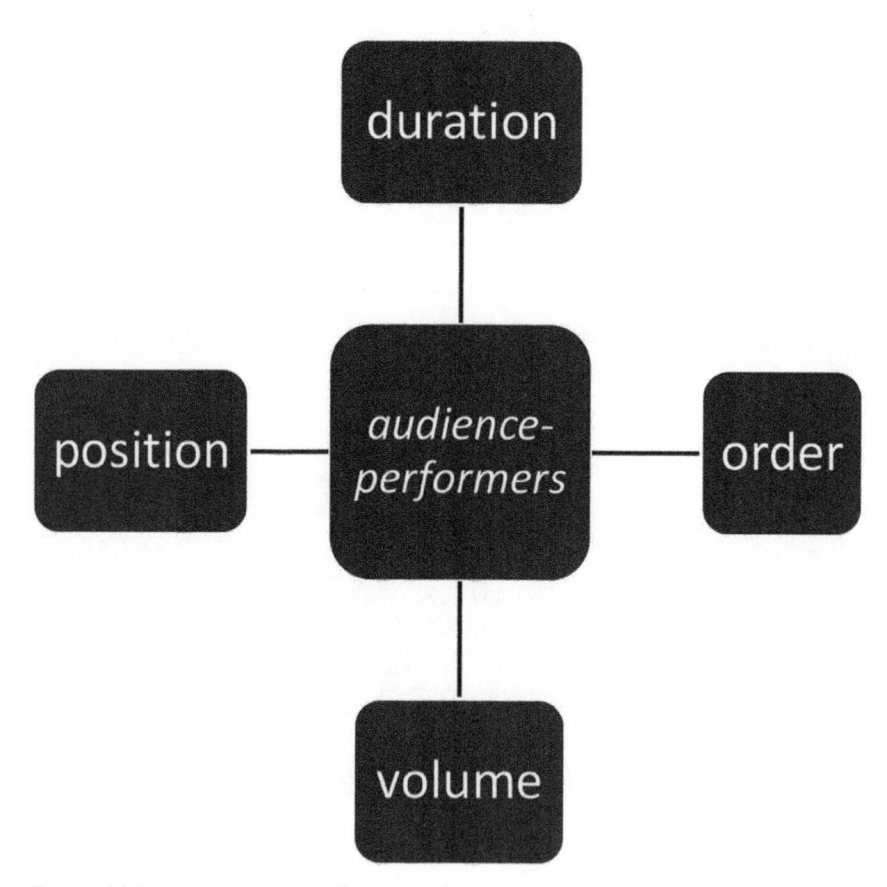

Figure 20.9 Deeper Love Audience-Performer Agency

The *Deeper Love* Soundpad App builds on the research carried out by Lee and Freeman (2013) using a networked musical instrument application that they had developed for mobile phone called *echobo* that audience members could download and perform on instantly, engaging with other members of the audience and generating sound that contributed to the performance. As with *echobo*, the *Deeper Love* Soundpad App sits in a hybrid rank within Freeman's taxonomic system of participatory performance modes (Freeman, 2005, pp.757–760) affording both the distributed sound of a sound transmitter (audience as sound transmitter) and unmediated performance to the audience (audience as performer).

As with the audience-performers, the audience-soloists using the WiiMote controllers have a degree of agency (Figure 20.10) over how much of the sample is triggered, the order in which the samples are triggered, the metric positioning of each trigger point and the potential for retriggering and sample combination to form completely new melodic, rhythmic and textural material. However, with the ability to create both motivic development and also rhythmic displacement, only the audience-soloists have the capacity to apply some of the improvisational techniques of the non-interactive instrumentalist or 'scatting' jazz vocalist.

As with *The Singularity*, the *Deeper Love* pilot in September of 2018 at the 'Crosstown Traffic' conference at the University of Huddersfield had no additional musicians; however, some of the subsequent performances

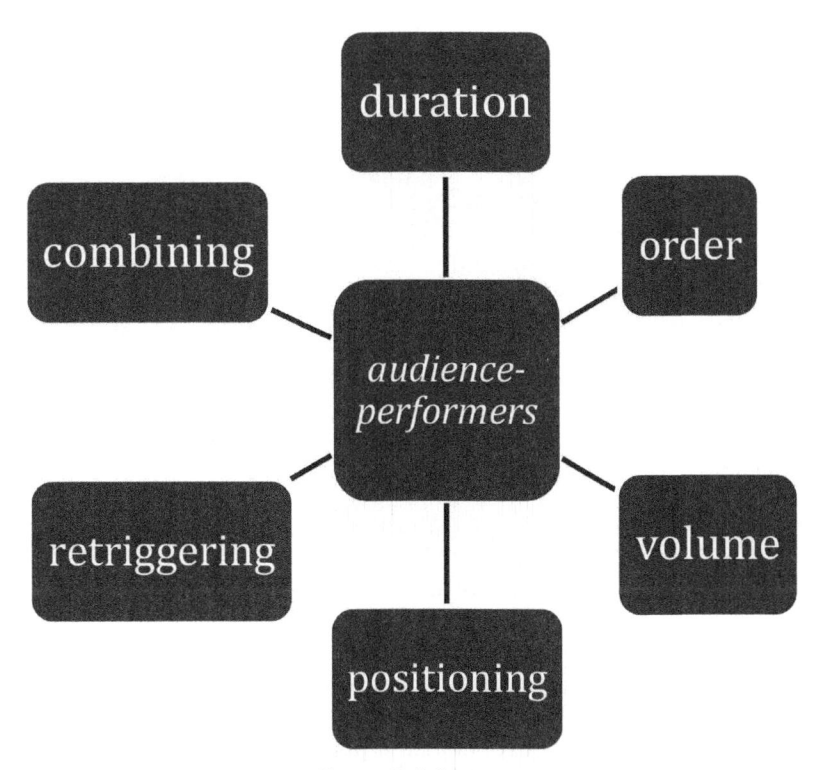

Figure 20.10 Deeper Love Audience-Soloist Agency

Figure 20.11 Deeper Love Performance at Area 51, University of Westminster

Figure 20.12 Deeper Love Performance 2 at Area 51, University of Westminster

of *Deeper Love* used live musicians in addition to the author (Figure 20.11). For the first three performances (Figure 20.12) at the Area 51 performance space (University of Westminster in December 2018, February and March 2019) a saxophonist, a percussionist, electric bass player and electric guitarist were added. A novel addition to industry-standard sound reinforcement at the third performance was the placing of two radio microphones in the audience area. This extra reinforcement allowed the audience-performers to amplify the sound coming from their iPhone speakers at appropriate times.

There is a video available of this performance available for streaming on YouTube at https://youtu.be/oRYjKNtZvlA. The performances at the East Grinstead Jazz Club, and the Toulouse Lautrec jazz club in Kennington just featured the author plus the audience-performers and the audience-soloists.

20.5 PERFORMANCE PROTOCOLS

As with *The Singularity,* the lead performer for *Deeper Love* functions as the musical director/conductor/MC of the performance, leading the on-stage musicians, audience-performers and audience-soloists as well as setting up and managing the equipment and software. At the start of the performance, the performer follows the instructions listed below which involve finding two volunteer audience-soloists, encouraging the audience to download and to use the app and explaining the app's functionality and the performance process.

Performance Instructions:

1. Ask the audience to download the *Deeper Love* Soundpad App and explain the app's functionality and the performance process
2. Find two volunteer audience-soloists
3. Give WiiMotes to audience-soloists plus verbal instructions on WiiMote function
4. Explain composition structure to audience-soloists and audience-performers
5. The lead performer triggers the Ableton Live scenes and cues solo sections. Each audience-soloist goes in turn – short exploration followed by a musical dialogue with the lead. This is followed by the audience-performers
6. During the second audience-participation segment, the lead performer cues the sound engineer to fade out the master fader
7. The lead performer cue musicians, audience-performers and audience-soloists to stop playing

Contrasting with the performance of *The Singularity* for which each of the audience-soloists were given a set of colour-coded performance protocols and technical instructions to read before the performance, all the *Deeper Love* instructions were delivered verbally thus meeting three of the eight principles (informal, immediate and natural) that the technological infrastructure for this project was based on.

The audience-performers were asked to download the app at the beginning of the event with posters in the performance space displaying the app's name to make the process straightforward. Following this the audience-performers were asked to open up the app, turn the volume up on their iPhones and were then told about triggering the sounds from the 5x5 grid. It was also suggested that they should move around during the audience-participation segment, and on the final Area 51 performance to use the radio microphones positioned in the performance.

20.6 METHODOLOGY, RESULTS AND EVALUATION

The process of collecting data from the audience-performers and audience-soloists to address the research questions has been approached in a variety of ways. A number of relevant methodological approaches follow.

Monson (1998) uses both ethnographic and journalistic interviewing techniques in a study on the interactivity that takes place between the musicians performing during a jazz performance. She is sensitive to the issues raised by the entextualisation of both spoken and musically transcribed content and presents her findings under a series of themed headings.

Sawyer and DeZutter (2009) study the process of distributed creativity within an improvisatory theatre group. Distributed creativity takes place when a 'shared creative product' is produced by a group of people working together. The group processes that generate unexpected outcomes in the context of distributed creativity are known as 'collaborative emergence' (Sawyer, 2003), which is "a defining characteristic of social encounters that are improvisational because only when the outcome is not scripted can there be unpredictability and contingency" (Sawyer and DeZutter, 2009, p.82).

Exploration of both distributed creativity and collaborative emergence were applicable to *Deeper Love*. The analytical methodology of choice applied within Sawyer and DeZutter's research is 'interaction analysis', a method of studying repeated patterns of observable behaviour using the medium of digital video. However, interaction analysis is probably less suited to the relatively small movements generated by audience-performers and audience-soloists such as tapping a smartphone icon, pressing a switch on a games controller or even pressing down a note on a keyboard, than the broader gestures and vocal utterances of an improvising actor.

The quantification of real-time interactions in improvisation is a research instrument yet to be developed, but a more fruitful direction for this research may be drawn from Breel (2015) in a paper that focuses on audience agency in participatory performance. Breel's methodology takes its inspiration in part from participatory action research (PAR), described by Kind, Pain and Kesby as being "a socially constructed reality within which multiple interpretations of a single phenomenon are possible by both researchers and participants" (cited in Breel, 2015, p.371). Using PAR as a tool creates an opportunity for the researcher to use a variety of methodologies and engage in research processes that afford collaborative knowledge production. The second element in Breel's methodology is drawn from interpretative phenomenological analysis (IPA) research which:

combines a phenomenological perspective of embodied, situated experience with a hermeneutic approach, encouraging awareness that experience is necessarily already interpreted when expressed and in IPA is then interpreted again by the researcher . . . IPA focuses on the attempt to make meaning out of the experience through interpretation.
(Breel, 2015, p.372)

Breel's research utilises three survey instruments:

1. A questionnaire to try to identify which performance elements were most meaningful
2. A creative response to the performance
3. Individual interviews to add more detail to the responses to the questionnaire

This research utilises the first and third instruments from Breel (2015) as the creative response option was not suitable in a jazz concert and club environment.

Quantitative data has been gathered through the use of several instruments including group-administered self-completion questionnaires, with qualitative open-ended interviews expanding on the quantitative results. All the studies were cross-sectional in nature with the individuals sampled for the questionnaire being self-selecting from the attendees at the four *Deeper Love* audience research events. The collection of information from performers and audience follows a mixed-method approach integrating both qualitative and quantitative data from a pragmatic perspective.

The Launch Event was held on 10 December 2018 in the Area 51 performance space at the University of Westminster. The performance had been publicised through the university with an open invitation to staff and students to what was a free of charge and non-ticketed event. There were approximately thirty standing attendees with at 70:30 female to male gender split, most of whom were of student age and with five older attendees drawn from members of the university staff. Nearly all of the audience owned iPhones running IOS 12 or later and were able to move around the room and participate. Whilst some interesting results emerged from this event, other research performances were scheduled so that the data could be tested in a variety of contexts.

The second performance (Figure 20.13) was held on 18 December 2018 at the East Grinstead Jazz Club. There were forty-three audience members seated at tables and therefore unable to move around freely during the performance, with an equal gender split and an average age of sixty. Only nine members of the audience filled in questionnaires as notably most of them did not own recent iPhones or have a model that runs IOS12, the minimum operating system to run the *Deeper Love* Soundpad App. Some expressed resentment that the app wasn't available for the Android operating system.

Toulouse Lautrec jazz club in Kennington, London was the venue for the third performance which took place on 19 December 2018 in front of

Figure 20.13 Deeper Love Performance 2 – East Grinstead Jazz Club

fifteen audience members of mixed gender and an average age of approximately fifty-five. The audience was seated at tables for this performance and the audience members were again unable to move around the room. At this performance only three people submitted the questionnaire and there were issues with finding enough audience members who had access to iPhones.

On the 23 February back in Area 51 at the University of Westminster another performance was held in front of an audience of applicants to the university and their guests. It was not run as an audience research event, but as a technical experiment responding to a handwritten comment on one of the questionnaires from the first performance. The comment read: "volume for the parts would help create more sense of agency and cohesion", referring to the volume of the samples being triggered from the app. Two radio microphones were positioned in the audience section of Area 51 to reinforce the sound level from the iPhones and to allow audience-performers to move as close to the amplification as they wished. This sound reinforcement made a noticeable difference to the level of the sounds being played from the iPhone. Comments relating to the use of the extra amplification from the sound technicians at the event included "That worked really well" and "Yeah, that was really cool".

The final audience research event took place on 20 March 2019 again at Area 51 to an audience of university applicants and their guests. As with the previous *Area 51* event the audience was standing and able to move around freely. The same sound reinforcement for the iPhones was used as on the 23 February performance. The audience of twenty-four members had a 50:50 gender split and was mostly comprised of sixteen- and seventeen-year-olds with some middle-aged parents in attendance. This audience with its high level of young people had an iPhone usage of 71%.

20.7 QUESTIONNAIRE

The responses to the questionnaire completed by the audience-performers at the four *Deeper Love* audience-research events have been turned into percentages with data having been collected from fifty-five individuals in all with high response rates from all participants. The data has also been summed (Table 20.3) to give an overview of the findings. Even with the results from the four audience research events combined this is still a relatively small data set to draw conclusions from and as so should be approached with some caution. However, with some comparisons between the summed responses and those from each audience research event it should be possible to see some trends emerging. A seven-point Likert scale has been used to report on the responses with 1 representing *Strongly disagree* and 7 *Strongly agree*.

Table 20.3 Audience Questionnaire Summed and Calculated as Percentages

Question and results							Total respondents
I felt a sense of agency during the performance							
1	2	3	4	5	6	7	54
2%	0%	3%	7%	20%	24%	44%	
My participation made a contribution to the work							
1	2	3	4	5	6	7	54
4%	5%	9%	20%	17%	17%	28%	
I did not feel that other audience participants made a contribution to the work							
1	2	3	4	5	6	7	54
22%	22%	15%	20%	8%	9%	4%	
I felt that the interactive moments in the work were meaningful							
1	2	3	4	5	6	7	53
4%	6%	7%	17%	23%	24%	19%	
I enjoyed being able to make a contribution to the work							
1	2	3	4	5	6	7	55
0%	0%	2%	11%	28%	22%	37%	
I felt that participation via the technology was easy to access							
1	2	3	4	5	6	7	54
7%	2%	4%	5%	24%	19%	39%	
I felt a bond with the other participants							
1	2	3	4	5	6	7	54
4%	11%	13%	17%	19%	18%	18%	
I felt a relationship with the performers							
1	2	3	4	5	6	7	55
2%	5%	13%	16%	15%	27%	22%	

Responses

*"I felt a sense of agency during the performance
(i.e. the ability to make free choices in respect to
your contribution)"*

At both the Area 51 launch event and at the Toulouse Lautrec event there were no negative choices at all. These responses indicate that a large majority of the audience-performers did feel a sense of agency during the performance.

"My participation made a contribution to the work"

The tendency towards the neutral is partly explained by the results coming from the two smaller sample sets with two out of the three Toulouse Lautrec responders opting for this option as did 37% of the eight East Grinstead responders. There may have been an issue with the older participants at these two events not finding the technical elements of the participation particularly easy to manage and this is borne out to a certain extent by the data relating to the sixth question that relates to ease of access to the technology.

*"I did not feel that other audience participants
made a contribution to the work"*

The Toulouse Lautrec and East Grinstead participants again bucked the trend with 66% of the Toulouse Lautrec and 75% of the East Grinstead responders on the neutral or negative side of the question. Some participants mentioned that they found this question confusing which may have created some false answers.

*"I felt that the interactive moments in the
work were meaningful"*

A possible explanation for this might be that the younger audiences at the Area 51 events were more receptive to the research than the participants for the Toulouse Lautrec event where 67% made the neutral choice, and at East Grinstead where 37% made the neutral choice with the same percentage of participants on the negative side of the scale.

*"I enjoyed being able to make a contribution
to the work"*

The positive results extrapolated from this data bode well for future work in this area since this theme is central to this research. However, it is important to bear in mind any possible bias in these responses as well as understanding that caution must be applied because of the relatively small sample size.

"I felt that participation via the technology was easy to access"

82% of the summed participants were on the positive side of the scale however 50% of the East Grinstead audience were either neutral or on the negative side of the proposition suggesting that despite enjoying the process, many of them were unable to access the app because of their lack of an iPhone running OS12 or later. In future research making the app platform agnostic by creating code and building the app for both the iOS and Android platforms may be a way of addressing the lack of ease of technological access reported by many of the East Grinstead respondents.

"I felt a bond with the other participants"

This outcome may stem from the fact that the East Grinstead audience-performers were seated and unable to move around the room; but with all the Toulouse Lautrec participants who were also seated being either neutral or on the positive side of the spectrum it would take further research to verify this conclusion.

"I felt a relationship with the performers"

There is an interesting comparison with the 54% of the East Grinstead respondents who also selected the negative side of the scale. With the Toulouse Lautrec results being based on only three returned questionnaires it is hard to draw many conclusions from those results in isolation; however, with the larger East Grinstead sample there seems to be a correlation between the higher level of negative scale results and the lack of mobility in the room, the age of the respondents and the lower iPhone to Android ratio displayed by those participants.

20.8 INTERVIEWS

Three qualitative open-ended interviews were undertaken with audience-soloists from the first Area 51 audience research event, the East Grinstead and the Toulouse Lautrec events. The first was carried out face to face and the second two by phone. The data was analysed using thematic analysis (Braun and Clarke, 2006) with six broad themes emerging.

Considering the holistic analysis of all data implies the following. No major changes need to be made to performance protocols although there are issues with both the harmonic makeup of compositions and the rhythmic elements of any triggered material that need to be carefully managed. An affordable, scalable and accessible technological framework has been developed which has been tested in real-world *gig* conditions and found to be reliable and robust thus opening up the field to other practitioners across popular music. The development of compositional and performance protocols enabled the research to move from the arena

Table 20.4 Results of thematic analysis

Theme	Comment
Ease of accessing the participatory process via the technology.	All interviewees supported the idea that the participatory process had been easy to access.
Level of audience-soloist agency.	There was a generally positive response to the theme of audience-soloist agency.
Feeling blended into the performance.	This theme focused on the level of integration into the performance that the audience-soloists felt they had experienced. Most comments supported the idea that there had been a good level of integration.
Sonic dialogue	Evidence of a sonic dialogue between the audience-soloists and the musicians emerged supported by audience-soloist.
Bonding with the other participants.	This theme was extrapolated from a number of comments.
Were the interactive moments in the work *meaningful* musically?	This addressed the potential of the research to be extended and to create a "meaningful" musical experience. One audience-soloist noted that "It was like a demo of what could be . . . it could branch out into something more . . . if it was done at a bigger scale with crowds and stuff like that . . .".

of an academic conference to the real-world context of a jazz club. The development of the app created a potentially limitless scaling up of the numbers of audience-performers.

To evaluate the success of the technological infrastructure for this project it is necessary to revisit the eight principles that guided its construction. It set out to be:

1. informal
2. interesting
3. immediate
4. accessible
5. natural
6. necessary
7. affordable
8. scalable

Principles 3, 4 and 5 are met by the responses to the questionnaire question "I felt that participation via the technology was easy to access" to which 82% of the summed participants were on the positive side of the scale. The scalability and free of charge nature of the app address principles 7 and 8, and the evidence for principles 1 and 2 comes from the 'informal' nature of the event itself, far away from the classical-music concerts described in Small (1998) and by the engagement of the audience-performers and audience-soloists throughout the event and comments such as "There's a lot of potential there". In regard to principle 6, developing an affordable and accessible technological infrastructure for IMP within jazz is embedded in the core of this research, and is taken from an identified gap in research.

Revisiting the Lee and Freeman (2013) set of criteria to enable a successful audience participatory experience, it can be seen that as with *The Singularity*:

1. Participation was easily accessible
2. Gestures from the audience were turned into a single musical composition
3. Audience-soloists had no reservations about participating
4. Audience-soloists were motivated to perform and sustained interest in their participation
5. Audience-soloists in some instances identify a clear relationship between their gestures and the musical outcomes

20.9 FUTURE WORK

Further investigation and experimentation into the way IMP can be integrated within popular music genres and other areas of interactive performance is strongly recommended. Future research might be broadly divided into three areas:

1. Technical improvements and developments
2. New compositional concepts
3. Therapeutic contexts

A number of ideas for developing the Soundpad App have emerged during the research process.

- Having the buttons on the app play back different samples for each song
- Being able to turn the sound of the app on and off remotely via a data automation system
- Sending new samples to the app at each interactive moment via a device automation system (Hagins and Hawkinson, 2013) or using remote virtualisation technology (Zhao *et al.*, 2013)
- Being able to trigger more than one button on the app at once
- Having the app display instructional messages

These improvements should increase the practicality of using the app through the duration of a complete performance as well as aiding the artist in controlling the interactive performance soundscape.

Further experimentation needs to take place in the area of reinforcement for the sounds triggered by the app using smartphones. Part of this would entail assessing the utilisation of the app at a larger concert, festival or stadium gig to see if it is more effective in those environments with a mass, full-house audience than in a club or small concert context. This area of research could see the realisation of McLuhan's (2001, p.22) proposal that the mass audience becomes a "creative participating force".

Future studies could be undertaken to develop novel compositional concepts using IMP. Building on Levin (2001), CoSiMa (2016) Lee and Freeman (2013), audience-performers within a performance context could be mobilised to be the prime source of sound generation with other performers improvising around and responding to these audience-generated soundscapes.

Some investigation would be warranted to explore the feasibility of using technologies such as the Soundpad App or the WiiMote for triggering pre-prepared samples in the field of music therapy or other therapeutic interventions that involve music, sound production or performance. Extending the research of Hunt *et al.* (2004), the therapeutic application of IMP could be analysed to see if it allows all performance participants to operate on a level playing field.

20.10 CONCLUSION

Although the current study is based upon a small number of participants and despite its exploratory nature, the findings contribute to knowledge by adding to the growing body of literature on IMP, and by providing novel contributions to the performance practice of popular music. This research adds to existing knowledge by providing for the first time a study of the application of IMP to the contemporary jazz genre, meeting Hödl *et al.*'s (2012, p.236) definition of IMP: "when a spectator can take part or at least make a contribution in a live concert through a technically driven system".

The findings add to the existing literature on IMP through an analysis of IMP when applied to a popular music genre that has specific performance protocols and compositional and improvisational structures. The creation of a technical framework to enable the research performances has provided a template that can be used or adapted by other researchers or practitioners entering the field.

REFERENCES

Berio, L. (1958). *Sequence I for Solo Flute*. Universal Edition. Available from https://www.youtube.com/watch?v=jAeoS8DoxY8 [Accessed 27 April 2018].

Biles, John Al. (2007) 'Improvising with genetic algorithms: GenJam'. In *Evolutionary Computer Music*, edited by Eduardo Reck Miranda. Springer Science & Business Media.

Breel, A (2015) Audience agency in participatory performance: a methodology for examining aesthetic experience. *Participations: Journal of Audience & Reception Studies*, 12 (1), 368–387.

Braun, V. and Clarke, V. (2006). Using thematic analysis in psychology, *Qualitative Research in Psychology*, 3 (2), 77–101.

Cook, P. (2001). Principles for designing computer music controllers, in ACM SIGCHI *New Interfaces for Musical Expression* (NIME) Workshop, Seattle, WA.

CoSiMa (2016) 'Hack the Audience', *Hack the Audience @ MTF Berlin*. Available at: http://cosima.ircam.fr/tag/concert/ (Accessed: 15 September 2020).

Freeman, J. (2005). Large Audience Participation, Technology, and Orchestral Performance. *Free Sound, Proceedings of the International Computer Music Association*. San Francisco, CA, 757–760.

Hagins, J. and Hawkinson, A. (2013). Distributed control scheme for remote control and monitoring of devices through a data network. *Google Patents*, available online from https://patents.google.com/patent/US9462041B1/en [Accessed 8 August 2019].

Hexler (2019). TouchOSC. *Hexler.net*, available online from https://hexler.net/software/touchosc [Accessed 3 March 2019].

Hit Songs Deconstructed (2019). Highlights from The State of the Hot 100 Top 10: 2018 in Review. *Hit Songs Deconstructed*, available online from https://www.hitsongsdeconstructed.com/highlights-from-the-state-of-the-hot-100-top-10/?ocode=2018Trend&utm_source=HSD&utm_campaign=2018Trend&utm_content=2018Trend&cmp=1&utm_medium=E [Accessed 12 April 2019].

Hödl, O., Kayali, F. and Fitzpatrick, G. (2012). Designing interactive audience participation using smart phones in a musical performance. *Non-Cochlear Sound*, 9 (14). Ljubljana, Slovenia. 9–14 September 2012, 236–241.

Hunt, A., Kirk, R. and Neighbour, M. (2004). Multiple media interfaces for music therapy. *IEEE MultiMedia*, 11 (3), 50–58, available online from doi: 10.1109/MMUL.2004.12 [Accessed 8 August 2019].

Lee, S., and Freeman, J. (2013). echobo: A Mobile Music Instrument Designed for Audience to Play. *NIME*, available online from http://www.nime.org/2013/program/papers/day3/poster3/291/291_Paper.pdf [Accessed 9 June 2017].

Levin, G. (2001). *Dialtones*. Audio available from http://www.flong.com/storage/experience/telesymphony/ Artist's statement at http://www.flong.com/storage/experience/telesymphony/index.html#background [Accessed 9 June 2017].

Love, S. (2012). An approach to phrase rhythm in jazz. *Journal of Jazz Studies*, 8 (1), 4–32, available online from https://jjs.libraries.rutgers.edu/index.php/jjs/article/view/35/39 [Accessed 18 April 2019].

McLuhan, M. (2001). *The Medium is the Massage*. Corte Madera: Ginko Press.

Monson, I. (1998). Oh Freedom: George Russell, John Coltrane, and Modal Jazz. In: Nettl, B. and Russell, M. (eds.) *In the Course of Performance: Studies in the World of Musical Improvisation*. Chicago: University of Chicago Press.

OSCulator (2020) *Home | OSCulator*. Available from: https://osculator.net/ (Accessed: 15 September 2020).

Paterson, J., Toulson, E. R., Lexer, S., Webster, T., Massey, S. and Ritter, J. (2017). Interactive digital music: enhancing listener engagement with commercial music. In: Hepworth-Sawyer, R., Hodgson, J., Toulson, R. and Paterson, J. L. (eds.) *Innovation in Music II*. Bath: Future Technology Press, 193–209.

Rosenkransa, G. (2010). Maximizing user interactivity through banner ad design. *Journal of Promotion Management*, 16 (3), 265–287.

Rubbra, Edmund (1953). String Quartet No. 2 in E flat, Op. 73: An Analytical Note by the Composer. *The Music Review*, 14, 36–44.

Rzewski, F. and Verken, M. (1969). Musica Elettronica Viva. *The Drama Review: TDR*, 14 (1), 92–97.

Sawyer, R. K. (2003) *Group Creativity: Music, Theater, Collaboration*. Mahwah, NJ: Psychology Press.

Sawyer, R. and DeZutter, S. (2009). Distributed creativity: How collective creations emerge from collaboration. *Psychology of Aesthetics, Creativity, and the Arts*, 3 (2), 81–92.

Small, C. (1998). *Musicking: The Meanings of Performing and Listening*. Hanover, NH: Wesleyan University Press.

Taylor, B. (2017) A history of the audience as a speaker array. In *Proceedings of the International Conference on New Interfaces for Musical Expression*. Copenhagen, Denmark: Aalborg University Copenhagen, 481–486. doi: 10.5281/zenodo.1176324.

Toulson, E. R. and York, A. (2018). Deeper Love Soundpad App, *Apple App Store* (website), available online from https://apps.apple.com/us/app/deeper-love-soundpad/id1441139504 [Accessed 20 September 2018].

Yang, Y. and Coffey, A. J. (2014) Audience valuation in the new media era: Interactivity, online engagement, and electronic word-of-mouth value. *International Journal on Media Management*, 16(2), pp. 77–103. doi: 10.1080/14241277.2014.943899.

York, A. (2019). Transforming musical performance: the audience as performer. In: Hepworth-Sawyer, R., Hodgson, J., Paterson, J. L. and Toulson, R. (eds.). *Innovation in Music: Performance, Production, Technology and Business*. New York: Routledge, 3–23.

Zhao, D., Qing Cheng, Y., D'Sa, R. and Schwartz, D. (2013). Remote virtualization of mobile apps. *Google Patents*, available online from https://patents.google.com/patent/US9451043B2/en [Accessed 8 August 2019].

21

The online composer–audience collaboration

Luis Ramirez

21.1 INTRODUCTION

Online platforms are increasingly blurring the boundaries between composers, listeners and performers through collaborative environments for musical creativity. Traditionally, audiences may be engaged when listening to music, but they do not impact its creation during the creative process. New approaches to music composition through these platforms have the potential to forge creative collaborations with audiences and allow them to become active participants in the conception of a work.

There is a substantial amount of research on the creative process of the composer, and there has been an increasing interest in detailing the relationship between composer and performer. Yet, there is little research about the dynamics between the composer and listener. There are several examples of research where the focus is on audience participation. For example, in "Large Audience Participation, Technology, And Orchestral Performance", Freeman postulates three categories of audience's interaction with the performance: as performers, sound transmitters, or influencers (Freeman 2005); and in "A Web Application for Audience Participation in Live Music Performance: The Open Symphony Use Case" (Zhang et al. 2016) and "Designing Interactive Audience Participation Using Smart Phones in a Musical Performance" (Hödl et al. 2012), the authors detail different mechanisms with which audiences can guide the outcome of a live performance by voting on pre-determined musical attributes via a smartphone app.

Additionally, several composers such as Frederic Rzewski, Iannis Xenakis, and John Cage have incorporated participatory dynamics from the audience into their pieces since the 1960s in the form of claps, vocalizations, or producing other sounds. Some examples include John Cage's work for audience-operated turntables *33–1/3* (Cage 1969) or several of Murray Schafer's works like *Patria*, where Schafer demands from the audience "active involvement in the performance and places an intrinsic responsibility on the participants and their actions in order to achieve a successful performance experience" (Galloway 2011).

While some composers have embraced the audience as a potential creative resource, many others maintain the posture of the composer as the sole source of the musical material. This creates a clear division in the ways a musical work is conveyed to an audience, creating a "dichotomy between participatory and non-participatory interactions" (York 2019). Yet, unless the work is improvisational in nature, the participatory aspects rarely cross into existing within the creative process of the composer. All the previously mentioned examples are cases in which the audience's participation occurs only during a live performance of the work. The research presented here focuses on two cases where the involvement occurs as part of the compositional creative process, and therefore fixed in the final product. More importantly, these interactions enrich the aspects of community and identity between artists and listeners.

Thanks to the internet and online video-sharing platforms, composers can directly interact with their listeners and fans, and this relationship is in sharp contrast to the usual dynamics between the performer and the listener. This research will focus specifically on Jacob Collier and Andrew Huang, two artists who make use of these online resources to collaborate with their audience by requesting compositional material from them to implement it into their songs.

This crowd-sourced music is not a novel phenomenon, but due to the popularity of these musicians it is now a recurrent dynamic online. Huang, a Toronto-based musician and YouTube personality, is known for his "Fan Mash" series, where he produces a song by processing fan-submitted short videos of random sounds. Collier, a Grammy-winning multi-instrumentalist based in London, England, became widely popular by producing complex reharmonizations from fan-submitted melodies and livestreaming the arranging process for his listeners.

These two young artists have in common a platform for interacting and submitting content; they both share their compositional process as a video and receive audience feedback before, during, and after the creative process. This results in a stronger sense of participation and identity with their audience, ultimately leading to a stronger community. This research analyses how these two musicians use these platforms to invite their audience into their creative process and it provides a detailed description of their corresponding approaches to audience collaboration. In Collier's case the result is a livestreamed video and in Huang's case a produced video, hosted in their own channels respectively. In addition, this research postulates eight layers of discourse that can be analysed for further insight into the dynamics between composers and online audiences, and as a tool for understanding and interpreting the mechanisms of digital interactions.

21.2 ANDREW HUANG

Andrew Huang is a Toronto-based musician and YouTube personality. His music spans a multitude of styles and genres and he is constantly expanding the boundaries of traditional music performance and production with his skills as a multi-instrumentalist, vocalist, producer, composer, and sound designer. One thing that stands out about his music is the innovative way of turning ordinary objects into instruments for his "song challenges", a series of videos where he produces a song based on audience suggestions by processing fan-submitted short videos of random sounds using everyday objects as instruments. His success has landed him several sponsorship opportunities, where companies like Google, LG, and Sony have partnered with him (Huang 2019) to create a song with the sounds of their products as a fresh new way of marketing to attract younger demographics.

In his video *How to make TRACKS and not just LOOPS* (Huang 2018b) published on February 12, 2018, Huang gives viewers advice in working the second part of tracks and how to avoid falling for the common bad habit of making loops that do not develop further. He finds an incomplete song project selected by his followers and decides to add a drop, so he goes to Twitter and tweets: "I need some random short sound effects. Feel free to tweet me back with any sound you've made that you don't mind me using. If you've got video of it too I'll take it!" (Huang 2018c). Huang leaves the submission open for one hour, after which he gathers his favourite sounds. This video mentioned is the first time he showcases the clips that people sent to him, presenting the result at the very end – a heavy dubstep-like groove combined with a video montage of all the videos people sent of themselves. Three days later, Huang uploaded the video titled "How I made a drop with random sounds you sent me" (Huang 2018a) where he explains in depth his creative process of editing and arranging the sounds. The main objective with this video is to explain the tricks and methods he used for editing and processing the sound bites. The sounds that the users submitted are varied, from the sounds of keys hitting a table, a water bottle hitting someone's face, or a sword being unsheathed. This is the video that will be analysed below.

21.3 JACOB COLLIER

Jacob Collier is a Grammy-winning multi-instrumentalist based in London, England. He has been recognized as one of the most innovative musicians of our time, hailed as "jazz's new messiah" (Lewis 2015). Not only is he pushing the limits of his music in compositional terms with his intricate and complex productions, he is also breaking new ground with the use of technology in music performance. Collier's journey began by uploading multi-track performances of himself to his YouTube channel. His fame and recognition on the internet eventually led him to Quincy Jones, who is now his manager and mentor.

Collier became widely popular online by producing complex reharmonizations from fan-submitted melodies and livestreaming the arranging process for his listeners. In 2016, Collier used the crowdfunding site Patreon to support the release of his album, *In My Room*, and created the #iHarmU campaign (JazzRefound 2016), where donors of $100 or more were able to send him 15-second melodies that he would harmonize and post on his Instagram and YouTube channel. The campaign greatly increased his following, and added some notable patrons, including British Jazz artist

Jamie Cullum, Ben Folds, and Kevin Olusola of the a cappella group Pentatonix (JazzRefound 2016). One of these patrons was Chris Costa, and Collier livestreamed his reharmonization of Costa's material on YouTube on 2 March 2018 (Collier 2018b) releasing the video to his Instagram page four days later (Collier 2018a).

This video is the third and most recent #iHarmU livestream by Collier, and his methodology has remained consistent throughout other livestreams. In his livestreams, he drafts his ideas on a Logic Pro X template prepared with several audio and MIDI tracks pre-loaded. The template is divided into four large regions: for vocals, bass, drums, and other instruments. Costa' submission was in two short parts, a melodic one and a spoken one. The lyrics are an excerpt of Costa' own song "The Masterplan": "My body was placed in a land of melody who decided for me [. . .] I want to see who did the Masterplan" (Chriscostamusic 2016).

Collier begins working with Costa's video and audio as the only initial sources, and as he explores different possibilities, he narrates his plans to the audience, recording his ideas by singing or with a MIDI device. The viewers can react and give him feedback in real time, which Collier sometimes incorporates into his creative decisions. It is important to note that this video was streamed shortly before YouTube's platform was able to record the chat commentary as they were happening live, so unfortunately the live interactions Collier had with the chat were not preserved. The comments left on the video were left after the video stream was uploaded to his channel.

One of the unique factors that allows Collier to have this dynamic with his audience is because of the remarkable speed of his workflow. A composer's creative process is rarely documented in this setting due to its usual secrecy and varying time frames depending on the composer. Collier has the advantage of being able to do exactly what he envisions thanks to his competence with the software, aural skills and musicianship. What the audience is seeing is akin to a laboratory, where Collier knows exactly how every instrument and formula works but is constantly experimenting with new results. Due to the density and complexity of his musical gestures, or what Collier calls "maximalism" (Shapiro 2018), it can take a long time to externalize his ideas even at this pace. Nevertheless, throughout the entire three hours of this livestream there were very few things that changed once he had recorded them.

One clear example of his creative thinking and constant perspective of the larger conception of the work occurs during the first few minutes of the stream, from [00:14:50] to [00:15:22] (Collier 2018b). During this period a lot of the aforementioned factors are reflected: musical and technological virtuosity, recording multiple tracks at a fast pace, and long-term planning by combining reversed audios with spoken, sung, and blabbed words to create a rich texture and colourful rising effect. A few moments later he expresses that the cacophonic juxtaposition of these elements is not random – it is connected to the sentence in the lyrics: "I want to know who did the masterplan", and Collier explains that the intention behind these layers is to portray multiple contenders behind the creation of this masterplan.

Table 21.1 Timeline of Collier's Livestream

Sections	Transition	First Section	Second Section	Final revisions
Mood	Sweeping Rise	Pastoral Waltz	Frenzy Funk	Groovy
# of tracks	~49	~129	~237	~245
Timecode	00:00:00–00:23:00	01:08:00	01:58:00	03:12:17

Despite of the long livestream, Collier works in a systematic and structured way, with a clear outline of what the overarching plan is going to be for this arrangement. Table 21.1 illustrates a summarized timeline of the entire livestream.

21.4 EIGHT LAYERS OF DISCOURSE

Whether it is a livestream or a video that has been published to their channel, the key principle is that the artists are in constant communication with their audience. However, there are certain advantages and disadvantages depending on the medium and approach. A livestream has the benefit of including more participatory elements and extended exposure to the composer's creative dynamics. On the other hand, the editing aspect of a fixed video makes the content more accessible and digestible for a broader audience. In both forms there are several layers of discourse, which collectively create an environment in which the viewers can immerse themselves. The following are the categories identified when comparing both artists' videos.

21.4.1 Visual interface

An important factor of Huang's brand is the editing style of his videos. Most commentators praise his aesthetic decisions, and this high-quality production is a combination of professional cameras, tracking shots, time-lapses, coloured LED lights, and various other cinematographic elements. This presentation packages the video as a high-quality product, making it more memorable.

On the other hand, the streaming setup of Collier's video consists of four different camera shots: a main one showing the Logic Pro X window where the tracks are laid out; a wide shot of himself and his room at the top right corner where he addresses the audience; an overhead shot that shows both the keyboard MIDI interface and his computer keyboard; and the streaming software window, basically a mirror of the streamed scene itself. This covers virtually every possible visual channel to maximize the connection with the viewers. The audience can see his space, his keyboard shortcuts and speed of workflow, the pitches he inputs, and what he is seeing on his screen. In addition, Streamlabs, the platform that Collier uses for donations and subscriptions, shows a notification on screen – a small animation of

Collier cheering – whenever a new user subscribes or donates to him, enticing others to do so. This multi-dimensional interface allows the viewer to be fully immersed in Collier's world.

21.4.2 Educational/technical

YouTube is an excellent platform for educational content, and Huang uses his channel to teach his viewers about gear, composition, tricks, or generally any musical advice that he can share from his experience. Although Collier mainly uses his channel to post his music videos, he also explains concepts or tools used during his workflow during livestreams, whether technical terms of audio production or explaining certain effects he has discovered over the years.

In the case of Huang's video (Huang 2018a), he walks the viewers through the specific techniques used for this excerpt of music:

- Editing: trimming down audio to use only the portion of the sound that is usable [01:09].
- Pitch Shifting: making the sound higher or lower, in two categories:
  - Melodies: using sounds with a defined pitch and shifting them around to create a melodic line [02:13].
  - Pitch Modulation: includes automation, or a moving parameter giving it continuous movement [02:51].
- Equalization: increasing or decreasing a specific region of the frequency spectrum [03:13].
- Layering: combining elements with similar timbres to create a larger sound [04:25].
- Other combinations of these techniques.

In Collier's video, he describes several audio techniques throughout the stream: how he uses panning to spread the sound [00:10:45]; how to create a sweep effect with his mouth and tremolo effect [00:18:12]; how the latch automation works [01:54:57]; or how to stretch an audio file using specific macros and shortcuts [00:22:08], among others.

21.4.3 Hardware and software

In order to examine the behaviour of the audience, a brief analysis of the comments is necessary. The comments left on both videos were read one by one and grouped into three overarching categories after recurring characteristics emerged between both versions. The three categories are *Praise*, *Observations*, and *Music Related*. After labelling the comments it is fair to assume a large proportion of these audiences are music gear enthusiasts, keenly interested in the tools that both Huang and Collier use, since gear and sound libraries are among the most common topics of discussion in the video. This category includes discussions about both hardware – microphones, computer, audio interface, etc. – and software – Digital Audio Workstation, sample libraries, plugins and effects, etc. A reasonable assumption for this interest is the sense of identity and relatability that these artists inspire in the viewers who may want to follow their steps.

Huang is famous for using modular synthesizers, and although he does not use one in this video, he adds a full list of his gear to every video's description, including audio and camera gear. In terms of software he constantly recommends Ableton Live, and during the video he mentions several distortion plugins and other effects used with this programme.

Collier mentions different products he uses during several moments, usually accompanied by a short review. In this video he mentions his recently acquired microphones [00:06:54], his recent purchase of Trilian, a bass module [00:09:24], the Crystallizer plugin by soundtoys, which adds reverse effects and textures [02:43:30], and the use of Altiverb [00:10:14], a reverb plugin that simulates the acoustic qualities of real spaces, among others.

21.4.4 Methodology

Huang describes the methodology for this drop (Huang 2018b) in three stages: he begins with a sample collection, in this case facilitated by his Twitter followers. He then edits each sample and makes them as musical as possible. The final stage is the production of the drop and all the aesthetic decisions involved.

In Collier's case, near the beginning of the video he announces that this arrangement will be groove-based, because the video contains more rhythmic potential than harmonic potential. When he records himself singing individual notes within a chord, he does not require the use of notated music or any other aid. He follows a quick strategy of recording on one track at a time, moving quickly from one to the next one until the chord is fully recorded. Sometimes he will record a specific pitch more than once to give it extra weight, voicing the chord like a pianist would. During the stream he constantly alternates between recording different instruments, keeping virtual instruments to a minimum. The real instruments he used were: bowed double bass, electric bass, piano, electric guitar, glockenspiel, drum set, acoustic guitar, bouzouki, several bells, tambourine, claps, melodica, djembe, and his voice. The only virtual ones he used were pizzicato strings, Celtic harp, and three audio samples – bubbles, an avalanche, and glass breaking. Despite his fast pace, he allows himself some time to make his intentions clear, sometimes verbalizing his ideas and others simply humming the desired musical gesture. By the end of the video, Collier has accumulated over 240 tracks of audio.

21.4.5 Creativity

This category encompasses discussions of philosophical aspects of each artist's creative process. In Huang's video his creativity is displayed as a finalized product. Whilst he does show the strategies for the final product, he does not show the procedure. In his video, the result itself is the creative aspect, whereas in Collier's case the creativity is witnessed as a process. Collier also likes to share his experience in relatable metaphors. During his livestream (Collier 2018b) he says things like "the best way to learn is by trying stuff out" [01:10:00] or points out the difference between a "bubble thing" and a "bubble-flavoured thing" [00:23:42] when he adds certain textures to colour larger-scale gestures. Quite frequently he emphasizes the value of one's individuality with quotes like "Be yourself, everybody else is taken" [01:19:04], and at a point even acknowledges when something finally achieves the "Jacob Collier" sound [02:56:33]. He shares many pieces of advice so often that it is common to find commenters who refer other viewers to the timecode of their favourite quotes as can be seen in this comment: "1:52:10 unexpected life lesson. You are smart on so many levels Jacob" (poeven 2019).

21.4.6 Personality

Huang has been regularly uploading videos to his channel since 2006 and his personal brand has solidified through the years, alongside a unique visual editing style to his videos. He is also rather active in Twitter and Instagram, allowing his followers to have multiple vantage points to his personality. Nevertheless, it is worth noting that Youtubers are known for heavily curating and editing their videos to fit a manufactured self that resonates with the viewers (Parkin 2018; Saul 2016).

One unique aspect of the livestream format is the access to Collier's raw personality. His mannerisms are constantly in the spotlight, and traits of his character are manifested in his humour and distinctly British accent, features that are brought up frequently in the comments: "The way this guy talks is so posh" (ANIMALxBTKx 2018). Some notable moments during the livestream are when he shares his philosophy about love and human interaction and not letting it be compressed or rushed [01:52:30], when he does something quirky to acknowledge people subscribing and tipping [00:24:03], or when he emulates a hyperbolic reaction from his viewers when playing an unorthodox chord progression [01:27:01]. Collier was wearing a dinosaur onesie during the stream which by itself says a lot about his demeanour.

21.4.7 Musical

Since Huang takes a more educational angle to his video, most of the specifically musical aspects were discussed above as techniques. However, he does mention other musical factors such as the fact that he uses three additional sounds for the mix – a kick drum and two different snare drums – or how the context for this drop is within the framework of a techno song.

On the other hand, Collier is known for his dense theoretical knowledge and incorporating it into his music. He gained a lot of popularity with several YouTube interviews about music theory, earning him a large following of theory enthusiasts, particularly in the jazz community (Lee 2017a, 2017b). Naturally, he does mention some theoretical concepts and techniques during the stream: he talks about Steve Reich and uses one of his minimalism techniques [00:45:32]; he explains the difference between just intonation and equal temperament by showing two instruments with a similar timbre but tuned respectively [02:37:15]; and he explains the "tintinnabuli" concept as bells ringing [02:38:27].

21.4.8 Conversational

This connection to the viewers is an informal type of discourse, merely to address certain questions from the chat or to provide observations on any given topic. Although this layer is not present in Huang's video, there is a lot activity happening "behind the scenes" in his Twitter feed or Instagram page. Twitter and Instagram are the main platforms where he corresponds with his community, whether to get ideas for new videos or to request random sound effects.

In Collier's case, he communicates in real time with his audience and request their input during the livestream. Some examples of Collier's interactions are: when he gets reminded by his viewers that he has not saved the project yet after accumulating over 200 tracks [01:08:44]; when he realizes that the viewers are sharing their ages in the chat he participates and adds his own age as well [01:09:11]; or when he asks the viewers in the chat which chord progression they prefer and waits for their response to record the most popular choice [01:27:33].

These conversational aspects extend to discussions within viewers in the comments, sometimes discussing certain elements of the stream, or talking about unrelated topics. These exchanges are important because they break the hierarchical dimensions typically ascribed to the dynamics between artists and fans. It preserves the human feel despite it being a virtual connection.

21.5 CONCLUSIONS

The interactions between composer and audience have never been as rich and honest as they can be with the internet. Also unprecedented is the ability to connect with millions of people from the comfort of your home. Online platforms for video sharing are becoming critical tools that can strengthen both the creative process of composers and the appreciation of the audience.

While there is research into audience participation for music performances, there is a clear distinction between audiences being involved as performers during a live setting or as creative sources during the creative process. The online interactions facilitate a creative symbiotic environment where the artist receives instant input and a sense of community, unlike the usual solitude of the compositional process, and the listeners achieve a unique level of intimacy with the creator and a sense of belonging in the final product. Their feedback is not simply used as an inspiration for the creator but as an active ingredient.

By exploring the eight layers of discourse presented, researchers can paint a broader image of the online dynamics between the composer and the audience. These layers can inform relationships not typically found through other mediums. This valuable data could dramatically improve the interpretation of digital interactions and should not be neglected.

Andrew Huang and Jacob Collier are two musicians that embrace video platforms as a new kind of stage to showcase their work and connect directly with their listeners and viewers. These two artists have different but equally valid approaches to engaging and collaborating with their viewers. In this ever-evolving music-making landscape, their methods are worthy of analysis and consideration for other creators to connect in deeper ways with their audience.

REFERENCES

ANIMALxBTKx. (2018). Comment on: *#IHarmU LIVE Ft. Chris Costa!* [Online video]. Available at: https://www.youtube.com/watch?v=gEHoeaA-NjU&lc=UgzOtOimPZqpsbQ3WXl4AaABAg [Accessed 9 April 2019].

Cage, J. (1969). *33–1/3*. New York: Edition Peters.

Chriscostamusic. (2016). *Chris Costa – The Master Plan (Video)*. [Online video]. Available at: https://youtu.be/-B8WTDA9eiU [Accessed 4 April 2019].

Collier, J. (2018a). *#IHarmU ft. @chriscostamusic ! The fruits of Friday's livestream :) Three cheers to Chris for an awesome melody! Many more [. . .]*. [Instagram]. 6 March. Available at: https://www.instagram.com/p/BgAAW60ni6o/ [Accessed 4 April 2019].

Collier, J. (2018b). *#IHarmU LIVE Ft. Chris Costa!* [Online video]. Available at: https://youtu.be/gEHoeaA-NjU [Accessed 4 April 2019].

Freeman, J. (2005). "Large Audience Participation, Technology, And Orchestral Performance" In *Free Sound*, 757–760. Proceedings of the International Computer Music Association. San Francisco, CA: International Computer Music Association (ICMC). Available at: http://distributedmusic.gatech.edu/jason/publications/pdf_files_of_publications/large_audience_participatio.pdf [Accessed 9 March 2020].

Galloway, K. (2011). "Sounding Nature, Sounding Place": Alternative Performance Spaces, Participatory Experience, and Ritual Performance in R. Murray Schafer's Patria Cycle. Available at: https://tspace.library.utoronto.ca/handle/1807/26175, p. 21 [Accessed 9 March 2020].

Hödl, O., Kayali, F. and Fitzpatrick, G. (2012). "Designing Interactive Audience Participation Using Smart Phones in a Musical Performance", Available at: https://www.researchgate.net/publication/262178344_Designing_Interactive_Audience_Participation_Using_Smart_Phones_in_a_Musical_Performance [Accessed 9 March 2020].

Huang, A. (2019). *Brands*. [Online]. Available at http://andrewhuang.com/brands [Accessed 4 April 2019].

Huang, A. (2018a). *How I Made a Drop with Random Sounds You Sent Me*. [Online video]. Available at: https://youtu.be/M021RSApMXs [Accessed 4 April 2019].

Huang, A. (2018b). *How to Make TRACKS and Not Just LOOPS* [Online video]. Available at: https://youtu.be/NEy9L7zyrGE [Accessed 4 April 2019].

Huang, A. (2018c). *This Track Is Coming along! I Need Some Random Short Sound Effects. Feel Free to Tweet Me Back with Any* [. . .]. [Twitter]. 9 February. Available at: https://twitter.com/andrewhuang/status/962041924377964544 [Accessed 4 April 2019].

JazzRefound. (2016). *Jacob Collier, Enfant prodige of the year.* [Online]. Available at: https://jazzrefound.it/2016/en/artista/jacob-collier/ [Accessed 4 April 2019].

Lee, J. (2017a). *Interview: Jacob Collier (Part 1)* [Online video]. Available at: https://youtu.be/DnBr070vcNE [Accessed 4 April 2019].

Lee, J. (2017b). *Interview: Jacob Collier (Part 2)* [Online video]. Available at: https://youtu.be/b78NoobJNEo [Accessed 4 April 2019].

Lewis, J. (2015). *Jacob Collier review – jazz's new messiah.* [Online]. Available at: https://www.theguardian.com/music/2015/jul/03/jacob-collier-review-ronnie-scotts-jazz-new-messiah [Accessed April 4, 2019].

Parkin, S. (2018). The YouTube Stars Heading for Burnout: 'The Most Fun Job Imaginable Became Deeply Bleak'. *The Guardian*. [Online]. 8 September. Available at: https://www.theguardian.com/technology/2018/sep/08/youtube-stars-burnout-fun-bleak-stressed [Accessed 4 April 2019].

poeven. (2019). Comment on: *#IHarmU LIVE Ft. Chris Costa!* [Online video]. Available at: https://www.youtube.com/watch?v=gEHoeaA-NjU&lc=Ugxg-O2mI6uFwDwmiDx4AaABAg [Accessed 16 June 2019].

Shapiro, A. (2018). *Jacob Collier Makes Staggering, Complex Music Feel Effortless.* [Online]. Available at https://www.npr.org/2018/12/12/675594631/jacob-collier-makes-staggering-complex-music-feel-effortless [Accessed 4 April 2019].

Saul, H. (2016). Sam Pepper: YouTuber Claims His Entire Online Persona Is Fake in Video after Deleting Everything Bar One Tweet. *The Independent*. [Online]. Available at: https://www.independent.co.uk/news/people/sam-pepper-youtuber-claims-his-entire-online-persona-is-fake-in-video-after-deleting-everything-bar-a6895246.html [Accessed 4 April 2019].

York, A. (2019). "Transforming Musical Performance: The Audience as Performer" in *Innovation in Music: Performance, Production, Technology, and Business*, edited by Russ Hepworth-Sawyer, Jay Hodgson, Justin Paterson, and Rob Toulson, New York: Routledge, pp. 3–23.

Zhang, L., Wu, Y., Barthet, M., and International Conference on New Interfaces for Musical Expression. (2016). "A Web Application for Audience Participation in Live Music Performance: The Open Symphony Use Case", Available at: https://qmro.qmul.ac.uk/xmlui/handle/123456789/12500 [Accessed 9 March 2020].

22

New instruments as creativity triggers in composer–performer collaboration

Agata Kubiak-Kenworthy

22.1 INTRODUCTION

Six Spiders (a musical piece for electric violin, voice, electric guitar and electronic drone by Bartosz Szafranski) serves as a clear example of the *New Instrument* collaboration type. The piece of music was written for (chapter author and violin performer) Agata Kubiak, engaging the soloist in simultaneous vocal and instrumental expression, with the electric guitar and drone parts serving as a background accompaniment. The piece was commissioned by the performer in early 2016 and rehearsals commenced in October the same year. Both the performer and the composer were keen to explore particular issues behind composition and collaboration in this individually tailored piece of music. Six Spiders and the process of working on it became a fertile ground for their research into composition and new music performance.

This chapter begins with a Background section, which looks at a historical context of composer-performer collaboration and new instrument research. It explains the role some of the tools used (the seven forms of creative change suggestions (Kubiak-Kenworthy, 2020)) play in the analysis of data. It also mentions most recent research contributions in this area. The following Data Analysis section explains the data collection process and methods used to analyse and contextualise the research findings. The Discussions and Conclusion sections look into particular examples of the analysed data. Here, the crucial role that verbal communication played in this collaboration can be seen. The presented examples show how the novelty of the material and questions around playability influenced the 'playing' versus 'talking time' in rehearsals. The reader can also observe clear examples of certain creative change suggestions (Kubiak-Kenworthy, 2020) being favoured by the collaborators. It is also explained how the disjointed character of rehearsals correlated with more creative suggestions from participants.

22.2 BACKGROUND

This chapter presents a specific component of a larger research project, which developed two typologies to analyse the nature of creative interaction between performers and composers collaborating on new works (Kubiak-Kenworthy, 2020). The case studies in this work relate primarily to string players but there is no reason why these results should not be applied to other areas of performance practice. The study relates to the ways in which performers contribute to the development of new works through the revising and rehearsal process. The first typology categorises seven different forms of creative change that happen during rehearsals:

a. mistakes being spotted,
b. simplification being offered,
c. choice being offered,
d. intention being clarified,
e. experiment being proposed,
f. moments when creative change happens spontaneously, and
g. editorial changes.

The second typology relates to five varying circumstances of composer-performer collaborations. These are divided into:

1. Traditional Collaboration,
2. Workshop Collaboration,
3. Hybrid Collaboration,
4. New Instrument Collaboration and
5. Experimental Collaboration.

Both of these typologies arose from an analysis of the data which was gathered from the interviews and the observations of the projects that were conducted (ibid). This chapter will focus on the New Instrument collaboration type.

The New Instrument approach is not a very common type of musical collaboration, but despite its rare occurrence, it has a potential to make major contributions to the entire domain of contemporary classical music. Historically the development of new instruments together with the improvement and non-standard use of the already existing instruments have been a powerful inspiration for many composers. For example, the evolution of brass instruments was undoubtedly one of the main factors behind the changing sounds of orchestral music between Baroque and late Romanticism. The development of a grand piano and its influence on keyboard music is an example of which we are also familiar. One should also mention saxophone and ondes martenot, among others. Looking at more current examples, Neil Heyde's collaboration with Brian Ferneyhough falls under same category. The role of STEIM (an Amsterdam-based centre for research and development of new instruments) is not to be missed when discussing current development in the New Instrument Approach. In this type of collaboration it is necessary for the composer to be present from the very first rehearsal. The music often uses a combination of traditional and innovative notation. Despite the score being mostly completed before the first rehearsal, it is prone to anything between minor and severe modifications. The key element of the collaborative practice is the discovery of the 'new instrument', with all its opportunities and the boundaries it has to respect. As mentioned by Christopher Redgate:

> Any musical instrument carries with it a well-defined body of knowledge that includes its usable range, available techniques, performance practices, distinctive sound and areas that are technically problematic. Such knowledge informs composers and provides the boundaries of what is and is not good compositional practice.
>
> (Redgate, 2017, p.141)

A lack of historical reference can cause the first draft of a piece to represent either a 'too safe' or 'too risky' approach, therefore the prevalence of creative change categories [b], [c], [d] and [e] is most common. Establishing possible new solutions on the new instrument stimulates inventiveness through creative problem solving. Christopher Redgate in his 'Composition changing instruments changing composition' writes about working on a new uniquely designed oboe:

> Demonstration and discussion often reveal whether new sounds can be obtained, and the composers may then include these in their compositions. . . . A further challenge is created when a composer appropriates sounds that he or she has heard in a performance, or seen in a score, and then uses them in another context. In order to develop good fingerings, and to test out their feasibility it is essential to have as wide a range of such contexts as possible, and the process of learning works with such demanding features involves the performer with problem-solving the execution of extreme passages.
>
> (Redgate, 2017, p.148)

22.3 DATA ANALYSIS

During this research, data was collected from audio and video recordings of the entire rehearsal process in the Kubiak/Szafranski collaboration and the interview with the composer. The collaboration lasted for over one year and five rehearsals were documented. The interview with the composer was conducted after the premiere of the piece and none of the hypotheses of the author were shared with the composer before or during the collaboration. Data from video and audio recordings was transcribed in full and analysed using NVivo software. Analysis consisted of mapping themes of conversation during the rehearsal process, timing musical activities and categorising creative change suggestions according to the aforementioned typology of seven types (Kubiak-Kenworthy, 2020). The languages used in all rehearsals included Polish and English, therefore translation of Polish quotes is provided when necessary. Details of linguistic nature were carefully analysed but will not be mentioned in this chapter as specifics of bi-lingual communication are not at the centre of interest for the author in this chapter.

22.4 DISCUSSIONS

One of the main aims of this research was to try to identify and analyse which aspects of the working environment and social behaviour (such as communication) might have most influence on the creative process. It is known that engaging in new music performance creates a unique opportunity for direct dialogue between the composer and performer and yet "very little attention has been paid to the performer's potentially significant mediation between composer and the piece" (Fitch and Heyde, 2007).

Having access to data from the entire process of collaboration on *Six Spiders* gives us the opportunity to gain insights into exactly how significant the role of the performer is under these circumstances. As in most cases, the composer is not a specialist performer on either the violin or the voice. This, in combination with a complete lack of references to any 'violin and voice' works, called for a different attitude towards the rehearsal process. The approach taken was more of a workshop/rehearsal in style and bore similarities to the one mentioned by Fitch and Heyde in their paper "'Recercar' - The Collaborative Process as Invention" (2007).

Despite big differences between the rehearsal lengths (ranging from 58–127 minutes), the time spent playing music remained almost unchanged (varying between 19–24 minutes), as shown in Figures 22.1 and 22.2.

This might be explained by the feeling of over saturation with the music; it was mentioned by both the performer in connection to having to invent a new practice routine to suit the piece and the composer experiencing similar difficulty when working on the piece in the earlier stages.

Agata (performer): From my point of view this is a completely different case . . . I had to approach it completely different to any other piece piece that I've ever learned.

Bartek (composer): Because you practically constantly have two brain in use, right?

Agata: mhm . . . yep! And when such intense focus takes over, even when I'm just practicing at home, I can't play for longer than half hour or forty minutes at once, as everything starts to muddle up for me . . . I'm starting to read the wrong line on the wrong instrument and so on haha

Bartek: Oh! This is very interesting as I have to admit I felt really similar when I was composing it, you know?
(Kubiak/Szafranski collaboration, Rehearsal no.5 transcription, translated by Agata Kubiak)

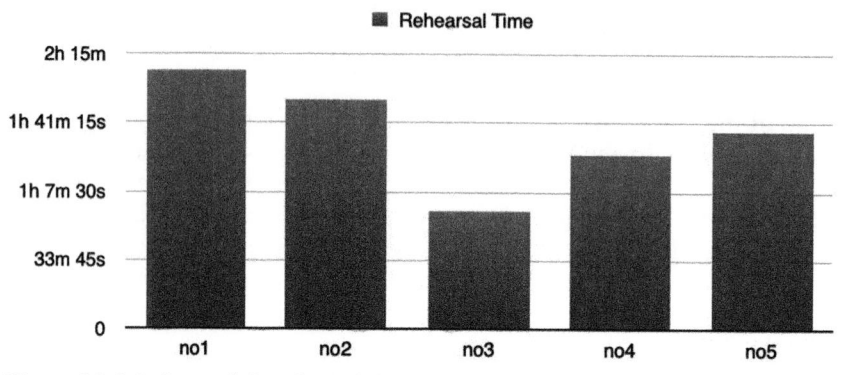

Figure 22.1 Rehearsal time in Kub/Szaf

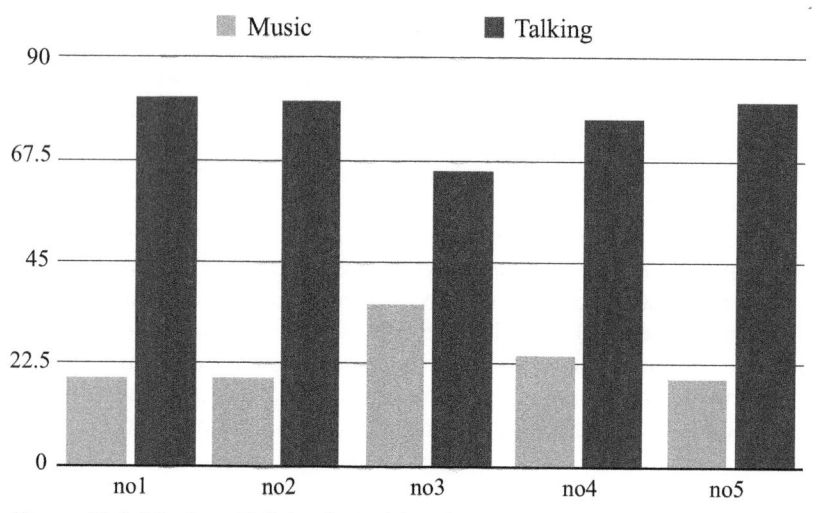

Figure 22.2 Music vs Talking in Kub/Szaf

The phenomenon could be blamed on the particular novelty of the material. The piece was written for the new instrument that is 'violin-voice'. When facing the questions associated with defining what is possible within a new performance situation, narrowing down what the problems might be seems crucial:

> problem construction is a particularly important influence on creative problem solving in ill-defined domains, where the pertinent goals, pertinent parameters, requisite information, and available solution strategies are unknown or poorly articulated.
>
> (Mumford et al., 1994, pp.8–9)

This also brings to mind the creative problem-solving theory by Wallas (1926), which laid the foundations for the later discoveries of Gordon (1973), Rubenzer (1979) and Moriarty and Vandenbergh (1984) to name a few. Wallas' proposed model of creative thought involved four different stages (preparation, incubation, illumination and verification) with the 'stage 2 – incubation' being the main innovation to the previous theory formulated by Dewey (1910). The need for the incubation of musical ideas could be the reason for such disassociation between the rehearsal time and music playing time.

In the *Six Spiders* Kubiak/Szafranski collaboration, the 'new instrument' is the performance of voice and violin by a single player and the composer was raising questions related to playability from the beginning of the first rehearsal:

Bartek: I did my best to check that they were playable, but to some extent it was just . . . the material
Agata: It's just the couple of them that are a big stretch, but apart from that . . . it's ok
Bartek: Right . . . that's . . . I know that . . . I suppose a lot of it will be the question of checking how comfortable are all the bits to play because you have to play and sing and so the point of it is not to have . . . not to leave anything in there that . . . that could distract you from just focusing on on on . . . well . . . doing two things at once'.
　　　　(Kubiak/Szafranski collaboration, Rehearsal no.1 transcription)

At the end of the same rehearsal a conversation, tackling difficulties behind writing for and performing on a new instrument, took place:

Bartek: Ok, yes . . . thanks, I will make your life even more difficult then
Agata: Let's be honest . . . I'm already singing and playing, how much more difficult can it get?
Bartek: That's the problem . . . you're looking to fill a gap in the repertoire, but of course composers are crazy, so . . . so rather than just filling a gap you're just suddenly gonna get very challenging way of filling the gap in the repertoire rather than just having something . . . something in there, so . . .
Agata: yeah, but I think that's what makes it real, doesn't it? Because normally when you write something you wouldn't think about being limited by the performer . . . that wouldn't be your first thought . . . If it's physically playable . . . if it's physically something that you would do, you would want to try it, at least and see then maybe in the process if we see something is too complicated and it doesn't work after I practised it for few weeks or something . . .
Bartek: You just don't do it yeah . . .
Agata: . . . but I think at that stage when I'm just starting to practice it, we could put more stuff in and just see if I can do it, cause otherwise . . . I don't like the idea of giving up before you try, so . . .
Bartek: yeah . . .
Agata: it's nice to try things and just see if you can make it happen . . .

Bartek: And I think it's the whole question of creating new repertoire now, in the 21st century and not trying to be . . .
Agata: We haven't got anything to base it on.
    (Kubiak/Szafranski collaboration, Rehearsal no.1 transcription)

As mentioned before the important characteristic of a New Instrument Collaboration is prevalence of creative categories [b], [c], [d] and [e].

There were 14 occurrences of category [b] within 5 documented rehearsals. An example from Rehearsal no.1:

Agata: mmmmm . . . I guess I was wondering about entries, when I'm playing that figure, cause obviously I'm syncing things up and that will be the biggest challenge for me with singing and playing, so moments of entries and note changes and things . . . I was wondering how accurate where that falls. . .
Bartek: On that one it was . . . it was pretty instinctive as I was composing so happy to move it onto the beginning of the bow
Agata: Oh Ok!
Bartek: So it'll fall onto the second beat
Agata: So it's not that it falls somewhere in-between these?
Bartek: No, I don't think so, it was how it instinctively . . .
    (Kubiak/Szafranski collaboration, Rehearsal no.1 transcription, change no.2, category [b])

There were 6 occurrences of category [c]. Below we can see an example from Rehearsal no.2:

Agata: aaa . . . that's a pizz as well? or is it an open? [*demonstrates*]
Bartek: Oh . . . both at once? that might be a . . . yeah! both at once is amazing . . . ok! mhm . . . I need a pencil . . . I like it! I should use it most of the time . . . So I'll change it to a longer note and at some point during it there will be a left hand pizz.
    (Kubiak/Szafranski collaboration, Rehearsal no.2 transcription, change no.1, category [c])

There were five occurrences of category [d] and [e]. We can use the fragments below as an example of each:

Bartek: Yeah . . . cause what I had before was this single note that was kind of a . . . [*demonstrates*] this sort of pizz, but it didn't work, it's too ?? too much . . . but this technique was something that I picked up from people talking about an orchestral . . . [*Agata demonstrates*] . . . Actually that's very good . . . yeah . . . that was . . .
Agata: Three string it would be . . .
Bartek: No, that was on a single note, on the top note of the chord *Agata demonstrates*
Bartek: But then whether you can do it when you [*points at position*] when you're here . . . maybe it's trickier, isn't it?
Agata: But you know what . . . why not, why not to do it there
Bartek: yeah?
Agata: If it's just the one note I can pluck . . . I can catch one here

Bartek: Yeah, it's just the top note of the chord . . . exactly when you see the dynamics [*Agata demonstrates*]

Bartek: Yes . . . This, I want, it's a very good effect . . . it supposed to be with a delay, it's very . . . interesting . . . And can you do that once you've . . . When you plucked the bigger chord can you do that at a certain time interval? Because I'm not worried that you . . . that other strings are muted after the cord cause the delay picks them up [*Agata demonstrates*]

Bartek: That's great . . .

        (Kubiak/Szafranski collaboration, Rehearsal no.2 transcription, change no.7, category [d])

Bartek: Let's say you would play . . . I don't know . . . only the beginning without this tremolando, just the chords(. . .)The charms of digital technology [*Agata demonstrates*] There is something appealing about it, I won't lie . . . it will then allow you to focus on singing.

Agata: Wow! It just keeps getting easier.

        (Kubiak/Szafranski collaboration, Rehearsal no.4 transcription, translation Agata Kubiak, change no.5, categories [e] and [b])

This last example is particularly interesting. This aspect of movement no.4 was featured twice already in previous rehearsals and implementing this final change puts it exactly back where it started. These decisions resulting in a creative 'full circle' might seem like a waste of time. One should not forget how crucial the role of possible experimentation is in creative ideation. Finding a solution through trying out and eliminating all other possibilities is also a good strategy, when it comes to creative problem solving. As Basadur (1994, p.256) puts it: "In contrast, even if they do not work, experimenting with such ideas provides further learning and the potential stumbling upon new and unexpected outcomes and opportunities".

Another aspect of New Instrument Collaboration is experimenting with notation of the piece. The performer's feedback becomes crucial in designing a new way of visually representing the music. The next change described below, was initiated by the performer and was crucial to the development of the video score used later. It reshaped the way the second movement was notated permanently and it was inspired by the performer's shorthand notation. This change reduced the amount of pages of the second movement from seven to four.

Agata: (. . .) if I just show you . . . literally what I've done with the counting here

Bartek: Every time after the chord?

Agata: Every time something is changing . . . so like here it goes and it goes but something is changing so I start counting again . . . so if something is changing if you could put it again

Bartek: put the group in again and repetitions

Agata: then it makes sense for me to . . .

        (Kubiak/Szafranski collaboration, Rehearsal no.2 transcription, change no.4, category [b])

This was a great example of solving the page turning problem present in the initial rehearsals. As Fitch and Heyde (2007) also mention, while referencing Karttunen (1999): "the performer's role is usually confined to the discovery of practical 'solutions' to music ideas ('problems') that have already been posed by the composer". They also mention a particularly analogous example of altering the notation: "I was struck by the way in which the 'simpler' notation allowed attention to be focused on the spoken text" (Fitch and Heyde, 2007).

The prevalence of category [b] in all five documented rehearsals does not imply that all simplifications are accepted by each side of the collaboration. One of the dangers the New Instrument Collaboration is cautious suggestions of simplification that underestimate the possibilities of the new instrument and overestimate the need to make the music 'more playable' for the performer. Below we can see a few examples of misjudged attempts.

Bartek: The one thing that . . . I mean . . . I don't want to do it if I don't have to . . . I could put time signatures in, appropriate time signatures in
Agata: Oh . . . don't worry about it. . .
(Kubiak/Szafranski collaboration, Rehearsal no.2 transcription, change no.5, category [b])

Agata: But it's cool, I'm slowly starting to get used to it.
Bartek: I can get rid of these lyrics
Agata: No, no . . . it's ok.
(Kubiak/Szafranski collaboration, Rehearsal no.3 transcription, translation Agata Kubiak, change no.1, category [b])

Bartek: That's all . . . and by the way there is one thing I had on my mind previously and I forgot about it . . . to take the . . . to take the vocal line an octave down has been a little bit on my mind
Agata: mhm
Bartek: And I wonder if in terms of . . . just keeping it at this quite low dynamic and the slow crescendo it would just be more . . . come more naturally . . . if it's lower
Agata: We'll need to try with a microphone really . . . cause if it's gonna be lower we won't be able to . . . it won't be like piercing through everything else that we're doing
Bartek: it won't . . . it won't . . .
Agata: . . . we wouldn't really hear it
Bartek: ummm . . . cause I mean . . . it sounds really nice . . . are you not strained by those really soprano things?
Agata: no . . . not really . . . to be honest I haven't been looking that much into dynamics yet, just trying to learn the notes for now.
Bartek: yeah . . . that's great . . . let's just leave it . . . that's great. . .
Agata: We can always change it later if we don't like it . . .
Bartek: yeah.
(Kubiak/Szafranski collaboration, Rehearsal no.2 transcription, change no.3, category [b])

Another interesting phenomenon is captured in the example below. New Instrument Collaboration calls for an increased presence of the composer and turns the rehearsals into an almost workshop like space.

The following creative idea was one of the most interesting ones, as it was difficult to determine whom to credit for it. The performer had some initial difficulty with remembering pitch to the vocal note within a busy violin passage in the second movement. While demonstrating the motif, she plucked the open A string with her left hand in order to find the vocal note needed for the next entry and not stop the flow of the violin line. The composer picked up on this 'addition', and enjoyed the sound of it so much that it developed into a recurring motif within the whole second half of the second movement. This is quite an accurate example of a joint creative initiative based around something that otherwise would have been dismissed as a mistake, if the composer was not present during the rehearsal.

Bartek: I could either notate that left hand pizz in or. . .
Agata: hahaha, you've noticed my sneaky note checking
Bartek: No! But that . . . it's good! It's just I just didn't think of the fact that it's . . .
Agata: That I can do that?
Bartek: It's just there! so we can put that in or we can just say do it. . .
(. . .)
Agata: . . . so maybe something like that? [*demonstrates*] It's not gonna disturb me cause I'm counting that way anyway and I can just hold my A on top of it, it's not gonna be a problem, so like [*demonstrates*]
Bartek: You've just composed it for me . . . That's very good . . .
(Kubiak/Szafranski collaboration, Rehearsal no.1 transcription, change no.7, category [f])

This brings to mind a comparison of how such process takes place when 'the composer' and 'the performer' are represented as the same person. This fragment of a statement by Francis Bacon shines some light onto the disjunctive nature of the creative process in arts: "but suddenly the lines that I'd drawn suggested something totally different and out of this suggestion arose this picture. I had no intention to do this picture. I never thought of it that way" (Francis Bacon, quoted by Sylvester, 1975).

The role of 'accidents' in the creative process is very often hidden. When it comes to creative 'accidents' in music, there must be many that never develop into an idea. One should not forget that the rehearsal situation described in the *Six Spiders* project was very unique. It is very rare that the composer is present throughout the entire rehearsal process and is able to witness and sometimes latch on creatively to such 'accidents' as the left-hand pizzicato motif described above. As mentioned, the author finds the classification of creative initiative difficult to determine in this case. The sound itself was initiated by the performer but picking up on and morphing the sound idea into an important part of the movement was due to the composer.

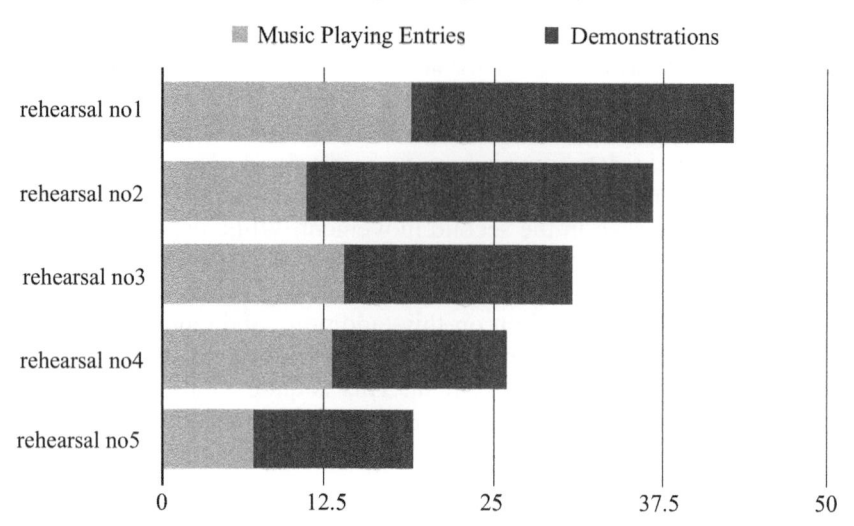

Figure 22.3 Music Entries and Demonstrations in Kub/Szaf

The last aspect of the New Instrument Collaboration is connected with the rehearsal structure and style. There seems to be a connection between the musical invention process (creative changes observed) and how the moments of playing music are distributed throughout the rehearsals. We noticed already that 'music playing time' did not differ much between all five cases, but the way these events are spaced out does differ greatly. A brief explanation of the author's classification of event is in order here. The aforementioned 'music playing time' refers to any music playing activity longer than ten seconds. Musical activities shorter than ten seconds are classified as 'demonstrations'. 'Music entries' refer to any musical activity lasting longer than ten seconds. Figure 22.3 shows a breakdown of such 'demonstrations' and 'music playing entries' throughout five rehearsals.

We can see that there is a clear tendency for both demonstrations and music entries to decrease as the piece becomes more familiar. The more disjointed structure of music activities in the initial rehearsals could also be stimulating the creative process. As Dudek and Cote (1994) also suggest maintaining the openness of structure for longer can be very beneficial in creative thinking. Francis Bacon, approached by Sylvester, mentions:

> Originality is an emotional essence, a disposition to capture in its net the novel, the fresh, the quivering, the writhing essence of lived reality. As soon as it takes form it loses life, becomes fixed and thus obsolete, no longer an equivalence. The creative process is an emotionally involved extension of a continual search until the artist puts down the tools and declares the problem to be solved.
> (Francis Bacon interviewed by Sylvester, 1975)

Accordingly, one can strongly hypothesise that structuring the rehearsal time as a constant back and forth of small musical interludes and conversation about the piece would be the most fertile ground for creative ideas to grow. Once the music playing interludes become longer but less frequent, the chance for feedback, experiment and demonstration diminishes. As both the composer and the performer settle upon a certain version, a certain interpretation of the movement in question, the implementation of changes and ideas becomes more difficult. The music then becomes much harder to morph, like paint that's almost dry or clay that's almost settled. It is clear that the most important, structural, musical and interpretational changes happen in the first period of rehearsals. It was also then, and only then, that the phenomenon of 'joint suggestions' took place. One should not claim that it would be impossible to re-shape the piece of music at later stages, but it is right to expect that it would be more difficult.

22.6 CONCLUSION

This chapter presents 'Six Spiders' by Bartosz Szafranski as an example of the New Instrument collaboration type. In this type of collaboration, increased composer's presence and increased verbal communication play a crucial role. Engaging one performer in two different roles as well as the composer's performance role were responsible for individuals' 'over-expression' and 'thinking out loud'. Data showed how verbal communication exceeded any musical activity in every rehearsal. An increase in the disjointed character of musical entries and demonstrations correlated with increased creative change suggestions from participants. Leaving gaps in musical activities allowed for commentary, real time feedback and creative opinion exchanges between the performer and composer. When looking at creative change suggestions, one can identify definite prevalence of category [b] – simplification being offered, [c] – choice being offered, [d] – intention being clarified and [e] – experiment is proposed. Many of the necessary interactions between the parties were connected with: lack of historical repertoire references, questions around playability, need for innovative score presentation, use of sound modifying tools. The collaboration between Kubiak and Szafranski lasted for over one year and out of five documented rehearsals, the initial two were identified as the most creatively fertile period. This research provides valuable information on how to structure composer/performer collaborations for most productive results. It gives insight into which practices increase creative input from participants and how to best manage valuable rehearsal time in similar collaborations. The New Instrument approach can become a catalyst for idea generation, creative problem solving and experimentation, as long as a back-and-forth dialogue between participants is available.

REFERENCES

Basadur, M. (1994). Managing the Creative Process in Organizations, *Problem Finding, Problem Solving and Creativity*. New Jersey, Ablex Publishing Corporation, pp. 237–268.

Dewey, J. (1910). *How We Think*. Boston, MA: Health.

Dudek, S.Z. and Cote, R. (1994). Problem Finding Revisited. *Problem Finding, Problem Solving and Creativity*. New Jersey, Ablex Publishing Corporation, pp. 130–152.

Gordon, R. (1973). Reflections on Creation, Therapy, and Communication. *Art Psychotherapy*, 1, pp. 109–112.

Fitch, F.J. and Heyde, N. (2007). 'Recercar': The Collaborative Process as Invention. *Twentieth-century Music*, 4 (1), pp. 71–95.

Karttunen, A. (1999). Discovering the Music around Me. *Finnish Music Quarterly* 2, pp.16–21.

Kubiak-Kenworthy, A. (2020). Composer-Performer Collaborations in New Music Compositions: Suggestions for Change Versus Authorship. *Music and Practice Journal*.

Moriarty, S.E. and Vandenbergh, B.G. (1984). Advertising Creatives Look at Creativity. *Journal of Creative Behaviour*, 18, pp. 162–174.

Mumford, M.D., Reiter-Palmon, R. and Redmond, M.R. (1994). Problem Construction and Cognition: Applying Problem Representations in Ill-Defined Domains. *Problem Finding, Problem Solving and Creativity*. New Jersey, Ablex Publishing Corporation, pp. 3–39.

Redgate, C. (2017). Composition Changing Instruments Changing Composition. *Distributed Creativity, Collaboration and Improvisation in Contemporary Music*. Oxford: Oxford University Press, pp. 141–154.

Rubenzer, R. (1979). The Role of the Right Hemisphere in Learning and Creativity: Implications for Enhancing Problem Solving Ability. *Gifted Child Quarterly*, 23, pp. 78–100.

Sylvester, D. (1975). *Francis Bacon interviewed by David Sylvester*. New York, Pantheon Books.

Wallas, G. (1926). *The Art of Thought*. New York, Harcourt Brace.

23

"My avatar and me"

Technology-enhanced mirror in monitoring music performance practice

Giusy Caruso, Luc Nijs and Marc Leman

23.1 INTRODUCTION

The digitization of movement and sound used in empirical studies for music performance analysis increasingly provides useful data to musicians engaged in the evaluation of their own performance practice (Goebl *et al.*, 2014). Musicians traditionally use different 'mirroring' tools that can assist them in this process of self-reflection (Caruso *et al.*, 2016). A typical example is the use of a simple mirror to observe and adjust posture in real-time while playing and to improve the correlation between the corporeal movement and the production of sound. Other mirroring tools are video and audio-recording devices, which have the double function of reproducing and documenting a performance.

In artistic research, the outcomes of this mirroring process are usually reported in written or oral narrative self-descriptions (Borgdorff, 2012; Bruner, 1986) grounded in the phenomenological approach of the *reflective practice methods* (Schön, 1984). However, within the community of artist-researchers, a debate is ongoing on whether the integration of rigorous empirical methods is valuable or even desirable in shaping the reflective processes in search for validity, reliability and credibility of artistic findings (Hannula *et al.*, 2005). In turn, empirical studies on music performance are mainly based upon monitoring and quantifying practice through such a biofeedback technology capable of generating and processing real-time visual and audio data (Wanderley *et al.*, 2005). For instance, motion-capture technologies offer new possibilities to study gestural involvement in performance by quantitatively tracking a variety of gestural qualities, such as displacement, velocity, acceleration and quantity of movement. Moreover, these technologies become the musician's mirror 2.0, allowing duplication of the performer's body in an augmented reality by turning the captured gestural information into a digital 3-D model of the performer (avatar). However, do these quantitative data and the possibilities they create have an added value to musician-researchers? Can this empirical approach be implemented in music-performance practice? Ultimately, can a mixed methodology contribute to the development of the monitoring process in music performance practice?

Methods that combine arts and sciences in music performance have not been thoroughly explored yet (Lapointe, 2016). Only a limited amount of empirical (e.g. Desmet *et al.*, 2012; Coorevits *et al.*, 2016) and artistic studies (e.g. Schacher *et al.*, 2015; Dries, 2017) considered this possible integration.

To contribute to the debate, this chapter proposes an empirical approach to monitoring music performance practice as developed at IPEM, Institute of Psychoacoustic and Electronic Music of Ghent University (Caruso, 2018). The aim of the study was to investigate whether quantitative data can be useful for artistic practice and, conversely, to see whether the artistic insights can offer new outlooks to empirical studies on music performance (Doğantan-Dack, 2012; 2015). The main question is how to associate quantitative results to qualitative artistic findings and vice versa. With this association, technology can be applied as a mirroring tool that can augment the monitoring of music performance practice, hence the idea of "technology-enhanced mirror". For this reason, a mixed methodology, which integrates subjective (qualitative/top-down approach) and objective (quantitative/bottom-up approach) perspectives, was conceived. As this methodology involves the artist performer, it was called "performer-based analysis method" in Caruso *et al.* (2016).

This chapter will briefly describe this mixed methodology, conducted by the performer-researcher, and illustrate possible implementation of the technology-enhanced mirror. This approach is seen as a step towards further studies that will open new frontiers for the innovation in music performance practice and research.

23.2 MIRRORING TECHNOLOGY IN MUSIC PERFORMANCE PRACTICE

For centuries, musicians have searched for means to enhance their practice and make it more effective and efficient. Besides innovative methods in practicing, different technological tools have assisted musicians in enhancing body awareness (Gallagher, 1986) and optimizing body posture.

The simplest tool for monitoring gestures in music performance has always been a mirror. Musicians are used to looking into a mirror to observe and evaluate themselves playing in order to adjust their gestures and posture, and to find alternative modes of execution. For example, Claudio Arrau stated in Von Arx (2014, p. 18), "I put a mirror next to my piano [. . .] I began to notice the rotation, the vibration, the use of arm weight, and so on. . .".

Awareness of gestural involvement in music performance practice plays a fundamental role in the development of musical skills (Leman, 2007, 2016). However, the image in a mirror provides visual information about gesturing, which is difficult to grasp, due to the fact that musicians have to watch and interpret what happens *in* the mirror while playing. At the end of the 19th century, the pianist and pedagogue Marie Trautmann Jaëll worked with a sequence of photographs, showing some moments of a piano performance, to study her pupils' gestures (Caruso, 2016). Later on, the invention of audio and video recordings gave the opportunity to reproduce a complete performance after the execution, which is commonly adopted by musicians nowadays. However, from the perspective of enhancing music performance practice, both audio and video recordings can be considered as immature technologies in view of new, more sophisticated tools.

Advances in the analysis of video-recorded gestures offers new ways to handle recorded performances (Castellano *et al.*, 2008). For example, the motion capture (mocap) recording of a performing musician offers a complex but highly intriguing new way of monitoring and interpreting gestures (Goebl *et al.*, 2014). Well known to film and gaming production, motion capture not only enables the reproduction of natural movements of a person as video, but it also provides accurate and detailed 3-D data on body postures and gestures (Jakubowski *et al.*, 2017). First of all, the captured images offer a 3-D perspective compared to 2-D video (which can only be frontal or lateral etc.), allowing possibilities for rotating and seeing the recorded performance from different viewpoints, as if one walks around the performer. Secondly, the analysis of the 2D-images was until recently based on subjective inspection, rather than on computational tools. Recent developments in technology offer a promising increment by providing 3D-visualization of the body in performance, together with techniques for the analysis of the movements and posture in 3D, as displacement, velocity and quantity of motion (Goebl *et al.*, 2014). The possibility of using such motion-capture data for gestural analysis has turned motion-capture technology into one of the most used methods in empirical studies on music performance (e.g. Davidson, 1993; Dahl & Friberg, 2007; Nusseck & Wanderley, 2009; Desmet *et al.*, 2012). Therefore, nowadays musicians can benefit from the use of this cutting-edge technology to potentiate and refresh their music performance practice.

Inspired by the possibilities offered by this new means to monitor, augment and, as such, enhance the traditional mirror in performance practice, an empirical study on piano performance was conducted at IPEM with a 3D-video recording equipment (Caruso, 2018). The goal was two-fold. On the one hand, this study aimed to help musicians to refine their own performance practice and develop their own artistic process (Cook, 1999; Yih, 2013). On the other hand, this study aimed to better understand the relationship between gestures, sound and interpretation. The first goal is more artistically oriented – sharpening artistic feelings and intuitions. The second goal is more scientifically oriented – at sharpening the understanding of the relation between gesture and intentionality in piano performance. This scientific approach ultimately leads to knowledge that is useful for other musicians, and it will lead to other methods based upon the 'mirroring' technology in the future.

23.3 QUANTITATIVE DATA AS A METAPERSPECTIVE FOR MUSIC PERFORMANCE ANALYSIS

Engaging in reflective practice (Schön, 1984) implies that musicians have to document and evaluate the different stages of their artistic process (including practice and performance). Most importantly, by eliciting knowledge concerning the artistic process itself and its outcomes, such documentation provides a metaperspective, i.e. offering the performer a third-party perspective of their work. Being a practice associated with other practices (e.g. practicing on the instrument or analysis), documentation may precede or follow a public performance and has always a powerful impact on the artistic process as a whole.

One way of documenting one's artistic practice is by 'written narrative description' (Bruner, 1986). The act of writing implies simultaneity of thinking and doing, i.e. observing the world and immediately (re)creating it (Hannula *et al.*, 2005). Another way of documenting the artistic process is based on scientific methods based on the quantitative data provided by technology, which can furnish different external viewpoints – the metaperspective – to support the subjective viewpoint (*first-person perspective*) of a music performance. In this way, technology appears as an 'augmented mirror' able to add new value to the musicians' self-reflection upon their practice.

To explore this new arena – and with a transferable and future-facing, user-friendly methodology, a performative experiment was set up by using software to perform a detailed analysis of sound and bodily engagement. To understand the relationship between physical actions (gestures) and interpretation (as intentional actions) in piano playing; video, audio and motion-capture recordings of a piano performance were considered. Finally, multimodal annotation software was applied to facilitate the comparative analysis and alignment of qualitative and quantitative data. This implementation defines the above-mentioned 'performer-based analysis method' (Caruso *et al.*, 2016), which was developed to form a better understanding of the complex relation between gestures, sound and musical interpretation.

23.3.1 Method

In order to investigate the evolution of gestures relative to the evolution of the musical interpretation, several consecutive interpretations of selected fragments of a contemporary piano-piece were recorded during the performative experiment. The participant in this study was a concert pianist (the first author) trained in classical music performance with a high-level of expertise in contemporary music performance.

To ensure the ecological validity of the performance space, the experiment was conducted in a concert hall (the Miry Zaal at the Royal Conservatory of Ghent) using a Steinway grand piano. To encourage spontaneous playing in the experiment and invoke the natural feeling of a public concert, a video recording was used. The performative experiment was recorded with two video cameras (lateral and top view) and a microphone. In addition, the performer's movements were tracked by the OptiTrack Motion Capture System. These cameras emit infrared light which markers on the body reflect, and these reflections are in turn is picked back up by cameras (at a sampling rate of 100 Hz) so that the markers' dynamic position in 3D

Figure 23.1 The markers placed on the body of the pianist and on the boundaries of the piano (Caruso 2018, p. 61)

space can be calculated. Six such cameras were positioned in a hexagonal configuration on a fixed rig. Eighteen markers were placed on the pianist's upper body (three on the head, three on each hand, three on the back and three on each elbow – see Figure 23.1). Furthermore, four markers were positioned on the boundaries of the keyboard in order to have its reference in the visualization of the motion-capture recording.

Because the performer was also analysing her own performance, a retrospective *thinking aloud procedure* was used to make her own artistic reflection more explicit and systematic. The performer/researcher looked back at the development of her gestural process by verbally explaining and demonstrating at the piano the evolution of her movement in relation to her interpretation, as reported in the *verbatim* (Caruso, 2018, pp. 213–215). Thus, she showed the differences between her initial intuitive approach (implicit understanding of score) and the developed approach (explicit understanding of the score after the deliberate practice). Before and after the think aloud session (including performance of the fragments), the whole piece was played throughout. The recording of the spontaneous performance of the piece was used as a point of reference to see whether the presupposed causal sequence of stimuli and expressive responses were biased during the explanation of the fragments. The analysis and observation carried out from the perspective of musical intentions were conceived of as states that cause gestural patterns in relation to the interpretation.

The qualitative top-down process consisted of a multimodal analysis of music and movement through the annotations that the pianist made during her artistic process. She outlined her performance practice in a written performance model and video annotation. The performance model implied the structural analysis of the music (form, sub-phrases) combined with a collection of subjective observations on the interpretative cues (tempo, phrasing, dynamics, timbre) and their technical implementation (e.g. fingerings) (see also Chaffin & Imreh, 2001). The video annotation was based on a coding system to describe the motor strategies (gestural approach) linked to specific musical patterns. This gestural coding system was conceived by watching at the archived video recordings of previous performances (see Bloom's (1953) *video stimulated recall*). On the basis of this observation and video annotation, it was possible to differentiate performance-related movements into sound-producing, technical and expressive gestures and, consequently, to relate structural, interpretative, and technical aspects of the score to the different involved gestures. This annotation framework (performance model and video annotation) served also as a protocol for the verbal description of the fragments performed during the actual performative experiment.

The quantitative bottom-up approach offered a way to segment the performance gestures (Desmet *et al.*, 2012), through motion capture and sound data. The goal of this bottom-up approach was to fuel the performer's *first-person perspective*, based on reflection in and on action during practice and performance, with a *third-person perspective* elicited by the visualization and analysis of the motion capture data. The aid of technology allowed the performer/researcher to objectify the image of her body. The extracted kinematic variables, such as velocity and acceleration made an empirical comparison of the two performance models possible. In this way, the performer's embodied musical intentions and expressiveness were detected on mapping and measuring the performative movements (Leman, 2016, 2007).

The combination of the subjective analysis (qualitative feedback), on the basis of the performance model and video annotation, with the quantitative measurement of the gestures and sound (quantitative feedback), enabled the performer to investigate systematically how the gestural articulation in performance changes in relation to the expressive intentions embedded in the score. To monitor and evaluate her gesture, the pianist had the opportunity to observe her *avatar* reproduced by the motion capture system and to analyse the quantitative data on sound in relation to her artistic interpretation and expectations. Thus, this performer-based analysis method (Caruso *et al.*, 2016) was conceived to align qualitative and quantitative data and to improve the performance (see Figure 23.2).

In this approach, the performer-based analysis is supported by technology as a mirror that provides top-down and bottom-up enhanced performance feedback system. Obviously, the feedback is re-injected in the artistic process that defines and shapes the expressive intention of the performer. The mirror thus becomes a tool in a reinforcement dynamic within the artistic process.

"My avatar and me"   361

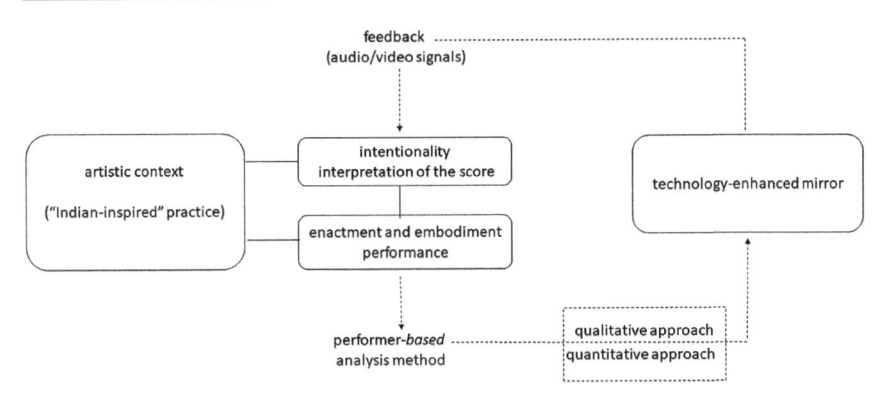

Figure 23.2 This scheme summarizes the stages of the performer-based analysis method

Source: Caruso (2018, p. 71)

23.3.2 Gestural analysis for body awareness

In preparing and installing the motion-capture technology, the pianist faced many technological and methodological challenges. A preliminary run was needed to find the right setting of cameras and markers. Normally, musicians are used to just one or two cameras for the video capture of their performance. Instead, the motion-capture system demands a precise configuration and calibration of a number of infrared cameras (up to eight and even more different cameras), depending on the kind of movements one wants to record (e.g. arms, hands) in order to be able to explore its full power. Finger movements, for example, were not recorded in this experiment. To accurately track the performer's body movements, reflective markers had to be positioned on the body to avoid occlusion

Figure 23.3 The body of the pianist as visualized by the motion capture system in the three-dimensional performance space

and reflection. This requires a robust positioning strategy of both cameras and markers, based on the artist-researchers' experiential knowledge about bodily engagement in performance (self-perception) and on adequate practical understanding of the motion-capture system.

This challenge provoked the pianist to deeply reflect on the morphology of her body while performing in a determined way.

To set the cameras and the markers, she carefully watched the video footages of her previous performances to have a major consciousness of her gestural approaches to the piano. This observation helped to decide on which parts of the body the reflective markers were placed. The motion-capture systems generates a 'stick figure' through which the performer's bodily behaviour is represented over time in video. This skeleton-like visual representation on the basis of interconnected dots can be seen as an *avatar* of the performer (see Figures 23.3 and 23.4), allowing interconnection of the first and third person perspectives. Compared to a normal mirror or simple video camera, even at this stage, the pianist could work on gestures in a more accurate and intuitive manner through observation of her body performing from different perspectives.

The motion capture system thus allows musicians to have a multiperspectival image of one's body in performance, by zooming in and out the joints or moving and rotating their avatar – it acts as a mirror that allows focusing on specific body parts – from multiple angles. Moreover, the capture recording has the advantage that it generates data concerning the motion tracking. This makes it an additional tool for a detailed research on music performance and for the transmission of knowledge.

Dealing with the motion-capture data requires specific computational skills. The raw data, representing movements – not of the entire body but of the markers attached to the body, have to be exported to another software package such as a bespoke script in Matlab, in order to process the time-based series of these data. This study explored different ways of processing the data, both in terms of data extraction and data analysis. From the motion capture of the performative experiment, the pianist extracted videos from different angles and processed the data with the software Physmo2 for frame-by-frame video analysis of motion (Barraclough, 2011). Physmo2 provided raw data concerning the horizontal and vertical displacements (x-y) of gestures. From these data, the velocity and acceleration of the body parts selected for this research were calculated.

Figure 23.4 The avatar of the pianist's body seen through in the virtual space from multiple perspectives (Caruso 2018, p. 118)

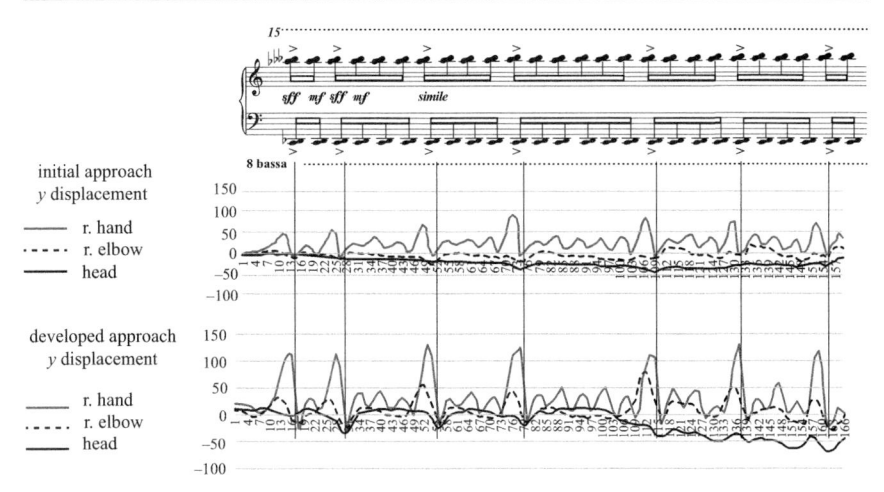

Figure 23.5 A comparison between the initial performance approach (1) and the developed performance approach (2) of right hand, right elbow and head (showing vertical displacement of the markers) related to a fragment of the score

Source: Caruso (2018, p. 91)

Figure 23.5 provides an illustration of the average displacement of markers on different body parts along the y-axis (vertical displacement) of the Mocap system and the score taken as a point of reference.

The results here show the change in coordination and embodiment in the developed performance approach after the period of training, compared with the initial performance approach (Furuya, & Altenmüller, 2013; Thompson & Luck, 2012).

These data constituted an alternative representation of a performance, which supports the verbal self-reflection.

23.3.3 Audio analysis: visual inspection and quantitative analysis

In a similar way to how motion-capture technologies can augment and thereby complement traditional video recordings to obtain feedback and to evaluate one's performance, musicians' use of simple audio-recording devices can also be augmented and complemented with digital tools to this end. In this study, we used Sonic Visualizer, an open-source application for viewing, analysing and annotating audio files (Cannam *et al.*, 2010). The use of this tool for visualization and analysis of sound facilitates detailed analysis of performance. For example, after importing a sound file, the software displays its waveform allowing the user to select fragments of the performance in a very precise way. Moreover, by adding dedicated plug-ins to the software, specific types of analysis can performed such as detecting note onsets (both automatically or through manual annotation), calculating timing and dynamics (such as the energy of the signal

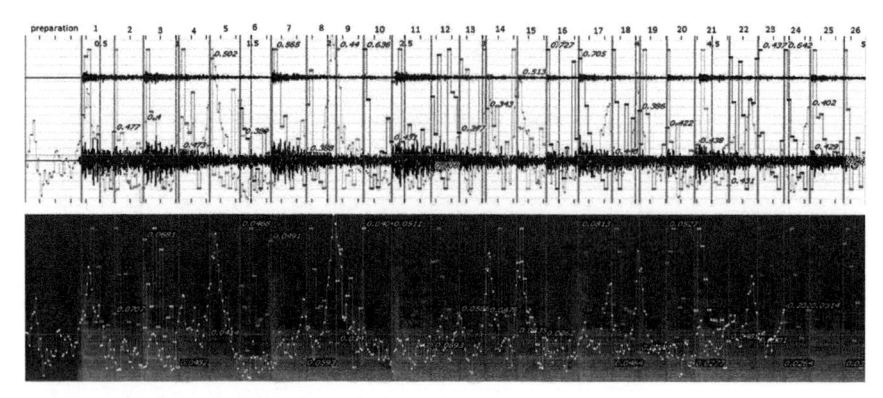

Figure 23.6 An example of audio analysis from Sonic Visualizer by selecting the waveform and spectrogram views per 26 note onsets of the fragment in Figure 23.5.

Source: Caruso (2018, p. 114)

approximated by computing the root-mean-square (RMS)) and providing spectrograms over the given segment. In the study by Caruso *et al.* (2018), duration and dynamics were extracted to add to the dataset around performance.

Working with the audio analysis of the different performance fragments, the pianist has an additional visual cue to test the sound result, and an excerpt can be seen in Figure 23.6. It is interesting to consider that, even in an empirical context, only performers and not scientists can give an artistic interpretation of the quantitative results. Comparing quantitative data on dynamics of the initial performance and the developed performance, for instance, was a stimulating discovery to observe why there were subtle differences between both approaches in relation to the score and the interpretation. For example, the energy of each note of a dynamic rhythmical phrase was analysed and compared in the initial execution (blue lines) and in the developed execution (orange lines) of Figure 23.7. The score notation in the top panel is taken as a reference point.

The pianist's intention was, indeed, to give different sound and energy to the accented notes by modifying her gestural approach. However, as reported in the verbatim of the experiment, the pianist attested she had the impression that the more exaggerated gestures of her developed approach could provide a more resonant timbre more easily, compared to the more restrained gestures of the initial approach (Caruso, 2018, p. 215). As shown in the Figure 23.7, it is evident that the last three groups from the score presented a different sound result (major in the initial approach). This quantitative result made the pianist think on how she should adjust her gestures to efficiently maintain her performance until the end. Thus, this example of the mirroring process explains how quantitative data can add elements to improve musicians' intuitions on and qualitative descriptions of their performance.

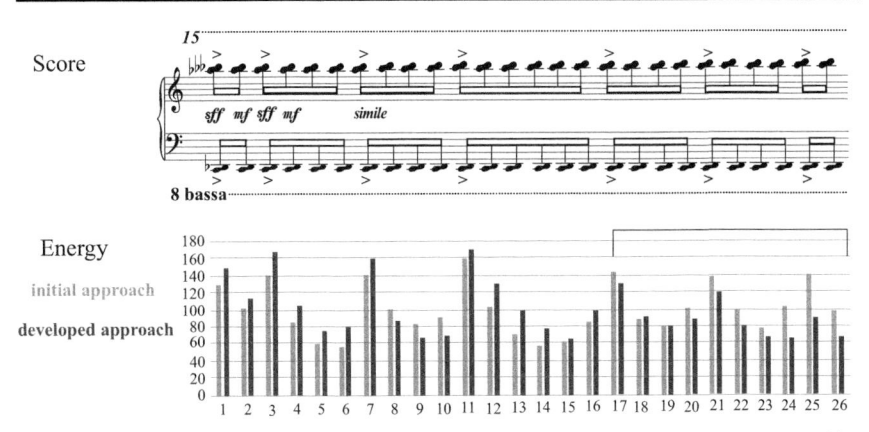

Figure 23.7 The lower panel shows a graphical representation of the energy (the root-mean-square (RMS)) calculated by Sonic Visualiser

Source: Caruso (2018, p. 115)

23.3.4 Integration of qualitative and quantitative analysis

Once the audio and motion-capture data were prepared and analysed, the qualitative and quantitative data could be related to each other, for example, using the multimodal annotation software ELAN (Wittenburg et al, 2006; ELAN, 2020). In this software, it is possible to import video recordings, audio tracks and data gathered from the motion capture (displacement, velocity and acceleration) and link them as streams together. The system then enables one to navigate in the multimedia data streams. Self-reflections on the score can be inserted and then verified through a parallel configuration of all the measurements (video, audio and motion) and accurately associated with specific pitches and gestures through annotation. In this way, ELAN also becomes a further augmented mirror where all the parameters from the performance are systematically displayed in detail. Thus, body movements can be accurately associated with the level of the note onsets or score topology. The gestures that were retrieved and categorized through coded video-observation and annotation can also be aligned with the duration and dynamics of the sound. This can all be triangulated against the expectation reported in her performance model.

The scenario presented in this ELAN project is an example on how quantitative data can complement qualitative approach, and vice versa, and a specific example can be seen in Figure 23.8. Video, audio, motion tracks, and segmentations are aligned. All the segments, that show progression over time in the video, audio and segmentation views, can be played. The upper panel shows the video, the middle panel shows the audio track and the lower panel shows the segmented annotation made by the pianist. The parallel configuration of the computed sound and gestures aligned with qualitative observations has the advantage to give musicians, who want to carry on a research on their performance, a complete and more precise picture on what they are producing.

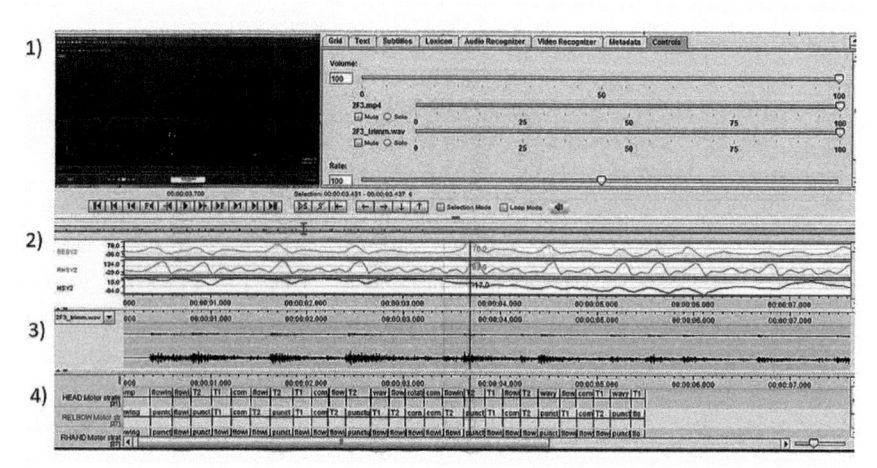

Figure 23.8 This screenshot, taken from one of the ELAN projects, shows the parallel configuration of four layers in analysing the developed performance of the piano fragment in Figure 23.5. The quantitative measurements are displayed in the following order from up: 1) the video; 2) the motion tracks (displacement) of head, right hand, and right elbow; 3) the audio waveforms; 4) the qualitative descriptions shown in the segmented annotations made by the performer according to her performance model structure

Source: Caruso (2018, p. 87)

23.4 GENERAL DISCUSSION AND CONCLUSION

This chapter presents a pioneering model of a technology-enhanced mirror to monitor music performance in order to intensify reflective practice. In recent decades, the artistic process, especially in music performance, has become an area of common interest for performers/researchers and scientists. On the one hand, performer-researchers need tools to enhance the monitoring of their practice and, on the other hand, scientists want to better understand the meaning of raw data concerning gestures in music performance in relation to specific musical structures.

In this study, a pianist's reflective practice was supported using a 'performer-based analysis method' (Caruso *et al.*, 2016), in which a top-down qualitative description of performance was combined with a bottom-up quantitative analysis using motion, visual and audio feedback. Such a feedback enriches the artistic process and contributes to define the expressive intention of the performer. By adopting a quasi-scientific approach, combining qualitative and quantitative methods in close connection to the artistic intuitions of the performer, the findings are the result of integrating art and science. We believe that this combination of art and science is fruitful, both for the artistic development of a performance and for the scientific development of an embodied interaction technology.

Importantly, this art-science approach contributes to fully acknowledge the unicity or the *aura* of a performance. Our study always adopted an artistic stance, always taking the score and the pianist's interpretation as a point of reference. Technologies such as the motion capture system for gestural analysis, Sonic Visualizer for the audio analysis and ELAN for the systematic annotation of the results, were used to enable and support the pianist to verify her interpretation and artistic intuitions related to her corporeal engagement and sound production. In this way, measurements of gestures and sound constitute quantitative issues that enabled the pianist to reach a major awareness of her performance. Quantitative data can offer a metaperspective for one's own analysis of a performance and provide information for a better understanding of one's own gestures and intentionality. Furthermore, they constitute an alternative way, to the narrative and written methods, to document and transmit knowledge about the embodied interaction in an artistic context.

In short, the art-science approach proposed in this chapter may be useful to support the description and evaluation of the artistic process and to identify the relation between gestures and sounds. Furthermore, it shows how the performers' perspective is needed in music-performance analysis to connect empirical data to musical structures. Ultimately, the performers can benefit from this method by becoming aware of the ways in which this connection can be established. However, this research work needs to be extended to other musicians in order to become a user-friendly tool for practicing. We believe that this pioneering approach, conducted by one pianist, may be of benefit to more performers. This may also lead to an increased reliability of this method that can be also applied in music education. We do not make any claim that the idea of technology-enhanced mirror can be easily applied. The use of technology still has many limitations. Nevertheless, this approach shows the potential to reinforce musicians' practice in checking their personal reflection and in improving their efficiency when performing. In this challenge, musicians should acquire the language of science and the competences of technical disciplines, data generation and processing (Coessens *et al.*, 2009).

So far, our studies are examples of how technology can be applied in the observation of music performance replacing the traditional mirror, audio or video devices. The utility of the quantitative data is definitely meant to support musicians' self-reflective approach. It illustrates how technology can contribute to renovating the traditional general approach to music performance analysis. The idea of a technology-enhanced mirror to monitor music performance is an example of how art and science can join forces, and how the digitization of movement and sound with subsequent computational methods constitute cutting-edge tools in support of both musicians' artistic practice and the generation and transmission of knowledge.

REFERENCES

Barraclough, J.K. (2011). Phys - Video Motion Analysis [Computer Software] http://physmo.sf.net.Benjamin, Walter: *L'opera d'arte nell'epoca della sua riproducibilità tecnica. Arte e società di massa* (1936), Einaudi, Torino, 1991.

Bloom, B. S. (1953). Thought-processes in lectures and discussions. *The Journal of General Education*, 7(3), pp. 160–169.

Borgdorff, H. A. (2012). *The conflict of the faculties: perspectives on artistic research and academia*. Amsterdam: Leiden University Press.

Bruner, J. S. (1986). *Actual minds, possible worlds*. Cambridge, MA: Harvard University Press.

Cannam, C., Landone, C., & Sandler, M. (2010) Sonic Visualiser: An Open Source Application for Viewing, Analysing, and Annotating Music Audio Files. Proceedings of the ACM Multimedia 2010 International Conference.

Caruso, G. (2016). La femme au toucher ineffable : la pianiste, pédagogue et chercheuse Marie Trautmann, épouse Jaëll. In *Cahiers internationaux de symbolisme*, (C. LEJEUNE, Ed.)143-144-145 (Genre), pp. 27–42.

Caruso, G., (2018). Mirroring the intentionality and gesture of a piano performance: an interpretation of 72 Etudes Karnatiques pour piano, [Ph.D. Dissertation], Ghent University Press.

Caruso, G., Coorevits, E., Nijs, L., & Leman, M. (2016). Gestures in contemporary music performance: a method to assist the performer's artistic process. In *Contemporary Music Review*, Volume 35, Issue 4–5: Gesture-Technology Interactions in Contemporary Music.

Castellano, G., Mortillaro, M., Camurri, A., Volpe, G., & Scherer, K. (2008). Automated analysis of body movement in emotionally expressive piano performances. *Music Perception*, 26, pp. 103–119.

Chaffin, R. & Imreh, G. (2001). Comparison of Practice and Self-Report as Sources of Information About the Goals of Expert Practice. *Psychology of Music*, Vol. 29, N. 1, pp. 39–69.

Coessens, K., Crispin, D., & Douglas, A. (2009). *The artistic turn: A manifesto*. Ghent, Belgium: Orpheus Institute. Leuven University Press.

Cook, N. (1999). Analysing Performance and Performing Analysis. *Rethinking Music*, Vol. 8, pp. 239–261.

Coorevits, E., Moelants, D., Östersjö, S., & Gorton, D. (2016). Decomposing a composition: On the multi-layered analysis of expressive music performance. In M. Aramaki, R. Kronland & S. Ystad (Eds.), *Lecture notes in computer science (LNCS): Post-proceedings of the 11th International Symposium on CMMR* (n.p.). Berlin: Springer.

Dahl, S. & Friberg, A. (2007). Visual perception of expressiveness in musicians' body movements. *Music Perception*, 24(5), 433–454.

Davidson, J. W. (1993). Visual perception of performance manner in the movements of solo musicians. *Psychology of Music*, 21(2), 103–113.

Desmet, F., Nijs, L., Demey, M., Lesaffre, M., Martens, J. P., & Leman, M. (2012). Assessing a clarinet player's performer textures in relation to locally intended musical targets. *Journal of New Music Research*, 41(1), pp. 31–48.

Doğantan-Dack, M. (2012). The art of research in live music performance. *Music Performance Research*, 5, pp. 34–48.

Doğantan-Dack, M. (2015). *Artistic practice as research in music: theory, criticism, practice*. Oxford: Oxford University Press.

Dries, K. (2017). *"Voyages" – Dualism in artistic research and performance of a saxophone player. An Interdisciplinary approach*. VUB, Brussels.

ELAN (Version 5.9) [Computer software]. (2020). Nijmegen: Max Planck Institute for Psycholinguistics. Retrieved from https://archive.mpi.nl/tla/elan.

Furuya, S. & Altenmüller, E. (2013). Flexibility of movement organization in piano performance. *Frontiers in Human Neuroscience*, 7(July), 173.

Gallagher, S. (1986). Body image and body schema: A conceptual clarification. *Journal of Mind and Behaviour*, 7(4), pp. 541–554.

Goebl, W., Dixon, S., & Schubert, E. (2014). Quantitative methods: Motion analysis, audio analysis, and continuous response techniques. In D. Fabian, R. Timmers, & E. Schubert (Eds.), *Expressiveness in music performance: Empirical approaches across styles and cultures* (pp. 221–239). Oxford: Oxford University Press.

Hannula, M., Suoranta, J., & Vaden, T. (2005). Artistic research: theories, methods and practices. Published by Academy of Fine Am, Helsinki, Finland and University of Gothenburg/ArtMonitor, Gothenburg, Sweden 2005.

Jakubowski, K., Eerola, T., Alborno, P., Volpe, G., Camurri, A., & Clayton, M. (2017). Extracting Coarse Body Movements from Video in Music Performance: A Comparison of Automated Computer Vision Techniques with Motion Capture Data. In *Frontiers in Digital Humanities*, 4(June), 9. http://doi.org/10.3389/fdigh.2017.00009.

Lapointe, F.J. (2016). On the Role of Experimentation in Art (and Science). *Journal of the New Media Caucus* | ISSN: 1942-017X, V.12 N.01. http://median.newmediacaucus.org/research-creation-explorations/6095-2/ (Accessed on 26/09/2017).

Leman, M. (2007). *Embodied music cognition and mediation technology*. Cambridge, MA: MIT Press.

Leman, M. (2016). *The expressive moment: How interaction (with music) shapes human empowerment*. Cambridge, MA: MIT Press.

Nusseck, M. & Wanderley, M.M. (2009). Music and motion – how music-related ancillary body movements contribute to the experience of music. *Music Perception*, 26(4), pp. 335–353.

Schacher, J.C., Järveläinen, H., Strinning, C., & Neff, P., (2015). Movement Perception in Music Performance - A Mixed Methods Investigation. *Proceedings of the International Conference on Sound and Music Computing, SMC'15*, Maynooth, Ireland.

Schön, D. (1984). *The reflective practitioner*. Basic Books: New York.

Thompson, M. & Luck, G. (2012). Exploring relationships between pianists' body movements, their expressive intentions, and structural elements of the music. *Musicae Scientiae* 16(1), pp. 19–40.

Von Arx, V.A. (2014). *Piano lessons with Claudio Arrau: A guide to his philosophy and techniques*. New York: Oxford University Press.

Wanderley, M.M., Vines, B.W., Middleton, N., McKay, C., & Hatch, W. (2005). The musical significance of clarinetists' ancillary gestures: An exploration of the field. *Journal of New Music Research*, 34(1), pp. 97–113.

Wittenburg, P., Brugman, H., Russel, A., Klassmann, A., & Sloetjes, H. (2006). ELAN: A professional framework for multimodality research. *Proceedings of LREC 2006*, Genova, Italy, 1556–1559.

Yih, A. (2013). Connecting analysis and performance: A case study for developing an effective approach. In *Gamut* 6/1 (Special feature: A music-theoretical matrix: essay in honor of Allen Forte, Part IV). New Found Press.

24

Creative considerations for on-screen visuals in electronic pop music performances

Kirsten Hermes

24.1 INTRODUCTION

Electronic music is at the forefront of contemporary recording practice and digital audio workstation (DAW)-based productions dominate the current popular song charts (Strachan, 2017, pp. 44–46). Many of these productions are created by layering software instruments and samples and cannot usually be reproduced on the fly in the same way as they were created in the studio.

Laptops have become a common tool in electronic music performances due to their powerful capabilities of real-time audio manipulation, however they lack visual feedback for the audience (Correia et al., 2017, pp. 1–8). Equally, not all audience members will understand the functionality of hardware tools such as MIDI controllers, effects units or DJ decks. Many will not know when and how performers are interacting with these systems, how the systems respond and what constitutes a performance mistake (Correia et al., 2017, pp. 1–8; Gurevich and Fyans, 2011, pp. 166–175; Berthaut et al., 2013). This means that in the live performance of electronic popular music, effective musical expression and communication is reduced due to a lack of visual agency and liveness (Canfer, 2017, pp. 100–112).

Audience members depend on visual information to make judgements about music performance (Tsay, 2013, pp. 14580–14585) and this information can significantly inform the perception of properties such as emotion, tension, phrasing and intensity (Gurevich and Fyans, 2011, pp. 166–175). Boltz (2013, pp. 217–234) states that when visuals and audio are presented together, they can influence how each is perceived and the intended emotion of a composition can be more clearly and unambiguously communicated to an audience via an audiovisual versus an audio- or visual-alone presentation. The impact of visual cues on auditory perception is also demonstrated by the McGurk effect, where the perception of a syllable can be altered when a video of a different spoken syllable is shown (McGurk and Macdonald, 1976, pp. 746–748). Overall, added visual information can likely bridge the gap between what is seen and heard in an electronic music performance. One way to achieve this is through the use of on-screen visuals, which this chapter focuses on.

Currently, there is a lack of studies that analyse the effectiveness of live visuals (Correia et al., 2017, pp. 1–8). According to Cooke (2010, pp. 193–208), live media performance remains under-theorized because it sits in between traditional modes of production and performance and "because it is still a relatively 'new' form of new media". Correia et al. (2017, pp. 1–8) assess what constitutes an effective use of visuals in electronic art music (e.g. relating to the audience perception of performance interface parameters), however this is likely to be different for commercial popular music, due to differences in venues sizes and types, the performance intent, the audience demographic and the music itself. Therefore, the aim of the current study is to investigate creative considerations for on-screen visuals in popular electronic music performances. The following questions are addressed:

- How can visuals be created and played back during the live performance?
- How can a relationship be established between what is seen and heard?
- What challenges and affordances can arise from working with visuals?

To answer these questions, a range of case studies are considered and connected with the author's own performance practice. This is backed by existing research in branding theory, musicology and audiovisual perception. The existing approaches for creating and playing back visuals are briefly summarized in 2. The practice-led case study is introduced in Section 24.3. In Section 24.4, possible ways in which visuals and sound can form a conceptual unit in live performance are explored, using the author's own creative practice and additional case studies as evidence.

24.2 HOW CAN VISUALS BE CREATED AND PLAYED BACK DURING THE LIVE PERFORMANCE?

There are a multitude of ways in which live visuals can be created. This includes camera footage and 3D graphics, both of which can be either prepared or generated during the performance. Established electronic pop artists usually work with visual production companies for the creation of their visuals (Ponsford, 2014). Professional video jockey's (VJs) are artists that create and mix video – live and synced to the music – in clubs or at concerts; a practice that has emerged in the 70s and 80s (Faulkner, 2018). VJs can edit clips together on-the-fly to accompany improvised electronic music performances, for example, video production company the Light Surgeons do this in their work with Chase and Status and the Cinematic Orchestra (Ponsford, 2014).

Less established artists have the option to create their own visuals, however this is accompanied with several challenges. Firstly, artists need to acquire skills in the area of video production, which may not be part of their skill set. Secondly, commonly used electronic music performance tools do not usually make live visuals a core part of their functionality. For example, *Ableton Live* does not offer a straightforward drag-and-drop functionality for video segments to be triggered alongside music loops in the *session view* (Ableton, 2019). Thirdly, the need to control both sound and visuals live is more complicated than controlling the sound alone.

In addition to the option of using filmed footage, countless pieces of graphics software exist that can be used for creating live visuals. These range from specific music visualizers to re-purposed Games engines. The node-based audio programming environment *Max/MSP* is accompanied by the visual processing platforms *Jitter* and *Vizzie* (Cycling '74, 2019). *Moditone* (2018) is a node-based workstation for building procedurally generated graphics algorithms to accompany live music and *Isadora* (2019) is a graphic programming environment with emphasis on real-time manipulation of digital video. Generative graphics can either be programmed from scratch or based on pre-made patches. For instance, Federico Foderaro (2019) creates live visual programmes specifically for musicians working in *Jitter*.

Pieces of 3D graphics software such as *Cinema4D*, *Maya* and *Houdini* can be used in order to create and animate complex visual scenes from scratch. Games engines such as *Unity* or *Unreal Engine* can be employed in order to build custom music visualizers. For example, *Chunity* is a custom programming environment for the creation of interactive audiovisual software (Atherton and Wang, 2018), based on the *ChucK* programming language and *Unity* game engine.

There are also options for using artificially intelligent tools. Steenbrugge's "Neural Synesthesia" (2019) machine learning project specializes in generating new data from a given training set, automatically generating eerie moving images ranging from photorealistic faces and animals to cartoon characters. Olowe et al. (2016) are in the process of developing a new music visualizer using pre-mixed, independent multitracks and audio feature extraction. A challenge with using generated graphics is that depending on the software, CPU demands can be high. Prepared video clips are easier to store and play back but are somewhat more restrictive in that they are more difficult to alter live.

Usually, visuals are shown on screens surrounding the stage but they can also be projected onto buildings and the performers themselves. CuteCircuit (2019) create wearable technologies, such as a "Sound Shirt" and a mini skirt with integrated screens that artists can wear and load visuals into, as an extension of their stage persona. In projection mapping, objects, persons and buildings act as a display surface for video projection. For example, futuristic Japanese electronic pop trio Perfume wore matching white dresses in their 2013 live performance of "Spending All My Time". In the drop of the piece, vivid and colourful graphics are projected onto the dresses, creating an augmented reality where humans and technology blend into one.

24.3 NYOKEË: A PRACTICE-LED CASE STUDY

In order to gain a clearer idea of the challenges and affordances associated with the use of live visuals, the case studies presented in the following sections are combined with a practice-led research approach. Under the moniker Nyokeë, the author is an audiovisual artist inspired by video games, Japanese Kawaii culture and her synaesthesia (see section 24.4.2). In order to capture the nostalgia of old video games consoles in songs, an outdated 90s *Gameboy* is recorded through an *Arduino* via MIDI keyboard input. The resulting chiptune sound is imported into *Logic Pro X* and embedded in electronic pop tracks alongside recorded vocals, software synths (such as *Plogue Chipsounds*, a chiptune software emulation synth and *Sylenth*, a popular EDM synth) and hardware synths (i.e. a *Dave Smith Prophet* and a *Roland JDXA synth*). The aim here is to create a track that matches the creative vision and artistic intent as closely as possible, layer by layer. As a result, it is impossible to perform the tracks live in the same way as they were created in the studio, requiring for this to be planned separately. Nyokeë's live performances (Figure 24.1) usually take place at Anime and Games events in the UK and abroad. This requires plane travel, meaning that a portable and durable setup is preferred. Therefore, Nyokeë uses a laptop and three MIDI controllers (Figure 24.2) in addition to the live vocals in order to play the music and prepared live visuals as follows.

A stem mixing approach is employed (Figure 24.3), whereby the finished productions are broken down into loops, for example *kick*, *bass*, *other drums*, *music*, *lead* and *added elements*, each for the verse, chorus and bridge parts. These loops are triggered with a *Launchpad* controller in *Ableton Live*. Additional one-shots (risers, falls, drum breaks and chiptune Foley elements) are triggered through a *Traktor Kontrol F1* MIDI controller and an *Akai MPK mini* keyboard controller. Lastly, *Ableton Live* software effects, including high and low pass filters, reverb, distortion and beat slicing, are mapped to the rotary and fader controls on the *F1*. Within Ableton Live, the third-party plugin *Ebosuite* (2019) is used in order to trigger prepared video clips alongside the music. By triggering a *scene* in

Figure 24.1 Nyokeë performing live with visuals

374   Kirsten Hermes

Figure 24.2 Nyokeë's MIDI controller setup

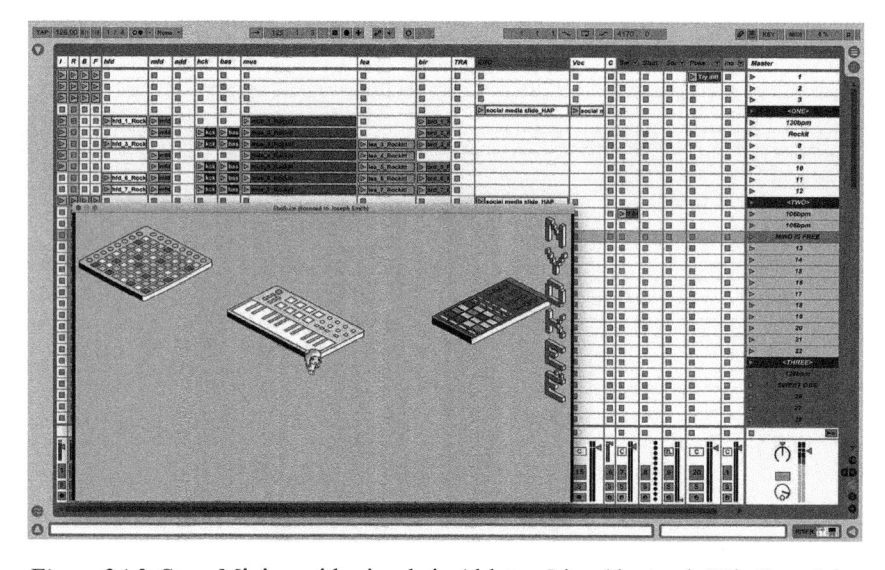

Figure 24.3 Stem Mixing with visuals in Ableton Live (the track "Ebo" contains the video segments)

Ableton Live, groups of loops and the accompanying video snippet begin to play back and continue looping, until other clips are triggered instead. This allows for flexibility and improvisation during the live performance, where the visuals automatically adapt to the music.

Nyokeë's visuals reflect the game aesthetic of the music, consisting almost entirely of pixelated animations and voxel-based scenes. Voxel graphics represent scenes in terms of data points that are situated on a regularly spaced, 3D-grid. The data points are often shown as cubes with different colours and textures. Since many games (such as *Minecraft*) are based on this technology, the aesthetic has clear game connotations. Nyokeë visual scenes show bright and colourful landscapes, sweets, fictional characters and lyrics; and sometimes reference popular video games. This is combined with Japanese Kawaii and Anime culture, borrowing from artists such as Kyary Pamyu Pamyu and Femm. Some songs are accompanied by camera-filmed visuals (e.g. "Serendipity") that show Nyokeë dancing. Between songs, a still image of Nyokeë's social media and website links is shown ("www.nyokeemusic.com"). All visuals are created by author in *Cinema4D*, *Photoshop*, *Premiere Pro* and *Magicavoxel* and are streamed to live venue projectors from the laptop via HDMI. Nyokeë adds choreography and Japanese street fashion inspired outfits.

24.4 HOW CAN A RELATIONSHIP BE ESTABLISHED BETWEEN WHAT IS SEEN AND HEARD?

Gow (1994, p. 255) asserts that music videos should not be judged based on their audio or video content alone but that the synergy between the two has a strong impact on the overall affective power. He observes that there appear to be 'empirical semiotics' for popular music, whereby syntactical characteristics of the music are linked to the visual. The same is likely the case for live visuals – it is not the music or visuals alone that determine the success of a performance, but rather their compatibility. The current section discusses what constitutes a successful match between what is seen and heard in the live performance. In Section 24.4.1, methods for amplifying performer and audience actions through visuals are presented. In Section 24.4.2, the creation of cross-sensory concepts is discussed. The creation of a narrative context is discussed in Section 24.4.3 and lastly, Section 24.4.4 presents visuals as a tool for branding.

24.4.1 Amplifying performer and audience actions

Gesture is a fundamental element of a successful performance as it helps to communicate liveness to an audience (Joaquim and Barbosa, 2013, pp. pp. 89–106). In fact, visual performance cues can outweigh auditory performance cues in terms of audience ratings of expressivity (Vuoskoski et al., 2016, pp. 457–471). Live video projections can show audience members how the music is created and thus help bridge the physical distance between performers and audience members (Correia et al., 2017, pp. 1–8). In this way, the agency and intentionality of the performing musician can be connected to the agency of the machine systems (Canfer, 2017, pp. 100–112), contributing to "immediacy" (Correia et al., 2017, pp. 1–8).

In large venues, these visual cues can be lost to far away audience members. Therefore, a close-up live video feed can help amplify the musicians' facial expression, movement and instrumental performance. For example, the recent US EDM festival Tomorrowland attracted some 200,000 visitors that were able to witness Armin van Buuren's trance DJ performance through a live video feed, projected onto several gigantic screens (Van Buuren, 2019). This was combined with a dramatic light show.

Drone footage of the audience is also often integrated, e.g. in Weirdcore's work for Aphex Twin (Bourton, 2017). This helps keep audience engaged, as concert goers can hope for a short moment of fame, where they momentarily become part of the performance itself. Often, a live feed of both the performers and audience is combined with other, prepared elements. Depeche Mode's Performance at Nos Alive (2017) combined live performance footage with neon-coloured animal stills. In his Made in America tour (2014), Kanye West could be seen rapping and moving on big screens, combined with geometrical shapes, colour effects and cinematic elements. Taylor Swift's Houston Live show (2017) combined live footage of dancers and Taylor Swift herself with geometric patterns and abstract landscapes. Close-up shots of the singer's face added an element of intimacy.

The visual amplification of performance parameters can also take place in a more abstract way, for instance by visually reinforcing the use of innovative performance tools. Björk's ambitious 2011 work "Biophilia" used a number of bespoke musical instruments, including a large Tesla coil lightning machine, suspended above the stage. Musical director Matt Robertson operated this through a controller keyboard via *Ableton Live* (Björk, 2011). On-screen visuals showed imagery of lightning on a black background, reinforcing the visual effect of the Tesla coil itself. In her Prismatic World Tour (2014), Katy Perry dramatically emerged from a pyramid consisting of screens for the song "Roar", wearing a neotribal-inspired holographic skirt and crop top featuring geometric shapes. This "prism" theme is repeated in the dancer's fashion and the visuals shown on the screens. Here also, on-stage performance parameters are amplified in the visuals.

In the case of Nyokeë, the song lyrics are displayed on-screen for a number of songs. This helps audience members better understand the context and is particularly useful for performances of covers and remixes, where audience members are invited to sing along. For the performance of the song "Serendipity", Nyokeë performs a dance choreography which can also be watched in the accompanying music video, creating a collage of real-life and recorded dancing.

Figure 24.4 Live visuals that amplify performance parameters

24.4.2 Creating cross-sensory concepts

Humans can understand and communicate cross-sensory concepts. This connection is explained in the phenomenon known as *ideasthesia*, where a concept or idea can be perceived through several senses. For example, the concept of harshness can be represented through sharp transients in audio, jagged lines in visuals and through rough textures haptically. Fast-moving music can be mapped to fast-moving visuals. Nikolić (2016, pp. 38–49) defines *ideasthesia* as a phenomenon in which activation of concepts produces phenomenal experience. He asserts that "art happens when the intensities of the meaning produced by a certain creation and the intensities of the experiences induced by that creation, are balanced out" (ibid). In addition to the intrinsic multisensory connections described in ideasthesia, *synesthetes* have sensory-like experiences to a stimulus that otherwise would not induce such experiences (Jürgens and Nikolić, 2012, pp. 1–18).

Overall, it is possible for an artistic concept and its audiovisual representation to match in a way that humans intrinsically understand. In this way, AV artists can create a "total artwork" or "Gesamtkunstwerk" that makes sense as a whole, or in other words a "hypermediacy (Correia et al., 2017, pp. 1–8). This interconnection between sound and image is sometimes apparent (for example, when music visualizers represent the speed or frequency content of a piece) and at other times intuitive (ibid). This connection is often explicitly explored in electronic art music. In an interview with Ableton (Blanning, 2017), Frank Brentschneider explains that his approach to live visuals is characterized by matching and synchronizing abstract geometrical patterns to his music, such as flashing and moving bars, dots, lines and numbers. He specifically avoids visuals that tell a story or look too cinematic. While not as explicitly discussed, this synergy between sonic and visual energy also can be observed in commercial, popular music performances, for example, in Comix' 3D animation for

Axwell and Sebastian Ingrosso's Billboard Magazine "Best Live Show" award-winning performances in 2014. The visuals showed explosions of colour and abstract moving shapes that are synced to the high-energy dance music (Ponsford, 2014). The same was the case in Comix' visuals for Avivii's "True Tour" (ibid).

Most Nyokeë songs are upbeat and energetic, which is also expressed in the live visuals. The author experiences synaesthesia, associating colour and movement with sound. Chiptune sounds usually have bright rainbow colours, while warm, low-frequency timbres tend to be dark in colour. Equally, chord progressions can influence the colour perception. Following this, the author attempts to colour-match the visuals and sound. Further, the overall dynamic flow of a piece is associated with movement in space. As a result, many choruses and drops are accompanied by rapidly switching images, lights and symbols that flash in time to the music. In other segments, the virtual "camera" moves quickly through 3D graphics landscapes and cityscapes (Figure 24.5), sometimes rotating around its own axis, to convey a feeling of flying. The aim here is to create a holistic, multisensory experience that conveys movement and energy across both senses.

24.4.3 Providing a narrative context

Many electronic live music performances tell stories that are reflected in their on-screen visuals. Billie Eilish's 2019 Coachella performance and her "When We All Fall Asleep, Where Do We Go?" tour shared the theme of American Horror (Comix, 2019). The matching on-screen visuals, created by Comix, show eerie woodland scenes, clusters of restless eyes, hands forming tense claws and faces of monsters, all presented in red, black and white. Comix (2019) assert on their website showreel that "working with Cour Design and Fireplay who provided the stage and

Figure 24.5 Fast "camera" movement in Nyokeë's live visuals

lighting design, we put together a show that would terrify the audience, in the best possible way".

J-Pop star's Kyarie Pamyu Pamyu's 2018 live show in Camden's Coco was based around the theme of a Japanese Pop culture Halloween party. Dancers in elaborate costumes became fantasy creatures, marrying Kawaii culture and traditional Japanese mythology. The theme was also reflected in the on-screen visuals – the show began with a short movie of a haunted house.

Folktronica band Laikipia used narrative music video segments to accompany their 2017 performance at the Hospital Club in London. In the videos, the band members enact a group of adventurers living in nature. Cuts in the visuals were precisely synced to the music, which consisted of acoustic folk elements, EDM synthesizer timbres and tribal rhythms. In their Nos Alive Festival performance in Lisbon (2017), Bonobo made use of earthy, imaginary 3D landscapes and abstract nature themes, supporting the African elements in their ambient electronic music.

When Nyokeë performs to tech-savvy audiences at games conventions and chiptune events, they tend to be intrigued by the electronic music performance tools used. At anime conventions, however, audience members appear to be particularly interested in the fashion, dancing and surrounding narrative. Reinforcing the retro game and "Kawaii" theme visually helps both audiences understand the context for the music.

24.4.4 Using live visuals as a branding tool

Frith asserts that pop music is "produced commercially for profit, as a matter of enterprise not art" (Frith, 2001, p. 94). Therefore, commercial considerations usually inform the choice of live performance visuals. For many musicians, live music has become their main source of income (O'Reilly *et al*. 2013, pp. 201–222), with additional income generated through merchandise sold at concerts. Accordingly, live music is up to ten times more expensive than recorded music (ibid). Despite the rising cost of concert ticket sales, fans attend live music events in order to share the experience with likeminded others, to demonstrate fan worship and to discover support acts, making live popular music a successful business (Brown and Knox, 2017, pp. 233–249).

In a highly competitive market, remarkable and unusual products are more likely to succeed and therefore, it is at least initially more effective to target a niche than the mainstream market (Godin, 2003). Having successfully targeted a specific market segment, popular music performances can subsequently be mass marketed to the general public (O'Reilly *et al*. 2013, p. 91). Since music promotion has largely shifted from radio to internet, social media and co-branding (Macy *et al*. 2016), the visual artist image has become particularly important. In line with this, *YouTube* has become the second largest online search engine. Macy et al (2016) assert that strong brands are authentic and consistent and engage and interact with their audience continuously, communicating their values, personality and style. Following this, it appears reasonable for artists to also reinforce their artist identity through live visuals. The following examples can all be viewed on YouTube.

EyeSupply's Carlo Ruijgers spent a year designing the visuals for Armin van Buuren's six-hour-plus "Armin Only" shows (Ponsford, 2014). This includes a huge logo of the word "Armin", reinforcing the performer's brand. For smaller acts, on-screen logos and social media links can be used to help audience members remember the artists' name and to invite them to stay in touch (Figure 24.6). An example of this is gender fluid PC Music artist Dorian Electra's performance of their track "Flamboyant" at the Go West Festival in Los Angeles (2019).

Progressive House star Deadmau5 admits "We all hit play. It's no secret. When it comes to 'live' performance of EDM . . . that's about the most it seems you can do anyway. It's not about performance art" (Golden, 2012). Instead, the visual appeal in Deadmau5's performances is created through his unique "mouse" stage persona. Musicians do not only play music, but they play roles (Auslander, 2009, pp. 303–316). In line with this, the producer wears a glowing mouse helmet in all of his live performances. His on-screen live visuals consist of geometric shapes and variations of the mouse theme, always reinforcing the visual brand (e.g. Deadmau5, 2019). Another famous example is presented by the cartoon characters the Gorillaz which also feature in the band's live performances.

The creation of fictional stage personas is taken to the extreme in Hatsune Miku's brand – an imaginary blue-haired, 16-year old Japanese anime girl that appears on stage as a hologram, accompanied by real-live musicians (Miku, 2017). Similarly, as promotion for the multiplayer online battle arena video game *League of Legends* (LoL), the imaginary girl group K/DA was created. The group consists of four animated female characters ("champions") that represent playable in-game avatars (Ahri, Akali, Evelynn and Kai'Sa). K/DA's track "Popstars" was performed at the LoL championship tournament Opening Ceremony in Incheon hosted by *Riot Games*, bringing together real and fictional musicians. Chiptune rock band Please Loose Battle incorporate VJing in their performances, using several screens. One screen is a retro monitor with a simple, "cute", animated 8-bit face that responds to audience reactions and the music itself by showing a range of simple emotions (Please Lose Battle, 2018).

Figure 24.6 Nyokeë's social media still (shown between songs)

Nyokeë's visual image is based on Kawaii culture and retro games and includes Nyokeë wearing a big head bow as a "visual trademark" (Figure 24.1). This "brand" is reinforced visually at all times. Since not all musicians create visuals, being an audiovisual artist in itself has attracted positive feedback and has helped lead to ongoing international performance opportunities. The website and social media still between songs can additionally help transform interested audience members into social media followers (Figure 24.6).

24.5 DISCUSSION OF THE AFFORDANCES AND CHALLENGES OF USING LIVE VISUALS

The preceding sections have shown several advantages of using live on-screen visuals. The key challenge is to ensure that the visuals and music performance match. Badly timed or seemingly unrelated visuals likely take away from a successful music performance by diffusing the overall message. The creation and playback of visuals lies outside the skill set of many musicians. Furthermore, as many performances include improvisation, the track length and structure are not always known in advance, requiring visuals that react to the music. However, having to control both visual and sonic elements in a live performance can be confusing for some performers. A DIY approach requires a greater time investment, while hiring a VJ is an additional cost that not all musicians can afford. Furthermore, streaming live visuals from a computer increases the overall risk of equipment failure, due to additional CPU demands and more processes running at the same time.

It is often difficult to test the visuals in the venue before the performance day, especially for touring musicians. This can lead to a performance result that differs from the original creative intention. In the case of Nyokeë, in some venues, the screen was placed in a separate location from the stage and the author observed audiences watching the screen, rather than the performer. Some performers may choose to "hide" behind their visuals but others risk "competing" with the visuals, as is the case for Nyokeë, since her performances also incorporate expressive dance choreographies. In some venues, the bright light from the screen overpowered the atmosphere in the room. As additional equipment is required, there is also a greater risk of technology failing. The author has experienced problems with venue HDMI protocols on multiple occasions, where the visuals would not play back as expected and required last-minute trouble shooting, adding to the overall anxiety before the performance.

Despite these challenges, having complete control over a creative product can be highly rewarding. The author naturally associates visual scenes with music and therefore, the combined live performance setup allows for a more complete artistic expression. If the author was to employ a collaborator to create her visuals, they would probably not quite match her own vision. It would also be more difficult to implement changes or to reuse material flexibly. In this way, the creation of an audiovisual product invites artists to think about their craft more holistically. While it can be difficult to create visuals and sound that match, artists that have creative control over all aspects of their audiovisual product are also more likely to garner acclaim (Valsesia *et al.* 2016, pp. 897–914).

24.6 CONCLUSION

Carefully layered studio productions can be difficult to perform live, due to the fact that they cannot be reproduced live in the same way as they were created. On-screen visuals can add an element of "liveness" to the performance. The questions in the introduction can now be answered, as follows.

How can visuals be created and played back during the live performance?

Artists can either take a DIY approach or work with VJs and visual production companies. Visuals can either be based on camera-filmed footage or 3D graphics. Filmed footage can be prepared or captured live. Similarly, graphics visuals can be rendered prior to a performance or be generated on the fly. They can be created in specific music visualization tools, games engines or high-end graphics software; and even make use of AI. Visuals can be shown on screens or be projected onto buildings and the performers through projection mapping.

How can a relationship be established between what is seen and heard?

The synergy between audio and video is important. This can be achieved by amplifying on-stage and audience actions, for instance through a live video feed. Visuals can turn music performances into holistic, multisensory experiences through abstract representations of the music in colour and shape, or by providing an additional narrative context. The artist image and visual branding can be formally integrated in the live performance. This can even include the creation of virtual characters. Promotional materials and social media links can be shown on-screen to help audience members memorize an artist's name and to garner interest in their online presence.

What challenges and affordances can arise from working with visuals?

On-screen live visuals can be an expressive medium for creating a holistic, creative output. They can bridge the gap between what is seen and heard in electronic music performances. The key challenge is to create visuals that successfully match the music. Many musicians lack the funds to pay for a VJ. Being a self-taught graphics artist can be challenging and time consuming. However, having complete control over an audiovisual product is creatively rewarding being able to create both music and accompanying video footage gives artists an extended platform for creative expression. Therefore, music artists are encouraged to consider a visual audiovisual approach to live performance.

REFERENCES

Ableton (2019) "Working with Video" (website) available online from https://www.ableton.com/en/manual/working-with-video/ [Accessed November 2019].

Atherton, J. and Wang, G. (2018) Chunity: Integrated Audiovisual Programming in Unity. In: *Proceedings of the International Conference on New Interfaces for Musical Expression*, Vol. 2018, June, pp. 102–107.

Auslander, P. (2009) Musical Persona: The Physical Performance of Popular Music. In: Scott, D. B. (ed.), *The Ashgate Research Companion to Popular Musicology*, Surrey, Ashgate, pp. 303–316.

Berthaut, F., Marshall, M. T., Subramanian, S. and Hachet, M. (2013) Rouages: Revealing the Mechanisms of Digital Musical Instruments to the Audience, *Proceedings of The International Conference on New Interfaces for Musical Expression 2013*, Daejeon, Seoul.

Björk (2011), [performance] Biophilia, international.

Blanning, L. (2017) A/V Interchange: Performing Music with Visuals, available online from https://www.ableton.com/en/blog/performing-music-with-visuals/ [accessed November 2019].

Boltz, M. G. (2013) Music Videos and visual influences on music perception and appreciation: Should you want your MTV? In: Tan, S. L., Cohen, A. J., Lipscomb, S. D. and Kendall, R. A. (eds). *The psychology of music in multimedia.* Oxford, Oxford University Press, pp. 217–234.

Bonobo (2017) [performance] Nos Alive, Lisbon, Portugal.

Bourton, L. (2017) "It's a psychological Overload": Weirdcore on creating Aphex Twin's Live Visuals, It's Nice That (website), available online from https://www.itsnicethat.com/features/weirdcore-aphex-twin-field-day-050617-miscellaneous [accessed November 2019].

Brown, S. and Knox, D. (2017) Why go to pop concerts? The motivations behind live music attendance. *Musicae Scientiae*, Vol. 21, No. 3, pp. 233–249.

Canfer, T. (2017) Visual Agency and Liveness in the Performance of Electronic Music, In: Hepworth-Sawyer, R., Hodgson, J., Paterson, J. and Toulson, R. (eds.) *Innovation in Music: Performance, Production, Technology and Business*. London: Routledge, pp. 100–112.

Comix (2019) "Work" (website), available online from https://www.thisiscomix.com/work [accessed November 2019].

Cooke, G. (2010) Start making sense: Live audio-visual media performance. *International Journal of Performance Arts and Digital Media*, Vol. 6, No. 2, pp. 193–208.

Correia, N.N., Castro, D., and Tanaka, A. (2017) The Role of Live Visuals in Audience Understanding of Electronic Music Performances, Proceedings of the 12th International Audio Mostly Conference on Augmented and Participatory Sound and Music Experiences – AM '17. ACM Press, London, pp. 1–8.

CuteCircuit (2019) Wearable Technology, Fashion Technology, available online from https://cutecircuit.com [accessed November 2019].

Cycling '74 (2019) What is Max? available online from https://cycling74.com [accessed November 2019].

Deadmau5 (2019) [performance] Cube V3 Live, Creamfields, Santiago, Chile.

EboStudio (2019) Ebosuite – Turn Ableton Live into an audio-visual instrument, available online from https://ebosuite.com [accessed November 2019].

Electra, Dorian (2019) [performance] Flamboyant, Go West, Los Angeles, USA.

Ephtracy (2019) "MagicaVoxel", (website) available online from [accessed November 2019].

Faulkner, M. (2018) *VJ: Audio-Visual Art and VJ Culture*. Laurence King Publishing, London.

Foderaro, F. (2019) "Federico Foderaro" (website) available online from https://www.federicofoderaro.com [accessed November 2019].

Frith, S. (2001) Pop music. In: S. Frith, W. Straw and J. Street, (eds.), *The Cambridge companion to pop and rock*. Cambridge: Cambridge University Press, pp. 93–108.

Godin, S. (2003) [TED talk] How to Get Your Ideas Spread, available online from http://www.ted.com/talks/seth_godin_on_sliced_bread.html [accessed November 2019].

Golden, E. (2012) Is Deadmau5 Right? The "We All Hit Play" Debate. DJ Tech Tools, July, 2.

Gow, J. (1994), Mood and meaning in music video: The dynamics of audiovisual synergy. *Southern Communication Journal*, Vol. 59, No. 3, pp. 255–261.

Gurevich, M. and Fyans, A.C. (2011) Digital Musical Interactions: Performer-system Relationships and Their Perception by Spectators. *Organised Sound*, Vol. 16, No. 2, pp. 166–175.

Joaquim, V. and Barbosa, Á (2013) Are Luminous Devices Helping Musicians to Produce Better Aural Results, or Just Helping Audiences Not To Get Bored? In: Verdicchio, M. and Carvalhais, M. *xCoAx 2013: Proceedings of the First Conference on Computation, Communication, Aesthetics and X*. Bergamo, Italy, pp. 89–106.

Jürgens, U.M., and Nikolić, D. (2012). Synaesthesia as an Ideasthesia – cognitive implications. In: Söffing, C. and Sinha, J.R. (eds.), *Synesthesia and Children - Learning and Creativity*. Kassel University Press, Kassel, Germany, pp. 1–18.

Kyarie Pamyu Pamyu (2018) [performance] Kyarie Pamyu Pamyu Live at Coco Camden, London, UK.

Laikipia (2017) [performance] Laikipia at the Hospital Club, London, UK.

Macy, A., Rolston, C., Allen, P., and Hutchison, T. (2016) *Record Label Marketing*, Third Edition. New York, Focal Press.

McGurk, H. and Macdonald, J. (1976) Hearing lips and seeing voices. *Nature*, 264(5588), pp. 746–748.

Miku, Hatsune (2017) [performance] World is Mine, Project DIVA Live, international.

Mode, Depeche (2017) [performance] Nos Alive, Lisbon, Portugal.

Moditone (2018) Wire, available online from https://www.moditone.com/wire [accessed November 2019].

Nikolić, Danko (2016), Ideasthesia and Art. In: Gsöllpointner, K., Schnell, R., Karla, R. (eds.) *Digital Synesthesia*. De Gruyter, Germany, pp. 38–49.

Olowe, I., Barthet, M., Grierson, M., and Bryan-Kinns, N. (2016) FEATUR.UX: An approach to leveraging multitrack information for artistic music visualization. In: *Proceedings of the International Conference on Technologies for Music Notation and Representation (TENOR)*. Cambridge, UK.

O'Reilly, D., Larsen, G. and Kubacki, K. (2013) *Music, Markets and Consumption*. Oxford, Goodfellow Publishers Ltd.

Perfume (2013) [performance] Spending All My Time, DOME Level 3 Tour, Japan.

Perry, Kary (2014) [performance] Prismatic World Tour, international.

Please Loose Battle (2018) [performance] Chip Bit Day, Manchester, UK.

Ponsford, M., (2014) "See the music: How astonishing visuals are revolutionizing concert experience" (CNN website), available online from http://edition.cnn.com/2014/11/20/world/the-greatest-stage-spectacles-on-earth/index.html [accessed November 2019].

Steenbrugge, Xander (2019) [video series] Neural Synaesthesia, available online from [accessed November 2019].

Strachan, Robert (2017) *Sonic Technologies. Popular Music, Digital Culture and the Creative Process*. New York, Bloomsbury.

Swift, Taylor (2017) [performance] Taylor Swift Live, Houston, USA.

Troikatronix (2019) Isadora, available online from https://troikatronix.com [accessed November 2019].

Tsay, C.J. (2013). Sight Over Sound in the Judgment of Music Performance. *Proceedings of the National Academy of Sciences of the United States of America*, Vol. 110, No. 36, pp. 14580–14585.

Valsesia, F., Nunes, J.C., and Ordanini, A. (2016) What Wins Awards Is Not Always What I Buy: How Creative Control Affects Authenticity and Thus Recognition (But Not Liking). *Journal of Consumer Research*, Vol. 42, No. 6, pp. 897–914.

Van Buuren, Armin (2019) [performance] Tomorrowland Festival, Boom, Belgium.

Vuoskoski, J.K., Thompson, M.R., Spence, C., and Clarke, E.F. (2016) Interaction of Sight and Sound in the Perception and Experience of Musical Performance. *Music Perception: An Interdisciplinary Journal*, Vol. 33, No. 4, pp. 457–471.

West, Kanye (2014) [performance] Made in America, Los Angeles, USA.

Part IV

Music business and artist development innovation

25

Towards a quantum theory of musical creativity

Matthew Lovett

25.1 INTRODUCTION

Writing about music has never felt so urgent to me. Much of my recent work has been concerned with the way in which music – whether we like to think of it as a creative practice, an industry, or, in the words of Jacques Attali, an 'immaterial pleasure' (Attali, 1985: 5) – is evolving; as familiar approaches to making, listening to, sharing and thinking about music are disrupted by technological change. As such, it is important to preface this chapter by framing it as part of a wider project that takes an experimental approach, on one hand, to developing insights into the nature of musical creativity, and on the other, to building a conceptual toolkit that can be used to describe music, along with processes involved in making it.

In the book *Meeting the Universe Halfway*, the theoretical physicist Karen Barad, presents a wide-ranging analysis of quantum physics that redefines the relationship between the movement of electrons and everyday acts of thinking and making things, thereby generating a materialist-realist philosophical model which she describes as 'agential realism' (Barad, 2007: 177). Her analysis enables her to place the act of making in a dynamic relationship with a broader consideration of the nature of time, suggesting that at a fundamental level, things are not simply made against a backdrop of constant time, but that things and time are created as part of an ever-changing topology of what she calls 'spacetimematter' (Barad, 2007: 177). In addition, the book argues for an holistic conception of making that Barad terms 'intra-action', that encompasses the impacts and impressions that are 'made' by particle collision, along with archetypal human mark-making, through to the production of both human consciousness and the universe itself (hence the ambition of the book's title). As a musician, what interests me about Barad's work in this area, is that by extension, we can draw some conclusions about how the production of music can also be understood in the light of what we could call 'quantum thinking'. In what follows, via a close reading of a number of Barad's key terms and concepts, I set out to forge some basic principles of a quantum theory of musical creativity.

25.2 QUANTUM THINKING IN CONTEXT: SPECULATIVE REALISM AND NON-PHILOSOPHY

In putting forward a case for a quantum theory of musical creativity, the chapter is designed to recognise that such a theory is not only simply a contention, rather than an explanatory formulation that can stand for all time, but also, that it is only 'a snapshot of a snapshot'. In other words, the ideas presented here reflect their own locatedness in time, along with their inability to apprehend anything more than a fragment of the critical and philosophical debates that are continually emerging from a range of global thinking practices. Just as any piece of music could be seen to be a composer's or a performer's 'best approximation' of all that is available to them at a given moment in time, so too does any formulation of thought represent a theorist's best attempt to harness and apply a range of available formulations in a way that is intended to shed new light and offer new perspectives on – in this case – creative music practice.

The chapter is not intended as a philosophical genealogy, but there are two key innovations in contemporary thought that provide a useful context for Karen Barad's work, demonstrating not only that there is a shared ancestry between recent practices in scientific and philosophical thinking, but also, that there is a conceptual landscape where shared ideas and themes – if not particular terms and strategies – are clearly in evidence. Barad's book was published in 2007. That same year, a set of philosophical debates and ideas began to emerge around the idea of 'Speculative Realism', after the 'Speculative Realism Workshop' was held at Goldsmiths, University of London (Urbanomic, 2007). The workshop brought together four key theorists, Ray Brassier, Graham Harman, Iain Hamilton Grant and Quentin Meillassoux, and in hindsight can be seen as a point of departure for much of what has informed current debate regarding materialist-realist thought.

Speculative Realism has come to stand for set of heterogeneous ideas and ambitions within continental philosophy and is a term that has enabled a wider set of thinkers to begin to interrogate a particular way of orienting human thought to the world. In their own way, each of the four workshop participants formulated a perspective that facilitated the 'speculative turn' wherein it is understood that human thought is able to conceive of that which is not the product of human thought. This was the premise that gave the workshop, and the subsequent movement its name; the notion that beyond human thought, there is an absolute reality that does not have a provenance in that thought. Meillassoux's book, *After Finitude*, explored this contention extensively, and one of his lasting contributions to the Speculative Realist debate was the idea that there is a 'Great Outdoors' to thought: that which is available to human imagination, but is wholly not the product of human imagination (Meillassoux, 2008: 7). As we shall see when we encounter Barad's work, this sense of internal-externality is also a feature of her vision for agential realism, albeit couched in a markedly different way, indicating a wider recognition of this conundrum that goes beyond the scope of pure philosophy. Although debates have moved on, the influence of Speculative Realism can still be discerned in the work of a range of contemporary theorists, including Reza Negarestani (2014, 2018) and Timothy Morton (2013, 2018), whose work continues to investigate the complex relationship between human thought and the world of lived experience.

Where the Speculative Realists argued that human thought must be able to access something which is fundamentally 'outside' it, another continental philosopher, François Laruelle, whose career spans the early 1970s up to the present day, had also been engaged in a similarly radical project to develop the idea of 'non-philosophy'. Across two relatively recent books, *The Concept of Non-Photography and Photo-Fiction, A Non-Standard Aesthetics*, Laruelle formulated the term 'photo-fiction', a concept designed to express the view that 'the photo is not a degradation of the World, but a process which is "parallel" to it' (Laruelle, 2011: 19). Laruelle's wider project is beyond the scope of this chapter, but importantly, his innovations in this area do allow for a considerable orientation to towards creative practice, and his suggestion that we are 'waiting for perhaps a music-fiction' (Laruelle, 2012: 2), indicates the value that his insights might have for a study of music making. In *Photo-Fiction*, Laruelle also takes up an extended engagement with quantum theory, putting forward a sustained narrative that connects creative practice with his own conception of superposition:

> [Photo-fiction] produces a fusion as superposition ... of the camera on one hand and philosophical discourse on the other, or even still of the photographer and the philosopher.
>
> (Laruelle, 2012: 11–15)

Although Laruelle does not use the term 'superposition' in the strict sense that we shall encounter in Barad's work, he nevertheless clearly acknowledges that it is a means of recognising and communicating how, at the moment a photograph is taken, a fusion occurs, of all of the component parts of that photographing moment. The camera, the photographer, the discourse of the discipline, the theoretical insights that set the determining features of the framing process; all this and more are in superposition, meaning that the outcome of the photographing process is, for Laruelle, temporarily unknowable.

At the same time that this contingent of continental philosophers had been engaged in developing speculative realist and non-philosophical treatises, Karen Barad had been exploring other aspects of poststructuralist theory and wedding it to her own background in theoretical physics. However, what emerges from her work is a set of conceptual tools and analytical frameworks that demonstrate remarkable commonality with many of the conclusions arrived at by those working in Speculative Realist and non-philosophical discourses.

25.3 DIFFRACTION AND ENTANGLEMENT

Barad's project presents a set of technical terms and concepts that are drawn from quantum physics and uses them as a basis for building her own epistemological and ontological model of 'agential realism'. Underpinning almost all of the narratives that run throughout *Meeting the Universe Halfway* is Barad's articulation of the work of two physicists, Niels Bohr and Erwin Schrödinger, and the book draws on Bohr's work relating to the 'wave-particle duality paradox' (Barad, 2007: 83), and Schrödinger's conclusions about the relationship between entanglement and observation (Barad, 2007: 276).

In simple terms, the wave-particle paradox refers to Bohr's theoretical conclusions about the nature of electrons that he draws from his now famous 'two slit' thought experiment. Bohr did not perform this experiment, as he lacked the necessary resources, nevertheless, he painstakingly mapped out the imagined components and conditions. In this hypothetical, 'gedanken' experiment, a series of electrons are fired individually from a source towards two slits that stand in front of a screen that captures and show the final positions of the electrons (Barad, 2007: 267). In version one of the experiment, the arrival of the electrons is displayed on the screen in an interference pattern that suggests that a wave has hit the screen, rather than a series of individual particles. However, the electrons have been fired individually so this interference should not be possible. For Bohr, this suggested that the electrons had travelled through both of the two slits simultaneously. In the second version of the experiment, one of the two slits is adjusted in such a way that it is possible to detect which of the two slits the electrons have travelled through. This experiment, which has come to be known as the 'which-path' experiment, further complicates the situation. In this version, the electrons do arrive at the screen in a particle-like diffusion pattern. Barad refers to this as a 'mixture' (rather than an interference pattern, or a diffraction pattern), wherein each electron has a determinable position (Barad, 2007: 264). What Bohr's experiment aimed to demonstrate, and what later experiments with quantum optics have proved, is that atomic and subatomic matter exhibits both particle-like and wave-like behaviour depending on how it is being observed (Barad, 2007: 307). It is this phenomenon that sits at the very heart of quantum theory, and it is the underlying principle that Barad draws on throughout the book.

Barad also makes a sustained engagement with the concept of diffraction, which for her, denotes the way in which waves overlap and disturb each other:

> Diffraction is a phenomenon that is unique to wave behaviour. Water waves exhibit diffraction patterns, as do sound waves, and light waves. Diffraction has to do with the way waves combine when they overlap and the apparent bending of and spreading out of waves when they encounter an obstruction.
>
> (Barad, 2007: 28)

Indeed, from the examples she gives here, through to the wave-like behaviour of quantum objects, at the core of her work is a commitment to understanding the fundamental mechanics of the material world in terms of a diffractive ontology. In a technical sense, superposition occurs when the amplitudes of two overlapping waves combine to create a resultant wave, indeed for Barad, 'diffraction patterns are evidence of superpositions' (Barad, 2007: 83). Diffraction is categorically different from interaction, and Barad's wave-based ontology operates on the principle that there is no pre-existing form or identity that gives shape or direction to a wave. Instead, everything that we understand to be the real world is the result of wave diffraction. As the basic building blocks of the world, it is therefore important to recognise that waves are not 'things', waves are disturbances; they are diffractions that continually overlap with other waves.

The nature of entanglement is also central to the model of quantum physics that Barad builds, and another foundation for her approach is the idea that 'space, time and matter do not exist prior to the intra-actions that reconstitute entanglements' (Barad, 2007: 74). In this regard, she moves more fully into an analysis of the key principles of quantum theory itself. But what is an entanglement? An entanglement, Barad informs us, which is a feature of quantum rather than classical physics, 'is a generalisation of a superposition to the case of more than one particle' (Barad, 2007: 270). Thus, if superposition denotes the combination of overlapping waves, then entanglement denotes a situation where particles interact (or 'intra-act'), and it becomes impossible to account for individual particles, separate from their *entangled* state.

A vital consequence of Barad's reading of entanglement and diffraction, is that there is no difference whatsoever between the realms of the 'discursive' and the 'material' (Barad, 2007: 63). In Barad's account – which here draws on the work of both Michel Foucault and Judith Butler – both matter and meaning result from diffraction of meaning and matter; there is no categorical separation. Furthermore, Barad's ontological model is topological, and she proposes another neologism – 'spacetimemattering' (Barad, 2007: 179) – as a means to convey this fully entangled process that results in the production of time, space, matter and meaning. Also worth noting is Barad's view that there can be no distinction between the 'quantum' world of atomic and subatomic diffraction, and the world that we normally experience (a world traditionally described in terms of so-called 'classical physics'). The distinction is not a matter of *type*, it is simply a matter of *scale*: Barad's point is simply that atomic and subatomic behaviour is too small for humans to recognise. Thus, everything that exists – and everything that we experience – is the product of entanglement at a quantum level (Barad, 2007: 279). With the production of meaning and matter couched in such a way, the implications for thinking about the production of music as both a material phenomenon and a discursive practice are clearly considerable.

25.4 INDETERMINACY AND COMPLEMENTARITY

The problematic nature of objects is another fundamental part of Barad's modelisation process. In this context, she works through a set of principles and concepts that relate to entanglement, indeterminacy, superposition and complementarity; often extending or modifying the contributions and ideas of Niels Bohr. Bohr is not without his critics in the wider field of theoretical physics, and indeed Barad acknowledges certain 'ambiguities' in his work with regard to 'correspondences [. . .] between theory and reality' (Barad, 2007: 122–123). I shall therefore make use of Barad's references to Bohr in the spirit in which she herself uses his work: as fundamental to current knowledge and understanding, but not without its limitations.

As she works deeper into the problematic nature of substance and determination that lies beyond a normally appreciable experience of the world, Barad brings into play the concept of complementarity:

> Bohr's indeterminacy principle can be stated as follows: the values of complementary variables (such as position and momentum) are not simultaneously determinate. The issue is not one of unknowability per se; rather it is a question of what can be said to simultaneously exist.
> (Barad, 2007: 118)

Throughout *Meeting the Universe Halfway*, Barad makes reference to the fundamental impossibility of measuring 'the position of a particle' (Barad, 2007: 109). If we wish to measure a particle, then we must be able to accurately account for its position, a measurement which itself can only be accurately captured if we also take into account the particle's momentum. However, following Bohr's principle, Barad informs us that a particle's position 'is determinate if and only if it is measured using a fixed platform'; whilst momentum can only be 'defined by an apparatus with a moveable platform' (Barad, 2007: 112). Barad also introduces the concept of 'complementarity', describing it as 'the impossibility of drawing any sharp separation between an independent behaviour of atomic objects and their interaction with the measuring instruments' (Barad, 2007: 308). What is at stake for Barad is that, because of complementarity, it is impossible to accurately measure anything, or precisely determine its exact position. In her exposition of Bohr's analysis of the problematic nature of measurement, Barad describes the way in which position 'must be defined by the circumstances required for its measurement' (Barad, 2007: 111). Given what we now understand as the all-encompassing nature of quantum physics – that it is a theory which explains all of how the material world functions, not just selected parts of it – this 'measurement problem' must therefore have a bearing both at the quantum level, and at the level of everyday experience. Thus, it is important for us to recognise that any act of measurement will always impact on the object that is being measured.

Having laid the groundwork for how to understand the problematic nature of measurement, Barad then extends her analysis to put forward a claim about ontology. Acknowledging that it is impossible to measure things without the measurement apparatus impacting on the things that are being measured 'entails a rejection of the classical metaphysical assumption that there are determinate objects with determinate properties and corresponding determinate concepts with determinate meanings' (Barad, 2007: 127). Fundamentally, Barad is suggesting that, because it is impossible to measure something without creating problems and contradictions (as demonstrated by the impossibility of measuring position and momentum simultaneously), it must follow that there can never be an ultimate or absolute meaning for something. Measurement, and therefore meaning, must always be indeterminate. This is not to say that objective statements cannot be made about the world, for as we shall see, her agential realist model is designed to engage with that particular problem. However, objectivity is more complex than simply imagining that there are actually existing things-in-themselves.

One of the critical outcomes of Barad's analysis of measurement is the contention that meaning is always something that comes into effect once something is being measured (or experienced). Meaning cannot exist in and of itself, because there is never a definite point where indeterminacy does not exist; in other words, there is literally no absolute and definite point, or moment, of complete determination (of meaning). Thus, Barad informs us, all of the components that make up the measurement-experience are what qualify as a 'phenomenon' (Barad, 2007: 139). In this sense, we can begin to understand Barad's ideas in relation to Laruelle's work on superposition, and indeed what we have already seen Barad exploring in terms of diffraction. Whether we are discussing a photograph or a piece of music, created artefacts – just like particles – do not have an objective or inherent meaning; there is always something indeterminate about them, and what is more, our act of listening cannot but help be framed by our own inherent indeterminacies, which manifest as certain 'ways of listening'. Indeed, taking Barad's point further, it is also essential to recognise that we ourselves are superpositions and processes of diffraction. Just as there is no absolute sonic object that we might choose to listen to, neither is there an absolute vantage point that we are listening from. Our listening is an entangled process that itself is both indeterminate and a constantly reforming topology: the things we listen to and the process of listening continually reformat the way that we listen, or in Karen Barad's words, 'we are part of that nature that we seek to understand' (Barad, 2007: 26).

25.5 APPARATUS AS INSTRUMENT; MEASURING AS MAKING

With these core components for engaging with quantum theory, we can now begin to apply a more theoretical approach to considering the possible consequences for musical creativity. As we have seen, whenever a measurement takes place, there is always some form of interaction between the measuring device and that which is measured. In other words, the act of measuring disturbs what is being measured and influences the results of the measurement. Barad's analysis of the nature of measurement and of measuring devices, or apparatuses, is therefore of huge value when thinking about creative processes. Not only does this aspect of her work provide insight into how an apparatus might interact with the object of measurement, but it also enables us to further (re)define how we understand what 'measurement' might mean.

A conventional view of measurement would suggest that a device of fixed dimensions and properties is used to measure another fixed object whose dimensions we do not yet know. However, what Barad's analysis of quantum behaviour shows is that, not only is it impossible to make a measurement without impacting on the object being measured, but that there can be no such thing as a determinate object. Barad provides a number of practical examples to illustrate the problematic nature of measurement in practice, including Don Eigler's use of a scanning tunnelling microscope, a device used to 'sense the presence of an individual atom' (Barad, 2007: 355), along with the experiments conducted by Scully *et al.* using 'quantum erasers' (Barad, 2007: 310). These experiments were designed to further interrogate the wave-particle paradox by first monitoring the movement of photons being emitted by an atom, and then erasing that information. The result was that, as with the 'which-path' experiment, when photons are observed as particles, then they behave as particles, and when they're left undetected, or when any trace of detection is erased, then they behave as waves.

This paradoxical behaviour gives rise to Barad's contention that measuring is a form of mark-making. Whilst it remains the case that 'measurement' is not the same as 'making', Barad nonetheless enables us to understand that measurement to some extent involves construction and fictioning, and in this way, her work brings together notions of making, marking and measuring, to create a continuum of productive principles. What is more, she extends the point to suggest that mark-making is a form of meaning-making. It is this relationship that enables Barad, as we have seen, to draw a line that connects discourse and matter, thus presenting us with the idea that the discursive and the material are each completely involved in the formation of the other.

Barad frequently returns to the phrase 'marks on bodies' (Barad, 2007: 232), which is a reference to the way in which one body, or thing, interacts with another body, and in so doing a trace of that interaction is left on each body. The example of the scanning tunnelling microscope demonstrates this in a practical way, whereby the same technology that is used to sense an atom can also be used to manipulate an atom, so for Barad there is a very real question around the relationship between sensing and mark-making. What is more, the phrase 'marks on bodies' directly correlates with Barad's claim about the entangled nature of matter and meaning; such that marks on bodies become the ultimate trace of the superposition of the discursive and the material. In a detailed exposition on the nature of apparatuses, Barad stresses the importance of recognising the deep involvement that measuring apparatuses have with the objects of measurement. Indeed, she contends that 'concepts obtain their meaning in relation to a particular physical apparatus' (Barad, 2007: 120), and as part of a list of attributes of apparatuses, she suggests that 'apparatuses produce differences that matter – they are boundary-making practices that are formative of matter and meaning, productive of, and part of, the phenomena produced' (Barad, 2007: 146). So saying, Barad's affirmation of the non-neutrality of apparatuses indicates that not only do we come to see something in a particular way because of the way that we are looking at it, but, because there was not a determinate thing that existed before the point of observation; the apparatus of observation is actually part of the thing that is being observed. The apparatus therefore not only influences the thing that is observed, it produces it. This is the intrinsic 'boundary-making' property of the apparatus, which from an opposite viewpoint can be taken to mean that any instrument – a guitar for example – can be thought of as an apparatus of measurement. A guitar is not only a luthier's 'best approximation' of acoustics, harmonic theory, woodwork, metalwork and electronics, but when used to create music, it is also the musician's measurement apparatus to take a reading and express the results of their understanding of and facility with a number of discourses, including harmonic theory, manual dexterity, melody writing, chord voicing, stylistic knowledge to name just a small number of variables that are pertinent to playing an acoustic guitar. Making a guitar and making a piece of music are acts of 'boundary making', and a guitar and a piece of music are phenomena in the way that Barad describes. Both are the result of a significant number of material and discursive practices, and both can be said to 'produce' the guitarists and the listeners that engage with them. A human who has learned to play the guitar, could be said to have been 'guitarred', and someone who has either written a piece of music or had a focused experience of listening to a piece of music could be said to have been 'musicked'. This blurring of the boundaries between the observation device and the observed is critical to a broader understanding of the implications of using quantum theory to think about creativity and the production of meaning. It is worth quoting Barad at length to see the extent of her vision in this regard:

> Since there is no inherent distinction between object and instrument, the property measured cannot meaningfully be attributed to either an abstract object or an abstract measuring instrument. That is, the measured value is neither attributable to an observation-independent object, nor is it a property created by the act of measurement. [Therefore] measured properties refer to phenomena, remembering that the crucial identifying feature of phenomena is that they include "all relevant features of the experimental arrangement".
>
> (Barad, 2007: 120)

This passage demonstrates that it is the measurement process itself, including all of the issues that complementarity throws up, that comprises and defines 'real' experience. The fact that an experience is not observer-independent, does not make it less real, or less authentic. Rather, it is this very act of complicity between measurement and measured that produces the 'real' phenomenon. And to return once more to 'marks on bodies', it is therefore vital to recognise that making and playing guitars, and making and listening to music are all phenomena that reveal that music does have a part to play in the reconfiguring of bodies. But this does not grant music any special status: music, just like every other phenomenon, cannot help but continually do this.

If we accept Barad's significant problematisation of the nature of determinable bodies, and the intertwined nature of observer-observed interactions, then how do we make an account for objective reality? There are certain resonances between Barad's perspectives on the relationship between creative processes and entanglements and Laruelle's ideas about the production of photo- and music-fictions via superposition. However, her commitment to the deep entwinement and interdependence of the world's material and discursive components does suggest that Meillassoux's radical innovations to prove the existence of an actually existing objective real that sits *outside* of human thought, may bear some reconsideration.

25.6 OBJECTIVITY, INTRA-ACTION, AGENTIAL REALISM

To complete this construction of a beta 'quantum toolkit', we can therefore turn to Barad's perspectives on objectivity, which will include an acknowledgement of her broader ambition to construct a new philosophy-physics. What becomes clear from Barad's questioning and analysis of critical theory and the collected histories of quantum physics, is that, for her, these lines of enquiry always fall short of their real potential to construct a far more radical view of the mechanics of the world. Rather than falling short herself of a fuller articulation of what could be called a 'radical objectivity', she instead develops two terms - 'intra-action' and 'agential realism' – in order to describe and explain what an ontology based on quantum theory could look like. Of paramount importance here, is that Barad argues against one of the most widely recognised theories in quantum physics, the theory of wavefunction collapse, as immortalised in the image of 'Schrödinger's Cat'. The cat in question was in fact another gedanken experiment, designed by Schrödinger to illustrate how, upon observation – similar to Bohr's 'which-path' experiment – a wave would 'collapse' into an observable state. The famous analogy is that, prior to observation, depending on whether or not poison has been released into a box in which a cat has been sealed, the said cat is both alive and dead. Schrödinger's point was that the 'blurring' that takes place at the microscopic level, wherein a wave does not exhibit particle-like behaviour until it is observed (or 'collapsed'), cannot hold at the macroscopic level of 'everyday' reality (Barad, 2007: 276). Barad reports that for Schrödinger, it was 'quite ridiculous' to think that it would be possible to imagine a cat in a box existing in a manner that was analogous to a uncollapsed subatomic wave, and the experiment was designed to illustrate this (Barad, 2007: 276–7).

However, Barad, steps beyond Schrödinger's – or indeed Bohr's – terms of reference to claim that 'there is no "collapse" that transforms a superposition or entanglement . . . into a definite state upon measurement' (Barad, 2007: 345); we do not step out of an entangled state to observe the world in an objective manner. In short, the collapse never happens. Instead, the world is a relentless series of entanglements and superpositions – diffractions – that simply involve each other in a never-ending continuum of topological change. To return to an earlier analogy, what we might have previously understood to be a collapse of a wave into a particle formation, is instead simply a 'snapshot' of a moment. Understanding entanglement and superposition as constituent parts of an ongoing topology means that, not only do we see particles rather than waves because we are looking for particles, but the entire moment within which the snapshot occurs is also produced by the taking of the snapshot. Again, this is what Barad means by the term 'spacetimemattering', in that everything about the registering of particles on a screen in Bohr's hypothetical experiment is simultaneously the product and the producer of a point on a topology. This provides us with another compelling opportunity to think about music. As an explicitly time-based activity, a piece of music not only has a duration, which can be measured against already-existing clock-time, but it also creates its own topological timeframe. In this regard, we can understand how music happens within a given temporal timeframe which is itself a phenomenon, but music also creates the time that it exists in, which is to say that music makes 'marks on bodies' in the way that it 'times' our experience and 'times' the world. A composition understood as a time-based sonic phenomenon will clearly draw on a wide range of available materials, but it is Barad's contention that the phenomenon consists of specific components such as location, environment, time of day, listening equipment that do not simply affect the quality of 'the listening experience', but determine the nature of the phenomenon. It is a question of recognising what the experience of listening to a piece of music is. As a phenomenon, it is not something that is limited to the relationship between a listener and a set of sounds. Instead, the entanglement that forms the topological moment of listening to a piece of music will always be comprised of multiple parts, of which the listener and the music itself are just a small number.

To return to the subject of objectivity, Barad is clearly aware of slipping all-too-too easily into a solipsistic mode, and points out that although 'there is no absolute condition of exteriority to secure objectivity [. . .] this doesn't mean that objectivity is lost. Rather, objectivity is a matter of exteriority-within-the-phenomenon' (Barad, 2007: 345). So, saying Barad affirms that the non-human and non-subjective are still radically present within phenomena. What is more, we are part of that exteriority, and at the same time, it is part of us and the things that we make. Because there are no determinate 'things' in the world, with inherent properties, then it is difficult to apprehend such an 'exteriority-within-the-phenomenon', but Barad counters this by referring back to the idea of mark-making:

> Objectivity is a matter of accountability to marks on bodies. Objectivity is not based on an inherent ontological separability, a relation of absolute exteriority, but on an intra-actively enacted agential separability, a relation of exteriority within phenomena.
>
> (Barad, 2007: 340)

Recognising that exteriority is not an already-existing phenomenon, Barad makes use of the notion of intra-activity to convey how exteriority is produced within a diffractive process. Intra-action is different from interaction, in that interaction suggests that two or more self-contained bodies are engaging with each other, whereas intra-action speaks of a process whereby two or more bodies are produced as a result of their overlapping. Again, the importance of Barad's commitment to the simultaneous processes of producing and being produced cannot be over-emphasised here, and it is her contention that humans, as much as pieces of music, are entanglements and superpositions, rather than clearly delineated and sealed formations, which means that we do not ever stop being bound up and produced by the other entanglements that we become entangled with.

Exteriority and agency are thus key to Barad's model, and she stresses that in an agential realist model, 'agency is not aligned with human intentionality or subjectivity [...] Crucially, agency is a matter of intra-acting; it is an enactment, not something that someone or something has' (Barad, 2007: 177–8). Again, Barad returns to the notion that exteriority and agency are produced by certain, local conditions, and that just as a phenomenon encompasses all of the elements that led to its production, which means that it could exist at no other point in space and time than where it happens to be, then so too is exteriority absolutely conditioned by its time and place of emergence. Thus, a subjective experience of a phenomenon is therefore part of the objective instantiation of that phenomenon. In Barad's model, subjective experience is part of a coming-into being of an objective exteriority, and vice-versa. With reference to the way in which apparatuses produce boundaries and delineations, Barad defines a measurement as an 'agential cut', and states that such a cut,

> provide[s] a contingent resolution of the ontological inseparability within the phenomenon and hence the conditions for the objective description: that is, it enables an unambiguous account of marks on bodies, but only within the particular phenomenon.
>
> (Barad, 2007: 348)

This passage contains all of the relevant components of the agential realist model: the components of a phenomenon and the phenomenon itself are contingent, there is no underlying, absolute reason for things being the way they are; the components of a phenomenon are inseparable, and as much as they come together to produce a given phenomenon, each component is concurrently producing and being produced by every other component; every phenomenon is particular, and although there is no underlying, pre-existing cause or reason for a phenomenon existing in a particular way, a phenomenon cannot be other than it is, the component parts make it what it is in all of its specificity; and finally the agential cut produces an unambiguous account, because it is a measurement both of the phenomenon, and of the production of the phenomenon, and in so doing, the agential cut acknowledges its own role in that production process. Thus to an extent, Barad is building a model that acknowledges the problems of comprehending and engaging with that which is contextual and located, and at the same time completely contingent.

25.7 CONCLUSIONS

We are, and will always be, inside phenomena. We can never look at, or listen to the world from the outside, although the outside is always part of any phenomenon that we make. What is essential for thinking about musical creativity in terms of quantum theory is that we recognise the importance of locatedness and specificity. Making and listening to a piece of music involves a vast number of components, and yet it will always be 'this' piece of music that we make or listen to, and only 'this' piece. Making a piece of music draws on all available resources, perhaps in a way that we had not previously recognised, and this making process 'cuts' into the world, leaving traces that affirm that for all we might want to think that listening to music is a matter of personal taste, music 'musics' us. Barad informs us that the physicist Max Planck understood energy to be 'quantised' and exchanged in discreet amounts, often too small for us to register. She also says that 'we don't notice the furniture being rearranged in a room when we switch the light on', although strictly speaking, this is what is happening (Barad, 2007: 108). Whilst its effects might be too small to notice at times, not only is music part of the world we make, but it is part of the world that makes us; indeed, *music makes the world that makes us*. Although this chapter has only provided an initial mapping of opportunities for generating a quantum theory of music, it is clear that thinking about music in terms of superposition, entanglement, exteriority, topology and mark-making can recalibrate a number of seemingly familiar narratives.

BIBLIOGRAPHY

Attali, J. 1985. *Noise: The Political Economy of Music*. University of Minnesota Press: Minneapolis and London.

Barad, K. 2007. *Meeting the Universe Halfway: Quantum Physics and the Entanglement of Matter and Meaning*. Duke University Press Books: Durham and London.

Brassier, R. 2007. *Nihil Unbound Enlightenment and Extinction*. Palgrave Macmillan: Basingstoke and New York.

Bryant, L., Srnicek, N., Harman, G. (eds). 2011. *The Speculative Turn: Continental Materialism and Realism*. re.press: Melbourne.

Laruelle, F. 2011. *The Concept of Non-Photography*. Urbanomic and Sequence Press: Falmouth and New York.

Laruelle, F. 2012. *Photo-Fiction, a Non-Standard Aesthetics*. Univocal Publishing: Minneapolis.

Laruelle, F. 2013b. *Dictionary of Non-Philosophy*. Univocal Publishing: Minneapolis.

Laruelle, F. 2013a. *Philosophy and Non-Philosophy*. Univocal Publishing: Minneapolis.

Meillassoux, Q. 2008. *After Finitude*. Continuum: London & New York.

Morton, T. 2013. *Hyperobjects: Philosophy and Ecology after the End of the World*. University of Minnesota Press: Minneapolis and London.

Morton, T. 2018. *Being Ecological*. Penguin Books: London.
Negarestani, R. 2008. *Cyclonopedia: Complicity with Anonymous Materials*. re.press: Melbourne.
Negarestani, R. 2014. 'The Labor of the Inhuman', in Mackay, R and Avanessian, A (eds). 2014. *Accelerate: The Accelerationist Reader*. Urbanomic: Falmouth.
Negarestani, R. 2018. *Intelligence and Spirit*. Urbanomic and Sequence Press: Falmouth and New York.
Urbanomic, 2007. Speculative Realism: A One Day Workshop. Available at https://www.urbanomic.com/event/speculative-realism-a-one-day-workshop/ (accessed March 2020).

26

Observing mood-based patterns and commonalities in music using machine learning algorithms

Jeffrey Lupker and William J. Turkel

26.1 INTRODUCTION

The availability of large musical datasets such as *The Million Song Dataset* (Bertin-Mahieux *et al.* 2011) has made it possible for researchers to take a 'big data' approach to various styles of western music. In a paper entitled "Measuring the Evolution of Contemporary Western Popular Music", Serrà *et al.* (2012) describe changes and trends related to pitch transitions, the homogenization of the timbral palette, and loudness levels that have shaped pop music over the past sixty years. They also suggest that past songs could be modernized by altering their characteristics to reflect trends of the modern era. Can similar methods be applied to different classifications of music? Instead of examining massive datasets of pop music over 65 years, can these methods be used to look at any genre of music and perhaps even more interestingly, moods? Moods are increasingly becoming the main method of music playlist consumption with listeners opting for more precise categorizations such as "music to raise your spirits" or "atmospheric rock to help you focus" as opposed to more generic classifications like jazz or rock. *Spotify* co-founder Daniel Ek echoed this statement saying "music is moving away from genres" at a company event before later acquiring *The Echo Nest*, the company which provided them the means to algorithmically group music by mood (Eriksson *et al.* 2019). Using datasets created by *The Echo Nest* and Spotify, are the songs grouped according to mood characterized by underlying patterns or metrics similar to those found by Serrà and colleagues?

Pitch vectors that occur commonly in songs that were categorized as having a particular mood are likely those associated with the key of a song. Transition networks were studied between these vectors in order to determine which vectors are network hubs and whether moods favor particular paths between certain pitch vectors. Furthermore, the occurrences of uncommon pitch vectors were examined and less frequently used transitions to explore places where songs deviate from the standard template and to test whether certain moods deviate more from common pitch vectors and transitions than others. Although Serrà and colleagues showed that pop music does indeed follow certain templates across a span of more than half a century, they also showed that there is room for innovation to attract listeners. This study intended to understand how moods might affect music composition by either allowing for or obstructing innovative use of pitch. This study is part of an ongoing research project focused on developing artificial intelligence systems that can aid music composition in the creation of new mood-based music.

26.2 BACKGROUND AND RELATED WORK

As noted above, Serrà *et al.* (2012) make use of current music information retrieval technologies and big data available to them through *The Million Song Dataset* (Bertin-Mahieux *et al.* 2011) to answer questions regarding similarities and differences between new and old pop music. This vast dataset allows researchers to acquire algorithmically determined characteristics of a song's various musical or informative descriptors. Serrà and colleagues collected year annotations and audio descriptors of almost 465,000 different recordings (2012, p. 1). The audio descriptors they focused on were loudness, pitch and timbre. As the focus was on pitch transitions pertaining to mood at this stage in the research, the following provides a brief overview of only their pitch-related studies.

In five-year batches, they collected lists of beat-consecutive chroma vectors per song from *The Million Song Dataset*. A chroma vector has twelve real-numbered values (each ranging from 0 to 1) which reflects the prominence of each of the twelve chromatic pitches over the course of a small segment, usually lasting no longer than a second (Jehan, 2014). Each vector begins on the pitch 'C' and continues in chromatic order (C#, D, D#, etc.) until all twelve pitches are reached. In order to study the relative frequency of chromatic transitions, they applied a thresholding function to each chroma vector, rounding real values to binary ones and zeros. Instead of a vast number of real-numbered chroma vectors, they now had a large set of pitch codewords. Since each of the twelve components can be either 0 or 1, there are $2^{12} = 4096$ possible pitch codewords. The codeword for a chroma vector that has a prominent 'C' pitch but no other prominent notes is 100000000000. Serrà and colleagues then made a tally of all of the observed transitions between codewords, regardless of direction. That is to say that they represented the transition from the codeword containing only pitch 'C' to one containing only pitch 'G' the same as a transition going from a codeword containing only pitch 'G' to one containing only pitch 'C.' There are millions of such possible transitions.

One consequence of this thresholding operation is that it filters out sonic material that may or may not be harmonically relevant. This might consist of harmonics, resonating timbral features, or other frequency elements that exist in the sonic space, but perhaps were not the actual 'played' note. From this vocabulary of pitch codewords and the frequency of transitions from one to the next, they were able to make observations about the usages of certain pitch or pitch transitions during different eras of the last 60 years of pop music. One such observation is that although the system can in principle describe very dense networks of possible transitions, empirically they are sparse. There are a limited number of transitions which actually occur between codewords "allowing for musical recognition and enjoyment as this capacity is grounded in our ability for guessing/learning transitions" (Serrà et al. 2012, p. 3).

This particular observation is one that directed the investigation during the early stages of finding codeword transition relationships that characterize the moods happy and sad. First, given the claim that a constrained list of possible pitch transitions benefits the listener's ability to recognize and thus enjoy a piece of music, could there be further constraints placed upon these transition networks that enable listeners to recognize mood? Second, what other distinctive musical qualities might be derived by adjusting the threshold upwards into the region between 0.5 and 0.9? Do some settings work better than others for mood-based classification?

Past research involving the training of machine learners to make musical key predictions using averaged chroma feature vectors taken from audio files have shown that indeed a varying threshold level will affect musical outcomes. These papers have found, for example, that the accuracy levels for predicting key from a song's audio file fluctuated as the threshold of acceptable pitches was modified (Lupker & Turkel, 2020; Finley & Razi, 2019; Mahieu, 2017).

Figure 26.1a shows a simple example where beat-consecutive codewords from the intro to the Beatles song "Let It Be" (Lennon & McCartney, 1970) have been turned into MIDI note data and their durations. In this example, the lowest purple line (MIDI note) corresponds to the pitch 'C' with every subsequent step up representing one half step (C#, D, D#, etc.). By changing the threshold rate, different pitches emerge, and it becomes very clear that care must be taken when making inferences from this type of big data-derived pitch information. At the threshold level of 0.5, some chromatic notes that are not found within the actual chord progression appear. At the threshold level of 1.0, on the other hand, the representation contains only singular notes representing a quasi-melody and bass. With this latter threshold, it would be difficult to make connections with chord data. For this work, it was important to understand that melody pitches or chord progression transition networks would not be tracked independently, but rather involve a blend of the two. This wasn't an issue, as the study was concerned with how all of these pitch features come together to sound happy or sad, and what connections between them represent that.

Making large-scale claims using chroma feature vectors can potentially be misleading as the entire frequency range of an audio file will be squashed into these twelve component vectors, including non-pitched instruments such as drum kits. A MIDI pitch representation of beat-specific codewords from the intro to "Billie Jean" by Michael Jackson (1983) demonstrates potential shortcomings (Figure 26.1b). Here the system forces a solo drum beat into the chroma vectors as well as it can. The result is a meaningless collection of pitch clusters that will create spurious transitions in pitch transition networks. Considering the fact that many songs have various percussive elements in them, it's necessary to be conscious of the ways that unpitched or noisy audio elements can degrade

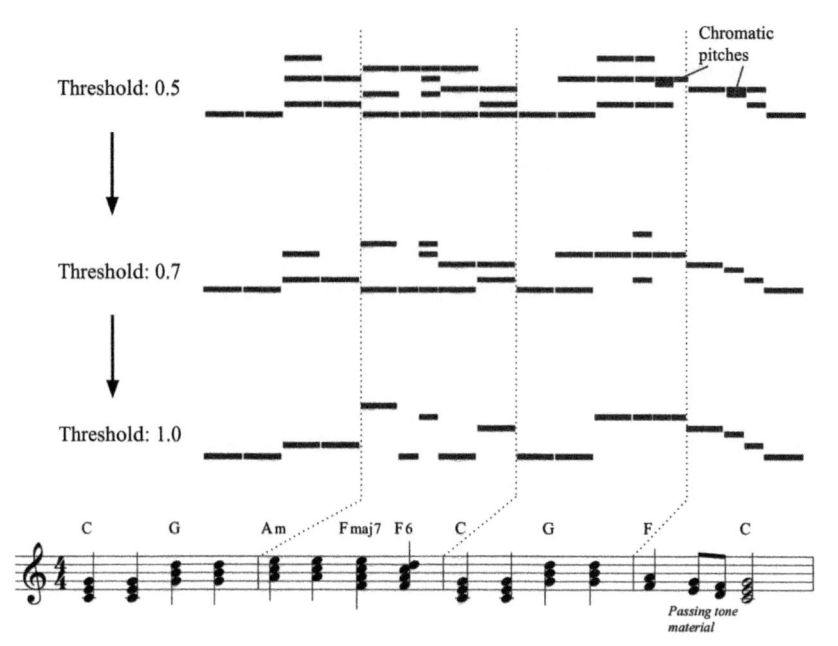

Figure 26.1a MIDI note representation of beat-consecutive codewords from the intro of "Let It Be" by The Beatles

Figure 26.1b MIDI note representation of the solo drum beat intro to "Billie Jean" by Michael Jackson

algorithmically derived measures of pitch, especially when big data are used to make musicological claims. With this in mind, an effort was made to test all of the chroma vector data as it pertains to mood using the five thresholds 0.5, 0.6, ..., 0.9. This allowed observations in which distinctive pitch qualities appear at different thresholds that still contain some harmonic content and to assess how these qualities relate to the two separate moods.

26.3 PROCESSING DATA FOR MACHINE LEARNING CLASSIFICATION

Spotify's *Web API* (which contains the acquired *The Echo Nest* datasets) was accessed in order to collect a large dataset of songs related to the moods happy and sad through playlists created either by Spotify developers or users. Organizing music by mood is a popular method of consumption and provides a relative consensus into what moods certain songs elicit. The popularity of playlists, measured by subscription numbers, drove certain playlists to the top of returned searches, creating an "agreed upon" selection of mood-based songs. A list of 2,300 unique songs per mood could then be obtained from a collection of the top-fifty playlists according to the search terms of "happy" and "sad." Beyond offering data on curated playlists, the API offers analysis info on various musical features, much like *The Million Song Dataset* does. According to the developers of the "The Echo Nest," the API acquired and repurposed by Spotify, the metadata for each song "contains a complete description of all musical events, structures, and global attributes such as key, loudness, time signature, tempo, beats, sections, harmony" (Jehan, 2014, p. 5). This available metadata allowed for the creation of a codeword vocabulary and pitch transition networks according to mood, determined by methods akin to those developed by Serrà and colleagues.

A machine learning algorithm was employed to find distinctions between these two datasets. As this is a binary classification problem, logistic regression can be used to search for the optimal features in each dataset by which to make predictions (Goodfellow *et al.* 2017). Following standard practice, some data was used to train the machine learners and some was withheld to test their performance, then repeated with different randomly selected training and testing sets. High accuracy during testing would reflect the fact that there are reliably detectable mood-based features to be found at the level of pitch codeword transitions. The availability of music-related big data has made supervised machine learning like this a popular method in current research.

Supervised learning algorithms require an input of training data containing independent features and a labeled output from which it can draw associations (Goodfellow *et al.* 2017). The labels of happy and sad (happy = 0, sad = 1) were already determined from the obtained datasets described above. Even using pitch codewords, the number of potential features is vast. There are almost 17 million possible transitions (4096^2 since direction is kept, unlike Serrà and colleagues). In the collection of 4600 songs, 40,000 pitch codeword transitions were observed for each mood, which is substantially fewer but still far too many features. To reduce this to a manageable number, the following preprocessing steps were taken:

1. Remove any self loops (i.e., pitch codewords that transition to themselves).
2. Remove any pitch codeword transition that only occurs in the songs of one mood but not the other.
3. For each remaining transition, count the number of times it occurs in happy songs and the number of times it occurs in sad ones, and divide the smaller of the two numbers by the larger. Intuitively, the closer this ratio is to one, the less discriminative the feature is, as it is more likely to be found in both happy and sad songs.

4. Sort the transitions by the ratio calculated in the previous step, and take the 200 with the smallest value. These are the pitch codeword transitions that can appear in either happy or sad songs, but are much more likely to be found in songs of one mood than the other.

This resulted in 200 features that could be used to train the logistic regression algorithm. The process was repeated with pitch codeword thresholds of 0.5, 0.6, 0.7, 0.8 and 0.9.

26.4 TESTING AND RESULTS

For each of the pitch codeword thresholds, the different data was randomly split to use 75% for training the logistic regression algorithm and 25% for testing. Testing the model after training returned extremely high accuracy levels for each threshold value: all were slightly above 99% accuracy. Figure 26.2 shows the exact accuracy levels of each threshold value with a peak occurring at a threshold value of 0.7. Finding the peak at this particular threshold level is interesting when compared with the earlier example involving "Let It Be." In this example (Figure 26.1a), a threshold value comparable to the methods used by Serrà *et al.* or lower resulted in unwanted chromaticism, while a threshold set too high resulted in too little pitch data. Figure 26.1a suggests that around a threshold of 0.7 instances of chromaticism are removed while keeping a fair amount of desirable harmonic content. Thus it seems reasonable to assume that this will affect the outcome positively when training machine learning programs by yielding the greatest amount of desired pitch content, while eliminating undesirable content. One area of interest is the machine learning algorithm's ability to predict at such a high level of accuracy given the likelihood that unwanted pitches permeate the datasets, as shown in the "Billie Jean" example. Since it is probable that many of the songs contain drum beats, and thus unwanted chromaticism, one can hypothesize that the logistic regression algorithm is able to take this into account. While a human would look at the score of the songs and ignore the drum beat in their analysis, the computer represents the frequencies of the drum beat in a different manner. Future research will attempt to address chroma feature vector variance that results from percussive sounds and propose methods of filtering it out for clearer depictions of pitch transition networks.

26.5 MOOD-BASED COMMONALITIES

The ability to distinguish music as happy or sad to a high degree of accuracy from pitch content alone is an exciting start into classifying a variety of moods according to this method. A secondary area of interest was what the top highly connected codewords common to each mood might reveal. The top codewords of each mood can be thought of as hubs in the transition network, with repeated paths through them as the song progresses. These hubs theoretically could provide a basic framework for a mood-based song and in training later AI algorithms to aid a composer writing

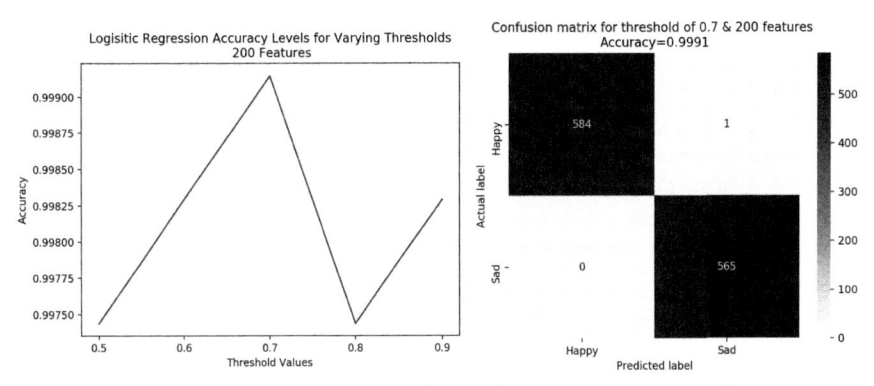

Figure 26.2 Accuracy levels found for each level of testing. The resultant confusion matrix for the dataset related to 0.7 threshold value is shown on the right

new mood-based music, this is probably the first suggestion it would give. Given the connectivity of these top codewords pertaining to mood, one would expect to find them in any particular song deemed happy or sad.

If the earlier example of "Let It Be" is considered to be a decidedly happy song (as it was found in one of the fifty happy playlists), the hypothesis can be tested to see if not only if these codewords exist, but how well-connected they are in this example. Figures 26.3a and 26.3b represent pitch transition networks for the codeword threshold values of 0.7 and 1 respectively. Both graphs reflect all transitions between codewords with an arrow indicating the direction of one codeword to the next. In Figure 26.3a, the codeword threshold of 0.7 was used as it has shown to give the best balance of harmonic representation by removing unwanted chromaticism and while still keeping a fair amount of essential harmonic content for this song. The transition network for the pitch codeword threshold of 1.0 was also graphed to check if the main hubs remain after filtering out a high level of pitch content (Figure 26.3b). The top five highly connected hubs for happy were determined to be 'E,' 'D,' 'G,' 'B' and 'A' which correspond to codewords 128, 512, 16, 1 and 4 respectively (in order from most connected to least). With these hubs being integral features for the mood happy, it was presumed that they would play a significant role in "Let It Be." Figures 26.3a and 26.3b show these top five codewords are found within each transition network and that the majority of them are found heavily involved in both examples. In Figure 26.3a, the codewords 16, 128 and 512 are found very close to the middle, representing high connectivity as they are continually featured throughout the song. Figure 26.3b again shows how important these three codewords are to the song even at the highly pitch-filtered threshold of 1. The fourth codeword also shows more connectivity than it does in the preceding example with a threshold value of 0.7. This might reflect the use of the aforementioned pitch "constraints" so a listener can recognize patterns (Serrà *et al.* 2012) in certain types of music, in this case pertaining to mood. If the assumption is made that the vocals are likely the most prominent feature of this song and therefore that the melody's pitches are most reflected in each codeword, it could be hypothesized that the most highly connected codewords for a mood are often featured in the melody. It would be interesting to test whether this is typically the case, and if so, whether frequently occurring codewords appear in the melody alongside lyrics that reflect a similar sentiment, as a sort of a mood-reinforcement. Currently, this suggestion is left for future research.

While it is clear that the framework for pitch transitions in this song are closely related to the top codewords found from the happy dataset, this does not hinder the use of innovation. While the top codewords found in the middle of the graph show high levels of inter-connectivity, there are around thirty instances of once-visited codewords which surround these commonalities. These codewords might provide instances of chromaticism, modulation or other novel techniques which break-away briefly from the main chord progression or melody in a tasteful way. Provided the framework of happy hubs constrains the majority of the transitions, the song will likely remain sounding happy. Further study into these infrequent transitions could provide another method by which AI algorithms

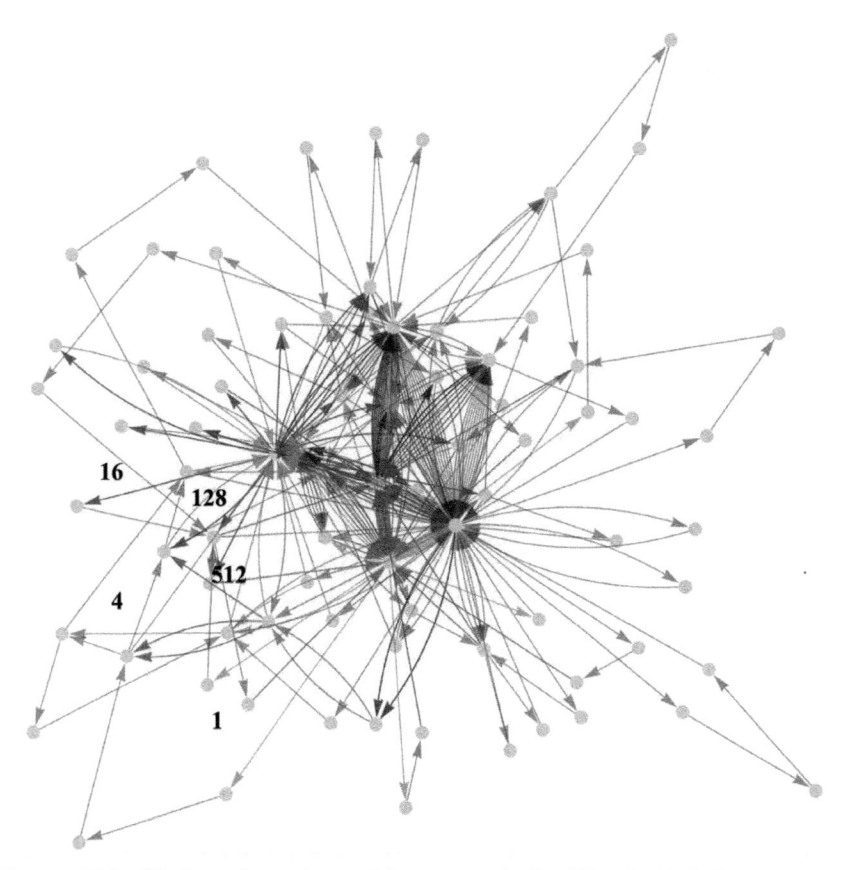

Figure 26.3a Pitch codeword transition network for "Let It Be" (Lennon & McCartney, 1970) with a threshold value of 0.7

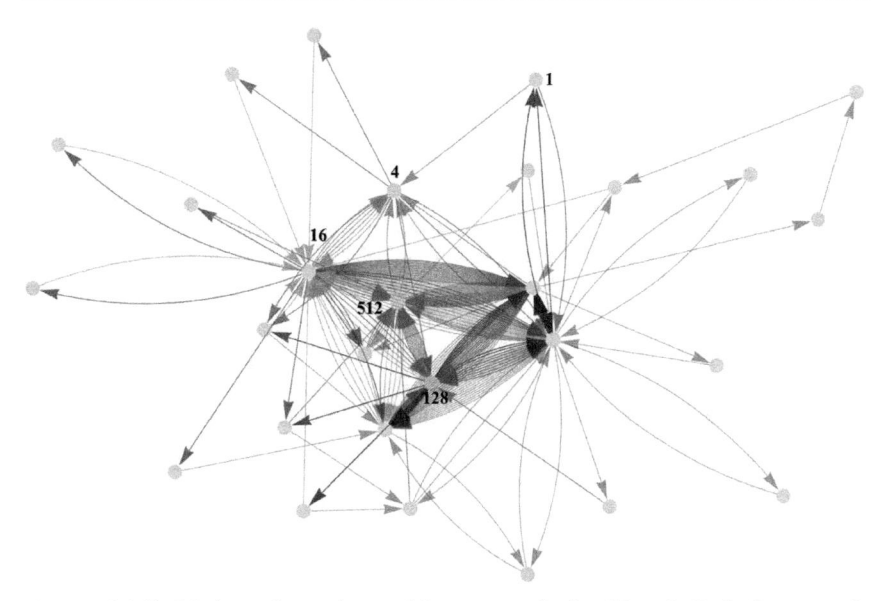

Figure 26.3b Pitch codeword transition network for "Let It Be" (Lennon & McCartney, 1970) with a threshold value of 1

aimed at mood-based composition could offer suggestions on where to "depart from the norm" in the creation of new innovative music.

26.6 CONCLUSIONS AND FUTURE RESEARCH

The highly accurate results in mood classification between happy and sad using underlying pitch transition networks provides an optimistic start for the classification of further mood descriptors. Future research will expand on this binary classification system to incorporate many more mood descriptors. Testing the logistic regression algorithm with data retrieved using varying levels of pitch codeword thresholds also provided information on how to best access pitch data using a codeword threshold of about 0.7. This allowed for claims based on pitch transitions that had removed unwanted chromaticism while still preserving a fair amount of important harmonic content. Observing accuracy results from the logistic regression tests further showed the codeword threshold value of 0.7 to be the most indicative of stable and usable pitch content. However, even with these results, one area of concern still comes from the high prominence of unwanted chromaticism. This chromaticism is likely a result of overtones and non-pitched instruments such as drum kits or other auxiliary percussion affecting the prominence of certain pitches in the chroma vector. Further steps that could be taken with this are to examine spectrogram representations of the frequencies from the audio samples using convolutional neural networks (CNNs). Since the issues that pertain to the squashing of a wide array of frequencies into a simple twelve-value vector, this might allow for pinpointing of areas of interest, or separate unwanted frequencies. There might also be a way to make use of the algorithmically determined timbral vectors that can be accessed through Spotify's *Web API*.

Since convolutional neural networks learn from spatial hierarchies of patterns increasing in complexity with each level (Chollet, 2018), the attempt would be to pinpoint the layer or layers containing percussive features. Finding these hidden modules or patterns is a complicated task for humans given the high complexity of the input source but is something that computers do comparatively well as found in well-documented image-based examples of CNNs such as 'DeepDream' (Mordvintsev *et al*. 2015b) or 'Inception' (Mordvintsev et al., 2015a). Using 'Inception' networks or modeling the CNN after the 'DeepDream' example, further attempts could be made to draw out these underlying features to make more accurate comparisons between moods.

In observing top codewords pertaining to the mood happy in "Let It Be," it was also shown that top-related codewords can play a vital role in providing a pitch transition framework. In this example and others, it was found that a fair amount of innovation in mood-based music is still available with the use of uncommon transitions. Provided that the balance between the important mood codeword hubs outweighs those less important to a particular mood, the overall mood of the song should be unaffected. Future research will aim to incorporate this work into the creation of AI algorithms which can aid a composer during the compositional process on the creation of new mood-based music.

REFERENCES

Bertin-Mahieux, T., Ellis, D., Whitman, B., & Lamere, P. (2011). The Million Song Dataset, *Proceedings of the 12th International Conference on Music Information*, Miami.

Chollet, F. (2018). *Deep Learning with Python*. Shelter Island, Manning Publications, pp. 120–159.

Eriksson, M., Fleischer, R., Johansson, A., Snickars, P. & Vonderau, P. (2019). *Spotify Teardown: Inside the Black Box of Streaming Music*. The MIT Press, London, pp. 64–65.

Finley, M. & Razi, A. (2019). Musical Key Estimation with Unsupervised Pattern Recognition, *Proceedings from IEEE 9th Annual Computing and Communication Workshop and Conference*, Las Vegas.

Goodfellow, I., Bengio, Y. & Courvile, A. (2017). *Deep Learning*. The MIT Press, London, pp. 137.

Jackson, Michael. (1983). Billie Jean, *Thriller*. Apple, London. Available online from https://open.spotify.com/track/7iN1s7xHE4ifF5povM6A48?si=Sz7Ar-EjRmyX5Y5aD cYuRg

Jehan, T. (2014). *Analyzer Documentation: The EchoNest*. Somerville: The Echo Nest Corporation, p. 5.

Lennon, John & Paul McCartney. (1970). Let it be, *Let it be*. Epic, Los Angeles. Available online from https://open.spotify.com/track/5ChkMS8OtdzJeqyybCc9R5?si=73DrspjISde9RT-72IsEaQ

Lupker, J. & Turkel, W. J. (2020). Music Theory, the Missing Link Between Musical Big Data and Artificial Intelligence, accepted to *Digital Humanities Quarterly*.

Mahieu, R. (2017). Detecting Musical Key with Supervised Learning, unpublished manuscript.

Mordvintsev, A., Olah, C. & Tyka, M. (2015b). Inceptionism: Going deeper into neural networks, in *Google Research Blog*. Available online from http://googleresearch.blogspot.de/2015/06/inceptionism-going-deeper-into-neural.html

Mordvintsev, A., Olah, C. & Tyka, M. (2015a). DeepDream - a code example for 34 visualizing Neural Networks, in *Google Research Blog*. Available online from https://research.googleblog.com/2015/07/deepdream-code-example-forvisualizing.html

Serrà, J., Corral, Á., Boguñá M., Haro M. & Arcos, J. Ll. (2012). "Supplementary Information: Measuring the Evolution of Contemporary Western Popular Music," *Scientific Reports* Vol. 521, No. 2.

Serrà, J., Corral, Á., Boguñá M., Haro M. & Arcos, J. Ll. (2012). Measuring the Evolution of Contemporary Western Popular Music, *Scientific Reports*, Vol. 521, No. 4.

27

The role of contests and talent shows as part of the artist development process within the music industry

Stefan Lalchev and Paul G. Oliver

27.1 INTRODUCTION

Artist development is a very delicate and complex process, which has been completely re-shaped over the last two decades. With major changes happening within the global music industry, initiated by the physical sales decline in the early 2000s – followed by the numerous mergers and acquisitions (Gordon, 2015; Rogers, 2010) – labels are not necessarily interested in long-term investments anymore, focusing mainly on quick and guaranteed success. The switch to a so-called 'synthetic' approach (Ripken, 2011) has resulted in major aspects of the initial stages of the artist development process being left for individual artists themselves to deal with – including getting exposure and building a fan base – so that labels can minimise the once-normal risk of making a bad investment (Wikstrom, 2009).

Providing an opportunity for getting instant exposure and building a large fan base, contests and talent shows have often been considered by young artists as a potential shortcut to a successful music career (Kjus, 2017). However, despite such concepts, especially the televised ones (i.e. The Idols, The X Factor, The Voice), they have been the subject of many analyses (Ganguly, 2019); although, as yet, no study has provided conclusive evidence to define the significance and applicability of talent shows as a clear step of an artist's development process.

On the other hand, musical talent development has also been the subject of research for decades (Petersen, 2017), but while those studies have discussed many theoretical approaches along with their applicability and limitations, they have not clearly referred to and defined the role of contests and talent shows either.

Addressing this potential gap in research, the main aim of this study is to define the role of live contests and talent shows in today's music industry, both as a stage of the artist development process, and as a potential form of business, through the perspectives of both music artists and entrepreneurs.

27.2 BACKGROUND

27.2.1 The theoretical background of talent development

In recent years, "there has been a lot of 'buzz' about the term *talent development*" (Olszewski-Kubilius and Thomson, 2015, p.49) as a "theoretical movement in the field of giftedness and gifted education" (Dai, 2017). Although in general, talent development "may mean very different things to different people" (Olszewski-Kubilius and Thomson, 2015, p.49), there appears to be a general consensus on the necessity of "recognising and nurturing" the talent, instead of simply "identifying and labelling" individuals as 'gifted' (Schroth *et al.*, 2011).

Another commonality between theories, concepts, and models relates to talent development found in its close relation to the psychological development of individuals and their psychosocial skills (Bloom, 1985; Csikszentmihalyi, 1996). For members of the public it might be quite easy to notice someone's outstanding performance in a certain field, but what often remains unnoticed is the set of mental qualities that enable the individual to demonstrate, when necessary, what he or she is truly capable of (Subotnik, 2015). While psychosocial skills may not be a substitute for individual talent or dedication to a specific activity, they are no less important. Indeed, such skills have been considered as being key to successful talent development (MacNamara and Collins, 2009; MacNamara *et al.*, 2006; Olszewski-Kubilius, 2000), and as Worrell (2010) points out, although aptitudes of psychosocial skills may vary, significant improvements can be achieved through teaching and learning.

Remaining on the topic of the theoretical background of talent development, perhaps one of the most popular theories, which has influenced many others, is the one established by Bloom in 1985 (Garces-Bacsal, 2014). As a result of the analysis of the talent development process of highly successful individuals in different areas, he establishes a model that reveals the talent development as a three-step process, with each of the steps having its own specific place in the hierarchy (Bloom, 1985). According to this model, the first step, or stage, of the process is when the individual is first being exposed to a certain field or activity in the context of play; then in the second stage that exposure turns into a form of systematic training and instructed practising; and then the third and final stage is the stage of commitment and mastery (Garces-Bacsal, 2014; Swanwick, 2001). Later, this theory has served as the basis for further developed programmes, such as Renzulli's Schoolwide Enrichment Model, according to which, the talent development process is similarly divided into three phases, but are referred to as types of enrichment: the first type being related to exploration; the second type is related to practicing under formal instructions; and the third type is related to autonomy and self-direction (Renzulli and Reis, 1994).

Another factor that researchers consider to play a key role in the talent development process is motivation (Garces-Bacsal, 2014; Oreck *et al.*, 2000). Depending on the source of the motivation, it can be classified as one of two distinctive types: intrinsic or extrinsic. As their name suggests, intrinsic motivation originates from internal sources, while extrinsic motivation originates from external ones, but an alternative and more accurate way of describing the difference between them, would be in the context of talent development in particular. Juniu *et al.* (1996) explain that intrinsic motivation can be observed when the individual finds complete satisfaction just by being involved in the activity itself, while extrinsic motivation exists when the individual's reason to aim for success is in the expected rewards or recognition of one's achievement.

More recently, a significant number of research publications discuss the still not fully explored and multifaceted nature of talent development in the specific context of a framework for viewing giftedness and the education of gifted individuals (Dai, 2010; Dai and Chen, 2014; Subotnik, Olszewski-Kubilius, and Worrell, 2011), which puts an emphasis on "the deliberate cultivation of psychosocial skills supportive of high achievement, persistence, and creativity rather than leaving these to chance" (Olszewski-Kubilius and Thomson, 2015, p.49).

27.2.2 Talent development in the musical domain today

At first, when put in the context of the musical domain, such theories seem applicable. Their first stages could easily be related to most people's first experiences with music, often at a very early age (Mills, 2003), then the second stages clearly resemble the time when the individual practices and develops under the supervision of a mentor (Ericsson, Krampe, and Tesch-Romer, 1993), and the final stages are those when the musicians apply their skills to create a style of their own (Ericsson and Lehmann, 1996). However, in reality things are not at all that simple, perhaps due to the mass popularity of the conception that a musician is "born not made", and success in music simply depends on a person's predisposition (Rickard and Chin, 2017; Tan *et al.*, 2014).

Despite the fact that many researches have attempted to explore talent development as a key to success in the musical domain (Petersen, 2017), in most cases, numerous flaws have been found, which have made such models and conclusions very limited in terms of applicability. As Garces-Bacsal (2014) states, "most theories on talent development assume that a young artist would have access to the resources required for one to advance in the domain". Similarly, Petersen (2017) adds that most studies "have been taken in Western settings". Such flaws are an interesting phenomenon, given the fact that there have been research studies focused on the importance of social context to the success in music (Mills, 2003; Moore *et al.*, 2003; Sloboda *et al.*, 1996; Winner and Martino, 2000). In addition to the abovementioned flaws, certain theorists have also criticised some of the traditional musical development conceptions, claiming that formal instruction is not even always necessary for a person to achieve mastery and succeed in the musical domain (O'Neill, 2002; Rickard and Chin, 2017; Sloboda, 2005).

What makes it all even more complicated is when business gets involved and talent development is being analysed in the specific case of performing artists as part of the current music industry environment. The natural and logical link between the music industry and the artist development process, for many years, have been the so-called artist and repertoire (A&R) executives, described by Rogers (2010) as "once the most powerful career in the music business [. . .], charged with finding new acts for record labels, signing them to contracts, and then supervising their artistic development". However, as in pure business terms, A&R is another segment of a label's structure (Baskerville and Baskerville, 2017), which has been highly affected by all the major changes in the industry from the last couple of decades, including the 'Digital Storm' (Wacholtz, 2017) and the large number of buyouts and mergers (Gordon, 2015; Rogers, 2010). As a result, the once powerful A&Rs, who were often allowed to sign and develop artists, without referring to the opinions of others (Negus, 1992) have had to switch to a new model of work, ruled by the philosophy that "you are only as good as your last recording" (Wikstrom, 2009, p.129). This means that A&Rs have had to deal with poor sales performance of an artist costing them their job (Rogers, 2010). Michael Alago, a major A&R with a massive career, and Ritch Esra, former A&R director at Arista Records, both confirm that "there's not artist development anymore" (cited in Rogers, 2010). In an industry, where labels want to reduce risks – and are very cautious when it comes to signing artists (Harrison, 2017) – A&R people are simply forced to search for well-developed acts with an established fan base and experience (Wikstrom, 2009). As Sutherland (2018) explains, A&R is being replaced by research and development, meaning that data simply takes over artist development, replacing the 'organic' approach (Negus, 1992) with a 'synthetic' one (Ripken, 2011).

27.2.3 Talent shows and contests

With the artist development process being entirely left for the artists themselves to deal with – they need to find the best ways not only to develop their talent – but also to build their fan base and gain the necessary experience, as explained above, which would potentially help them get to the next level. One way for an artist to obtain both of these assets, for many years, has been through talent contests (Dyer 1973; Shepherd *et al.*, 2003). Dating back to the early days of radio programming, at first low-budget stations were used to showcase cheap content, as explained by Shepherd *et al.* (2003), whereby talent contests and talent shows, in fact, contributed to the successful beginnings of many stellar careers, including Frank Sinatra's after the Major Bowes' Original Amateur Hour.

There are a number of ways in which talent shows and contests could be perceived and analysed in terms of the role they play in the artist development process. From a theoretical perspective, referring back to the abovementioned models by Bloom (1985) and Renzulli (Renzulli and Reis,

1994), contests and talent shows could potentially be seen as either stage two or stage three. In the majority of cases, talent shows and contests do not require original material, but even prefer well-known hits to be performed (Kjus, 2017), which can easily be seen as a form of imitation, that has been theoretically defined to have certain educational and developmental benefits (Mills, 2003). Furthermore, as stage two consists of deliberate training and refinement of performance under the instructions of a coach or a mentor, contests could in fact be perceived as a real-life testing platform in front of actual audience. On the other hand, being seen by many artists as a shortcut to a successful career, considering the opportunities of record deals, and the huge exposure and celebrity make-over (Ganguly, 2019), contests and talent shows could also easily fit within the definition of stage three, in which all skills and training are being translated into a distinctive style (Ericsson and Lehmann, 1996). Despite a plethora of research and case studies (Coutas, 2006; Ganguly, 2019; Holmes, 2004; Kjus, 2009, 2017; Redden, 2010; Reijnders *et al.*, 2007; Stahl, 2004) – exploring and analysing certain aspects related to talent shows, contests, and contestants – none of them seems to clearly determine the exact role of such productions in the context of the artist development process.

Businesswise however, the case is slightly different. Contests and talent shows, big televised ones especially, and their business structures, have been the subject of discussion within a number of publications (Ganguly, 2019; Kjus, 2017; Redden, 2010).

In an interview from 2001, then A&R at BMG, Simon Cowell shares some interesting thoughts about 'A&R-ing' and artist development in general. He claims that he always takes risks with new acts, that he would never ever research a record before it is released, and that the only thing he trusts is his "gut instinct" (Cowell in Sorin, 2001). Also, when asked about the way he sees his future in the following five to ten years, Cowell's response is: "I hope I will still be doing this" (Cowell in Sorin, 2001). Not only did Simon Cowell's future turn out to be different from his own predictions, but in fact a project, in which he was involved, and which started the same year of 2001, significantly affected the artist development process worldwide. Simon Fuller and Simon Cowell – both experienced British music professionals, at the time working for BMG – created a concept that "redefined the idea of promoting unknown talents via television" (Kjus, 2017, p.1016). As Fuller claimed, that concept, called *Idols*, would create new stars, who would not need any support from radio or tastemakers, as "they would already be famous" through major TV exposure (Chapman, 2014). Aiming to not only discover the talents, but also build them a celebrity status with a substantial fan base, the show was supposed to exchange the 'hit-and-miss' approach with a guaranteed success by engaging an audience directly (Bower, 2012). This approach turned out to be very popular, as the single released by the first Idols winner, Will Young, became the fastest-selling debut single ever in the UK (Kjus, 2017).

The concept's tremendous success has been followed up by a number of similar programmes, which have been produced in more than 50 countries worldwide, and their contribution to musical culture has even become the topic of research studies (Meizel, 2011). However, despite their early glory, and claims to be a genuine platform for talent discovery, it has become apparent that some contestants are being selected due to their applicability to specific commercial characteristics or celebrity brand coding (Fairchild, 2007; Kjus, 2009). The decreasing sales, and abandonments of contest winners have led to significant levels of scepticism amongst contestants, including the fact that many of them claim to be better off losing the contest (Kjus, 2017). Collins (2008) simply defines this process as the creation of "dispensable celebrities". Furthermore, many publications highlight the unfairness incorporated within the business model of talent shows, including exploitation of contestants' free labour (Bonner, 2003; Redden, 2010) and prioritising the need for "good TV" over actual talent showcase (Kjus, 2017).

Forman (2012) sees contemporary talent shows as a simple reflection of programmes from the 1940s and the 1950s, but in business terms, the new concepts prove themselves as a well-designed machine with revenue streams that include advertising, sponsorship, merchandising, licence fees, televoting, and more (Redden, 2010). However, despite being labelled as the entertainment phenomena of the 2000s, the decrease in ratings and interest from both contestants and audience (Kjus, 2017) logically lead to the question of whether musical talent shows and contests are still a viable investment from an entrepreneurial, or even business, perspective today.

27.3 DESIGN AND METHODOLOGY

The research has a very specific, and quite unusual, multifaceted nature, which combines topics related to both the artists' perspectives on talent development, and the entrepreneurs' motivation as contest organisers – including the profitability of these projects – which is considered the business aspect most relevant to the aim of the study. Therefore, a well-developed strategy is required in terms of the study's design and methodology, and the appropriate choice of specific methods to be used. Drawing inspiration from previously undertaken research, related to artist development within the context of the music industry (Negus, 1992; Stratton, 1981, 1983; Zvaan and Bogt, 2009), for this research interviews were conducted as the method for primary data collection, especially because their qualitative nature makes them more efficient in providing insight into the different, unique, and complex aspects of the artists (Rostan, 2003). The interviews have been designed in two different versions, one applicable to artist respondents, and another one to be conducted with entrepreneurs.

27.3.1 Sampling

With the main research question and the project's aims in mind, a careful selection has been made for interviewees. Following the non-probability purposive sampling approach (Blaxter *et al.*, 2001), for each of the two interview structures (artistic and entrepreneurial), ten respondents have been selected and invited to participate, being assured that their identities will remain confidential. For each of the two groups of respondents, the researcher has aimed to recruit interviewees with a variety of professional experience, in order to diversify the sample and ensure reasonable levels of objectivity. Nevertheless, participants also had to meet certain criteria, as follows:

- Criteria for artist respondents:
  - Extensive live performing experience;
  - Experience as participant in big or small scale, regional or national, live singing contests;
  - Televised talent show contestant, who has reached the big live concerts stage.
- Criteria for entrepreneur respondents:
  - At least ten years of professional experience in any area of the music industry;
  - Formal qualifications related to music, music education, or performance;
  - Experience as an organiser of one or more singing contests (national or international) with at least two successfully completed editions.

The specific criteria for both the artists and the entrepreneur's respondent groups derive from the main research question and the overall interview design. These aim to ensure that interviewees will not only be able to answer the questions and find them applicable to their own circumstances; but also have an experience, which is rich and diverse enough to enable them to express well-informed opinions, from which the research would benefit. Furthermore, in the entrepreneurs' case, the criteria for music experience and formal qualifications aim to ensure that, as the research primarily investigates the role of contests and talent shows in the process of artist development, the interviewees will have a good understanding of the artistic side of musical development and how it is being affected by their activity as entrepreneurs.

27.3.2 Interview guideline

The data, which the researcher was trying to gather through interviews, was mostly related to the respondents' experience in the context of their music-related biography (Petersen, 2017). However, despite the fact that, in such cases, the unstructured narrative interview is usually the preferred approach (Blaxter *et al.*, 2001), this study relies on strictly structured interviews instead. Nevertheless, as the study aims to not only investigate musical talent development, but to also give voice to creative individuals and learn about their life experiences, the qualitative feel of the interviews has been preserved. This has facilitated a more in-depth understanding (Csikszentmihalyi, 1996; Garces-Bacsal, 2014; Gruber and Wallace,

1998; Horowitz and Webb-Dempsey, 2002), which has been achieved through the use of open-ended questions. While this approach usually results in semi-structured interviews, where the interviewer is in a position to further facilitate the process throughout the interview, this has not been found achievable in this case, due to the physical distance between the interviewer and the interviewees. Therefore, the interviews have been conducted in written form.

In accordance with the research's aim and objectives, the questions forming the interviews were designed to gather information from the respondents on the following topics:

- Experience in the musical domain (as an artist or entrepreneur);
- Reasons for the career choices made and sources of motivation for development;
- Perception of artist development;
- Perception of the importance of singing contests and talent shows;
- Their opinion on the business aspects of the projects;
- Career goals and expectances.

The interviews have been conducted with the assistance of a dedicated online platform. In cases when a specific respondent has not felt comfortable about the interview being conducted in English, a version translated in the respondent's native language has been used, and their answers have been translated back in English subsequently in preparation for the data analysis stage. Factors related to personal background, such as gender or ethnicity, have not been included in the sampling process, as those have not been considered to be relevant to, or in any way affecting, the participants' responses in the context of this research.

27.3.3 Method of analysis

Apart from the physical distance between the researcher and the respondents, another reason for the tight-structured interview design was to facilitate the analysis stage. To some extent relying on the approach of grounded theory (Abramson and Mizrahi, 1994; Strauss and Corbin, 1998), the interviewee's responses have been analysed going through the stages of open coding, axial coding, and selective coding. During these stages, the main themes were identified first, then connections and interrelations between fragments were established, and, finally, the essence of the responses has been summarised in a way that corresponds with the aims and objectives, and the main research question.

The coding and analysis have been completed by the researcher himself, without the use of a specialised coding or data analysis software. The artists' and the entrepreneurs' answers have been coded and analysed separately due to their different perspectives and the differences in the structure of the interviews respectively. One of the main priorities throughout the whole process has remained the high importance of the accurate interpretation of responses and the context in which they have been given (Blaxter *et al.*, 2001).

27.4 DATA ANALYSIS AND RESULTS

27.4.1 Artists' perspectives

What is their musical background?

The analysis has not been able to reveal the existence of a 'typical background' of the talent show contestant. When asked about their age at the time of auditioning, their answers vary from being 15 to 27 years old. However, 9 out of 10 respondents have had at least 6 years of vocal training, under the instruction of vocal coach. Interestingly though, another commonality between 8 out of the 10 respondents is the fact that they had only attended no more than three other singing contests before auditioning.

How was the decision for auditioning was made?

There has been a strong agreement among all the respondents that they have made the decision to audition themselves for the reason of just trying it out. While four respondents mention being further persuaded by friends or colleagues to take part, only one mentions discussing the step with a vocal coach and family members.

Did they know what to expect?

All respondents state that they have been aware to a certain extent what to expect. Although some share that they have not expected certain disappointments, all respondents confirm that they do not regret taking part, and if able to go back now, would take part again. A strong agreement among all the interviewees has been observed that being part of the show has remained one of their most memorable experiences to date, and they have really enjoyed it.

How did the show affect their development?

Interestingly, all the respondents state that the talent show has not been the factor, which has turned them into 'professionals', with a few of them stating that they have only felt professional once they got their music degrees or when they started earning a living out of music. However, they all admit that being part of the show has been a life-changing experience, which has opened their eyes to what being a professional in the music industry actually is. The majority of people define 'becoming a professional' as a long process of development and gaining experience, however, other key attributes which stand out include: hard work, preparation, persistence, responsibility, discipline, and the ability to focus quickly and efficiently. Only one respondent's answer is on the negative side, being convinced by personal observations on the show that vocal mastery is of low significance to a music career and development at the end of the 2010s. However, in terms of their development, 9 out of 10 respondents state that the show has allowed them to make a progress through the TV exposure, the experience gained, and the new valuable contacts made.

How do they perceive the business aspect of talent shows?

All respondents unanimously state that the big talent shows are profitable businesses that make money from the contestants' labour, but the majority of them in fact find this acceptable, considering it 'part of the deal' that consists of a number of mutual benefits for both parts. On the other hand, one respondent claims that the money-making contestant-exploiting machines are not the TV producers, but the record companies that take over the artists' development after the show, and refers to unfair and enslaving contract terms. What could be summarised as an overall theme here, is that respondents are generally aware of the show's business aspects, but decide to take part regardless.

Why contestants rarely have success in the music industry afterwards?

Among the responses, three reasons for the talent show contestants' career failure stand out as the most common ones, which have been mentioned each by approximately an equal amount of respondents. Two of those reasons are business-related: the short-term and superficial nature of the talent show concept itself; and the music market environment, which especially in small countries can be extremely restrictive. The third reason however is related to the fact that many young performers may be really talented, but are just not ready for a professional career, due to lack of certain personal, professional, mental, and psychosocial skills, or due to having wrong priorities.

How important are contest and talent shows for the development of young artists?

While in the answers to the initial questions there seems to be an agreement among the majority of respondents that contests and talent shows are not always a necessary step, in the rest of their answers, where they provide some reasoning, the opinions get divided. While a small majority define the contests as a school that teaches the young artist essential skills and has a positive impact on their development, other individuals state that they are not for everyone, they are only for really gifted and well-trained singers, and also that they negatively affect the artist development, as music is not supposed to be a competition, and stage experience can be gained also from concerts.

Are they currently professionally related to music?

All the respondents confirm that they are still professionally related to music, and 9 out of 10 people are still active music artists. It is the minority of them, however, defining their artist career as their main source of income.

27.4.2 Entrepreneurs' perspectives

When and why have they started organising contests?

Having started out as organisers anywhere from 2 to 23 years ago, for 8 out of 10 respondents, the reason to start organising contests is because they provide an exposure platform to young talents. In some cases, they have felt that there has been a necessity of another contest, due to other contests' quality not being high enough. In other cases, they have simply been concerned about the lack of such event in their local region. Only three of the respondents admit that this decision has been made for personal career purposes.

How old are the artists who take part in their contests?

While the lower age threshold for contestants slightly fluctuates, they tend to be in the range of three to five years old. On the contrary, however, the reported upper thresholds are extremely different, starting from 21, and going all the way up to 85 years of age.

Where is the place of contests in the artist development process?

A clear agreement among the respondents is that contests are a vital part of the artist development process, which for some people could be related to their business engagement with such projects. The majority of respondents point out almost identical factors that are beneficial for the artist, with the main ones being stage presence or experience, confidence/mental stability, exposure, and new industry contacts. However, one respondent specifically adds that only high-quality contests are actually beneficial to the artists. Other interesting points, raised by individual respondents, are that contests should only take place in the appropriate cultural and educational centres, and that contestants should consider taking part right after completion of the basic levels of singing tuition.

What are their biggest challenges?

According to 8 out of 10 respondents, the main challenge is the difficulty of securing the necessary financial support from sponsors and local authorities. This support allows the organisers to focus on further developing their concepts, keeping them up to date with the relevant industry trends. Some of the respondents also share that they find it challenging to keep their contests interesting and attractive to contestants and audiences. Only one respondent shares that their team has an established working process and hasn't personally met significant difficulties. Interestingly, another respondent points out as the main challenge the big interest from low-quality contestants.

Are contests a viable business form?

While the majority of respondents claim in a similar fashion that their projects do not really generate any profit, the entrepreneurs seem to be on very different opinions in regards to whether they see business potential in such projects. A few respondents define only the televised talent shows as a form of business, but one respondent points out that even non-televised live contests could potentially benefit the local economy. Only three respondents explain that contests could be both supporting artists and being successful business models, but two of them add that it all depends on the organiser's priorities.

What is the future of contests and talent shows?

On this question, there seems to be no trending answer, but instead the respondents seem to be on either of three equally represented sides. The first group predicts a bright future for contests and talent shows, as they see a growth in the public interest. The second group of respondents expect these projects to keep their current state of exposure platforms that allow young artists to perform in front of different audiences. The third group, however, claims that most of the contests' concepts and quality levels are not up to date with the music industry trends and requirements, so there need to be major changes for such projects to continue their existence.

How do they see their future as organisers?

Interestingly, despite the not so optimistic overall expectancies about the future of contests, the respondents seem to be all positive about their own future as organisers. Some of them admit that they keep finding it more and more difficult, but all of them confirm that they would like to keep working on their projects, even if that includes introducing certain changes to them, as clarified by some of the interviewees.

27.4.3 Results

By considering and analysing all the gathered research data, as presented in the previous parts of this section, and by identifying and establishing strong inter-relations between different data segments, in an attempt to answer the main research question by fulfilling the set aim and objectives, the study has come to the following overall results:

Contests and talent shows do have an important place in the artist development process

The majority of respondents, both artistic and entrepreneurial, define singing contests as highly beneficial to the development of an artist. In a quite similar fashion both groups of respondents highlight that taking part in contests is one of the best ways for a young performer to start building skills related to stage presence, performing confidence, mental stability, as well as being an excellent opportunity for getting exposure and making useful industry contacts, which are essential steps that young artists should make by themselves as early as possible, if willing to start a professional career in the current music industry environment (Wikstrom, 2009).

In terms of the specific places of contests and talent shows as a step of the development process of the artist, based on all responses, a conclusion can be drawn that the two concepts are quite different from each other, therefore should be treated differently in terms of their role in the talent development process. Based on the responses, non-televised contests should be more suitable as part of the second stages of both Bloom's (1985) model and the Renzulli's Schoolwide Enrichment Model (Renzulli and Reis, 1994), consisting of practicing under the guidance of a coach, and improving certain performance aspects (Ericsson, Krampe, and Tesch-Romer, 1993). Furthermore, the research confirms that contests contribute to the 'psychosocial skills learning' (Worrell, 2010), which can be of key importance to the individual's successful talent development (MacNamara and Collins, 2009; MacNamara *et al.*, 2006; Olszewski-Kubilius, 2000).

On the other hand, talent shows seem to be considered the appropriate step for more experienced performers, whose development is more related to the talent development models' stage three, consisting of autonomy and self-direction, and perceived as the time for artists to develop their own style (Ericsson and Lehmann, 1996). At this stage, the artist should also be actively looking to get more exposure and start building a fan base (Wikstrom, 2009), and, as confirmed by the research data, the televised talent shows seem to be one of the best ways to obtain those (Chapman, 2014).

Contests and talent shows have a clear business potential, but an unclear future

The majority of the research respondents seem to be on the opinion that contests and talent shows should be treated differently, taking into account the differences in their financial aspects. However, at the same time, when all the opinions are being cross-compared to the published sources, the perception of their current state and predictions for their future seem quite similar.

With regards to contests, the entrepreneurial respondents state that they don't make any profit, and almost all of them find it challenging to secure the necessary finances for the production of the events. Therefore, quite understandably they express their concerns about the future of contests and the changes needed for them to remain contemporary and attractive. At the same time, however, the respondents seem to be predominantly optimistic about their future in the field, and some of them clearly express their opinion that with good planning, competent management, and enough persistence, such projects could in fact turn into profitable ones without compromising the quality.

The case with talent shows is slightly different, as all respondents along with numerous published sources (Ganguly, 2019) confirm the huge business potential of such concepts. And despite that they are often being criticised for their business model relying on the free labour of contestants (Redden, 2010), and for not treating contestants fairly (Kjus, 2017), the majority of this research's respondents, who are experienced as finalists in such talent shows, have clearly stated that have not just enjoyed their time on the show, but also find the terms of participating acceptable, considering the potential benefits for the contestants. Despite these positive findings, however, the reported decrease in ratings, record sales, and interest from both contestants and audience (Kjus, 2017) cast some doubts on the success and profitability of these concepts in future.

27.5 CONCLUSION AND RECOMMENDATION

This investigation has addressed a gap in research, concerning the role of contests and talent shows in the context of the artist development process and their viability as a business form. Analysing the matter from both music artists' and entrepreneurs' perspectives, the study suggests that it is not only contests and talent shows that have their specific and very important roles as part of the artist development process. By truly supporting young talents, and with a well-developed long-term strategy, such concepts could also be profitable for businesses.

Nevertheless, the research in this form does include some limitations, mainly affecting its scope, as the current resources available have only allowed the researcher to conduct the study in one specific location, and despite cross-comparing the research findings with those of related international research publications, the study's limitations could potentially question the applicability of its findings on an international level. Therefore, further research, conducted on a much larger-scale, with a bigger sample of international participants, could be considered beneficial for providing a more certain answer to the research question.

REFERENCES

Abramson, J. and Mizrahi, T. (1994) "Examining Social Work/Physician Collaboration: An Application of Grounded Theory Methods", in Riessman, C. (ed.) *Qualitative Studies in Social Work Research*. Thousand Oaks, CA: Sage, pp. 28–48.

Baskerville, D. and Baskerville, T. (2017) *Music Business Handbook and Career Guide*. 11th ed. California: SAGE Publications.

Blaxter, L., Hughes, C., and Tight, M. (2001) *How to Research*, 2nd edn. Buckingham: Open University Press.

Bloom, B. (ed.) (1985) *Developing Talent in Young People*. New York: Ballantine Books.

Bonner, F. (2003) *Ordinary Television: Analysing Popular TV*. London: Sage.

Bower, T. (2012) *Sweet Revenge: The Intimate Life of Simon Cowell*. London: Faber and Faber.

Chapman, N. (2014) The Fuller Picture: The Simon Fuller Story. BBC documentary, broadcast on Radio 2, 26 June.

Collins, S. (2008) "Making the Most Out of 15 Minutes: Reality TV's Dispensable Celebrity", *Television & New Media*, 9(2), pp. 87–110.

Coutas, P. (2006) "Fame, Fortune and Fantasy: Indonesian Idol and the New Celebrity", *Asian Journal of Communication*, 16(4), pp. 371–392.

Csikszentmihalyi, M. (1996) *Creativity: Flow and the Psychology of Discovery and Invention*. New York: Harper Perennial.

Dai, D.Y. (2010) *The Nature and Nurture of Giftedness: Anew Framework for Understanding Gifted Education*. New York, NY: Teachers College Press.

Dai, D.Y. (2017) "Envisioning a New Foundation for Gifted Education: Evolving Complexity Theory (ECT) of Talent Development", *Gifted Child Quarterly*, 61(3), pp. 172–182.

Dai, D.Y. and Chen, F. (2014) *Paradigms of Gifted Education*. Waco, TX: Prufrock Press.

Dyer, R. (1973) *Light Entertainment*. London: BFI Publications.

Ericsson, K., Krampe, R., and Tesch-Romer, C. (1993) "The Role of Deliberate Practice in the Acquisition of Performance", *Psychological Review*, 100, pp. 363–406.

Ericsson, K. and Lehmann, A. (1996) "Expert and Exceptional Performance: Evidence of Maximal Adaptation to Task Constraints", *Annual Review of Psychology*, 47, pp. 273–305.

Fairchild, C. (2007) "Building the Authentic Celebrity: The "Idol" Phenomenon in the Attention Economy", *Popular Music and Society*, 30(3), pp. 355–375.

Forman, M. (2012) *One Night on TV Is Worth Weeks at the Paramount: Popular Music on Early Television*. London: Duke University Press.

Ganguly, L. (2019) "Global Television Formats and Their Impact on Production Cultures: The Remaking of Music Entertainment Television in India", *Television & New Media*, 20(1), pp. 20–35.

Garces-Bacsal, R.M. (2014) "Alternative Pathways to Talent Development in Music: The Narrative of an Eminent Filipino Singer-Songwriter", *Gifted Child Quarterly*, 58(3), pp. 231–242.

Gonneau, E. (2011) "It's Time Artists Took Centre Stage of the Music Business Again", MIDEM Blog, 28 November. Available at: http://blog.midem.com/2011/11/emily-gonneau-its-time-artists-took-centre-stage-of-the-music-business-again/ (Accessed: 17 December 2018).

Gordon, S. (2015) *The Future of the Music Business*. 4th ed. Milwaukee: Hal Leonard Books.

Gruber, H. and Wallace, D. (1998) "The Case Study Method and Evolving Systems Approach for Understanding Unique Creative People at Work", in Sternberg, R.J. (ed.) *Handbook of Creativity*. New York: Cambridge University Press, pp. 93–115.

Harrison, A. (2017) *Music the Business*. 7th edn. London: Virgin Books.

Holmes, S. (2004) "Reality Goes Pop! Reality TV, Popular Music, and Narratives of Stardom in Pop Idol", *Television & New Media*, 5(2), pp. 147–172.

Horowitz, R. and Webb-Dempsey, J. (2002) "Promising Signs of Positive Effects: Lessons from the Multi-arts Studies", in Deasy, R.J. (ed.) *Critical Links: Learning in the Arts and Student Academic and Social Development*. Washington, DC: Arts Education Partnership, pp. 98–101.

Juniu, S., Tedrick, T., and Boyd, R. (1996) "Leisure or Work? Amateur and Professional Musicians' Perception of Rehearsal and Performance", *Journal of Leisure Research*, 28, pp. 44–56.

Kjus, Y. (2009) "Idolizing and Monetizing the Public: The Production of Celebrities and Fans, Representatives and Citizens in Reality TV", *International Journal of Communication*, 3, pp. 277–300.

Kjus, Y. (2017) "Harmonious or Out of Tune? Cooperation Between the Television Industry and the Music Business in Talent Contests of the 2000s", *Media, Culture & Society*, 39(7), pp. 1011–1026.

MacNamara, A. and Collins, D. (2009) "More Than the 'X' Factor! A Longitudinal Investigation of the Psychological Characteristics of Developing Excellence in Musical Development", *Music Education Research*, 11, pp. 377–392.

MacNamara, A., Holmes, P., and Collins, D. (2006) "The Pathway to Excellence: The Role of Psychological Characteristics in Negotiating the Challenges of Musical Development", *British Journal of Music Education*, 23, pp. 285–302.

Meizel, K. (2011) *Idolized: Music, Media and Identity in American Idol*. Bloomington, IN: Indiana University Press.

Mills, J. (2003) "Musical Performance: Crux or Curse of Music Education?", *Psychology of Music*, 31(3), pp. 324–339.

Moore, D., Burland, K., and Davidson, J. (2003) "The Social Context of Musical Success: A Developmental Account", *British Journal of Psychology*, 94, pp. 529–549.

Negus, K. (1992) *Producing Pop – Culture and Conflict in Popular Music*. London: Hodder and Stoughton.

O'Neill, S.A. (2002) "The Self-identity of Young Musicians", in Hargreaves, D.J., Miell, D., and MacDonald, R.A.R. (eds.) *Musical Identities*. Oxford: Oxford University Press, pp. 79–96.

Olszewski-Kubilius, P. (2000) "The Transition From Childhood Giftedness to Adult Creative Productiveness: Psychological Characteristics and Social Supports", *Roeper Review*, 23, pp. 65–71.

Olszewski-Kubilius, P. and Thomson, D. (2015) "Talent Development as a Framework for Gifted Education", *Gifted Child Today*, 38(1), pp. 49–59.

Oreck, B. *et al.* (2000) *Artistic Talent Development for Urban Youth: The Promise and the Challenge*. Storrs, CT: National Research Center on the Gifted and Talented.

Petersen, S. (2017) "Talent development in Chinese and Swiss music students", *International Journal of Music Education*, 36(2), pp. 230–243.

Redden, G. (2010) "Learning to Labour on the Reality Talent Show", *Media International Australia*, 134(1), pp. 131–140.

Reijnders, S. *et al.* (2007) "Community Spirit and Competition in Idols: Ritual Meanings of a TV Talent Quest", *European Journal of Communication*, 22(3), pp. 275–292.

Renzulli, J. and Reis, S. (1994) "Research Related to the Schoolwide Enrichment Triad Model", *Gifted Child Quarterly*, 38, pp. 7–20.

Rickard, N.S. and Chin, T. (2017) "Defining the Musical Identity of 'Nonmusicians'", in MacDonald, R., Hargreaves, D.J., and Miell, D. (eds.) *Handbook of Musical Identities*. Oxford: Oxford University Press, pp. 288–303.

Ripken, J. (2011) "Readjusting Artist Development", Johannes Ripken Music Industry Blog, 6 December. Available at: http://www.johannesripken.com/readjusting-artist-development/ (Accessed: 12 January 2019).

Rogers, P. (2010) "A&R Star Makers: The Vanishing Gatekeepers", *LA Times*, 2 November.

Rostan, S.M. (2003) "In the Spirit of Howard E. Gruber's Gift: Case Studies of Two Young Artists' Evolving Systems", *Creativity Research Journal*, 15(1), pp. 45–60.

Schroth, S.T. et al. (2011) "Talent Development: From Theoretical Conceptions to Practical Applications", in Cross, T.L. and Cross, J.R. (eds.) *Handbook of Counselors Serving Students With Gifts and Talents*. Waco, TX: Prufrock Press Inc., pp. 39–52.

Shepherd, J. *et al.* (eds) (2003) *Continuum Encyclopedia of Popular Music of the World*. London: Continuum.

Sloboda, J. (2005) *Exploring the Musical Mind*. Oxford: Oxford University Press.

Sloboda, J. *et al.* (1996) "The Role of Practice in the Development of Performing Musicians", *British Journal of Psychology*, 87, pp. 287–309.

Sorin, S. (2001) Interview With Simon Cowell, A&R at BMG for Westlife, Five. Available at: http://www.hitquarters.com/index.php3?page=intrview/2001/October23_2_32_21.html (Accessed: 15 December 2018).

Stahl, M. (2004) "A Moment Like This: American Idol and Narratives of Meritocracy", in Washburne, C. and Maiken, D. (eds) *Bad Music: The Music We Love to Hate*. New York: Routledge, pp. 212–232.

Stratton, J. (1981) "Reconciling Contradictions: The Role of the Artist and Repertoire Person in the British Record Industry", *Popular Music and Society*, 8(2), pp. 90–100.

Stratton, J. (1983) "Capitalism and Romantic Ideology in the Record Business", *Popular Music*, 3, pp. 143–156.

Strauss, A. and Corbin, J. (1998) *Basics of Qualitative Research: Techniques and Procedures for Developing Grounded Theory*. Thousand Oaks, CA: Sage.

Subotnik, R.F. (2015) "Psychosocial Strength Training: The Missing Piece in Talent Development", *Gifted Child Today*, 38(1), pp. 41–48.

Subotnik, R.F., Olszewski-Kubilius, P., and Worrell, F.C. (2011) "Rethinking Giftedness and Gifted Education: A Proposed Direction Forward Based on Psychological Science", *Psychological Science in the Public Interest*, 12, pp. 3–54.

Sutherland, M. (2018) A&R, Not R&D: Why the Music Biz Shouldn't Let Data Take Over Artist Development. Available at: http://www.musicweek.com/opinion/read/a-r-not-r-d-why-the-music-biz-shouldn-t-let-data-take-over-artist-development/074182 (Accessed: 10 December 2018).

Swanwick, K. (2001) "Conference Keynote: Musical Development Theories Revisited", *Music Education Research*, 3, pp. 227–242.

Tan, Y.T. *et al.* (2014) "The Genetic Basis of Music Ability", *Frontiers in Psychology*, 5, p. 658.

Wacholtz, L. (2017) *Monetizing Entertainment*. London: Routledge.

Wikstrom, P. (2009) *The Music Industry, Music in the Cloud*. Cambridge: Polity Press.

Winner, E. and Martino, G. (2000) "Giftedness in Non-academic Domains: The Case of the Visual Arts and Music", in Heller, K.A., Monks, F.J., Sternberg, R.J., and Subotnik, R.F. (eds.) *International Handbook of Giftedness and Talent*. Oxford: Elsevier, pp. 95–110.

Worrell, F.C. (2010) "Psychosocial Stressors in the Development of Gifted Learners with Atypical Profiles", in VanTassel-Baska, J.L. (ed.) *Patterns and Profiles of Promising Learners From Poverty*. Waco, TX: Prufrock Press, pp. 33–58.

Zvaan, K. and Bogt, T.M.F (2009) "Research Note: Breaking into the Popular Record Industry", *European Journal of Communication*, 24(1), pp. 89–101.

28

Music

Leeds – supporting a regionalised music sector and scene

Paul Thompson and Sam Nicholls

28.1 INTRODUCTION

Over the last two decades, local authority and city governance have: 'expressed a growing interest in placing culture at the core of urban development strategies' (UNESCO, 2016). Culture is used as part of urban regeneration strategies to: 'create a new cosmopolitan image. In an atmosphere of growing interurban competition, increasing mobility of capital and the waning importance of physical location factors, cities now profile themselves by investing in the cultural and creative sectors' (Van der Hoeven & Hitters, 2019: 263). Popular music, and the activity that surrounds it, has become a significant part of these culture-led regeneration strategies (Ross, 2017) where music events for example are used to help cultivate inclusivity, promote social cohesion or to reinvigorate urban spaces (Cohen, 2013; Holt & Wergin, 2013). As an extension of one-off or a series of curated events, a 'Music City' is a term that describes an urban environment that has the ideal conditions to take advantage of the cultural and musical fabric to support and nurture its musical economy (Baker, 2017; Terrill, Hogarth, Clement, & Francis, 2015). A 'Music City' emphasises elements of creative development and business growth, placemaking and tourism, access to music-making and music events as well as supporting the existing music scene.

Since the formation of Berlin's Club Commission in 2001, and following the dissolution of Regional Development Agencies (RDAs) in 2012, UK local government's remit has expanded to include the stimulation and support of regionalised music sectors and scenes. These support opportunities have taken different forms such as sector-led initiatives and government imposed leadership structures in order to improve aspects of the music economy such as protecting a city's night-time economy and developing access to music education and a link to the wider skills agenda. Some UK cities have formulated City Region Music Boards (i.e. London, Greater Manchester, Liverpool and Sheffield) to help provide a more formal and unified strategy to influence music policy and provide consultancy on a local level and implement a regional music strategy. The city of Leeds however, which is situated in the North of England, originally developed a dedicated culture strategy alongside the region's proposed bid to become European Capital of Culture in 2023. In light of the UK's imminent exit from the European Union, and subsequently the disqualification of Leeds from the bidding process, Leeds City Council declared 2023 as a year of culture with a determined approach to improve its arts and culture offering. In addressing music as part of this offering, Leeds City Council consulted with the newly formulated independent organisation 'Music:Leeds', which has now undertaken a strategic partnership with Leeds City Council in establishing programmes with funding from national bodies including Arts Council England and PRS Foundation, as well as wider support from other major music industry bodies such as UK Music and Association of Independent Music.

This chapter discusses a range of strategies and initiatives that have been implemented across the city of Leeds (UK) with a critical evaluation of the ways in which models from other European cities, feedback and opinion from music professionals, consultation from government officials in Leeds and guidance documents from professional bodies and global consultancy agencies (i.e. Sound Diplomacy and the International Federation of the Phonographic Industry) have been implemented in the development of the city's strategy to stimulate music activity around Music:Leeds' three core areas of activity: Creative Development and Business Growth; Placemaking and Tourism; Access to Music.

28.2 CONTEXT

A city's Creative and Cultural Economy (CCE) has been defined as: 'any human activity that embodies symbolic meaning or is shaped by cultural factors that can be construed as contributing to the cultural vitality of the city' (Hutton, 2004: 91). Musical activity is therefore part of a broader creative sector that includes the Arts, design, fashion and bespoke manufacturing (Baird & Scott, 2018) but forms a fundamental part of the global CCE agenda. Live music in particular is a central focus for development within numerous city and local authority CCE strategies because it is a significant contributor to the urban cultural economy. For example, the economic value of live music in the UK accounts for almost 25% of the music industry's £4.5 billion contribution to the UK economy (UKMusic, 2018: 8). City and local authorities on the whole have come to recognise that music activity and specifically live music is a crucial indication of a city's cultural and economic vitality, a city's attractiveness as a place to live, and an important stream of employment for modern musicians and occupations that support music-making in a digital era (Holt, 2010).

Strategies around emphasising the creative sectors of a city have taken many forms over the lifespan of their implementation but have typically centred upon urban live music policy (Behr, Brennan, & Cloonan, 2016; Evans, 2009; Gibson and Stevenson, 2004; Hudson, 2006). Some policies around music activity in cities have been shown to be part of a broader cultural strategy (Hutton, 2009; O'Connor and Shaw, 2014) or formed part of an approach to address noise, gentrification or zoning of the night-time economy within a local authority's urban planning policy (e.g. Gibson & Homan, 2004; Homan, 2008; Homan, 2010; Homan, 2014; Strong, Cannizzo, & Rogers, 2017). There are CCE policies that are often arguably 'neo-liberal economic policies rather than cultural policies' (Atkinson & Easthope, 2009: 69). For example, strategies that side-line creators and artists, emphasise short-lived rather than sustainable cultural activities, or creating further precariousness in an already precarious labour market, are indicators of a neo-liberal economic approach that overlook the interconnected cultural factors beyond the purely economic (Koefoed, 2013; Pratt, 2008; Scott, 2006; Vivant, 2013; Zukin, 1987). Consequently, there are differing approaches to designing and implementing CCE strategies and this is often because different actors such as policy makers, consultancy firms and music industry support organisations have differing views and interests when emphasising the importance of live music within these CCE strategies.

Despite these differences, a number of common approaches, methods and policies have been implemented across the world to create 'Music Cities' in which 'hard' and 'soft' institutional policies are introduced to support live music activity. For example, as part of a $45million grant, the national music funding body of Canada (Music Canada, 2016) developed a series of short-term, medium-term and long-term strategies in which music was integrated with the connected areas of tourism, heritage, city development and urban planning for the city of Toronto (City of Toronto Strategic Plan, 2016; Hracs, 2009). Live music activity is supported through 'hard' institutional policy which relates to issues of noise for live music venues/zones within new or existing urban developments and 'soft' institutional implementation in which a dedicated live music office was set up as a central point of contact for musicians, venue owners and promoters to access information relating to: 'noise attenuation, liquor licensing, and building code issues. Here government departments, music businesses and non-profit music related entities share space, ideas and strategies at one location' (Baird & Scott, 2018: 3).

The city of Brisbane in Australia is a unique example within its country because it has ring-fenced the Fortitude Valley area of the city as a dedicated entertainment precinct (Burke & Schmidt, 2013), which has been described as: 'a bohemian enclave of creative arts, music and culture' (Baird & Scott, 2018: 3). In order to preserve the area's character, Brisbane City Council designed the 'Valley Music Harmony Plan' (Valley Sound Machine, 2004) that allowed the council to monitor noise levels, implement specific plans for infrastructure and deploy more effective approaches for policing. Hard institutional policy included notifying potential residents to the area to expect above average noise levels and implementing compulsory soundproofing and additional noise attenuation measures for new residential builds (Baird & Scott, 2018).

Finally, Nashville in the United States has already established itself as a Music City and the 'Home of Country Music' but in the face of the economic effects of gentrification and culture-led urban renewal, The Mayor's office of Nashville has taken a hard and soft institutional approach. Firstly, it has created a merchant advisory group that comprises of representatives from government, business, non-profit organisations and the heritage and tourism sectors. The advisory grouped labelled 'The District' focuses on areas and/or buildings of particular cultural significance to the city of Nashville and strives to extend heritage status to them (The District, 2015). Secondly, Nashville's music city council, the Country Music Association (CMA) and the Nashville entrepreneur centre have joined together under Nashville's 'Project Music' (Nashville Music Council, 2016) to distribute start-up grants to small emerging businesses (Nashville Next City Plan, 2015).

In their survey of global music cities Baird and Scott noted that an ideal Music City should include strategies involving the re-regulation of space, Imagineering, governance, and supply. On this last point they argue that an ideal music city requires: 'Deep engagement with musicians and related creative sector professionals. Such supply-side policies aim to refine the human capital of industry actors through education, training and up-skilling (Scott, 2013)' (2018: 5). They further explain that 'hard' institutional forms may include: 'the development of contestable grants to incentivise music production, videos and touring; or to underwrite festivals and events, industry conferences and professional development' (ibid). The 'soft' institutional forms, Baird and Scott argue, work to encourage musicians and associated professionals to think in a more entrepreneurial way. They suggest soft forms might include: 'organizing professional development, industry awareness, networking and performance events, such information sharing' (ibid). This 'upskilling' approach they argue can be 'implemented in conjunction with other arts strategies through community and youth engagement programs (Scott & Craig, 2012)' (ibid).

28.3 MAPPING THE MUSICAL ECONOMY OF LEEDS

Prior to the formulation of Music:Leeds, a mapping exercise throughout 2017 was undertaken by the initial members of the team. This involved first surveying the number of music businesses, organisations or people currently operating in Leeds and the surrounding area. Existing phone or business directories, Internet searches, recommendations from managers, promoters, venue owners and musicians alongside a publicised open call to individuals and organisations, were all used to compile a dedicated directory of music activity in the region. The businesses, organisations or people that support and work with artists and musicians in Leeds were then categorised using the areas set out by Complete Music Update (CMU, 2018):

- Music Creation
- Live Performance
- Music Marketing and Fanbase Building
- Artist Business Services
- Music Heritage and Tourism
- Music Education and Participation

This data was compiled into a database to create a holistic view of the musical economy of Leeds. The mapping exercise uncovered some notable aspects of the Leeds music economy in particular the area of 'Live Performance', which showed it was a vibrant part of the sector with 215 music venues in operation under a Leeds postcode. The type and function of these live music venues ranged from large venues operated by multinational corporations, full-time independent music venues to suburban pubs with singular weekly live music events.

In the area of 'Artist Business Services' the mapping exercise identified a number of record labels based in the city ranging from large independent labels with a national profile to smaller micro-independent labels. Although a true number of smaller micro-independent labels was difficult to fully determine it was estimated that there were fewer than 10 Leeds-based record labels that were recognised as formal businesses or companies supporting less than 10 full-time-equivalent jobs. The mapping exercise identified a large number of self-distributing artists not attached to a record label, which indicated a large number of music creators in the city who were potentially retaining the rights to their work by not contracting it to third parties. Connected to this point it was found that although there are a handful of successful companies managing associated publishing rights in the field of film and television, the commercial popular music sector has no bespoke publisher in the city. The lack of business representation in this area could limit the potential for local music creators to fully exploit their works and gain wider exposure; particularly within the lucrative field of music synchronisation, which is not served by PROs, who at least collect performance and mechanical copyrights for music creators. Finally, the mapping exercise highlighted the lack of legal services for musicians and music operations in the city with no music lawyers or representatives. This may indicate that there is not enough work to support a music lawyer in the city and that the primary elements of the music economy are more independent or DIY-centric than commercial.

28.4 ESTABLISHING MUSIC:LEEDS

Data from the mapping exercise was critical in highlighting the wealth of musical activity in the city of Leeds and that despite a lack of formal structure and sporadic local authority economic support, the music sector and scene is prospering. In spite of this, there are three principal considerations. Firstly, the consideration of sustainability and the ways in which this bourgeoning scene be supported long term. Secondly, the consideration of representation and the methods by which the interests and issues of music businesses, organisations and people can be represented to local authorities. Finally, cooperation and the means by which a collective approach can be organised and managed to help meet some of the challenges involved in supporting a regional music sector and scene.

There are a number of existing models for establishing a mechanism for supporting the music sector within a city; for example, some UK cities have formulated City Region Music Boards (i.e. London, Greater Manchester,

Liverpool and Sheffield) to help provide a more formal and unified strategy to influence music policy and provide consultancy on a local level and implement a regional music strategy. Some cities and regions have created roles within local government such as dedicated music officers or to establish a dedicated music office (i.e. Brighton) that supports music activity in all areas of the economy. Alongside the region's proposed bid to become European Capital of Culture in 2023, the city of Leeds originally developed a broader culture strategy of which music was only a part. In light of the UK's potential exit from the European Union, and subsequently the disqualification of Leeds from the bidding process, Leeds City Council declared 2023 as a year of culture with a determined approach to improve the offer of arts and culture across the city. The findings from the mapping exercise were presented to Leeds City Council and used to advocate for developing a more holistic and strategic approach to support music activity in the city. In a bid to be visible, non-partisan and representative of all areas of the musical economy, Music:Leeds was initiated as an independent organisation to act as a conduit for consultation between local music businesses, individuals and services, and Leeds City Council to begin to create a framework for support to the music sector of Leeds.

The first of many consultation events managed and run by Music:Leeds was held at Leeds Town Hall in the Autumn of 2017 in which key individuals, business and services from the local music sector highlighted in the mapping exercise were invited to attend. In an attempt to actively engage as much of the music community as possible, representatives from each of the six areas (Music Creation, Live Performance, Music Marketing and Fanbase Building, Artist Business Services, Music Heritage and Tourism, Music Education and Participation) were invited to "listen, think, shout and contribute to a day that will help develop a mandate to connect and support music in the city at all levels" (Music:Leeds, 2017). The event included addresses and provocations from Tom Riordan (Chief Executive, Leeds City Council), Cllr Blake (Leader, Leeds City Council), Michael Dugher (CEO, UK Music) alongside sector development experts Sound Diplomacy and individuals working to create models to sustain and promote the music sectors of other cities and regions including Amsterdam, Aarhus, Liverpool and Brighton. The large-scale consultation forum further helped to establish Music:Leeds as an independent organisation "to act as a centralised point to support, develop, grow and promote music in the city across all levels, genres and cultures" (ibid).

28.5 ENGAGING THE MUSIC ECONOMY OF LEEDS

Following the 2017 event, Music:Leeds created online networks, including social media channels, an email list and online forums to create a framework for communicating future events, opportunities and news from the sector. Throughout 2018, Music:Leeds were able to host a series of events that addressed the issue of gender equality in the music industries, music industry insights and a series of skills workshops for musicians. These events featured a networking element that also provided an opportunity for diverse parties from the local music community to meet and discuss potential collaborations. Further consultation with representatives from the music economy of Leeds was undertaken at the 2019 City Music Forum which served as an opportunity for Music:Leeds to present its initial activity and encourage representatives from the sector to present their own topics for discussion within smaller breakout focus groups. In total, 12 distinct topics were put forward for discussion, that were then published in a round-up document, which were as follows:

- Funding, education and accessibility
- Stickability: How can Leeds develop more music businesses? How can we keep talent in Leeds?
- Supporting promoters
- Why is music in Leeds so white?
- Combatting groping, sexual harassment and violence at live music events
- Leeds music history
- Music Tourism and Leeds
- How to start a collective – from competition to collaboration
- Access to live music for children and young people
- The relationship between health and music
- Apprenticeships/training routes in music/music related and creative skills
- How to avoid plans for music in Leeds from becoming a self-congratulatory exercise and genuinely encouraging external contributions and development?

These events arranged by Music:Leeds served to engage the: 'musicians and related creative sector professionals' (Scott, 2013) more deeply from across the musical economy of Leeds. The issues, needs and opportunities discussed at events were then further grouped into three specific areas that Music:Leeds could help to address:

- Creative Development and Business Growth in Leeds
- Placemaking and Tourism in Leeds
- Access to Music in Leeds

The first of these, 'Creative Development and Business Growth' was underpinned by findings from the database, which identified clear areas of strengths and areas for development in both volume and scale for music organisations in the city. In particular, the mapping exercise highlighted a lack of music businesses that could support pathways for emerging music industry entrepreneurs and professionals to establish themselves and/or new businesses in the city relating to the music economy. Some participants on the day of the forum argued that an absence of established pathways often leads to a talent drain to other cities; specifically to London and the South East of England.

The second area identified through engagement with the music economy of Leeds was 'Tourism and placemaking', which relates to the benefits a successful music sector can have in both attracting visitors to the city and retaining talent within the music sector and across the broader workforce. Engagement with the musical economy of Leeds showed that although Leeds is highly regarded for having strong longstanding relationships to events and brands (e.g. within the House music scene and the Back to Basics club night, the Pop Punk scene and the Slam Dunk festival, the DIY and Punk Rock music scene with Cops & Robbers), it doesn't currently have a clear and cohesive reputation for its music offering. Representatives from Leeds' music scene underlined that there is a need to create a defining narrative that can raise the national profile of the music sector of Leeds, which is not defined by a 'sound' but by a sense of independence, and diversity as a tangible asset.

Music economy engagement identified a final area 'Access to Music' in which representatives across the city region highlighted three particular aspects of accessibility that should be addressed in Leeds's current provision:

1. Access to music-making and music events. It is typically community, charity or non-profit organisations that lead the way in access to music-making and musical development but there are still a range of musical, geographical, socio-economic barriers and physical barriers for all ages in the city; specifically disabled and impaired music makers and audience members.
2. Access and representation. Issues of diversity and representation within the musical economy; specifically at leadership level, is vital to help meet the needs of the diverse cultural communities of Leeds and the global workforce more broadly.
3. Access to opportunities. Improving the local musical economy will also increase access to opportunities of development, employment and engagement with the musical economy. This may also include the ability to help recognise opportunities in order to be able to access them.

28.6 INFLUENCING THE MUSIC ECONOMY OF LEEDS

Strategic engagement with representatives across the musical economy of Leeds allowed Music:Leeds to address particular aspects of the musical economy of 'Creative Development & Business Growth', 'Placemaking and Tourism' and 'Access to Music'.

'Creative Development & Business Growth' is the area in which Music:Leeds has had the most visible influence on the musical economy of Leeds. This is through the early career artist development programme called 'Launchpad', which groups together 20–30 local and national music organisations, businesses and live events to support emerging artists. Funding for Launchpad was generated to support this activity from the National Lottery through Arts Council England and PRS Foundation as a Talent Development Partner. This has crucially helped to create a tangible network of support organisations for anyone involved in music in the region. The secondary impact of developing partnerships with such a wide range of local music festival and organisations is that a tangible network of local organisations has become visible to any artists accessing the Launchpad initiative. By artists engaging with these direct and overtly desirable opportunities (e.g. a sought after festival slot), Music:Leeds have been able to signpost and disseminate a wider range of opportunities, both from organisations within Leeds, as well as national bodies to include major arts / music funders to emerging artists in the region.

Music:Leeds has also contributed to the area of 'Placemaking and Tourism' through strategic engagement with Leeds Enterprise Partnership (LEP), Leeds City Council & Leeds 2023. The Leeds City Region European Structural and Investment Funds (ESIF) Strategy published in 2014 only mentions music once – however, through its developing relationship with local government, Music:Leeds has contributed to the music industry section of the city-wide strategy for 2020 onwards. Unlike Liverpool that has focused on the Beatles, or Nashville with Country Music, Leeds lacks a unifying and tangible focus for its music heritage. However over the last 10 years, momentum has been growing with numerous exhibitions including 'Leeds Music History' and 'One Foot In The Rave', with support from Leeds City Council to Leeds Business Improvement District (BID). Music:Leeds' contribution to the city-wide strategy draws upon the key areas of these exhibitions to develop a strategy to create a notable identity for music in Leeds, celebrating its past and present to help profile the city of Leeds as a musical destination for future tourists, audiences, music makers and those that support the music economy.

Through the building of networks and strategic partnerships to amplify opportunities, Music:Leeds has also contributed to the area of 'Access to Music'. For example, The Launchpad Project was designed solely to have a direct impact on artists in the region, but engagement with the initiative plays a role in building a noticeable network of music industry individuals and organisations in the city, which has contributed to making music opportunities more accessible, whilst establishing role models and developing the sector and artists. Music:Leeds Launchpad also provides opportunities for artists (musicians and music creators) of any genre and style to access support through a combination live performance, studio recording, one-to-one mentoring, conference, talks and workshop aimed at increasing knowledge and skills of those who attend. Artists are invited to apply via an open call, which was distributed as widely as possible. Strategic partnerships were made with local festivals to provide live opportunities and this encouraged a diverse range of artists to apply and amplify the opportunities that were on offer to a diverse audience.

Music:Leeds has also engaged with specific activity to address widespread issues around diversity and inclusivity and following collaborative events with Brighter Sound, a Gender Rebalance Equality Action & Advisory Team (GREAAT) has been convened to increase and promote opportunities for women and people of marginalised gender in the city.

This has led to showcase and social events throughout the year, and enabled collaboration across different organisations working within the sector. Additionally, through analysis of its database of music businesses, Music:Leeds has helped to engage venues across the city in addressing sexual harassment at live music events (in collaboration with Dr Rosemary Hill's Healthy Music Audiences project) and improve venues' online information for disabled and deaf audience members in line with Attitude Is Everything's Access Starts Online guidance. Examples include working with Brighter Sound on Both Sides Now to create more opportunities for female music creators, running consultation supported by Attitude is Everything to improve the access information for live music venues in the city and collaborating with Dr Rosemary Hill on work to address sexual harassment at live music events.

Importantly, the formation of Music:Leeds has provided an opportunity for widespread organisational cooperation in raising the profile of music activity both within the city, and on a national level. This has allowed more sophisticated projects to take place with more awareness for our audiences and practitioners.

28.7 CONCLUSIONS AND FURTHER WORK

A 'Music City' describes an urban environment that has the ideal conditions to take advantage of the cultural and musical fabric to support and nurture its musical economy (Baker, 2017; Terrill, Hogarth, Clement, & Francis, 2015). A 'Music City' emphasises elements of creative development and business growth, placemaking and tourism, access to music-making and music events as well as supporting the existing music scene. Supporting the regionalised music sector and scene of Leeds began with a mapping exercise to identify the individuals, groups, organisations and businesses working within the music economy of the city.

Data from the mapping exercise was crucial in highlighting the diversity of musical activity in the city of Leeds and that despite a lack of formal structure and sporadic local authority economic support, the music sector and scene is prospering. However, three principal challenges and issues were highlighted; that of sustainability, representation and cooperation. After a consultation event in 2017, the orgnaisation Music:Leeds was formed and developed a series of regular events to engage the music industries of Leeds and the UK more broadly. Further consultation was undertaken at 2019 City Music Forum, which reinforced a number of issues highlighted three specific areas of development that Music:Leeds can help to address:

- Creative Development and Business Growth in Leeds
- Placemaking and Tourism in Leeds
- Access to Music in Leeds

Music:Leeds has had the most visible influence on the musical economy of Leeds. This is through the early career artist development programme called 'Launchpad' local and national music organisations, businesses and live events to support emerging artists. Through its developing relationship with local government, Music:Leeds has developed the music industry section of the City-Wide Strategy for 2020 onwards to influence the area of 'Placemaking and Tourism' and, importantly, Music:Leeds has helped to increase awareness of issues of access and inclusivity within the musical economy of Leeds through the curation of a diverse range of events across the region. Music:Leeds were able to facilitate this work and maximise the impact of these projects because of the critical engagement with representatives from across the musical economy of Leeds and building relationships with them through consultations in the City Music Forum.

The activity of Music:Leeds activity to date has been informed by mapping data, consultative events and action research through delivery of its programme tied to its funding. Further work on evaluating these aspects is needed to fully assess the impact of these activities and how they can inform a structure and pathway through to 2023 and beyond. These include the need to effectively support and sustain a fit for purpose music eco-system that facilitates emerging artists and music industry professionals, a diverse workforce and increasing music activity opportunities. There is also a need to define a narrative for what music in Leeds represents, to create an inclusive identity that all those engaged with music in the city can respond to, and equally project, and that equally harnesses the power of the city's music heritage.

REFERENCES

Atkinson, R., & Easthope, H. (2009). The Consequences of the Creative Class: The Pursuit of Creativity Strategies in Australia's cities. *International Journal of Urban and Regional Research*, 33(1), 64–79.

Baird, P., & Scott, M. (2018). Towards an Ideal Typical Live Music City. *City, Culture and Society*. https://doi.org/10.1016/j.ccs.2018.03.003.

Baker, A.J. (2017). Algorithms to Assess Music Cities: Case study—Melbourne as a music capital. *SAGE Open*, 7(1), 1–12.

Behr, A., Brennan, M., Cloonan, M., Frith, S., & Webster, E. (2016). Live Concert Performance: An Ecological Approach. *Rock Music Studies*, 3(1), 5–23.

Burke, M., & Schmidt, A. (2013). How Should We Plan and Regulate Live Music in Australian Cities? Learnings from Brisbane. *Australian Planner*, 50(1), 68–78.

City of Toronto Strategic Plan (2016). Available at: http://www.toronto.ca/legdocs/mmis/2016/ed/bgrd/backgroundfile-90615.pdf, accessed date: 2 December 2019.

Cohen, S. (2013). "From the Big Dig to the Big Gig": Live Music, Urban Regeneration and Social Change in the European Capital of Culture 2008. In C. Wergin, & F. Holt (Eds.). *Musical Performance and the Changing City: Post-industrial Contexts in Europe and the United States* (pp. 27–51). New York: Routledge.

Complete Music Update (CMU) (2018). Available at: https://completemusicupdate.com/, accessed date: 2 December 2019.

Evans, G. (2009). Creative Cities, Creative Spaces and Urban Policy. *Urban Studies*, 46(5–6), 1003–1040.

Gibson, C., & Homan, S. (2004). Urban Redevelopment, Live and Public Space, Cultural Performance and the Re-making of Marrickville. *International Journal of Cultural Policy*, 10(1), 67–84.

Gibson, L., & Stevenson, D. (2004). Urban Space and the Uses of Culture. *International Journal of Cultural Policy*, 10(1), 1–4.

Holt, F. (2010). The Economy of Live Music in the Digital Age. *European Journal of Cultural Studies*, 13(2), 243–261.

Holt, F., & Wergin, C. (2013). Introduction: Musical performance and the Changing City. In F. Holt, & C. Wergin (Eds.). *Musical Performance and the Changing City: Post-industrial Contexts in Europe and the United States* (pp. 1–24). New York: Routledge.

Homan, S. (2008). A Portrait of the Politician as a Young Pub Rocker: Live Music Venue Reform in Australia. *Popular Music*, 27(2), 243–256.

Homan, S. (2010). Governmental as Anything: Live Music and Law and Order in Melbourne. *Perfect Beat*, 11(2), 103–118.

Homan, S. (2014). Liveability and Creativity: The Case for Melbourne Music Precincts. *City, Culture and Society*, 5(3), 149–155.

Hracs, B.J. (2009). Beyond Bohemia: Geographies of Everyday Creativity for Musicians in Toronto. In T. Edensor, D. Leslie, S. Millington, Steve, & N. Rantisi (Eds.). *Spaces of Vernacular Creativity: Rethinking the Cultural Economy* (pp. 75–88). London: Routledge.

Hudson, R. (2006). Regions and Place: Music, Identity and Place. *Progress in Human Geography*, 30(5), 626–634.

Hutton, T.A. (2004). The new economy of the inner city. *Cities*, 21(2), pp.89–108.

Hutton, T. (2009). *The New Economy of the Inner City: Restructuring, Regeneration and Dislocation in the 21st century Metropolis*. London: Routledge.

Koefoed, O. (2013). European Capitals of Culture and Cultures of Sustainability: The Case of Guimaraes 2012. *City, Culture and Society*, 4(3), 153–162.

Music:Leeds (2017) https://www.musicleeds.com/leedstownhall, accessed date: 2 October 2020.

Music Canada (2016). The Mastering of a Music City – Leveraging Best Practices from Austin, Texas. March 2016. Available at: http://musiccanada.com/wp-content/uploads/2014/07/AcceleratingToronto%E2%80%99s-Music-Industry-Growth-%E2%80%93-Leveraging-Best-Practices-from-Austin Texas.pdf, accessed date: 2 December 2019.

Nashville Next City Plan (2015). Arts and Cultural Land Use Planning including Music Row. Available at: www.nashvillenext.net, accessed date: 2 December 2019.

Nashville Music Council (2016). Available at: http://www.nashville.gov/Mayors-Office/Priorities/Economic-Development/Programs-and-Services/Music-City-Music-Council.aspx, accessed date: 2 December 2019.

O'Connor, J., & Shaw, K. (2014). What Next for the Creative City? *City, Culture and Society*, 5(3), 165–170.

Pratt, A. (2008). Creative Cities: The Cultural Industries and the Creative Class. Geografiska Annaler - Series B: *Human Geography*, 90(2), 107–117.

Ross, S. (2017). 'Making a Music City: The Commodification of Culture in Toronto's Urban Redevelopment, Tensions between Use-Value and Exchange-Value, and the Counterproductive Treatment of Alternative Cultures within Municipal Legal Frameworks'. *Journal of Law and Social Policy* 27: 116–153.

Scott, A. J. (2006). Creative Cities: Conceptual Issues and Policy Questions. *Journal of Urban Affairs*, 28(1), 1–17.

Scott, M. (2013). *Making New Zealand's Pop Renaissance: State, Markets, Musicians*. London: Routledge.

Scott, M., & Craig, D. (2012). The Promotional State 'After Neo-liberalism': Ideologies of Governance and New Zealand's Pop Renaissance. *Popular Music*, 31(1), 143–163.

Strong, C., Cannizzo, F., & Rogers, I. (2017). Aesthetic Cosmopolitan, National and Local Popular Music Heritage in Melbourne's Music Laneways. *International Journal of Heritage Studies*, 2(2), 83–96.

Terrill, A., Hogarth, D., Clement, A., & Francis, R. (2015). Mastering of a Music City. Available at: http://www.ifpi.org/downloads/The-Mastering-of-a-Music-City.pdf.

The District (2015). Available at: http://thedistrictnashville.org, Accessed date: 2 December 2019.

UKMusic (2018). Measuring Music. Available at: https://www.ukmusic.org/news/measuring-music-2018, accessed date: 2 December 2019.

UNESCO (2016). Issue Paper on Urban Culture and Heritage. Presented at *The United Nations Conference on Housing and Sustainable Urban Development*, Quito, Ecuador, 17–20 October. Available at: http://www.unesco.org/new/fileadmin/MULTIMEDIA/HQ/CLT/pdf/ISSUE-Paper-En.pdf, accessed date October 2020.

Valley Sound Machine (2004). Available at: https://www.brisbane.qld.gov.au/planning-building/planning-guidelines-tools/other-plans-projects/valley-special-entertainmentprecinct/

valley-sound-machine, Accessed date: 2 December 2019.

Van der Hoeven, A., & Hitters, E. (2019). The Social and Cultural Values of Live Music: Sustaining Urban Live Music Ecologies. *Cities* 90 (2019) pp. 263–271.

Vivant, E. (2013). Creatives in the City: Urban Contradictions of the Creative City. *City, Culture and Society*, 4(2), 57–63.

Zukin, S. (1987). Gentrification: Culture and Capital in the Urban Core. *Annual Review of Sociology*, 1(1), 129–147.

Index

Page numbers in **bold** refer to figures, page numbers in *italic* refer to tables.

360 degrees videos 129

Ableton 210; CV Tools 164
Ableton Live 136–137, **137**, 138, 213–214, 250, 252, 253, 258, 312, **312**, 337, 371–372, 373, **374**, 375, 376
A Capella (Rundgren) 73, 74
accessibility 439; hardware 107; Internet of Things music system 115–117, **115**; sonic-play instruments 229–230
Accessible Digital Musical Interfaces 220; *see also* sonic-play instruments
accidents, role of 351
acousmatic sound 190
acoustic signatures 21–22
actor-network theory 20–21
Adams, Kyle 39
Adkins, M. 214
A-D-S-R installation 206–217; compositional output 213–214; convolution reverb 214; future developments 217; haptic feedback 210, 216; image-to-sound process 211–213, **211**; mapping image to sound 208–209; physical artefacts 215–216, **215**; SUBPAC 209–210, 211 216; system 210–213, **210**, **211**, **212**; vibrotactile experiences 209–210
advance fee scammers 236
aesthetic-causal alliance 186
agency 400
agential realism 391–392, 400
ambient music 214
ambient sound 192, 202
AmbiFreeVerb 2 136
Ambisonic Guitar System: *see* GASP: Guitars with Ambisonic Spatial Performance

Ambisonics 129
Ample Projects 277
Analogue Shift Register 162, 165
Anand, N. 291
Anthony, B. 30
anti-Semitism 242
Aphex Twin 376
apps and app-based music 77–78, *78*, 279–280; CopierMaschine 165–171; *Notes* 280; Soundpad 313, **315**, 316, 317
arousal potential 60–61, 65, 67
arrangements 7
arranging, Motormouth project 63
Arrau, C. 356
art: hacking as 241–243; and politics 240–241
artificial intelligence 282–283, 284, 285, 372, 382
Artism Ensemble project 219, 223, 224
artist and repertoire (A&R) executives 417, 418
artist development 414–427, 439–440; artists' perspectives 422–424; business involvement 417; contests and talent shows 414, 417–427; current situation 416–417; entrepreneurs' perspectives 424–425; and exposure 414; flaws 416–417; motivation 416; predisposition 416; process 414, 415; psychosocial skills 415, 426; Schoolwide Enrichment Model 415, 426; theoretical background 415–416
artistic identity 258
Art of Noise 61
Arts Council England 433, 440
assemblages 184–185

445

attachment 260–271; audience engagement 263–265; emotionally rooted interaction 265–268; Emotional Memory Impact Groups 262–263, 270–271; fan engagement 268–269, 269–271; narrative anchoring 263; recipient-complemented content 260–262; supporting media techniques 265–268, 270–271
attitudinal enhancement 60–61
audience: attachment 260–262; collectivity 265; composer collaboration 331–340; and electronic music visuals 375–376; emotional attachment 262–263; emotionally rooted interaction 265–268; Emotional Memory Impact Groups 270–271; feedback 339; interaction categories 331; mental wellbeing 261; performative actions 267; recipient-complemented content 260–262; visual information 370
audience engagement 263–265, 268–269, 269–270
audience experience 252
audience participation: audience-performer agency 316–317, **316**, **317**; data and data analysis 320–327, *326*; *Deeper Love* 306, 309–311, **309**, **310**, *310*; design and implementation 309–311, **309**, **310**, *311*; as digital collaborators 306–328; future work 327–328; interactive 278–280; methods 308; performance protocols 319–320; ranks of 307; research performances 308; *The Singularity* 309, 310, 311, 312, 319–320, 327; technical infrastructure 312–314, **312**, **313**, **314**, **315**, 316–319, **316**, **317**, **318**; thematic analysis *326*
audience-performer agency 316–317, **316**, **317**
audience responses, live electronic music performance techniques 256–257
Audinate 89, 91, 95, 104
Audinate Brooklyn II Dante 97–98
audio description 195
audio plugins 24
audio processors 114–115, **114**
audio-visual conditioning 64–65
auditioning 422
auditory perception, visual cues 370

Augmented Musical Instruments (#MIs) 146; aural invasiveness. 147; background 148–149; control precision 157–158; effects 151; evaluation 153–158, **154**, *154*; feel 155–156; freedom of playing 147; future development 158–159; gestural controllers 146; gestural data mapping 149–150, 150–153; instrument choice 147–148; interface comparison 153–154, **154**; interface ranking 154–155, *154*; invasiveness 156, 159–160; learning curve 147, *153*, 154–155, 156, 156–157; methodology 152–153, **152**, **153**; and pianistic virtuosity 146–160; Reach system 146, 149–150, **149**; software 159; sound balancing 158; transparency 157; user testing **150**, **152**, **153**; user testing limitations 158
augmented reality 280–281, 284, 285
Austin, Dallas 23
Australia 434
Austrian Research Institute for Artificial Intelligence 283
authenticity 25; electronic music performance techniques 249, 249–250
A Wizard, A True Star (Rundgren) 73

Badfinger, *Straight Up* 71
Baird, P 435
Bakan, M. 219
Baker, Fred T. 139–140
bansuri flutes 8–10
Barad, K. 389–401
Barrett, N. 177
Bat Out of Hell (Meat Loaf) 71–72, 73
Bauman, Z. 290
BBC Music 276
BBC Philharmonic 280
beat-consecutive codewords 404–405, **406**
beat-making 38
Becker, Walter 7
Beck, Jeff 83
Begany, G. M. 91, 100, 103
Benjamin, W. 267
Bennett, J. 184, 185, 188, 189
bereavement 206–207, 217
Berlin 432
Berlyne, D. E. 56, 60, 61
Bhamra, Kuljit 4–6, **5**; bansuri flute edit process 10–11; bansuri flute recordings

Index

8–10; final mix 14–15; harmonica session 11–12; overdubbing additional guitars 11; review session 12–14; studio 6; studio recordings 6–8
big data 403
BigHit Entertainment 261
BIGmack 222
Biophilia (Björk) 77–78, 82
Björk 376; *Biophilia* 77–78, 82
blackmail 236, 238, 238–239
Bloom, B. 417, 426
Bloom, Harold 76
Blue Ripple 136
bodies, primacy of 178–179
body awareness 356, 361–363, **361**, **362**, **363**
body posture 356
body work 178
Bohemian Rhapsody (film) 12
Bohr, N. 392, 393–394, 398
Bomb Squad, The 80
Bonenfant, Y. 216
Bonobo 379
Brackett, D. 25
Braga, Alex 282–283
Branch, Alan 115, 116, 119
branding 338, 379–381, **380**
Brauer, Michael 27, *28–29*, 30–32, *31*
Braun-Thürmann, H. 291
Brazil, E. 197
Breel, A 320–321
Brentschneider, F. 377
Brisbane 434
British Paraorchestra 273
Bromham, B. 24
Bromham, Gary 115, 116–117, 119
Brown, Ross 189
Brubaker J.R. 206
Brunvoll, Mari Kvien 175
BTS 260–271; audience engagement 263–265; emotionally rooted interaction 265–268; Emotional Memory Impact Groups 262–263, 270–271; fan engagement 268–269, 269–271; narrative anchoring 263; performative strategies 263–264; pop-up store 268; recipient-complemented content 260–262; "Speak Yourself" tour 263–265, 269–270; supporting media techniques 265–268, 270–271
Bussy, P. 248
Butler, J. 393

Cage, John 331
Campbell, Bill 115, 118, 119–120
Canada 434
Carboni, M. 284
Carot, A. 89, 91
Carter, D. 17, 23, 25–26
Caruso, G. 356, 366
Caudell, Tom 280–281
Chafe, C. 91
Chafe, Chris 90
Chion, Michel 190, 191, 192, 202
Christian, Robin 9–10
chromaticism 408, 411
chroma vectors 404
Churches, Tim 165
Ciani, Suzanne 168
Ciciliani, M. 208
City Region Music Boards 432
classical art-music, Germany 290–302; free ensembles 290, 291, 293–302; orchestra scene 292–293; presumed crisis 290, 290–291, 296; small (chamber) orchestras 290, 291, 293, 296–297, 301; theoretical framework 291–292
Classical Concept of the Future 298–299
classical music, live: and artificial intelligence 282–283, 284, 285; augmented reality 280–281, 284, 285; contemporary practices 274–283; and electronic music 275–276; incorporating digital technologies 273–285; mixed reality visual displays 280–282; and mobile devices 278–280; and video projections 277–278; virtual reality 281–282, 284, 285
Clearmountain, Bob 80–81
Cloud Booths 91
cloud, the 90
CNN 412
Coffey, A. J. 313–314
collaboration 345–353; composer-audience 331–340; composer-performer 342–353; creative 175; cultural 11; data analysis 353; discussions **345**, **346**, **352**, 353; importance 26; Internet of Things music system and 119; long-distance 89–104; New Instrument 342–353; power struggles 13–14; problem-solving 346–347; remote 10–11; role of the performer 345, 349–350; and sonic signatures 17, 25–26; typology 343

collaborative emergence 320
Collier, Jacob 332, 333–335, 335–340, *335*
Collins, Karen 190, 191
Collins, Phil 64
Collins, S. 419
Comix 378–379
commercial viability 12–14
communication 8
complementarity 393–395, 397
Complete Music Update 435–436
composer-audience collaboration 331–340; Collier 332, 333–335, 335–340, *335*; comments 336; conversational 339; creativity 337–338; crowdfunding 333; educational/technical 336; feedback 339; hardware and software 336–337; Huang 332, 332–333, 335–340; methodology 337; musical 338–339; personality 338; visual interface 335–336
composer-performer collaboration 342–353; data analysis 344, 353; discussions 345–353, **345**, **346**, **352**, 353; problem-solving 346–347; role of the performer 345, 349–350; typology 343
compositional aesthetics 177
compositional affordances 57
composition, structuring 7
compression 74
computer crime: *see* security engineering
concerts: rituals 298; traditional 297
contests and talent shows 414, 417–427; age threshold 424; artist respondents 420; artists' perspectives 422–424; auditioning 422; business aspects 423; business case 418, 425, 426–427; challenges 424; concept 418; contestants' career failure 423; data analysis 421–422, 422–427; entrepreneur respondents 420; entrepreneurs' perspectives 424–425; expectations 422; future of 425, 427; impacts 422–423; importance 423, 425–426; interviews 420–421; methodology 419–422; role 417–418, 424, 425–426, 427; sampling 419–420; success 418–419
context 61, 67
convolutional neural networks 411–412
Cooke 371

Cook, Perry 279
CopierMaschine app 165–166; performance approaches 167–171; USP 170
copyright 237, 243
Correia, N.N. 371
CoSiMa 328
Costa, Chris 334
Cote, R. 352
Country & Eastern (album): arrangements 7; bansuri flute edit process 10–11; bansuri flute recordings 8–10; final mix 14–15; harmonica session 11–12; inclusion of an engineer 8; jam session 6; notepad 4–5; origins 4–6; overdubbing additional guitars 11; repairs 7; review session 12–14; studio recordings 6–8; and trust 5, 10–11, 11
country music 25, 434–435
Court, H. 195
Covach, John 19
Cowell, Simon 417–418
Craig, Carl 276
Crawford, G. 284
Creative and Cultural Economy 433–434
creative change, typology 343
creative collaboration 175
creative ownership 26
creative process, and cultural differences 3
creative thought 346–347
creativity 117–118, 121, 337–338; distributed 320; quantum theory of 389–401
creativity triggers 342–353
critical race theory 40
cross-sensory concepts 377–378, **378**
crowdfunding 333
crowd-sourced music 332
cultural assimilation 11
cultural collaboration 11
cultural differences: and the creative process 3; mediation 3–15
cultural identity 241
cultural influences 4
cultural integrity 11
cultural manipulation 235
cultural policies, Germany 290–291
cultural transference, mediation 3–15
cultural values: consensus 4; friction 4; mediation 3–15; power struggle over 13–14

Index

culture 432; production of 291
culture strategy 432–433
Culver, Max 188
Cunningham, M. 248
CuteCircuit 372
cyber security: *see* security engineering
cyber-threats 235–237

Dadaism 56
Daedelus 248
Dallali, Dominic 140
Dante Audio Over IP 89, 91, 103–104; Grandmaster Clock 94, 96; single subnet system 93–94, **93**; two subnet system 94, **95**; two zone system 95–97, **96**
Dante Domain Manager 93, 94, 95, **95**, **96**, 97–98; two zone system 102
Darlington, A 248
data value 238
Davis, R. 17, 26, 30
Deadmau5 380
DeepDream 412
Deeper Love 306; Ableton Live session 312, **312**; audience-performer agency 316–317, **316**; compositional construction 309–311; data and data analysis 320–327, *326*; Dorian mode **309**; Double Bass Ostinato **309**; interviews 325–327; lead performer 319; performance protocols 319–320; performance rig 313, **313**; performances 317–319, **318**, 321–322, **322**; questionnaire 323–325, *323*; Sonic Element Control *311*; Soundpad App 313, **315**, 316, 317; structure *310*; technical infrastructure 312–314, **312**, **313**, **314**, **315**, 316–319, **316**, **317**, **318**; thematic analysis *326*; vocal melody **310**; WiiMote controllers 313, **314**
Deleuze, G. 184
Depeche Mode 376
Derby, University of 125
Derek and the Dominos 65
Dewey, J. 346
DeZutter, S. 320
dialogue 191
diffraction 391–393
digital collaboration, audience 306–328; audience-performer agency 316–317, **316**, **317**; data and data analysis 320–327, *326*; *Deeper Love* 306, 309–311, **309**, **310**, *310*; design and implementation 309–311, **309**, **310**, *311*; future work 327–328; methods 308; performance protocols 319–320; ranks of 307; research performances 308; *The Singularity* 309, 310, 311, 312, 319–320, 327; technical infrastructure 312–314, **312**, **313**, **314**, **315**, 316–319, **316**, **317**, **318**; thematic analysis *326*
Digital Musical Instrument 147
Digital Projection Mapping 277–278
digital security: *see* security engineering
digital technologies: artificial intelligence 282–283, 284, 285; augmented reality 280–281, 284, 285; categories 273; contemporary classical music practices 274–283; costs 284–285; electronic music 275–276; incorporating 273–285; mixed reality visual displays 280–282; mobile devices 278–280; use 273; video projections 277–278; virtual reality 281–282, 284, 285
dimensionality 146
disabled users, design approaches 219–220; *see also* sonic-play instruments
disclosure 240
disco music 25
Disney 239–240
dispensable celebrities 419
distributed creativity 320
distributed music 307–308
DJing 248
Docherty, Harry 102–103
Dowling, Patrick 165
Drettakis, G. 189
Drucker, P. 291
drum sequencer 250–251
drum sounds, sonic recontextualization 63
Dudek, S.Z. 352

economic value, music 433
editing 7, 336
editorial control 10–11
Eigler, D. 396
Eilish, Billie 378
Eimert, Herbert 275
Ek, Daniel 403
ELAN 365, **366**, 367
Electra, Dorian 380
Electro Continuo approach 172
electronic music 275–276, 370

electronic music performance techniques 247–258; audience experience 252; audience responses 256–257; authenticity 249, 249–250; background 248–249; challenge 247; DJing 248; drum sequencer 250–251; further research 258; live 247–258; loop sequencer 251–254, **253**, *254*, **255**, 257; methodologies 248–249; on-stage aesthetics 255–256, **255**; performance system 249–250; personal perspective 257–258; touch screen controller 251

electronic music visuals 370–383; affective power 375; amplification of performance parameters 375–376, **376**; audience and 375–376; as branding tool 379–381, **380**; challenges 381–382, 382–383; creation 371–372, 382; cross-sensory concepts 377–378, **378**; literature review 371; MIDI controller setup **374**; narrative context 378–379, 382; Nyokeë case study 372–373, **373**, **374**, 375, 376, 378, **378**, 379, **380**, 381; play back 372, 382; relationship to audio 375–381, **377**, **378**, **380**, 382; stem mixing approach 373, **374**

Elektronische Musik 275

emotional attachment 262–263

emotionally rooted interaction, supporting media techniques 265–268

Emotional Memory Impact Groups 262–263, 270–271

emotional response 216

empirical semiotics 375

EnCue app 280

engineers 8, 9, 18; signature 22, 32–33; test mixes phase 30–32, *31*; training 27–32; video tutorials analysis 27, *28–29*

enhanced CDs 76–77, *77*

ensemble reflector 295–296, 299–300

Ensemble Resonanz 295, 298, 299

entanglement 391–393, 398, 399

environment 45

equalization 336

equipment, sonic identity 17, 19–21

Essl, G. 148

European Union, Article 13 237

Evans, Matthew D.F. 206–207, 210, 214, 216, 217

Everhart, D. 91

experimentation 349
exposure 414
expression, freedom of 9
exteriority 399–400
extramusical gestures 147
EyeSupply 380

Facebook 206–207, 281
Fagan, Donald 7
Fairlight CMI 61
Faithful (Rundgren) 73–74
Faithless 249
fake news 235
familiarity 60–61, 65, 66, 67
Fancafe 261
fan-created content 261
fans: attachment 260–271; audience engagement 263–265; collective experience 264; collectivity 265; emotionally rooted interaction 265–268; Emotional Memory Impact Groups 262–263, 270–271; engagement 268–269, 269–271; mental wellbeing 261; recipient-complemented content 260–262; self-affirmation 265–266
Farinella, D.J. 9
Farnell, A. 189, 202
Feitis. R. 178
Felbick, L. 293
Ferguson, P. 92–93, 95
Ferneyhough, B. 343
Fernström, M. 197
Ferreira, P. 252
field recordings: potential for 58; recontextualization of 56–67
first order surrogacy 65
Fisher, M. 84
Fisher, T. 284
Fitch, F.J. 345, 349–350
Focusrite 103
Focusrite Rednet 104
Foley sound 191
Forman, M. 419
Fortune Magazine 241
Foucault, M. 393
freedom 72, 300
free ensembles 290, 291, 293–296, 300; concert venues 299; number 293–294; performative practices 296–302; repertoire 297–298
freeform jamming 164
Freeman, J. 307, 317, 327, 328, 331

Index

Friday (Jonesy in the Jag) (Motormouth project) 57
Frid, E. 220, 227
Frith, S. 379
Fry, G. 190
Fuller, Simon 418

Gabriel, Peter, *MusicTiles* 77, 82
game industry, security engineering 239
game music 78
Garces-Bacsal, R.M. 416
Gardner, Eric 75
GASP Auditory Scenes 137
GASP: Guitars with Ambisonic Spatial Performance 125–142; Ambisonic send effects 135–136; arpeggiation 135, **136**; Auditory Scenes 137; directivity pattern vs distance control 131–132, **132**; encoding equations 132, *133*; expansion to 3D 141; frequency band splitting 142; gain versus angle plots 134, **134**; guitars 127–129; hardware 126, **126**; key features 126–127, **127**, **128**; lab interconnections **128**; live performance control 142; playback modes 129; post-production reflections 139–141; Signal Flow Overview **127**; signal processing elements 130; spatialisation 129–131, **130**, 134–135, **135**; Spread, Angle, Distance effects and control 138, **139**; system control 136–138, **137**; system detail 126–138, **127**, **128**, **130**, **132**, *133*, **134**, **135**, **136**, **137**, **139**; system overview 125–126; system rationalisation 141; timbralisation 131–132, **132**, *133*, 134–135, **134**, **135**
genre, stylistic influences 24–25
geographical barriers: breaking 89–104; context 90–91; dual stream approach 92–93, **92**; erasing 100; single subnet Dante system 93–94, **93**; two subnet Dante system 94; two zone Dante system 95–97, **96**
Germany 291–292; classical art-music 290–302; cultural policies 290–291; free ensembles 290, 291, 293–302; orchestra scene 292–293, 301; presumed crisis 290, 290–291, 296; small (chamber) orchestras 290, 291, 293, 296–297
Gerzon, Michael 129
gestures and gestural analysis 361–363, **361**, **362**, **363**, 367: mapping 149–150; monitoring 356–357; user testing 150–153
gestural controllers 146
Gibson, D. 42
Gibson, M. 206–207
Gillespie, M. 17, 22
GitHub 165
Glass, Phillip, *REWORK_* 77, 82
Glory Days (Motormouth project) 57
Gogerly, Simon 115, 117, 119–120, 120
Goldberg, David 40–41
Golden, E. 249
Gottinger, B. 17, 19–20, 20, 21, 22
Gow, J. 375
Great Britain, alternative classical music scene 293
Green, D. 189
Grokgazer 80
grounded theory 421–422
Guattari, F. 184
GuitArpeggiator 135, **136**
Gurevich, M. 91

hacking 235, 241–243
hacktivism 236, 242
Hallyu 3.0 260–262, 270
haptic experiences 209
haptic feedback 210, 216
Harding, P. 32
hardware 89, 116, 121; accessibility 107, 116–117; Ambisonic Guitar System 126, **126**; composer-audience collaboration 336–337
harmonic distortion 19
Harrison, Jerry 80–81, 182, 183, 186
"Hearing Loss / Cold Atlantic" (Wynne) 215, 216
hegemony 9
Herbert, Matthew 56, 58, 64
Heyde, N. 343, 345, 349–350
Hip Hop 24–25, 37–53, 79–80; analysis problems 39; literature review 39–41; meta levels 44; mix perspective 42; phonographic otherness 41–46, **45**, *47–48*, **49**, 50–52, *52*; poetic-aesthetic issues 37–38; production 46; sample-based aesthetic 52–53; sonics-feeling-output triangle 38; source material 37–38
Hislop, I. 242
Hitters, E. 432
Hodgson, J. 22

Hödl, O. 328, 331
Hooley, Jack 140
Houston Symphony Orchestra 282
Howaldt, J. 291
Howlett, M. 17, 23, 23–24, 26
Huang, Andrew 332, 332–333, 335–340
Huart, Warren 20

Ideas of Noise installation 230–231
ideasthesia 377
idol-factory phenomenon 261–262
image: mapping to sound 208–209; and sound 190, 192, 210, 213
Inception 412
indeterminacy 393–395
influence agents 235
information warfare 240–241
Initiation (Rundgren) 74
innovation: approach to 70–86; dialectics of 301; theoretical framework 291–292
Innovation In Music Conference 89
Instagram 339
interaction styles, sonic-play instruments 226–227
interactive art *see A–D-S-R* installation
interactive music 70, 306–328; audience-performer agency 316–317, **316**, **317**; categories 76; data and data analysis 320–327, *326*; *Deeper Love* 306, 309–311, **309**, **310**, *310*; definition 306; design and implementation 309–311, **309**, **310**, *311*; future work 327–328; history 76–79, *77*, *78*; listener control 81–82; methods 308; *No World Order* (Rundgren) 79, 79–86; performance protocols 319–320; ranks of 307; research performances 308; *The Singularity* 309, 310, 311, 312, 319–320, 327; technical infrastructure 312–314, **312**, **313**, **314**, **315**, 316–319, **316**, **317**, **318**; thematic analysis *326*
Interactive (Prince) 77
INTERIOR 188, 195–201, **198**, **199**, **200**, 201–202, **201**
internal-externality 390
"Internal Garden" (Wiggan) 209
Internet of Things 106
Internet of Things music system 106–121; and accessibility 115–116, **115**, 116–117; availability 120; background 106–107; collaboration and 119; creative benefits 117–118, 121; cultural benefits 118–119, 121; development 108, **108**, 109–111, **110**, **111**; educational benefits 119–120; and engagement 116–117; enterprise benefits 119; hardware/software appreciation 116; methodology 108, **108**; music production concept 109, **109**; processing techniques 109–111; processing tools 114–115, **114**; producer evaluations 111–120, **113**, **114**, **115**; production environment 113–114, **113**; reliability concerns 120; research aims 107; research questions 107–108; resource limitations 120; viability 121; workflows 117
Internet Service Providers 237
internet, the 237, 298–299, 332; fan-created content 261
intertextuality 73–74
intra-action 398–400
invisible producer, the 23
IPEM, Institute of Psychoacoustic and Electronic Music 356, 357
Izhaki, R. 18

Jack-Trip 91
Jacobsen, H. 291
Jaëll, M.T. 356
Jamboree (Griffiths) 230
jam sessions 6
Jarre, Jean Michel 248
Jarrett, M. 23
Jay-Z, *Magna Carta* 77
Jehan, T. 407
Jitter 372
Johannes Kepler University 283
John Deere 242
Jones, C. 247, 248
Jones, Netia 277
junge norddeutsche philharmonie 296, 299
Juniu, S. 416

Kajikawa, Loren 40
Karttunen, A. 349–350
Kawakami, Fukushi 162
K/DA 380
Keith, C., Keith, C. 109
Kent, University of 4
keyboard interfaces 146, 148–149

Kim, Y. 260
Kirn, P. 250
Knapp, B. 196
Kobayashi, R. 208
Konzerthausorchester Berlin 282
Kopp, B. 84
K-pop 260–262, 260–271; audience engagement 263–265; emotionally rooted interaction 265–268; Emotional Memory Impact Groups 262–263, 270–271; fan engagement 268–269, 269–271; performative strategies 263–264; queuing 265; recipient-complemented content 260–262; supporting media techniques 265–268, 270–271
Kraft, Robert 86
Kraftwerk 248
Krims, Adam 40
Kubiak, Agata 342–353
Kulturorchester 293, 300

Lacey, L. 106
Laikipia 379
laptops 370
Laruelle, F. 391, 395
Launchpad Project 440–441, 441–442
Law, J. 184
layering 336
Leeds City Council 433, 433–434
Leeds music economy 432–442; accessibility 439; Artist Business Services 436; benefits 439; challenges 441; City Music Forum 441, 442; City-Wide Strategy 442; context 433–435; core areas of activity 433; Creative and Cultural Economy 433–434; culture strategy 432–433; engagement 437–439; influencing 439–441; Launchpad Project 440–441, 441–442; mapping 435–436, 441; Music:Leeds 433, 436–437, 437–439, 439–441, 441–442; policies 433–434
Lee, S. 317, 327, 328
Leslie, Donald 176
Levine, Aaron David 80, 81
Levine, Larry 22
Levin, Golan 279, 307, 328
Lightman, Richard **5**; bansuri flute edit process 10–11; bansuri flute recordings 8–10; final mix 14–15; harmonica session 11–12; overdubbing additional guitars 11; review session 12–14; studio recordings 6–8
Liljedahl, Mats 190, 191
limitations 85–86
Linear Feedback Shift Register 165–166
liquid orchestras 290, 292
listening 44–45; idealised 176; primacy of 298; tactile 178
listener control 81–82
live electronic music performance techniques 247–258; audience experience 252; audience responses 256–257; authenticity 249, 249–250; background 248–249; DJing 248; drum sequencer 250–251; further research 258; loop sequencer 251–254, **253**, *254*, **255**, 257; methodologies 248–249; on-stage aesthetics 255–256, **255**; performance system 249–250; personal perspective 257–258; touch screen controller 251
LiveNote app 279
livestreaming 334–335, 335, *335*, 336, 338, 339
Living Sound Pictures 213
local authorities 432
locatedness 401
LOLA 91, 92, **92**, 95
London Contemporary Music Festival 293
London Contemporary Orchestra 283, 284
London Symphony Orchestra 284
Long Way to Grandma's (Motormouth project) 57, 58
loop points 250–251
loop sequencer 251–254, **253**, *254*, **255**, 257
Lord-Alge, Chris 20, 27, *28–29*, 30–32, *31*
Los Angeles Philharmonic 277
loudspeakers and loudspeaker design 20; accuracy 176; aesthetic-causal alliance 186; as an assemblage 184–185; and compositional aesthetics 177; cone-less speaker drivers 179–180, **180**; cone-less speaker transducers 175; context 176–178; diaphragm characteristics 181; diffusers 176; materials 179; and post-acousmatic composition 175–186; and

post-acousmatic compositional approach 178–179; RayGun 195; *Speaker Park* designs 179–181, **180**; *Speaker Park* spatial strategy 181–184, **182**

machine learning 148, 403–412; accuracy 411; background 404–406; beat-consecutive codewords 404–405, **406**; chroma vectors 404; codewords 408–411, 412; codeword transition relationships 404–405; convolutional neural networks 411–412; data processing 406–408; future research 411–412; mood classification 408–411, **410**, 411, **411**, 412; pitch transition networks 409, **410**, **411**; pitch vectors 403; shortcomings 405–406, **406**; testing and results 408, **409**; thresholding operation 404–405; threshold levels 408; training data 407
McLardy, Jamie 103
McPherson, A. 146
McRobbie, A, 301
Macy, A. 379
Maeterlinck, Maurice 195, 196–197, 200
Magna Carta (Jay-Z) 77
Malcolm, Calum 90
malleability, sound 189
Mandelson, Ben 5
mark-making 396
Marl, Marley 38
Marshall, Wayne 38
Massey, H. 9
Matthews, K. 209
Max/MSP 372
meaning-making 396
measurement, and quantum theory 394–395, 395–398
Meat Loaf, *Bat Out of Hell* 71–72, 73
mediation 3–15; Country & Eastern (album) 5–15; producers 3–15
Meillassoux, Q. 390
Menger, P.-M. 301
mentorship: mentor choice 27; practice-based approach 18, 27–32, 32–33; study methodologies 18; test mixes phase 30–32, *31*; video tutorials analysis 27, *28–29*
merchandise 264–265, 268
meta-music 37, 40
metric displacement 311
microphones 21

Miku, Hatsune 380
The Million Song Dataset 403, 404, 407
Mills, Jeff 276
miming 64–65
mirroring technology 355–367; 3-D models 355; art-science approach 366–367; audio analysis 363–364, **364**, **365**; development 356–357; gestural analysis 361–363, **361**, **362**, **363**, 367; gesture monitoring 356–357; methodology 356, 358–360, **359**, **361**; motion-capture 355–363, **359**, **361**, **362**, **363**; qualitative and quantitative analysis integration 365, **366**; quantitative data 357–358, 367
Mitchell, Joni 71
mixers, stylistic influences 24–25
mixing: actor-network theory 20–21; audio plugins 24; processes 30–32, *31*; and sonic signatures 18, 20–21, 22; task 18; templates 32; top down 32
mixMacros 32
mobile devices 278–280
Moby 249
Moditone 372
modular synthesizers 337
Moir, Zack 90, 92–93, 103
Monahan, Gordon 177
Montpellier Philharmonic Orchestra 276
moods 403, 404, 407, 408–411, **410**, 411, **411**, 412
Moore, A. 20, 25
Moriarty, S.E. 346
Morton, T. 392
Morton, Timothy 181
motion-capture 355–363; 3-D model 355; advantages 357; avatar **361**, **362**, **362**; challenges 361–362; gestural analysis 361–363, **361**, **362**, **363**; markers 358–359, **359**, 361–362, 363, **363**; methodology 356, 358–360, **359**, **361**; quantitative data 357–358
motivation 3–4, 416
Motormouth project 56–67; analysis 65–67; arranging 63; background 57–58; cars 57; drum sounds 63; *Long Way to Grandma's* 58; mixing and production 63–64; noise into music 58–62; novelty factor 56–57, 64–65; *Playing Tonight* 58, 65–67; raw material 61; sonic cartooning 64, 65, 66, 67; synth sounds 62–63

Mudede, Charles 37, 44
multisensory experience 206–217
Multi-Story Orchestra 293
Mumford, M.D. 345
music: economic value 433; role of 270
Musica Elettronica Viva 307
musical borrowing 39
musical creativity: agential realist model 400; conceptual landscape 389; entanglement and diffraction 391–393; indeterminacy and complementarity 393–395; internal-externality 390; quantum theory of 389–401
musical datasets 403, 404
Musical Instrument Digital Interface 147
musical style 17
Music Cities: *see* Leeds music economy
music economy: accessibility 439; Artist Business Services 436; benefits 439; challenges 441; context 433–435; core areas of activity 433; Creative and Cultural Economy 433–434; culture strategy 432–433; engagement 437–439; influencing 439–441; Leeds 432–442; mapping 435–436, 441; policies 433–434; support 433, 436–437
musicking 220–221
Music: Leeds 433, 436–437; activity 442; City-Wide Strategy 442; engagement 437–439; influence 439–441; Launchpad Project 440–441, 441–442; strategic engagement 440
music performance analysis: art-science approach 366–367; audio analysis 363–364, **364**, **365**; body awareness 361–363, **361**, **362**, **363**; development 356–357; digitization 355; empirical approach 356; gestural analysis 361–363, **361**, **362**, **363**, 367; gesture monitoring 356–357; methodology 356, 358–360, **359**, **361**; mirroring technology 355–367; motion-capture 355–363, **359**, **361**, **362**, **363**; narrative self-descriptions 355, 358; performer-based analysis method 366; qualitative and quantitative analysis integration 365, **366**; quantitative data 357–358, 367; thinking aloud procedure 359
music production: context 90–91; definition 91; environment 113–114, **113**; Internet of Things concept 109, **109**; Internet of Things music system

development 109–111, **110**, **111**; long-distance 89–104
music sector, support 436–437
Music Tech Fest 307–308
music technology, accessible design 219–232; challenge of 220; child-led 220, 221, 224; constraints 224–227, **225**; openness 222–224, **223**; sensor choice 223–224, **223**; testing 221
MusicTiles (Gabriel) 77, 82
music videos 375
Musii 228
musique concrète 57, 79, 177, 275

Nack, Estee 43
narrative anchoring 263
narrative context, electronic music visuals 378–379, 382
Nashville 21, 434–435
National Lottery 440
Negarestani, R. 391
Netsky 249
networked music performance 89–104; audio stream 91; benefits 90; Cloud Booths 91, 100–101, **101**, 102, 103; commercial 90; context 90–91; device synchronisation **98**, 99; dual stream approach 92–93, **92**; Grandmaster Clock 94; Ground Control 100–101, **101**; hardware and software 89; Local Area Network 100; local subnets 93; network connection 97, 97–98; network jitter 97, 98–99; shared headspace 100; single subnet Dante system 93–94, **93**; terminology 100–102; two subnet Dante system **95**; two zone Dante system 95–97, **96**, 102; virtual space 100–102, **101**; Voice Over IP 91; Wide Area Network 100
New Instrument collaboration 342–353; background 342–344; data analysis 344, 353; demonstrations 352; discussions 345–353, **345**, **346**, **352**, 353; experimentation 349; key element 344; presence of the composer 351; role of the performer 349–350
Newman, N. 242
Nikolić, Danko 377
Nil, B. 191–192
Nilsson, M. 197
noise: arousal potential 60–61; context 61; definition 58–59; familiarity 60–61; into

music 58–62, 67; repetition theory 60; repurposed 56; sampling 59–60
nostalgia 118
Notes app 280
No World Order (Rundgren) 70, 79, 79–86; achievement 83–85; influences 79–80; lessons from 85–86; listener control 81–82; musical fragments 80–81; music collage 73; producers mixes 80–81; programming 80; reaction to 82–83; release 70; themes 79
Nyokeë 372–373, **373**, **374**, 375, 376, 378, **378**, 379, **380**, 381

Oakland Symphony 281, 285
objectives, producers 5
objectivity 398–399, 399
Olowe, I. 372
Olszewski-Kubilius, P. 415
on-screen visuals, electronic music 370–383; affective power 375; amplification of performance parameters 375–376, **376**; audience and 375–376; as branding tool 379–381, **380**; challenges 381–382, 382–383; creation 371, 382; cross-sensory concepts 377–378, **378**; literature review 371; MIDI controller setup **374**; narrative context 378–379, 382; Nyokeë case study 372–373, **373**, **374**, 375, 376, 378, **378**, 379, **380**, 381; play back 372, 382; relationship to audio 375–381, **377**, **378**, **380**, 382; stem mixing approach 373, **374**; video mixing 371
on-stage aesthetics, electronic music performance techniques 255–256, **255**
Orchester im Treppenhaus 295, 299
originality 352
otherness 52; definition 43–46; featuring 46, *47–48*, **49**, 50–51, *51*
ownership 17, 26

Pamyu, Kyarie Pamyu 379
participatory action research 320
Paterson, J. 20–21, 32, 76, 308
Paul, Les 83
Paxman, Mike 9–10
P.C.C.O.M. Manifesto (Herbert) 58
peer-to-peer information sharing 237
people, sonic signatures of 22–23
Perez-Lopez, A. 125
performance approaches, Shift Registers 167–171
performance efficiency 367
performance parameters, amplification of 375–376, **376**
performance techniques, electronic music 247–258; audience experience 252; audience responses 256–257; authenticity 249, 249–250; background 248–249; challenge 247; DJing 248; drum sequencer 250–251; further research 258; live 247–258; loop sequencer 251–254, **253**, *254*, **255**, 257; methodologies 248–249; on-stage aesthetics 255–256, **255**; performance system 249–250; personal perspective 257–258; touch screen controller 251
performer-based analysis method 366
Perini, A. 209
Perry, Katy 376
personal brand 338
personality 338
Petersen, S. 416
Peterson, R.A. 291
Philadelphia Orchestra 279
Phillips Research Labs BBD 162–163
phonographic otherness 52; definition 43–46; featuring 46, *47–48*, **49**, 50–51, *51*; hearing 41–43; mix perspective 42; sample characteristics 51, *51*
phonographic sound 37–38
photo-fiction 391
photographs and photography: contextual information 213; future developments 217; haptic feedback 206, 210; image-to-sound process 211–213, **211**; mapping to sound 208–209; multisensory experience 206–217; power 206; promise of 207; raster scanning 213; sonification 206, 207, 208–209; vibrotactile experiences 209
Photosounder 208
PiaF 148
pianistic virtuosity: and Augmented Musical Instruments (#MIs) 146–160; aural invasiveness. 147, 148–149; control precision 157–158; effects 151; evaluation 153–158, **154**, *154*; feel 155–156; freedom of playing 147; gestural data mapping 149–150, 150–153; instrument choice 147–148;

interface comparison 153–154, **154**;
interface ranking 154–155, *154*;
invasiveness 156, 159–160; learning
curve 147, *153*, 154–155, 156, 156–157;
methodology 152–153, **152**, **153**;
Reach system 146, 149–150, **149**;
sound balancing 158, 158–159; user
testing 146, **150**, **152**, **153**; user testing
limitations 158
Pickering M. 45
Pignato, J. M. 91, 100, 103
Pigott, Jon 175, 179–180
pitch shifting 336
pitch transition networks 409, **410**, **411**
pitch vectors 403
Planck, M. 401
playback loops 62–63
playing, freedom of 147
Playing Tonight (Motormouth project) 57,
58, 65–67
politics, and art 240–241
post-acousmatic composition: approach
178–179; and loudspeaker design
175–186
post-acousmatic compositional approach
178–179
post-modern producers 118
power struggles 5, 13–14
pre-release ransom 237–238
Presley, Elvis 21
Preston, Leo 175
Prince, *Interactive* 77
Princeton Laptop Orchestra 279
Pritchard, S. 284
procedural audio, theatre: *see*
theatre, procedural audio
procedural generation 189–190
processing tools 114–115, **114**
producers: communication 8; consensus
4; Country & Eastern 5–15, **5**; cultural
influences 4; disagreements 7; friction
4; hegemony 9; hierarchical positioning
3; mediation 3–15; objectives 5; power
struggle 13–14; power struggles 5; role
10; sonic signatures 22–23; stresses
of recording 9–10; stylistic influences
24–25; and trust 5, 10–11, 11;
vision 10
producer's vision 10
production 46
production authorship, identifying 22–23
profitability 5, 243

prop sound 191–192, 195
Pro Tools Cloud Collaboration 92–93, **92**
PRS Foundation 433, 440
psychosocial skills 415, 426
Pullin, G. 219–220, 220
Pysiewicz, A. 142

Quadraphonics 129
quantization algorithms 166
quantum theory: and agency 400; agential
realist model 400; and apparatus
396–397; complementarity 393–395,
397; conceptual landscape 389;
diffraction 391–393; entanglement
391–393, 398, 399; exteriority 399–400;
indeterminacy 393–395; internal-
externality 390; intra-action 398–400;
and measurement 394–395, 395–398; of
musical creativity 389–401; objectivity
398–399, 399; spacetimemattering 393,
399; wave collapse 398–399; wave-
particle paradox 391–393
Queen 12
queuing 265

ransomware 238
rap music 40
Rappak, Roman 139
raster scanning 213
RayGun 188, 192–193, **193**, **194**, 195,
201–202
Reach system 146; aural invasiveness.
147, 148–149; control precision
157–158; effects 151; evaluation
153–158, **154**, *154*; feel 155–156;
freedom of playing 147; gestural data
mapping 149–150; instrument choice
147–148; interface comparison 153–154,
154; interface ranking 154–155, *154*;
invasiveness 156, 159–160; learning
curve 147, *153*, 154–155, 156,
156–157; methodology 152–153, **152**,
153; overview 149–150, **149**; sound
balancing 158, 158–159; user testing
146, 150–153, **150**, **152**, **153**; user
testing limitations 158
recipient-complemented content
260–262
recontextualization, of field recordings
56–67
recording medium, signal path to 20
recording, stresses of 9–10

recording studios: acoustic properties 17; and sonic signatures 21–22
Red Fort Studios 8
Redgate, C. 344
reflective analysis 12–14
reflective practice methods 355, 357–358
regional music strategy: Artist Business Services 436; benefits 439; challenges 441; context 433–435; core areas of activity 433; Creative and Cultural Economy 433–434; culture strategy 432–433; engagement 437–439; influencing 439–441; Leeds 432–442; mapping 435–436, 441; policies 433–434; support 433, 436–437
Reich, Steve 339
Reid Shippen, F. 27, *28–29*, 30–32, *31*
Reitzell, Todd 116, 117, 119
remote surrogacy 65, 67
Renzulli, J. 415, 417, 426
repetition theory 60
respect 14
Resurface Audio 103
*REWORK_* (Glass) 77, 82
Reynolds, S. 248
Robertson, Matt 376
rock music 25
Rogen, Seth 240
Rogers, P. 417
Rolf, Ida 178
Roma Tre University 282–283
Rose, Ethan 176
Rosenkransa, G. 308, 316
Rose, Tricia 39
Rosner, Tal 278
Rouzic, M. 208
Royal Philharmonic Orchestra 281–282
Rubenzer, R. 346
Rudimental. 249
Ruijgers, Carlo 380
Rundgren, Todd: achievement 83–85; approach to innovation 70–86; *A Capella* 73, 74; career 70–76, *72, 75*; *Faithful* 73–74; freedom 72; *Initiation* 74; innovations 73–76, *75*; intertextuality 73–74; musical style 71; *No World Order* 70, 73, 79, 79–86; *Runt* 73; *Second Wind* 74; *Something/Anything* 73, 74; *A Wizard, A True Star* 73
Runt (Rundgren) 73

Rushdie, Salman 241
Rzewski, F. 307

S&H function 163
Saario, Antti Sakari 175, 178, 181, 183
SadhuGold 41–43
Sahai, S. 189
sample-based practices 37–53, **45**, 59–60; literature review 39–41; meta levels 44; mix perspective 42; narrative/aesthetic 50–51; phonographic otherness 41–46, **45**, *47–48*, **49**, 50–52, *52*; phonographic sound 37–38; poetic-aesthetic issues 37–38; pragmatic 50–51; processing choices 50–51; production 46; sample layers 46, *47–48*, **49**, 50; sonics-feeling-output triangle 38; source material 37–38; typology 40
sample-creating 38
sample layers 46, *47–48*, **49**, 50
samplers 59
Sanglid, T. 56
Sawyer, R. 320
Sawyer, R. K. 26
"Scanline: fp" (Kobayashi) 208
scanline synthesis 208–209
Schaeffer, Pierre 57, 275
Schafer, Murray 331
Scheps, Andrew 27, *28–29*, 30–32, *31*
Schloss, Joseph 39–40, 52, 53
Schmidt Horning, S. 17, 21
Schoolwide Enrichment Model 415, 426
Schrader, Barry 162
Schrödinger's Cat 398
Schultz, R.L. 178
Scott, M. 435, 438
Seaboard 147, 148; control precision 157–158; evaluation 153–158, **154**, *154*; feel 155–156; interface comparison 153–154, **154**; interface ranking 154–155, *154*; invasiveness 156, 159–160; learning curve *153*, 154–155, 156, 156–157; sound balancing 158, 158–159; user testing 150–153; user testing limitations 158
Seay, T. 17, 19, 20, 21
second order surrogacy 65, 65–66
Second Wind (Rundgren) 74
security engineering 235–244; advance fee scammers 236; blackmail 236, 238, 238–239; cyber-threats 235–237; data value 238; deeper game 239–240;

disclosure 240; game industry 239; hacking 235, 241–243; historical errors 236–237; information warfare 240–241; perpetrators 235–236; and politics 240–241; pre-release ransom 237–238; ransomware 238; Stuxnet attack 236; unique issues 238–239; vulnerability 235, 235–236; watermarking technologies 238
self-reflection 11, 367
Serge Synthesizer System 162
Sermon, Eric 44
Serrà, J. 403, 403–404, 404, 405, 407
Sewell, A. 46
shared headspace 100
Shift Registers 162–173; analogue 162, 165; buffer length 166–167, 172–173; clock cycle 164; clock sources 171, 172; combinatorial approach use case 169–170, 172; control voltage (CV) tools 164; CopierMaschine app 165–166; design elements 166–167; flexibility 168; four voices use case 168–169; freeze function 166–167, 170, 172–173; gate sources 171; history 162–163; improvisation 168; Linear Feedback 165–166; logical-operator module 171; mixer levels 169; o_C module 165, 172; oscillators 169–170, 172; output 163–164; performance approaches 167–171, 172; performance kit list 167–168; plugins 162–173; probability module 171; quantization algorithms 166, 172; randomness 164; S&H function 163; scale mask 166; single oscillator with filter use case 170–171; trigger sources 171; variety 163–164
Shim, Ae-Gyung 261–262
Shocklee, Hank 37–38
signature sounds 19
Si-Hyuk, Bang 271
'Six Spiders' (Szafranski) 342–353; background 342–344, 344; data analysis 353; discussions 345–353, **345**, **346**, **352**, 353
Skidmore, Mat 116, 117
Skoog 222, 224
Skype 91, 102
Sletteland, Roar 175
Slonimsky, N. 166
small (chamber) orchestras 293, 296–297

Smalley, D. 56, 64–65, 178
smartphones 308
Smile 12
Smith, G. 92–93
social media 206–207, 269–270, 273
soft haptics 202
software 107, 116; composer-audience collaboration 336–337; INTERIOR 199, **200**
Something/Anything (Rundgren) 73, 74
song writing, improvising 162–173
"Sonic Bed London" (Matthews) 209
sonic cartooning 64, 65, 66, 67
sonic exploration 57
sonic identity 26; equipment 17, 19–21
sonic otherness, definition 43–46
sonic-play instruments 219–232; accessibility 229–230; application 230–231; challenge of 220; child-led sessions 220, 221, 224; constraints 224–227, **225**; cues 229; directionality 228, **229**; engagement 225–226; first prototype 220–221, **221**; interaction styles 226–227; layouts 224–225; medical biases 220; ongoing research 231, **231**; openness 222–224, **223**, 230, 231; output 225–226; playing styles 222, **223**; pre-configuration 226, 229–230; second prototype 221–222, **221**, 225–226, 227, 228, 229–230; sensor choice 223–224, **223**; sensory coherence 227–228, 231–232; testing 221, 225–226, 229; visual feedback 228
sonic recontextualization 56–67; analysis 65–67; arranging 63; cartooning 64, 65, 66, 67; drum sounds 63; mixing and production 63–64; noise into music 58–62; novelty factor 56–57, 64–65; raw material 62; synth sounds 62–63
sonic signatures 17–33, 45–46; audio plugins 24; and collaboration 17, 25–26; creation framework 27–32, *28*, *31*; definition 17–18, 19; equipment 17, 19–21; external factors 23–24, *26*, 32; importance 32; internal factors *26*, 32; literature review 17–18; and mentorship 32–33; mentorship phase 18, 27–32; and mixing 18, 20–21, 22, 25; and musical style 17; ownership 17, 26; of people 22–23; and recording studios 17,

21–22; study methodologies 18; stylistic influences 24–25; taxonomy 19–24
Sonic Visualizer 363, **364**, 367
sonification 206, 207, 208–209
Sony 235
Sony Pictures Hack, 2014 237, 240, 241
sound: acousmatic 190; ambient 192, 202; dialogue 191; film 190; and image 190, 192, 206–217, 210, 213; malleability 189; mapping image to 208–209; materiality 178; physicality of 175; scanline synthesis 208–209; spatialisation 177; in theatre 188–189, 190–192; video games 190; visualised 190
sound balance 158
sound effects (prop sounds) 191–192, 195
sound spatialisation 125
Sound Symphony (Independent Arts Projects) 230
Sound to Music project 219
source material, distortion 64
space: negotiating 8; possession of 6; understanding 125; use of 21–22
spacetimemattering 393, 399
spatialisation 177
spatialisation systems 125
Speaker Park project 175–186; aesthetic-causal alliance 186; as an assemblage 184–185; compositional intent 179; concert 175; context 176–178; creative collaboration 175; funding 175; loudspeaker design 179–181, **180**; post-acousmatic compositional approach 178–179; spatial strategy 181–184, **182**
specificity 401
Spector, Phil 22, 23, 74
spectromorphological gestural surrogacy 56, 64–65, 65–67
spectromorphology 178
Speculative Realism 390–391
Spotify 403, 406–407, 412
Staffel, Tim 12
staging, stylistic conventions 25
Stanford Mobile Phone Orchestra 279
Stang, D. J. 56, 60, 61
Staszak, J. F. 43
Steely Dan 7

Steenbrugge, Xander 372
STEGREIF.orchester 296, 297, 298, 298–299, 299
STEIM 343
stem mixing approach 373, **374**
Stockhausen, Karlheinz 275–276
Straight Up (Badfinger) 71
Strummi 224
stylistic influences, sonic signatures 24–25
SUBPAC 209–210, 211, 216
Surkov, Vladislav 240
surrogacy 65, 65–67
Sutherland, I. 281
Swift, Taylor 376
Sydney Symphony Orchestra 277
symbolic meaning 40
synesthetes 377
synthesisers 74
Szafranski, Bartosz 342–353

tactile listening 178
talent contests: *see* contests and talent shows
talent development: *see* artist development
Talent Development Partners 440
tape effects 73
taste 271
Taylor, B. 307–308
technological black box, the 184–185
theatre, procedural audio 188–202; ambient sound 192, 202; audio description 195; dialogue 191; future work 202; INTERIOR 188, 195–201, **198**, **199**, **200**, 201–202, **201**; limitations 201–202; localisation solution 195; music 192; procedural generation 189–190; RayGun 188, 192–193, **193**, **194**, 195, 201–202; sound 188–189; sound categorisation 190–192; sound effects (prop sounds) 191–192, 195
Theatres Trust 189
Théberge, P. 21, 57, 79
thinking aloud procedure 359
third order surrogacy 65, 66–67
Thomas, Marcel 281
Thomson, D. 415
Thorseth, Veronica 175
Tin Men and the Telephone 279
Tomorrowland 376

Index

Toronto 434
TouchKeys 148; control precision 157–158; evaluation 153–158, **154**, *154*; feel 155–156; interface comparison 153–154, **154**; interface ranking 154–155, *154*; invasiveness 156, 159–160; learning curve *153*, 154–155, 156, 156–157; sound balancing 158, 158–159; user testing 150–153; user testing limitations 158
touch screen controller 251
Toulson, R. 76
Trueman, Dan 279
Trump, Donald 242
trust 5, 10–11, 11
Tudor, David 177, 178
Turing, Alan 282
Turnbull, D. 184
Tuuri, K. 221
Twitter 261, 339

UK Music and Association of Independent Music 433
Ullmer, B.A. 197
United States of America 434–435

Valle, Andrea 178
van Buuren, A. 376
Vandenberg, B.G. 346
Van der Hoeven, A. 432
Verron, C. 189
VESBALL 228, 229
video games 78, 189, 190
video jockeys 371
video projections 277–278
video-sharing platforms 332
Vienna 277
virtually extended music studio 106
virtual reality 129, 130, 202, 209, 281–282, 284, 285
visual cues 375–376; auditory perception 370
visual information, audience 370
visual interface 335–336
visualised sound 190
vital materialism 184
Vizzie 372
vococentrism 191

Voice Over IP 91
Von Arx, V. A. 356
VOSIS 209

Wallas, G. 346–347
Walt Disney Concert Hall 277
Wang, Ge 279
Ward, David 139
Was, Don 80–81
watermarking technologies 238
Watson-Verran, H. 184
Webb, R. 285
Webb, S. 280
Weheliye, A. G. 44, 44–45
Weinzierl, S. 142
wellbeing 261
Westergaard, Kurt 241
West, Kanye 376
Westside Gunn 41–42
Whalley, I. 106
White, Jack 86
Who's Afraid Of The Art Of Noise (Art of Noise) 61
Wiggan, J. 209
Wilde, Dan 115, 118, 119
Willner, Hal 80–81
Wilson, Mark 107
Wolfgang app 280
"Wooden Waves" (Perini) 209
workflows 117
working environment 291
Worrell, F.C. 415
Wynne, J. **215**, 216

Yang, Q. 148
Yang, Y. 313–314
Yecies, B. 261–262
York, A. 307, 332
YouTube 281, 334, 336, 338–339, 379–380

Zagorski-Thomas, S. 17, 19, 20–21, 21, 22, 25, 45–46, 64
Zajonc, R. B. 56, 60–61
Zak, A. 17, 20, 22, 23, 24–25, 52
Zappa, Frank 71
Zappi, V. 146
Zhang, L. 331

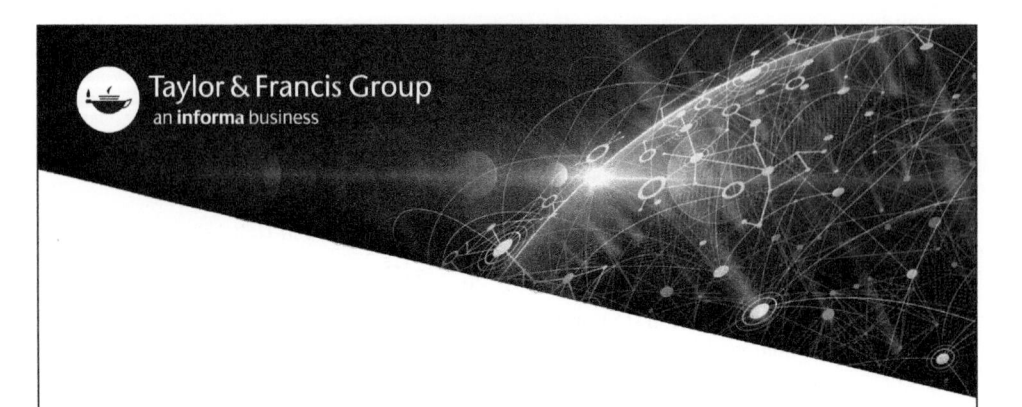

9780367363376